Software engineering with C++ and CASE tools

Michael J. Pont

University of Leicester

 **ADDISON-WESLEY**

Harlow, England • Reading, Massachusetts • Menlo Park,
California • New York • Don Mills, Ontario • Amsterdam • Bonn
Sydney • Singapore • Tokyo • Madrid • San Juan • Milan
Mexico City • Seoul • Taipei

Cover designed by Chris Eley
Typeset by Meridian Colour Repro, Pangbourne
Text designed by Sally Grover

Printed and bound in the United States of America

First printed 1996. Reprinted 1997

ISBN 0-201-87718-X

British Library Cataloguing in Publication Data
A catalogue record for this book is available from the British Library.

Library of Congress Cataloging in Publication Data
Pont, Michael J.
      Software engineering with C++ and CASE tools / Michael J. Pont.
           p.   cm.
      Includes bibliographical references and index.
      ISBN 0-201-87718-X (alk. paper)
        1. Software engineering.   2. C++ (Computer program language)
      3. Computer-aided software engineering.   I. Title.
      QA76.758.P66   1996   95-49889
      005.13'3--dc20   CIP

Software engineering with C++ and CASE tools

This book is respectfully dedicated to the memory of my grandfather, Philip Roy Pont, who died at the age of 92 on 15 April 1995, without ever growing old.

Preface

This book focuses on the engineering of substantial bespoke systems: that is, on the development of specialized software products for a single or limited number of clients. For all but the most trivial of projects, this development will be carried out jointly by a team of engineers.

My specific objectives in writing are as follows:

- to provide a pragmatic introduction to the field of software engineering;

- to compare and contrast the three major software development strategies in widespread use at the present time: process-oriented ('structured') development, data-oriented development and object-oriented development;

- to introduce the C++ programming language, and to illustrate, through a series of substantial case studies, the engineering of C++ programs for a broad spectrum of software projects, from decision support systems to real-time embedded systems;

- to demonstrate the practical benefits of computer-aided software engineering (CASE) by including a high-quality CASE tool with the book, and making use of this tool for all examples in the text.

Readers are assumed to be professionally interested in some aspect of software engineering. They may, for example, be practising software engineers trained in COBOL or FORTRAN and wishing to update their skills. They may be software engineering, computer science or electronic engineering students, or lecturers on such programmes. Readers are expected to have had some previous high-level programming experience, but no specific experience with C or C++ is assumed. Within a university or college environment, the material may be found most suitable for intermediate-level (second year in the UK) students, perhaps following a short introductory programming course.

The material in the text has been thoroughly 'field tested', having formed the basis for a number of commercial training courses which I have presented over several years. It has also been used in my university undergraduate and postgraduate teaching, first in the Department of Computer Science at the University of Sheffield, and more recently in the Department of Engineering at the University of Leicester.

Instructor's Guide

To make it easier for you to use *Software Engineering with C++ and CASE Tools* in a university or college environment, an Instructor's Guide, written by Andrew J. Norman, Vasanthi Sundaramoorthy and Michael J. Pont, is available from Addison-Wesley. The guide provides solutions to many of the exercises, plus some further examples. It also contains suggestions for conducting various types of software engineering courses, and for associated practical work.

The CASE tool included with this book is produced by SELECT Software Tools. If you wish to use the SELECT CASE tool for university or college teaching, then you may be interested to know that SELECT Software Tools offer a very substantial discount on academic site licences for a full network version of the single-user CASE tool included in this package. You can contact the company as follows:

> SELECT Software Tools
> Westmoreland House
> 80–86 Bath Road
> Cheltenham
> Gloucestershire GL53 7JT
> UK

or,

> SELECT Software Tools
> Suite #84 Brookhollow Office Park
> 1526 Brookhollow Drive
> Santa Ana
> California 92705
> USA

Compact disk

The code for the SELECT CASE tool itself (executable files) is included on the compact disk (CD) attached inside the back cover. Details of how to install the CASE tool are given in Appendix A. With the exception of the first study (which is concerned solely with programming), the case studies employ this tool. All of the associated diagrams and files are included on the CD. Details of how to install the case study files are given in Appendix C.

Copies of all the C++ programs given in the text (source files) are also included on the CD. The samples have been tested with a number of compilers, including the Microsoft Visual C++ compiler (v4.2), the Borland C++ compiler (v3.5), and the Watcom C++ compiler (v10.5). Details of how to install the code samples are given on the CD in the file 'READ_ME.WRI' in the root directory.

Video

A video introduction to object-oriented programming based on the material in this book is available from the University of Leicester. The video, created by Eric Worrall and the author, provides a comparison of process-oriented, data-oriented and object-oriented programming styles, with a particular emphasis on object-oriented techniques. It can be used effectively by companies as well as universities and colleges as part of a software engineering training programme.

Further details of the video, including samples, are available on the CD enclosed with this book. Further information is also available on the World Wide Web (http://www.engg.le.ac.uk/Cplusplus/video/).

The road goes ever on and on...

You are reading 'Edition 1.1' of *Software Engineering with C++ and CASE Tools*: that is, Edition 1.0 with a small number of corrections and updates. To ensure that future editions provide the information you need, I'd be delighted to hear of your experiences (good or bad) using the book. I can be contacted either by post (via the publishers, please), or much more efficiently by e-mail at the address given at the end of this preface.

Edition 1.0 of *Software Engineering with C++ and CASE Tools* has already resulted in a large number of people contacting me: I'll continue to do my best to respond personally and promptly to every communication.

Acknowledgements

In a project such as this, one name appears on the cover, but the book only exists because of the efforts of others behind the scenes. It is a pleasure, therefore, to be able to publicly thank those who have been involved in bringing this work to fruition.

I thank all my friends and colleagues at Sheffield University and Leicester University for many helpful discussions: Fernando Schlindwein and Derek Andrews both deserve special mention. I thank John Fothergill both for his encouragement, and also for enlightening me about the roots of the engineering profession. The book wouldn't have appeared at all without the active support of Barrie Jones, then Head of the Department of Engineering in Leicester. Particular thanks are also due to Andrew Norman, without whom the C++ examples in this book would include many more bugs than they do. Pop Sharma and Andy Willby each deserve a medal for surviving many debugging sessions.

This book has arisen, in part, from my experiences with software development on a number of research projects over the past ten years, mainly involving the computer simulation of parts of the human auditory nervous system. This work would not have been possible without the support of a great many people, among them Bob Damper, Phil Green and John Frisby. Particular thanks are also due to my long-suffering post-graduate students – David Sewell, Chen Pang Wong, Kien Seng Wong and Eric Worrall – for putting up with absence of their supervisor (in mind when not in body) during the gestation of this text in the past 12 months. Thanks are also due to David for his help with several of the code examples, to Kien Seng for the screen shot in Chapter 14, and to Chen Pang and Eric for their work on the appendices.

I thank everyone – university students and those from industry and elsewhere – who have endured my courses in programming and software engineering over recent years, for asking tough questions and teaching me a great deal in the process. Thanks are particularly due to Maheboob S. Ahmad, Daniel Grimwade, Vasanthi Sundaramoorthy, Graham Cottle, Noel John Bernatt, Y.K. Ng, Lee Pasifull, Stuart Urban, Tony Vickers and Daniel Yeoh for useful comments on the evolving manuscript.

I thank Emanuela Moreale for taking the trouble to provide a detailed review of the whole of an early draft of the manuscript, and Gordon Pont and Andrew Pont for useful comments on an even earlier draft. I thank the (anonymous) reviewers of the evolving manuscript for many helpful suggestions.

I thank Simon Plumtree at Addison-Wesley for believing in this large, complicated project and getting it off the ground. Also at Addison-Wesley, Sheila Chatten spent many weeks dealing patiently with my frequent email queries, and generally keeping the book on the rails. In 'Edition 1.0', I neglected to thank Margaret Macknelly of Margaret Macknelly Design who did a great job with the many figures: thank you! With the departure of Simon Plumtree and Sheila Chatten from A-W after 'Edition 1.0', Sally Mortimore and Fiona Kinnear have inherited this project: without their effort and encouragement, this reprint would never have appeared.

I thank the staff at Select Software Tools: in particular, the book could not have appeared in this form without the efforts of Virginia Bray.

I thank Bruce Springsteen for writing and recording 'Greetings from Asbury Park NJ'.

I thank all the folk at Leicester Software Engineering – Jane, Stephanie and Harry – without whom none of this would have been possible.

Last, and most of all, I thank Sarah, my partner and my best friend. After several years which we have both shared with 'The Book', any sanity I have left is entirely due to her.

Michael J. Pont
Leicester, May 1997
E-mail: M.J.Pont@sun.engineering.leicester.ac.uk
URL: http://www.engg.le.ac.uk/home/Michael.J.Pont/

Contents

Introduction

Beginning at the end

1.1 What is software engineering?

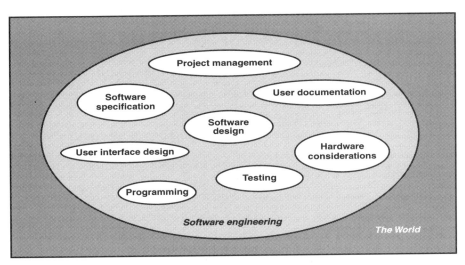

Figure 1.1 Programming is a comparatively small component of the software engineering field. Some of the other parts (including, for example, software specification and design) are equally important.

Although precise figures are difficult to obtain, software engineering is probably the most rapidly expanding field of modern engineering; certainly it is one of the most exciting and challenging areas in which an engineer may choose to specialize. Despite this there is still rather a lot of confusion, and not just outside the engineering profession, over the meaning of the job title 'software engineer'. After all, isn't an engineer someone who gets their hands oily fixing your car? It follows, since software has something to do with computers, and most cars don't yet contain computers, that the term **software engineering** appears almost wholly contradictory.

The confusion probably arises not only because software engineering is a comparatively young discipline, but also because people tend to assume that the word engineer is derived from the word 'engine'. In fact, the word engineer, like the word ingenious, originated from the Latin word *ingeniosus*. The person who mends your car may be an ingenious mechanic, but a true engineer is best described as someone who is 'marked by a special aptitude for discovering, inventing or contriving' *(Longman Dictionary of the English Language)*.

Even people who understand that a software engineer has nothing to do with crankshafts or carburettors tend to assume that software engineering is synonymous with programming, but this is not the case either: the discipline encompasses not only programming (Figure 1.1), but all the stages involved in the development of large software products.

Perhaps because of a misperception that software development is an easy thing to do, only between 20 and 35% of companies in the UK 'engineer' the software they produce (Clifton and Sutcliffe, 1994, p.401),* while in the US the corresponding figure may be less than 15% (Coad and Yourdon, 1991, p.191). The consequences of such an informal approach are very real: in the UK alone, problems with software development cost the economy in the region of £2 billion per annum (Norris *et al.*, 1993).

1.2   Engineering quality software

The goal of software engineering is to produce what is sometimes referred to as **quality software**. Quality software is not something that is easy to achieve, for reasons that we will begin to consider in this chapter, but is a goal well worth striving for. This goal might be defined as follows:

- Quality software performs precisely as required, under all circumstances.
- Quality software is entirely 'bug-free'.
- Quality software is delivered on time.
- Quality software is delivered within budget.

The purpose of this book is to help you to develop, using C++, software products that meet these quality aims. We shall focus primarily on bespoke software engineering: that is, on the development of specialized software products for a single or limited number of clients. For all but the most trivial of projects, the development will be carried out jointly by a team of engineers.

Traditionally, the software engineering process that the team follows has been viewed as a series of steps – a **waterfall** – where results flow, sequentially, from one stage to the next (Figure 1.2). The process typically begins with a telephone call, in which your potential client gives a loose outline of the problem in hand. Next, you will take part in a series of more detailed discussions, during which you must ascertain what the detailed requirements for the system actually are. Following such discussions, you draw up a rigorous specification of the problem: such a specification lays out explicitly what the proposed software product must do, and will usually, along with budget details and agreed time scales, form the basis of a contract between your company and your client. Armed with such a specification, you are in a position to consider the data structures and the algorithms you will require in order to satisfy the specification: together,

---

* Details of books referred to in the text are given in Chapter 34, Bibliography.

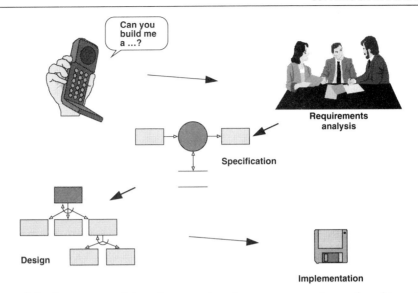

Figure 1.2   An overview of the software engineering process, sometimes referred to as the 'waterfall model'.

these elements constitute the design of your system. Finally, you need to take the design, and translate this into a working product, using C++, possibly in conjunction with other programming components.

This book will consider each of the above stages, and examine how these can most effectively be used to facilitate the production of software which aims to meets all the quality requirements outlined above.

1.3   But hang on a minute ...

By now, you may be looking at Figure 1.2 in horror. After all, if you are reading this book, you have probably already done a little computer programming. What, you may be wondering, is all this nonsense about 'analysis' and 'design'? Surely these are just a waste of time? Wouldn't it be much more productive simply to get on and build the thing, rather than sitting around talking about it?

As someone said at the start of a recent course run by the author:

> *'With the computer in my study, my six-year-old daughter can write a working Basic program in less than five minutes. Obviously, writing a large program is going to take a bit longer, which is precisely why it's a good idea not to waste time on woolly design theories, and instead to get down to writing the program as soon as possible – isn't it?'*

Now, this is a perfectly valid point of view, but it is also very *wrong*! Yes, it is easy to write small programs, but when it comes to writing larger programs, the situation gets much more complex. Specifically, the quotation above implies a 'model' of program development much like the one shown in Figure 1.3.

Such a linear model may appear intuitively attractive, but in practice the relationship between program size and design complexity can easily become something

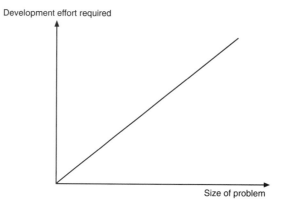

Figure 1.3   A linear model of program development.

more like the **Hacker's Curve** shown in Figure 1.4. As this figure illustrates, it is often found that the development of small programs is straightforward, but once the programs grow in size and complexity, the development effort can begin to increase dramatically. Of course, there is no way of *proving* that the software development process takes this form (and 'size of problem' and 'development effort required' are rather ill-defined concepts anyway) but a small thought experiment should help to demonstrate that this model is on the right tracks.

1.4   A thought experiment

Consider that you are asked to remember two numbers (say 2 and 5): you can do this without any difficulty. Now try three numbers (say 2, 5, 67): this should still present no problems. You can probably easily remember 10 numbers without undue stress, but would it be twice as hard for you to remember 20 numbers? Would it be *10 times* as hard for you to remember 100 numbers correctly? Or well-nigh impossible (Figure 1.5)?

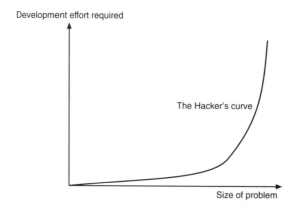

Figure 1.4   A more realistic model of program development.

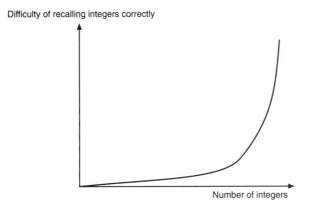

Difficulty of recalling integers correctly

Number of integers

Figure 1.5 Remembering collections of integers.

The same problem confronts you when you write a 10-line computer program: it is easy to remember, and to check (for example) which variables have still to be declared. In a 3000-line program, the process gets more difficult, and by the time you reach 30 000 lines, the problem is intractable.

Just to make matters more complicated, suppose your company was to develop a new software product involving, say, 100 000 lines of code, perhaps for an air traffic control system. No one individual could develop the whole system: this would simply take too long. In addition, a well-organized software house will already have developed other products, probably sharing many of the features of the current system. Since the previous code will, naturally, have been thoroughly tested and debugged, it makes excellent sense to 'recycle' the existing code wherever possible. In these situations, the programmers in the team will be integrating the code they develop with code, either new code or recycled code, developed by other people. In such circumstances, programmers simply cannot remember all the details of previous code, because they may well not have written it.

It is not possible to say how big a design task must be undertaken, or how many lines of code a program has to have, before the 'linear' relation between problem size and program size breaks down, but most people who think that there is a linear relationship between these entities have never had to build a large system.

The good news is that you are not necessarily constrained to follow such a model of program development. Let us stick with the thought experiment for a moment, and flesh out some of the details. Suppose you were (for some obscure reason) required to listen to and later recall a list of 1000 numbers recited over the radio. Naturally, you wouldn't actually try to remember the numbers, but you would write them down as they were read out. Then, when you were required to recall the numbers again, you would simply read out the numbers from your list. If the list was 10 numbers long, it might take you (say) 10 seconds to write down the numbers, and a further 10 seconds to read them out again, a total of 20 seconds: if the list was 1000 numbers long, the process might take you 2000 seconds. What you have done, therefore, is to reduce the complexity of your problem, resulting once again in a more easily manageable relationship between the size of your problem and the effort of obtaining a result (Figure 1.6).

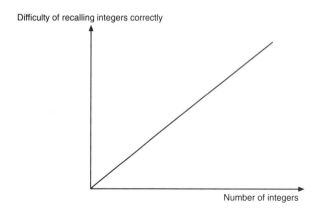

Figure 1.6 The result of using some basic tools (in this case, paper and a pencil) to help in the memory task.

In an engineering situation, just as piece of paper and a pencil was used in the thought experiment, a form of *aide-mémoire* is required by all engineers. In a real situation, the engineer uses a variety of techniques to help spread the complexity of the problem, and to communicate details of the final design with the client. Just as you would not expect a civil engineer to begin a construction of a bridge without first drawing up a plan of the proposed structure, you should not expect a software engineer to begin construction of a complex product without first going through the stages of analysis and design outlined above, and using an appropriate notation to record the results of each stage.

In the thought experiment above, a pencil and paper are used as very basic tools to aid in the completion of the required task. In all branches of engineering, the use of tools, from computer-aided design packages to spanners, is widespread. In many cases, the use of such tools seems like 'common sense', just as the idea of writing down the numbers in this thought experiment is quite blindingly obvious. Laying aside the hyperbole, the acronyms and exaggerated claims, much of software engineering is also common sense. Moreover, software engineering consists of no more and no less than a set of tools and techniques with three central aims: to make the development of quality software a more predictable, rapid and reliable process.

For very simple programs (falling on to the initial, linear, portion of the Hacker's Curve), we don't need to pay any heed to good software engineering practice. However, it is unlikely that in your career as a software engineer you will be asked to develop many such trivial programs: most real-world problems require rather more than a pencil and paper to solve.

1.5 Quality software in the real world

The leap between simple programs and the real world can be a substantial one. For instance, the software supporting the US Space Shuttle programme consists of some *three million* lines of code, including computers on the ground controlling the launch and the flight and 100000 lines of code in the shuttle itself (Pfleeger, 1987). To put

We begin to fill in the details of SADIE in Part I, beginning with an introduction to the use of C++ functions to develop large programs. As mentioned above, programming is really only the final scene in a much longer software engineering opera. Nonetheless, it is with programming, rather than high-level issues of requirements analysis or software design, that we are concerned in this early part of the book. This 'back to front' approach is necessary because, while we might like to assume that our analysis and (particularly) design models can be made implementation independent, this is would be a rather naïve assumption. For instance, use of an object-oriented design model (discussed in Part III) implicitly assumes that the implementation language provides support for a feature known as inheritance, whereas many popular languages (such as C, Ada, COBOL and FORTRAN) provide no such support, making it at least more difficult and occasionally impossible to develop a clean implementation of the specified design.

In Part I, we therefore begin by covering the basics of process-oriented C++ programming in a manner that will provide good preparation for the task of using this language to develop the larger systems we consider throughout much of the rest of the book. We will also consider other essential parts of the implementation process, including programming from a process-oriented design, and the essentials of program testing. The focus then switches to a higher level as the process of analysis is considered, culminating in a specification of the system requirements sometimes referred to as the essential, or logical, model. Here, the techniques required to ascertain and record the detailed requirements for a software system are explored in depth. Some simple systems are first considered then, in later chapters, more substantial, interactive systems are examined. We are then ready to take a closer look at process-oriented design, and at the development of what is sometimes called the implementation, or physical, model.

Throughout Part I, the emphasis is on process-oriented development: such an approach is widely used and is appropriate where systems have comparatively simple data requirements. In Part II, we build on the earlier material and consider how a data-oriented approach can be employed to develop isolated data systems: that is, software products involving storage and manipulation of more complex data, often stored in an external database. Here we consider both implementations in C++ and other techniques involving relational database systems and Structured Query Language (SQL). We examine entity-relationship modelling techniques, and explore how the same techniques can aid in the development of hybrid systems, such as substantial decision support and executive information systems.

In Part III, we go on to explore ways in which systems can be produced using object-oriented development techniques. Here we are concerned with systems making much greater use of user-defined data types. In fact, the central feature of object-oriented development is the use of C++ classes to implement data types that become as much a part of the language as the simple built-in types. As before, Part III builds on, rather than replacing, the material presented earlier.

Throughout the book, we will follow the fortunes of an up-and-coming software engineering company (Leicester Software Engineering) as it specifies, designs and develops software systems for use in a bell foundry, for detecting yetis in the Arctic Circle, for stock control, and for controlling bank cash machines. The examples are varied, and are as substantial and complete as is practical within the confines of a book such as this. They are intended to demonstrate how quality software can be developed using SADIE.

In the appendices, you will find a guide to the installation and use of the SELECT CASE tool, plus a series of tutorials to help you learn how to use this package in an effective manner.

1.11   Conclusions

In this chapter, we have introduced software engineering, CASE tools and SADIE, and we have outlined some of the reasons why C++ is an appropriate language to use at the implementation stage of modern software projects.

In Chapter 2, we'll provide some further details of the software engineering process, and introduce the company that will be used to illustrate the case studies in this book – Leicester Software Engineering.

2 Leicester Software Engineering

2.1   Introduction

In order to illustrate the software engineering and programming techniques discussed in this book, we present a number of case studies describing some of the projects undertaken by a small software house called Leicester Software Engineering (Figure 2.1). In this chapter, we briefly introduce Leicester Software Engineering, and consider how the company operates.

2.2   LSE company structure

Leicester Software Engineering (LSE) is a small software house, specializing in the development of bespoke packages, computer training and general software consultancy for a range of companies throughout the UK and mainland Europe. The turnover of the company in 1995 was slightly more than £1 400 000.

LSE has four employees: the managing director (who prefers simply to be called 'Boss'), two software engineers (Jane, who specializes in analysis; and Stephanie, who specializes in design) and one programmer (Harry). The management structure of the company is shown in Figure 2.2.

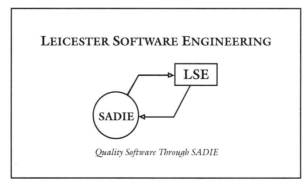

Figure 2.1   The Leicester Software Engineering company logo.

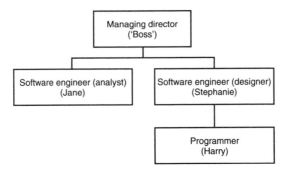

Figure 2.2 Management structure of Leicester Software Engineering.

LSE are based in a rather smart area of Leicester known as Birstall. Boss has a large office on the second floor of the building, Jane and Stephanie each have their own room on the first floor, and Harry has a desk next to the coffee machine on the ground floor. Jane is paid a salary of £45 000 a year, Stephanie is paid £37 000, and Harry £21 000: no one knows how much Boss earns, but he dresses well and drives a very expensive car.

No one is quite sure how Boss earns his money either, because he doesn't generally seem to do very much. When people contact LSE, it is Jane, Stephanie and Harry who work together to deliver the required software products.

2.3 A typical scenario

Most clients contact the Leicester Software Engineering by telephone in the first instance: these calls are put through to Jane. If, after an initial brief discussion, Jane thinks the job is one that LSE can profitably take on, she usually arranges a meeting with the prospective clients in order to find out more about it.

Jane is a software engineer, but her main task is one of analysis (Figure 2.3). Generally, the process of analysis can be defined as follows: 'examination and identification of the constituents of a complex whole and their relationship to one another'. As far as software engineering is concerned, analysis involves finding out, through discussions with the customer, what functions the specified product is expected to perform, how quickly it must respond, how much data it must deal with and so on. We will have more to say about the analysis process later; for now, we just need to appreciate that it is a non-trivial information gathering exercise, crucial to the success of the project.

It is also important to realize that, while Jane learned how to program (in COBOL) when studying for a degree in computer science at the University of Glasgow, she has done no programming in the last 10 years. Her job is not to program, nor even to say how the product will work: her job is 'simply' to develop a detailed logical model of the system, saying *what* the software product should do when it is complete. We can summarize this as follows:

The analyst develops the logical model (the 'what' model) based on discussions with the client.

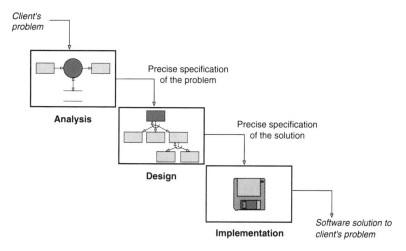

Client's problem

Precise specification of the problem

Analysis

Precise specification of the solution

Design

Implementation

Software solution to client's problem

Figure 2.3 An overview of the software engineering process. As we will see, this overview is somewhat idealized; however, it will serve the purposes of our initial discussion here.

When Jane has agreed a specification for the job with the client, she passes a copy of this specification to Stephanie. Stephanie's job is to translate Jane's logical model into a 'how' model: the physical model. That is, she has to develop a design specification, saying how the requirements identified by Jane are to be achieved. Stephanie tends not to deal with the clients directly: if she has any questions, she usually makes contact through Jane.

We can summarize Stephanie's role as follows:

The designer develops the physical model (the 'how' model) based on the logical model.

Again, Stephanie does no programming. She did learn to program (in C++, as it happens) a few years ago, but she doesn't use much of her programming knowledge on a day-to-day basis. The physical model that Stephanie constructs should, in theory at least, be suitable for implementation in almost any programming language. Her model specifies precisely what components the program should be assembled from, and what each component should do. She does not write the code to implement the product.

Harry, of course, knows how to program in C++. Harry isn't terribly smart, but he doesn't need to be: in LSE his job is very strictly defined, and he isn't expected to have many bright ideas. For each of the components Stephanie has defined in her physical model, Harry writes some C++ code, often in the form of a C++ function or class. He tests each component of the program when he has written it, and makes sure it corresponds to Stephanie's specification. When he has finished all the components, he assembles them together into a single program. At this stage, he calls in Stephanie to make sure that she is happy that the complete program matches her model. When these in-house tests are complete, Jane takes the complete prototype to the clients.

We can summarize Harry's role as follows:

The programmer develops the software based on the physical model.

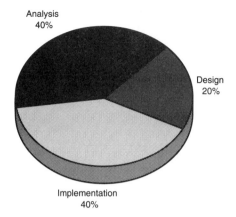

Figure 2.4 How LSE divide up their time on a general software project. Note that 'implementation' here (and throughout the book) is assumed to refer to both coding and testing.

Finally, though it is difficult to be precise, Jane estimates that the time required by LSE to complete each of these analysis, design and implementation stages is as shown in Figure 2.4. What the pie chart shows is that, for some arbitrary but *substantial* project, LSE's initial analysis may occupy about 40% of the project time scale, followed by about 20% for design and a final 40% for implementation (including testing).

2.4   A more realistic software development model

We presented the simple 'waterfall model' in Chapter 1, and implied in our discussions above that this is the approach adopted at LSE. This isn't quite true.

While attractive on paper, the simple waterfall model is, in practice, unduly simplistic. The main reason for this is that people who know little about computer technology (and these, after all, are the people most likely to need you to work for them) don't know what they want the software product to do, beyond a general outline, until you have built this product for them. Clearly, this is a question of 'chicken and egg'.

So, what does a more realistic picture of software development look like? We still need to carry out analysis and design phases (otherwise we are simply reinventing the Hacker's Curve), but we don't finish each stage completely before embarking on the next (Figure 2.5). What this figure attempts to illustrate is that, in the real world, the various steps of analysis, design, implementation and testing seldom happen in a single perfect sequence. Typically, what you have is an iterative process, whereby you start with an initial analysis of the problem, do a rapid design, then code-up, test and demonstrate (to your client) a prototype. The user may be asked to comment on the results of earlier phases, but is generally most interested in the prototype system. Seeing the prototype also reassures the user that she is getting something for money, and invariably raises a few comments, along the lines of: 'Well, that's basically okay: but it would be better if you could also make it do ...'

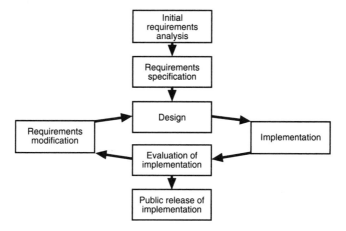

Figure 2.5 A rapid prototyping model of software development, illustrating the iterative way in which many real products are developed.

This approach shown in Figure 2.5 is known as **rapid prototyping** (or rapid application development), and is the approach Jane and her team use for most projects.

2.5 Two main system categories

LSE find that the products they are asked to develop generally fall into one of two broad categories (Figure 2.6):

- technical systems

- information systems

Less commonly, LSE staff are asked to develop 'hybrid systems'; that is, systems using components from both technical and information systems. For example, an important class of product which integrates complex data with complex processing is that of **decision support systems**, a topic we consider in Part II.

We consider the features of technical systems and information systems in turn below.

2.5.1 Technical systems

An example of a technical system might be a single-lead electrocardiogram (ECG) monitor. Such systems are used following heart surgery to monitor continuously the heartbeats of patients. Typically, the system will be about the size of a Sony Walkman and will be worn on a belt at the patient's waist. The system will have a single electrode attached to the surface of the patient's chest. The 'computer' at the heart of

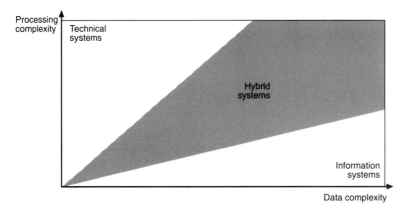

Figure 2.6 The 'spectrum' of different types of software product. At one end of this range are technical systems, at the other end are information systems. Hybrid systems share features from both ends of the spectrum.

the monitor will consist of a small microprocessor (perhaps a Motorola 68HC05B6 or similar device) along with a small amount of memory.

In general cases, technical systems have the following distinguishing character-istics:

- As in the ECG monitor here, the processing carried out by the system may be complex, and will frequently have to be conducted in real time (that is, very rapidly).

- In contrast to the complex processing requirements, the data processed by a tech-nical system is often very simple, though there may be a lot of it. For example, in the ECG monitor, the data may well consist of a stream of integers representing the heart activity at various instants of time.

- As in the above ECG monitor, in traffic light control systems, vehicle engine management or air traffic control, the system may be **safety-critical**: if the soft-ware fails or does not perform as required, people may be injured or killed.

- Many technical systems are also embedded systems: they run not on general-purpose desktop computers or workstations, but on single-board computer systems (see Chapter 15).

- Technical systems very often have little or no user interface: the ECG monitor may well simply have a single flashing LED on the top to reassure the user that everything is connected and working; a buzzer might sound if a problem was detected, or if the patient was over-exerting herself.

2.5.2 Information systems

An example of an information system might be a tendering support system (TSS) for a large company manufacturing replacement 'double glazed' windows for people living in older houses. Companies or private customers would ring the company and ask for a quotation. The salesman, after a site visit, would enter into the system details of the size of the windows, the type of frames required, the type of glass required, along with any additional features such as doors, security fitments, and so on. The TSS would then interrogate the company database to obtain current prices and stock levels for the required items. The database might also contain information on time taken to assemble windows of a particular kind, including up-to-date charges for labour and tax. The TSS would provide the required 'tender'.

In general cases, information systems frequently have the following distinguishing characteristics:

- In contrast to the simple data requirements of technical systems, the data processed by an information system is often complex. For example, in the TSS above, the data will include not only current prices for all the required components (metal, different cuts of timber, various kinds of glass, and so forth), but also labour costs, details of staff availability and other current orders. Only with all such information will the system be able to estimate costs and delivery times with any accuracy.

- As in the TSS, the processing carried out by the system may be comparatively simple.

- Many information systems are required to run on, and/or to access information stored on, a wide range of mainframe, mini and desktop computer systems.

- Generally, the information systems carry business information and – while these data are undoubtedly of great importance – a system crash is likely to result 'only' in court action against the software engineer, not in a loss of life.

- Traditional information systems have a simple text-based user interface, but more modern systems may have a sophisticated graphical user interface, requiring the use of a mouse and incorporating features like 'pull-down' menus.

2.6   LSE and SADIE

So far, we've seen that Leicester Software Engineering are asked to build at least two types of software systems (information systems and technical systems). We have argued that to build either type of system, Jane and her team start by doing some analysis, followed by some design, then finally some coding. Usually, for the reasons laid out in Section 2.4, they then demonstrate a prototype to their client. After analysing the feedback they receive from such a presentation, they go on to refine their system specification during another analysis phase.

What we have not yet explained, however, in more than very general terms, is what exactly these various terms mean. For example, just what is 'analysis'? So far, all we've said is that the process involves 'examination and identification of the constituents of a complex whole and their relationship to one another'. This isn't really much help. We might legitimately start asking some tough questions, along the lines:

- Given a general problem, how do we start analysing it?

- How do we know that two analysts, given the same problem to investigate, will arrive at a similar solution?

- How can we manage a group of analysts?
- When should we stop analysing and start designing?
- How do we know we've got the design right?
- When do we start coding?

Simple Analysis, Design & Implementation (SADIE), introduced in the last chapter and described throughout this book, attempts to provide answers to such questions. As the name suggests, SADIE incorporates aspects of software development from initial contact with the client, to implementation and testing of the prototype product.

SADIE is a methodology, which simply means a 'set of methods': specifically, SADIE consists of three overlapping methods. Each of these methods is, in turn, a 'recipe' rather than an algorithm: that is, each method consists of a list of steps which beginning 'chefs' will probably wish to follow closely, and which those with more experience will generally 'adjust to taste'.

To understand SADIE, you need to appreciate that the central aim of each of the methods is to build a model of the system we are trying to construct. The models are each represented using a standard graphical notation, examples of which are given below.

SADIE thus has two components:

- a set of (three) methods, designed to help the software engineer translate the initial outline user requirements into a series of increasingly detailed models of the system being developed;
- a notation for representing the above models.

As the company logo suggests (Figure 2.1), Leicester Software Engineering is a strong advocate of the SADIE methodology. Using SADIE, Jane views the whole of the software engineering process as a model-building activity. She starts with a very hazy idea of the product LSE are trying to construct and, during analysis, constructs her first logical model of the system. This model is then refined (by Stephanie) to give a more detailed physical model. Finally, during the implementation phase, Harry builds a final complete 'model' (in source code, usually C++), of a system that is usually destined to become object code. Jane doesn't pretend that SADIE provides all the answers, but she does believe that it helps LSE develop quality software (as defined in Chapter 1).

We begin to describe SADIE in more detail below.

2.7 One methodology, three different methods

To cope with the development of a range of possible software systems (discussed in Section 2.5), SADIE incorporates three related methods, as illustrated in Figure 2.7. Each of the methods (process-oriented, data-oriented and object-oriented) involve the engineer viewing the problem domain in a slightly different way, and constructing appropriate logical and physical models of the system.

These three different system development strategies and the corresponding models are described in detail throughout this text: an overview of each method is given below.

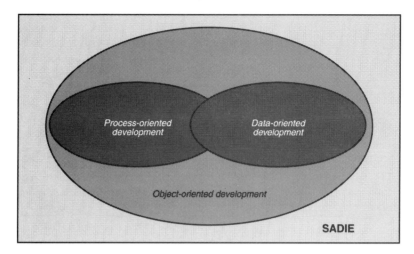

Figure 2.7 The three software development approaches supported by the 'Simple Analysis, Design & Implementation' (SADIE) methodology discussed in this book.

2.7.1 Process-oriented software development

Process-oriented (P-O) SADIE involves thinking about a product in terms of the processes it must perform. Process-oriented methods are sometimes known as **Structured methods** (usually with a capital 'S'). The final program is constructed largely of functions.

P-O development involves the construction of logical and physical process models. Typically, for example, a logical process model will centre around the construction of a hierarchy of dataflow diagrams, like that shown in Figure 2.8. We consider process-oriented software development in Part I.

2.7.2 Data-oriented software development

Data-oriented (D-O) SADIE overlaps with P-O SADIE (see Figure 2.7). Instead of focusing on the processing to be performed by the software product, D-O development emphasizes the **data** that will be processed. Such data are usually complex in nature and may be physically isolated from the rest of the program in some form of external database.

D-O development involves the construction of data models, which in turn usually consist of one or more entity-relationship diagrams, like that shown in Figure 2.9. Note that D-O development will also frequently involve the construction of related process models, like that already shown in Figure 2.8.

We shall consider data-oriented software development in Part II.

2.7.3 Object-oriented software development

Object-oriented (O-O) software development builds on both P-O and D-O development (see Figure 2.7). O-O techniques provide a rich set of additional tools to the software engineer (for example, see Figure 2.10), tools that become particularly important when

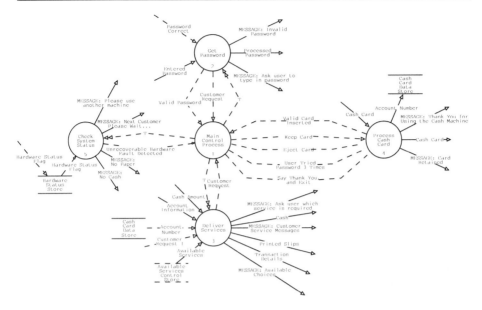

Figure 2.8 A sample dataflow diagram. Such diagrams are an important part of the process model developed during the analysis phase of a process-oriented software development. Ultimately, each of the 'bubbles' on the dataflow diagram may become a C++ function.

developing very large systems, and which may make it easier to 'recycle' code between projects.

We shall consider object-oriented software development in Part III.

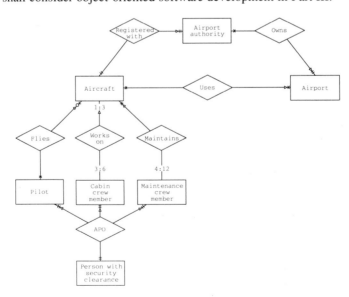

Figure 2.9 Part of the data model for an airport security system, including both association and aggregation relationships. In the final implementation, each entity on the diagram (represented by a rectangle) may become a 'table' in a database. Note that APO stands for 'A Part Of': it denotes the fact that a Person entity will form part of, for example, a Pilot entity.

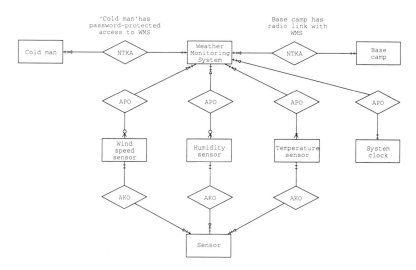

Figure 2.10 The class-relationship diagram for a simple weather monitoring system. Here again, as in Figure 2.9 we have associations and aggregation relationships: we also have a new inheritance relationship, represented as 'AKO'. AKO stands for 'A Kind Of'.

2.8 Conclusions

This chapter has introduced Leicester Software Engineering (LSE), the company at the heart of the case studies in this book. It has also outlined SADIE, the approach used at LSE to develop their systems.

We can conclude by raising an obvious question following from the discussions here: given a particular piece of software to build, which method should be used? Unfortunately, there is no easy answer to this. For example, process-oriented methods are very widely used for developing technical systems (see Section 2.5.1). However, object-oriented techniques are also appropriate in such situations. In very general terms, code developed using a process-oriented approach may run more efficiently (that is, faster) that the equivalent code developed in an object-oriented manner. Such factors may or may not be important for your particular project.

We shall be in a better position to answer this question in Part III.

Exercises

2.1   Consider one or more different engineering disciplines: for example, chemical engineering, civil engineering, electronic engineering, and so on. How do individual engineers in your chosen field(s) implement analysis and design strategies? Are the techniques they use compatible with software engineering? If not, why not?

2.2   Reverse engineering is a fascinating area of study. At one level, it means trying to reproduce, from an executable program, the original source code. The aim of such an exercise is to alter the original source code enough to disguise the product, then resell it.

The aim of this exercise is not to encourage you to embark on such an illegal activity, but to encourage you to experiment with a more innocent form of reverse engineering. Consider the spell checker in your favourite word processor or some similar software package. Now, try to reverse engineer a completely unambiguous **specification** for this package that you could pass to a software designer for development – ultimately, into an identical working program.

If your specification is sufficiently rigorous, then it should be possible for someone to design and code a spell checker from your description without asking any questions. In addition, it should also be possible to explain what the spell checker does to someone who is not computer literate.

Remember: the specification is a 'what' document, not a 'how' document. Your answer should not contain any design or implementation information.

2.3 SADIE is by no means the only method of software development. To put the material in this book in context, it is worth considering some other techniques. If you have access to a technical library, see how many other 'methodologies' you can unearth: the bibliography in Chapter 34 may provide a useful starting point.

3 Goodbye, cruel world!

3.1 Introduction

A central aim of this text is to illustrate, in a single volume, an integrated engineering methodology that encompasses all stages of software development, from conception (in the mind of the analyst) to implementation (at the hands of the programmer). For reasons we outlined at the end of Chapter 1, we shall 'begin at the end', with a discussion of basic programming concepts. Our main focus in this text will, of course, be on the use of C++ as an implementation language, a choice we explained in Chapter 1. In the remainder of the Introduction, we describe some basic features of the C++ language and begin to explore the use of C++ for what is sometimes called 'programming in the small'.

If you are already an experienced programmer, you may wish to skim-read this chapter and Chapter 4, as we go right back to basics.

3.2 The origins of C++

As you are aware, a computer is merely a device capable of performing computations (that is, 'crunching numbers') and making logical decisions. A programming language is in turn simply a means of telling a computer what to do (Figure 3.1). However, all computers are 'stupid' in that they always do precisely what they are told, and they will only accept instructions in a very simple numeric language known as **machine code** or **object code** (Figure 3.2). Machine code is often referred to as a low-level language, which simply means that you need a vast list of machine code to do anything even vaguely useful. To make matters worse, machine code is not **portable**, a shorthand way of saying that machine code developed for one computer must be completely rewritten for use on different hardware.

As computers grew more popular, the problems with writing in machine code grew more acute, and medium-level languages called assembly language were developed. Assembly is, in retrospect, considered to be the first generation of true programming languages (usually abbreviated as 1GL). Instead of numbers, assembly language uses English-like instructions to represent the elementary operations carried out by the computer (Figure 3.3). It follows from the discussions above that to use these assembly

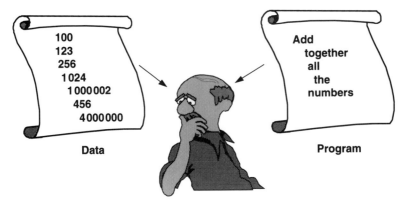

Figure 3.1 A schematic view of a simple computer system. The microprocessor – the central processing unit – is told by the program how to process some items of data in a useful way.

```
74   12
80   3F   00
80   3C   0D
A4
EB   F8
74   03
```

Figure 3.2 An example of a program in machine code. Note that, despite appearances, the code is numerical: the numbers are in hexadecimal (base 16) notation, which uses A to represent 10, B to represent 11, up to F which represents 15.

language programs, translators called assemblers are required to convert the instructions from a language the programmer can read into a machine code the computer can 'understand'. Because they are a step removed from raw machine code, assembly languages are more portable than their lower-level counterparts, but it still takes considerable effort to develop programs in assembly language, and still more work to convert such programs to run on a different computer.

The next generation of languages (2GLs) were designed to further speed up the programming process. The translator programs that convert such high-level language programs into machine language are called compilers (or, less commonly, interpreters). One statement in a high-level language will typically correspond to many tens of lines

```
MOV   AH,   2
MOV   DL,   7
INT   21H
CMP   INDEX,   4
MOVSB
JMP   034E
```

Figure 3.3 An example of code written in assembly language.

of machine code. High-level language programming is quicker and less error-prone than writing assembly language or machine code. As a result, very few people now write machine code at all. However, assembly language is still used, not often to write complete programs but generally to 'hand optimize' pieces of code that may, for example, need to run as quickly as possible (such as in telecommunications, image-processing or signal-processing work). Typically, assembly language routines will be called as functions from the main program code, written in a 2GL (or later) programming language.

Examples of important 2GLs include FORTRAN and COBOL. FORTRAN (FORmula TRANslator), was developed in 1954 and is still widely used for a large number of scientific and engineering applications (Figure 3.4). COBOL (COmmon Business Oriented Language) was developed in 1960, and is still used for approximately half of all business software.

Next, we come to the third generation, and languages such as (standard) Pascal, Ada and C (Figure 3.5). The gulf between 3GLs and their second-generation counterparts is not as vast as that between, say, COBOL and assembly language, but it is a significant one. 3GLs are process-oriented programming languages. Process-oriented languages allow the programmer to lay out the code in a manner that makes it easy for the programmer to read and debug. Most significantly, process-oriented languages encourage the programmer to create programs from small, named blocks of code known as functions: we'll discuss the use of functions as program building-blocks in Part I.

Beyond 3GLs, the numbering of language generations becomes a matter of fierce debate. The general industry definition of a fourth-generation (4GL) language is that it should be characterized by its 'non-procedural' nature: that is, the 'programmer' specifies what is to be done by the program, not how this result is to be achieved. Current 4GLs are aimed at data-oriented software development, a process we discuss in Part II. The database programming language 'Structured Query Language' (SQL) can be viewed as a 4GL: this language, which can be used effectively in conjunction with C++, is discussed further in Chapter 20.

Finally, we come to what can be viewed as the fifth generation of programming languages. These are languages which support an object-oriented style of programming and code development. Examples of 5GLs include Smalltalk, a variety of object-oriented extensions to Pascal: and, of course, C++.

The C++ language was developed by Bjarne Stroustrup early in the 1980s, at Bell Laboratories in the US (Stroustrup, 1991). C++ is essentially a **superset** of C: that is to say, everything you can do in C you can do in C++. However, C++ is also 'a better C': it is easier for new programmers to learn to develop 'C-style' programs in C++ than it was in C, as well as for experienced programmers to build more reliable programs more quickly. Of greater significance, as we will see in Part III, C++ also provides many rather more interesting extensions to C++, which give the support for object-oriented software development necessary to classify this language as a 5GL.

```
          DO 200 A = 1,2
          TEST(A) = EXP (-C/AVERAGE(A))
          IF (AVERAGE(A).LE.V) THEN X = Y
          ELSE X = Z
    200   CONTINUE
```

Figure 3.4 An example of code written in FORTRAN.

```
/* File: hello.c
   A program to print "hello, world"
   Written by MJP: 12 August, 1993. */

#include <stdio.h>

int main(void)
    {
    printf("hello, world");
    return 0;
    }
```

Figure 3.5 An example of code written in C.

Note that while 5GLs (as described above) are currently the 'most advanced' languages in widespread use, it would be naïve and foolish to assume that a complete history of programming can now be written. For example, agent-oriented software development is a new form of software development which is attracting considerable interest at the present time, not least because it can be used very effectively with '6GLs', like Java, to develop applications for the World Wide Web. Further details of agent-oriented development are given in Appendix K.

3.3 A first C++ program

In order to gain experience of any new programming language, there is a long-standing tradition that your first program should print a few words on the screen. The tradition is a good one: in order to perform such a comparatively simple task, you need to understand the most basic elements of your chosen programming language: equally important, however, is the fact that writing your simple program will introduce you to the use of the particular program editor, the linker and the compiler needed with all your later work.

Program 3.1 is our first simple C++ program.

```
// A program to print "Goodbye, cruel world!"
// Written by MJP: 1 January, 1996
// Source is: 03_01.CPP

#include <iostream.h>

int main()
    {
    cout << "Goodbye, cruel world!";
    return 0;
    }
```

Program 3.1 A first C++ program that displays the words 'Goodbye, cruel world' on the computer screen. (☺)

Program 3.1 generates the following output:

```
Goodbye, cruel world!
```

Note in particular the use of the modulus operator (%), and the results of integer division.

3.6 Input and output

In general, the most implementation-specific components of any program are concerned with access to external devices, such as keyboards, screens, and disks. C++, in common with many other languages, does not include facilities for communicating with such devices in the language itself. Instead, the (stream) input and output routines are not strictly part of the language itself, but depend on the stream **class library** provided with the implementation: we consider class libraries in greater detail in Part III.

As already mentioned, each source file that refers to the iostream I/O facilities must contain the line:

```
#include <iostream.h>
```

before the first reference to any of the facilities from this library.

We look at some of the essential features provided through iostream.h in the following sections.

3.6.1 The stream insertion operator revisited

Now that we have looked at the declaration of integer and floating-point variables, we are in a position to consider how we can exert greater control over the way that information is displayed on the screen and, for instance, how we can generate output in tables or control the number of decimal places that are displayed.

Let's begin with a simple example program that prints out the values of a few integers (Program 3.5):

```
// Playing with cout and <<
// Source is: 03_05.CPP

// Must include this header file
#include <iostream.h>
int main()
    {
    // Declare two integer variables
    int Int1, Int2;

    // Print out a few integer constants
    cout << 1;
    cout << 2;
    cout << 3 << endl;

    // Assign values to our integer variables
    Int1 = 11;
    Int2 = 22;

    // Print out the values of the variables
    cout << Int1 << endl;
    cout << Int2 << endl;

    /* Finally, print out the value of the
       variables again, more informatively */
```

```
cout << "Int1 = " << Int1 << " and Int2 = " << Int2 <<
endl;

return 0;
}
```

Program 3.5 The use of cout and the stream insertion operator. (☺)

The output from Program 3.5 is as follows:

```
123
11
22
Int1 = 11 and Int2 = 22
```

The operation of most of this program is straightforward. If we consider the most complex section, then the operation of the rest of the program should become clear. Consider the following lines:

```
/* Finally, print out the value of the
   variables again, with more info. */
cout << "Int1 = " << Int1 << " and Int2 = " << Int2 << endl;
```

The first two lines are comments, followed by extensive use of the stream insertion operator. The main thing to note is that the stream insertion operator works equally well with string constants and integer data, even if these different types are mixed in the same statement.

Note that programmers with a background in C would have probably written this program without making use of the endl manipulator at all. Instead, they would have used a 'new line' escape sequence, written '\n', to achieve the same result.

Thus, the following lines are *approximately* equivalent:

```
cout << Int1 << endl;
cout << Int1 << '\n';
```

Note that the lines are only 'approximately' equivalent because endl invokes an immediate flushing of the output buffer, while '\n' does not: however, in 99% of practical circumstances, no differences in output will be observed.

As well as the new line escape character, some of the other escape sequences that C++ provides are also useful. Some other examples are given in Table 3.4.

Escape sequence	Meaning
\n	'New line' (that is, carriage return, line feed)
\r	Carriage return (no line feed): that is, overwrite the current output line
\b	Backspace
\t	Tab
\'	Output single quotation mark
\"	Output double quotation mark

Table 3.4 A selection of useful escape sequences.

```
int Answer;      // Value UNDEFINED
Answer = 0;      // Value DEFINED
```

Alternatively, you can declare and (explicitly) initialize your variables at the same time, if you wish:

```
int Answer = 0; // Value DEFINED
```

The above points are illustrated in Program 3.10.

```
// Initializing Variables
// Source is: 03_10.CPP

#include <iostream.h>

int main()
    {
    int Int1, Int2 = 2001;

    // Print out the values of the variables
    // NB. Value of Int1 is undefined
    cout << "Int1 = " << Int1 << " and Int2 = " << Int2 << endl;

    return 0;
    }
```

Program 3.10   Initializing, and not-initializing, variables. (☺)

Note that the line:

```
int Int1, Int2 = 2001;
```

initializes `Int2` to 2001: `Int1` is *not* initialized (to 2001 or anything else).

One sample run from Program 3.10 is shown below (note the value of `Int1`):

```
Int1 = 3959 and Int2 = 2001
```

Here is another sample run (note the *different* value of `Int1`):

```
Int1 = 18415 and Int2 = 2001
```

In theory, were we to run the program a thousand times, we could obtain a thousand different answers: the precise values obtained will vary between systems.

We consider the initialization, scope and storage class of variables in greater depth in Chapter 6.

3.7.2   Read-only variables

It is good programming practice to define names for numerical constants, and to use the names (rather than numbers) throughout the program. In C++, this process is usually best carried out through the use of **read-only variables**.

To illustrate the use of such a variable, suppose we wish to write a program to calculate the amount of interest due on an investment. Throughout the program, we may well need to know the current interest rate. If this interest rate is (say) 7.00%, we could go through our program writing '0.07f' every time we needed this information (the significance of the 'f' was discussed in Section 3.6.1), as follows:

```
int main()
    {
    ...
    Interest_due = Capital * 0.07f;
    ...
    Saving = Reserve * 0.07f;
    ...
    }
```

However, if the interest rate changed to 8.00%, we would then have to go back through the program again, replacing all the original values. For a realistic program, this replacement process would be tedious, and error prone: if, just once, we mistyped the interest rate, or forgot a replacement, the impact on the calculations we perform could be immense, and costly.

An obvious solution would be to use a float variable, which we might sensibly call Interest_rate, to store the current interest rate value, as follows:

```
int main()
    {
    float Interest_rate = 0.07f;
    ...
    Interest_due = Capital * Interest_rate;
    ...
    Saving = Reserve * Interest_rate
    ...
    }
```

The use of a variable to store the interest rate value is an obvious and better solution. However, suppose we are debugging the program at a later date and we accidentally leave a new line in the program:

```
int main()
    {
    float Interest_rate = 0.07f;
    ...
    Interest_due = Capital * Interest_rate;
    ...
    Interest_rate = 9.0f; // Debugging statement...
    ...
    Saving = Reserve * Interest_rate;
    ...
    }
```

As the above fragment illustrates, there is still the possibility that we can (usually inadvertently) change the value of Interest_rate later in the program. To avoid this possibility, we can use a 'read-only variable' (sometimes confusingly referred to as 'constant variables') to represent symbolic constants. Such read-only variables make use of the C++ const modifier, as shown below:

```
int main()
    {
    const float INTEREST_RATE = 0.07f;
    ...
    Interest_due = Capital * INTEREST_RATE;
    ...
    Saving = Reserve * INTEREST_RATE;
    ...
    }
```

Note that it is customary in C++ (and therefore good programming practice) to use all capital letters for identifiers that represent constants.

In this example, if we try to include a line in our program:

```
INTEREST_RATE = 0.09f;
```

then the compiler will immediately generate an error message, indicating that we are trying to change the value of a 'constant object'.

3.7.3   Where to declare variables

In C, and many other structured, typed, programming languages, the programmer is forced to declare all variables at the start of the block of code in which they are to be used, before any executable statements. In simple programs (where no user-defined functions are used), this means that all variables have to be declared at the start of main().

While, in general, it is good programming practice to follow this same pattern in C++, the programmer is not constrained to do so. Instead, while variables must still be declared, this declaration need only take place immediately before first use of the variable in the program. For example, Program 3.11 shows another version of Program 3.9 discussed earlier in this chapter.

```
// Addition program - version 2
// Source is: 03_11.CPP
#include <iostream.h>
int main()
    {
    cout << "Enter first integer : ";
    int Int1;
    cin >> Int1;
    cout << "Enter second integer : ";
    int Int2;
    cin >> Int2;
    int Sum_of_Int1_and_Int2 = Int1 + Int2;
    cout << "The sum of " << Int1
        << " and "        << Int2 << " is "
        << Sum_of_Int1_and_Int2;
    return 0;
    }
```

Program 3.11   Exploiting the facility in C++ to declare variables just before they are used. This style is not recommended. (☺)

In general, programs should follow the following guidelines:

- If variables are used frequently throughout a program (or function) then the variables should be declared at the beginning of the program (or function).

- If variables are 'temporary'– that is, are used only in a few lines of code in the same part of the program – then they should be declared near to the point where they are used.

3.8 Conclusions

In this chapter, we've looked at some of the essential features of all C++ programs. Before you read any further you should, if possible, put some of this material into practice by trying to write some simple C++ programs for yourself. The exercises that follow will help get you started.

In the final introductory chapter, we go on to look at some important control statements and related operators.

Exercises

3.1 Type in the 'Goodbye, cruel world!' program. Modify the program so that it prints out your name.

3.2 Type in Program 3.9. Make sure that the program works. Modify the program so that it sums two floats instead of two integers. Print out the result on the screen, displaying only one decimal place after the point.

3.3 Write a program to confirm that the values given for the C++ binary operators in Table 3.3 are correct.

3.4 Generalize your solution to Exercise 3.3 so that it calculates results for any numbers chosen by the user.

3.5 Write a program `DIVIDE.CPP`. The program should prompt the user for two integer values (for example, 5 and 2), and store these values in two integer variables. The program should then divide the two integers, to give a real number (in this case 2.5 *not* 2). The result should be printed on the screen, displaying three decimal places.

3.6 Write a C++ program to prompt the user for a real number. The program should calculate and print out (with suitable supporting text): (a) the area of a circle with this radius; (b) the circumference of a circle with this radius; and (c) the volume of a sphere with this radius.

In each case, the results are required to a precision of three decimal places, and should be neatly set out in the form of a table.

The following formulae may jog your memory:

$$a = \pi r^2$$
$$c = 2\pi r$$
$$v = \frac{4}{3}\pi r^3$$

Where: a is the area of a circle with radius r; c is the circumference of a circle with radius r; and v is the volume of a sphere with radius r.

4 Taking control

4.1 Introduction

In Chapter 3, we looked at the basic components of all C++ programs. However, in order to be able to create anything useful, you also need to know something about control statements and related operators, the subject of this chapter.

4.2 Some important operators

We begin by looking at relational operators, logical operators, increment and decrement operators, and the ways in which multiple operators can be combined together.

More experienced programmers should note that the operators we consider here (as well as those considered in Chapter 3) can be **overloaded** to enable their use with user-defined, class-based types. Details of this process are given in Part III.

4.2.1 Binary operators

Binary operators are in general the most straightforward of C++'s operators: we shall therefore consider these before we look at unary operators in the next section.

As we saw in Chapter 3, binary operators act upon two operands. Note that binary operators are sometimes referred to as dyadic operators.

Relational operators

Relational operators allow the comparison of two values, yielding a result which depends on whether the comparison is TRUE or FALSE. A TRUE result yields a result of 1 (`int`), while a FALSE result yields a result of 0.

The relational operators are given in Table 4.1.

Operator	Meaning
>	greater than
<=	less than or equal to
>=	greater than or equal to
NB! ☞ ==	equal to
<	less than
!=	not equal to

Table 4.1 C++'s relational operators. Note that the representation of the 'equal to' operator (==) is distinct from than that of the assignment operator (=).

These operators are most frequently used in if statements (described in Section 4.4.1).

Logical operators

There are three logical operators AND (&&), OR (||) and the unary operator NOT (!). These logical operators work with logical values (TRUE and FALSE) allowing the combination of relational expressions.

For example: if (int) variable x has a value of 2:

!0	has value TRUE
(x > 1)	has value TRUE
!(x > 1)	has value FALSE
((x > 1) && (x < 4))	has value TRUE
((x >= 2) || (x < 0))	has value TRUE
((x >= 2) && (x < 0))	has value FALSE

Note that the operators && and || will **short circuit**, so that once the truth or falsehood is established, the remaining expressions will *not* be evaluated. For example, in the following example:

    ((x >= 2) || (x < 0))

if x >= 2 evaluates to TRUE, then there is no need to evaluate the expression x < 0 (and C++ will not do so).

4.2.2 The nature of truth

As far as C++ is concerned the world is a simple place in which every expression is either FALSE or TRUE. More specifically, C++ views source code according to the following rule:

- An expression which evaluates to zero (0) is FALSE;

- An expression which evaluates to *any* non-zero value is TRUE.

This can lead to some subtle errors. Just as expressions involving the relational operator ('==') have a value (TRUE or FALSE), assignment expressions (using '=') also have a **value** (which is the value of the left hand side after the assignment). To illustrate this, consider Program 4.1.

```
// Using == and =
// Source is: 04_01.CPP
#include <iostream.h>
int main (void)
    {
    int x = 3;

    cout << (x == 3) << endl;
    cout << (x == 2) << endl;

    cout << (x = 3) << endl;
    cout << (x = 2) << endl;

    return 0;
    }
```

Program 4.1 Illustrating the difference between '==' and '='. (☺)

The output from Program 4.1 is as follows:

```
1
0
3
2
```

To understand this code, remember that, '*x* == 3' is a **question**: the programmer is asking, in effect, 'is *x* equal to 3?'. Such a question can have only two possible answers
'yes' (coded as 1 in C++), or 'no' (coded as 0). By contrast, '*x* = 3' is an assignment
statement: an instruction to set the value of *x* to 3. Simply because of the way the C++
language is defined, this assignment also has a value (in this case 3), and is also TRUE
as far as C++ is concerned.

We'll see some examples of the errors caused by confusing '==' and '=' later in
this chapter.

Another side-effect caused by the above features of the language is that the use
of the NOT operator (written '!') is not reversible. Thus, for example, !!x, where x is
some non-zero integer variable, is not equivalent to x. This is illustrated in Program 4.2.

```
// Using the ! operator
// Source is: 04_02.CPP
#include <iostream.h>
int main ()
    {
    int x = 3;              // x is "TRUE"

    cout << !x << endl;     // !x is "FALSE"
    cout << !!x << endl;    // !!x is "TRUE"
    cout << ((!!x) == x);   // !!x == x is "FALSE"

    return 0;
    }
```

Program 4.2 Illustrating the use of the ! operator. (☺)

The output from Program 4.2 is as follows:

```
0
1
0
```

4.2.3 Unary operators

Unary operators act upon a single operand. They are sometimes referred to as monadic operators.

Unary versions of + and –

C++ supports unary versions of the plus (+) and minus (–) operators, so that the programmer can write (probably without thinking about it), +123 or –456.

++ and – – operators

This is an area that often causes confusion for new C++ programmers. The unary operators, increment (++) and decrement (– –), are single operators that add or subtract 1 from any value. The addition or subtraction can be done either *before* or *after* evaluation of the expression. The following examples illustrate the use of the increment operator:

```
sum = a + b++;
```

This adds a and b, assigns the result to sum, *and only then* increments b by 1. Similarly, consider the following statement:

```
sum = a + ++b;
```

This increments b by 1, *then* adds a and b together, and assigns the result to sum.
Program 4.3 illustrates the use of these operators:

```
// Playing with Pre- and Post-Increments
// Source is: 04_03.CPP

#include <iostream.h>

int main()
    {
    int Num1;

    Num1 = 10;
    cout << "Num1   = "  << Num1              << endl;
    cout << "Display and POST-increment Num1 : ";
    cout << "Num1++ = "  << Num1++             << endl;
    cout << "Num1   = "  << Num1              << endl << endl;

    Num1 = 10;
    cout << "Num1   = "  << Num1              << endl;
    cout << "Display and PRE-increment Num1 : ";
    cout << "++Num1 = "  << ++Num1             << endl;
    cout << "Num1   = "  << Num1              << endl << endl;

    return 0;
    }
```

Program 4.3   Playing with the pre- and post-increment operators. (☺)

4.2.5   Combining operators

C++ allows programmers to use an abbreviated method of writing expressions that contain multiple operators. The assignment operator (=) can be combined with the above operators (unary, binary, increment, decrement).

Most expressions of the form

```
<variable1> = <variable1> <operator> <variable2>;
```

can be replaced by

```
<variable1> <operator> = <variable2>;
```

For example:

```
a = a + b;
a = a % b;
```

can be condensed to

```
a+=b;
a%=b;
```

4.3   Iteration

Strictly, numerical iteration involves successive approximation of a required final value, with the aim of reducing some measure of error (between required and calculated values) successively with each step. The iterative process is terminated when an error criterion is satisfied.

In computer programming, iteration simply involves the repeated execution of one or more statements until some condition is satisfied. Iteration in C++ is accomplished with the while, do and for statements.

4.3.1   The while loop

The while loop is the most general loop: anything you can do with a do loop or a for loop you can also do with while (though one of the other approaches may result in neater code).

The general format of the while loop is:

```
while (expression)
    statement;
```

The **expression** is evaluated and if TRUE (see Section 4.2.2) the **statement** is executed: this process is repeated until expression is FALSE (if ever).

As with all the loops, a single statement can be replaced by a **compound statement**. That is:

```
{
// Any number of statements...
// ...each ending with a semicolon.
}
```

Program 4.7 illustrates the use of the `while` loop.

```cpp
// Program to find the average of some student exam marks
// Source is: 04_07.CPP

#include <iostream.h>
#include <iomanip.h>

int main()
    {
    float average_score;
    int class_size = 0, score, total_score = 0;

    cout    << setiosflags(ios::fixed);

    cout    << "Program to Calculate Average Exam Mark\n"
            << "----------------------------------------\n\n";
    cout    << "Marks must be in the range 0 - 100\n\n";
    cout    << "Enter mark for student number "
            << class_size + 1
            << " (type -1 to end) > ";
    cin     >> score;

    while(score != -1)
       {
       total_score += score;
       class_size++;
       cout    << "Enter mark for student number "
               << class_size + 1
               << " (type -1 to end) > ";
       cin     >> score;
       }
    average_score = (float) total_score / class_size;
    cout    << "\nAverage was " << average_score
            << " in a class of " << class_size << " students";

    return 0;
    }
```

Program 4.7   Program to find the average of some student exam marks using a `while` statement. Note that the program is not robust: it will crash if the user enters 0 marks. (☺)

A typical output from Program 4-7 is as follows:

```
Program to Calculate Average Exam Mark

Marks must be in the range 0 - 100

Enter mark for student number 1 (type -1 to end) > 5
Enter mark for student number 2 (type -1 to end) > 2
Enter mark for student number 3 (type -1 to end) > 8
Enter mark for student number 4 (type -1 to end) > -1

Average was 5.000000 in a class of 3 students
```

Let's consider how Program 4.7 works. First, we declare some variables to be used in the program, and read in some data:

```
float average_score;
int class_size = 0, score, total_score = 0;

cout    << setiosflags(ios::fixed);

cout    << "Program to Calculate Average Exam Mark\n"
        << "--------------------------------\n\n";
cout    << "Marks must be in the range 0 - 100\n\n";
cout    << "Enter mark for student number "
        << class_size + 1
        << " (type -1 to end) ?> ";
cin     >> score;
```

Next, we have the while statement itself. The basic structure is quite simple:

```
while(score != -1)
   {
   ...
   }
```

We have already read in a value for variable score: the while statement dictates that, if this value is not equal to '–1' (a code value which we presume is not a valid student mark, and which we use to indicate that the user wishes to quit the program) then the statement block following the while header will be executed.

If we assume for the moment that the user doesn't immediately type '–1', then we move on to consider the statements in the while body:

```
total_score += score;
class_size++;
cout    << "Enter mark for student number "
        << class_size + 1
        << " (type -1 to end) ?> ";
cin     >> score;
```

Again, these statements are, on their own, straightforward. Note, however, that we must prompt the user for a new score at the end of the while loop: this value of score will then be tested against the loop continuation condition (score != -1), at which point the loop will either be terminated, or repeated.

In theory, the program could be run indefinitely, looping again and again: in practice, the user will eventually run out of marks to type in, or get bored and choose to quit anyway. When this happens, the program calculates the average:

```
average_score = (float) total_score / class_size;
```

and then prints out the results:

```
cout    << "\nAverage was " << average_score
        << " in a class of " << class_size << " students";
```

Testing Program 4.7

This is our first useful program. We can test to see if the program works correctly with some simple test data:

```
Program to Calculate Average Exam Mark

Marks must be in the range 0 - 100

Enter mark for student number 1 (type -1 to end) > 0
Enter mark for student number 2 (type -1 to end) > 0
Enter mark for student number 3 (type -1 to end) > 0
Enter mark for student number 4 (type -1 to end) > -1

Average was 0.000000 in a class of 3 students
```

So far so good.

```
Program to Calculate Average Exam Mark

Marks must be in the range 0 - 100

Enter mark for student number 1 (type -1 to end) > 10
Enter mark for student number 2 (type -1 to end) > 20
Enter mark for student number 3 (type -1 to end) > 30
Enter mark for student number 4 (type -1 to end) > 40
Enter mark for student number 5 (type -1 to end) > 50
Enter mark for student number 6 (type -1 to end) > -1

Average was 30.000000 in a class of 5 students
```

The program seems to work. Finally, what happens if we change our minds after starting to run the program?

```
Program to Calculate Average Exam Mark

Marks must be in the range 0 - 100

Enter mark for student number 1 (type -1 to end) > -1
**************** CRASH!!!! *************
```

This problem arises because on this line

```
average_score = (float) total_score / class_size;
```

we are trying to divide the `total_score` by 0: theoretically, the result is infinite: no matter how powerful your computer, this operation will cause an error and (usually) crash the program. We consider ways of trapping such errors in Chapter 9.

A simple way to avoid this situation using a selection statement: we illustrate this in Section 4.4.2. We also explore some more substantial test strategies in Chapter 11.

Structuring your programs

In Chapter 3, we mentioned that C++ is a free format language. This useful feature of the language enables the programmer to lay out his or her code in a 'structured' manner. Now that we have begun to consider control statements, we are in a position to consider just what a structured program layout actually looks like.

The output from Program 4.10 is as follows:

```
Value of number is 10
Value of number is 8
Value of number is 6
Value of number is 4
Value of number is 2
Value of number is 0
```

Of course, C++ allows us to use variables to control how often a loop is executed. In Program 4.11, for example, the user is prompted to type in two numbers used to control the count range.

```
// Counting with a variable-length for loop
// Source is: 04_11.CPP

#include <iostream.h>

int main()
    {
    int number, low, high;

    cout << "Count program\n";
    cout << "-----------\n\n";

    cout << "Low value (0 - 10) ? : ";
    cin >> low;

    cout << "High value (0 - 10) ? : ";
    cin >> high;

    cout << endl;

    for (number = low; number <= high; number++)
        {
        cout << "Value of number is " << number << endl;
        }
    return 0;
    }
```

Program 4.11 Counting with a variable-length for loop. Note that the program contains no error checking: if the user mistakenly swaps the high and low values, the program will not count down, but will do nothing. (☺)

A typical run of Program 4.11 gives this output:

```
Count program

Low value (0 - 10) ? : 4
High value (0 - 10) ? : 9

Value of number is 4
Value of number is 5
Value of number is 6
Value of number is 7
Value of number is 8
Value of number is 9
```

Note that in Program 4.11, no attempt is made to restrict the range of numbers typed in by the user. If the user types in a 'low' value higher than the 'high' value, then the program will not count down (as the user might expect). Instead, because the loop control condition in the `for` header is never satisfied, the loop does not execute.

This possibility is illustrated in the following program output:

```
Count program

Low value  (0 - 10) ? : 5
High value (0 - 10) ? : 4
```

We shall be in a position to make this program more flexible when we have investigated C++ selection statements later in this chapter.

In the meantime, consider yet another variation on the important `for` loop (Program 4.12):

```cpp
// Counting up with a for loop - FAULTY VERSION
// Source is: 04_12.CPP

#include <iostream.h>

int main()
    {
    int number;

    for (number = 0; number <= 5; number++);
        {
        cout << "Value of number is " << number << endl;
        }

    return 0;
    }
```

Program 4.12 A program which illustrates a common programming error. Note the extra ';' at the end of the `for` loop header. (☺)

Program 4.12 gives this output:

```
Value of number is 6
```

This erroneous output arises because, as far as the compiler is concerned, the `for` loop ends with the semi-colon at the end of the header. Only the statements before that semi-colon (in this case none!) are executed under the control of the header. Only when the loop has finished are the following block of statements executed.

The program also illustrates another important point that occasionally catches out new programmers. The count in this case runs from 0 up to 5, yet the value printed here is 6.

We can understand why a value of 6 is printed if we consider how the loop operates. Remember that after executing the block of statements (or, in this case, executing no statements), the loop control variable is incremented. After the increment is applied, the continuation condition is checked: the loop terminates when this condition is no longer satisfied. In this case, the loop is executed with a control value of 5; this value is then incremented (to 6), and the loop continuation condition is checked, and fails. The program then continues with number set to a value of 6, as illustrated by the output obtained.

Finally, consider one last simple `for` loop (Program 4.13):

```cpp
// Summation with a for loop
// Source is: 04_13.CPP

#include <iostream.h>
#include <iomanip.h>

int main()
    {
    int number;
    int sum_int = 0;
    long sum_long_int = 0;
    float sum_float = 0.0f;
    double sum_double = 0.0;

    // Can "count down" as easily as counting up
    for (number = 1000; number >= 0; number -= 3)
        {
        sum_long_int += number;
        sum_int += number;
        sum_float += number;
        sum_double += number;
        }

    cout << setiosflags(ios::fixed);
    cout << setprecision(1);

    // Print out the results
    cout << "Sum (stored as an int) is    " << sum_int
                                            << endl;
    cout << "Sum (stored as a long int) is " << sum_long_int
                                            << endl;
    cout << "Sum (stored as a float) is    " << sum_float
                                            << endl;
    cout << "Sum (stored as a double) is   " << sum_double
                                            << endl;

    return 0;
    }
```

Program 4.13 Summing up numbers with a `for` loop. (☺)

The output from Program 4.13 is as follows:

```
Sum (stored as an int) is    -29441
Sum (stored as a long int)is 167167
Sum (stored as a float) is    167167.0
Sum (stored as a double) is  167167.0
```

This time the problem is not really the fault of the `for` statement. Here we use the `for` loop to calculate the sum of a series of numbers {1000, 997, 994, ... }. We

several copies of this sum, storing the results as an integer, a long integer, a float and a double. If we accept a majority decision, then the answer is 167 167.

In the case of the result stored as an integer, however, we get a different answer. Why? If you think back to our first discussion of integers, you'll remember that on most systems the maximum value that can be stored in an `int` is often about 32 000, which is a lot less than the result here. The integer variable `sum_int` does its best, but it simply can't store integers this large.

One of the 'charms' of C++ is that it allows you, the programmer, the flexibility of writing such erroneous programs. Remember that Program 4.13 did not crash, and that the compiler did not generate any errors: in different circumstances, you might well not have been aware that there was a problem, until, for example, your program started issuing cheques for negative salary amounts.

4.3.4 'Where to declare' revisited

In Chapter 3, we argued that, if variables are temporary or used only in one isolated area of a program, then they should be declared close to the point at which they are used.

A good example of the application of this general rule often arises through the use of the `for` loop. For example, rather than writing:

```
int number;

...

for (number = 1000; number >= 0; number -= 3)
    {
    ...
    }
```

most C++ programmers would write:

```
...

for (int number = 1000; number >= 0; number -= 3)
    {
    ...
    }
```

that is, they would declare the loop control variable (`number`) in the `for` header. In most circumstances, the loop control variable is a temporary variable, with influence on in the local code area: 'in header' declarations are then an excellent idea.

It is important to realize why this declaration works, however, so that you're not tempted to try using something like this:

```
while(int x > 0)
    {
    ...
    }
```

which *won't* work.

To understand the difference, you have to remember that any variable can only be defined once in the program. In the `for` loop, the initialization (`number = 1000`) only takes place once, and a combined definition and initialization (`int number = 1000`) therefore works in most circumstances. In the `while` loop, the test (`x > 0`) is performed once for every circuit of the loop: an attempt at definition (int x > 0) in such circumstances means (implicitly) that the programmer is trying to redefine variable x, something which the compiler will not allow.

4.3.5 Nested `for` loops

One particularly common programming construct is known as a 'nested' loop, a term which simply means a 'loop within a loop'.

Program 4.14 shows a nested `for` loop in operation.

```
// Nested for loops
// Source is: 04_14.CPP

#include <iostream.h>

int main()
    {
    for (int outer = 1; outer <= 3; outer++)
        {
        cout << "outer : " << outer << endl;

        for (int inner = 4; inner <= 6; inner++)
            {
            cout << " inner : " << inner << endl;
            }

        }

    return 0;
    }
```

Program 4.14 Nested `for` loops. Note that the structure of the program in the listing reflects the flow of control when the program runs. (☺)

The output from Program 4.14 is as follows:

```
outer : 1
        inner : 4
        inner : 5
        inner : 6
outer : 2
        inner : 4
        inner : 5
        inner : 6
outer : 3
        inner : 4
        inner : 5
        inner : 6
```

Note the indentation used in the nested `for` loop. As we discussed in Section 4.3.1, if you want to avoid spending your life debugging, then your program layout should reflect the operation of your program. In this case, the basic structure is:

```
int main()
    for (outer …)
        for (inner …)
```

reflecting the fact that, within the `main()` function, the outer `for` loop is the most important statement: under control of this outer loop, depending on the conditions, an inner `for` loop may also execute.

If we had laid the program out as shown in Program 4.15, then the structure would have implied (incorrectly) to the reader that first loop `a` is executed to completion, then loop `b` is executed to completion: this impression would have been, of course, erroneous, and may well have slowed or confused any later program maintenance or upgrade tasks.

```
// Badly structured nested for loops
// Source is: 04_15.CPP

#include <iostream.h>

int main() {
for (int a = 1; a <= 3; a++) {
cout << "a : " << a << endl;
for (int b = 4; b <= 6; b++) {
cout << " b : " << b << endl;
}} return 0; }
```

Program 4.15 Nested `for` loops. Note that the structure of the program does not reflect the flow of control: such program style should be avoided. (☹)

4.3.6 The do loop

The generic format of the `do` loop is:

```
do statement while (expression);
```

This differs from the `while` loop in that the statements in the `do` loop always execute at least once. An example is shown in Program 4.16.

```
// Playing with the do/while structure
// Source is: 04_16.CPP

#include <iostream.h>

int main()
    {
    int counter = 10;

    do {
        cout << counter << " ";
        } while (--counter >= 1); // Don't forget the ;

    return 0;
    }
```

Program 4.16 Using a `do` loop. (☺)

The output from Program 4.16 is as follows:

```
10 9 8 7 6 5 4 3 2 1
```

Note that omission of the final semi-colon after the 'while' test is a common error for inexperienced C++ programmers.

4.4   Selection statements

Selection statements choose – from among one or more alternatives – the action that the computer is to carry out. The selection is based on the value of a control expression.

C++ provides two selection statements: the if-else statement, and the switch statement.

4.4.1   The if...else statement

The general format of the if...else statement is:

```
if (expression)
     statement1;
else
     statement2;
```

where expression must again resolve to an **integer** value. If this **value** is non zero (TRUE) then *statement1* is executed, otherwise *statement2* is executed.

In simple cases, we can reduce this to:

```
if (expression)
     statement1;
```

omitting the else clause. As before, *statement1* and/or *statement2* can be replaced by compound statements.

Program 4.17 illustrates the use of this statement.

```
// Playing with the if...else statement
// Source is: 04_17.CPP

#include <iostream.h>

int main()
    {
    int Int1, Int2;

    cout << "Type two integers, then <RETURN> : ";
    cin >> Int1 >> Int2;

    /* This is the recommended layout for nested
       if-else statements: related if and else
       components should line up */
    if (Int1 == Int2)
        {
        cout << Int1 << " is equal to " << Int2 << endl;
```

```
            }
        else
            {
            if (Int1 > Int2)
                {
                cout << Int1 << " is greater than " << Int2 << endl;
                }
            else
                {
                // Int1 < Int2 (by default)
                cout << Int1 << " is less than " << Int2 << endl;
                }
            }
        return 0;
        }
```

Program 4.17   Playing with the `if…else` statement (☺)

A typical output from Program 4.17 is as follows:

```
Type two integers, then <RETURN> : 6 9
6 is less than 9
```

Understanding the `if` statement

As we have seen, the `if` statement can take the simple form:

```
if (expression)
    {
    /* expression evaluates to TRUE
        - i.e. a NON-ZERO value
            so do statements listed here. */
    }
```

Here, the expression may well involve one of the binary operators listed above, for example:

```
if (x >= 3)
    {
        ...
    }
```

However, the following code fragment is also perfectly valid (if not very useful):

```
if (3)
    {
        ...
    }
```

In this case, since the integer constant '3' is non-zero, the block of code under the `if` header would *always* execute.

To take this a little further, consider the error made by all C++ programmers at some point, of writing an if statement as follows:

```
if (x = 3)
    {
    ...
    }
```

The reasons why this statement compiles and runs were discussed in Section 4.2.2.

To illustrate the erroneous use of '=' in a more realistic situation, let's look at another, almost identical, version of the if-else program we considered above (Program 4.18).

```
// Playing with the if...else statement
// Source is: 04_18.CPP

#include <iostream.h>

int main()
    {
    int Int1, Int2;

    cout << "Type two integers, then <RETURN> : ";
    cin >> Int1 >> Int2;

    // NOTE: "=" cf. "=="
    if (Int1 = Int2)
        {
        cout << Int1 << " is equal to " << Int2 << endl;
        }
    else
        {
        if (Int1 > Int2)
            {
            cout << Int1 << " is greater than " << Int2 << endl;
            }
        else
            {
            // Int1 < Int2 (by default)
            cout << Int1 << " is less than " << Int2 << endl;
            }
        }
    return 0;
    }
```

Program 4.18   Incorrect use of the assignment operator. (☹)

The output from four separate runs of Program 4.18 shows that it is not operating correctly:

```
Type two integers, then <RETURN> : 5 5
5 is equal to 5
```

```
Type two integers, then <RETURN> : 1 0
0 is less than 0
```

```
Type two integers, then <RETURN> : 1 3
3 is equal to 3
```

```
Type two integers, then <RETURN> : 100 1
1 is equal to 1
```

```
Type two integers, then <RETURN> : 2001 0
0 is less than 0
```

You need to be aware of this potential problem to avoid errors in your own programs.

Using error flags in `if` statements

A common feature of C++ programs is to control selection and loop statements through 'flag' variables. By way of example, consider Program 4.19.

```cpp
// Demonstrating error flags
// Source is: 04_19.CPP
#include <iostream.h>
int main()
    {
    int error_flag_set = 1;
    if (error_flag_set)
        {
        cout << "Error detected";
        }
    else
        {
        cout << "No errors detected";
        }
    return 0;
    }
```

Program 4.19   Introducing control flags. (☺)

In Program 4.19, control of the program hinges on the value of the variable `error_flag_set`. As we have seen previously (Section 4.4.1), if this 'flag' has a value of 0 (that is FALSE), then the 'else' statement will be triggered, giving the output 'No errors detected'. For all other values of `error_flag_set` (as is the case here) an output of 'Errors detected' will be produced.

4.4.2   Using loops *and* selection statements

It most realistic programs, a combination of loops and selection statements will be used. Program 4.20 illustrates one possible combination.

```
// Program to find the average of some student exam marks
// Updated version - works with 0 students
// Source is: 04_20.CPP

#include <iostream.h>
#include <iomanip.h>

int main()
    {
    float average_mark;
    int class_size = 0, mark, total_mark = 0;

    cout << setiosflags(ios::fixed);
    cout << setprecision(2);

    cout << "Program to Calculate Average Exam Mark\n"
         << "-------------------------------\n\n";
    cout << "Marks must be in the range 0 - 100\n\n";

    do
        {
        cout << "Enter mark for student number "
             << class_size + 1
             << " (type -1 to end) ?> ";
        cin  >> mark;
        } while ((mark < -1) || (mark > 100));

    while(mark != -1)
        {
        total_mark += mark;
        class_size++;
        do
            {
            cout << "Enter mark for student number "
                 << class_size + 1
                 << " (type -1 to end) ?> ";
            cin  >> mark;
            } while ((mark < -1) || (mark > 100));
        }

    if (class_size)
        {
        average_mark = (float) total_mark / class_size;
        cout << "\nAverage was " << average_mark
             << "% in a class of " << class_size << " students";
        }

    return 0;
    }
```

Program 4.20   An improved version of Program 4.7. (☺)

Trying two simple test runs suggests that Program 4.20 works correctly:

```
Program to Calculate Average Exam Mark

Marks must be in the range 0 - 100

Enter mark for student number 1 (type -1 to end) ?> 60
Enter mark for student number 2 (type -1 to end) ?> 60
Enter mark for student number 3 (type -1 to end) ?> 200
Enter mark for student number 3 (type -1 to end) ?> 60
Enter mark for student number 4 (type -1 to end) ?> -1

Average was 60.00% in a class of 3 students
```

This time, having zero students causes no errors, just a normal termination of the program.

```
Program to Calculate Average Exam Mark

Marks must be in the range 0 - 100

Enter mark for student number 1 (type -1 to end) ?> -1
```

4.4.3 The `switch` statement

It can often improve the readability of your program to replace repeated `if..else if..else if..` constructs with a single `switch` statement. This statement has the general format:

```
switch (expression)
    {
    case const-expr:
        statements;
        break; // Optional (but usual)
    case const-expr:
        statements;
        break; // Optional (but usual)

    ...
    default:
        statements; // Optional
    }
```

Each case is **labelled** by one or more integer-valued constants. If one of these case labels matches the expression value, execution begins with the statements following the matching label. Because 'cases' are simply labels, it follows that execution continues from one case to the next unless explicit action is taken to prevent this: the `break` statement, discussed in more detail in Section 4.4.4, is the usual way of achieving this.

The 'default' case label is optional, but generally useful: if one is present, execution will begin at the default statement if none of the other matches is satisfied. If there is no default label in such circumstances, then no statement is executed (Program 4.21).

```
// Playing with the switch() statement
// Source is: 04_21.CPP

#include <iostream.h>

int main()
    {
    int number;

    // Tell the user what the program does
    cout << "Convert Integers to Strings Using Switch\n";
    cout << "-------------------------------- \n";

    // Ask the user for a small integer
    cout << "Type in a number (1 - 4), then <ENTER> : ";
    cin >> number;

    // Now for the switch statement
    switch(number)
        {
        case 1:
            // User typed '1'
            cout << "One!";
            break;
        case 2:
            // User typed '2'
            cout << "Two!";
            break;
        case 3:
            // User typed '3'
            cout << "Three!";
            break;
        case 4:
            // User typed '4'
            cout << "Four!";
            break;
        default:
            // Don't know what the user typed
            cout << "???";
        }

    return 0;
    }
```

Program 4.21   Using the `switch` statement. (☺)

The output from Program 4.21 on three separate runs is as follows:

```
Convert Integers to Strings Using Switch
Type in a number (1 - 4), then <ENTER> : 4
Four!
```

```
Convert Integers to Strings Using Switch
Type in a number (1 - 4), then <ENTER> : 3
Three!
```

```
Convert Integers to Strings Using Switch
Type in a number (1 - 4), then <ENTER> : 7
???
```

The function of the break statements is clarified by comparing the operation of Program 4.21 with that of Program 4.22.

```cpp
// Playing with the switch() statement
// Source is: 04_22.CPP
#include <iostream.h>
int main()
    {
    int number;

    // Tell the user what the program does
    cout << "Countdown Program\n";
    cout << "-------------- \n";

    // Ask the user for a small integer
    cout << "Type in the number of seconds till launch (1 - 4) : ";
    cin >> number;

    // Now for the switch statement (with only one "break")
    switch(number)
        {
        case 4:
            // User typed '4'
            cout << "\nFour!\n";
        case 3:
            // User typed '4' or '3'
            cout << "\nThree!\n";
        case 2:
            // User typed '4' or '3' or '2'
            cout << "\nTwo!\n";
        case 1:
            // User typed '4' or '3' or '2' or '1'
            cout << "\nOne!\n";
            cout << "\nLift Off!\n";
            break;
        default:
            // Don't know what the user typed
            cout << "\nCountdown aborted.";
        }
    return 0;
    }
```

Program 4.22 Using the switch statement without break. (☺)

The output from Program 4.22 is as follows:

```
Countdown Program
Type in the number of seconds till launch (1 - 4) : 4
Four!
Three!
Two!
One!
Lift Off!
```

The usefulness of the switch statement is illustrated by repeating Program 4.21, this time replacing the switch with an if-else ladder (Program 4.23). The output is as before.

```cpp
// Replacing switch with if-else
// Source is: 04_23.CPP

#include <iostream.h>

int main()
    {
    int number;

    // Tell the user what the program does
    cout << "Convert Integers to Strings Using if-else\n";
    cout << "----------------------------------------\n";

    // Ask the user for a small integer
    cout << "Type in a number (1 - 4), then <ENTER> : ";
    cin >> number;

    if (number == 1)
        {
        // User typed '1'
        cout << "One!";
        }
    else
        {
        if (number == 2)
            {
            // User typed '2'
            cout << "Two!";
            }
        else
            {
            if (number == 3)
                {
                // User typed '3'
                cout << "Three!";
                }
            else
```

```
                    {
                    if (number == 4)
                        {
                        // User typed '4'
                        cout << "Four!";
                        }
                    else
                        {
                        // Don't know what the user typed
                        cout << "???";
                        }
                    }
                }
            }
        return 0;
        }
```

Program 4.23   Repeating Program 4.21 using an `if-else` ladder. (☺)

4.4.4   Jump statements

C has three jump statements: `break`, `continue` and `goto`.

Before we consider these statements, a word (or two) of warning:

> *The* break, continue *and* goto *statements are inherently 'unstructured', and can lead to very confusing code if used extensively.*

We'll be in a better position to understand why such a warning is necessary at the end of the chapter.

Using break **and** continue

The `break` statement can be used with all three loop statements and, as seen above, with the `switch` statement, but not with the `if...else` statement. It permits the quick and easy exit from a loop, before the end is reached, and allows the exit from a `switch` statement.

Similarly, it is sometimes necessary to skip the rest of a loop and start again at the top. The `continue` statement allows this (Program 4.24).

```
// Using the break and continue statements in a for structure
// For illustrative purposes only !
// Source is: 04_24.CPP

#include <iostream.h>

int main()
    {
    int loop_control;

    for (loop_control = 1; loop_control <= 10; loop_control++)
        {
        if (loop_control == 4)
            {
```

```
                cout << "About to 'continue' to head of loop...\n";
                continue;
                }
            if (loop_control == 8)
                {
                cout << "About to 'break' out of loop
                        altogether...\n";
                break;
                }
            cout << "Loop value is now : " << loop_control << endl;
            }
    cout << "\nNote that '4' was not printed.";
    cout << "\nNote that break aborts the loop, not the
            program.";

    return 0;
    }
```

Program 4.24 Using the `break` and `continue` statements in a `for` structure (☹)

The output from Program 4.24 is as follows:

```
Loop value is now : 1
Loop value is now : 2
Loop value is now : 3
About to 'continue' to head of loop...
Loop value is now : 5
Loop value is now : 6
Loop value is now : 7
About to 'break' out of loop altogether...

Note that '4' was not printed.
Note that break aborts the loop, not the program.
```

Using `goto` (if you must)

Use the `goto` statement sparingly. Often you will find that programming purists will react violently to the mere sight of a single such statement in your code. However, the `goto` statement has its *occasional* uses: in particular, it provides a reasonably elegant way of escaping from a labyrinth of deeply nested `for` loops.

Program 4.25 and Program 4.26 illustrate the problem, while Program 4.27 provides a solution using `goto`. Remember, however, that it is *always* possible to avoid using `goto` and you should generally do so.

```
// Playing with the break statement
// Another example
// Source is: 04_25.CPP

#include <iostream.h>

int main()
```

```
{
// The break statement exits the
// NEAREST CLOSING in for, while
// and do-while loops (as well as
// switch statements)
for (int i = 1; i <= 3; i++)
     { // Outer loop
     for (int j = 1; j <= 3; j++)
          { // Inner loop
          if ((i == 2) && (j == 2))
             {
             cout << "*** BREAK! ***\n";
             break;
             }
          cout << i << " " << j << endl;
          } // Inner loop
     } // Outer loop
return 0;
}
```

Program 4.25   Trying to escape from nested loops (v1.0). (☺)

The output from Program 4.25 is as follows:

```
1 1
1 2
1 3
2 1
*** BREAK! ***
3 1
3 2
3 3
```

The break statement (itself unstructured) allows us only to escape from one level of the loop: if we want to escape out of the nested loop altogether, we need a more drastic solution. One possibility is to use multiple break statements, as illustrated in Program 4.26.

```
// Playing with the break statement
// Another example
// Source is: 04_26.CPP

#include <iostream.h>

int main()
     {
     for (int i = 1; i <= 3; i++)
          { // Outer loop
          for (int j = 1; j <= 3; j++)
               { // Inner loop
               if ((i == 2) && (j == 2))
                  {
```

```
                            cout << "*** BREAK! ***\n";
                            break;
                            }
                        cout << i << " " << j << endl;
                        } // Inner loop
                if ((i == 2) && (j == 2))
                    {
                    cout << "*** BREAK! ***\n";
                    break;
                    }
                } // Outer loop
        return 0;
        }
```

Program 4.26 Trying to escape from nested loops (v2.0). (☺)

The output from Program 4.26 is as follows:

```
1 1
1 2
1 3
2 1
*** BREAK! ***
*** BREAK! ***
```

The other, and often more elegant, way of escaping from deeply nested loops is to use the goto statement: Program 4.27 demonstrates the technique.

```
// Playing with the GOTO statement
// Source is: 04_27.CPP

#include <iostream.h>

int main()
    {
    // The goto statement allows
    // us to exit completely from
    // the nested loop
    for (int i = 1; i <= 3; i++)
        { // Outer loop
        for (int j = 1; j <= 3; j++)
            { // Inner loop
            if ((i == 2) && (j == 2))
                {
                cout << "*** GOTO! ***\n";
                goto loop_break;
                }
            cout << i << " " << j << endl;
            } // Inner loop
        } // Outer loop
    loop_break:
```

```
            cout << "The end of structured programming...\n";
        return 0;
        }
```

Program 4.27   Trying to escape from nested loops (v3.0). (☺)

The output from Program 4.27 is as follows:

```
    1 1
    1 2
    1 3
    2 1
    *** GOTO! ***
    The end of structured programming...
```

4.4.5   For ever...

Consider the following `for` loop:

```
    ...
    for(;;)
        {
        ...
        ...
        }
    ...
```

This code is valid, but the loop is infinite. In general, such loops are better replaced by a `while` equivalent, but you may see examples of `for` loops used in this way, and should understand how they operate.

In order to escape from such a loop, you would require to use a jump statement (Program 4.28).

```
// Playing with the infinite for loop
// Source is: 04_28.CPP

#include <iostream.h>

int main()
    {
    const int PASSWORD = 1234;
    int guess;

    for (;;)
    {
    cout << "Type the password : ";
    cin >> guess;

    if (guess == PASSWORD)
        {
        cout << "Correct password received.";
        break;
```

```
              }
          }
      return 0;
      }
```

Program 4.28 An infinite `for` loop ((☹))

The output from Program 4.28 is as follows:

```
      Type the password : 1243
      Type the password : 2001
      Type the password : 673
      Type the password : 1234
      Correct password received.
```

4.5 Advanced operators

We conclude this chapter by considering two of C++'s more complex operators: the conditional operator and the comma operator.

4.5.1 The conditional operator

C++ also has an operator for selection: the conditional operator. This is the only trinary operator in C++: its three operands are separated by the symbols '?' and ':' as follows:

```
      expression-c ? expression-t : expression-f
```

Here, *expression-c* is the control expression; its value determines which of the following expressions (*expression-t,* or *expression-f*) will be evaluated. If *expression-c* yields TRUE, *expression-t* is evaluated and its value is returned by the conditional operator. If *expression-c* yields FALSE, *expression-f* is evaluated and its value is returned.

For example, the following expression yields the maximum of the values of *m* and *n*:

```
      (m >= n) ? (m) : (n)
```

So that we can assign this maximum value to *x* with the following line:

```
      x = ((m >= n) ? (m) : (n))
```

Note that the parentheses are optional, but generally improve the readability of the code (and you should therefore use them!).

4.5.2 The comma operator

We often need to evaluate a series of expressions sequentially (one after another). We can usually do this by writing a separate expression statement for each expression. Sometimes, however, we need to evaluate several expressions where only one expression is allowed: in such cases we use the comma operator.

The comma operator is a powerful feature of C++ programming, which can cause some confusion when you first encounter it. It is used between multiple expressions inside a set of parentheses. These expressions are evaluated from left to right and the entire expression assumes the value of the last one evaluated. This means that the following assignment statement (which is syntactically correct, but not very useful)...

```
comma = (100,23,56,0);
```

assigns a value of 0 to the variable comma (assuming, of course, that comma has previously been declared appropriately).

You may by now be wondering where you would actually use such a feature. In fact, the comma operator is most often used in a for structure, where it enables the programmer to use multiple initialization and/or multiple increment expressions. The for statement format allows one expression for initializing a variable, and one expression for incrementing a variable. By using the comma operator, however, each of those expressions can be made up of sub-expressions that initialize or increment different variables.

For example, consider Program 4.29 and its output.

```
// Playing with the comma operator
// Source is: 04_29.CPP

#include <iostream.h>

int main()
    {
    cout << "Celsius\tFahrenheit\n"
         << "----- \t--------- \n";
    for (int c = 0, f = 32; c <= 100; c +=10, f = (c * 9)/5 + 32)
        {
        cout << " " << c << "\t" << " " << f << endl;
        }
    return 0;
    }
```

Program 4.29 An example of spaghetti C++ code. (☺)

The output from Program 4.29 is as follows:

```
Celsius    Fahrenheit
0          32
10         50
20         68
30         86
40         104
50         122
60         140
70         158
80         176
90         194
100        212
```

Here, the initialization expression is familiar from the start of many programs:

```
int c = 0, f = 32
```

This line, of course, declares integer variables *c* and *f*, and initializes them as indicated. After each execution of the controlled statement, the expression:

```
c +=10, f = (c * 9)/5 + 32
```

increments *c* by 10, and performs a more complex calculation to derive the appropriate value of *f*.

To summarize, the comma operator can be a useful feature of C++: however, it also allows you to write code that, while it may be efficient, is often difficult to understand. Use it sparingly!

4.6 Conclusions

When you have practised using the features of C++ outlined in this chapter, you will be in a position to write substantial, **monolithic**, C++ programs.

In Chapter 6, we go on to look at ways in which you can break up your programming problems into more easily manageable chunks, and solve the resulting subproblems using C++ functions. This procedure lies at the heart of the process-oriented software development technique.

We shall begin to explore process-oriented software development in Part I, starting with a short case study.

Exercises

4.1 Make sure that Program 4.7 works, and then modify it so that it finds the average of exactly 10 marks, using a `for` statement in place of the `while` statement.

4.2 Make sure that Program 4.22 works as intended, and then modify it so that it uses `if...else` statements in place of the `switch` statement.

4.3 In this chapter it was asserted that the use of the `goto` statement can always be avoided. Demonstrate that this is the case by rewriting program Program 4.27 without using *any* of the break statements: your modified program should work precisely as before. How elegant and readable do you think your `goto`-less code is? Which version would be easier to debug?

4.4 Write two short programs that add up a list of integers (of unspecified length) typed in by the user. The programs should, as far as the user is concerned, be identical. However, one should be written using an infinite `for` loop (as described in Section 4.4.5), while the other should use no jump statements.

4.5 Write a C++ program that prompts the user to type in an integer. The program will then calculate and print out the **absolute value** of that integer twice. The first calculation will use an `if...else` statement, and the second will use the conditional operator. Your program should generate output similar to the following:

```
Type an integer: -1
The absolute value (using if-else) is: 1
The absolute value (using the conditional operator) is: 1
```

4.6   Write a C++ program that will prompt the user to type in five integers, then will print out the values of the largest and of the smallest.

4.7   As part of the software for the next European election, you are asked to write a program that prompts the user to type in four numbers, each between 1 and 20. The marks represent the number of seats won by four political parties in some (arbitrary) constituency. The output of your program should be a histogram representing the election result: for instance, if the user types in 10,3,7,15 as the data, then the program should generate the following output.

```
PARTY 0: **********
PARTY 1: ***
PARTY 2: *******
PARTY 3: ***************
```

4.8   The factorial of a positive integer n ($n!$) is equal to the product of the positive integers from 1 to n. Write a C++ program that calculates the factorials of the integers from 1 to 5, printing the results out neatly in a table.

4.9   In the UK, income tax is calculated as follows (year 1994/95):

First £3445	No tax
Next £3000	20% tax
Next £20 700	25% tax
Remainder	40% tax

For example, someone earning £4445.00 would pay no tax on the first £3445.00, and 20% on the remaining £1000.00: a total of £200.00 tax. Write a C++ program to calculate the tax due on any arbitrary salary.

4.10 Write a C++ program that calculates and prints the sum of all the even integers between 33 000 and 35 000.

PART I

Process-oriented software development

5 Case study:
Harry Hacker (Programming) Ltd

5.1 Introduction

Software engineering means building software solutions to other people's problems. As we saw in the introductory chapters, the problems for which the engineer is asked to develop solutions are usually substantial ones and, as a consequence, all engineering methodologies begin by trying to analyse the initial problem into 'sub-problems' of a more manageable size. Similarly, all methods involve the programmer writing code modules to solve each sub-problem, modules which will ultimately be synthesized: that is, assembled together to provide a solution to the original problem. The central differences between the three different software engineering methods considered in Parts I to III of this book lie, firstly, in the way the initial problem is analysed (a process we will begin to consider in Chapter 12), and secondly, in the type of program components which are used to construct the solution.

The most widely used software engineering methods are process-oriented (or structured) methods. From the perspective of the programmer, process-oriented methods involve assembling programs from C++ functions.

We begin this part of the book by considering a brief fable from the archives of Leicester Software Engineering (introduced in Chapter 2) to illustrate the need for functions.

5.2 The scenario

In the recent recession, times have been rather hard at Leicester Software Engineering (LSE), and there has been little work about. Harry Hacker, the company programmer, had been filling in his time tidying up the company database, when he discovered (by accident, he claims) the wages file. Unable to resist reading through the pay details (see p. 16), Harry realized that his salary was much lower than that of everyone else in the company.

Stung by this discovery, Harry decides that he can go it alone. He immediately resigns from LSE and sets up his own rival software house (Figure 5.1).

GOTO

Harry Hacker (Programming) Ltd

for GREAT programs – CHEAP and FAST

Figure 5.1   The Harry Hacker (Programming) Ltd company logo.

Harry manages to rent a small office, in an inexpensive part of town. After two weeks in business, the telephone has never rung, he's had no work, and hasn't eaten for two days. Harry is starting to get a little desperate, and even beginning to regret leaving LSE.

Without warning, the telephone does ring: on the phone is Conrad Kreet, from Anderson Building Construction (ABC) Ltd. Mr Kreet wants Harry Hacker (Programming) Ltd to write them some software. Naturally, Harry jumps at the chance.

He asks for further details ...

5.2.1   The initial specification

ABC are in the office building business. Their clients, they have found, like to have their offices carpeted before they move in. Originally, ABC used to employ another company to fit the carpets, but now they have decided that they can do this job 'in house' and make a little more money on each office building they sell.

ABC's problem appears to be a very simple one. The office buildings they construct have several rooms (typically three). Each room is to be carpeted with the same carpet material. ABC will make the measurements of each room in the building (length and width, in metres). They want a program to take the room measurements from each room, and calculate the area of each type of carpet that they require for the building as a whole.

5.2.2   Harry's solution

Having had a quick think about what ABC require, Harry sits down and applies himself to producing Program 5.1.

```
// Carpet Area Calculation v1.0
// Source is: 05_01.CPP

#include <iostream.h>

int main()
    {
    float width, length;

    cout << "\nROOM 1\n";
    cout << "Type in width (in metres) <RETURN>: ";
    cin  >> width;
    cout << "Type in length (in metres) <RETURN>: ";
    cin  >> length;
    cout << "Area of carpet for Room 1 is: "
         << width * length << endl;
```

```
cout    << "\nROOM 2\n";
cout    << "Type in width (in metres) <RETURN>: ";
cin     >> width;
cout    << "Type in length (in metres) <RETURN>: ";
cin     >> length;
cout    << "Area of carpet for Room 2 is: "
        << width * length << endl;

cout    << "\nROOM 3\n";
cout    << "Type in width (in metres) <RETURN>: ";
cin     >> width;
cout    << "Type in length (in metres) <RETURN>: ";
cin     >> length;
cout    << "Area of carpet for Room 3 is: "
        << width * length << endl;

return 0;
}
```

Program 5.1   Harry Hacker's C++ program for calculating the area of carpet required in an office v1.0. (☺)

The program gives the following output during a single test run:

```
ROOM 1
Type in width (in metres) <RETURN>: 3
Type in length (in metres) <RETURN>: 2
Area of carpet for Room 1 is: 6

ROOM 2
Type in width (in metres) <RETURN>: 4.5
Type in length (in metres) <RETURN>: 3.2
Area of carpet for Room 2 is: 14.4

ROOM 3
Type in width (in metres) <RETURN>: 3.1
Type in length (in metres) <RETURN>: 4
Area of carpet for Room 3 is: 12.4
```

Harry rushes back to ABC and shows them the results. Conrad Kreet is very impressed by the speed of Harry's programming, and generally happy with the way the program works: the only thing is, he has decided that ABC need to put carpet on the *ceiling* of the offices as well as on the floor. Apparently, Mr Kreet says, their business customers prefer their offices this way.

Harry shakes his head a bit at this, but ABC are paying, so he bites his tongue. He goes back to his dingy office and quickly alters his program (Program 5.2).

```
// Carpet Area Calculation v2.0 (includes ceiling…)
// Source is: 05_02.CPP

#include <iostream.h>
int main()
    {
    float width, length;
```

```
cout   << "\nROOM 1\n";
cout   << "Type in width (in metres) <RETURN>: ";
cin    >> width;
cout   << "Type in length (in metres) <RETURN>: ";
cin    >> length;
cout   << "Area of carpet for Room 1 is: "
       << 2 * width * length << endl;

cout   << "\nROOM 2\n";
cout   << "Type in width (in metres) <RETURN>: ";
cin    >> width;
cout   << "Type in length (in metres) <RETURN>: ";
cin    >> length;
cout   << "Area of carpet for Room 2 is: "
       << 2 * width * length << endl;

cout   << "\nROOM 3\n";
cout   << "Type in width (in metres) <RETURN>: ";
cin    >> width;
cout   << "Type in length (in metres) <RETURN>: ";
cin    >> length;
cout   << "Area of carpet for Room 3 is: "
       << width * length << endl;

return 0;
}
```

Program 5.2   Harry Hacker's C++ program for calculating the area of carpet required in an office v2.0. (☹)

Harry's modified program produces the following output:

```
ROOM 1
Type in width (in metres) <RETURN>: 1
Type in length (in metres) <RETURN>: 1
Area of carpet for Room 1 is: 2

ROOM 2
Type in width (in metres) <RETURN>: 1
Type in length (in metres) <RETURN>: 1
Area of carpet for Room 2 is: 2

ROOM 3
Type in width (in metres) <RETURN>: 1
Type in length (in metres) <RETURN>: 1
Area of carpet for Room 3 is: 1
```

Again, Harry demonstrates his program to Conrad Kreet who is very happy with it, and pays up immediately, in cash. Harry leaves the ABC offices grinning broadly, wishing that his former colleagues at Leicester Software Engineering could see him now.

5.2.3 The aftermath

After a rather boisterous evening celebrating his first success, during which he consumed rather too much champagne, Harry is still sleeping peacefully at 11 o'clock the next morning when the telephone rings. On the phone is Mr Kreet, who tells Harry that ABC will be commencing legal proceedings against Harry Hacker (Programming) Ltd.

They've been using Harry's program, they say, and it is not giving them enough carpet to complete the job. They are furious! Aghast, Harry turns to his code. Sure enough, he realizes that when altering the code he managed to make a mistake in the Room 3 calculation... Harry knows his new company is finished. Swallowing his pride, he picks up the phone, dials Leicester Software Engineering, and asks for his old job back.

5.3   You need to use functions

The small example in this chapter is rather tongue-in-cheek, but the underlying problem is a frequent one in real world programming situations: unless you are careful when you edit your code, it is easy to introduce further errors. The problem in this case was exacerbated by the fact that the program was not tested before it was delivered to the client (we shall consider testing in depth in Chapter 11). Yet the need for testing, and the likelihood that such tests would fail, was greatly increased because of the *unstructured* way in which the program was developed, or in this case 'hacked'.

To engineer this simple program, one needs to use functions. A function can be viewed as a block of code with a name. We might represent this schematically as shown in Figure 5.2. We can execute the named block of code simply by including the function name in our program, a process usually referred to as **calling** the function.

Functions are so important that all C++ programs contain at least one, called `main()`. In addition to `main()`, software developed in a process-oriented or data-oriented manner will consist of a series of layers of clearly defined functions. We'll have a lot more to say about these ideas throughout the remainder of Parts I and II, but we can summarize them for now as follows:

> *Software that is engineered using a process- or data-oriented method will consist of many independent functions, each with a clearly defined task to perform. No function will have side-effects. No function will serve more than one task, and no single task will be split between functions.*

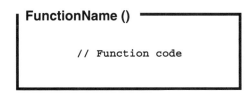

Figure 5.2   A schematic representation of a simple function.

There are three important reasons why we wish to have our programs written in this form:

- When a problem occurs in a program assembled from independent functions (and errors always occur, because programmers are human) then the error can be easily detected and often corrected (by the program itself) before a catastrophic system failure occurs.
- During implementation of your programs, the use of independent functions means that you can edit and correct any errors you do find, without introducing further problems.
- The small amount of extra effort involved in producing code from independent functions is often repaid many times over because such functions are easy to reuse again and again in subsequent projects.

We consider these ideas throughout this part of the book. In the case study here, what Harry *should* have done was write a single C++ function to calculate the area of the carpet required in a given room. He should then have called this function several times in his program. With only one copy of the area calculation code to work with, he'd have been much less likely to go wrong when he made subsequent alterations to the code.

For example, Program 5.3 is an improved version of Program 5.2. The new version has a user-defined function to break up the program into two 'bite-sized' chunks.

```cpp
// Carpet Area Calculation v3.0 - more structured version
// Source is: 05_03.CPP

#include <iostream.h>

// Function prototype for Calculate_Area()
float Calculate_Area(int);

int main()
    {
    int room, num_rooms;
    float total_area;

    cout << "Carpet Area Calculation\n";
    cout << "-------------------------\n";

    cout << "How many rooms (0 = QUIT)? : ";
    cin >> num_rooms;

    for (room = 1; room <= num_rooms; room++)
        {
        // Keep a running total of the carpet area
        total_area += Calculate_Area(room);
        }

    if (num_rooms > 0)
        {
        cout << "\n\nTotal area of carpet required = "
            << total_area << " square metres.\n\n";
        }

    cout << "Finished.";

    return 0;
    }
```

```
/ ***********************************************************
 *                                                         *
 * FUNCTION: Calculate_Area                                *
 *                                                         *
 * OVERVIEW: Calculate carpet area for one room.           *
 *                                                         *
 ********************************************************** /

float Calculate_Area(int room_no)
    {
    float width, length, area;

    cout << "\nROOM " << room_no << "\n";
    cout << "Type in width (in metres) <RETURN>: ";
    cin  >> width;
    cout << "Type in length (in metres) <RETURN>: ";
    cin  >> length;

    area = width * length * 2; // Covering ceiling too.

    cout << "Area of carpet for Room " << room_no
         << " is: " << 2 * width * length << endl;

    return area;
    }
```

Program 5.3   A more structured program for calculating the area of carpet required in an office v3.0. (☺)

The output from Program 5.3 is as follows:

```
Carpet Area Calculation
How many rooms (0 = QUIT)? : 0
Finished.
```

```
Carpet Area Calculation

How many rooms (0 = QUIT)? : 2

ROOM 1
Type in width (in metres) <RETURN>: 2
Type in length (in metres) <RETURN>: 3
Area of carpet for Room 1 is: 12

ROOM 2
Type in width (in metres) <RETURN>: 4
Type in length (in metres) <RETURN>: 2
Area of carpet for Room 2 is: 16

Total area of carpet required = 28 square metres.

Finished.
```

Program 5.3 is presented without further comment at this time: we'll consider the details in subsequent chapters.

Conclusions

This chapter has presented our first short case study, and has attempted to illustrate the need to structure even very small programs in an appropriate manner.

We begin to consider how to write functions of the sort previewed in Program 5.3 in the next chapter.

6 Writing C++ functions

6.1   Introduction

In the last chapter, we saw what can happen if you try to squeeze all the code for your program into a single `main()` function. Here we explore ways of avoiding such problems by breaking up monolithic programs into a collection of self-contained C++ functions. We look at the best ways of writing such functions for yourself, and then see how to combine them into robust programs.

As we'll see throughout this book, the key to creating quality software (as defined in Chapter 1) is to think *defensively*. This means accepting that errors will occur in your applications, and acting to minimize their impact on the people using your software. When developing programs with a process-oriented method, the correct use of functions is the singlemost important way of achieving this goal.

6.2   Another Look at `main()`

Before considering other functions, it is worth taking a closer look at one function we have already used extensively: the `main()` function. For example, consider the following code fragment:

```
int main(void)
    {
    cout << "hello";
    return 0;
    }
```

Here, `main()` *returns a value* of zero (to the operating system) upon normal completion of the program. If the program runs and terminates normally, the value of zero will be returned; if the program does not terminate normally, then a value not equal to zero could be returned. The value can be used by the operating system to determine what has happened to the program, and you should therefore generally include return values in your programs.

To make use of the return value, you must first tell the compiler what *type* of data the `main()` will return:

```
<return_code_type> main(void)
    {
    ...
    return <return_code>;
    }
```

Here `<return_code_type>` specifies the type of the variable `<return_code>`. Generally, an integer value is used to code the type of error, so that the shell of `main()` becomes:

```
int main(void)
    {
    ...
    return 0;
    }
```

However, if you are determined not to return a value from `main()`, the following fragment will also compile and run successfully on most compilers:

```
void main(void)
    {
    cout << "hello";
    }
```

Here, the type of data returned by `main()` is `void`, which means that no data are returned: in these circumstances, `main()` should not include a return statement at all. Note that if you miss out the (first) `void` in the above heading, and write:

```
main(void)
    {
    ...
```

then the compiler will assume that you intend `main()` to return an *integer* value (not void) value. As usual, it is generally better programming practice to be *explicit*.

Finally, note that in the examples here we have included a second `void` in the heading:

```
...main(void)
```

This second use of `void` says that `main()` is a function without any parameters; we consider functions with parameters in detail throughout much of the remainder of this chapter. The use of this second `void` is optional, but if you omit it, then this time a `void` value will be assumed. As many new graphical operating systems don't readily support `main()` functions with parameters (also known as command line parameters) it is now relatively uncommon to need anything but `void` at this point, and most C++ programmers simply leave the brackets empty. We won't make use of `main()` functions with parameters in this book; if you need such a facility, you should investigate `argc` and `argv` in the documentation provided with your compiler.

6.3   A first simple function: `Sadie()`

We're now in a position to consider our first 'real' function. The following useful function will display 'I love SADIE!' on the screen every time it is called:

```
int Sadie()
    {
    cout << "I love SADIE!";

    return 0;
    }
```

Here, `Sadie()` is the function name. The block of code within the function body is delimited with a pair of curly braces { and }.

If we look first at the beginning of the function header, *viz.*

```
int Sadie …
```

we can see that this takes precisely the same form as the header for `main()`. As with `main()`, the use of `int` means that the function returns an error code, and we have the facility to indicate to the calling function that an error has occurred in `Sadie()`. It is important to note that, although we shall not explicitly make use of the values returned by our functions in early examples, we see in Section 6.10 that appropriate use of such values can allow the detection, isolation and *correction* of errors *before* they get out of hand. Again, we explore these ideas further in later chapters.

Note also that, in addition to their application in error detection and recovery, we shall find other uses of the return value in later sections.

6.4   Declaration vs definition revisited

In Chapter 3 we emphasized the difference between declaration and definition of variables. We saw then that declarations indicate both the type and the name of the variable without allocating memory, while a definition allocates a block of memory large enough to hold the variable. We also saw that all variables had to be declared before they were used. As we see here, functions too must have declarations.

The general form of a C++ program developed using a process-oriented method is illustrated in Figure 6.1, which shows that our process-oriented C++ program will consist of `main()`, preceded by the **declarations** of our user-defined functions, and proceeded by their **definitions**. Within `main()` calls will be made to these functions.

The function definitions take exactly the same form as the code for the `Sadie()` function considered in the previous section:

```
// This is the definition of Sadie()
int Sadie()
    {
    cout << "I love SADIE!\n";

    return 0;
    }
```

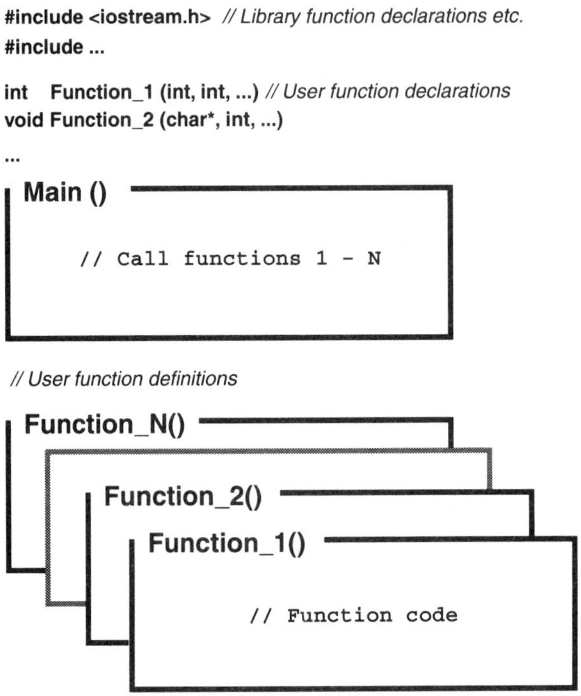

```
#include <iostream.h>  // Library function declarations etc.
#include ...

int   Function_1 (int, int, ...) // User function declarations
void Function_2 (char*, int, ...)

...
```

Main () ─────────────

    // Call functions 1 - N

// User function definitions

Function_N() ─────────────

    Function_2() ─────────────

        Function_1() ─────────────

            // Function code

Figure 6.1   A schematic representation of a general process-oriented C++ program. Note that in most situations, the various functions and associated components will be distributed across more than one source file, a process we consider in Chapter 10.

Like variable definitions, function definitions consume memory, and involve the 'construction' of a 'code object'. Similarly, function declarations (more generally referred to as function prototypes) are simply an extension of the idea of variable declarations. Declarations do not involve the construction of objects, and do not consume memory. The main purpose of declarations, as we discussed in Chapter 3, is to allow the compiler to perform type checking.

To understand function declarations, we need to complete our explanation of variable declarations. As we saw in Chapter 3, most variable declarations are also definitions. Here is an example of a variable declaration that is not a definition:

```
extern int x;
```

This definition does not allocate memory for variable x, it simply says to the compiler: 'if you come across any mention of variable x, then bear in mind that x is an integer'. The extern keyword (which we consider in more detail in Chapter 9), means that x is defined elsewhere in the program (in fact, it means that x will be defined in a different source file, a possibility we discuss in Chapter 10).

If we have made the above declaration of x and, later in the program, we try to assign a real value to this variable, such as:

```
x = 3.1415;
```

the compiler will indicate, through a type mismatch error, that we have made an error. Such type checking can seem trivial and a nuisance at first, but for realistic programming situations it can also save a great deal of time and avoid potential loss of information. For example, in the above case, if no errors were detected by the compiler and we ran the program in ignorance, using a value of 3 for *x*, instead of the given value, then the impact on the results from our program could be profound. Moreover, if and when we did realize that something was amiss, tracking down the error could be very time-consuming without help from the compiler.

A similar argument applies in the case of function declarations, the general form of which is:

```
<return-code-type> function-name (type parameter1-name,
                                  type parameter2-name,
                                  ...
                                  type parameterN-name);
```

We consider functions with parameters later in this chapter. For now, we can consider a slightly simpler function declaration:

```
<return-code-type> function-name ();
```

Just as in the case of predefined data items, function declarations are used by the compiler to check that what you have said you are *going to do* with a function and what you *actually do* are consistent. For example, we could have a function declaration like the following:

```
int test1();
```

If, subsequently, our function took the following form, then the compiler would quite rightly complain:

```
float test1()
    {
    ...
    ...
    return 3.14;
    }
```

As Figure 6.1 suggests, most C++ programs also use library functions provided with the implementation to perform a range of useful tasks, from basic I/O functions to mathematical calculations (we discuss the range of library functions available, and ways of making effective use of them, in Chapter 9). These functions also require declarations, which are made accessible via the #include directive. Note that #include is not a C++ statement: it is an instruction to the C++ pre-processor. For example, the line

```
#include <iostream.h>
```

is an instruction to the C++ pre-processor to include a copy of the file iostream.h at this point in the code. The iostream.h file contains, among other things, declarations for the various functions used to provide I/O facilities in most C++ programs. We discuss header files in more detail in Chapter 9.

Finally, note that just as we can have variable declarations that are also definitions, we can have function declarations that are also definitions, by rearranging our program (Figure 6.2). The only advantage of this structure is that you do not have to write function declarations (a process which takes only a few seconds). The structure is not widely used, and is not recommended. A significant drawback with this program structure is that it makes it considerably more difficult to exploit C++ support for separate compilation, frequently used in large projects, particularly where teams are involved. As noted above, we discuss separate compilation in Chapter 10.

6.5   Calling a simple function

We are now in a position to write a complete test program around our `Sadie()` function (Program 6.1).

```cpp
// Test program for Sadie() function
// Source is: 06_01.CPP

#include <iostream.h>

// The declaration of Sadie()
int Sadie();

// This is the definition of main()
int main ()
    {
    // Call Sadie()
    Sadie();

    return 0;
    }
// This is the definition of Sadie()
int Sadie()
    {
    cout << "I love SADIE!\n";

    return 0;
    }
```

Program 6.1   A test program for the user-defined `Sadie()` function. (☺)

Program 6.1 gives the following output:

```
I love SADIE!
```

Program 6.1 is structured in the same way as Figure 6.1, with `main()` preceded by the declaration of `Sadie()` and followed by its definition.

To understand how this program works, first consider the line:

```
Sadie();
```

In this code fragment, we *call* the function `Sadie()`. This generates our 'I love SADIE!' output, then returns control back to the main program. If we had wanted to write the text on the screen three times, we do not need (as in the Chapter 5 example)

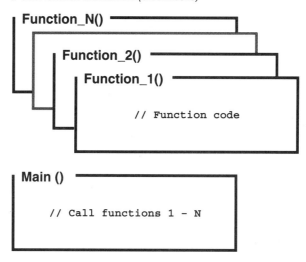

#include <iostream.h> // *Library function declarations etc.*
#include ...

// *User function declarations (& definitions)*

Function_N()

Function_2()

Function_1()

```
// Function code
```

Main ()

```
// Call functions 1 - N
```

Figure 6.2 A schematic representation of a process-oriented C++ program, restructured to avoid the need for separate function declarations. This program structure is not recommended.

to repeat the underlying code three times, but merely to call the same piece of code by writing:

```
Sadie();
Sadie();
Sadie();
```

6.6 Call by value

The above very simple example is all very well, but real functions need to do more than print out messages; they also need to process data. A vital consideration when writing C++ programs, therefore, is that we can transfer data to our functions in a *controlled* manner.

When we pass variables (data) to a function using 'call by value' we transmit not the variables themselves, but the *value* of the variables: that is, we pass of copy of our original data, and hang on to the original. From a common sense point of view, this sounds a reasonable strategy. You don't send valuable documents through the post unless you absolutely have to: if you have the choice, it's much safer to send a photo-copy. From a defensive programming point of view, this is also an excellent idea: no matter what the function does, and even if it goes drastically wrong, it is unlikely to be able to alter (or destroy) our original data.

We'll consider how call by value is implemented in C++ through an example (Program 6.2). This example takes two integers, squares each one, and finds the sum of the result.

```
// Program to find the sum of the squares of two numbers
// Source is: 06_02.CPP

#include <iostream.h>

// Function declaration
int Sum_of_Squares (int, int);

int main()
    {
    int Num_1 = 1;
    int Num_2 = 2;

    // Call function Sum_of_Squares
    Sum_of_Squares (Num_1, Num_2);

    return 0;
    }
/**************************************************************
 * FUNCTION: Sum_of_Squares                                  *
 *                                                           *
 * OVERVIEW: To print out the sum of the squares             *
 *           of a and b (both integers).                     *
 **************************************************************/
int Sum_of_Squares (int a, int b)
    {
    int square1 = a*a;
    int square2 = b*b;

    cout << "Number 1 is : " << a << endl;
    cout << "Number 2 is : " << b << endl;
    cout << "Sum of Squares is : " << square1+square2 << endl;

    return 0;
    }
```

Program 6.2 A 'sum of squares' program. (☺)

Program 6.2 gives the output:

```
Number 1 is : 1
Number 2 is : 2
Sum of Squares is : 5
```

Let's now see how the program works, starting with the function Sum_of_Squares():

```
/**************************************************************
 * FUNCTION: Sum_of_Squares                                  *
 *                                                           *
 * OVERVIEW: To print out the sum of the squares             *
 *           of a and b (both integers).                     *
 **************************************************************/
int Sum_of_Squares (int a, int b)
    {
    int square1 = a*a;
    int square2 = b*b;
```

```
cout << "Number 1 is : " << a << endl;
cout << "Number 2 is : " << b << endl;
cout << "Sum of Squares is : " << square1+square2 << endl;
return 0;
}
```

The first thing to note is that this function has a meaningful name, telling someone using the code what its purpose is. The next thing to note is that the definition itself has a 'banner' giving a brief overview of the function. Both name and banner should make it easier to remember six months later what a particular piece of code does, and should help other people understand your programs. Both should also make it easier to reuse functions in later programs.

Next, we have, as before, an error-code of type `int`, and a corresponding return value:

```
int Sum_of_Squares(...)
    {
    ...
    ...
    return 0;
    }
```

Turning to the function parameters, we can see that, in line with the general function header format considered in Section 6.4, there are two parameters listed, a and b, which are both of type `int`:

```
int Sum_of_Squares(int a, int b)
    {
    ...
    ...
    }
```

It is important to note that this heading includes the **definition** of parameters a and b. It is also essential that we draw a distinction between the **formal parameters** of the function header, and the **actual parameters** (or arguments) used when the function is called. In particular, note that the (formal) parameters listed in the function header are of type `int`, with names a and b. However, when the function is called, its actual parameters are called Num_1 and Num_2:

```
int Num_1 = 1;
int Num_2 = 2;
// Call function Sum_of_Squares
Sum_of_Squares(Num_1,Num_2);
```

As far as the compiler is concerned, all that matters is that the *type* of the function's arguments matches the type of the function's parameters. This fact is emphasized when we consider the declaration for Sum_of_Squares(), which gives only the types of the function parameters, and gives no names at all:

```
// Function declaration
int Sum_of_Squares (int, int);
```

Note that we can include names in the declaration. For example, we could write:

```
int Sum_of_Squares (int a, int b);
```

or, equally well:

```
int Sum_of_Squares (int ignore_me, int and_me);
```

In either case, the names will be ignored by the compiler. Because inclusion of the names implies (incorrectly) that some form of checking may be conducted on these names, it is usual to omit them.

The end result is that the program works, and is robust. We can illustrate this last point by making some modifications to Program 6.2, as shown in Program 6.3.

```
// Demonstration of Call by Value
// Source is: 06_03.CPP

#include <iostream.h>

// Function declaration
int Sum_of_Squares2(int, int);

int main()
    {
    int Num_1 = 1;
    int Num_2 = 2;

    // Call function Sum_of_Squares2()
    Sum_of_Squares2(Num_1,Num_2);

    cout << "\n\nBack in main: Number 1 is : " << Num_1 << endl;
    cout << "Back in main: Number 2 is : " << Num_2 << endl;

    return 0;
    }
/******************************************************************
 * FUNCTION:    Sum_of_Squares2()                                 *
 *                                                                *
 * OVERVIEW:    To print out the sum of the squares               *
 *              of a and b (both integers).                       *
 ******************************************************************/
int Sum_of_Squares2(int a, int b)
    {
    int square1 = a*a;
    int square2 = b*b;
    cout << "Number 1 is : " << a << endl;
    cout << "Number 2 is : " << b << endl;
    cout << "Sum of Squares is : " << square1+square2 << endl;

    // Changing values of a,b
    a = 10;
    b = 20;
    cout << "Number 1 is : " << a << endl;
    cout << "Number 2 is : " << b << endl;

    return 0;
    }
```

Program 6.3 A modified version of Program 6.2. (☺)

Program 6.3 generates the following outputs:

```
Number 1 is : 1
Number 2 is : 2
Sum of Squares is : 5

Number 1 is : 10
Number 2 is : 20

Back in main: Number 1 is : 1
Back in main: Number 2 is : 2
```

The changes made in Program 6.3 have no impact on the operation of the program, but they do confirm one important point: no matter what changes we make to the value of our formal parameters a and b within the function Sum_of_Squares2(), the corresponding actual parameters Num_1 and Num_2 are not changed.

In conclusion, call by value is a safe way of passing information to functions: this is the technique to use, unless you have good reason not to.

6.7 Local and global scope

Let's consider one more version of Program 6.2 (Program 6.4):

```
// Demonstration of Call by Value
// Source is: 06_04.CPP

#include <iostream.h>

// Function declaration
int Sum_of_Squares2(int, int);

int main()
    {
    int a = 1; // NB!!!
    int b = 2;

    // Call function Sum_of_Squares2()
    Sum_of_Squares2(a,b);

    cout << "\n\nBack in main: Number 1 is : " << a << endl;
    cout << "Back in main: Number 2 is : " << b << endl;

    return 0;
    }
/****************************************************************
 * FUNCTION: Sum_of_Squares2()                                 *
 *                                                             *
 * OVERVIEW: To print out the sum of the squares              *
 *           of a and b (both integers).                       *
 ****************************************************************/

int Sum_of_Squares2(int a, int b)
    {
    int square1 = a*a;
    int square2 = b*b;
```

```
        cout << "Number 1 is : " << a << endl;
        cout << "Number 2 is : " << b << endl;
        cout << "Sum of Squares is : " << square1+square2 << endl;

        // Changing values of a,b
        a = 10;
        b = 20;
        cout << "Number 1 is : " << a << endl;
        cout << "Number 2 is : " << b << endl;

        return 0;
        }
```

Program 6.4   Another modified version of Program 6.2. (☺)

Program 6.4 generates the following outputs:

```
    Number 1 is : 1
    Number 2 is : 2
    Sum of Squares is : 5

    Number 1 is : 10
    Number 2 is : 20

    Back in main: Number 1 is : 1
    Back in main: Number 2 is : 2
```

The output from Program 6.4 is exactly the same as the output from Program 6.3 and, as before, we see that no matter what changes we make to the value of our formal parameters within the function Sum_of_Squares2(), the corresponding actual parameters are not changed.

This time, however, both the formal parameters and the actual parameters have the same name (both are called a and b). This may seem strange: surely we can't have two variables of the same name? For example, if we try to compile a code fragment:

```
    ...
    int a;
    int a; // Can't do this!
    ...
```

then the compiler will object, saying something like 'multiple definition of a'.

The answer is that we can have as many variables as we like, all called the same thing, as long as only one of these variables is in **scope** at the same time. The concept of variable scope is closely linked to what are often called local and global variables, which we can sum up as follows:

Local variables are invisible outside the function in which they are defined, while global variables are visible throughout all functions in the program.

For example, Program 6.5 illustrates the scope of various local and global variables.

```
    // Demonstration of scope of local and global variables
    // Source is: 06_05.CPP
    #include <iostream.h>
```

```
// Function declaration
int Function1();

int Global1 = 1;
int Global2 = 2;

int main()
    {
    int Local1 = 3;
    int Local2 = 4;

    cout << "In Main: Global1 = "       << Global1 << endl;
    cout << "In Main: Global2 = "       << Global2 << endl;
    cout << "In Main: Local1 = "        << Local1  << endl;
    cout << "In Main: Local2 = "        << Local2  << endl;

    Function1();

    cout << "\nBack in Main: Global1 = " << Global1 << endl;
    cout << "Back in Main: Global2 = "   << Global2 << endl;
    cout << "Back in Main: Local1 = "    << Local1  << endl;
    cout << "Back in Main: Local2 = "    << Local2  << endl;

    return 0;
    }

int Function1()
    {
    int Local1 = 20;
    int Local3 = 30;

    Global1 = 2001;

    cout << "\nIn Function1: Global1 = " << Global1 << endl;
    cout << "In Function1: Global2 = "   << Global2 << endl;
    cout << "In Function1: Local1 = "    << Local1  << endl;
    cout << "In Function1: Local3 = "    << Local3  << endl;

    return 0;
    }
```

Program 6.5 A program that demonstrates the scope of local and global variables. (☺)

The output from Program 6.5 is as follows:

```
In Main: Global1 = 1
In Main: Global2 = 2
In Main: Local1 = 3
In Main: Local2 = 4

In Function1: Global1 = 2001
In Function1: Global2 = 2
In Function1: Local1 = 20
In Function1: Local3 = 30

Back in Main: Global1 = 2001
Back in Main: Global2 = 2
Back in Main: Local1 = 3
Back in Main: Local2 = 4
```

In very general terms, what Program 6.5 does is to declare some variables, and assign to them certain values. When `main()` is called, the values of some of the variables are printed out, then `Function1()` is called, when the value of a global variable is changed, and more values are printed. Finally, control of the program returns to `main()`, and the values are printed out again.

More specifically, consider first the global variables. The program has two such variables (`Global1`, `Global2`) which are defined *outside* `main()`. `Global1` and `Global2` are initialized with values of 1 and 2 respectively. The program then proceeds as follows:

(1)   In `main()` the values of `Global1` and `Global2` are printed. Their values are, as expected, 1 and 2.

(2)   `main()` calls `Function1()`.

(3)   Inside `Function1()`, the value of `Global2` is printed out. Again, viewed from within this function, its value remains at 2. However, also within `Function1()`, `Global1` is assigned a value of 2001. Printing out the value of `Global1` from within `Function1()` confirms that this change of value has taken place.

(4)   With the completion of `Function1()`, the program returns to `main()`. Again, the values of `Global1` and `Global2` are printed out, showing that while `Global2`'s value has remained unchanged throughout the program, the value of `Global1` has maintained the value assigned to it in `Function1()`.

Thus, we see that the **global** variables (that is, variables defined outside `main()`) are accessible **globally**, both by `main()` and by (all) other functions in the program.

Turning now to the **local** variables, the operation of the program is as follows:

(1)   In `main()` two local variables are declared, `Local1` and `Local2`. These variables are initialized with values of 3 and 4 (respectively), and the values are printed out.

(2)   `main()` calls `Function1()`.

(3)   In `Function1()`, two new local variables are declared, again called `Local1` and `Local3`. They are assigned values of 20 and 30 respectively, and their values are printed out. Note that the compiler is perfectly happy to allow this (apparent) redefinition of variable `Local1` within `Function1()`.

(4)   With the completion of `Function1()`, the program returns to `main()`. Here the values of variables `Local1` and `Local2` are again printed out. The value of `Local1` is seen to be 3 (not 20) as far as `main()` is concerned. The value of `Local2` is also unchanged at 4.

The implication of the operation of Program 6.5 is that we don't need call by value after all: we can make our programs much easier to write by using global variables everywhere. For example, we can rewrite our sum of squares program to take advantage of this new feature (Program 6.6).

```
// Demonstration of Global Variables
// Source is: 06_06.CPP
#include <iostream.h>
```

```cpp
// Global variables
int a = 1;
int b = 2;

// Function declaration
int Sum_of_Squares3();

int main()
    {
    // Call function Sum_of_Squares3()
    Sum_of_Squares3();

    cout << "\n\nBack in main: Number 1 is : " << a << endl;
    cout << "Back in main: Number 2 is : " << b << endl;

    return 0;
    }
/*****************************************************************
* FUNCTION: Sum_of_Squares3()                                   *
*                                                               *
* OVERVIEW: To print out the sum of the squares                 *
*           of global variables a and b (both integers)         *
*****************************************************************/
int Sum_of_Squares3()
    {
    int square1 = a*a;
    int square2 = b*b;
    cout << "Number 1 is : " << a << endl;
    cout << "Number 2 is : " << b << endl;
    cout << "Sum of Squares is : " << square1+square2 << endl;

    // Changing values of a,b
    a = 10;
    b = 20;
    cout << "Number 1 is : " << a << endl;
    cout << "Number 2 is : " << b << endl;

    return 0;
    }
```

Program 6.6 An example of very poor programming style. (☹)

Note that Program 6.6 carries a very strong health warning. To understand why, we can compare it with the basic guidelines introduced at the end of Chapter 5:

> *Software that is engineered using a process- or data-oriented method will consist of many independent functions, each with a clearly defined task to perform. No function will have side-effects. No function will serve more than one task, and no single task will be split between functions.*

Simply through the use of global variables, Sum_of_Squares3() manages to break our first, and most important, guideline: it has **side-effects**. This is illustrated when we look at the output from the Program 6.6:

```
Number 1 is : 1
Number 2 is : 2
Sum of Squares is : 5

Number 1 is : 10
Number 2 is : 20

Back in main: Number 1 is : 10
Back in main: Number 2 is : 20
```

From this output, it is clear that changes made to (global) variables a and b within Sum_of_Squares3() are reflected in main(). To see why these side-effects are significant, we need to consider what we are trying to achieve by following these guidelines. As we stated at the end of Chapter 5, there are three reasons why we wish to have our programs written in this form:

- When a problem occurs in a program assembled from independent functions (and errors always occur, because programmers are human) then the error can be easily detected and often corrected (by the program itself) before a catastrophic system failure occurs.

- During implementation of your programs, the use of independent functions means that you can edit and correct any errors you do find, without introducing further problems.

- The small amount of extra effort involved in producing code from independent functions is often repaid many times over because such functions are easy to reuse again and again in subsequent projects.

By using global variables, all of these advantages are lost, as follows:

- When functions have side-effects, they are not independent. When we use global variables, and an error occurs, say, in the control of one of the fermentation vessels in a system for a company brewing beer, we don't know whether that error may be due to a problem in the function (say) Main_fermentation_control(), or whether it arises because of a change in a global variable in some distant and totally unrelated part of the part of the program.

- If you do isolate the source of an error in a system where functions are not independent, then correcting this error is likely to involve altering a global variable. This fact may lead to new errors, errors which are impossible to predict, and which may only become apparent several weeks later.

- It is very difficult to recycle functions which are not independent. For example, the Sum_of_squares3() function from Program 6.6 can only be used in programs with global variables called a and b. If we wanted to use several functions in our programs, they might all require global variables with different names. We can embark on a tedious process of editing all the relevant functions, trying to make them all compatible. However, as we do this, we shall probably introduce more errors. In addition, one of the advantages of recycling code is that the code will already have been thoroughly tested: if we edit the functions, we have to repeat all of the test procedures again.

Overall, there is no justification for making extensive use of global variables in your program. Just like `goto` statements (introduced in Chapter 3), use of global variables is not consistent with a robust, defensive programming style.

However, just as we saw with `goto` statements, there is one set of circumstances where use of global variables can be justified, and used with reasonable safety. This is where your program requires the use of read-only variables (as described in Chapter 3).

For example, where many functions in your program need to know the current value of business interest rates, you might declare a global `const float` as follows:

```
...
const float INTEREST_RATE = 7.0f;
...
int main()
    {
    ...
```

The use of such constant global variables carries the risk of few side-effects, because the value cannot be altered anywhere in the program. Strictly, even this use of global variables should be avoided, but global read-only variables are widely used in real systems.

6.8 Call by reference

There are three good techniques for passing information to and from C++ functions: call by value, call by reference, and call by address. In general, for reasons we have already considered, call by value is the preferred technique: what call by value will not do, however, is allow us to *return* data to the calling function. This is usually achieved using **call by reference**. We consider call by reference in this section.

Call by address is a more advanced, and complex, technique, which you will probably use less frequently: we defer discussion of this topic until Chapter 8.

6.8.1 General use of reference variables

In order to make effective use of call by reference, we need first to understand the features of reference variables. For example, consider the following code fragment:

```
float float1;                // Type is float
float& float1_REF = float1;  // Type is float&
```

This fragment illustrates several important points:

- Here, `float1` is an (ordinary) floating-point variable, while `float1_REF` is a floating-point **reference variable**.

- Reference variable types are, as in this example, denoted by the base type, with an additional '&' postfix. Thus, here, `float1_REF` is of type `float&`.

- Note that you may see code written:

  ```
  float &float2 = float1;
  ```

  This notation is ambiguous, and not recommended. Here, it implies that the name of the variable is `&float2` and the type is `float`. Both are incorrect!

- References allow one identifier to be declared as an alternative name (alias) of another. For example, here float1_REF is an alias for float1: a change to either variable will affect the value of both.

- From the above, it is clear that changing the value of a reference variable has side-effects. Because of this, it is good programming practice to give reference variables distinct and consistent names: we use the '_REF' postfix to denote such variables.

- The name of the object for which the identifier provides an alternative name is specified when the reference is initialized: it *cannot* be subsequently changed.

- Note that only one reference variable can be declared per line: the following two declarations of float1_REF and float2_REF are *not* equivalent:

```
float& float1_REF = float1, float2_REF = float3; // WRONG!!

float& float1_REF = float1; // OK
float& float2_REF = float3; // OK
```

Program 6.7 demonstrates some of these important points.

```
// Playing with reference variables
// Source is: 06_07.CPP

#include <iostream.h>

int main()
    {
    float float1 = 1.11f;
    float float2 = 2.22f;
    float& float1_REF = float1;

    cout << " float1           : " << float1      << endl;
    cout << " float2           : " << float2      << endl;
    cout << " float1_REF       : " << float1_REF  << endl;

    // Changes only the VALUE of float1_REF
    float1_REF = float2;
    float2 = 3.33f;

    cout << "\n float1          : " << float1      << endl;
    cout << " float2           : " << float2      << endl;
    cout << " float1_REF       : " << float1_REF  << endl;

    return 0;
    }
```

Program 6.7 Illustrating the simple use of reference variables. (☺)

Program 6.7 generates the following output:

```
float1 : 1.11
    float2 :        2.22
    float1_REF :    1.11

    float1 :        2.22
    float2 :        3.33
    float1_REF :    2.22
```

You might be wondering just why you would ever want to use these features. In fact, reference variables are of value mainly in formal parameter lists (that is, in function headings), as we'll see below.

6.8.2 Using reference parameters

As an alternative to sending copies of data to our functions using call by value we can, in effect, 'send the data itself', using call by reference (Program 6.8).

```
// Program to find the sum of the squares of two numbers
// Using call by reference
// Source is: 06_08.CPP

#include <iostream.h>

// Function declaration
int Sum_of_Squares4(int, int, int&);

// No global variables !

int main()
    {
    int Num_1 = 1;
    int Num_2 = 2;
    int Result;

    // Call function Sum_of_Squares4
    Sum_of_Squares4(Num_1, Num_2, Result);

    cout << "Sum of Squares is : " << Result;

    return 0;
    }
/*****************************************************************
 * FUNCTION:    Sum_of_Squares4                                  *
 *                                                               *
 * OVERVIEW:    To calculate the sum of the squares              *
 *              of a and b (both integers) returning the         *
 *              result via reference variable sum_REF            *
 *****************************************************************/
int Sum_of_Squares4(int a, int b, int& sum_REF)
    {
    int square1 = a*a;
    int square2 = b*b;

    cout << "Number 1 is : " << a << endl;
    cout << "Number 2 is : " << b << endl;
    sum_REF = square1 + square2;

    return 0;
    }
```

Program 6.8 The sum of squares program, using call by reference. (☺)

Program 6.8 generates the following output:

```
Number 1 is : 1
Number 2 is : 2
Sum of Squares is : 5
```

Though the output from the program is the same as before, the internal operation is a little different. First of all, consider the header of the function Sum_of_Squares4():

```
int Sum_of_Squares4(int a, int b, int& sum_REF)
    {
    ...
    }
```

On this occasion, we have not only integer variables a and b as before, but also a further integer *reference* variable, sum_REF. This is just like the reference variables considered in Section 6.8.1: this time (implicitly) sum_REF is initialized to the corresponding actual parameter when the function is called. Thus, in this particular program, we are in effect doing the following when we call the function:

```
int& sum_REF = Result;
```

Within the function, we can treat sum_REF just like any other integer variable, as in:

```
sum_REF = square1 + square2;
```

As is clear from the output of the program, the assignment also alters the value of Result, in main().

Turning finally to the function declaration, we can see that once again we need inform the compiler only of the type of data to expect (in this case two integers and an integer reference):

```
// Function declaration
int Sum_of_Squares4(int, int, int&);
```

As we have seen previously, we do not need to provide the names of the particular data items. If we do provide these names, then the compiler will ignore them.

6.9   ASIDE: Scope rules and storage class

It is important to realize that the scope rules we considered earlier in this chapter don't simply apply when using functions: even in monolithic C++ programs you need to be aware of both the scope and the storage class of your variables. We'll consider each of these issues in turn.

6.9.1   Scope rules

Consider Program 6.9.

```
// Scope and nested for loops
// Source is: 06_09.CPP

#include <iostream.h>

int main()
    {
```

```
for (int i = 1; i < 3; i++)
      { // Start of block 1
      for (int j = 1; j < 3; j++)
            {
            cout << i << '\t' << j << endl;
            }
      } // End of block 1
for (i = 1; i < 3; i++)                // i is *not* redefined here
      { // Start of block 2
      for (int j = 1; j < 3; j++)   // j is redefined here
            {
            cout << i << '\t' << j << endl;
            }
      } // End of block 2
return 0;
}
```

Program 6.9 Illustrating scope rules in (rather useless) single-function program. Note that the inner loop control variable (j) must be redefined in the second set of nested `for` loops, because the original variable goes out of scope at the point labelled 'End of block 1' (☺).

In particular, note that the inner loop control variable (j) is defined in both groups of nested `for` loops. By contrast, note that the outer loop control variable i is defined only once, at the start of the first `for` loop.

The reason for this apparent anomaly is that C++ has very tight scope rules: specifically, the scope of any variable extends only within the **block** in which it is defined, where a block is defined by opening and closing braces ({ and }). In Program 6.9, j is first defined within the block controlled by the first outer loop: the beginning of this loop is labelled '// Start of block 1', and the end is labelled '// End of block 1'. Because the second set of nested for loops happens after j has passed out of scope – that is, after the label '// End of block 1' – then these variables no longer exist and new variables (of the same name) must be defined again.

The same is not true of the variable i: this is defined within the main() function body, and is therefore within scope for the whole of this function.

Finally, note that we can artificially create (anonymous) code blocks in programs, should we wish to do so, simply by including 'floating' pairs of braces. For instance, consider Program 6.10.

```
// Further demonstration of scope rules
// Source is: 06_10.CPP

#include <iostream.h>

int Global1 = 1;

int main()
      {
      int Local1 = 1;
      int Local2 = 2;
      int Local3 = 3;
```

```
cout << "In Main: Global1 = "    << Global1    << endl;
cout << "In Main: Local1 = "     << Local1     << endl;
cout << "In Main: Local2 = "     << Local2     << endl;
cout << "In Main: Local3 = "     << Local3     << endl;

// Start of Block 1
{
    int Local1 = 9999;
    int Local2;

    cout << "\nIn Block 1: Global1 = "   << Global1    << endl;
    cout << "In Block 1: Local1 = "      << Local1     << endl;
    cout << "In Block 1: Local2 = "      << Local2     << endl;
    cout << "In Block 1: Local3 = "      << Local3     << endl;
}
// End of Block 1

cout << "\nIn Main: Global1 = "    << Global1    << endl;
cout << "In Main: Local1 = "       << Local1     << endl;
cout << "In Main: Local2 = "       << Local2     << endl;
cout << "In Main: Local3 = "       << Local3     << endl;

return 0;
}
```

Program 6.10 Further illustrating scope rules in single-function programs. (☺?).

The output from Program 6.10 on a typical run is as follows:

```
In Main: Global1 = 1
In Main: Local1 = 1
In Main: Local2 = 2
In Main: Local3 = 3

In Block 1: Global1 = 1
In Block 1: Local1 = 9999
In Block 1: Local2 = 13880
In Block 1: Local3 = 3

In Main: Global1 = 1
In Main: Local1 = 1
In Main: Local2 = 2
In Main: Local3 = 3
```

First of all, note that Global1 maintains its value throughout the program: it is always in scope, because it is defined outside the body of main(). Note also that the other local variables generally behave as if 'Block 1' was a function. In particular, note that Local2 (redefined within Block 1, but not initialized) has an undefined value within this new block.

An important exception to the rule that anonymous code blocks behave like named blocks (that is, functions) is illustrated by examining the way Local3 behaves inside the anonymous block; within a function, Local3 would be out of scope, and its value could not be printed.

This example will repay careful study. While you may never have cause explicitly to include floating blocks within your programs, typing mistakes can cause errors to appear which, unless you understand C++'s scope rules, can be difficult to track down.

Finally, consider Program 6.11. In this example, it is worth noting that we can override some of the usual C++ scope rules by making use of the scope resolution operator (::).

```
// Playing with the unary scope resolution operator
// Source is: 06_11.CPP

#include <iostream.h>

int number = 10;

int main()
    {
    int number = 5;

    cout << "Local number = "   << number << endl
         << "Global value = "   << ::number << endl;

    return 0;
    }
```

Program 6.11   Using the scope resolution operator. (☺)

The output from Program 6.11 is as follows:

```
Local number = 5
Global value = 10
```

The scope resolution operator allows the programmer to access a global variable even when a local variable of the same name is in scope. We see further uses for this operator in Part III.

6.9.2   Storage class

Let's now turn to consider the storage class of variables. It is important to realize that C++ tags all variables not just with a type (for example, int, double, char, and so on) but also with a **storage class**. While the type of your variables is something that we have considered, storage class is slightly more subtle, and many programmers are not even aware of its importance.

There are two fundamental storage classes (automatic and external) and two additional classes (register and static). Variables declared within function bodies are, by default, automatic. When the block is entered, the system allocates memory for automatic variables (from the stack, as discussed further in Chapter 7). Variables created in this way are not implicitly initialized (to zero or anything else).

External variables are declared outside functions, and are assigned memory on a permanent basis (for the duration of the program). External, 'global', variables are initialized to zero.

The distinction between automatic and external variables is illustrated in Program 6.12.

```
// Initialization of Automatic and Extern Variables
// Source is: 06_12.CPP

#include <iostream.h>

// Int1, Int2 declared outside a function body
int Int1, Int2 = 2001; // Storage class "extern" (external)

int main()
    {
    // Int3, Int4 declared within function main()
    int Int3, Int4 = 1234; // Storage class "auto" (automatic)

    // Print out the values of the variables
    cout << "Int1 = " << Int1 << " and Int2 = " << Int2 << endl;
    cout << "Int3 = " << Int3 << " and Int4 = " << Int4 << endl;

    return 0;
    }
```

Program 6.12 Initialization of automatic and extern variables. (☺)

The output from Program 6.12 is as follows on two runs:

```
Int1 = 0 and Int2 = 2001
Int3 = 10303 and Int4 = 1234
```

```
Int1 = 0 and Int2 = 2001
Int3 = 9727 and Int4 = 1234
```

The storage class `register` is a *request* to the compiler to store the associated variable in one of the computer's registers. Though there are limited numbers of registers available, these are very fast memory locations and their judicious use can result in a speed improvement. Note that it is not possible to find the address of (and hence use pointers with) register variables. Program 6.13 illustrates the use of register variables.

```
// Initializing register variables
// Source is: 06_13.CPP

#include <iostream.h>
#include <time.h>

int main()
    {
    int automatic_int;
    register int register_int;

    const long NUM_PASSES = 100000000;
    double elapsed_time;

    time_t start_time, stop_time; // time_t is defined in time.h

    // METHOD ONE
    cout << "Starting calculation - please wait...\n";
```

```
start_time = time(NULL);

for (long pass = 0; pass <= NUM_PASSES; pass++)
    {
    automatic_int = 10;
    }
stop_time = time(NULL);
elapsed_time = difftime(stop_time, start_time);
cout << "Automatic, time (in seconds) : " << elapsed_time << endl;

// METHOD TWO
start_time = time(NULL);

for (pass = 0; pass <= NUM_PASSES; pass++)
    {
    register_int = 10;
    }
stop_time = time(NULL);
elapsed_time = difftime(stop_time, start_time);
cout << "Register, time (in seconds) : " << elapsed_time << endl;

return 0;
}
```

Program 6.13 Illustrating the use of register variables. Note that such speed improvements cannot be relied upon. (☺).

The output from Program 6.13 on a typical run is as follows:

```
Starting calculation - please wait...
Automatic, time (in seconds) : 73
Register, time (in seconds) : 61
```

Program 6-13 uses, among others, the time() library function to determine accurately the duration of the various calculations. This simple use of time() is largely self explanatory, and we will not describe this function further here: if you are interested, you will find details of time(), along with a wide range of other useful functions, in Chapter 9.
Note the following:

- There may be restrictions on the *type* of data you can store in a register: typically one cannot store data which occupies more memory than an int.

- As the number of registers on any computer system is limited, the use of the register keyword is a request to the compiler: it may not always be carried out.

- As different computers have different numbers of registers available, the results obtained may vary between systems.

- In many cases, a good optimizing compiler will already make use of register variables as much as possible. The compiler may be able to do this better than you can...

Finally, use of the `static` storage class means that local variables (declared within a block) can retain their values when that block is re-entered. Like external variables, static variables are initialized to zero by the system. Memory is reserved for static variables for the lifetime of the program, not just the lifetime of the function in which they are declared.

Program 6.14 illustrates the use of static variables.

```cpp
// Demonstration of static variables.
// Source is: 06_14.CPP
#include <iostream.h>

// Function declaration
int Test_Static();

int main()
    {
    int x;

    x = Test_Static();
    x = Test_Static();

    x = Test_Static();
    x = Test_Static();

    return 0;
    }

int Test_Static()
    {
    int Auto_int;           // Automatic
    static int Static_int;  // Static

    Auto_int++;
    Static_int++;

    cout << "\nIn Test_Static:  Auto_int = "<< Auto_int << endl;
    cout << "In Test_Static: Static_int = "  << Static_int << endl;

    return 0;
    }
```

Program 6.14   Illustrating the use of static variables. (☺)

Program 6.14 generates the following outputs on two typical runs:

```
In Test_Static:    Auto_int = 4305429
In Test_Static: Static_int = 1
In Test_Static:    Auto_int = 4305429
In Test_Static: Static_int = 2
In Test_Static:    Auto_int = 4305429
In Test_Static: Static_int = 3
In Test_Static:    Auto_int = 4305429
In Test_Static: Static_int = 4
```

```
In Test_Static:    Auto_int = 4289045
In Test_Static: Static_int = 1

In Test_Static:    Auto_int = 4289045
In Test_Static: Static_int = 2

In Test_Static:    Auto_int = 4289045
In Test_Static: Static_int = 3

In Test_Static:    Auto_int = 4289045
In Test_Static: Static_int = 4
```

6.10 Detecting and correcting errors

We present below (Program 6.15) another version of the 'sum of squares' program that makes more effective use of the function return value to allow for error recovery.

```cpp
// Program to find the sum of the squares of two numbers
// This time with error detection & recovery
// Source is: 06_15.CPP

#include <iostream.h>
#include <limits.h>

// Function declaration
int Sum_Of_Squares5(int, int);

int main()
    {
    Int Num1, Num2;
    int Return_value;   // Stores return value

    do
        {
        cout << "Type first number : ";
        cin >> Num1;
        cout << "Type second number : ";
        cin >> Num2;

        // Call function and check return code value
        Return_value = Sum_Of_Squares5(Num1, Num2);
        } while (Return_value != 0);

    return 0;
    }
/****************************************************************
* FUNCTION:    Sum_Of_Squares5()                               *
*                                                              *
* OVERVIEW:    To calculate and display the sum of the         *
*              squares of a and b (both integers).             *
*                                                              *
* RETURNS:     0  on normal completion.                        *
*              1  if sum of squares exceeds INT_MAX.           *
****************************************************************/
int Sum_Of_Squares5(int a, int b)
    {
    float SOS_float = ((float) a * a) + ((float) b * b);
    if (SOS_float > INT_MAX)
```

```
        {
        // Numbers too large: can't represent result as int
        cerr << "\n*** Numbers too large! ***\n\n";
        return 1;   // return 1 to indicate error
        }
    else
        {
        cout << "Sum of squares is : " << SOS_float;
        return 0;   // return 0 - everything is OK
        }
    }
```

Program 6.15 The sum of squares program, using error detection and recovery. (☺)

Program 6.15 generates the following outputs on two sample runs:

```
Type first number : 10
Type second number : 10
Sum of squares is : 200
```

```
Type first number : 1000
Type second number : 1000

*** Numbers too large! ***

Type first number : 100
Type second number : 100
Sum of squares is : 20000
```

The first thing to note is that the function checks to see whether the numbers entered by the user are sufficiently small to be represented as an integer. It does this by using the float variable SOS_float to store the result of the calculation:

```
float SOS_float = ((float) a * a) + ((float) b * b);
```

This result is then compared with INT_MAX: this (as first mentioned in Chapter 3) is an implementation-dependent read-only variable, defined in the header file limits.h. Typically, the file limits.h will include the line:

```
#define INT_MAX  32767   // maximum value of an int
```

Note that #define is (as we will see in Chapter 8, p. 191) one way of creating numerical constants. To make use of INT_MAX, or the corresponding INT_MIN value, the header file limits.h must be included in your program.

In Program 6.15, the calculation cannot simply be carried out with an integer since, by definition, no integer can store a value greater than INT_MAX, and the test could never fail. If test has a value less than INT_MAX, then the function operates in the same way as previous examples: where test exceeds this value, a return value of 1 is used to indicate an error. Note also that the error message generated in these circumstances is directed to cerr and not cout. In most cases, cerr and cout represent the user's screen, but this may not always be the case. For example, some operating systems (notably UNIX) allow the user to direct the program outputs to a file. In these circumstances, all outputs sent to cout will be directed to the file, but outputs sent to cerr will still appear on the screen. Usually this is useful behaviour, and `cerr` is therefore frequently used for error messages in larger programs.

Note how the return value is used in the calling function to 'recover' from the error:

```
do
    {
    cout << "Type first number : ";
    cin >> Num1;
    cout << "Type second number : ";
    cin >> Num2;
    // Call function and check return code value
    Return_value = Sum_Of_Squares5(Num1, Num2);
    } while (Return_value != 0);
```

Here, while a return value of 1 is produced by `Sum_of_Squares5()`, this value will be assigned to the variable `return_value`, and the program will keep prompting the user for valid inputs.

We'll see some more realistic uses for this useful error correction strategy in later chapters. We'll also look in more detail at the `return` statement in Chapter 8 (p. 184).

6.11 Using the `const` modifier in function headers

We used the `const` modifier in Chapter 3 to produce read-only variables. This modifier is also very widely used in function headers, as we will see here.

6.11.1 Using `const` value parameters

Consider the `Sum_Of_Squares6()` function:

```
/*******************************************************************
 * FUNCTION: Sum_Of_Squares6                                       *
 *                                                                 *
 * OVERVIEW: To calculate the sum of the squares                   *
 *           of a and b (both integers) returning the              *
 *           result via reference variable Sum_REF.                *
 *******************************************************************/
void Sum_of_Squares6(int a, int b, int& Sum_REF)
    {
    int Square1;
    int Square2;

    a = 0; // Debug statement;

    Square1 = a * a;
    Square2 = b * b;

    Sum_REF = Square1 + Square2;
    }
```

Here, with the line,

```
a = 0;   // Debug statement;
```

we modify the value parameter a before making the calculation. Such a modification is, of course, valid C++, but is very rarely necessary in a well-written program (and in this case is definitely **not** necessary). Errors of this nature can be extremely difficult to spot during debugging.

Usually we wish to avoid this possibility: we can do so very effectively by making use of the const modifier in the function heading, as follows:

```
/*****************************************************************
 * FUNCTION: Sum_Of_Squares7                                     *
 *                                                               *
 * OVERVIEW: To calculate the sum of the squares                 *
 *           of A and B (both integers) returning the            *
 *           result via reference variable Sum_REF.              *
 *****************************************************************/
void Sum_Of_Squares7(const int A, const int B, int& Sum_REF)
    {
    int Square1;
    int Square2;

    A = 0;   // WON'T COMPILE!!!!

    Square1 = A * A;
    Square2 = B * B;

    Sum_REF = Square1 + Square2;
    }
```

As the comments suggest, this new version of the function won't compile.

As a general rule, you should always use the const modifier with value parameters.

6.11.2   Using const reference parameters

Despite all our earlier comments in this chapter, professional programmers don't always use value parameters in their code. This is because value parameters always (necessarily) involve making copies of the data you wish to use, and making such copies may have a large impact on the speed of your program. Where speed of execution is important, you will usually find it more effective to use 'constant call by reference': that is, to use reference parameters, with the const modifier, to gain all of the advantages of call by value, without the overhead of copying the parameters each time you call the function.

Program 6.16 illustrates the advantages of this technique.

```
// Fast access to functions using const refs
// Source is: 06_16.CPP
#include <iostream.h>
#include <time.h>

// Function declarations
int Function1(const double, const double);
int Function2(const double&, const double&);
```

```
int main()
    {
    double temp1 = 1.0, temp2 = 2.0;
    const long NUM_PASSES = 10000000;
    double elapsed_time;

    time_t start_time, stop_time; // time_t is defined in time.h

    // METHOD ONE
    start_time = time(NULL);

    for (long pass = 0; pass <= NUM_PASSES; pass++)
        {
        Function1(temp1, temp2);
        }
    stop_time = time(NULL);
    elapsed_time = difftime(stop_time, start_time);
    cout << "Value, time (in seconds) : " << elapsed_time << endl;

    // METHOD TWO
    start_time = time(NULL);

    for (pass = 0; pass <= NUM_PASSES; pass++)
        {
        Function2(temp1, temp2);
        }

    stop_time = time(NULL);
    elapsed_time = difftime(stop_time, start_time);
    cout << "Reference, time (in seconds) : " << elapsed_time << endl;

    return 0;
    }
int Function1(const double A, const double B)
    {
    double x = A;
    double y = B;

    return 0;
    }

int Function2(const double& A_REF, const double& B_REF)
    {
    double x = A_REF;
    double y = B_REF;

    return 0;
    }
```

Program 6.16 Using constant references for fast function access. (☺)

The output from Program 6.16 is as follows:

```
Value, time (in seconds) : 41
Reference, time (in seconds) : 36
```

Note that, when passing a very small amount of data (say a single character) it may be faster to use (true) call by value: in most other circumstances, where speed is important, constant call by reference is a faster, and equally safe, technique. Note that, at heart, the speed increases arise through the use of pointers, a topic we consider in Chapter 7. We shall see further uses for the `const` modifier in Chapter 8.

6.12   Conclusions

In this chapter, we've seen that functions, and particularly the passing of data to and from functions, need to be handled with care, if a reliable program is to be developed and subsequently maintained.

We can summarize the material in this chapter in the form of 10 guidelines to help you produce a successful process-oriented implementation. These are not absolute, but you should, nonetheless, have a good reason for breaking them!

(1)   Don't write monolithic programs, that is, programs comprising of only a `main()` function. Break your programs up into a number of small self-contained functions.

(Note that we have, quite deliberately, not attempted to present any guidelines for decomposing your program into individual functions: such a decomposition arises as the end result of the earlier stages of SADIE. These topics are the focus of much of the remainder of this part of the book.)

(2)   If the analysts and designers have done their job, the design specification will include appropriate descriptions of a number of independent functions, each with a clearly defined task to perform. None of the specified functions will serve more than one task, and no single task will be split between functions. If these conditions are not satisfied, then no attempt should be made to implement the design: it should be returned to the design team for rework.

(3)   The *ideal* function is one with no parameters. Such an ideal function is completely isolated from the outside world. Sadly, functions without parameters are usually of limited utility.

(4)   Don't be tempted to write parameterless functions and then 'slip' them data through the use of global variables. Such a function is as (un)structured as a monolithic program, and probably less reliable because anyone looking at the code is lulled into a false sense of security. To be more pragmatic, passing constant data to functions as global variables, if used sparingly and fully documented, is usually acceptable.

(5)   You should always write functions on a 'need to know' basis. Let your functions have access only to the data which they 'need to know' about allow your functions only the degree of access to their parameters that they absolutely must have.

(6)   It follows from point 5 that you should use call by value wherever possible: that is, where the calling function does not need to modify the data it is supplied with. In general, you should always use the `const` modifier in conjunction with value parameters. This prevents, for example, erroneous values being in advertently used within a function due to careless modification of a value parameter.

(7)   If the speed of your program is important, consider using 'constant reference' parameters in place of the 'constant value' parameters described in point 6. Use of register variables *may* also help speed up your code.

(8)   If your called function must return data to the calling function, then use call by reference (reference variables), this time without the `const` modifier.

(9)   Use the return value from your functions wherever possible to indicate when errors have occurred, and to allow for error recovery.

(10)   For maximum portability, send error messages to `cerr`, rather than `cout`.

We expand on these guidelines in later chapters.

Exercises

6.1   Write a program that asks the user to type in a real number. Print out the number using a function called `Print_Float()`. Don't use *any* global variables, use call by value.

6.2   Write a program with two functions. The first (`Get_Int()`) will ask the user to type in an integer. The second (`Print_Int()`) will print out the number that the user typed in. Use call by reference in `Get_Int()`, and call by value in `Print_Int()`.

6.3   Repeat Exercise 6.2, this time asking the user to type in single characters (instead of integers).

6.4   Repeat Exercise 6.2 again, this time using call by reference in *both* the `Get_Int()` and the `Print_Int()` functions. Explain why, although this solution works, it may be bad programming practice. Explain how the use of `const` modifiers can make this a reasonable solution.

6.5   Repeat Exercise 6.2 one last time, using global variables everywhere! Explain why, although this solution also works, it is *always* very bad programming practice.

6.6   Write a program that works as a simple calculator, prompting the user for two integers, and asking whether he or she wants to add or subtract them. The program should have a `main()` function of course, and at least two other functions (`Add_Num()` and `Subtract_Num()`). Make sure you use the return value from these functions in an appropriate way.

        The program should generate outputs in the following form:

```
Simple calculator

First number >          5
Operation (+ or -) >  +
Second number >         4

ANSWER :                9
```

```
Simple calculator

First number >          100
Operation (+ or -) >  -
Second number >         90

ANSWER :                10
```

```
Simple calculator

First number >          100
Operation (+ or -) >  *

<<< OPERATION * NOT DEFINED >>>

Operation (+ or -) >  +
Second number >         80

ANSWER :                180
```

6.7   Write a C++ function `Multiple()` that takes two integer parameters. If the first parameter is a multiple of the second (e.g. 4 is a multiple of 2; 9 is a multiple of 3), then the function will return a value of 1, otherwise the function will return a value of 0. Write a C++ program to test this function.

6.8   Write a C++ program `PRIME.CPP` that will calculate the first 100 prime numbers. The program should use the function `Multiple()` written in Exercise 6.7.

6.9   Consider the output from Program 6.14 (pp. 126–7). On all compilers the values of the static variable within the function will be the same, but the values of the automatic variable can vary depending on the way that memory use is optimized. Explore this program using your own compiler, and investigate how the results change as you alter the options used: for example, try optimizing for small code size, and compare this with code compiled for maximum speed. Explain the different results you obtain.

7 Pointers and arrays

7.1 Introduction

An understanding of pointers is essential if you are to understand C++ programs written by other people and if you are going to program well in this language yourself. Much of this chapter will therefore be devoted to this important topic and to the closely related subject of arrays.

To understand pointers, however, we need to consider some basic features of memory organization.

7.2 Memory organization

Consider the memory structure for a fictitious computer system shown in Figure 7.1. When the computer is started, the operating system is loaded into working memory (RAM) first: this process is usually, as far as the user is concerned, completely automatic. When the user then runs a program, the program code is loaded from disk, along with any necessary data for processing. At the same time, an additional area of working memory (usually known as the stack) is reserved. It is in this area that local variables and function arguments will be stored. Finally, the remaining memory not so far used is classed as the 'free store': if you, the programmer, know what you are doing, then you can use this memory too to make your programs more efficient (a process discussed in Chapter 18).

This still isn't the end of the story. The above explanation assumes that you will be programming for a desktop computer of some description. For the programmer, and his or her program, such an environment is a benign one. In an embedded system, by contrast, the microprocessor is generally 'naked'; that is, there is no operating system or BIOS (Basic Input Output System) in the conventional sense (Figure 7.1). Since both BIOS and operating system are, anyway, just another software layer, this does not present a fundamental problem but it does mean the programmer has more to do. We have more to say about embedded system development in Chapter 15.

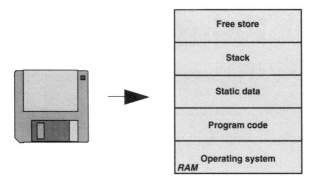

Figure 7.1 Memory structure on a simple desktop computer system while a program is running.

7.2.1 Bits and bytes

Let's consider the memory of the computer in slightly more detail. A computer memory can only store binary digits (**bits**), that is 0s and 1s. All data items must therefore be represented in some form of binary code, each containing a certain number of bits. To simplify the storage and retrieval of data items, these memory bits are grouped into **memory locations**, each with a unique **memory address**. In a common byte-oriented memory (such as that used on the IBM PC and most other computer systems), the smallest memory location contains eight bits, or one **byte** of storage, and each byte has a unique address, illustrated in Figure 7.2.

7.2.2 Storing characters in memory

Suppose we want to store a character at memory location '301' in the above computer system. Clearly, since the computer can only store numbers, we need a code for representing this character as a number.

One common character code is known as the ASCII code, a fragment of which is reproduced in Table 7.1.

The ASCII code represents each character as a single byte, so in our byte-oriented memory scheme we can store a single character at each memory location. If we store the character 'a' at memory location '301', the computer's memory becomes something like that shown in Figure 7.3.

Address	Contents							
...	–	–	–	–	–	–	–	–
304	1	0	0	1	1	1	1	1
303	0	0	1	1	1	1	0	0
302	1	1	0	0	0	0	0	1
301	1	0	1	0	1	0	0	0
...	–	–	–	–	–	–	–	–

Figure 7.2 A segment of byte-oriented memory. Note that each **byte** (rather than each **bit**) has its own unique address, shown in decimal notation here though, of course, they would be stored in binary notation on the computer.

Address	Contents							
...	–	–	–	–	–	–	–	–
304	–	–	–	–	–	–	–	–
303	–	–	–	–	–	–	–	–
302	–	–	–	–	–	–	–	–
301	0	1	1	0	0	0	0	1
...	–	–	–	–	–	–	–	–

Figure 7.3   Storing the character 'a' in memory location '301' of a fictional computer, using one possible binary representation of the ASCII character code.

Number	Character
65	A
66	B
67	C
68	D
...	...
97	a
98	b
99	c
100	d
...	...

Table 7.1   Part of the American Standard Code for Information Interchange (ASCII) character set.

As we have seen, each location in memory is an 8-bit byte on most computer systems. Now, with these 8 bits, we can store 2^8, that is 256, distinct values. This range is more than adequate for many European languages, but inadequate for many Eastern languages. Rudd (1994) provides details of C++ multibyte characters and wide characters that allow you to solve this problem.

7.2.3   Storing integers and other data

As we saw above, we can store only 256 distinct values in a single memory location. Now, suppose we wish to store integers: this means (depending on the code we used) that we could represent numbers from 0 to 255, or from –127 to + 128. Clearly, we are very likely to want to use integers outside these ranges!

The solution is to use multiple adjacent bytes of memory to represent single pieces of data. As mentioned previously, the size (in bytes) of the various data types is implementation specific, but the values given in Table 7.2 are typical of those used found on a desktop computer system. Note that, in each case, when we talk about the *address of* a particular data item, we mean the address at which the *first byte* of information is stored.

It is left as an exercise to work out the range of signed and unsigned integers that can be accommodated by each of these types.

Type	Size (in bytes)
char	1
short	2
int	2 or 4
long	4

Table 7.2 Typical sizes (in bytes) of some simple data types.

7.2.4 The `sizeof` operator

One way of determining the number of bytes required to store various data types on your own computer system is to use the unary `sizeof` operator, the use of which is illustrated in Program 7.1.

```
// Demonstrating the sizeof operator
// Source is: 07_01.CPP

#include <iostream.h>

int main()
    {
    cout << "A char uses          " << sizeof(char)
                         << " byte(s) of memory\n";
    cout << "A short int uses     " << sizeof(short)
                         << " byte(s) of memory\n";
    cout << "An int uses          " << sizeof(int)
                         << " byte(s) of memory\n";
    cout << "A float uses         " << sizeof(float)
                         << " byte(s) of memory\n";
    cout << "A double uses        " << sizeof(double)
                         << " byte(s) of memory\n";

    return 0;
    }
```

Program 7.1 Using the `sizeof` unary operator. (☺)

The output from Program 7.1 is as follows (on an IBM PC compatible):

```
A char uses         1 byte(s) of memory
A short int uses    2 byte(s) of memory
An int uses         2 byte(s) of memory
A float uses        4 byte(s) of memory
A double uses       8 byte(s) of memory
```

On a RISC-based Sun Sparcstation (UNIX Workstation), the output is as follows:

```
A char uses         1 byte(s) of memory
A short int uses    2 byte(s) of memory
An int uses         4 byte(s) of memory
A float uses        4 byte(s) of memory
A double uses       8 byte(s) of memory
```

Program 7.1 reveals that a `char` variable requires only a single byte of storage, while even a `short int` uses twice as much memory (but see Section 7.2.5). In addition, the two runs of Program 7.1 also tend to confirm the implementation-dependent nature of the C++ language that we first mentioned in Chapter 3. We consider other ways of detecting and correcting for such variations in Chapter 9.

7.2.5 Bytes and words

Consider that we are trying to develop a piece of C++ code which must both run very quickly and use very little memory. We have in the code some loops that require small numerical values (0–100). Because we know that, as far as C++ is concerned, a `char` variable is part of the set of integer data types (and that all data is stored numerically), we decide to use `char` variables to hold the loop control values, rather than the integer equivalents. In this way, we feel, we'll save some memory (at least one byte per loop), and because we're moving less data in and out of memory, we'll probably produce faster code too.

Thus, we decide, our code will feature several loops along the following lines:

```
for (char c = 0;  c <= 100;  c++)
    {
    ...
    }
```

where the 'integer' loop equivalent would, of course, be as follows:

```
for (int i = 0;  i <= 100;  i++)
    {
    ...
    }
```

Now, while it is true that the 'character' loop will compile and run, this is almost certainly a very bad idea. This is because most computer systems don't manipulate data in bytes, but work with larger blocks of memory arranged in what are usually called 'words'. A word of memory on a desktop computer, for example, will frequently be two bytes in size. Any computer will be at its most efficient when manipulating data in word-sized blocks. To exploit this efficiency, all data is usually aligned by the C++ compiler on what is known as **word** boundaries. Thus, on our desktop system mentioned above, all data items may begin (say) at odd-numbered memory locations.

What this means is that if we have 2 (1-byte) character variables to store they will be likely to consume not 2 bytes but 4 bytes of memory, which is precisely the same as 2 (2-byte) integers. Of course, it is no coincidence that the `int` data type will be 2 bytes in size on a desktop machine with a word size of 2 bytes, and 24 bytes on a machine with a 24-byte word size. In C++, the size of the `int` variable is deliberately chosen by the compiler writer to match the word size of the machine being used.

The bottom line is that there is very seldom any advantage to be gained by using character variables in place of the integer 'equivalents'. In general, such an exercise will prove counter-productive. Note, however, that using an integer variable in place of a long int (or, say, a double) will generally save memory, and possibly cause a large increase in the speed of your code.

Some of these ideas are illustrated in Program 7.2. Note that the timing functions used in this program were first used in Chapter 6 (p. 125), and will be discussed further in Chapter 9.

```cpp
// Access times for various data types
// Source is: 07_02.CPP

#include <iostream.h>
#include <time.h>

int main()
    {
    const long NUM_PASSES = 2000000;

    double elapsed_time;
    time_t start_time, stop_time; // time_t is defined in time.h

    // Using char
    start_time = time(NULL);

    int x = 0;
    for (long pass = 0; pass <= NUM_PASSES; pass++)
        {
        for (char char1 = 0; char1 <= 100; char1++)
            {
            x++;
            }
        }
    stop_time = time(NULL);
    elapsed_time = difftime(stop_time, start_time);
    cout << "Using char, time (in seconds) : "
        << elapsed_time << endl;

    // Using int
    start_time = time(NULL);

    x = 0;
    for (pass = 0; pass <= NUM_PASSES; pass++)
        {
        for (int int1 = 0; int1 <= 100; int1++)
            {
            x++;
            }
        }
    stop_time = time(NULL);
    elapsed_time = difftime(stop_time, start_time);
    cout << "Using int,  time (in seconds) : "
        << elapsed_time << endl;

    // Using long
    start_time = time(NULL);

    x = 0;
    for (pass = 0; pass <= NUM_PASSES; pass++)
        {
        for (long int1 = 0; int1 <= 100; int1++)
            {
            x++;
            }
        }
```

```
stop_time = time(NULL);
elapsed_time = difftime(stop_time, start_time);
cout << "Using long, time (in seconds) : "
    << elapsed_time << endl;

return 0;
}
```

Program 7.2 Comparing the speed of access to variables of different size. (☺)

The output from Program 7.2 is as follows:

```
Using char, time (in seconds) : 60
Using int,  time (in seconds) : 48
Using long, time (in seconds) : 86
```

Note carefully the results obtained here: although the precise figures obtained will, of course, vary according to the speed of hardware used to run the program, the relative differences in speed are realistic. That is, regardless of the hardware or compiler used, it generally proves substantially *slower* to use character data in this situation in place of an integer equivalent. In addition, it is unlikely that the use of character data will offer a saving in memory.

7.3 Assigning values to variables

Now that we know a bit more about the representation of data in memory, we can begin to consider what happens when we assign values to variables, as in Program 7.3.

```
// Source is: 07_03.CPP
// Useless
int main ()
    {
    int x;
    x = 3;
    return 0;
    }
```

Program 7.3 Assigning values to integer variables. (☺)

Program 7.3 will compile successfully, and will also run, doing (apparently) nothing. Let's consider what is actually happening.

First of all, with the line

```
int x;
```

the programmer is asking the compiler to allocate a piece of memory (from the stack), large enough to hold an integer (type `int`). Let's assume that our compiler allocates 4 bytes for an `int`, then what is actually happening is that a 4-byte area of memory is reserved, and labelled 'x', as illustrated in Figure 7.4.

Label	Address	Contents							
...	...	–	–	–	–	–	–	–	–
(x-continued)	415	?	?	?	?	?	?	?	?
(x-continued)	414	?	?	?	?	?	?	?	?
(x-continued)	413	?	?	?	?	?	?	?	?
x	412	?	?	?	?	?	?	?	?
...	...	–	–	–	–	–	–	–	–

Figure 7.4 Declaring a 4-byte `int` on a fictional computer. Note that the contents of the memory, before we initialize the variable, could be anything at all.

It is very important to note two things:

- As we have seen previously, the initial value of (automatic) variables is unknown. We can now see where the 'random' value arises from. In this case, if we were to print out the value of x, the computer will, quite reasonably, interpret the (binary) number presently in memory as an integer, and display this value. The result will always be an integer, but will not (except by chance) be 0. This is because C++ does not generally 'empty' memory locations of their previous contents when a new variable is defined. For instance, if – just before running Program 7.3 – you had been using your word processor, memory locations 412 to 415 could have been used to store part of your latest novel. Of course, the text would have been stored in binary notation, and C++ can quite happily interpret the 0s and 1s as integers, real numbers, characters, etc.

- When we run this program, we don't know what the actual address used to store variable x will be on any individual computer, or even on any individual program run. Most of the time we don't need to know, of course, and we just refer to the contents of this location by the label 'x': however, as we see below, this is not always the case.

If we now consider the next stage of this program, on the line

```
x = 3;
```

we assign to the variable x a value of 3. Now our memory diagram looks as shown in Figure 7.5.

Label	Address	Contents							
...	...	–	–	–	–	–	–	–	–
(x-continued)	415	0	0	0	0	0	0	0	0
(x-continued)	414	0	0	0	0	0	0	0	0
(x-continued)	413	0	0	0	0	0	0	0	0
x	412	0	0	0	0	0	0	1	1
...	...	–	–	–	–	–	–	–	–

Figure 7.5 Assigning a value of 3 to the 4-byte `int` variable x. (Note that the code used to represent the data is not intended to be representative of a realistic coding scheme: it is for illustrative purposes only.)

And that's it: the program run is complete. The program apparently does nothing, but behind the scenes there has been considerable activity, and our initially 'random' value of *x* has been changed to a known value.

However, as noted above, one thing we still don't know is the actual address in memory occupied by variable *x*. Should we actually wish to find this address we could do so using **pointers**. We consider why we might want to do so below.

7.4 Pointers

Having considered how memory is organized, we are finally in a position to consider what pointers actually are, and what they can do for us.

7.4.1 What are pointers?

Returning to our earlier example, we assign a value of 3 to the 4-byte int variable *x* (Figure 7.6).

The pointer to the variable *x* is the address of the memory location at which the variable *x* is stored: in this case, for our idealized computer system, the pointer to *x* is the address '412'.

Thus pointers are used to say *where* in memory a particular item of data is stored, rather than saying *what* the value stored in the memory location actually is.

7.4.2 How do you use pointers?

There are two key operators that allow us to use pointers in C++:

- The *address-of* operator (&) returns the *address* (NOT the value) of a given variable. Thus &x is the address in memory of the variable x.

- The *indirection* operator (*) returns the variable to which a pointer variable points. Thus *ptr returns the character to which the pointer (ptr), of type char, points.

The use of these operators is illustrated in Program 7.4.

Label	Address	Contents							
...	...	–	–	–	–	–	–	–	–
(x-continued)	415	0	0	0	0	0	0	0	0
(x-continued)	414	0	0	0	0	0	0	0	0
(x-continued)	413	0	0	0	0	0	0	0	0
x	412	0	0	0	0	0	0	1	1
...	...	–	–	–	–	–	–	–	–

Figure 7.6 Assigning a value of 3 to the 4-byte int variable *x* in a fictional computer system.

```
// A first look at pointers
// Source is: 07_04.CPP

#include <iostream.h>

int main()
    {
    int* q_PTR;         // q_PTR can store the ADDRESS of an integer
    int q;              // q can store the VALUE of an integer

    q = 100;            // Assign to q a value 100

    q_PTR = &q;         // Assign to q_PTR the ADDRESS OF q

    cout << q << "\n";// Display q's value directly
    cout << *q_PTR;     // Display q's value using a pointer

    return 0;
    }
```

Program 7.4   A first look at pointers. (☺)

The output from Program 7.4 is as follows:

```
100
100
```

Note the use of the variable name 'q_PTR' for the integer pointer used in this example. Of course, the name of such variables is entirely up to the programmer: however, it is often essential to know that you are dealing with a pointer variable when you come to debug a program, and consistent variable names like this can be a great help.

The next example, Program 7.5, illustrates that the use of pointers is not simply a read-only process.

```
// Another look at pointers
// Source is: 07_05.CPP

#include <iostream.h>

int main()
    {
    int* q_PTR;             // q_PTR is an integer pointer variable
    int q;                  // q is simply an integer variable

    q = 100;                // Assign to q a value 100
    q_PTR = &q;             // Assign to q_PTR the ADDRESS OF q

    cout << q << "\n";      // Display q's value directly
    cout << *q_PTR << "\n"; // Display q's value using a pointer

    *q_PTR = 123;           // Alter value of q, VIA POINTER

    cout << q << "\n";      // Display q's value directly
    cout << *q_PTR;         // Display q's value using a pointer

    return 0;
    }
```

Program 7.5   Using pointers to read from and write to memory. (☺)

The output from Program 7.5 is as follows:

```
100
100
123
123
```

Note that the type of the integer pointer variables used in the above example is 'int*', and the name of the variables is q_PTR. In some books you may see equivalent declarations written:

```
int *q_PTR;      // q_PTR is an integer pointer variable?
```

While such declarations are valid, you should resist the temptation to write your declarations in this way. Such a declaration *implies* to the reader of your code that the type of the variable is 'int' (it isn't: it is integer *pointer*), and that the variable's name is '*q_PTR' (it isn't: it is q_PTR). The situation is of course very similar to the declaration of reference variables in the last chapter. As with reference variables, you can only declare pointer variables 'correctly' by making one declaration per line.

The final example program here (Program 7.6) illustrates that, if you need to, you can display the address in memory at which your data is being stored. Note that the memory locations on your computer may vary from those shown.

```
// Displaying memory addresses using pointers
// Source is: 07_06.CPP
#include <iostream.h>
int main()
  {
  float     f;
  float*    f_PTR;
  // The address of f is assigned to i_PTR
  f_PTR = &f;
  // The value 1234.5 is assigned to f
  f = 1234.5f;
  // Print out some values
  cout << "Address of f              : " << &f << endl;
  cout << "Value of f                : " << f << endl;
  cout << "Value of f_PTR            : " << f_PTR << endl;
  cout << "Value pointed to by f_PTR: " << *f_PTR << endl;
  return 0;
  }
```

Program 7.6 Displaying memory addresses using pointers. (☺)

The output from one run of Program 7.6 is as follows:

```
Address of f              : 0x1e14
Value of f                : 1234.5
Value of f_PTR            : 0x1e14
Value pointed to by f_PTR : 1234.5
```

Note that the prefix '0x' indicates that addresses are given in hexadecimal notation ('hex' was briefly discussed in Chapter 3).

7.4.3 Why use pointers?

Now that we know what pointers are, and how to use them, let's consider why we would want to do such a thing. In fact, we have little choice: we have to use pointers because the use of such variables is integral to C++.

In practice, pointers are used in several ways:

- Pointers can be used to point to different data elements and different data structures, by changing the address the pointer contains (that is, performing pointer arithmetic). Thus, for example, a **linked list** of structures can be traversed with only one pointer. We consider this topic in Chapter 18.

- Pointer are used in conjunction with **dynamic memory allocation**, allowing the creation of new variables while the program is running. We consider this topic in Chapter 18.

- Pointers are used extensively in **function calls by address**. We have to postpone a detailed consideration of why this should be until Chapter 8.

- Pointers can be used to access individual elements in arrays of data. Accessing array elements in this way can be fast compared with normal array indexing.

We return repeatedly to the use of pointers throughout the remainder of this book. More immediately, we shall consider arrays in the next section and we shall see that the subjects of arrays and pointers are intimately related.

7.5 Arrays

An array is composed of a series of elements of a single data type. Most high-level languages, including C++, allow arrays to be defined. The array is (usually) declared at the start of the program or function so that the compiler is aware of *the number of elements* in the array and the data *type* of those elements.

We begin our discussion by looking at simple one-dimensional arrays.

7.5.1 One-dimensional arrays

We might represent an array of five elements as shown in Figure 7.7.

Some typical array declarations are:

```
int      results[20];      // array of 20 integers
float    weights[10];      // array of 10 floats
```

Note that:

- The brackets [] identify the variable as an array and the number in the brackets indicates the number of elements in the array.

- The first element always has the subscript or index 0: thus for the array results[] declared above, the individual (int) variables making up the array are results[0], results[1], results[2], ..., results[19].

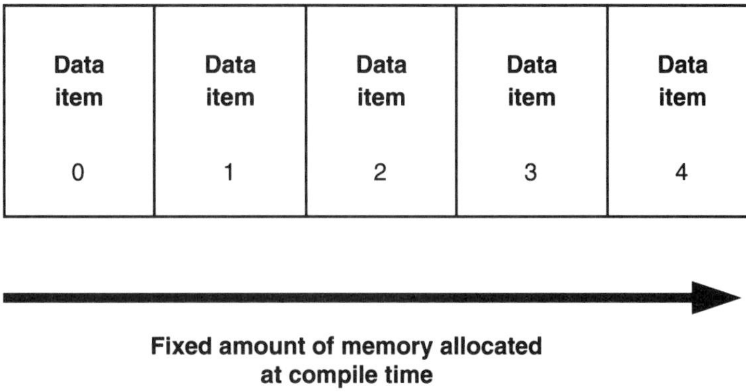

**Fixed amount of memory allocated
at compile time**

Figure 7.7 A schematic representation of an array of five elements.

● The data type indicates to the compiler the memory space required per element. It is very important to realize that the array is stored in a *single*, *continuous* block of memory: the compiler uses the information about the size of the array and the type of the elements in the array to allocate an appropriate block of memory to this data structure.

Example

In the exercises at the end of Chapter 4, you wrote a program to display results from a European election. To illustrate the use of arrays, let's look at a possible solution to this problem.

To remind you, the problem was as follows:

As part of the software for the next European election, you are asked to write a program that prompts the user to type in four numbers, each between 1 and 20. The marks represent the number of seats won by four political parties in some (arbitrary) constituency. The output of your program should be a histogram representing the election result: for instance, if the user types in 10,3,7,15 as the data, then the program should generate the following output:

```
PARTY 0: **********
PARTY 1: ***
PARTY 2: *******
PARTY 3: ***************
```

To solve this problem, we'll use an array of integers to store the results for each party. This array, which we'll call results[], will form the heart of our solution (Program 7.7).

```
// Using arrays: Solution to election problem
// Source is: 07_07.CPP
#include <iostream.h>
int main()
    {
    int results[4];
    // Get results
```

```
            for (int party = 0; party <= 3; party++)
                {
                do
                    {
                    cout << "Type result (between 1 and 20) for Party
                            number "
                        << party << "?> ";
                    cin >> results[party];
                    } while ((results[party] < 0) || (results[party] > 20));
                }
            // Display results in specified format
            for (party = 0; party <= 3; party++)
                {
                cout << "\nPARTY " << party << " : ";
                for (int stars = 1; stars <= results[party]; stars++)
                    {
                    cout << "*";
                    }
                }
            return 0;
            }
```

Program 7.7 Displaying a simple histogram using arrays. (☺)

A typical output from Program 7.7 is as follows:

```
Type result (between 1 and 20) for Party number 0> 13
Type result (between 1 and 20) for Party number 1> 30
Type result (between 1 and 20) for Party number 1> 20
Type result (between 1 and 20) for Party number 2> -1
Type result (between 1 and 20) for Party number 2> 6
Type result (between 1 and 20) for Party number 3> 19

PARTY 0 : *************
PARTY 1 : *******************
PARTY 2 : ******
PARTY 3 : *******************
```

Without the array, we would have had to declare four separate integer variables (say, result0, result1, result2, result3) and used these in our calculation. Because we couldn't use array indexing, we would probably have had to write a program almost four times as long to read in and display these data.

Initializing arrays

Note that we can initialize an array when we define it, as shown in the following example:

```
    float    Float_Array[3] = {12.3, 45.6, 78.9};
```

Following this definition, Float_Array[0] has a value 12.3, Float_Array[1] has a value 45.6 and Float_Array[2] a value 78.9.

When you wish to initialize all the elements of an array to 0 or some other value, then the situation gets a little more complex. Program 7.8 illustrates this situation.

```cpp
// Initialization of arrays
// Source is: 07_08.CPP

#include <iostream.h>

// A1 declared outside main() function
int A1[3]; // Storage class "extern" (external)

int main()
    {
    // A2, A3, A4 declared within function main()
    int A2[3];              // Storage class "auto" (automatic)
    int A3[3] = {1,2};      // Storage class "auto"
    int A4[4] = {0};        // Storage class "auto"

    // Print out the array contents
    cout << "\t\tA1\t\tA2\t\tA3\t\tA4\n";
    for (int i = 0; i < 3; i++)
        {
        cout << i << "\t\t" << A1[i] << "\t\t" << A2[i]
             << "\t\t" << A3[i] << "\t\t" << A4[i] << "\n";
        }

    return 0;
    }
```

Program 7.8   Initializing, and not initializing, arrays. (☺)

The output from Program 7.8 is as follows:

	A1	A2	A3	A4
0	0	13563	1	0
1	0	11	2	0
2	0	11551	0	0

As the output reveals, the initialization of automatic and external arrays follows the same basic rules that we saw in Chapter 6: that is, external arrays (such as A1[]) have elements initialized to zero, while automatic arrays (such as A2[]) are not initialized.

Note, however, that A3[], defined and initialised with the line:

```cpp
int A3[3] = {1,2}; // Storage class "auto"
```

has the first two (of three) elements initialized to '1' and '2', as expected. In such circumstances, as is the case for the third element here, all remaining elements in the array are also initialized, to a default of zero.

It follows from the above that we can initialize a whole array to '0' as with the line:

```cpp
int A4[4] = {0}; // Storage class "auto"
```

7.5.2 Multi-dimensional arrays

We can have arrays of any type, including integers, floating point numbers, characters, and even arrays of arrays. Arrays of arrays are, in effect, multi-dimensional arrays and have many uses.

Suppose, for example, we are asked to write some software to determine the most active salesperson in a particular company. As part of the program, we need to store the data given in Table 7.3.

	Q1	Q2	Q3	Q4
Ireland	450	375	456	460
Scotland	234	275	325	403
Wales	102	103	92	57

Table 7.3 Sales figures for mobile phones in Ireland, Scotland and Wales for 1995. Results are given individually for each quarter.

Table 7.3 has three rows and four columns. We could represent this data in C++ as follows:

```
const int ROWS      = 3;
const int COLUMNS   = 4;

int Sales[ROWS][COLUMNS]  =   {{450,375,456,460},
                               {234,275,325,403}
                               {102,103, 92, 57}};
```

Note how the initial data is laid out, and that we cannot write:

```
int Sales[ROWS, COLUMNS]; // *** WRONG!!! ***
```

Now, if we wanted to change the value of the table entry at row 2, column 3 to, say, 10, we would, bearing in mind that C++ always indexes from 0, write:

```
Sales[1][2] = 10;
```

We'll consider some further features of 2-D arrays when we consider arrays and pointers in Section 7.6.2.

7.6 Pointers and arrays

As we have mentioned, pointers and arrays are intimately related: now we can begin to see the nature of this relationship. One important reason for understanding this relationship is that speed improvements can result when the underlying pointer representation is exploited.

7.6.1 One-dimensional arrays

If, for example, we declare an array of integers as:

```
int numbers[3] = {12,14,16};
```

then both numbers and &numbers[0] represent the memory address of the first element of the array numbers[].

If we also declare an integer pointer, Int_PTR, as follows:

```
int* Int_PTR;
```

then we can assign Int_PTR to point to the start of the array numbers[] as follows:

```
Int_PTR = numbers;
```

or

```
Int_PTR = &numbers[0];
```

Following either of the above statements, then *Int_PTR has a value of 12.

We can then change the value of the first element of this array (to, say, 25) using the indirection operator, as follows:

```
*Int_PTR = 25;
```

We can also access the remaining elements of this array in a similar manner, by using pointer arithmetic. For instance, to set the contents of the three arrays elements to values of 10, 20 and 30, we could use the following code fragment:

```
*(Int_PTR + 0) = 10;
*(Int_PTR + 1) = 20;
*(Int_PTR + 2) = 30;
```

Here, the idea of, for example, 'adding 1' to the value of the pointer variable does *not* mean that we are adding one byte to the address pointed to. Instead, C++ knows the kind of data pointed to by the pointer (from the original pointer declaration) and will add the appropriate number of bytes to our address so that Int_PTR + 1 points to the address at which the next data item in the array is stored.

Accessing array elements in this manner may result in faster executable code: we consider this topic in Section 7.6.3. The price paid, however, is that the code may not be easy for less experienced C++ programmers to understand, and in writing the code even experienced programmers are likely to inadvertently introduce errors.

Program 7.9 illustrates the main points discussed here.

```
// Accessing array elements using pointer arithmetic
// Source is: 07_09.CPP
#include <iostream.h>
int main()
    {
    int Numbers[3] = {11,22,33};
    int* Num_PTR;
    int Sum_of_Numbers;

    // METHOD ONE
    Sum_of_Numbers = 0;

    // Set Num_PTR to start of array
    Num_PTR = Numbers;
```

```
for (int i = 0; i <= 2; i++)
    {
    Sum_of_Numbers += *(Num_PTR + i);
    }
cout << "Sum is (the hard way) " << Sum_of_Numbers << endl;
// METHOD TWO
Sum_of_Numbers = 0;
for (i = 0; i <= 2; i++)
    {
    Sum_of_Numbers += Numbers[i];
    }
cout << "Sum is (the easy way) " << Sum_of_Numbers << endl;
return 0;
}
```

Program 7.9 Using pointer arithmetic with arrays. (☺)

The output from Program 7.9 is as follows:

```
Sum is (the hard way) 66
Sum is (the easy way) 66
```

Note that a central problem with C++'s 'flexible' approach to arrays is that there can be no bounds checking. What this means is that the programmer is free to make a declaration like this:

```
int numbers[3] = {12,14,16};
```

followed by a statement like this:

```
numbers[300] = 45;
```

or even like this:

```
numbers[-5] = 23;
```

What happens is that, although the programmer has declared numbers[] to be a three-element array, the compiler will simply convert any reference to this array into the equivalent pointer notation, without making any checks as to the upper and lower 'bounds' of the data.

You may be wondering why C++, in many ways a sophisticated high-level language with strict type-checking, would allow such an obvious loophole. The answer lies in C++'s historical roots. In C++'s predecessor, the C language, arrays were developed to exploit auto-increment pointers that existed on primitive computer systems. When C++ was developed, the decision was made to keep the new language upwardly compatible with (ANSI/ISO) C code: to change the array data structure in C++ to provide support for bounds checking would have gone against this decision.

This does not mean, however, that you cannot used bounded arrays with your programs. In Chapter 25, we describe a new class-based array data type that is easy to produce, and does offer bounds checking.

7.6.2 Two-dimensional arrays

Pointer arithmetic can, of course, be used with arrays of more than one dimension. In order to use pointers, we first need to know how our arrays are stored in memory.

Let's suppose we have a 2-D array two_d[][] of characters. It will be stored in memory as shown in Figure 7.8.

Label	Address	Contents							
...	...	–	–	–	–	–	–	–	–
two_d[1][1]	13517	?	?	?	?	?	?	?	?
two_d[1][0]	13516	?	?	?	?	?	?	?	?
two_d[0][1]	13515	?	?	?	?	?	?	?	?
two_d[0][0]	13514	?	?	?	?	?	?	?	?
...	...	–	–	–	–	–	–	–	–

Figure 7.8 How elements of a 2-D array two_d[] are stored in memory. Note that the array is not initialized so the contents are unknown.

Suppose that we declare our 2-D array as follows:

```
two_d[ROWS][COLUMNS]
```

where ROWS and COLUMNS are integer constants specifying the array dimensions. We can then access any arbitrary element in row r, column c of this array using any of the following equivalent expressions:

```
two_d[r][c]
*(two_d[r] + c)
*(*(two_d + r) + c)
*(*two_d + (r * COLUMNS) + c)
```

These various possibilities are illustrated in Program 7.10.

```
// Investigating 2-D array pointers
// Source is: 07_10.CPP

#include <iostream.h>

int main()
    {
    const int ROWS    = 2;
    const int COLUMNS = 3;
          int data    = 0;
          int two_d[ROWS][COLUMNS];

    for (int r = 0; r < ROWS; r++)
        {
        for (int c = 0; c < COLUMNS; c++)
            {
            two_d[r][c] = data++;

            cout << "two_d[" << r << "][" << c << "] = "
                 << two_d[r][c]                 << " ( "
```

```
                        << *(two_d[r] + c)              << " "
                        << *(*(two_d + r) + c)          << " "
                        << *(*two_d + (r * COLUMNS) + c) << " )\n";
            }
        }
    return 0;
}
```

Program 7.10   Using pointers to access elements of a 2-D array. (☺)

The output from Program 7.10 is as follows:

```
two_d[0][0] = 0    ( 0 0 0 )
two_d[0][1] = 1    ( 1 1 1 )
two_d[0][2] = 2    ( 2 2 2 )
two_d[1][0] = 3    ( 3 3 3 )
two_d[1][1] = 4    ( 4 4 4 )
two_d[1][2] = 5    ( 5 5 5 )
```

We have already seen that, for a 1-D array (let's call it one_d[]) both &one_d[0] and simply one_d are equivalent representations of the memory locations at which the array begins.

For two-dimensional arrays, the situation is slightly more complex. As before, &two_d[0][0] gives the address at which the array begins in memory. However, two_d is now a pointer to an array whose elements are two_d[0] and two_d[1]: in other words, two_d is a *pointer to a pointer*. Further, two_d[0] is a pointer to two_d[0][0], and two_d[1] is a pointer to two_d[1][0].

We can summarize these important relationships as shown in Table 7.4. Note that this does not mean that a two-dimensional array requires additional storage for 'an extra set of pointers'. We can confirm this using the sizeof operator (Program 7.11).

two_d *is a pointer to…*	two_d[0]	*is a pointer to…*	two_d[0][0]
	two_d[1]	*is a pointer to…*	two_d[1][0]

Table 7.4   Pointers and two-dimensional arrays.

```
// Checking sizes of arrays
// Source is: 07_11.CPP

#include <iostream.h>

int main()
    {
    int one_d[3];
    int two_d[3][3];

    cout << "1-D " << sizeof(one_d) << endl;
    cout << "2-D " << sizeof(two_d);

    return 0;
    }
```

Program 7.11   Using sizeof with 1-D and 2-D arrays. (☺)

Program 7.11 generates the following output:

```
1-D  12
2-D  36
```

Note that `sizeof` gives the size of the array in *bytes*: the output was produced on a 32-bit computer system. We'll use a further program to demonstrate the results in Table 7.4 in Section 7.7.1.

7.6.3 Speeding up array access

One important use of array access through pointer arithmetic arises when we pass arrays to functions, a topic we consider in Chapter 8. However, another important reason is that array access can be faster when carried out in this manner. Such factors can be of particular importance, for example, when you need to make a copy of a large array.

To illustrate this process, consider Program 7.12.

```cpp
// Copying multi-dimensional arrays using pointer arithmetic
// and "normal" indexing. Compares the speed of each technique.
// Source is: 07_12.CPP
#include <iostream.h>
#include <time.h>
int main()
    {
    const int     DIM1 = 10;
    const int     DIM2 = 10;
    const int     DIM3 = 10;

    const long    NUM_PASSES = 100000;

    int      Original[DIM1][DIM2][DIM3] = {0};
    int      Copy[DIM1][DIM2][DIM3];
    int*     Orig_PTR;
    int*     Copy_PTR;
    double   elapsed_time;
    time_t   start_time, stop_time; // time_t is defined in time.h

    // METHOD ONE
    cout << "Starting calculation - please wait...\n";
    start_time = time(NULL);

    for (long pass = 0; pass <= NUM_PASSES; pass++)
        {
        Orig_PTR = &Original[0][0][0];
        Copy_PTR = &Copy[0][0][0];
        for (int i = 0; i < DIM1; i++)
            {
            for (int j = 0; j < DIM2; j++)
                {
                for (int k = 0; k < DIM3; k++)
                    {
                    *Copy_PTR = *Orig_PTR;
                    Orig_PTR++;
                    Copy_PTR++;
```

```
                                                }
                                            }
                                        }
                                    }
            stop_time = time(NULL);
            elapsed_time = difftime(stop_time, start_time);
            cout << "Using pointers, time (in seconds) : "
                    << elapsed_time << endl;
            cout << "Starting second calculation - please wait...\n";

            // METHOD TWO
            start_time = time(NULL);

            for (pass = 0; pass <= NUM_PASSES; pass++)
                {
                for (int i = 0; i < DIM1; i++)
                    {
                    for (int j = 0; j < DIM2; j++)
                        {
                        for (int k = 0; k < DIM3; k++)
                            {
                            Copy[i][j][k] = Original[i][j][k];
                            }
                        }
                    }
                }
            stop_time = time(NULL);
            elapsed_time = difftime(stop_time, start_time);
            cout << "Using indexing, time (in seconds) : "
                    << elapsed_time << endl;

            return 0;
            }
```

Program 7.12 Copying arrays using normal indexing and pointers. (☺)

The output from Program 7.12 is as follows:

```
    Starting calculation - please wait...
    Using pointers, time (in seconds) : 78
    Starting second calculation - please wait...
    Using indexing, time (in seconds) : 171
```

As here, the pointer-based technique (which looks, if anything, less direct and more clumsy) is generally faster, mainly because we eliminate an address computation:

- When we write Numbers[i][j][k], the compiler turns this into the pointer-based equivalent:

```
    *(&Numbers[0][0][0] + (i * DIM2 * DIM3) + (j * DIM3) + k)
```

which requires several additions and, more importantly, several time-costly multiplications to locate the desired element.

● In the pointer version, the pointer is incremented each time we go through the loop: this can often be done as part of the machine instruction that dereferences the pointer, and no further calculation is necessary. At worst, a single addition is required.

7.7 Strings

Arrays and pointers are widely used in C++ to manipulate strings. As we shall see, all strings are arrays of characters, but not all arrays of characters are strings.

7.7.1 Using `char` variables

As we have seen in previous chapters, a single character, such as the 'Y' or 'N' answer to a question, is declared in C++ as follows:

```
char      Do_You_Want_To_Continue;
```

We might use such a variable as shown in Program 7.13.

```cpp
// Playing with char variables
// Source is: 07_13.CPP

#include <iostream.h>

int main()
    {
    char do_you_want_to_continue;
    for (int count = 0; count <= 10000; count++)
        {
        cout << "Count is " << count << endl;
        cout << "Do you want to continue counting (y/n) ? ";
        cin >> do_you_want_to_continue;
        if (do_you_want_to_continue == 'n')
            {
            break;
            }
        }
    cout << "Count aborted";
    return 0;
    }
```

Program 7.13 Using a simple character variable. (☺)

The output from Program 7.13 is as follows:

```
Count is 0
Do you want to continue counting (y/n) ? y
Count is 1
Do you want to continue counting (y/n) ? y
Count is 2
Do you want to continue counting (y/n) ? y
Count is 3
Do you want to continue counting (y/n) ? n
Count aborted
```

7.7.2 Simple strings

Use of character variables is straightforward. However, when it comes to strings, C++ provides no directly applicable type: instead, an aggregate data type must be assembled using an array of character variables. As we shall see, the lack of a simple string data type in C++ has some additional, wider-reaching implications: in particular, operations such as copying and comparing string data cannot be conducted as easily as similar operations on simple data types. We shall consider these issues in greater depth in Chapters 8 and 9.

A simple character (string) array might be declared as follows:

```
char    message[30];
```

Note that the [30] after message sets aside space for up to 29 characters, followed by a **null terminator**, (\0): this terminator is required if the character string is to be, for example, interpreted correctly by the stream insertion operator <<.

Program 7.14 illustrates the simple use of strings.

```
// Reading and Printing Character Arrays (Strings)
// Source is: 07_14.CPP

#include <iostream.h>

int main()
    {
    char line1[18] = "When I was young,";
    char line2[] = "Megan brought stone giants through the
                    centuries";
    char line3[] = "to fight back the darkness.";
    char* line2_PTR = &line2[0];
    char* line3_PTR = line3;

    cout << line1 << endl;
    cout << line2_PTR << endl;
    cout << line3_PTR;

    return 0;
    }
```

Program 7.14 Playing with some strings. (☺)

The output from Program 7.14 is as follows:

```
When I was young,
Megan brought stone giants through the centuries
to fight back the darkness.
```

In Program 7.14, the line:

```
char line1[18] = "When I was young,";
```

copies the string constant "When I was young," (seventeen characters in total), *plus a null terminator*, into the character array `line1[18]`.

The line:

```
char line2[] = "Megan brought stone giants through the centuries";
```

looks different (and more complicated) but is simply another example of C++ shorthand. This line is *directly equivalent* to the line:

```
char line2[49] = "Megan brought stone giants through the centuries";
```

The only difference is that, in the program, we let the *compiler* count the characters (and add one for a null terminator), while in the example above we do the count ourselves. As a general rule, it is better to be explicit, but you will see examples with 'empty brackets' in C++ code.

When it comes to displaying the strings, we use the character pointers in Program 7.14 to emphasize what is happening. For example, when we write:

```
cout << line1 << endl;
```

we are specifying that a *character pointer* should be displayed. If we had written such a line for an integer pointer (for example), we would have expected to have seen an *address* displayed (probably in hex).

However, in the case of character pointers, the stream insertion operator has a different default behaviour: instead of an address, the contents of the whole string (up to the null terminator) are displayed on the screen:

```
When I was young,
```

As we will see in Part III, the stream insertion operator is very powerful, and can perform a range of different actions depending on the type of data with which it is used. Importantly, the *programmer* can define the behaviour required when working with programmer-defined data types (see Chapter 27 for further details of this).

Of course, if you wish to display the address at which a string is stored in memory, you can do so; this will be illustrated in Program 7.17.

Finally, note that, just as you can have arrays of characters, C++ also allows the programmer to use arrays of strings: that is *arrays of* arrays of characters. We defer consideration of such features until Section 7.7.4.

7.7.3 More complex string I/O

The use of the identifiers `cin` and `cout` with strings is straightforward. However, as the following examples show, you need to understand the features of these identifiers if you are to use them in this way. In particular, you may quickly find that `cin` is not sufficiently flexible for your input requirements.

For example, consider Program 7.15.

```cpp
// Reading and Printing Character Arrays (Strings)
// Source is: 07_15.CPP

#include <iostream.h>

int main()
    {
    // Space for (up to) 5 characters, plus NULL terminator
    char short_char_array[6];

    // Space for (up to) a screen width of characters, + NULL
    terminator char long_char_array[81];

    // A pointer to the LONG array
    // (for illustrative purposes only)
    char* long_PTR = &long_char_array[0];

    cout << "Type a short string : ";
    cin >> short_char_array;

    cout << "The following string was stored : " << short_char_array
         << endl;

    cout << "Type a long string : ";
    cin >> long_PTR;

    cout << "The following string was stored : " << long_PTR << endl;

    return 0;
    }
```

Program 7.15 Revealing the limitations of simple input routines. (☺)

The output from Program 7.15 is as follows:

```
Type a short string : 1234
The following string was stored : 1234
Type a long string : 12345678
The following string was stored : 12345678
```

Here, you must be careful that the string you type is not too long, causing an array out of bounds error (discussed above in Section 7.6.1). In this event, unpredictable errors may occur (when C++ may overwrite areas of memory assigned to, say, other variables).

However, a more immediate problem is that `cin` (usually) terminates its strings when it encounters any spaces (strictly, any 'white space') in your input, as illustrated in the following output from Program 7.15:

```
Type a short string : Goran
The following string was stored : Goran
Type a long string : Goran Macleod
The following string was stored : Goran
```

To circumvent such problems, another input function `getline()` is much more flexible. We consider `getline()` and other useful string handling functions in Chapter 9.

7.7.4 Arrays of arrays of characters

As we have already mentioned, we can have arrays of pointers. One common use for this in C++ is to provide efficient storage for strings. For example, suppose we wish to store the following list of names:

```
Goran Macleod
Megan
Joe Bloggs
Alexander the Great
```

We could use a 2-D array of characters, declared and initialized as follows:

```
char names1[4][20] =
    { {"Goran Macleod"},
      {"Megan"},
      {"Joe Bloggs"},
      {"Alexander the Great"} };
```

However, this would be very inefficient, as we are forced to make each of the four rows of the array long enough to store the longest name (19 characters, plus null terminator). In effect, we have an array $4 \times 20 = 80$ bytes in size, when the total space we require is only 51 bytes. In a realistic situation, this could well mean that we were wasting up to 50% of the available computer memory.

A better alternative is frequently to use not a 2-D array of characters in such circumstances, but a 1-D array of *pointers*, where each array element points to the start of a string just long enough to hold the required data. In such circumstances, almost all of the 'wasted' memory from the above example can be recovered:

```
char* names_PTR[4] =
    { {"Goran Macleod"},
      {"Megan"},
      {"Joe Bloggs"},
      {"Alexander the Great"} };
```

These two possibilities are compared in Program 7.16.

```
// Arrays of pointers to strings
// Source is: 07_16.CPP

#include <iostream.h>
#include <stdio.h>
#include <iomanip.h>

int main()
    {
    char names1[4][20] =
        { {"Goran Macleod"},
          {"Megan"},
          {"Joe Bloggs"},
          {"Alexander the Great"} };
```

```
            char* names_PTR[4] =
                { {"Goran Macleod"},
                  {"Joe Bloggs"},
                  {"Megan"},
                  {"Alexander the Great"} };
        cout << "2-D array of characters:" << endl;
        cout << names1[0] << endl;
        cout << names1[1] << endl;
        cout << names1[2] << endl;
        cout << names1[3] << endl << endl;

        cout << "1-D array of pointers:" << endl;
        cout << names_PTR[0] << endl;
        cout << names_PTR[1] << endl;
        cout << names_PTR[2] << endl;
        cout << names_PTR[3] << endl << endl;

        return 0;
        }
```

Program 7.16 Arrays of pointers to strings. (☺)

The output from Program 7.16 is as follows:

```
    2-D array of characters:
    Goran Macleod
    Megan
    Joe Bloggs
    Alexander the Great

    1-D array of pointers:
    Goran Macleod
    Joe Bloggs
    Megan
    Alexander the Great
```

In a similar way, we can confirm that the results given in Table 7.4 are correct using Program 7.17.

```
// Arrays of pointers to strings
// Source is: 07_17.CPP

#include <iostream.h>
#include <stdio.h>
#include <iomanip.h>

int main()
    {
    char name[20] = "Goran";

    char names[4][20] =
        { {"Goran Macleod"},
          {"Megan"},
          {"Joe Bloggs"},
          {"Alexander the Great"} };
```

```
        cout << (unsigned int) name << endl;
        cout << (unsigned int) &name[0] << endl;
        cout << name << endl << endl;

        cout << (unsigned int) names << endl;
        cout << (unsigned int) names[0] << endl;
        cout << (unsigned int) &names[0] << endl;
        cout << (unsigned int) &names[0][0] << endl;
        cout << names[0][0] << endl;
        cout << names[0] << endl << endl;

        cout << (unsigned int) names[1] << endl;
        cout << (unsigned int) &names[1] << endl;
        cout << (unsigned int) &names[1][0] << endl;
        cout << names[1][0] << endl;
        cout << names[1] << endl << endl;

        cout << (unsigned int) names[2] << endl;
        cout << (unsigned int) &names[2] << endl;
        cout << (unsigned int) &names[2][0] << endl;
        cout << names[2][0] << endl;
        cout << names[2] << endl << endl;

        cout << (unsigned int) names[3] << endl;
        cout << (unsigned int) &names[3] << endl;
        cout << (unsigned int) &names[3][0] << endl;
        cout << names[3][0] << endl;
        cout << names[3] << endl << endl;

        return 0;
    }
```

Program 7.17 Confirming the results from Table 7.4. (☺)

Program 7.17 generates the following output:

```
13556
13556
Goran

13476
13476
13476
13476
G
Goran Macleod

13496
13496
13496
M
Megan
```

```
13516
13516
13516
J
Joe Bloggs

13536
13536
13536
A
Alexander the Great
```

Note that the addresses here are in decimal notation, not hexadecimal. This is achieved using the `(unsigned int)` cast operator, for example:

```
cout << (unsigned int) name << endl;
```

You may have to change the cast operator on your system, depending on the way memory is mapped. The example shown was run on an IBM PC, using a particular set of compiler options (notably 'small memory model'). In these circumstances, all memory in the computer is arranged in 64 Kbyte segments, and no memory address will exceed this value: this range of possible memory addresses matches the range of 'unsigned int' (on this system) precisely. Use of `unsigned int` works on the majority of systems: however, if your compiler uses a 'flat' memory model, you **may** need to change from `(unsigned int)` to, for example, `(unsigned long)`.

```
// Displaying pointer addresses
// See text: implementation dependent
// Source is: 07_18.CPP

#include <iostream.h>

int main(void)
    {
    double x = 0;

    cout << "                        x = " << x << endl;
    cout << "(unsigned int) &x = " << (unsigned int) &x << endl;
    cout << "                        &x = " << &x;

    return 0;
    }
```

Program 7.18 Illustrating the use of the cast operator with pointer variables. Note that, as discussed in the text, these results are implementation dependent. (☺)

Program 7.18 generates the following output:

```
                    x = 0
(unsigned int) &x = 14058
                    &x = 0x36EA
```

The easiest way to make your programs completely portable is to omit the cast operator altogether, and learn to read 'hex'.

7.7.5 On strings, arrays, pointers and constants

As we have discussed, C++ does not have a string data type. This has important implications: for example, while the programmer can, of course, simply copy one integer
variable to another:

```
...
int a,b = 4;
a = b;
...
```

the corresponding operation on a character string won't work:

```
...
char a[81], b[81] = "Hello";
a = b; // Can't copy strings like this!!!
...
```

Fortunately, the problems caused by the lack of a string data type can be largely alleviated if you are familiar with the character and string handling facilities provided with
all C++ compilers: we consider such features in Chapter 9.

Here, we'll look at the case where the 'you can't copy strings' rule is apparently
broken. For example, suppose we declare and *initialize* three character arrays and two
character pointers as shown in Program 7.19.

As you look at Program 7.19, remember that a string constant is simply another
array of characters (with a null terminator at the end), which will be, after compilation
and linking, stored somewhere in the resulting executable program. The important difference between this character array and a 'normal' character array is, however, that it
is *anonymous*. In general, only the compiler knows where the information has been
stored.

```
// Playing with character consts & c
// Source is: 07_19.CPP

#include <iostream.h>

int main()
    {
    int x; // An integer variable...
    // Some character arrays
    char Char_Array1[81] = "Help";                  // 1
    char Char_Array2[81] = {'H','e','l','p','\0'};  // 2
    char Char_Array3[] = "Help";                     // 3

    // Some character pointers
    char* Char_PTR = "Help";                         // 4
    char* Char_PTR2 = "Help";                        // 5

    cout << "Integer variable:\n";
    cout << (unsigned int) &x << endl << endl;

    cout << "Strings:\n";
    cout << Char_Array1 << endl;
    cout << (unsigned int) Char_Array1 << endl;
    cout << Char_Array2 << endl;
```

```
      cout << (unsigned int) Char_Array2 << endl;
      cout << Char_Array3 << endl;
      cout << (unsigned int) Char_Array3 << endl << endl;

      cout << "Character pointers:\n";
      cout << Char_PTR << endl;
      cout << (unsigned int) Char_PTR << endl;
      cout << Char_PTR2 << endl;
      cout << (unsigned int) Char_PTR2 << endl << endl;

      return 0;
      }
```

Program 7.19   Comparing character arrays and character pointers, and more. (☺)

The output from Program 7.19 is as follows:

```
    Integer variable:
    13586

    Strings:
    Help
    13504
    Help
    13422
    Help
    13416

    Character pointers:
    Help
    26
    Help
    31
```

The first thing to notice about this program out is that the addresses of the various variables fall into two groups the 'normal addresses' (13586, 13504, 13422, 13416) and the 'low addresses' (26, 31). The normal addresses (as shown by the integer variable) have values typical for the particular compiler and computer on which the program was developed. The low addresses reveal, however, that the string constants (declarations 4 and 5) are stored in a different area of memory.

The numbers also provide (circumstantial!) evidence of an important distinction between string and pointer initializations. When a character pointer is created and initialized, as in:

```
    // Some character pointers
    char* Char_PTR = "Help";                               // 4
```

then the value of the pointer is set to the address in memory at which the corresponding string constant is stored.

When, on the other hand, a string is initialized, as in:

```
    // Some character arrays
    char Char_Array1[81] = "Help";                         // 1
```

```
char Char_Array2[81] = {'H','e','l','p','\0'};    // 2
char Char_Array3[] = "Help";                      // 3
```

then the compiler does not simply change the address of the character array: instead, the string constant is copied into the character array: thus, there are two copies of the string in existence during the program run.

There are a few other things to note from Program 7.19. The second declaration above shows an alternative, less commonly used, way of initializing character arrays. Note that in this case it is necessary to explicitly include a null terminator in the initialization. Thus this type of initialization is useful if you require simply an array of characters and not a string. Remember, however, that an array of characters without a null terminator must generally be displayed on the screen character at a time (if necessary): the standard output routines assume that the arrays they are passed are terminated with a null character. The bottom line is that all strings are character arrays but not all character arrays are strings.

Note also that declarations 4 and 5 refer to different copies of the string constant 'help'. This compiler did not simply create one string constant and then set all the various pointer variables to the address of this single constant. Note that you cannot rely on this behaviour: it is implementation dependent (Stroustrup, 1991).

Finally, although you can (with many compilers) produce code that alters string constants, such as:

```
char* char_PTR = "Hello";

...

cout << "Type a sentence : ";
cin >> char_PTR;
```

this is bad programming practice, and the explicit declaration of a character array is to be much preferred in such circumstances.

One reason for this is that, using the first approach, the programmer may be tempted to write:

```
char* char_PTR;

...

cout << "Type a sentence : ";
cin >> char_PTR;
```

In this case, memory has been reserved only for a single, uninitialized, character pointer: the sentence typed by the user will overwrite unreserved memory areas, and often crash the program.

Character pointers are of greatest practical value when used in conjunction with dynamic memory allocation, a process considered in Chapter 18.

7.8   More advanced pointer topics

We close by considering two advanced features of pointers: generic pointers, and function pointers.

7.8.1 Pointing into the `void`

A pointer is more than a memory location. Because, as we saw in Section 7.2.3, most variables span more than a single memory location, to retrieve a particular piece of data, the system needs to know:

- the address in memory at which the first byte of the data item is stored, and,
- the size of the data item: that is, the number of bytes that must be fetched from memory.

Using pointers, we must have both location and size information, or the indirection operator cannot be used. Sometimes, however, it is useful to be able to stores not a complete pointer, but a generic or void pointer. A generic pointer stores only an address, with no type information. Such a pointer can be declared as follows:

```
void* generic_PTR;
```

A generic pointer must generally be used in conjunction with a cast operator, as we shall see in later examples. The use of generic pointers is discussed further in Chapter 9.

7.8.2 Pointers to functions

We have already seen that both code and data reside in physical memory when a program is executing. Just as, for example, we can calculate the starting address for an array of data in memory, we can also find the address in memory at which the executable code for any particular function begins: such function pointers can, in general, be manipulated in the same way as the data pointers we have so far considered.

The ability to locate the address of particular pieces of executable code in memory has wide implications for advanced C++ programs, such as the writing of system software (compilers, assemblers and interpreters), and is an invaluable feature of the language for such applications.

We see some practical uses of function pointers in Chapter 9. Program 7.20 illustrates some of the basic technicalities.

```
// Using function pointers
// Source is: 07_20.CPP

#include <iostream.h>

int squared(int, int&);

int main()
    {
    int a,b;
    int (* p)(int, int&); /* Declares p to be a pointer to fn with
                           *  int and int ref parameters
                           *  (returning an int) */
    int result_a, result_b;
    int* q;

    a = 7;
    b = 8;
    p = squared; // p has address of fn. squared()
    q = &a;
```

```
    cout << "Function code starts at address: " << p << endl;

    cout << "Data item a starts at address: " << q << endl;

    if (squared(a,result_a))
        {
        cerr << "WARNING: Error in function squared.";
        }

    if ((*p)(b,result_b))
        {
        cerr << "WARNING: Error in function squared.";
        }

    cout << a << " squared is " << result_a
         << " (using normal function call)\n";
    cout << b << " squared is " << result_b
         << " (using function pointer)\n";

    return 0;
    }

int squared(int a, int& b)
    {
    b = a * a;

    return 0;
    }
```

Program 7.20   An introduction to the use of function pointers. (☺?)

Program 7.20 generates the following output:

```
Function code starts at address: 0x0258
Data item a starts at address: 0x1b9a
7 squared is 49 (using normal function call)
8 squared is 64 (using function pointer)
```

As before, the addresses you see when you run this program will differ from those shown here, depending on the machine and compiler you are using.

The program operates as follows. In the statement:

```
int (* p)(int, int&);
```

variable p is declared to be a pointer to a function which has as parameters an integer and an integer reference, and which returns an integer. We need to include the brackets around '* p', otherwise, due to C++'s rules of precedence, we would not be declaring a function pointer but the prototype of a function (called p) which has as parameters an integer and an integer reference, and which returns an integer pointer. In effect, the declaration would be as follows:

```
int* p (int, int&);
```

or, explicitly:

```
int* (p) (int, int*);
```

Such a declaration is, in general, syntactically correct: but in this context it will not do what we require.

Returning to the correct declaration of the function pointer:

```
int (* p)(int, int&);
```

we can see that this pointer is, at a first glance, typeless. That is, it *appears* to be a void pointer (as discussed in Section 7.8.1). However, this is not a void pointer: with function pointers, the 'type' of the pointer depends on the number and type of the parameters (as well as on the type of the return value) of the function pointed to. For instance, if we wish to point to the function probably_not_very_structured(), with the prototype:

```
void probably_not_very_structured();
```

then we would declare our pointer, pnvs_FN_PTR (say) as follows:

```
void (* pnvs_FN_PTR)();
```

In each case, of course, the number of bytes required to store the pointer address depends on a number of complex factors, and we leave it up to the compiler to work out the size of the address for itself.

Returning to Program 7.20, we assign the function address to our function pointer with the line:

```
p = squared; // p has address of squared
```

which looks very similar to other pointer assignments we have seen, using arrays.

Now that we have uncovered the address at which the function code for squared resides, we can run this code through the statement:

```
if ((* p)(b,result_b))
    {
    ...
    }
```

which is very similar to the corresponding 'normal' function call:

```
if (squared(a,result_a))
    {
    ...
    }
```

Note that, in some circumstances, the use of virtual functions provides an elegant alternative to the use of function pointers: we discuss virtual functions in Chapter 29.

7.9 Conclusions

We have now looked at the essentials of pointers and arrays. We return repeatedly to these subjects throughout the remainder of the book.

In the next chapter, we go on to consider how arrays may be used with functions.

Exercises

7.1 Start by typing in the program below (or loading it from the CD):

```
// Source is: 07_21.CPP
#include <iostream.h>

int main()
    {
    int x, *y;

    cout << "Type in an integer: ";
    cin >> x;

    y = &x;

    cout << "The value of x is     " << x << endl;
    cout << "The address of x is " << &x << endl;
    cout << "The value of y is     " << y << endl;
    cout << "The value of *y is   " << *y;

    return 0;
    }
```

(a) Run the program, and note down the address in memory at which variable x is stored.

(b) The addresses are given in hexadecimal notation by this program. Modify the program so that the addresses are generated in decimal notation.

(c) Run the program twice more. Is the address of variable x the same each time? Should it be?

7.2 Start by typing in the following program (or loading it from the CD):

```
// Source is: 07_22.CPP
#include <iostream.h>

int main()
    {
    double test1[3] = {1.0,2.0,3.0};
    float   test2[3] = {4,5,6};
    int index;

    // print out the contents of the arrays
    for (index =0; index <=2; index+=1)
        {
        cout << "test1 array element " << index
            << " is " << test1[index] << endl;
        cout << "test2 array element " << index
            << " is " << test2[index] << endl;
        }
    cout << "\n\nAddress of start of test1 array is           "
        << test1
        << "\nAddress of second element of test1 array is "
        << &test1[1]
        << "\nAddress of start of test2 array is           "
        << test2
```

```
                  << "\nAddress of second element of test2 array is  "
                  << &test2[1];
        return 0;
        }
```

(a)   Note down the four addresses produced when the program is run. What do you notice about the memory addresses of the first and second elements of each of the arrays? What does this tell you, if anything, about the representation of numerical data used by this compiler?

(b)   Using the unary `sizeof` operator, verify your suspicions from part (a).

7.3   Write a C++ program (with a single `main()` function) that gives the user three chances to guess a stored password. Passwords may contain any mixture of six alphabetic characters and digits (e.g. alb2c3; 1h319d; DE34gh). The correct password should be stored as follows:

```
const char CORRECT_PASSWORD[7] = "aBc123";
```

7.4   Write a C++ program (with a single `main()` function) that prompts the user to type in two strings and prints out the longest one. For example, if the user enters "Pete" and "Josephine", the program should display "Josephine". The strings should contain only single digits and alphabetic characters. If both strings are the same length, then both should be printed on the screen. HINT: to find the length of the strings, look for the null terminator.

7.5   Write a C++ program (with a single `main()` function) that prompts the user to type in two strings and then joins (concatenates) the strings (with a space between) before printing out the result. For example, if the user types in "Joe" and "Bloggs" as the two strings, the program should print out "Joe Bloggs".

7.6   Write a C++ program to calculate the size of both the 1-D array of pointers and the 2-D array of characters in Program 7.16. Note: you will be able to use `sizeof` directly for the 2-D array, but will need to be more ingenious when it comes to the 1-D array.

7.7   Consider the following program:

```
// Source is: 07_23.CPP

#include <stdlib.h>
#include <iostream.h>
...

int main()
    {
    const int RANGE = 3; // Random numbers from 1 to RANGE
    int random_number;

    // Seed the random-number generator with the current time
    // so that the numbers generated will be different
    // every time we run.
    srand((unsigned)time(NULL));

    // Display 10 "random" numbers
    for(int i = 1; i <= 10; i++ )
```

```
        {
        random_number = 1 + (int)(1.0 * RANGE *
        rand()/(RAND_MAX + 1.0));
        cout << random_number << endl;
        }
    return 0;
    }
```

The `rand()` function is part of the library of functions provided with all C++ compilers: the library is discussed in more detail in Chapter 9.

The aim of this exercise is to use `rand()` to write a program that simulates the rolling of a six-sided die ('dice') 1000 times.

Your program should use a six-element array of integers to store the results obtained. The program should generate different results each time it is run, and should display the results in the form of a histogram like that used in Section 7.5.1.

8 A closer look at functions

8.1 Introduction

Now that we've covered the essentials of functions and pointers, we're ready to go on to look at some links between these two fundamental features of large C++ programs. The material in this chapter will enable us to pass arrays to functions, and to make full use of the enormous range of standard library functions included with all C++ compilers, a process we consider in Chapter 9.

We'll also consider recursive calls, and some useful, more advanced topics, including the use of inline functions, overloaded functions, and functions with variable numbers of arguments. We begin by examining call by address.

8.2 Call by address

Call by reference is an elegant way of passing data to and from functions. While call by reference relies (implicitly) on the use of pointers, the programmer need not be concerned with the complexities of de-referencing pointers and dealing with the address-of operator.

There are occasions when it is necessary to use a different technique to exchange information with functions: this technique is known as **call by address**. Call by address is particularly useful when passing arrays to functions. In addition, as call by address was the only way of performing (simulated) call by reference in C, there are many useful C library functions in daily use by C++ programmers which use call by address. As we see in the next chapter, it is likely that you will often want to recycle these library functions for use in your programs: to do so, you need to understand how call by address works.

The call by address technique relies on the use of pointers, as illustrated in Program 8.1.

```
// Program to find the sum of the squares of two numbers
// This time using call by address
// Source is: 08_01.CPP

#include <iostream.h>

// Function prototype
void Sum_of_Squares8(const int, const int, int*);

int main()
    {
    int Num_1 = 1;
    int Num_2 = 2;
    int Result;

    // Call function Sum_of_Squares8()
    Sum_of_Squares8(Num_1, Num_2, &Result);

    cout << "Sum of Squares is : " << Result << endl;

    return 0;
    }
/*****************************************************************
* FUNCTION:   Sum_of_Squares8                                   *
*                                                               *
* OVERVIEW:   To calculate the sum of the squares               *
*             of A and B (both integers) returning the          *
*             result via integer pointer sum_PTR                *
*****************************************************************/

void Sum_of_Squares8(const int A, const int B, int* sum_PTR)
    {
    int square1 = A * A;
    int square2 = B * B;

    cout << "Number 1 is : " << A << endl;
    cout << "Number 2 is : " << B << endl;

    *sum_PTR = square1 + square2;
    }
```

Program 8.1 It's that dreaded sum of squares program again, this time using call by address. (☺)

Program 8.1 generates the following familiar output:

```
Number 1 is : 1
Number 2 is : 2
Sum of Squares is : 5
```

Though the output from the program is the same as before, the internal operation is a little different, as we will see.

First of all, consider the header of the function Sum_of_Squares8():

```
void Sum_of_Squares8(const int A, const int B, int* sum_PTR)
    {
    ...
    }
```

On this occasion, we have (constant) integer value variables A and B as before, and also a further integer pointer, sum_PTR. Here, what we pass to the function is the address (and, implicitly, the type) of the variable to be altered within the function.

It is very important to appreciate that *the pointer address is itself passed by* **value** *to our function: we cannot return a different address to the calling program* (if you need to do so, you generally need to use a 'pointer to a pointer', a process we discuss in Section 8.5). However, it is still possible that, within our function, the address could be temporarily changed. The const modifier can prevent this: use of const with pointers is discussed in Section 8.3.

Within the function itself, the main change is that we must refer always to sum_PTR using the indirection operator (*), as in:

```
*sum_PTR = square1 + square2;
```

When we look at the manner in which the function is called, the situation becomes clearer:

```
Sum_of_Squares8(Num_1,Num_2,&Result)
```

Here we are passing the address of the variable Result (an int) to Sum_of_Squares8(). Recalling that the indirection operator and the address-of operator cancel one another, we can see that within the function when we write:

```
*sum_PTR = square1 + square2;
```

this is effectively:

```
*(&Result) = square1 + square2;
```

or:

```
Result = square1 + square2;
```

which is, of course, precisely what we require.

Turning finally to the function prototype, we can see that once again we need to inform the compiler only of the type of data to expect (in this case two integers and an integer pointer):

```
// Function prototype
int Sum_of_Squares8(const int, const int, int*);
```

As we have seen previously, we do not need to (and generally should not) provide the names of the particular data items. If we do provide these names, then the compiler will ignore them.

8.3 More on the `const` modifier

As we first discussed in Chapter 6, the use of the `const` modifier can add a useful extra layer of protection to our functions when using value or constant reference parameters. Clearly, when using pointers as function parameters we would wish to achieve the same degree of protection.

In general, use (or not) of the `const` modifier with pointers can take one of four forms:

- We can declare a variable pointer to variable data. This is the default situation: `const` is not used. If, for example, we pass an array address to a function in this manner then, within the function, the array address *could* be changed. This could result in disastrous side-effects if, following such a change, the function attempted to alter the array contents. An example of the declaration of a variable pointer to variable data is (of course) as follows:

```
int* int_PTR
```

- We can declare a variable pointer to constant data. In these circumstances, viewed in the context of a function, we can pass a pointer to our function, and cannot change the contents of the address pointed to. It will still be possible, however, to change the pointer address, and so read incorrect data. An example of such a declaration is as follows:

```
const int* int_PTR
```

- We can declare a constant pointer to variable data. Here we might want to pass the address of a data item (which will not change) to a function which will change the item's value. An example of such a declaration is as follows:

```
int* const int_PTR
```

  These declarations are easiest to read from right to left: here `int_PTR` is a constant pointer to a (variable) integer. Note also that this is the pointer equivalent of a reference variable.

- Finally, we can declare a const pointer to constant data. This is the safest solution: neither the pointer nor the contents of the address pointed to can be altered. An example of such a declaration is as follows:

```
const int* const INT_PTR
```

  Note that this is the pointer equivalent of a constant reference variable.

8.4 Arrays as function parameters

Passing arrays to functions is a common task. We begin by considering individual array elements, then go on to consider how complete multi-dimensional arrays can be passed between `main()` and other functions.

8.4.1 Individual array elements

Passing individual array elements to a function is carried out precisely as if the array elements were simple data types. For instance, Program 8.2 shows a modified version of the 'sum of squares' program, this time working with an array of data.

```
// Program to find the sum of the squares of two numbers
// This version works with array elements
// Source is: 08_02.CPP

#include <iostream.h>

// Function prototype
void Sum_of_Squares9(const int, const int, int&);

int main()
    {
    // Assigning values only to first two elements
    int Nums[3] = {1,2};

    // Call function Sum_of_Squares9
    Sum_of_Squares9(Nums[0], Nums[1], Nums[2]);

    cout << "Sum of Squares is : " << Nums[2] << endl;

    return 0;
    }

/****************************************************************
 * FUNCTION:   Sum_of_Squares9                                  *
 *                                                              *
 * OVERVIEW:   To calculate the sum of the squares              *
 *             of A and B (both integers) returning the         *
 *             result via integer-reference sum_REF             *
 ****************************************************************/

void Sum_of_Squares9(const int A, const int B, int& sum_REF)
    {
    int square1 = A * A;
    int square2 = B * B;

    cout << "Number 1 is : " << A << endl;
    cout << "Number 2 is : " << B << endl;

    sum_REF = square1 + square2;
    }
```

Program 8.2 Passing individual array elements to functions. (☺)

Here the use of individual array elements has neither added to the complexity of the code, nor, indeed, altered the function itself. As before, Program 8.2 generates the following outputs:

```
Number 1 is : 1
Number 2 is : 2
Sum of Squares is : 5
```

8.4.2 One-dimensional arrays

When we want to pass a whole array to a function, the situation gets a little more interesting. When an array is used as a function argument, C++ automatically resorts to call by address. In the 1-D case, what is passed to the function is the address of the first element of the array.

For example, Program 8.3 uses a function to sum the elements of a one-dimensional array, and then overwrites each of the elements in the array with the calculated result.

```cpp
// Passing a 1-D Array to a Function
// First version
// Source is: 08_03.CPP

#include <iostream.h>

// Function prototype for Sum_of_Elements()
void Sum_of_Elements(int Int_Array[3]);

int main()
    {
    int i, Int_Array[3] = {1,2,3};

    // Print out array Contents
    cout << "Just about to call Sum_of_Elements...\n";
    for (i=0; i < 3; i++)
        {
        cout << "Array element " << i << " is "
            << Int_Array[i] << endl;
        }
    // Call Sum_of_Elements
    Sum_of_Elements(&Int_Array[0]);

    cout << "\nAfter calling Sum_of_Elements...\n";
    for (i=0; i < 3; i++)
        {
        cout << "Array element " << i << " is "
            << Int_Array[i] << endl;
        }
    return 0;
    }

/******************************************************************
 * FUNCTION:   Sum_of_Elements                                    *
 *                                                                *
 * OVERVIEW:   To calculate the sum of the elements               *
 *             in a 1-D array.                                    *
 ******************************************************************/

void Sum_of_Elements(int Array[3])
    {
    int i, sum = 0;

    for (i=0; i < 3; i++)
```

```
        {
        sum += Array[i];
        }
    for (i=0; i < 3; i++)
        {
        Array[i] = sum;
        }
    }
```

Program 8.3 Passing a 1-D array to a function. (☺)

Program 8.3 gives the output shown below:

```
Just about to call Sum_of_Elements...
Array element 0 is 1
Array element 1 is 2
Array element 2 is 3

After calling Sum_of_Elements...
Array element 0 is 6
Array element 1 is 6
Array element 2 is 6
```

As the program output reveals, the program successfully sums the three elements of the array, and assigns the value calculated to each element of the array, before returning. Thus, clearly, we have achieved call by address, as required. Call by address is the default when passing arrays to functions in C++, and this makes good sense: typically, an array will be a large data structure, which would be costly (in terms of both memory and time) to copy during call by value.

However, if we look at the code for this program, it is not at all clear that the array is passed by address. For instance, looking at the function header for Sum_of_Elements():

```
// Function prototype for Sum_of_Elements()
int Sum_of_Elements(int Int_Array[3]);
```

it looks to a less-experienced C++ programmer as though we are actually passing an array (using call by value) to the function. In fact, what is actually passed to the function is the *address of the first element of the array*. To illustrate this, note that a C++ compilers will allow you to use the prototype above, but re-write the function header omitting the array dimension:

```
int Sum_of_Elements(Int_Array[])
```

All standard compilers will also compile (and run, correctly) a version with the following header:

```
int Sum_of_Elements(int*)
```

As always, it is good programming practice to make the operation of the code explicit. We can do this by rewriting Sum_of_Elements() as shown below:

```
/*****************************************************************
 * FUNCTION:    Sum_of_Elements2                                 *
 *                                                               *
 * OVERVIEW:    To calculate the sum of the elements             *
 *              in a 1-D array, and set each element             *
 *              of the array to this value.                      *
 *****************************************************************/

void Sum_of_Elements2(int* const Array_PTR, const int ARRAY_DIM)
    {
    int i, sum = 0;

    for (i=0; i < ARRAY_DIM; i++)
        {
        sum += Array_PTR[i];
        }

    for (i=0; i < ARRAY_DIM; i++)
        {
        Array_PTR[i] = sum;
        }
    }
```

As in this example, to help avoid 'out of bounds' errors, you should explicitly pass the dimension(s) of your arrays to your functions. As we will see below, this is a particularly important consideration with multi-dimensional arrays.

One point which we have previously discussed (Section 7.6.2), is that the sizeof operator can generally be used to determine the size of an array. When they realize this, some programmers think that they can use this operator to avoid the need to pass array dimensions to a function.

Program 8.4 illustrates that this approach will *not* work:

```
// Array sizes and sizeof
// Source is: 08_04.CPP

#include <iostream.h>

void Array_Function(const int* const);

int main()
    {
    int Numbers[3] = {11,22,33};

    cout <<  "Size of array (in main) is: "
         << sizeof(Numbers)/sizeof(int) << endl;

    // Call Array_Function()
    Array_Function(Numbers);

    return 0;
    }

void Array_Function(const int* const ARRAY_PTR)
    {
```

```
        cout << "Size of array (in function) is apparently : "
            << sizeof(ARRAY_PTR)/sizeof(int);
    }
```

Program 8.4 Using `sizeof` to calculate array dimensions. (☺)

The output from Program 8.4 is as follows:

```
    Size of array (in main) is: 3
    Size of array (in function) is: 1
```

Note that, within `Array_Function()`, the compile-time operator `sizeof` reveals only the size of the *pointer variable*, not the size of the array itself.

8.4.3 Multi-dimensional arrays

Like one-dimensional arrays, multi-dimensional arrays are passed to functions by address; specifically, via the address of their first element. However, in addition to this address (and the type of data stored) the function clearly has to also know some further details about the dimensions of array if it is to be able to access the appropriate elements in a useful manner.

In general, in order to avoid out-of-bounds problems with your arrays, you should explicitly pass not only the start address of your array, but the appropriate array dimensions. A final version of the element-summing example is given in Program 8.5.

```
// Passing a 2-D Array to a Function
// Source is: 08_05.CPP

#include <iostream.h>

// Function prototype for Sum_of_Elements_2D()
void Sum_of_Elements_2D(int* const, const int, const int);

int main()
    {
    int i,j, Int_Array[2][3] = {{1,2,3},
                                {4,5,6}};

    // Print out array Contents
    cout << "Just about to call Sum_of_Elements_2D...\n";
    for (i=0; i < 2; i++)
        {
        for (j=0; j < 3; j++)
            {
            cout << "Array element [" << i << "," << j
                << "] is " << Int_Array[i][j] << endl;
            }
        }
```

```
        // Call Sum_of_Elements_2D
        Sum_of_Elements_2D(&Int_Array[0][0], 2, 3);

        // Print out array Contents
        cout << "\nAfter calling Sum_of_Elements_2D...\n";
        for (i=0; i < 2; i++)
            {
            for (j=0; j < 3; j++)
                {
                cout << "Array element [" << i << "," << j
                    << "] is " << Int_Array[i][j] << endl;
                }
            }

        return 0;
        }

/*****************************************************************
 * FUNCTION:   Sum_of_Elements_2D()                              *
 *                                                               *
 * OVERVIEW:   To calculate the sum of the elements              *
 *             in a 2-D array, and set each element              *
 *             of the array to this value.                       *
 *****************************************************************/

void Sum_of_Elements_2D( int* const  Int_PTR,
                         const int   ROWS,
                         const int   COLUMNS)
    {
    int i,j, sum = 0;

    for (i=0; i < ROWS; i++)
        {
        for (j=0; j < COLUMNS; j++)
            {
            sum += *(Int_PTR + (i * COLUMNS) + j);
            }
        }

    for (i=0; i < ROWS; i++)
        {
        for (j=0; j < COLUMNS; j++)
            {
            *(Int_PTR + (i * COLUMNS) + j) = sum;
            }
        }
    }
```

Program 8.5 Passing a 2-D array to a function. (☺)

The output from Program 8.5 is as follows:

```
Just about to call Sum_of_Elements_2D...
Array element [0,0] is 1
Array element [0,1] is 2
Array element [0,2] is 3
Array element [1,0] is 4
Array element [1,1] is 5
Array element [1,2] is 6

After calling Sum_of_Elements_2D...
Array element [0,0] is 21
Array element [0,1] is 21
Array element [0,2] is 21
Array element [1,0] is 21
Array element [1,1] is 21
Array element [1,2] is 21
```

8.5 Returning values from functions

In Chapter 6 we looked at ways in which the return values from functions could be used to detect and correct errors. This is not the only use for return values: these function components can be used to return data as well as error codes.

We consider some of the possibilities in this section.

8.5.1 Returning data from function

The version of 'sum of squares' shown in Program 8.6 uses the return value both to return data, and to code for errors.

```cpp
// Program to find the sum of the squares of two numbers
// This time returning data and error code
// Source is: 08_06.CPP

#include <iostream.h>
#include <limits.h>

// Function declaration
int Sum_of_Squares10(const int, const int);

int main()
    {
    int Num_1;
    int Num_2;
    int Result;

    cout << "Two integers, please : ";
    cin >> Num_1 >> Num_2;

    Result = Sum_of_Squares10(Num_1, Num_2);

    if (Result < 0)
        {
        cout << "Sorry - result could not be calculated.";
        }
    else
        {
```

```
                     cout << "Result is " << Result;
                     }
                 return 0;
                 }
/****************************************************************
 * FUNCTION:   Sum_of_Squares10                                 *
 *                                                              *
 * OVERVIEW:   To calculate the sum of the squares              *
 *             of a and b (both integers) returning the         *
 *             result                                           *
 *                                                              *
 * RETURNS:    Sum of squares on normal completion.             *
 *             -1 if numbers too large                          *
 ****************************************************************/
int Sum_of_Squares10(const int A, const int B)
    {
    float test = ((float) A * A) + ((float) B * B);
    if (test > INT_MAX)
        {
        // Numbers too large: can't represent result as int
        return -1;
        }
    else
        {
        return (int) test;
        }
    }
```

Program 8.6   The sum of squares program, using the `return` statement for data and error detection. (☺)

Program 8.6 generates the following outputs on two sample runs:

```
Two integers, please : 1000 1000
Sorry - result could not be calculated.
```

```
Two integers, please : 8 9
Result is 145
```

Sometimes, returning data from functions in this manner can make your code easy to read. The technique is appropriate if no errors can occur (!), or if it is possible to interleave error codes and data in a useful way. For example, here the function always returns positive data values, and a negative return value can therefore be used to indicate that an error has occurred.

8.5.2   Two-way communication

You should also be aware that, although not generally recommended, it is possible to send data to functions via the "return" value. For example, consider Program 8.7.

```
// "Returning" refs from functions…
// Source is: 08_07.CPP

#include <iostream.h>

int& test();

int main()
    {
    cout << "x = " << test() << endl;

    test() = 3; // Note: sends value of 3 to 'x'…

    cout << "x = " << test() << endl;

    return 0;
    }

int& test()
    {
    static int x;

    return x;
    }
```

Program 8.7 Abusing the return value. (☹)

The output from Program 8.7 is as follows:

```
x = 0
x = 3
```

In Program 8.7, function test uses the integer *reference* return value to alter the value of x. Note that a similar result can be obtained using pointers.

This approach is not generally recommended as it can confuse the unwary. Nonetheless, we shall see some uses for it in a slightly different context in Part III.

8.6 Example: On strings, constants and functions

Passing strings to and from functions is a process that can cause confusion, particularly when there are string constants involved. Consider, for example, Program 8.8.

```
// Strings, pointers and functions
// Source is: 08_08.CPP

#include <iostream.h>

// All strings are of fixed size
const int STR_SIZE = 81;

int Check_Quote(char*);

int main()
    {
    char Quote[STR_SIZE] = " ";
```

```
    if(!Check_Quote(Quote))
        {
        cout << "Quote OK\n";
        }
    else
        {
        cout << "Not OK\n";
        cout << "Correct name is: " << Quote;
        }
    return 0;
    }
// Note: array dimensions fixed (not passed)
int Check_Quote(char* Quote_PTR)
    {
    char Attempt[STR_SIZE];
    Quote_PTR = "Alanis Morissette";

    cout << "Please complete the following (mis) quote : \n\n";
    cout << "\"I have heard the future of rock and roll, \n";
    cout << "and her name is ... ";

    // Use getline() to avoid whitespace problems
    cin.getline(Attempt, STR_SIZE, '\n');

    int Difference = 0;

    char* Ch1_PTR = Quote_PTR;
    char* Ch2_PTR = Attempt;

    while (!((*Ch1_PTR == '\0') || (*Ch2_PTR == '\0')))
        {
        if (!(*Ch1_PTR == *Ch2_PTR))
            {
            Difference = 1;
            }
        Ch1_PTR++;
        Ch2_PTR++;
        }

    return Difference;
    }
```

Program 8.8 Strings, pointers and functions. (☹)

On two separate runs, the executable code generated from Program 8.8 produces the following outputs:

```
Please complete the following (mis) quote :

"I have heard the future of rock and roll,
and her name is ... " Maria Callas
Not OK
Correct name is:
```

```
Please complete the following (mis) quote :

"I have heard the future of rock and roll,
and her name is … " Alanis Morissette
Quote OK
```

In fact, what the programmer probably wanted to produce was something like this:

```
Please complete the following (mis) quote :

"I have heard the future of rock and roll,
and her name is … " Maria Callas
Not OK
Correct name is: Alanis Morissette
```

So, why doesn't the program work?

First of all, note that we have used the getline() function:

```
cin.getline(Attempt, STR_SIZE, '\n');
```

to allow the program to read a line of text into the Attempt[] array without the 'white-space' problems we saw in Chapter 7. This program will therefore correctly read in strings containing (for example) spaces. We have more to say about getline() in Chapter 9.

The next thing to note is that the string comparison routine is imperfect:

```
int Difference = 0;

char* Ch1_PTR = Quote_PTR;
char* Ch2_PTR = Attempt;

while (!((*Ch1_PTR == '\0') || (*Ch2_PTR == '\0')))
    {
    if (!(*Ch1_PTR == *Ch2_PTR))
        {
        Difference = 1;
        }
    Ch1_PTR++;
    Ch2_PTR++;
    }
```

Here, the strings are compared, one character at a time, until the end of (**one of**) the strings is reached: we'll consider how this code could be improved in the exercises at the end of this chapter, but this isn't the reason why this program doesn't work correctly.

The problem arises because the programmer has assumed that the following code fragment:

```
…
int Check_Quote(char* Quote_PTR)
    {
    char Attempt[81];
    Quote_PTR = "Alanis Morissette";
    …
```

will change the value of Quote_PTR to point to the string constant 'Alanis Morissette' somewhere in memory. This will happen within the function but, as we discussed in Section 8.2, the character pointer Quote_PTR is itself passed *by value*: no matter how Quote_PTR is varied within the function, these changes *will not be reflected* in the copy of Quote_PTR (that is, in the contents of the Quote[] array) in main().

Thus, when a pointer is passed to a function (and the const modifier is not used), we can – within the function – change the **contents** of the memory location pointed to. Any changes made in this way are **permanent**, and will still be evident when we return from the function call. However, any changes we make to the **value** of the pointer variable itself (for example, by changing the address pointed to) will be **lost** when we return from the function call.

In this example, one solution is to explicitly copy the string constant, one character at a time, to the memory location beginning at address Quote_PTR. This is carried out in the following version of the Check_Quote() function:

```cpp
// Note: array dimensions fixed (not passed)
int Check_Quote(char* Quote_PTR)
    {
    char Attempt[STR_SIZE];
    char* correct_PTR = "Alanis Morissette";

    cout << "Please complete the following (mis) quote : \n\n";
    cout << "\"I have heard the future of rock and roll, \n";
    cout << "and her name is ... \" " ;
    // Use getline() to avoid whitespace problems
    cin.getline(Attempt, STR_SIZE, '\n');

    int Difference = 0;

    char* Ch1_PTR = correct_PTR;
    char* Ch2_PTR = Attempt;

    while (!((*Ch1_PTR == '\0') || (*Ch2_PTR == '\0')))
        {
        if (!(*Ch1_PTR == *Ch2_PTR))
            {
            Difference = 1;
            }
        Ch1_PTR++;
        Ch2_PTR++;
        }

    if (Difference)
        {
        // Copy correct version to Quote_PTR
        *Quote_PTR = *correct_PTR;
        while (!(*Quote_PTR == '\0'))
            {
            Quote_PTR++;
            correct_PTR++;
            *Quote_PTR = *correct_PTR;
            }
        }

    return Difference;
    }
```

Using this function the program works as required.

However, another possibility is to pass not a *pointer* to `Check_Quote()`, but a *pointer to a pointer*. Program 8.9 illustrates this approach.

```cpp
// Strings, pointers and constants
// Source is: 08_09.CPP

#include <iostream.h>

// All strings are fixed size
const int STR_SIZE = 81;

int Check_Quote(char**);

int main()
    {
    char   Quote[STR_SIZE] = " ";
    char* Quote_PTR = Quote;

    if(!Check_Quote(&Quote_PTR))
        {
        cout << "Quote OK\n";
        }
    else
        {
        cout << "Not OK\n";
        cout << "Correct name is: " << Quote_PTR;
        }
    }

// Note: array dimensions fixed (not passed)
int Check_Quote(char** Quote_PTR_PTR)
    {
    char Attempt[STR_SIZE];
    *Quote_PTR_PTR = "Alanis Morissette";

    cout << "Please complete the following (mis) quote : \n\n";
    cout << "\"I have heard the future of rock and roll, \n";
    cout << "and her name is ... \" " ;

    // Use getline() to avoid whitespace problems
    cin.getline(Attempt, STR_SIZE, '\n');

    int Difference = 0;

    char* Ch1_PTR = *Quote_PTR_PTR;
    char* Ch2_PTR = Attempt;

    while (!((*Ch1_PTR == '\0') || (*Ch2_PTR == '\0')))
        {
        if (!(*Ch1_PTR == *Ch2_PTR))
            {
            Difference = 1;
            }
        Ch1_PTR++;
        Ch2_PTR++;
        }

    return Difference;
    }
```

Program 8.9 Using pointers to pointers. (☺)

Note how Program 8.9 operates. The `Quote` array is declared as before. This time, however, an additional character pointer (`Quote_PTR`) is also declared. This variable stores the address of the start of `Quote`. It is the *pointer* to `Quote_PTR` that is passed to the modified function `Check_Quote()`:

```
...
char   Quote[STR_SIZE] = " ";
char* Quote_PTR = Quote;

if(!Check_Quote(&Quote_PTR))
     {
      ...
```

Within `Check_Quote()` we now have not a pointer variable (implicitly passed by value and therefore inalterable) but we have the address at which our pointer variable is stored. Therefore, with care, we can alter the contents of this memory address, and thereby make the pointer variable to point to our string constant, as required:

```
int Check_Quote(char** Quote_PTR_PTR)
     {
      ...
     *Quote_PTR_PTR = "Alanis Morissette";
      ...
```

Note that, rather than using (explicit) multiple indirection, it is sometimes possible to use references to pointers to achieve the same result: this possibility is addressed in the exercises at the end of this chapter. Also in the exercises, we will consider another solution using the new **string** data type available in standard C++.

In Chapter 9, we will look at ways of using library functions to eliminate many of the complexities of these programs.

8.7   Macros and inline functions

We saw in Chapter 3 that it is good programming practice to define names for symbolic constants, and to use the names (rather than numbers) throughout the program. As we saw, this process is usually carried out through the use of **read-only variables**.

Such read-only variables make use of the C++ `const` modifier, as shown below:

```
int main()
     {
     const float INTEREST_RATE = 7.0f;
      ...
     interest_due = capital * INTEREST_RATE;
      ...
     saving = reserve * INTEREST_RATE;
      ...
     }
```

However, this is not the only way to achieve the same result. From C, C++ has also inherited the pre-processor directive `#define`. As this directive is still useful in C++ programs, we will consider it briefly here.

At its simplest, `#define` can be used, like `const`, to define symbolic constants. For example, if we write in our program:

```
#define PI 3.14159265 // NOTE: NO ";", NO "="
```

followed later (in the same source file) by:

```
area = PI * radius * radius;
```

then pre-processor will expand this second line to:

```
area = 3.14159265 * radius * radius;
```

Note that, since PI is only #define-d and never truly defined, we have a slight saving in memory, compared with the corresponding const-based equivalent code. Since, unless space is really at a premium, the saving will usually be slight, most C++ programmers use the const version.

What #define and the pre-processor do is simply a 'search and replace' operation on your source file. If you think about this a little, you will realize that it is possible not simply to use this mechanism with symbolic constants, but also with (small) 'functions'. Code written in this way is known as a **macro**.

For example, consider the following example:

```
#define ABS(X) (((X) < 0)? -(X) : X)
```

Just as the use of #define to provide symbolic constants can save memory, the use of macros can also be efficient. With macros, the saving can be one of time. For example, when calling a function with parameters, the parameter values will (generally) need to be copied (onto the stack), the called function will execute, further copying will take place and the calling function will resume. If your program is time-critical, and you need to make many function calls, then it can be very tempting to use macros instead.

The first problem with macros, however, is that they need to be written with care (and that usually – as in the above example – means using many parentheses), or the 'search and replace' will have unpredictable results. A greater problem, however, is the lack of *any* form of type checking. Despite these drawbacks, many C programmers have found macros very tempting: in fact, as we shall see in Chapter 11, we shall have cause to make use of a macro (assert()) in many of our larger programs.

Generally, C++ provides an alternative to macros with most of the advantages and none of the drawbacks: this is the inline function. Just like a macro, inline functions are 'cut and pasted' to the appropriate line of code, giving no function call overheads. Unlike macros, however, inline functions have prototypes allowing parameter checks to be carried out. Note that the inline directive is a request, not a command: *in-lining* functions puts an overhead on the compiler, and cannot always be carried out, particularly for large functions. If you say 'inline' the compiler may or may not comply: depending on the environment you are using, you *may* get a warning message in such circumstances.

By way of example, we could rewrite our ABS macro as shown in Program 8.10.

```
// Using inline functions
// Source is: 08_10.CPP

#include <iostream.h>

inline int Abs(int);

int main()
```

```
        {
        cout << Abs(-0) << endl;
        cout << Abs(0) << endl;
        cout << Abs(-1) << endl;
        cout << Abs(1) << endl;
        cout << Abs(-2) << endl;
        cout << Abs(2) << endl;
        cout << Abs(-3) << endl;
        cout << Abs(3) << endl;
        cout << Abs(-4) << endl;
        cout << Abs(4) << endl;
        cout << Abs(-5) << endl;
        cout << Abs(5) << endl;

        return 0;
        }
    inline int Abs(int x)
        {
        return (((x) < 0)? -(x) : x);
        }
```

Program 8.10   Using inline functions. (☺)

The output of Program 8.10 is as follows:

```
0
0
1
1
2
2
3
3
4
4
5
5
```

Not surprisingly, the use of inline functions may have an impact on the size of your final executable program. Using Microsoft Visual C++ to compile Program 8.10 with the inline keyword results in an executable program 32 bytes larger than that produced using a 'normal' function. As always, what you gain on the swings, you lose on the roundabouts.

Note (for future reference): a function defined within the declaration of a class is inline by default (we consider classes in Part III).

Finally, note that rather than swithering between use of a macro or inline function to implement the ABS() operation, the best solution is not to write the function at all. In this case, as in many others, there are existing library functions already provided with your C++ compiler that can do the job. We'll look at several useful ways to avoid reinventing the wheel in Chapter 9.

8.8 Recursion

One important general feature of C++ that we have not yet mentioned is that the language supports recursion. A function is said to be recursive if one (or more) of its statements executes a call to itself.

Program 8.11 shows an example of a recursive routine used to calculate the factorial of an integer. Note that the factorials of, say, 3 and 6 (usually written 3! and 6!) are defined as follows:

$$3! = 3 \times 2 \times 1$$
$$6! = 6 \times 5 \times 4 \times 3 \times 2 \times 1$$

```cpp
// Demonstration of recursion
// Source is: 08_11.CPP
#include <iostream.h>
int Factorial(const int);
int main()
    {
    cout << Factorial(3);
    return 0;
    }


/*****************************************************************
 * FUNCTION:   Factorial()                                       *
 *                                                               *
 * OVERVIEW:   To calculate the factorial of N (int)             *
 *             returning the result directly                     *
 *****************************************************************/
int Factorial (const int N)
    {
    if (N == 1)
        {
        return 1;
        }
    else
        {
        return N * Factorial(N-1);
        }
    }
```

Program 8.11 A recursive C++ function. (☺)

Program 8.11 generates the following output:

```
6
```

8.9 Flexible functions

In this final section we consider three useful forms of 'flexible' function: overloaded functions, functions with default arguments, and functions with variable numbers of arguments.

8.9.1   Function overloading

Function overloading is usually viewed as an object-oriented programming feature: nonetheless, we consider it in this part of the book because it is of general use in process-oriented and data-oriented development.

Suppose, for example, that you need in a program to prompt the user for a valid integer, and keep looping until the user types in a valid response. You might call this function `Get_Int()`. Now, suppose you find that, later in your program, you need to have the user type in a valid character, then a valid string, then a valid double. This could result in writing many functions, all with different names, all doing the same thing, namely getting data from the user. Function overloading allows you to give all your functions the same name, and have the system choose an appropriate function to call (at compile time) based on the function arguments. In this way, we can hide some of the complexity of the program.

Program 8.12 illustrates this process. It contains three functions, all called 'Display()', intended to print three types of data on the screen.

```cpp
// Demonstrating "polymorphic functions"
// Source is: 08_12.CPP

#include <iostream.h>

//Prototypes
void Display(int);
void Display(char*);
void Display(double);

int main()
    {
    // Call the functions
    Display(123);
    Display("123");
    Display(123.0);

    return 0;
    }


void Display(int a)
    {
    cout << "The integer is " << a << endl;
    }
void Display(char* a)
    {
    cout << "The string is " << a << endl;
    }

void Display(double a)
    {
    cout << "The double is " << a << endl;
    }
```

Program 8.12   Demonstrating polymorphic (overloaded) functions. (☺)

Typical output from Program 8.12 is as follows:

```
The integer is 123
The string is 123
The double is 123
```

Note that functions to be overloaded must differ by more than just the type of their return values. This is necessary, because code might otherwise easily become ambiguous.

Thus, the following code fragment will *not* compile:

```
// Prototypes
void Display(int);
void Display(char*);
int Display(int);
```

8.9.2 Functions with default arguments

In addition to function overloading, C++ provides the facility for writing functions with default arguments. This can provide benefits similar to those of overloaded functions, with the added advantage that only one version of the function needs to be written.

Program 8.13 gives an example of a function with one 'normal' and two default arguments.

```
// Demonstrating default function arguments
// Source is: 08_13.CPP

#include <iostream.h>

void DefaultFn(int, int = 2, int = 3);

int main()
    {
    DefaultFn(1);
    DefaultFn(1,20);
    DefaultFn(1,25,30);

    return 0;
    }
void DefaultFn(int a, int b, int c)
    {
    cout << a << endl;
    cout << b << endl;
    cout << c << endl << endl;
    }
```

Program 8.13 Functions with default arguments. (☺)

The output of Program 8.13 is as follows:

```
1
2
3

1
20
3

1
25
30
```

In Program 8.13, `DefaultFn()` is called three times:

```
DefaultFn(1);
DefaultFn(1,20);
DefaultFn(1,25,30);
```

The first call uses both default arguments (specified in the function prototype). The second call uses only the second default value and the third call specifies all arguments. Note that you cannot use the default value for parameter two while specifying a value for parameter three; you must therefore think carefully about the order of your parameter lists. Note that you can, if you wish, have default values for all arguments.

8.9.3 Variable numbers of arguments

In addition to providing facilities for overloaded functions and functions with default arguments, C++ also provides facilities for producing a single function that can be called with different numbers of arguments. While such features can be useful, they are really historical artefacts, left over from very early versions of the C language. As a consequence, when using functions of this form, the compiler is unable to do any parameter type checking. Such programming constructs are 'unstructured' and, in almost all circumstances, exactly the same result can be achieved in a safer way using overloaded functions and/or default arguments. We shall therefore not consider functions with different numbers of arguments and you should refer to the macros `va_list()`, `va_start()`, `va_arg()` and `va_end()` in your compiler manual if you are convinced that your quality of life will suffer from a lack of such facilities.

8.10 Conclusions

Now that we have considered many of the important features of C++ functions, we are also in a position to make effective use of a wide range of library functions, a process we consider in the next chapter.

We can summarize the material in this chapter by updating our guidelines from Chapter 6.

(1) Don't write monolithic programs, that is, programs comprising only a `main()` function. Break your programs up into a number of small self-contained functions.

(Note that we have, quite deliberately, not attempted to present any guidelines for decomposing your program into individual functions: such a decomposition arises as the end result of the earlier stages of SADIE. These topics are the focus of much of the remainder of this part of the book.)

(2)   If the analysts and designers have done their job, the design specification will include appropriate descriptions of a number of independent functions, each with a clearly defined task to perform. None of the specified functions will serve more than one task, and no single task will be split between functions. If these conditions are not satisfied, then no attempt should be made to implement the design: it should be returned to the design team for rework.

(3)   The *ideal* function is one with no parameters, but this is not an ideal world. Don't be tempted to write parameterless functions and then 'slip' them data through the use of global variables. Functions using global variables always have side effects, and are never portable. That being said, passing *constant* data to functions as global read-only variables, if used sparingly and fully documented, is usually acceptable.

(4)   You should always write functions on a 'need to know' basis. Let your functions have access only to the data they must have: allow your functions only the degree of access to their parameters that they absolutely must have.

(5)   It follows from point 4 that you should use call by value wherever possible: that is, where the calling function does not need to modify the data it is supplied with. In general, you should always use the `const` modifier in conjunction with value parameters.

(6)   If the speed of your program is important, consider using 'constant reference' parameters in place of the 'constant value' parameters described under point 5. Use of inline functions and/or register variables *may* also help speed up your code (and an optimizing compiler may have already made use of these features on your behalf).

(7)   If your called function must return data to the calling function, then use call by reference (reference variables), this time without the `const` modifier.

(8)   If your function uses arrays, or must deal with pointers, then you must use call by address. When working with arrays, pass the address to the first element (by address) and the array dimensions (by value, or by constant reference). Remember: call by address is inherently more dangerous than call by reference, and must always be used with care. Always use `const` modifiers as much as possible.

(9)   Where it is practical and sensible to do so, use the return value from your functions to indicate when errors have occurred, and to allow for error recovery. Use the return value for data only if this makes the program much easier to read, and if there is either no possibility of errors occurring, or you can sensibly code error values in your data. Avoid the use of reference variables in return statements except in very limited cases: use of such variables to pass data can lead to *very* confusing code.

(10) For maximum portability, send error messages to `cerr`, rather than `cout`.

Exercises

8.1 Write a C++ program that contains two functions. The first function `Get_Function()` will prompt the user to type in her name (e.g. 'Susan Armstrong'), a double precision floating point number (e.g. 3.14), and an unsigned integer (e.g. 7). The second function `Display_Function()` will display on the screen all the data that the user typed in.

8.2 Repeat Exercise 8.1, this time using *only* call by address to pass all the information to and from the function (that is, both strings and numbers). Make appropriate use of the `const` modifier to ensure that the function is as safe as possible.

8.3 Repeat Exercise 8.2 again, but this time only ask the user to type in his or her name. Use the `return` statement from `Get_Function()` to pass the name to the calling function (this time `Get_Function()` won't need to have *any* parameters). HINT: you will probably need to make use of the `static` keyword.

8.4 Consider why having a function return a pointer to a local function variable is usually A (very) Bad Idea. Consider your solution to Exercise 8.3 in the light of your comments here…

8.5 What is wrong with the following simple string comparison routine (first met in Program 8.8)? Modify the routine as necessary to make it work correctly under all circumstances. Put your modified routine in a function, and write an appropriate test program to verify that the function works as required.

```
int Difference = 0;
char* Ch1_PTR = *Quote_PTR;
char* Ch2_PTR = Attempt;
while (!((*Ch1_PTR == '\0') || (*Ch2_PTR == '\0')))
    {
    if (!(*Ch1_PTR == *Ch2_PTR))
        {
        Difference = 1;
        }
    Ch1_PTR++;
    Ch2_PTR++;
    }
```

8.6 Write a program that contains three functions. Each function will be passed an integer value, the first using call by value, the second using call by reference and the third using call by address. Your program should compare the speed at which data is transferred using the different techniques. Are the differences significant? Satisfy yourself that you can explain the differences you observe. If your compiler has a disassembler, compare the assembly language versions of each function.

8.7 Repeat Exercise 8.6, this time passing 'long doubles' to each function. Similarly, repeat the exercise passing characters to each function. A usual heuristic is: 'It is faster to pass objects larger than integers to (and from) functions by reference or by address rather than by value'. Do your results from this and the previous exercise support this 'rule of thumb'? If not, it is probably because of the way your compiler optimizes the code it creates: see if you can explain how this optimization works.

8.8 We saw in Section 8.8 that C++ supports recursion. Re-write Program 8.11 so that it operates, without crashing, for any positive integer (in the range 1–32,000) chosen by the user. Test your program carefully.

8.9 Although recursion can seem a neat solution to some programming problems, it can also prove to be quite inefficient (in terms of execution time and memory usage). Explain why this is the case. Re-write your solution to Exercise 8.9, this time avoiding the use of the recursive function call. How would you compare the efficiency of the recursive and non-recursive techniques?

8.10 Rather than using multiple indirection ('pointers to pointers'), it is sometimes possible to use pointer references ('references to pointers'). Try to re-write the 'Alanis' quote program (Program 8.9) using pointer references.

The prototype for your new `Check_Quote()` function should look something like:

```
int Check_Quote(char*&);
```

8.11 If your compiler supports the `string` data type (included in the draft C++ standard), then you can reduce the complexity of Program 8.8 by using this data type. Starting with the function `main()` given below, write a new version of this Program 8.8 using C++ strings.

```
// Standard strings, pointers and functions
#include <iostream>
#include <string>

int Check_Quote(string&);

int main(void)
    {
    string Quote;

    if(!Check_Quote(Quote))
        {
        cout << "Quote OK\n";
        }
    else
        {
        cout << "Not OK\n";
        cout << "Correct name is: " << Quote << endl;
        }

    return EXIT_SUCCESS;
    }
```

9 The standard libraries

9.1 Introduction

Wherever possible, rather than writing your own functions, it makes sense to reuse code from one of the standard libraries included with all C++ compilers. Assuming you bought a good compiler, this code will have been thoroughly debugged, and will be well documented. It can be usually be distributed with your product without payment of royalties.

The idea is not new. When an electronics engineer builds a circuit, he or she doesn't generally reach for a handful of transistors, resistors and capacitors but, instead, looks through a set of data books to find an integrated circuit (that is, a pre-packaged computer chip, containing vast numbers of transistors and other components) that will do most of the hard work. In this rather simplified view of electronic product development, the job of implementation is reduced to selecting the correct components, and providing the electronic 'glue' to link them together.

For many years, people have been comparing the development of software products with the development of electronic products and bemoaning a perceived lack of 'software integrated circuits'. In this chapter, we consider some well-tested software ICs, in the form of C and C++ standard library functions.

9.2 Pragmatics

Before we look at the standard libraries, we need to consider some general practical matters.

9.2 Header files and `#include` revisited

Just as we had to write function prototypes for the user-defined functions introduced in Chapters 6 and 8, library functions also require prototypes. However, you don't need to write these yourself: they are provided for you in a range of existing **header** files which you can '#include' in your programs.

In general, related C++ functions are bundled together into code libraries (usually called `x.lib`, `y.lib`, and so on), associated with which there will be one (or more) header files. For example, when you use functions from the mathematics library (described below), you need to '#include' the header file 'math.h' in your program, as follows:

```
// Program using functions from math library

#include <math.h>
#include <iostream.h>
#include ...
int main()
    {
```

Note that, unfortunately, you won't usually find that, say, the compiled functions associated with header file 'ABC.H' are stored in a library file called 'ABC.LIB'. That is, there is *not* usually a simple one-to-one correspondence between header files and library files. Such is life!

We shall give the names of the corresponding header files as we consider some of the most useful library functions in this chapter.

9.2.2   Using extern "C"

We considered the extern storage class in Chapter 6. In addition to the simple (and often implicit) use of external variables, we can also use the extern keyword, along with a **string**, to tell the compiler that the linkage conventions of another language are to be used with some associated function prototypes.

The most common need for this is when using C library functions with C++ programs. For example, two useful C functions are getchar() and putchar(). With some C++ compilers, to use these functions, you need to say explicitly:

```
...
extern "C"
    {
    int getchar(void);
    int putchar(int);
    }
...
```

This problem arises because of function overloading. In C, no overloaded functions are allowed, so that when linking your programs, the system needs only to know the name of each function. In C++, however, the use (or potential use) of overloaded function names means that both the basic name of the function and details of any formal parameters must be stored. If you were to try and link library code generated using a C compiler with C++ code, then the linker may not be able to do its job, without being explicitly told that the library (C) code won't include overloaded functions.

That being said, with standard library functions (like, say, getchar()), few modern C++ compilers require the use of extern in this way by the programmer; instead, the developers have included any required extern statements in the appropriate header files.

However, if you (or your company) has been working in C and you want to continue to use 'home-made' C functions with your C++ programs you'll probably need to make use of extern, as shown above. If you're using a lot of functions, and the prototypes are (as is common) in header files, you can usually simply write:

```
...
extern "C"
{
#include "C_header_file1"
#include "C_header_file2"
#include "C_header_file3"
#include "C_header_file4"
...
```

Don't forget that the #include directive must start in column 1, as shown (that is, you *can't* indent the #include lines). This is because #include isn't a C++ statement (it's a pre-processor directive), and it doesn't adhere to the 'free format' nature of the language itself.

Ultimately, it may be possible to directly use external code not just from C, but from other languages as well, as follows:

```
...
extern "ADA"
    {
    int ADA_FN_1( void );
    int ADA_FN_2( int );
    }
...

...
extern "COBOL"
    {
    int COBOL_FN_1( void );
    int COBOL_FN_2( int );
    }
...
```

However, such links are not yet provided (at least in such a straightforward, portable, manner) by mainstream C++ compilers.

Note that it is possible to incorporate to assembly language in your C++ programs. To do so, you need to use the asm keyword, as follows:

```
...
asm
    {
    MOV   AH,  2
    MOV   DL,  7
    INT   21H
    CMP   INDEX,  4
    MOVSB
    JMP   034E
    }
...
```

Of course, details of the appropriate assembly language are very implementation dependent: if you wish to use such features, you should begin by consulting the documentation provided with your compiler.

9.3 Character and string handling

As we have seen, the lack of a safe array data type in C++ is one of the language's most endearing 'features', and one which has important implications for professional programmers. One of the serious side-effects of the pointer-based array representation is the lack of a dedicated string data type, which in turn means that string handling can become something of a chore.

For example, while the programmer can, of course, simply copy one integer variable to another:

```
...
int a,b = 4;
a = b;
...
```

the corresponding operation on a character string won't work:

```
...
char a[81], b[81] = "Hello";
a = b; // Can't copy strings like this!!!
...
```

Fortunately, the problems caused by the lack of a string data type can be largely alleviated if you are familiar with the character and string handling facilities provided with all C++ compilers.

9.3.1 First, capture your string

One of the most useful C++ input functions, which will form the basis of the robust input routines used in the larger programs in this book, is getline().

To remind you of one of the problems caused by basic C++ input routines, consider Program 9.1, which we first met in a slightly different form in Chapter 7.

```
// Reading and Printing Strings
// Source is: 09_01.CPP
#include <iostream.h>

int main()
    {
    char characters[81];

    cout << "Type a string : ";
    cin >> characters;

    cout << "You typed : \"" << characters << "\"";

    return 0;
    }
```

Program 9.1 Problems caused by using simple input routines. (☹)

A typical output from Program 9.1 is as follows:

```
Type a string : On my last morning on the island
You typed : "On"
```

The problem, as we saw in Chapter 7, is that 'white space' (spaces, tabs, as well as the '<enter>' or '<return>' key) all terminate the string. While there are various solutions to this problem, the most generally useful is the function getline(), illustrated in Program 9.2.

```cpp
// Reading and Printing Strings
// Source is: 09_02.CPP

#include <iostream.h>

int main()
    {
    char characters[81];

    cout << "Type a string : ";
    cin.getline(characters, 81, '\n');

    cout << "You typed : \"" << characters << "\"";

    return 0;
    }
```

Program 9.2   More flexible string input. (☺)

The output from Program 9.2 is as follows:

```
Type a string : On my last morning on the island
You typed : "On my last morning on the island"
```

A few noteworthy points:

- The getline() function is called by typing cin.getline(). This is because getline() is a member function of the cin object. These features, which are part of C++'s object-oriented repertoire, will be considered in more detail in Part III. For now, you should consider that the full name of the function is cin.getline().

- To use the getline() function, we had to specify the name of the character array we wanted to read into (that is, a character pointer, characters), the *maximum* number of characters we wanted to read (in this case 81), and the terminating character (in this case '\n'). Note that the third argument has '\n' as a default, so you don't need to explicitly include it. We'll consider alternatives to '\n' below.

- The function will add a null terminator at the end of your string, but you don't need to allow space for this when you specify the maximum number of characters: if you specify 81 characters, you'll get (up to) 80 characters, and a null terminator.

- The 'maximum characters' facility means that if you are using character arrays fixed at, say, 30 characters, they cannot be rendered 'out of bounds' (with possibly disastrous consequences) by an unduly energetic typist.

- Setting the terminating character to, say, 'X', means that the programmer still has to enter <RETURN> ('\n') at the end of the input line. However, the returned string will contain only the characters before the 'X'. If there is no 'X', then the function will keep reading input (including, if necessary, multiple '\n'), until the 'maximum characters' limit has been reached. Any extra characters, including the terminating character, will not be appended to your string: they may, however, be left in the input buffer (see Section 9.3.2).

Some of these possibilities are illustrated in Program 9.3.

```
// Reading and Printing Strings
// Source is: 09_03.CPP

#include <iostream.h>

int main()
    {
    char characters[26];

    cout << "Type a string ending in \'X\': ";
    cin.getline(characters, 25, 'X');

    cout << "You typed : \"" << characters << "\"";

    return 0;
    }
```

Program 9.3 Using `getline()` with a different terminator. (☺)

Some typical outputs from Program 9.3 are as follows:

```
Type a string ending in 'X': Hello again, EdinburghX
You typed : "Hello again, Edinburgh"
```

```
Type a string ending in 'X': Not only is this the last show
of the tour,
You typed : "Not only is this the las"
```

9.3.2   ASIDE: Problems with input buffering

Occasionally, you may find that certain combinations of input operations cause problems. Most problems arise because certain input functions can leave characters (notably the new line character, `'\n'`) in the input buffer. If this happens and you subsequently use `cin.getline()` your input stream may be terminated rather sooner than you expected.

For example, Program 9.4 reads in a number typed by the user, then attempts to use `cin.getline()` to read in a string. Since, however, the `cin >> num` statement leaves a `'\n'` character in the input buffer, the user is given no opportunity to type anything and the program terminates.

```
// Problems with input buffering
// Source is: 09_04.CPP

#include <iostream.h>

int main()
    {
    float num;
```

```
char name[81];
cout << "Type a float: ";
cin >> num;
cout << "Type your name : ";
cin.getline(name, sizeof(name));
cout << "\nHello " << name;
cout << "\nFinished.";
return 0;
}
```

Program 9.4 Problems with input buffers. (☹)

Typical output from Program 9.4 is as follows:

```
Type a float: 45.0
Type your name :

Hello
Finished.
```

One solution to this problem is to use `cin.ignore()` to discard any characters in the input buffer, up to and including the `'\n'`: this is illustrated in Program 9.5.

```
// Problems with input buffering
// Source is: 09_05.CPP
#include <iostream.h>
int main()
    {
    float num;
    char name[81];
    cout << "Type a float: ";
    cin >> num;
    // Throw away (up to) 100 characters
    cin.ignore(100,'\n');
    cout << "Type your name : ";
    cin.getline(name, sizeof(name));
    cout << "\nHello " << name;
    cout << "\nFinished.";
    return 0;
    }
```

Program 9.5 Solving problems with input buffers. (☺)

Typical output from Program 9.5 is as follows:

```
Type a float: 45.0
Type your name : Fish

Hello Fish
Finished.
```

Note also the use of the `sizeof()` operator in the `getline()` call in both programs 9.4 and 9.5: this is common and can be useful. Don't forget, however, that this may not work within functions (see Chapter 8).

Finally, `getline()` itself is not without problems, as indicated by Program 9.6.

```
// More buffering problems...
// Source is: 09_06.CPP

#include <iostream.h>

int main ()
    {
    const int SIZE = 10;
    char String[SIZE];

    // Note: string typed is too long...
    // (spare characters left in input buffer)
    cout << "Please type \"0123456543210 <RETURN>\" : ";
    cin.getline(String, sizeof(String));
    cout << String << endl;

    cout << "Please type \"0123456543210 <RETURN>\" : ";
    cin.getline(String, sizeof(String));
    cout << String << endl;
    cout << "Finished.";

    return 0;
    }
```

Program 9.6   More buffering problems. (☹)

The output from Program 9.6 is as follows:

```
Please type "0123456543210 <RETURN>" : 0123456543210
012345654
Please type "0123456543210 <RETURN>" : 3210
Finished.
```

In this program the user never gets the chance to type the second input string: instead the 3210 'left over' from the first input is substituted. This is because characters beyond the specified count are not discarded, but remain in the input buffer. Note that this result does vary between implementations.

Program 9.7 shows a working version of Program 9.6. Here we 'solve' the problem by always reading into a large buffer (which is never *likely* to overflow), and then copying the results afterwards using the standard library function `strncpy()`; note that `strncpy()` is discussed in Section 9.3.6. We don't pretend that this is particularly elegant solution, but it is portable and effective.

```
// More buffering problems solved (Note: crude but portable)
// Source is: 09_07.CPP

#include <iostream.h>
#include <string.h>

int main ()
```

```
{
    const int SIZE = 10;
    char String[SIZE];
    char tmp[81];      // Temporary (large) char buffer

    cout << "Please type \"0123456543210 <RETURN>\" : ";
    cin.getline(tmp, sizeof(tmp));
    strncpy(String, tmp, SIZE); // Standard library fn.
    cout << String << endl;

    cout << "Please type \"0123456543210 <RETURN>\" : ";
    cin.getline(tmp, sizeof(tmp));
    strncpy(String, tmp, SIZE);
    cout << String << endl;
    cout << "Finished.";

    return 0;
}
```

Program 9.7 Solving buffering problems (again). (☺)

The output from Program 9.7 is as follows:

```
Please type "0123456543210 <RETURN>" : 0123456543210
0123456543

Please type "0123456543210 <RETURN>" : 0123456543210
0123456543

Finished.
```

Please remember with all the above function calls: the stream class library has not yet been standardized and though it is (unfortunately) unlikely, the above behaviour may change when a standard is introduced.

9.3.3 Character checking library

Most of the character checking functions and macros are intended to allow the programmer to tell whether a particular character belongs in a specified data set. Since strings are character arrays, many of the character handling routines are equally applicable to both characters and strings. A list of the available test macros is given in Table 9.1.

Macro	*Test for...*
int **isalpha**(char)	Alphabetic ('A'–'Z' or 'a'–'z')
int **isdigit**(char)	Digit ('0'–'9')
int **isalnum**(char)	Alphanumeric (alphabetic or digit)
int **isgraph**(char)	Printable character except space (' ')
int **islower**(char)	Lowercase letter ('a'–'z')
int **ispunct**(char)	Punctuation character
int **isspace**(char)	White-space character
int **isupper**(char)	Uppercase letter ('A'–'Z')
int **isxdigit**(char)	Hexadecimal digit ('A'–'F', 'a'–'f', or '0'–'9')

Table 9.1 A selection of useful character testing macros. All return 1 (integer) if the test is satisfied, 0 otherwise. These macros require the `ctype.h` header file.

Examples of the use of some of these macros are given in Program 9.8.

```
// Demonstrating character testing functions
// Source is: 09_08.CPP

#include <iostream.h>
#include <ctype.h>

int main( void )
    {
    char ch[8] = {'A','k','.',')','$','&','9','0'};
    for(int index = 0; index <= 7; index++)
        {
        cout << ch[index];
        if (isalnum(ch[index])) cout << " ALNUM ";
        else cout << "        ";
        if (ispunct(ch[index])) cout << " PUNCT ";
        else cout << "        ";
        if (isdigit(ch[index])) cout << " DIGIT ";
        else cout << "        ";
        if (isxdigit(ch[index])) cout << " HEX ";
        else cout << "        ";
        if (isupper(ch[index])) cout << " UPPER ";
        else cout << "        ";
        cout << "\n";
        }
    return 0;
    }
```

Program 9.8 Demonstrating simple use of some character testing functions. (☺)

The output of Program 9.8 is as follows:

```
A ALNUM                     HEX UPPER
k ALNUM
.           PUNCT
)           PUNCT
$           PUNCT
&           PUNCT
9 ALNUM               DIGIT HEX
0 ALNUM               DIGIT HEX
```

9.3.4   Character conversion library

Another small collection of library macros allows the conversion of particular characters (Table 9.2). We make use of `toupper()` in Program 9.13.

Macro	Conversion
char **toupper**(char)	Convert character to upper case
char **tolower**(char)	Convert character to lower case

Table 9.2 A selection of useful character conversion macros. These macros require the ctype.h header file.

9.3.5 Converting strings

As we have seen, the simple input and output features provided in C++ are too basic for general use. The cardinal rule for robust programs is always to read strings from the keyboard, and never to read integers, real numbers, and so on. If you *always* use get-line() to read data into your prototype programs, you won't be going too seriously wrong. However, you'll not always want to have string data in your programs, so you will need to be able to convert your strings into different data types. We outline some of the possible ways of doing this in Table 9.3, and provide examples below.

Function		Conversion
int	**sscanf**(char* s, const char* format, ...)	Formatted conversion from an array of characters
int	**atoi**(const char*)	Convert a character array to integer (if possible)
double	**atof**(const char*)	Convert a character array to float (if possible)
long	**atol**(const char*)	Convert a character array to long (if possible)

Table 9.3 A selection of useful string conversion functions. The atox() functions require the stdlib.h header file, while sscanf() requires the stdio.h header file.

Using sscanf()

One useful string conversion function is sscanf(). The straightforward use of sscanf() is demonstrated by Program 9.9, where the library function is used to detect and 'catch' an int and a float 'hidden' in a text string.

```
// Demonstration of sscanf() library function
// Source is: 09_09.CPP

#include <iostream.h>
#include <stdio.h>

int main()
    {
    int integer;
    float real_no;
    char text_string[] = "100 3.141516";

    cout << "Demonstration of sscanf\n";
    cout << "-------------------\n";

    cout << "The text string is: \"" << text_string << "\"\n\n";
```

```
       if (sscanf(text_string, "%d", &integer))
           {
           cout << "The integer is: " << integer << "\n\n";
           }
       else
           {
           // sscanf returned zero
           cerr << "WARNING: No integers found.\n";
           }
       if(sscanf(text_string, "%d%f", &integer, &real_no))
           {
           cout << "The integer is: " << integer << endl;
           cout << "The real number is: " << real_no << endl;
           }
       else
           {
           // sscanf returned zero
           cerr << "WARNING: Specified numbers not found.\n";
           }
       return 0;
       }
```

Program 9.9 Use of the `sscanf()` library function to avoid program crashes. (☺)

The output of Program 9.9 is as follows:

```
Demonstration of sscanf
The text string is: "100 3.141516"
The integer is: 100
The integer is: 100
The real number is: 3.141516
```

Program 9.9 shows how `sscanf()` can be used to extract one or more data items of selected types from a text string.
In the line:

```
       if (sscanf(text_string, "%d", &integer))
```

the `sscanf()` function is used to scan the string `text_string[]`. The `%d` is a format specifier, which tells `sscanf()` which kind of data to search for in the input string. A list of some useful format specifiers is given in Table 9.4. From this table, we can see that the '`%d`' format specifier instructs the function to search `text_string[]` for an integer.

If an integer is found, it is assigned to the variable integer. When this happens, `sscanf()` returns an error code of 1 to indicate that one single integer was found in the input stream. Note that if `text_string[]` contained no integers, then `sscanf()` would return 0; if the string contains several integers, then `sscanf()` will return the number found. As the second part of the program shows, more than one data item can be extracted from the same string in the same way.

Format	Corresponding data type
%d	integer
%u	unsigned integer
%ld	long integer
%lu	long unsigned integer
%f	floating-point
%c	character
%s	string

Table 9.4 A selection of format specifiers.

Function sscanf() is a useful facility for your programs. We use it in several of the later, more substantial, programs in this book.

Using the atof() family

The atof() family of functions comprises atof(), atoi() and atol(). These functions are used to convert (if it is possible to do so) a character string into:

- a double-precision floating-point value (using atof());
- an integer value (using atoi()); or
- a long integer value (using atol()).

In each case, the functions stop reading the input string at the first character that they cannot recognize as part of a number of the appropriate type; this character may be the null character ('\0') terminating the string. Note also that these functions are good candidates for 'overloading' (discussed in Chapter 8); however, they were originally written in C, which did not allow more than one function to have the same name.

Note that a maximum string size of 100 characters can be handled by atof(). Finally note that, in contrast to many other functions (but like the 'isa' functions considered in Section 9.3.2), the return value is 0 if the conversion to the required type is *unsuccessful*, and non-zero otherwise.

The use of these functions is illustrated in Program 9.10.

```
// Demonstrating use of String Conversion Functions
// Source is: 09_10.CPP

#include <stdlib.h>
#include <iostream.h>

int main()
    {
    char* strings[4] = { "1234.56xyz",
                         "-2001 Leagues",
                         "35000",
                         "43.2E-07" };
    double    double_num;
    long      long_num;
    int       int_num;
```

```
        for (int test = 0; test < 4; test++)
            {
            cout << strings[test] << endl;
            int_num = atoi(strings[test]);
            cout << "Integer : " << int_num << endl;

            long_num = atol(strings[test]);
            cout << "Long    : " << long_num << endl;
            double_num = atof(strings[test]);
            cout << "Double : " << double_num << endl << endl;
            }

        return 0;
        }
```

Program 9.10   Using string conversion functions. (☺)

The output of Program 9.10 is as follows:

```
    1234.56xyz
    Integer      : 1234
    Long         : 1234
    Double       : 1234.56

    -2001 Leagues
    Integer      : -2001
    Long         : -2001
    Double       : -2001

    35000
    Integer      : -30536
    Long         : 35000
    Double       : 35000

    43.2E-07
    Integer      : 43
    Long         : 43
    Double       : 4.32e-006
```

As the examples illustrate, care needs to be taken with these functions if the results obtained are to be correct.

9.3.6   Basic string handling

Three essential string handling operations are copying, comparison and concatenation. We give an outline of useful functions that can perform each of these operations in Table 9.5, and provide examples below. Note that the type size_t is defined in the ANSI/ISO C standard as being equal to the size of the largest object supported by the compiler. It is defined in the stdio.h header file. In effect, depending on the system you are using, size_t is a synonym for either unsigned long or unsigned int.

Function		Conversion
char*	**strcpy**(char* copy, const char* orig)	Copy orig string to copy string, and return copy
char*	**strncpy**(char* copy, const char* orig, size_t n)	Copy at most n characters from original string to copy, and return the copy. If original string has less than n characters, pad the copy with '\0's
char*	**strcat**(char* string1, const char* string2)	Join string2 onto the end of string1; return string1
char*	**strncat**(char* string1, const char* string2, size_t n)	Same as above, but appends at most n characters from string2. Note that the resulting string1 will be terminated with '\0'
int	**strcmp**(const char* string1, const char* string2)	Compare string1 to string2. Return <0 if string1 < string2, 0 if the strings are equal, and >0 if string2 > string1
int	**strncmp**(const char* string1, const char* string2, size_t n)	Same as above, but compare at most n characters
size_t	**strlen**(const char* string)	Return length of string (excluding '\0')

Table 9.5 A selection of useful string handling functions. The functions require the string.h header file.

Copying strings

One way of copying strings is to do so 'by hand', as illustrated in Program 9.11.

```
// Copying strings by hand
// Source is: 09_11.CPP

#include <iostream.h>

int main()
    {
    char orig[81] = "The Man in the High Castle";
    char copy[81];

    cout << orig << endl;

    // copy strings - standard "trick"
    for (int i=0; copy[i] = orig[i]; i++);

    cout << copy << endl;

    return 0;
    }
```

Program 9.11 Copying strings 'by hand'. (☺)

The output of Program 9.11 is as follows:

```
The Man in the High Castle
The Man in the High Castle
```

All the work in this program is done in the `for` loop header:

```
for (int i=0; copy[i] = orig[i]; i++) ;
```

Note that the loop itself is empty (as indicated by the floating semi-colon). The original string is copied, one character at a time, till the null terminator is reached. After this has been copied, the loop condition is no longer satisfied, and it terminates.

The alternative way of copying strings is to use the library functions `strcpy()` (to copy the whole string), or `strncpy()` (to copy the first n characters of the string). Note that you may have to add a `null` terminator manually, if required, when using `strncpy()`. Use of these functions is illustrated in Program 9.12.

```cpp
// Copying strings using library functions
// Source is: 09_12.CPP

#include <iostream.h>
#include <string.h>

int main()
    {
    char orig[81] = "The Man in the High Castle";
    char copy1[81], copy2[81], copy3[81];

    cout << orig << endl << endl;

    strcpy(copy1, orig);
    strncpy(copy2, orig, 7);
    strncpy(copy3, orig, 7);
    copy3[7] = '\0';

    cout << copy1 << endl;
    cout << copy2 << endl;
    cout << copy3 << endl;

    return 0;
    }
```

Program 9.12   Copying strings using library functions. (☺)

The output of Program 9.12 is as follows:

```
The Man in the High Castle

The Man in the High Castle
The Man_È_☐_ÌE<E
The Man
```

Note the effect of displaying the second copy of the string, without a null terminator.

Comparing strings

The function strcmp() allows comparison of two strings. In Program 9.13 we use strcmp(), along with two other functions: strlen() to find the length of a string, and toupper() to convert a character to upper case.

```
// Using library functions for robust data input
// Source is: 09_13.CPP

// Use: strcmp, toupper, getline, sscanf, strlen
#include <string.h>
#include <iostream.h>
#include <ctype.h>
int main()
    {
    char line[81];
    char* c_PTR;
    int count = 0;
    char user_wants_to_continue; // Flag
    char answer;
    do
        {
        cout << "Type 'start', then <ENTER> to start count ";
        cin.getline(line, sizeof(line));

        // Convert input to upper case
        for(c_PTR = line; c_PTR < line + strlen(line); c_PTR++)
            {
            *c_PTR = toupper(*c_PTR);
            }
        } while (strcmp(line, "START"));
    do
        {
        // Start counting...
        cout << "Count is : " << count++ << endl;
        if (!(count % 2))
            {
            do
                {
                cout << "Do you want to continue (Y/N) : ";
                cin.getline(line, sizeof(line));
                answer = toupper(line[0]);
                } while ((answer != 'Y') && (answer != 'N'));
            user_wants_to_continue = (answer == 'Y');

            }
        else
            {
            do
                {
                cout << "Hit <RETURN> to continue ";
                cin.getline(line, sizeof(line));
```

```
                              } while (strlen(line));
                     user_wants_to_continue = 1;
                     }
                } while (user_wants_to_continue);
           return 0;
           }
```

Program 9.13 Robust data input using library functions. (☺)

A typical run of Program 9.13 generates the following output:

```
Type 'start', then <ENTER> to start count go
Type 'start', then <ENTER> to start count
Type 'start', then <ENTER> to start count Start
Count is : 0
Hit <RETURN> to continue
Count is : 1
Do you want to continue (Y/N) : h
Do you want to continue (Y/N) : y
Count is : 2
Hit <RETURN> to continue y
Hit <RETURN> to continue
Count is : 3
Do you want to continue (Y/N) : y
Count is : 4
Hit <RETURN> to continue
Count is : 5
Do you want to continue (Y/N) : n
```

Concatenating strings

Concatenating strings (that is, joining two strings together) is most easily carried out using the library function strcat(), as illustrated in Program 9.14.

```
// Concatenating strings using library functions
// Source is: 09_14.CPP

#include <iostream.h>
#include <string.h>

int main()
    {
    char part1[81] = "Flow my tears, ";
    char part2[81] = "the policeman said";
    cout << part1 << endl;
    cout << part2 << endl << endl;

    strcat(part1, part2); // Join part2 to end of part1
    cout << part1 << endl << endl;

    return 0;
    }
```

Program 9.14 Joining two strings together. (☺)

The output of Program 9.14 is as follows:

```
Flow my tears,
the policeman said
Flow my tears, the policeman said
```

9.3.7 Using `printf()` and `scanf()`

As a C++ programmer, you need to be aware that in C programs, cin and cout were not available, and that most input and output (in simple programs at least) was effected using the library functions printf() and scanf(). We provide an example (Program 9.15) of the use of these functions for completeness. Note that the parameters of both functions are similar to each other and to sscanf().

```
// Addition program
// Source is: 09_15.CPP

#include <stdio.h>

int main(void)
    {
    int x, y, z;

    printf("Enter first integer : ");
    scanf("%d", &x);
    printf("Enter second integer : ");
    scanf("%d", &y);

    z = x + y;

    printf("The sum of %d and %d is %d\n", x,y,z);

    return 0;
    }
```

Program 9.15 Using C's I/O functions in a C++ program. (☺)

A typical output from Program 9.15 is as follows:

```
Enter first integer : 3
Enter second integer : 4
The sum of 3 and 4 is 7
```

The program is straightforward, but the line:

```
printf("The sum of %d and %d is %d\n", x,y,z);
```

deserves some explanation.

Looking at the program output, we can see that the string is printed as it appears in the printf() call, except that the two '%d' parts of the string are not printed. Here, as for sscanf(), the '%d' is a format specification. There should be exactly one data item for each format specification listed in the format string, and the data types of these items must correspond to that in the specification. The items themselves can be variables, constants, expressions (or even further function calls). The output is written to the 'standard output' device, which is almost invariably the screen.

Here we can see that the format string tells the `printf()` function to expect two `%d`-type data items. Referring to Table 9.4, we can see that `%d` format specifier refers to integer data. Sure enough, in function call:

```
printf("The sum of %d and %d is %d\n", x,y,z);
```

we have three integers (x, y and z) listed immediately following the format string. The remainder of the program can be understood in much the same way.

If you are tempted to use a mixture of C and C++ I/O in your programs, a word of advice – don't! The buffering arrangements used by the C and C++ functions are different, a fact which can and will cause unpredictable results in your programs. If you are determined to use a mix, then look up the `sync_with_stdio()` function in your compiler documentation.

If you are tempted to abandon `cin` and `cout` completely in favour of `printf()` and `scanf()`, then don't do this either. The advantage of using the `iostream` library is that you, or someone else working with your code at a later date, will be able to overload the stream insertion and extraction operators, a useful process we discuss in Chapter 26.

9.4 Mathematical functions

Table 9.6 gives some brief details of functions included in the maths library. Some examples showing the use of these functions are given below.

Function	Description	Example
`sqrt(x)`	Square root of x	`sqrt(100.0) = 10.0`
`exp(x)`	e^x	`exp(1.0) = 2.718282`
`log(x)`	Natural log of x	`log(2.718282) = 1.0`
`log10(x)`	Log of x (base 10)	`log10(100.0) = 2.0`
`sin(x), cos(x), tan(x)`	Trigonometric functions	`sin(0.0) = 0.0`
`pow(x,y)`	x^y	`pow(2,7) = 128.0`
`floor(x)`	Rounds x to 'the largest integer not greater than x'	`floor(1.2) = 1.0` `floor(-1.2) = -2.0`
`ceil(x)`	Rounds x to 'the smallest integer not less than x'	`ceil(1.2) = 2.0` `ceil(-1.2) = -1.0`

Table 9.6 Some functions from the standard maths library. All parameters and return values are of type `double`. All need the `math.h` header file.

First of all, we use `ceil()` and `floor()` in Program 9.16 to convert real numbers to integers in a controlled manner.

```
// Demonstrating ceil and floor
// Source is: 09_16.CPP

#include <math.h>
#include <iostream.h>
```

```
int main()
    {
    double number;
    number = floor(3.7);
    cout << "The floor of 3.7 is "   << number << endl;
    number = floor(-3.7);
    cout << "The floor of -3.7 is "  << number << endl;
    number = ceil(3.7);
    cout << "The ceil of 3.7 is "    << number << endl;
    number = ceil(-3.7);
    cout << "The ceil of -3.7 is "   << number << endl;
    return 0;
    }
```

Program 9.16 Using the math library functions `ceil()` and `floor()`. (☺)

The output of Program 9.16 is as follows:

```
The floor of 3.7 is 3
The floor of -3.7 is -4
The ceil of 3.7 is 4
The ceil of -3.7 is -3
```

In Program 9.17, we make use of some further functions from the maths library to display a sine wave on the screen.

```
// Using maths library functions
// Source is: 09_17.CPP
#include <iostream.h>
#include <math.h>
int main()
    {
    float const PI = 3.141512657f;
    float radians;
    int amplitude, space;
    for (int degrees = 0; degrees <= 360; degrees+=15)
        {
        radians = 2 * PI * degrees/360.0f;
        amplitude = 31 + ((int) float(30.0 * sin(radians)));
        for (space = 0; space < amplitude; space++)
            {
            cout << " ";
            }
        cout << "*\n";
        }
    return 0;
    }
```

Program 9.17 Drawing a sine wave using the `sin()` function. (☺)

The output of Program 9.17 is as follows:

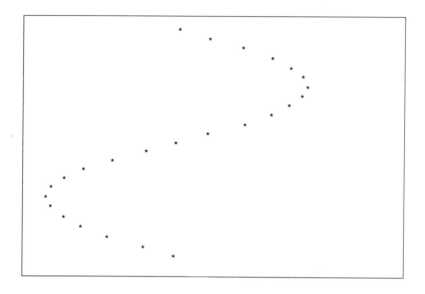

9.5 Sorting and searching

The C/C++ standard libraries contain two useful sorting and searching functions. Use of these library functions is one useful application of function pointers, considered in Chapter 7.

The qsort() function performs a generic 'Quicksort' on any type of 1-D array. The prototype for qsort() is:

```
void qsort(void*        array_start,
           size_t       num_of_elements,
           size_t       size_of_elements,
           int (*compare)(const void*, const void*));
```

The prototype uses a number of advanced C++ features discussed in previous chapters; it does, however, deserve some explanation.

The first parameter, array_start, gives the start address of the array of elements that we wish to sort. Note that since qsort() can sort data items of any type, array_start is a generic pointer (as discussed in Chapter 7).

The second parameter, num_of_elements, specifies the number of elements, stored in a continuous block of memory starting at address array_start, that we wish qsort() to sort. Note that to allow maximum portability, the type of this parameter is size_t (see Section 9.3.6).

Also of type size_t is the third parameter size_of_elements which specifies the size (in bytes) of the data elements in the array.

The final parameter is also the most interesting. This relates to the (user-written) function used to compare the individual elements during the sort process. Again as a consequence of the generic nature of qsort(), this parameter is actually a pointer to the comparison function, which in turn has two generic pointers as formal parameters.

We can best see how qsort() works by considering a simple example. Program 9.18 uses qsort() to arrange the elements of an array of integers in ascending order.

```
// Demonstrating standard sorting functions
// Source is: 09_18.CPP

#include <iostream.h>
#include <stdlib.h>

int compare(const void*, const void*);

int main()
    {
    int list[10] = {9,5,2,8,1,7,3,6,4,0};

    //display unsorted list
    for (int element = 0; element <= 9; element++)
        {
        cout << list[element] << " ";
        }

    cout << endl;

    qsort(list, 10, sizeof(int), compare);

    //display sorted list
    for (element = 0; element <= 9; element++)
        {
        cout << list[element] << " ";
        }

    return 0;
    }
int compare (const void* a_PTR, const void* b_PTR)
    {
    return *((int*)a_PTR) - *((int*)b_PTR);
    }
```

Program 9.18 Simple use of qsort(). Note the inclusion of the stdlib.h header file. (☺)

Program 9.18 generates the following output:

```
9 5 2 8 1 7 3 6 4 0
0 1 2 3 4 5 6 7 8 9
```

Note the use of the cast operator with the generic pointers within the comparison function.

C++ also provides a useful search function called bsearch(). As this works with sorted arrays only, it is frequently used in conjunction with qsort(). The prototype for bsearch() is:

```
void bsearch(void*        key
             void*        array_start,
             size_t       num_of_elements,
             size_t       size_of_elements,
             int (*compare)(const void*, const void*));
```

As you can see, the parameters of bsearch() are the same as those of qsort(), with the exception of the first. The first parameter in bsearch() is a generic pointer to the data for which the programmer wishes to search.

Use of bsearch() is straightforward, as illustrated by Program 9.19.

```cpp
// Demonstrating standard searching and sorting functions
// Source is: 09_19.CPP

#include <iostream.h>
#include <stdlib.h>

int compare(const void*, const void*);

int main()
    {
    int list[10] = {9,5,2,8,1,7,3,6,4,0};
    int key = 3;

    //display array contents
    for (int element = 0; element <= 9; element++)
        {
        cout << list[element] << " ";
        }

    cout << endl;

    qsort(list, 10, sizeof(int), compare);

    if (bsearch(&key, list, 10, sizeof(int), compare))
        {
        cout << key << " is in the array" << endl;
        }
    else
        {
        cout << key << " is NOT in the array" << endl;
        }

    return 0;
    }

int compare(const void* a_PTR, const void* b_PTR)
    {
    return *((int*)a_PTR - *((int*) b_PTR;
    }
```

Program 9.19 Simple use of bsearch(). Note the inclusion of the stdlib.h header file. (☺)

Program 9.19 generates the following output:

```
9 5 2 8 1 7 3 6 4 0
3 is in the array
```

9.6 Time and date functions

Often, your programs will need to know the current time and date. For example, if you were developing a system to process X-ray images recorded in a hospital environment, the clinicians using your product may well want to automatically store the date and time the images were taken along with patient information and the picture data themselves. In other circumstances, you may be more interested in the time that has elapsed between two events. For example, while developing the X-ray program above, you may need to accurately compare the speed of two filtering techniques on a range of different image types and sizes.

In these circumstances, you need the time function library. For example, consider first Program 9.20. Here, the library function time() is used. This function returns the number of seconds elapsed since midnight (00:00:00), 1 January 1970: this time is known as 'UNIX time' or Universal Coordinated Time (UCT).

Knowing the UCT, we can calculate dates, days, and so on, as required, or (as in Program 9.20) we can let the ctime() do the work for us. The function ctime() converts UCT – stored in a structure (a user-defined data type, discussed in Chapter 17) – into a character string. This string always contains 26 characters, as in the following example:

```
Mon Jan 01 09:01:25 1996\n\0
```

Note that a 24-hour time representation is used, and that the new line character ('\n') and the null character ('\0') occupy the last two positions of the string.

```
// Illustrating basic use of time() and ctime().
// Source is: 09_20.CPP

#include <time.h>
#include <iostream.h>

int main()
    {
    time_t current_time;

    // Find time and display.
    time(&current_time);
    cout << ctime(&current_time);

    return 0;
    }
```

Program 9.20 Simple use of time functions. (☺)

The output of Program 9.20 is as follows:

```
Mon Jan 01 08:37:21 1996
```

For recording elapsed time, a similar procedure is used. For instance, in Chapter 6, we used these facilities to compare the speed of access to register and automatic variables.

9.7   Abandoning the sinking ship

In previous chapters, we have occasionally made use of a useful standard library function called `exit()`. The function `exit()` allows the programmer to terminate a program if a catastrophic error occurs, or some condition necessary for the program's execution has not been satisfied.

The function has the following prototype:

```
void    exit(int error_code);
```

and uses the `stdlib.h` header file.

As we have seen, most operating systems use an error code (return code) of zero to indicate a normal program completion, with non-zero values used to indicate an abnormal termination. The following code fragment will abort a program, returning an error code of one to the operating system:

```
...
exit(1);
...
```

Like all 'jump' operations, `exit()` is inherently unstructured; use it with care.

9.8   Interrupts

Interrupts, as far as programmers are concerned, arise from unexpected or unpredictable events, either directly from hardware (such as a component failure or a disk write error) or from software-based problems (such as trying to divide by 0). Interrupts are sometimes referred to as signals.

When an interrupt is detected, then the programmer has three options:

(1)   to terminate the program (this is often the default behaviour);
(2)   to ignore the interrupt and carry on (for as long as possible);
(3)   to handle the interrupt, by causing control to pass to an interrupt handling function.

'Standard' C++ inherits from C the signal handling library, with header file `signal.h`. This provides facilities for detecting, among other things, floating-point exceptions (such as floating-point overflow), interactive attention signals (such as the user typing 'Control-C' at the keyboard) and memory violations (such as attempts to access invalid memory areas). Details of these features are given by Plauger (1992).

Interrupt handling is never portable, even with the 'standard' routines mentioned above. To make life even more interesting, with any particular C++ implementation there is usually a way of establishing your own interrupt handlers. For example, the 80x86 family of computers reserves the first 1024 bytes of memory for function pointers (see Chapter 7) used to access such handlers. Many of these locations are unused and, if you know what you are doing, you can create your own interrupt handling function, and place a pointer to this function in a spare location. Details of this process are very implementation dependent and well beyond the scope of this book.

We have more to say about the use of interrupts in later chapters.

9.9 Beyond the standard library: simple graphics

The 'graphical' output from Program 9.17 is too crude for anything but the most primitive prototype. What we want for many applications is some simple, flexible, high-resolution graphics functions. Unfortunately, as C++ is intended to be used on a huge variety of different hardware platforms, there is no standard graphics library; everything to do with graphics is implementation dependent.

To provide a feel for the use of basic graphics capabilities, consider Program 9.21.

```
// Demonstrating basic maths and MS graphics library functions
// Source is: 09_21.CPP
// NOTE: This program makes extensive use of implementation
//       dependent graphics functions. All function names
//       preceded by an underscore are Microsoft specific.
#include <graph.h>
#include <stdlib.h>
#include <conio.h>
#include <math.h>
#include <stdio.h>
int main()
    {
    char buffer[80];
    const float PI = 3.141512657f;
    double sum[362] = {0.0};
    int old_x, old_y;
    float radians;
    int x, y, color = 1;
    struct _videoconfig v;
    // Find a valid graphics mode
    if(!_setvideomode(_MAXCOLORMODE))
        {
        exit(1);
        }
    _getvideoconfig( &v );
    int x_max = v.numxpixels;
    int y_max = v.numypixels;
    // Calculate result
    for (long harmonic = 1; harmonic < 6; harmonic+=2)
        {
        for (int degrees = 0; degrees <= 360; degrees++)
            {
            radians = 2 * PI * degrees/360.0f * harmonic;
            sum[degrees] += sin(radians);
            }
        }
    double sum_max = -1000, sum_min = 1000;
    for (int degrees = 0; degrees <= 360; degrees++)
        {
        if (sum[degrees] > sum_max)
```

```
                    {
                    sum_max = sum[degrees];
                    }
                if (sum[degrees] < sum_min)
                    {
                    sum_min = sum[degrees];
                    }
                }
        // Display result
        old_x = 0;
        old_y = y_max / 2;
        _setbkcolor(1);
        for (degrees = 0; degrees <= 360; degrees++)
                {
                x = (int)((degrees/360.0) * x_max);
                y = y_max - (int)(((sum[degrees]-sum_min)
                               /(sum_max-sum_min))*y_max);
                _moveto(old_x,old_y);
                _lineto(x,y);
                old_x = x;
                old_y = y;
                }
        _settextposition(20,10);
        sprintf(buffer, "Sum of %d Odd Harmonics", harmonic/2);
        _outtext( buffer );

        return 0;
        }
```

Program 9.21   A program which adds a number of sine waves together and displays the results using Microsoft-specific graphics functions. (☺)

The output of Program 9.21 is as follows:

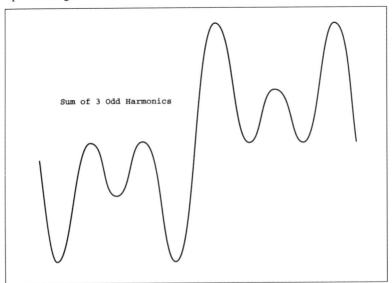

Sum of 3 Odd Harmonics

Program 9.21 is one of very few in this book to use implementation-dependent features. It is worth noting from the source code that the non-standard nature of the graphics functions is made explicit from the pre-underscored function names.

Note that the line

```
_getvideoconfig( &v );
```

calls a function to determine the current video screen mode. What is passed to the function is a C++ `struct`, a type of data structure we consider in Chapter 17.

9.10   Conclusions

We've considered a host of useful C and C++ functions and related features in this chapter, and yet we've scarcely scratched the surface. You can't use existing code or functions if you don't know what is available: there's no option but to study the standard C/C++ libraries, the extra libraries provided with your own compiler, plus further specialized books in your area. In the last case, the bibliography (Chapter 34) will help get you off the ground.

Exercises

9.1   Write a C++ function called `Convert_to_Upper_Case()` that takes a string of characters and converts it to UPPER CASE. Call the function in a C++ program so that the program works as follows:

```
What is your name? John Smith
Hello, JOHN SMITH
```

9.2   Extend your solution to Exercise 9.1 so that it includes an additional function called `Sensible_Name()`. In this function, a check is made to see if the user has typed in a sensible name: here, a sensible name is less than 30 characters long, and consists of only alphabetic characters or spaces. If the name is not 'sensible' the program should generate an output like the following:

```
What is your name? John 5
Hello, JOHN 5
(By the way, has anyone ever told you
that JOHN 5 is a very unusual name?)
```

9.3   Modify your solution to Exercise 9.1 so that it has an additional function which calculates the time of day. Using the information provided by this additional function, the program generates the following output:

```
What is your name? John 5
Good afternoon, JOHN 5
(By the way, has anyone ever told you
that JOHN 5 is a very unusual name?)
```

9.4   Rewrite your solution to Exercise 9.3, this time avoiding the use of *any* of the standard library functions (you may continue to use `cout`, etc.).

9.5   Modify the 'Quote' program from Chapter 8 so that it uses only single indirection, and makes maximum use of library functions.

9.6   Making use of the functions described in Section 9.3.4, write a set of overloaded C++ functions called `atox()` that will, where possible, convert a character string into:

●   a double-precision floating-point value

●   a single-precision floating-point value

●   a short integer value

●   an integer value, or

●   a long integer value.

Note that `atox()` should have two parameters, the first a character pointer (giving the start of the string to be converted) and the second a (reference) variable to which the result will be assigned.

9.7   Rewrite the 'sum of sine waves' (Program 9.21) to work with your compiler.

9.8   A bank wishes to introduce a new type of bank account. As they come to a decision about the precise terms they will offer, they require a program that will calculate the balance resulting at the end of a year when a customer deposits a sum at the beginning of the year, and leaves it to gather interest for the whole period.

They require a program that will allow them to specify the sum to be deposited, and will print out the balance at the end of the year, assuming that the interest is calculated monthly. The program will also ask for the annual interest rate, and will divide this figure by 12 to find the monthly rate to use in its calculations.

The bank wishes to use the following simple formula to calculate the monthly interest:

$b2 = b1 + (b1 \times \text{monthly interest rate})$

where:

$b2$ = balance at end of month;
$b1$ = balance at start of month.

Write a suitable program for the bank, using user-defined functions and library functions as appropriate. Modify your program so that it prints out two balances, one based on a monthly interest rate calculation, and one based on a daily interest rate calculation.

10 The physical process model

10.1 Introduction

We were rather dismissive of programmers in the introduction to this book, implying that the only honourable course of action open to such individuals is to strive to become a software engineer. Of course, this is entirely unfair. The reality is that good programming is as much art as science, and many of the best programmers are creative, intelligent, independently minded individuals who have joined the computing game for the sheer pleasure of solving difficult problems and creating interesting, novel solutions. It is this, above all else, that can make programming a fulfilling career choice.

Now, as you've guessed, there's a 'but' coming. The problem is that to complete a software contract requires more than creativity and raw programming ability. The client won't be impressed to learn that you've managed to shave a full three milliseconds off the time taken to compute function XYZ by using a modified version of Donald Knuth's PQR algorithm (even if this is ground-breaking stuff); the client simply wants the product as specified, on time and within budget.

If you view this from a management perspective, then the main concern is along the following lines:

> *'How do we ensure that the programmers actually deliver what we want them to deliver?'*

From a programmer's perspective, the corresponding gripe is:

> *'I built precisely what you asked me to build. If you wanted different, you should have told me different six months ago – not now.'*

The problem stems, in part at least, from communication difficulties. What we need is a way of making sure that managers, designers, clients and programmers can all understand one another. That is, we want to have a design for our system that is clear and unambiguous, that can be shown to and discussed with the client and then passed to the programmer for implementation. Thus, we require a way of representing our system that satisfies the following criteria:

- It must provide an unambiguous specification of the system to be constructed.
- It must be comprehensible by designer, programmer and client.

- It must be concise (if it's not, no one will read it).

- It must be straightforward and economical to produce.

These are not easy requirements to satisfy. We might summarize the above (if we wished to sound grandiose) by claiming that our intention is to provide a broadband 'channel of communication' between the designers and the programmers that removes ambiguity from the programmer's task, while still leaving room for that elusive spark of creativity that can turn a moribund uninspiring software product into a best seller.

One possibility would be to use a description in English (or French, Italian, or whatever) of the project. The problem is that descriptions in ordinary English are often ambiguous, and the whole point of producing a specification is that it should be free of ambiguity. If a specification is open to interpretation then it is also open to legal challenges in the event that problems occur. We might be able to avoid this if we create a very long document, but this will be both difficult to write and difficult to read: in effect, this is a 'narrowband' communication channel. Instead, we might choose to use a more restricted specification language, made up of some form of structured English. A very similar approach is taken by the legal profession, which has evolved its own version of English to cope with the ambiguities of ordinary language. The natural consequence is that legal English generally must be written and read by experts.

Another alternative is to use mathematics to record the system specification and design. There are a number of mathematical software development techniques in use, notably the Vienna Development Method (for example, Andrews and Ince, 1991) and Z (for example, Hayes, 1993). These do offer a precise and entirely unambiguous method of specifying software, and even of proving that a particular program matches a specification. However, such techniques are not widely used in practice, because – like structured English – they can generally only be properly understood by experts in the area.

The most general solution, and the one we use here, is to use a form of structured diagram to represent our systems. As we first saw in Chapter 2, the engineering of software may involve the creation of a range of Context diagrams, dataflow diagrams (DfDs) and class-relationship diagrams, in addition to the structure charts we describe in this chapter. The diagrams are backed up by a (structured English) description of the system being constructed, but even on their own they provide a great deal of information.

The use of diagrams in this way makes sense, because, as a species, we have evolved to digest visual information rapidly and efficiently. If you invite your friends to dinner at your new house, you might choose to describe the route as a long series of written instructions, but you'd be more likely to sketch a map; the latter approach will often be quicker and easier for both you and your guests.

In this chapter, we'll look at our first structured diagrams, as we consider the physical process model. This is used to specify software systems assembled from functions. The model itself consists of two main components: structure charts and process specifications (PSpecs). We'll investigate both in this chapter.

Let's be clear, however, before we start: structure charts and PSpecs are not developed by the programmer but by the *analyst* and *designer*. It is the analyst who determines the initial PSpecs, and the designer who draws up the structure charts and any further necessary PSpecs in so doing; we'll consider these stages of SADIE in Chapters 12 to 16. Here we are concerned only with the notation used; in Chapter 11 we'll see how this representation is translated into C++ code.

10.2   Structure charts

We begin our investigation of the use of diagrams in software development by exploring the features of structure charts in this section. The notation used for structure here and throughout this book is a common one, originally described by Larry Constantine and therefore often referred to as a 'Constantine chart'. Yourdon and Constantine (1978) provide a review of the original notation.

Note that all the structure charts in this chapter were produced using the CASE tool included with the book. If you want to explore the use of these charts with the tool, then you'll need to complete the installation described in Appendix A before you begin. Appendix I contains a tutorial describing how the charts can be created.

10.2.1   Example

Let's start by considering the structure chart for a calculator (Figure 10.1). The figure should be read as follows: running the 'Simple Calculator' program causes the 'Main' program module to be called. The 'Main' module itself then calls 'Display menu', which returns a (control) flag 'Choice'. Here 'Choice' will, we presume, indicate whether the user wishes to add some numbers, subtract some numbers, or quit (we return to this point below). Condition 'C1' then specifies that, depending on the value of 'Choice', module 'Main' may call 'Add numbers' or 'Subtract numbers'. The process of alternately calling the menu module and the user's chosen arithmetic module repeats (under the control of Condition C0) until the 'Quit' choice is made, at which point 'Main' returns a value to the operating system (presumably to indicate that the program completed normally).

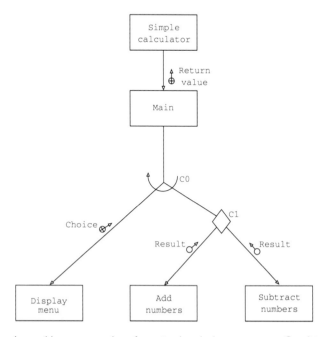

Figure 10.1   A possible structure chart for a simple calculator program. Conditions – C0: Keep calling 'Display menu' and the user's chosen arithmetic function, until 'Choice' is equal to 'Quit'; C1: Call 'Add numbers' or 'Subtract numbers' (or neither) depending on the value of 'Choice'

There are two particular points worth noting from this simple system. First, the possible values of 'Choice' are not explicitly shown in the structure chart; instead, such details belong in the data dictionary. Secondly, 'Main' will not necessarily call either the add or subtract module: the notation specifies that *both* modules will *not* be called on a particular iteration, but does not preclude the possibility that (if the user chose to quit immediately) neither module will be called.

In theory, the initial translation from a structure chart to a C++ program is straightforward: for each 'box' on the structure chart we create a corresponding C++ function. The general structure of the program is therefore simply represented by the structure chart. As we see in this chapter, in practice there's a little more to it.

10.2.2 General features of structure charts

Figure 10.2 gives some further details of the notation we shall use to represent structure charts. The following notes refer to Figure 10.2:

- The module Program Name is the top-level module. You can think of the Program calling the main module (here called Main), the equivalent of a C++ `main()` function. Note that, although the process is no longer common (and we have

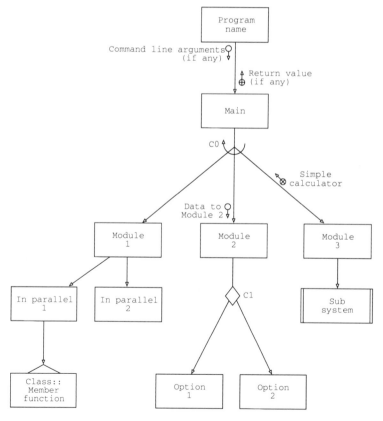

Figure 10.2 A structure chart showing the range of program features that can be represented in this notation (refer to the text for details).

not considered it in this book) it is possible for the `main()` function to take command line arguments: Stroustrup (1991) provides details of this process. Similarly, the Program may receive a return value from Main at the end of the run.

- Module Main calls modules Module 1, Module 2, and Module 3 in order.

- The curved call arrow below 'Main' module indicates that 'Module 1', 'Module 2', and 'Module 3' may be called, in order, over and over again. This process continues until (if ever) some condition, 'C0', is satisfied: this may be, for example, until the users opts to quit, or an error occurs, or a control signal is received. Details of C0 will usually be provided in a key on, or accompanying, the diagram (e.g. see Figure 10.1).

- The dotted call line from Module 1 to modules In Parallel 1 and In Parallel 2 means that these modules are executed *in parallel*: that is, both modules execute at the same time. To translate this design directly into code requires that your programming language and/or your operating system and/or your hardware support what is sometimes called 'multi-threaded' applications. Since such features are very implementation dependent, we won't discuss them further in this book.

- 'Module 2' can call modules 'Option 1' **or** 'Option 2', or neither. The particular module executed (if either) depends on the value of the condition 'C1' which – like C0 – will be detailed in a key.

- Module Sub system is parent to a further child structure chart (not shown), in exactly the same format as Figure 10.2. This allows us to split a complex design over as many pages as necessary.

- Most modules which are not subsystem modules will nonetheless still have children, in the form of process specifications (PSpecs). PSpecs provide details of the processing to be performed by the module: they are discussed in Section 10.3.

- All of the modules are named.

- Finally, the module 'Class::Member function' is used to represented a member function in the final implementation. Member functions are an essential feature of object-oriented C++ programs, as we will see in Part III. For completeness, we include details of the notation used to represent member functions here, but we won't discuss them further in this chapter.

10.3   Process specifications

As we have mentioned, along with one or more structure charts, we need an appropriate collection of process specifications (PSpecs) in order to unambiguously describe the system that we are attempting to develop.

In order to see how such process specifications should be interpreted, let's consider that we are given the design for a program intended to add two numbers. An appropriate structure chart, including a `Main` module and two further modules called `Get two numbers` and `Add two numbers`, is presented in Figure 10.3.

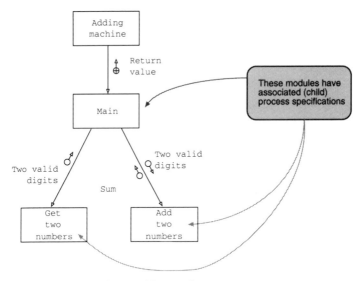

Figure 10.3 Structure chart for an adding machine.

Let's begin by considering an appropriate PSpec for the Get two numbers module (Figure 10.4).

The PSpec consists of four components:

- the header
- the body (optional)
- the pre-conditions
- the post-conditions

We consider each of these components in turn below.

@ IN   = User input
@ OUT = Request for two digits
@ OUT = Two valid digits

@PSPEC Get two numbers

Pre-condition:
    None

Generate a (Request for two digits)
Read the (User input)
When the user has typed in the required digits, then output these as
(Two valid digits)
Until then, keep prompting for the required input

Post-condition:
    Got (Two valid digits)

@

Figure 10.4 PSpec 'Get two numbers' from the adding machine example.

@OUT = Return value

@PSPEC Main

Pre-condition:
    None

Call Get two numbers
Call Add two numbers
Return (Return value) = 0

Post-condition:
    None

@

Figure 10.5 PSpec 'Main' from the adding machine example.

@IN = Two valid digits
@OUT = Sum

@PSPEC Add two numbers

Pre-condition:
    Got (Two valid digits).

Post-condition:
    (Sum) = sum of (Two valid digits)

@

Figure 10.6 PSpec 'Add two numbers' from the adding machine example.

For reference, we include the remaining two PSpecs from the physical process model in Figures 10.5 and 10.6.

10.3.1 The header

The PSpec header gives the name of the associated process, such as:

@PSPEC Get two numbers

The header also includes details of the inputs and outputs from the process, such as:

@IN = User input
@OUT = Request for two digits
@OUT = Two valid digits

Comparing the list of process inputs and outputs given on the function header, we should note that there is an apparent inconsistency between the structure chart, and the associated PSpec. This arises because the structure chart only shows the relationship between the various modules in the system; it does not show the information passed to the function via, for example, the keyboard or an external sensor. Neither does it show the information sent, for instance, to the computer screen, or to external actuators. Such information is shown on the dataflow diagram hierarchy (see Section 10.3.5).

Thus, the programmer needs to be aware that input and output flows not represented on the structure chart may have to be implemented using, for example, `cin` and `cout`.

10.3.2 The PSpec body

The body of the function describes the processing to be performed:

> Generate a (Request for two digits)
> Read the (User input)
> When the user has typed in the required digits, then output these as (Two valid digits)
> Until then, keep prompting for the required input

The programmer should find that there is enough information provided to enable implementation of the corresponding function.

Note that, by adopting a declarative approach to the creation of PSpecs, we say only what the inputs and outputs of the process are, and nothing about the processing required to achieve these results. This can be an effective approach, and is illustrated in Figure 10.6. As Figure 10.6 illustrates, declarative PSpecs do not have a 'body'. However, when dealing with larger or more complex processes, use of a pure declarative approach can become cumbersome and artificial.

We adopt a pragmatic approach to the creation of PSpecs in this text, and use a mixture of declarative and procedural styles.

10.3.3 The pre-conditions

In general terms, the pre-conditions specify the circumstances that must apply before this particular function can be correctly carried out. In this particular case, there are no pre-conditions.

> **Pre-condition:**
> None

More generally, the pre-conditions might specify that the value of 'Temperature' must lie between 1 and 1000. This case could be expressed as follows:

> **Pre-condition:**
> 1 <= (Temperature) <= 1000

Note that, in the final code, both the pre- and post-conditions may be translated into assertions (see Chapter 11).

10.3.4 The post-conditions

The post-conditions specify the conditions that will prevail when the function completes normally. Note that this implies that the pre-conditions were also satisfied.

In this case, the function will only be complete when two valid digits have been provided by the user:

> **Post-condition:**
> Got (Two valid digits)

10.3.5 ASIDE: Sneak preview of the logical process model

As we noted in Chapter 2, the job of the designer in most software houses is to generate some form of physical model of the system (a design specification) based on the logical model produced by the analyst. As we noted above, the programmers should expect to have at their disposal all the available information on the system they are asked to implement: if, as in this part of the book, they are taking a process-oriented approach to software development, then this means they will be provided with both physical and **logical** models. We should therefore consider the logical model of the adding machine; note that we present only an introduction here, deferring a detailed discussion until Chapter 12.

The logical model begins with a context diagram (Figure 10.7). This shows the 'Adding machine' process in the context of the external 'entities' (in this case the system 'User') with which it must interact. In general, terminators model the boundaries of the system. These are components that are essential to the operation of the product, but which the software engineer will not actually have to build herself.

The arrows to and from the terminators show the flow of 'data' to and from the 'Adding machine' process.

The next stage of the logical process model defines in more detail what happens within the 'Adding machine' process. This is done on the Level 1 DfD, 'under' the 'Adding machine' process (Figure 10.8). Notice that the same data items flow in and out of this DfD as did in the higher-level context diagram and that the terminators from the higher level are not shown here.

As before, the Level 1 DfD is 'inside' the Context diagram (Figure 10.8). The DfDs form a hierarchy, shown explicitly in Figure 10.9.

As we shall see, in real systems, there are frequently more levels 'inside' the Level 1 processes, and so on. For the bottom-level processes, the leaf nodes on the tree, the analyst draws up the process specifications (PSpecs). In this case, as we can see in Figure 10.9, there will be two PSpecs, both of which we have already seen: the 'Get two numbers' PSpec is given in Figure 10.4, and the 'Add two numbers' PSpec in Figure 10.6.

Note that the PSpecs form a 'bridge' between the physical and logical models of the system. Note also that the PSpec for 'Main' presented in Figure 10.5 is not part of the logical model: it is created by the designer, as we describe in Chapter 17.

However, PSpecs are not the only common feature of the logical and physical models; details of the data used in both models is provided through the **data dictionary**. An appropriate dictionary for this project is shown in Table 10.1 and data dictionaries are discussed in Chapter 12.

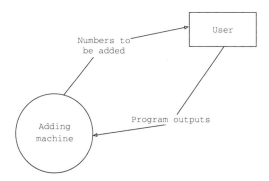

Figure 10.7   Context diagram for the adding machine.

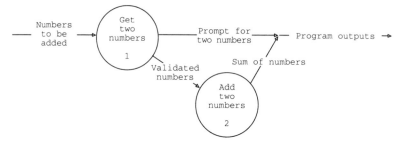

Figure 10.8 The Level 1 DfD for describing in more detail what goes on in the 'Adding machine' process.

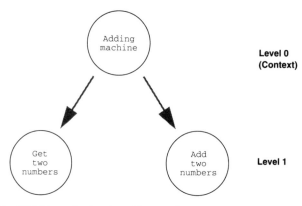

Figure 10.9 The DfD hierarchy for the adding machine.

Data name	Description	Type
Program outputs	Request for two digits + Sum	–
Request for two digits	\Polite request to user to type in two single-digit numbers \	char [81]
Sum	["0"|"1"|"2"|"3"|"4"|"5"|"6"|"7"|"8"|"9"] +(["0"|"1"|"2"|"3"|"4"|"5"|"6"|"7"|"8"|"9"])	char
Two valid digits	["0"|"1"|"2"|"3"|"4"|"5"|"6"|"7"|"8"|"9"] , ["0"|"1"|"2"|"3"|"4"|"5"|"6"|"7"|"8"|"9"]	char
User input	\User responses, possibly containing two valid single-digit integers \	char [81]

Table 10.1 Data dictionary for adding machine example.

Finally, as for the physical model, we have presented the logical model here as a fait accompli; for real systems, creation of such a model is a major undertaking, as we begin to see in Chapter 12.

10.4 An alternative structure chart notation

We should note that, of course, Figure 10.2 is not the only way to represent structure charts. For example, the Jackson structure chart shown in Figure 10.10 uses another popular notation.

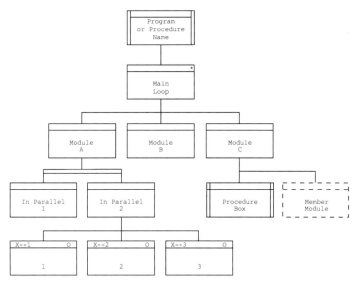

Figure 10.10 A structure chart showing the range of program features that can be represented in this notation (refer to the text for details).

The following notes refer to Figure 10.10:

- The module 'Program or Procedure Name' is the top-level module.
- The asterisk (*) in the corner of the module Main Loop shows that the modules Module A, Module B, and Module C are executed in a loop, in order, repeatedly.
- Modules In Parallel 1 and In Parallel 2 – connected by a double link – execute in parallel.
- Module In Parallel 2 can call modules 1 *or* 2 *or* 3. The particular module executed depends on the value of the control variable X: for example, if X is 2, then Module 2 will execute.
- Module Procedure Box is parent to a further child structure chart (not shown), in exactly the same format as Figure 10.10.
- Most modules which are not procedure boxes will nonetheless still have children, in the form of process specifications (PSpecs).
- Finally, a Member Module is used to represent a member function in the final implementation, as in Section 10.2.2.

You can produce Jackson structure charts with the CASE tool, and their use is described in Appendix I. The two notations are similar; however, we find Jackson-style charts less flexible than the Constantine-style equivalents. The type of chart you choose to use to represent your designs is, of course, up to you.

10.5 Conclusions

In this chapter, we've looked at the physical process model, in the form of structure charts and PSpecs, that a programmer can expected to work from. We consider the translation of such models into robust C++ programs in the next chapter.

Exercises

10.1 Use the CASE tool to reproduce the structure chart shown in Figure 10.1.

10.2 Use the CASE tool to reproduce the structure chart shown in Figure 10.2.

10.3 In the exercises at the end of Chapter 6, you wrote a program that worked as a simple calculator, prompting the user for two real numbers, and asking whether she wants to add or subtract them. The program had a `main()` function, and at least two other functions, (`add_num()` and `subtract_num()`).

The program generated outputs in the following form:

```
Simple calculator

First number >     5
Operation (+ or -) >  +
Second number >    4

ANSWER :     9
```

Use the CASE tool to draw up a structure chart for this program.

10.4 Use the CASE tool to draw up a structure chart for Program 9.12 (p.216).

10.5 Use the CASE tool to draw up a structure chart for Program 9.13 (p.217).

11 Implementation of the physical process model

11.1 Introduction

The implementation process is often dismissed by software engineering texts: once you have created the structure charts (described in Chapter 10), the authors imply, it is a simple matter to create the necessary code. Similarly, many programming books are correspondingly dismissive of the planning phases of software projects, and relegate issues of 'analysis' and 'design' to a final chapter or to an appendix.

Both approaches are equally foolhardy. At the risk of falling between two stools, we therefore take an even-handed view of planning an implementation issue throughout this book. In this chapter, we begin to build a bridge between the sometimes apparently disparate 'planning' and 'programming' camps by considering the issues involved in translating the design of a system into a reliable implementation.

11.2 The recipe

As with all other stages in the software engineering process, during the implementation phase it helps to have a 'recipe' to follow as you embark on your first projects. Assuming we have been provided with the physical process model (discussed in the last chapter), the following general approach is one effective way of producing the robust and well-tested software products we are striving for:

(1) One team member will start by implementing a **code framework** in stub C++ functions or CppSpecs; this process is described in Section 11.3.

(2) Responsibility for particular modules will then be allocated to the remaining team members. Each individual will see one or more modules through to completion. Each will take responsibility for all stages in the implementation of their module(s), and will consider issues such as portability (Section 11.5.2), error detection (Section 11.5.3) and error recovery (Section 11.5.4) as they do so.

(3) As each module is completed, it is tested for the first time. Testing, as we will see, is fundamental to the implementation process. During this period, each module will be tested to breaking point with an individual driver program (Section 11.7). Upon satisfactory completion of such tests, the completed module will replace its

corresponding stub in the framework to undergo further testing as a integral part of the evolving system.

(4)   Following completion of the framework, further testing is carried out. Initially, this will be in-house testing. This will be followed by broader tests and usually involve some type of field trial (Section 11.8).

For larger projects, a team rather than an individual may be responsible for each stage. Thus, for example, a team rather than an individual will produce the general framework. The individual (or team) producing the framework is also likely to be responsible, where appropriate, for the (graphical) user interface components. We consider user interface issues in Chapter 14.

The aim of this chapter is to describe the use of the above 'recipe' in greater depth.

11.3   The starting point

The starting point for any implementation is the physical model. The general guidelines presented in Section 11.2 apply to any of the three types of model (process, data or object models) which we consider in this book, but we shall focus in this chapter on implementation from a physical process model, as described in Chapter 10.

As an example, we'll use the physical process model of the 'Adding Machine', described in the last chapter; this system is, of course, too small to be of any practical significance, but it will allow us to consider all aspects of a complete system implementation in one chapter. For ease of reference, the structure chart and PSpecs for the Adding Machine are repeated below (Figures 11.1 to 11.4). Implementation of a larger system is described in Chapter 16.

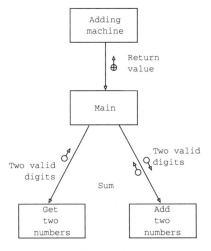

Figure 11.1   Structure chart for the adding machine example.

@ OUT = Return value

@PSPEC Main

Pre-condition:
    None

Call Get two numbers
Call Add two numbers
Return (Return value) = 0

Post-condition:
    None

@

Figure 11.2 PSpec 'Main' from the adding machine example.

@ IN = User input
@ OUT = Request for two digits
@ OUT = Two valid digits

@PSPEC Get two numbers

Pre-condition:
    None

Generate a (Request for two digits)
Read the (User input)
When the user has typed in the required digits, then output these as
(Two valid digits)
Until then, keep prompting for the required input

Post-condition:
    Got (Two valid digits)

@

Figure 11.3 PSpec 'Get two numbers' from the adding machine example.

@ IN = Two valid digits
@ OUT = Sum

@PSPEC Add two numbers

Pre-condition:
    Got (Two valid digits).

Add the (Two valid digits) together. Output the sum as (Sum).

Post-condition:
    (Sum) = sum of (Two valid digits)

@

Figure 11.4 PSpec 'Add two numbers' from the adding machine example.

11.4 Building the system code framework

When working on a large project, whether alone or as part of a team, it is useful to have a general code framework to work with. This framework, which can be compiled and run, will do nothing of any value initially but will, as individual functions are completed, tested and added in, begin to become more useful.

11.4.1 Writing CppSpecs

The initial code framework is assembled from 'stub' C++ function, or what we call **CppSpecs**. A CppSpec is simply a function with a complete interface, but incomplete 'internals'. For example, for our adding machine (Section 11.3), we would have a CppSpec like that shown in Figure 11.5 for the 'Get two numbers' module. The creation of the CppSpec framework involves very little additional work; all of the documentation, plus the function heading, and so on, will all be recycled in the working version of the system.

```
/ ****************************************************************
*                                                              *
*  CppSpec:     Get_two_numbers()                              *
*                                                              *
*  OVERVIEW:    Prompts the user for two positive digits       *
*               (0-9), returning the result via char           *
*               reference variables digit1_REF and             *
*               digit2_REF. Keeps prompting until valid        *
*               input is received.                             *
*                                                              *
*  PRE:         None.                                          *
*  POST:        Got two valid digits.                         *
*                                                              *
*  RETURN:      None.                                          *
*                                                              *
***************************************************************** /
void Get_two_numbers(char& digit1_REF, char& digit2_REF)
    {
    digit1_REF = 0;
    digit2_REF = 0;

    cout << "*** FUNCTION: Get_two_numbers()\n";
    cout << "*** Returning 0 and 0\n\n";
    }
```

Figure 11.5 The CppSpec (a form of stub C++ function) for the 'Get two numbers' module in the adding machine example.

11.4.2 Exploiting separate compilation

A valuable feature of the C++ programming language, and one which facilitates the rapid development of large programs, is the ability to arrange a single program in multiple source files and to combine all these files into a single **project**. These features are of particular value in the development of programs from code frameworks both by individual programmers and particularly by programming teams.

The advantages this feature confers are:

- It allow parts of the project to be worked on by several different people at the same time, in support of the general development approach described above.

- It means that each part of the project can be separately compiled. Thus, for example, if you change one line in one function, you need only recompile the single source file containing this line (a process which may take a few seconds) rather than all the source files (which may take many minutes or even hours …).

- It avoids the need to edit huge files.

Though, for the small programs we will consider in this book, the above 'advantages' may appear rather illusory, in large projects (>10 000 lines of code) on which 10 or more people may be actively employed, these features of C++ are essential.

To illustrate the essential features of separate compilation, consider Program 11.1 (in four parts) which gives a complete framework for the adding machine.

```
/******************************************************************
*                                                                *
*  HEADER: 11_01.H                                               *
*                                                                *
******************************************************************/
// Function prototypes
void Get_two_numbers(char&, char&);
int Add_two_numbers(const char, const char);

/******************************************************************
*                      *** END OF FILE ***                      *
******************************************************************/
```

Program 11.1 (a)   The header file '11_01.H' from the adding machine framework. (☺)

```
/******************************************************************
*                                                                *
*  SOURCE: 11_01a.CPP                                            *
*                                                                *
******************************************************************/
#include <iostream.h>
#include "11_01.H"          // Project header file

/******************************************************************
*                                                                *
*  FUNCTION: main()                                              *
*                                                                *
******************************************************************/
int main()
    {
    char digit1, digit2; // char is all we need here
    int result;

    cout << "The LSE Adding Machine Code Framework\n";
    cout << "--------------------------------\n\n";
```

```
        // Get two valid digits.
        Get_two_numbers(digit1, digit2);

        // Add valid digits
        result = Add_two_numbers(digit1, digit2);

        cout << "Sum is" << result;

        return 0;
        }
/*****************************************************************
*                        *** END OF FILE ***                    *
*****************************************************************/
```

Program 11.1 (b)   File '11_01a.CPP' from the adding machine framework. (☺)

```
/*****************************************************************
*                                                               *
*  SOURCE: 11_01b.CPP                                           *
*                                                               *
*****************************************************************/
#include <iostream.h>
#include "11_01.H"              // Project header file

/*****************************************************************
*                                                               *
*  CppSpec:     Get_two_numbers()                               *
*                                                               *
*  OVERVIEW:    Prompts the user for two positive digits        *
*               (0-9), returning the result via char            *
*               reference variables digit1_REF and              *
*               digit2_REF. Keeps prompting until valid         *
*               input is received.                              *
*                                                               *
*  PRE:         None.                                           *
*  POST:        Got two valid digits.                          *
*                                                               *
*  RETURN:      None.                                           *
*                                                               *
*****************************************************************/
void Get_two_numbers(char& digit1_REF, char& digit2_REF)
        {
        digit1_REF = 0;
        digit2_REF = 0;

        cout << "*** FUNCTION: Get_two_numbers()\n";
        cout << "*** Returning 0 and 0\n\n";
        }
/*****************************************************************
*                        *** END OF FILE ***                    *
*****************************************************************/
```

Program 11.1 (c)   File '11_01b.CPP' from the adding machine framework. (☺)

```
/*****************************************************************
 *                                                               *
 * SOURCE: 11_01c.CPP                                            *
 *                                                               *
 *****************************************************************/
#include <iostream.h>
#include "11_01.H"       // Project header file

/*****************************************************************
 *                                                               *
 * CppSpec:     Add_two_numbers()                                *
 *                                                               *
 * OVERVIEW:    Adds two digits (num1, num2)                     *
 *                                                               *
 * PRE:         num1,num2 are valid digits (chars)               *
 * POST:        sum = num1 + num2                                *
 *                                                               *
 * RETURNS:     sum                                              *
 *                                                               *
 *****************************************************************/
int Add_two_numbers(const char num1, const char num2)
    {
    cout << "*** FUNCTION: Add_two_numbers()\n";
    cout << "*** Returning 0\n\n";

    return 0;
    }

/*****************************************************************
 *                       *** END OF FILE ***                     *
 *****************************************************************/
```

Program 11.1 (d)   File '11_01c' from the adding machine framework. (☺)

Note that the details of project files vary: you will need to refer to the manual for your own compiler to see how to include these files in a project.

11.5   Creating robust functions

A constant focus in the earlier chapters of this book has been on the creation of robust functions: that is, 'bullet proof' functions, that are self-contained and have no side-effects. As we translate our PSpecs into C++ functions, there are three central issues which we must consider:

- software recycling
- portability
- error detection
- error recovery

11.5.1   Software recycling recycled

The first thing you should ask yourself before you write any code is whether you need to do so at all.

We have already considered this issue in Chapter 9, largely in connection with the standard C library provided with all C++ compilers. However, recycling is an equally important consideration when working with code of your own, when there are two related points to consider:

- How do we know whether we, or our company, have any suitable code available?
- How can we write code now suitable for reuse in future projects?

The short answer to the first question is that, unless you make an effort to document your code in a consistent manner, then it is unlikely that you will be able to find a particular code fragment again. You might begin, for example, by taking each function that you write, printing it out and clipping it into a ring binder. Stick with one function per page, and note down on the page where the machine-readable version of the function is stored.

Graduating from this simple approach, you may find it useful to computerize your function database, with cross-links between related functions, and complete programs stored too. Using an on-line version of the code database should allow you to search for particular functions by keywords.

Of course, the approach isn't limited to functions. Data structures (as discussed in Part II) and classes (Part III) are both equally well suited to the same treatment. Neither are we restricted to recording details of functions for which we have the source: you may also wish to include details of any library functions you have, such as the standard C library and any further libraries you have purchased.

The second related concern mentioned above was how you made your code suitable for recycling. In large part, this simply comes down to good and consistent programming style. This means that you must ensure that the systems for which you are responsible are constructed from code that is well documented (as far as possible, self-documented: see Chapters 3 and 4). You must ensure that meaningful variable names are used (Chapter 3), and a consistent code layout (Chapter 4) is adopted. You must ensure that the code is as portable as practical (discussed below, Section 11.5.2). You must ensure that assertions (Section 11.5.3) are used wherever possible and that appropriate use is made of function return values (Section 11.5.4). You must ensure that persistent data structures are well-normalized (see Part II), and that classes (see Part III) enforce a private data, public member functions rule. Finally, you must ensure that no code enters your products, or your database, without adequate testing.

Of course, nothing is free in this world, and following the above guidelines will take time. The nature of project deadlines means that time is always a luxury. Software recycling, when exploited effectively, can pay enormous dividends with the right software team; because software will be reused, it becomes worthwhile to invest a little more time getting it right, and if the code is well-written, it is worth recycling. You have to weigh up the pros and cons of the technique for yourself.

11.5.2   Basic portability issues

As we have seen (Chapters 3 and 4) the range of various C++ types is implementation dependent. You should be aware that the various standard header files contain more than simply function prototypes: also of value are a number of constant declarations specifying the ranges of, for example, integers and floats in a particular implementation. As your programs get more advanced, and if they need to be easily ported to different computer systems, you may need to make use of these facilities.

For example, the header files `limits.h` defines the maximum and minimum range for integers on a particular implementation, through the read-only variables `INT_MAX` and `INT_MIN`; we make use of these constants in some later examples in this chapter. In `floats.h`, similar ranges are defined for floating point data.

In addition, the `typedef` keyword provides a simple mechanism for creating 'aliases' for previously defined data types. The result can be programs that are both more readable, and more portable. For example, if our program requires positive integers in the range 0–50 000, then, on some systems, this will be an `unsigned int`; on others an `unsigned short int` would suffice. If we use `typedef` in our program (or header file) to declare the following alias:

```
typedef unsigned int int_TYPE;
```

then we can use this `int_TYPE` everywhere in our program that we require this implementation-specific type of integer. If we subsequently do port the software to a different system, we need only change one program line:

```
typedef unsigned short int int_TYPE;
```

and recompile our program; everything will then work as before.

Note that we shall see some further uses for `typedef` when we consider the creation of user-defined data types in Parts II and III.

11.5.3 Error detection

No matter how careful we are as software engineers, we know that errors will creep in and problems will occur. Sometimes there is a temptation to assume that one or two 'temporary' fixes to code won't do any harm, reassured perhaps by an assumption that if the fix doesn't work properly under all circumstances then 'the tests will pick it up'. However, programs beyond some 10 000 or 20 000 lines in size are difficult if not impossible to test exhaustively.

In all systems we ship, it is therefore our responsibility to *be responsible*, and to iron out as many bugs as possible during the course of the development process. However, as we see in Chapter 15, there are some systems where errors are of even greater concern. These are the wide and growing range of **safety-critical** systems, from real-time technical systems for car or aircraft control, to information systems used within a clinical environment to aid in medical diagnosis, in which software errors can cause injury or loss of life. For such systems the software engineer has a clear responsibility to ensure that the code is as bug-free as he or she can possibly make it. However, for such safety-critical systems, and all other systems, we need to accept that we shall miss errors, and we must ensure that that those bugs we do miss can do as little damage as possible.

To avoid reduce the number of errors that occur and reducing the propagation of those that do occur is the shared responsibility of all engineers in the team. As we see throughout much of the rest of this book, if our products are to be robust, then we need to "build in" robustness at all stages, from specification right through to the code itself.

Particularly relevant to our discussion on implementation in this chapter is the mechanisms C++ provides for error detection and recovery. The first of these – the macro `assert()` – is primarily useful for error detection during program development.

In addition to the use of assertions, error recovery can sometimes best be effected through the use of appropriate return values from your functions. We consider both of these possibilities below.

Basic use of `assert()`

The use of assertions as a component of good programming style has a long and illustrious history: Dahl *et al.* (1972) and Dijkstra (1973) provide more detail on this area than we cover here.

We shall focus on the use of `assert()` as a debugging tool during program development. Note that use of `assert()` requires the `assert.h` header file be included in the relevant parts of your program. For example, suppose – for some reason – the operation of our program depends on the fact that num1_REF has a value of 1. We can use `assert()` to confirm this, as follows:

```
assert(num1_REF == 1);
```

Here, if num1_REF does not have a value of 1, then our asserted condition will not hold. In these circumstances, the program will halt execution and a suitable warning message will be displayed on the screen. The precise form of the warning message varies between implementation, but it should at least include the line number (of the source code) at which the problem was detected.

An example of such an error message (generated from Microsoft Visual C++) is shown in Figure 11.6.

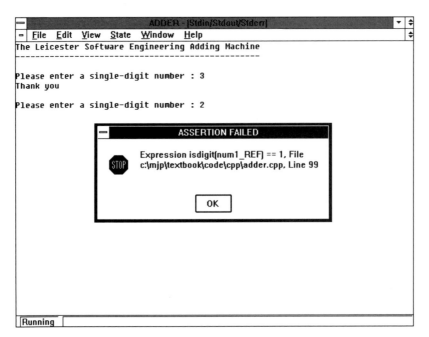

Figure 11.6 How a failed assertion appears to the programmer in Microsoft Visual C++.

Proper use of `assert()` can be of great value during program development. However, it is not usual to ship code (except for Alpha and Beta testing: see Section 11.8.2) with assertions included. This doesn't mean, however, that you have to embark on a tedious (and potentially error-prone) process of removing assertions before shipping. Instead, simply by including the following line in your code (ideally in a shared header file), you can ensure that the `assert()` macro will be ignored by the compiler:

```
#define NDEBUG // Turn off assertions
```

Note that the #define directive must appear before the `#include <assert.h>` line.

Using `assert()` with SADIE

The main use of `assert()` is to check pre- and post-conditions during code development. For example, one of the tasks of the programmer implementing the 'Add two numbers' module from Section 11.3 would be to generate suitable tests for the pre- and post conditions.

The function in Figure 11.7 illustrates the use of the `assert()` macro in this way. Figure 11.7 is a complete implementation of module 'Add two numbers', in C++.

```
/*************************************************************
 *                                                          *
 * FUNCTION:    Add_two_numbers()                           *
 *                                                          *
 * OVERVIEW:    Adds two digits (num1, num2)                *
 *                                                          *
 * PRE:         num1,num2 are valid digits (chars)          *
 * POST:        sum = num1 + num2                           *
 *                                                          *
 * RETURNS:     sum                                         *
 *                                                          *
 *************************************************************/
int Add_two_numbers(const char num1, const char num2)
    {
    int sum;
    // Check pre conditions
    assert(isdigit(num1) == 1);
    assert(isdigit(num2) == 1);
    // Add the digits
    sum = (int) num1 + (int) num2;
    // Check post condition
    assert((sum >=0) && (sum <= 18));
    return sum;
    }
```

Figure 11.7 A function using `assert()`.

Practical uses for `assert()`

Assertions are very useful in theory, but often difficult to use in practice. For example, we used a char variable to hold the single digits used in our adding machine example. Suppose we decide to modify the program, so that it works with integers. We might start by reworking the `Add_two_numbers()` function, as follows:

```
int Add_two_numbers(const int num1, const int num2)
    {
    int sum;
    // Check pre conditions
    assert(isinteger(num1) == 1);
    assert(isinteger(num2) == 1);
    // Add the integers
    sum = num1 + num2;
    // Check post condition
    assert((sum >= INT_MIN) && (sum <= INT_MAX));
    return sum;
    }
```

Here we've made some minor modifications. We've assumed we know the sizes of the largest and smallest integers we can store (INT_MAX and INT_MIN, respectively); this is a reasonable assumption (see Section 11.5.2). We've also assumed that we have available a function (or a macro) called isinteger() that returns a value of 1 if the relevant parameter is, in fact, an integer. This, unfortunately, is not a reasonable assumption. What isdigit() does is to take a character variable and determine whether the value of this variable falls within a specific part of the valid char range. By contrast, what we require our isinteger() function to do is take an integer and tell us if it is an integer: such a function can only ever return a value of TRUE. This is the case because, assuming your computer uses n byte integers, you can pick, at random, any n bytes of memory, and interpret the contents of those locations as a perfectly valid integer.

We could, however, try a different approach, similar to the one adopted in the original digit calculator. We could transmit all data between our functions in the form of strings, then use atoi(), for example, to convert the strings back to integers and/or as part of our assertion. We could do this, but to do so would only slow down our program and make the interfaces to our functions more complex than they need to be.

What this means is that we must take care when we use assertions in our code. Some useful applications are given below:

- If you are writing an input function, that is, one that obtains data from disk, from the keyboard, from a sensor or from a database, then think about how you might check that the data is valid. For example, from the keyboard, always read in from a string and use sscanf(), and the atox() functions (or write your own versions if these are insufficiently flexible, as they may well be) to check that the data is valid. When getting data from a sensor, you need to know how to detect a sensor error, and the range and format of the values that should expect to see. From a database, you need to check, for example, that the dates of birth you are reading don't suggest that your customers are thousands of years old ...

- Check that data sent to your function, and from your function are in range. For example, should the data be greater than 0? Are the array dimensions 0 or less?

- Similarly, check that the data returned from your functions are valid.

- If you are dealing with pointers, then make sure that these are not null values.

In the above example, involving the addition of two integers, we might end up with something like this:

```
int Add_two_numbers(const int NUM1, const int NUM2)
   {
   // Pre: data are appropriate
   assert(!(((num1 > 0)&&(num2 > 0)&&(num1 > INT_MAX-num2))
          ||((num1 < 0)&&(num2 < 0)&&(num1 < INT_MIN+num2)))));

   // Post: return value = x + y
   return num1 + num2;
   }
```

11.5.4 Error recovery

Using assertions is important in debugging, but does not correct errors. We'll address the
problem of error correction here: in particular, we will look at the use of function return
values for error recovery. You should note that one of the important features of the proposed ANSI C++ standard is a feature called **exceptions**: this can, in a similar way to the
use of return statements, help in error recovery. We reserve a discussion of exceptions
until Part III, as this technique is mainly (but not exclusively) used in O-O programs.

We first mentioned the use of return values from functions as an error recovery
mechanism in Chapter 6. As a slightly more practical example, consider function
Multiply() (Figure 11.8). This function returns an error code of 0 upon normal completion, and an error code of 1 if the user tries to multiply numbers that are too large for
the program to handle.

```
/************************************************************
*                                                          *
* FUNCTION:   Multiply                                     *
*                                                          *
* OVERVIEW:   Multiplies two integers (num1 * num2)        *
*             returning the result via result.             *
*                                                          *
* PRE:        num1,num2 are integers (not checked)         *
* POST:       result = num1 * num2 (not checked)           *
*                                                          *
* RETURNS:    0 = Normal completion                        *
*             1 = Product greater than INT_MAX             *
*               (result = 0)                               *
*                                                          *
************************************************************/
Multiply (const int NUM1, const int NUM2, int& result_REF)
   {
   float test;
   int error_code;

   test = ((float) NUM1 * NUM2);
   // INT_MAX - defined in LIMITS.H
   if (test > INT_MAX)
        {
        // product too large to represent as type int
        result_REF = 0;
        error_code = 1;
        }
```

```
        else
            {
            // Can represent product as int: do so
            result_REF = NUM1 * NUM2;
            error_code = 0;
            }
        return error_code;
        }
```

Figure 11.8   The `Multiply()` function, using error codes.

Note that in Figure 11.8 we do not use assertions. Note also that the program is imperfect; we illustrate the testing of this program in Section 11.7.

11.6   Fundamentals of testing

Consider the following scenario:

> For the past six months you've been implementing a piece of image-processing software. The software is designed to compare X-ray photographs from hospital patients. In each case, the first of the two photographs has been taken immediately following a hip replacement operation; the second X-ray photograph has been taken a month later. Your software is an important component of a decision support system intended to help the orthopaedic surgeon determine whether there has been any movement of the replacement (metal) hip joint relative to the femur (leg bone) to which it is attached. If there has been even the slightest movement at this early stage, then further tests (and possibly corrective surgery) are likely to be required. The project has been a challenging but interesting one, and you've worked hard at it. The resulting code is tightly written and well structured. Overall, at some 5000 lines long, it doesn't seem like a huge project, but the length of new code is deceptive because, working carefully, you've managed to use many of your previously written libraries.
>
>   You get a call from the hospital. The surgeon and his team have been trying your software. They've tested it thoroughly and carefully on a sizeable database of X-ray images. They've compared the predictions made by your system as to the need for surgery, with the actual results obtained by an experienced clinician. They have concluded that it would be more effective – and cheaper – to employ a naïve first year (fresher) medical student to inspect the images rather than rely on your system.
>
>   How do you feel?

It's a stupid question, of course. You feel angry. You feel disappointed. You feel that these technophobe doctors wouldn't know a good piece of software if it *bit* them. These things are all perfectly natural: programming is a creative process, and you are bound to feel aggrieved when someone criticizes your creation.

Now, these feelings may be natural, but they are also extremely significant. Too many software companies perceive that the only people who know enough about software to be able to test it are the programmers who wrote it. Since, clearly, such people have a vested interest – let's be charitable and say a 'subconscious' interest – in not finding 'bugs' in their code, they are the last people who should be doing the testing. In the above scenario, for example, rather than blaming the doctors, we should be asking why some of them weren't involved in testing a prototype at an earlier stage, and why – apparently – the hospital was simply presented with the final product as a fait accompli.

In some firms, an even more insidious solution is often in place. Here, a 'software test' team does the tests. Though superficially this may appear to be a major improvement, it may in fact be worse. In 90% of cases, the software test team (whether in-house or external) tests a large number of products a month. The team members frequently don't know all the details of the product: for instance, in the above scenario, the software house is unlikely to include any orthopaedic surgeons. When the test team doesn't know the details, someone else has to write the tests. Who do they get to write the tests but the programmers ... ?

To effect a change, we must first agree on a goal: that is, we need to establish just what we expect an *ideal* software test strategy to achieve:

- The test strategy detects all *design* flaws. (For example, the design specifies that the system will compress X-ray images using an inappropriate compression algorithm: the implementation may be perfect, but the program is still wrong).

- The test strategy detects all errors of *implementation*. (For example, the design specifies an appropriate algorithm for predicting share prices, but the algorithm has been coded incorrectly).

- The test strategy is equally effective on *all types* of software products.

- The test strategy costs *nothing* to implement.

- The test strategy takes *no time* to complete.

Clearly, we are unlikely to achieve *any* of these goals, and acknowledging that this is the case is fundamental to the development of reliable software. Yes, we must test our systems as thoroughly as possible, but we must also implement our systems so that errors which do occur will not propagate.

Given that you have design and analysis documentation, there are two fundamental approaches to testing, known as **White Box** and **Black Box** testing. Each set of these tests is a 'module' test, and should be carried out first on individual program modules (functions or classes) as they are written. While the programming team may well be the first to test their own software in this way, the job should – for the reasons described above – subsequently also be carried out by another team.

Note that, in all cases, good use of `assert()` to test pre- and post-conditions should have helped the programmer detect and correct many such problems during the development process.

11.6.1 White Box module testing

The procedure for White Box testing is illustrated schematically in Figure 11.9. To qualify as a White Box test, we assume that the test team have access to the program source code and are thereby able to see 'what makes your program tick'. White Box testing is largely carried out by hand.

Figure 11.9 In White Box testing, the tester has access to the source code and can therefore determine, for example, whether an appropriate algorithm has been used to implement a particular function (or program), and whether there may be certain input conditions that would give rise to unpredictable and/or unspecified outputs.

We would generally perform a White Box test in two stages, as follows:

- a basic code inspection
- use of software metrics

We consider each of these stages in turn below.

Basic code inspection

A basic code inspection involves reading through the code looking for errors. In doing so, there are two main questions that you need to address. The first is whether the approach (the algorithm) used is appropriate. The second is to ask whether the implementation is appropriate and efficient. That is, assuming the algorithm is appropriate, has it been implemented correctly?

It is impossible to provide any general guidance on the first phase of such tests. During the second phase, one aspect that the tester should consider is the various possible **logical paths** through the software, by looking at the ways in which all the various conditions and/or loops can operate.

For example, in the following fragment:

```
while(score != -1)
    {
    total_score += score;
    class_size++;
    cout << "Enter mark for student number "
        << class_size + 1
        << " (type -1 to end) ?> ";
    cin  >> score;
    }
```

the tester would need to ascertain that it was possible for the loop termination condition to be satisfied (it is).

Similarly, the tester would consider the operation and efficiency of the following structure:

```
if (Int1 == Int2)
    {
    cout << Int1 << " is equal to " << Int2 << endl;
    }
else
    {
    if (Int1 > Int2)
        {
        cout << Int1 << " is greater than " << Int2 << endl;
        }
    else
        {
        // Int1 < Int2 (by default)
        cout << Int1 << " is less than " << Int2 << endl;
        }
    }
```

For example, can all branches be reached? Are the features of each branch as intended?

It may seem that White Box testing could, in theory, detect all bugs; this is not the case. Programs with loops and conditions quickly suffer a 'combinatorial explosion' in which the number of possible paths though the software quickly becomes too large to test by hand in a practical time scale (for example, Pressman, 1992). Both software metrics (considered next) and Black Box testing (Section 11.6.2) can help address this problem.

Using software metrics

If, for example, we were producing nuts and bolts, then we could measure each as we produced it, and note that, say, 3% of our output was outside some pre-specified tolerance limit. We might then compare this to a figure of 6% obtained in the previous year, and conclude that recent changes made to the manufacturing system have been beneficial.

When we are developing software, such direct measurements are much more difficult to make: how, for example, do we ascertain that a particular function is better than another? Because of the difficulty of making measurements, many software developers take only indirect measures. Typically, this is carried out late in the development process, when the client is asked to comment on the prototype. Even where developers take the trouble to record the details of the client's comments, these are always difficult to interpret. If, for example, the client is not happy, then this *may* not have any implications for the quality of the software itself: instead, it may mean that the initial project requirements were not correctly identified.

Software metrics are measurements that can be made of software. Such metrics are sometimes used in conjunction with statistical analysis to allow predictions of, for example, the eventual size and cost of new software projects. Use of such techniques can also help to provide a focus to White Box tests.

For example, one of the most useful (and also most simple) measures that can be made at the module level is the size of the module. Typically, this is measured by counting the number of lines of code in the module, excluding lines which are blank or contain only comments. Common sense would dictate that the larger the module, the more likely it is to contain an error, and this is indeed the result obtained in practical studies

(Norris *et al.*, 1993). Thus, given a finite amount of time for testing, we can say that we should spend more time examining larger modules.

Of course, we can go further. For example, if we record – over a period of a few years – details of all the modules we produce, and find that all those involving interaction with a particular type of database, or with a particular piece of hardware, cause particular problems then we can again focus development and testing efforts in these areas in future projects.

During White Box testing, there are also other useful measures we can make at code level. For example, the McCabe cyclomatic complexity measure (McCabe, 1976) measures the number of decision alternatives in a program, and the Henry–Kafura measure (Henry and Kafura, 1981) provides an indication of the information flow. By making these and other measurements, many of which may be automated, then a set of useful data relevant to the type of projects developed in a particular company can be obtained. By making measurements during White Box testing, and comparing the results with those from previous projects, it is possible to predict where errors are most likely to occur, and to plan accordingly.

The use of software metrics is discussed in greater depth by Somerville (1996), who also provides a number of useful references to other work in this area.

11.6.2 Black Box module testing

Knowing the specified function that a product has been designed to perform, tests can be conducted to demonstrate that each function (and in turn the whole program) is fully operational. Specifically, Black Box testing is carried out at the function and program interface. For example, if we were to Black Box test the function `Multiply()` considered in Section 11.5.4, we would focus not on the code itself, but only on the process model and the function interface (Figure 11.11).

Figure 11.10 In Black Box testing, the tester has no access to the source code and must therefore determine, using an appropriate set of test data, whether the program or function satisfies the design criteria.

@ *IN = Two valid integers*
@ *OUT = Product*

@PSPEC Multiply

Pre-condition:
        Got (Two valid integers)

Multiply the (Two valid integers) together. Output the sum as (Product).

Post-condition:
        (Product) = product of (Two valid integers)

@

```
/****************************************************************
*                                                              *
* FUNCTION:    Multiply                                         *
*                                                              *
* OVERVIEW:    Multiplies two integers (num1 * num2)           *
*              returning the result via result.                *
*                                                              *
* PRE:         num1,num2 are integers                          *
* POST:        result = num1 * num2                            *
*                                                              *
* RETURNS:     0 = Normal completion                           *
*              1 = Product greater than INT_MAX                *
*                  (result = 0)                                *
*                                                              *
****************************************************************/
Multiply(const int num1, const int num2, int& result_REF)
...
```

Figure 11.11 PSpec 'Multiply', and the corresponding function header.

We are therefore concerned with testing a range of values of num1 and num2 ensuring that a correct value of result (as defined by the comments) is produced in each case.

As with White Box testing, we can quickly run out of time if we try to test every single value. For example, here we have approximately $(2 \times INT\_MAX)^2$ possible inputs to test: a minimum of approximately 4.3 thousand million tests. If each test took only one millisecond to perform, this test alone – on this trivial function – would take about 50 days to complete.

A good general solution, therefore, is to choose at random values that span the range of possible function inputs; typically, we might aim to test 10% of the input range in this way, usually using a simple driver program. This approach is outlined in the next section.

11.7   Using driver programs

The basic aim of testing is straightforward: we wish to push our code until it breaks (for example, see Myers, 1979). When we've pushed the code to breaking point, we either try to fix it so that it won't break in the future, or we document its limitations. Driver programs are a basic, implementation-independent way of performing Black Box tests to define the limits of our code.

The rationale for using drivers is simple: in a final program we may have a hundred or a thousand functions. Testing all the possible features of each function in such an environment is difficult to do, so we begin by testing each function in isolation from the rest, providing a range of inputs and checking that the outputs are correct. For example, let's take another look at our `Multiply()` function from Section 11.5.4 (Program 11.2).

```cpp
// Illustrating the use of drivers
// Source is: 11_02.CPP

#include <iostream.h>
#include <limits.h>

// Function prototype
int Multiply (const int, const int, int&);

int main(void)
    {
    long a,b; // N.B!!!
    int c;

    // Tell user what the program does
    cout << "Driver Program for Multiply Function\n";
    cout << "------------------------------\n";

int key[3] = {INT_MIN, 0, INT_MAX};

// First, test end points and any other key values
for (a = 0; a < 3; a+=1)
    {
    for (b = 0; b < 3; b+=1)
    {
    cout << key[a] << " x " << key[b] << " = "
    << (float) key[a] * key[b] << "\n";
    if (Multiply(key[a],key[b],c))
    {
    cout << "Numbers too large !!!\n";
    }
    cout << "Result : " << c << "\n\n";
    }
    }

// Now test (part of) the rest of the range
for (a = INT_MAX-1; a > INT_MIN; a-=20000)
    {
    for (b = INT_MAX-1; b > INT_MIN; b-=20000)
    {
    cout << (int) a << " x " << (int) b << " = "
```

```
                        << (float) a * b << "\n";
                if (Multiply((int) a, (int) b,c))
                    {
                    cout << "Numbers too large !!!\n";
                    }
                cout << "Result : " << c << "\n\n";
                }
            }
    cout << "Test complete.";
    return 0;
    }
/**********************************************************************
 *                                                                    *
 * FUNCTION:   Multiply                                               *
 *                                                                    *
 * PURPOSE:    Multiplies two integers (NUM1 * NUM2)                  *
 *             returning the result via result.                      *
 *                                                                    *
 * PRE:        NUM1,NUM2 are integers (not checked)                  *
 * POST:       result = NUM1 * NUM2 (not checked)                    *
 *                                                                    *
 * ERROR CODE: 0 = Normal completion                                 *
 *             1 = Product greater than INT_MAX                      *
 *                  (result = 0)                                     *
 *                                                                    *
 **********************************************************************/
Multiply (const int NUM1, const int NUM2, int& result_REF)
    {
    int error_code;
    float test = (float) NUM1 * NUM2; // NB float
    // INT_MAX - defined in LIMITS.H
    if (test > INT_MAX)
        {
        // product too large to represent as type int
        result_REF = 0;
        error_code = 1;
        }
    else
        {
        // Can represent product as int: do so
        result_REF = NUM1 * NUM2;
        error_code = 0;
        }
    return error_code;
    }
```

Program 11.2 Using drivers to test C++ programs. (☺)

The output of Program 11.2 is:

```
Driver Program for Multiply Function
-32767 × -32767 = 1.07368e+009
Numbers too large !!!
Result : 0

-32767 × 0 = 0
Result : 0

-32767 × 32767 = -1.07368e+009
Result : -1

0 × -32767 = 0
Result : 0

0 × 0 = 0
Result : 0

0 × 32767 = 0
Result : 0

32767 × -32767 = -1.07368e+009
Result : -1

32767 × 0 = 0
Result : 0

32767 × 32767 = 1.07368e+009
Numbers too large !!!
Result : 0

32766 × 32766 = 1.07361e+009
Numbers too large !!!
Result : 0

32766 × 12766 = 4.18291e+008
Numbers too large !!!
Result : 0

32766 × -7234 = -2.37029e+008
Result : 14468

32766 × -27234 = -8.92349e+008
Result : -11068

12766 × 32766 = 4.18291e+008
Numbers too large !!!
Result : 0

12766 × 12766 = 1.62971e+008
Numbers too large !!!
Result : 0

12766 × -7234 = -9.23492e+007
Result : -9020

12766 × -27234 = -3.47669e+008
Result : -764

-7234 × 32766 = -2.37029e+008
Result : 14468

-7234 × 12766 = -9.23492e+007
Result : -9020
```

```
-7234 × -7234 = 5.23308e+007
Numbers too large !!!
Result : 0

-7234 × -27234 = 1.97011e+008
Numbers too large !!!
Result : 0

-27234 × 32766 = -8.92349e+008
Result : -11068

-27234 × 12766 = -3.47669e+008
Result : -764

-27234 × -7234 = 1.97011e+008
Numbers too large !!!
Result : 0

-27234 × -27234 = 7.41691e+008
Numbers too large !!!
Result : 0

Test complete.
```

The output reveals that test for overflow is inadequate: specifically, where large negative numbers are produced, the test will fail.

This test could have been written:

```
// INT_MAX and INT_MIN - defined in LIMITS.H
if ((test > INT_MAX) || (test < INT_MIN))
```

Note that in this example, while we have tested a tiny fraction of the input range, we have made sure that the 'ends' of the range were tested, along with other key values (here 0 and 0).

11.8   Field trials

As will be clear from the above, software testing is an imperfect science. Ultimately, in most circumstances, long-term (or even short-term) use of the product by your clients or users can often pick up more problems than even the most enthusiastic and thorough test team will miss. Sometimes, but not always, this is because your clients will use your product in ways you had not anticipated.

Field trials should therefore become an important part of your development timetable. In general, these trials take the form of acceptance tests, or Alpha and Beta tests; we consider these possibilities below.

11.8.1   Acceptance testing

For one-off bespoke software projects, the developer can work with the client to iron out any unexpected problems. Such tests – usually known as **acceptance tests** – are carried out *after* the completion of the in-house test procedures. You should allow time in the project development cycle for such tests and any necessary reworking. Don't be tempted to skimp on your normal White and Black Box testing because you have an acceptance test coming up – bugs detected at this stage are embarrassing, and, if there are lots of them, can seriously undermine the confidence of the client in you product and in your company. Bluntly, the more bugs your client finds during acceptance testing, the less likely you are to get a repeat order.

Incidentally, if you are involved in bespoke software development, and use a rapid prototyping approach, you can avoid much of the nail-biting terror associated with acceptance tests late in the program cycle. In a curious way, it pays to have a few bugs in your early prototype system: if you have signed your client up for an expensive six-month project and roll out a working prototype one month in, your client is going to start wondering what you'll be doing for the next five months …

11.8.2 Alpha and Beta testing

When a major software house launches a new spreadsheet program, they expect to sell many thousands of copies. In such circumstances, acceptance tests become wholly impractical and a different form of field trial is required.

Alpha testing is a term usually used to refer to testing carried out 'in house'. The software developer may offer a reduced-fee licensing deal to valued customers who agree to take part in the first set of customer trials of a new product. These tests are usually conducted under the watchful eye of the developer.

After all necessary bugs have been repaired, the Beta testing can begin. Here, another group of customers test the pre-release versions of the software package. The Beta tests are always carried out by the customers themselves, installing and using the software just as if it was the finished product. Customers performing such trials can reasonably expect some form of payment for their efforts.

11.9 Conclusions

We conclude the chapter by presenting, in summary, an eight-step method which will use throughout the remainder of this part of the book to implement systems from a physical model.

(1) *Review and refinement of the physical model*
The design documents are reviewed, in order to gain an understanding of the system, and to correct any flaws in the physical model.

(2) *The system framework*
The code framework is created, using CppSpecs, based on the structure chart and the PSpecs. For some systems, a prototype hardware framework may also be required.

(3) *The preliminary modules*
The preliminary modules are created or, preferably, recycled from a code library. In either case, the resulting function will build on the CppSpecs, and will make reference to the physical model (particularly the PSpecs and the data dictionary).

(4) *Error detection and recovery*
The preliminary modules are extended, where necessary, through the addition of appropriate error detection and correction features.

(5) *Module tests*
The modules are tested, by the programmers, according to the test strategy produced by the design team. Modifications are made as required.

(6) *The prototype system*
The tested modules are assembled into a prototype system, as dictated by the structure chart(s).

(7) *System tests and maintenance*
The complete prototype is tested again, first by the programmers, and then by the test team, both working from the test strategy produced by the designers. The system is then subjected to user tests, including field tests and/or acceptance tests. The system is revised as necessary; any changes made during the testing and subsequent ongoing maintenance are recorded and reflected in the evolving process model.

Note that while the above guidelines build on the material presented here, we are not yet in a position to discuss the first and last stages of the above steps in any detail: they are presented now for the sake of completeness, and will be seen in practice in later case studies.

Exercises

11.1 One at a time, replace each of the CppSpecs from Program 11.1 with an appropriate C++ function (Figure 11.7 provides a start!). As you do so, test each function with an appropriate driver.

11.2 Alter your `Add_two_numbers()` function from Exercise 11.1 so that `assert()` is not used. Instead, use return codes enable error recovery. Write a driver program to confirm that the modified function works as required.

11.3 Repeat Exercise 8.1, this time placing each of the three program functions (`main()`, `Get_Function()` and `Display_Function()`) in separate source files. Put the prototypes for `Get_Function()` and `Display_Function()` into a header file (called, for example, `GET_DISP.H`), and `#include` this header file as required.

11.4 Consider the structure chart in Figure 11.12. Write some CppSpecs that are interrelated as suggested by Figure 11.12. Assemble the CppSpecs into a code framework.

11.5 Repeat Exercise 11.4 for the Jackson structure chart given in Figure 11.13.

11.6 Write a C++ program that implements the outline design given in Figure 11.14. Note the following:

- The program should work with integer values.
- Function F has the following specification: it multiplies odd numbers by 2 and divides even numbers by two.
- Function M has the following specification: it finds the absolute value of a given number. (The absolute value of +1 is +1, and the absolute value of −1 is +1).

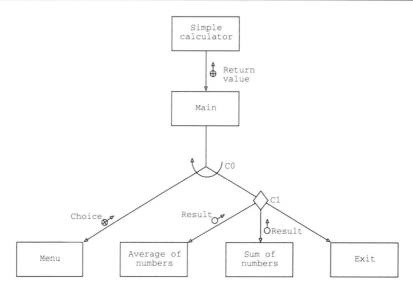

Figure 11.12 The structure chart for a two-function calculator

11.7 Consider how you might automate the collection and use of software metrics in a small software house.

11.8 For individual programmers, software recycling can be made easier by listing out functions on individual pieces of paper, and storing them in a filing cabinet. When a function is required, the existing body of code can be referred to and, where possible, recycled. Consider how you might (partially) automate or simplify the recycling of source code within a large software house. How would your system deal with code in pre-compiled libraries for which the source is not provided?

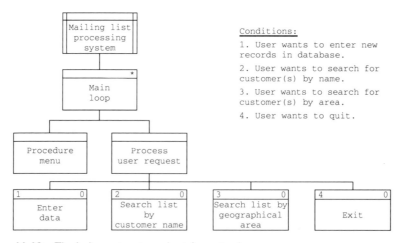

Figure 11.13 The Jackson structure chart for a simple system.

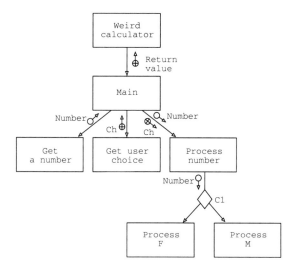

Figure 11.14 The outline design for a software system.

11.9 Following a small radiation leak, and a consequent public outcry over safety, the SuperSafe nuclear reactor has been temporarily closed by the UK Government. You have been called in, on behalf of the Government, to organize a series of tests of the reactor safety system. The safety system is software based.

Describe, in general terms, how you would go about testing such a system. What safety features would you include in the system (software or hardware) to convince a sceptical public that SuperSafe installation lives up to its name?

You will need to consider, for example, how the reactor safety would be controlled in the event of a power failure. In addition, if there was a substantial radiation leak, would this have an impact on the computers controlling the plant?

11.10 SADIE is a semi-formal, or structured, software development methodology. If you have access to a technical library, investigate techniques for formal software specification and development: two popular examples you may find details of are the Vienna Development Method (used in the US and elsewhere), and 'Z' (used in the UK and elsewhere).

As you will discover, formal software methods are based on (discrete) mathematics. In the context of our discussions on testing in this chapter, formal methods are of particular relevance because it possible to prove, mathematically, that a given piece of software matches the design, if the design has been expressed in a formal notation.

Consider how you could integrate formal methods (for example, VDM) into SADIE.

12 Process-oriented analysis

12.1 Introduction

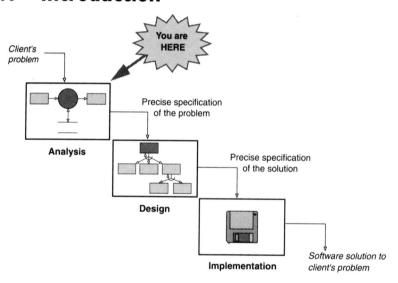

Figure 12.1 In our *Alice-in-Wonderland* approach to this part of the book, we've reached the top of the waterfall. Over the next few chapters, we'll work our way back to the bottom again.

In Chapter 11, we described an effective method that may be used to translate between the physical process model and C++ code. This process model is not spontaneously created: it arises as a result of work conducted by the design team, which in turn builds on the work of the company analysts. Over the next few chapters, we shall consider these earlier planning stages in detail.

In this chapter, we are primarily concerned with the analysis process, and with the creation of what is known as the logical process model. We review the main tools used in the development of simple systems, and include details of the support provided by the CASE tool for each. In Chapter 14, we extend the methods described here with some real-time features. By the end of Part I, we shall be in a position to complete the analysis, design and implementation of a more realistic software system.

12.2 Requirements analysis

The first stage of any project is usually called, rather portentously, **requirements analysis**. Requirements analysis involves talking to your prospective client to find out more about the contract in question.

There are a multitude of questions you need to begin to ask at this stage, falling into three broad and overlapping categories:

- *Business issues*
  - Is this a job your company has the expertise to handle?
  - Roughly how much will it cost your company to develop this product, allowing for all your usual business overheads?
  - Is the job sufficiently large to be profitable? That is, will the client be able and willing to pay for this product, allowing for all the development costs and a reasonable profit margin?
  - Is the job too large? Do you have sufficient staff to complete it within the deadline? If not, can you subcontract parts of it?
- *Logical issues*
  - What is the system to do?
  - What form of user interface is required?
- *Physical issues*
  - What hardware is the software to run on?
  - How fast must it run?
  - Is it single-user or network-based?

As far as the analyst is concerned, business and 'logical' issues are of greatest importance, in this order.

12.2.1 Business issues

First and foremost, you need to ascertain whether you and/or your firm are competent to handle the task in question. If the clients require a real-time control system for a coal-fired electricity generating station, and your previous experience is in information systems for the supermarket trade, then you must think carefully before taking on the task. Yes, it's 'all software', and a variety of jobs makes for an interesting working life. Broadening your experience also helps spread the business risk beyond a single market sector. However, the costs of recruiting or re-training staff at short notice to fill such a contract may, in the short term at least, cause your boss, your bank manager or your shareholders some concern.

The question of large projects, small firms and tight deadlines is also important. Too many firms still appear to believe that if they have a software project that starts to run late, then all they have to do is recruit some more people. When they do so, the most common result is that the project becomes even more delayed (Brooks, 1975).

If you believe your firm can handle the job, then you need to work out whether you can afford to. You'll know, or should know, how much it costs to keep your business afloat. In a small firm, this means the amount of money you have to make daily or monthly to pay the business rent, taxes and staff costs. In a large firm, the accountants may have done such calculations for you, leaving you with a standard daily or weekly charge for the staff involved. In either situation, you also need to know what your material costs will be, in terms of software or hardware required to complete the job.

The problem you will immediately face is that, inevitably, probably during your first meeting – certainly early in the project – your prospective client will want to know how much the job will cost. This is a difficult question to answer until you, and probably your designer(s) and programmer(s) have had a chance to sit down and discuss the logical and physical constraints on the system. Unless you or your firm have completed an identical job in the recent past, it is usually extremely difficult to make a realistic estimate of the project cost, until you have constructed the logical model of the system. At that time, armed with you own experience, and guidance from Barry Boehm's excellent book on the subject (Boehm, 1991), you should be able to estimate the total cost of the project.

Clearly, this presents you with something of a conundrum. To provide an accurate estimate of the project cost, you and your colleagues are likely to have to spend perhaps a week or more working on the project. Until you have provided such an estimate, your (still prospective) client may be, not unreasonably, unwilling to agree on a contract. There is no general solution to this problem. You or your firm may be able to afford to devote a week to the project without charge, knowing that these costs will be met if not by this contract, then by a later one. Alternatively, you and your prospective client may be able to agree on a 'cost plus profits' arrangement, whereby time and materials, plus agreed profits, are all charged to the client for the duration of the project. If you are well established, such an approach may be workable, but for newcomers few firms will be willing to write such a 'blank cheque'. Particularly for smaller firms, the most practical solution may be to agree on a small fixed fee (say £1000) for an initial analysis of the problem, with no commitment from the client to go beyond this if the resulting estimate or quotation is too large.

12.2.2 Creating the initial Context diagram

Assuming that you have resolved the initial business problems, then your next task is to ascertain the technical requirements. That is, you need to start modelling the system in question. The **Context diagram** is usually the first model to be constructed. It specifies the boundaries of the system: that is, it puts the system 'in context'.

The logical model is, or should, largely implementation independent. We emphasize this fact by beginning with an example that has nothing to do with software or computers: instead, it derives from the initial statement of requirements given below:

'Define, precisely, how one should go about preparing an omelette.'

As we'll see, SADIE is up to the task. For example, Figure 12.2 shows one possible context diagram for our 'recipe' example. This diagram shows the boundaries of the system ('Make omelette') which we are going to model. All systems have such a boundary: we cannot model the whole world. Such boundaries are represented by terminators ('Supermarket' and 'Hungry person').

Figure 12.3 presents two more realistic examples. Terminators should have associated with them a brief textual description, describing their role and function. This will usually be included in the data dictionary, which we consider below.

Note that there are often several potential terminators. In general, the initial choice of terminators in your system is an important one. Terminators are the most

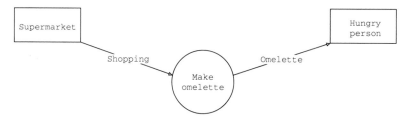

Figure 12.2 Context diagram for the recipe example.

important feature of the Context diagram and, whether you are building a technical system, information system or object-oriented system, the Context diagram is likely to be one of the first things you draw up.

Therefore:

An inappropriate initial choice of terminators can distort your understanding of the system under investigation and involve you in a vast amount of 'corrective surgery' at later stages of the project.

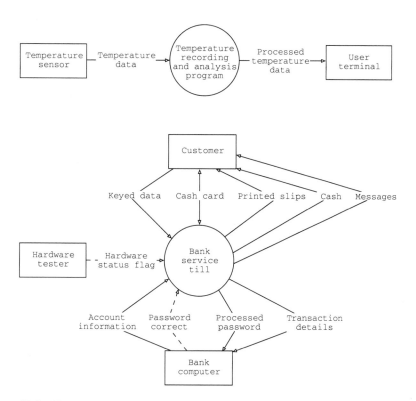

Figure 12.3 Two more representative examples of Context diagrams. The diagram at the top models a temperature monitoring system, while that at the bottom models a 'hole in the wall' bank auto teller machine (ATM). We will consider each of the underlying systems in detail during later case studies.

For this reason, it is worth spending a little time considering how a choice of terminators should be made. The first thing to note is that terminators are generally parts of the world (or models of the world) with which your system must interact, but which you won't actually have to build or program. Sometimes terminators represent pieces of hardware (for example, sensors or actuators) which your system will receive information from, or send control information to. On other occasions, terminators may represent the people using your system.

The particular terminators in your particular system will depend on the system perspective. For example, suppose our initial statement of requirements is as follows:

'Build a burglar alarm system.'

Given this imprecise statement, Figure 12.4 shows one valid Context diagram. This diagram implies that the system to be constructed will receive information from window and IR sensors, along with some further information from a control panel (which we assume is to be used by the home owner to set and reset the alarm). The system also sends information to a 'bell box' in order to wake the neighbours when a burglar is detected. Because the developer is never expected to construct the terminators, this model of the system further implies that the developer of the system intends only to build a system to process signals from a set of external sensors, these being perhaps bought 'off the shelf' or supplied by the client.

On the other hand, Figure 12.5 shows a different perspective on the 'same' system. Here, the software engineer has viewed 'Burglar', 'Home owner' and 'Neighbours' as the external entities. Since genetic engineering has not reached the point where one might expect to construct such people, we can accept that the system will, as before, only deal with data related to these external entities. This implies, as further DfD levels would no doubt reveal (see Section 12.4), that sensors and a control panel, and so on (which will presumably also be a feature of this burglar alarm system) will appear inside the boundaries of the single context diagram process bubble. Since they lie within the system boundary, Figure 12.5 implies that the software engineer intends to include these components in his or her system.

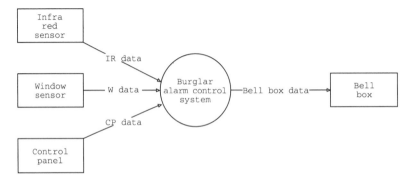

Figure 12.4   One possible Context diagram for a burglar alarm system.

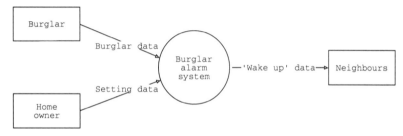

Figure 12.5 Another possible Context diagram for a burglar alarm system.

Note that, given the vague nature of the specification, we cannot say which, if either, of Figures 12.4 or 12.5 represents what the client requires. Only further discussions with the client could reveal this. We can see, however, that to begin work on either system without clarifying these requirements would be asking for trouble.

12.2.3 Specifying the user interface

In an ideal world, the analyst would not be concerned with issues of user interface design. In such a world, details of the interface (clearly part of the physical model of the system) would fall to the designer.

This is not an ideal world, and as a general rule, user interface issues need to be considered early in the lifetime of a project. Using SADIE, it is usual for discussions to take place with the client, involving sketches of the nascent user interface, at the same time that the context diagram and process list are created. The specification document itself will then include these sketches or perhaps some screen shots from an early prototype system.

When developing user interfaces, Sommerville (1996) proposes the following five guidelines:

- The interface should use terms and concepts which are familiar to the anticipated class of user.
- The interface should be appropriately consistent.
- The user should not be surprised by the system.
- The interface should include some mechanism which allows users to recover from their errors.
- The interface should incorporate some form of user guidance.

The above points provide worthwhile guidance for the development of general interfaces to your system, whether these are hardware, text-based or graphical in nature.

Hardware interfaces (for example, a collection of LEDs on the front panel of a system) come in all shapes and sizes and it is not possible to give any details of their implementation here. However, the general design guidelines above still apply in these circumstances. For example, the required control panel for our burglar alarm system might look something like that shown in Figure 12.6. Clearly, in the case of Figure 12.6, further explanation of the interface would be required; such an

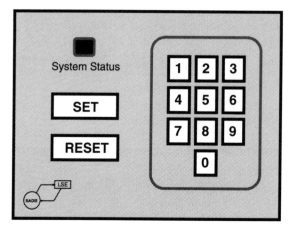

Figure 12.6 A sketch of the control panel for a burglar alarm (see text for details).

explanation, in words, is an important part of the process model. We discuss such documentation in Section 12.8.

We shall say little about the design of new text-based interfaces, as new designs in this area are not common. Galitz (1985) has much to say on these matters. His recommendations provide detailed guidelines for the design of screen layouts for general interface design and data input. For instance, he suggests where on a common 24-line text screen the error messages should appear (line 23, as it happens), and that the screen body should fill lines 3 to 22.

A suitable sketch of a software (text-based) interface to a simple menu-driven recipe program is given in Figure 12.7.

Increasingly, the GUI is replacing text-based interfaces for most desktop users; one of the reasons for this is that software incorporating such an interface can most easily satisfy Somerville's guidelines (given above). Of these, these foremost was as follows: 'The interface should use terms and concepts which are familiar to the anticipated class of user'. In many cases, this means that your program needs to conform to the user's expectations *for the particular environment* in which your program is operating.

```
                        LSE: Meal Maker


   MAIN MENU:

   1     Search for a recipe by name
   2     Search for a recipe by ingredients


   3     QUIT program.


   ?   :
```

Figure 12.7 A sketch of the main interface to a simple menu-driven recipe program.

At the time of writing, the three main GUI environments are Microsoft Windows, running on a variety of computer systems (Microsoft, 1992); X-Windows/Motif, running on UNIX workstations (Berlage, 1991); and, the Macintosh interface running on Apple computers (Apple, 1993). The texts cited provide some useful guidance on developing applications for each of these environments.

12.2.4 Creating the initial process list

The process list will be drawn up, with the context diagram, interface sketches and the initial business plan, during or soon after your initial contact with the prospective client. For example, the process list corresponding to the recipe we have been using to illustrate the material in this chapter is shown in Table 12.1.

Process name	Notes
Prepare frying pan	Put a small amount of butter in a frying pan. Heat the pan gently until the butter melts
Prepare omelette mixture	Break two eggs into a bowl then add a little milk and seasoning. Lightly whisk the ingredients to form the omelette mixture
Cook omelette	To the frying pan containing the melted butter add the omelette mixture and cook on a medium heat until the ingredients solidify. Your omelette is now ready

Table 12.1 Process list for the recipe example.

The importance of the process list is often underestimated; in fact, the process list itself is sometimes completely overlooked by users new to SADIE. This is a pity, because many experienced engineers find the construction of the initial list to be one of the most important, and challenging, parts of their job.

The process list does, or should, emphasize that the job of the software engineer is to create products that solve other people's problems. What makes this process interesting, and constantly new, is that you may know all the details of the latest computer technology but you won't necessarily know much about the business you have been called in to support. In an extreme case, you might be helping to automate the milking process for a herd of pedigree Highland cattle one week, and the next investigating ways of providing useful information to the desks of senior managers in a plant manufacturing baked beans. You won't get bored, but you will have to accept that you can never hope to be an expert in each business that you are called in to support.

In general, your lack of knowledge about the business in question is probably 'A Good Thing': you are then in a position to approach the problem with an open mind and develop a system without preconceptions or prejudices. Your job, in the initial stages of any new project, is to listen and learn, trying as you do so to identify all the key processes that the product is to provide.

By way of example, a provisional process list for the burglar alarm system (Section 12.2.2) is given in Table 12.2.

Process name	Notes
Set alarm	The system status LED will be green. The user will type in a number on the numeric keypad and press 'Set'. The system will check that the number matches the factory-set code. If it does then, after a 30-second delay to allow the user to leave the area, the system will be armed. In this state, the LED will be constantly red. If the entered code is incorrect, the LED will flash red, and a 'bleep' will sound every second for three seconds, after which the system will return to the 'green' state.
Detect intruder	While the alarm is set, do the following repeatedly: *Check IR sensor, Check window sensor, Check for tampering*.
Reset alarm	The system will be armed, and the approach of the user will have been detected. From the time of detection, the user will have one minute to reset the alarm. The status LED will be flashing red. The user will type in a number on the numeric keypad and press 'Reset'. The system will check that the number matches the factory-set code. If it does, then
Check IR sensor	Check the output of the infra red sensor. If it's high, then *Sound the Alarm*. Part of *Detect Intruder*.
Check window sensor	Check the output of the window sensor. If it's high, then *Sound the Alarm*. Part of *Detect Intruder*.
Check for tampering	A master key code is available. If this has been entered correctly, then the control panel may be opened for maintenance. If this code has not been entered then opening the panel will be interpreted as an attempt to interfere with the system, triggering *Sound the Alarm*.
Sound the alarm	Ring the bell in the bell box. Activate a flashing light too? Contact the police directly?

Table 12.2 Initial process list for a burglar alarm control system. The italicized terms in the notes are 'cross-references' to other processes.

The following guidelines may help you get off the ground:

- Successful requirements analysis necessitates that you should talk to the key people in the organization or company concerned. If you don't talk to the right people at some point during the analysis phase of the project, you're simply storing up expensive problems for the future. If you haven't organized a series of meetings with your client during the early days of the project, alarm bells should be ringing.

- Notwithstanding the comments above, it is equally important not to put off the start of construction of the main logical model until you prepared a totally perfect and beautifully formatted process list. Try not to get bogged down with details at the early stages, and don't worry if some of the details you have are initially rather hazy. The point of following a semi-formal method is that you won't be starting to 'code-up' from these initial details, and it is not difficult to make even substantial changes during the *analysis* phase of the project. As you complete the logical process model, many of the details will 'come out in the wash', or in the walkthrough (Section 12.2.5).

- Don't worry if there seem to be 'too many processes'; for a realistic system, you may identify a hundred or more processes at this time.

- Don't worry if the processes 'are of different sizes' or appear to 'overlap'. For example, we might initially have 'break eggs' and 'prepare omelette mixture' as independent processes in our recipe system. Such details will be resolved as you start to level the system. If in any doubt, don't be: add the process to the list, and make a note to yourself saying that Process X may ultimately become part of Process Y.

- It's easy to make the mistake that the most senior people in the company are also the key people. This often not the case. Senior management should know the general company strategy, and be able to provide an overview of a number of different projects. What they may not know are the fine details, or the very latest details, about the project with which you are involved. They may also have very busy schedules. Sometimes it's better, where necessary, to talk first to senior staff, then spend more time with people on the shop floor, in the dealing room, on the sales counters: people who are working with the project on a day-to-day basis.

- Finally, tread lightly. To you, this may be simply another contract, but to the people in the company concerned, you may be seen as extremely threatening. It may pay to know why you have been brought in, and what the implications are of your project. For example, if there's an in-house software team, then why aren't they doing the work? How will it impact on them if your project is successful, or if you fail? Or, if you are going to provide a new, efficient, computerized system, what will happen to those people involved with the current manual system, the very people that you will be interviewing?

  You may feel that such aspects of the job are none of your business and, if you ask, you may be told precisely this. However, such factors will naturally be of great concern to the people with whom you must interact, which may lead to a potential conflict of interest. If you understand the significance and implications of your efforts, you may be able to provide genuine reassurance to those involved.

Most engineers prefer simply to use a pad of recycled paper and a pen to draw up their process lists: others like to have this information included with the other files in their project, and to enter the information directly into their CASE tool. If you fall into the latter category, you'll be able to use process lists with the CASE tool if you install the standard SADIE project, described in Appendix C.

12.2.5 The walkthrough

Having sketched the interface to your system, drafted a context diagram, and scribbled a process list, you're ready to take stock. A widespread and cost-effective way (Norris *et al.,* 1993) of reviewing the system requirements is to perform a **walkthrough** (Yourdon, 1985; Yourdon, 1989; Hollicker, 1991).

A walkthrough is a 'thought experiment', whereby, either alone or (much better) in a team, you think about the way your developing product will perform. Walkthroughs can be considered as the first phase of testing, sometimes conducted long before you start coding, and often before you have even begun to record the system specification in any detail.

There are no rules to walkthroughs. The idea is that you imagine how users will use your system. As you do so, you may update your interface, process list and context diagram. We give a detailed example of a walkthrough in action in Chapter 16.

12.3 The dataflow diagram

Having completed the initial requirements analysis, your job is to complete the logical process model. The central component of this model is the **dataflow diagram** (DfD). We've already met a simple, specialized form of DfD in the form of the context diagram (Section 12.2.2).

The power, and success, of the dataflow diagram as a tool for modelling software problems arises in large part because of its simplicity: the DfD is easy to understand, and easy to use. An individual dataflow diagram is drawn from a restricted number of components (Figure 12.8), namely processes, terminators, dataflows and data stores.

Terminators appear only on context diagrams and were discussed in Section 12.2.2: they will not be considered further here. We shall consider each of the remaining components in turn.

12.3.1 Processes

Processes process: that is, they transform their incoming data (in some manner) to generate output data. Processes are represented on the DfD as circles or 'bubbles' (Figure 12.9). As in the examples shown in this figure, processes should have appropriate names. Just as in naming C++ functions, your processes should consist of a verb-object phrase such as: 'Cook omelette', 'Process image', 'Store prices', 'Calculate current overdraft limit'.

In addition, processes should be numbered. The numbers make it easy to relate different parts of the model together. Usually, each process on a particular diagram will be given an exclusive number. The numbering scheme is usually 1 to n, where n is the number of processes on the particular diagram. The numbering of processes is automatic when you use the CASE tool.

Figure 12.8 A dataflow diagram showing the components used in such diagrams.

Figure 12.9 Some processes from the recipe case study.

12.3.2 Dataflows

On their own, processes can do nothing without data to feed on. These data are represented by dataflows (Figure 12.10). Dataflows usually reveal themselves quite naturally as you develop the dataflow diagrams and consider the data required and generated by each process. Each dataflow is, of course, appropriately labelled; as we will see below, the data items will also be more rigorously defined in the associated data dictionary (see Section 12.6).

On your diagrams convention dictates that the flow of data should be from left to right. This simple convention makes your diagrams much easier to understand. Figure 12.11 illustrates what *not* to do.

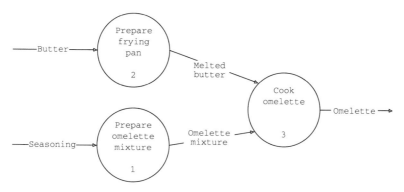

Figure 12.10 Part of a level 1 DfD for the recipe example, showing the dataflows into and out of three of the processes.

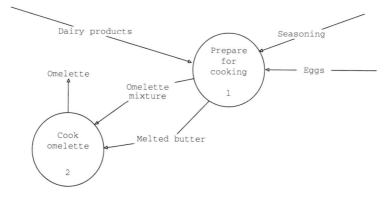

Figure 12.11 A version of the Level 1 DfD from the revised recipe example with an unstructured flow direction.

12.3.3 Stores

The DfD is not intended to provide information about the temporal relationship between processes on the diagram. That is to say, the DfD will not, without some further control features considered in Chapter 14, tell us anything about the order in which processes depicted on the DfD are called. Nonetheless, if the flow of data between any two connected processes is significantly asynchronous, we need to record this fact.

To illustrate the use of stores, consider part of the recipe system model shown in Figure 12.12. This models the fact that our 'shopping' is not necessarily processed immediately into an omelette. Instead, the ingredients are stored in a fridge or cupboard until required.

There are several general points we should note concerning the use of stores:

(1) The store does not process the information; you get *exactly* the same data out that you put in.

(2) You should not have data stores in your system with only input flows; the data must be read again, or it is worthless. Similarly, you should not have stores in your system with only output flows. The data must have originated somewhere. *Note:* a possible exception to this is stores that appear 'outside the walls' of your system: that is, on the context diagram (see Point 6).

(3) The same store can appear in many places in your DfD hierarchy; it may even appear more than once on the same diagram, particularly if this helps avoid a confusing spaghetti of dataflow lines.

(4) While it is likely that many of the stores on your diagram will become disk files in the final system, this is not necessarily the case. For instance, buffered data inputs may well be represented on the DfD as stores, and implemented in fast static RAM. The decision about implementation is generally taken by the designer/programmer rather than the analyst.

(5) In the 'Customers' example above, the store on the system is a repository for a single 'table' of data (we discuss database tables in Part II). It may be, however – particularly in a business environment – that the store is more than a simple table. Just as the code requirements of your system are ultimately decomposed into an interrelated collection of functions, the data requirements may be more efficiently represented (and implemented) as a *collection* of tables. In such

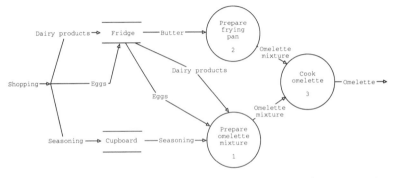

Figure 12.12 A level I DfD for the recipe example. The corresponding context diagram is given in Figure 12.2.

circumstances, the store on your DfD may represent, for example, not a single disk file but, at a higher level of abstraction, a whole relational database. When this is the case, the data dictionary is insufficiently flexible to model the data requirements effectively, and the dictionary will simply include a cross-reference to an additional modelling tool known as the entity-relationship diagram (ERD). We discuss these matters in greater depth in Part II.

(6) The same rules apply to stores as to other components of your system. If the store appears on the Context diagram, then this implies that it is part of the interface to your system: that is, the (data in the) store is to be manipulated by some other application(s), and may in fact represent a central data repository elsewhere in the company. If the store appears within the main process bubble, this generally implies that while your system may, for instance, export these data, an external program will not be able to directly manipulate them. These two possibilities are illustrated in Figure 12.13.

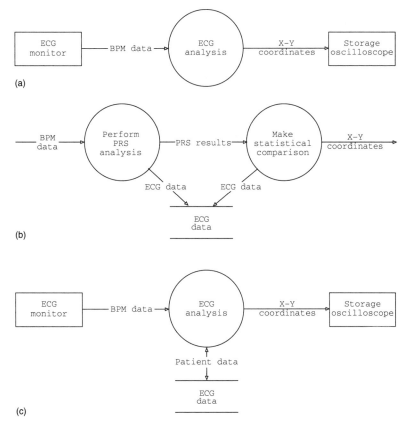

Figure 12.13 Outline process models for two systems with contrasting data requirements: (a) Context diagram for one version of a heart monitoring system. This system, represented by Level 0 and Level 1 DfDs, has an internal data store, containing information not directly available to the outside world. (b) Level 1 DfD for the system shown in (a) above. (c) Context diagram for a second heart monitoring system. This system, represented with a single Level 0 DfD, exchanges data with an external database, which may be simultaneously accessed by other programs.

We consider how stores are represented in the data dictionary in Section 12.3.3.

12.4 The DfD hierarchy

As we first saw in Chapter 10, the DfDs form a hierarchy. For example, at the highest level, we have the context diagram for the recipe 'system', one possible version of which is shown in Figure 12.2. As we have seen, this diagram shows the 'Make omelette' process in the context of the other entities with which it must interact.

Below the context diagram, we have the Level 1 DfD shown, for example, in Figure 12.12. Notice that the data items flowing into and out of this DfD also appear in the corresponding context diagram (Figure 12.2). The matching of the various dataflows between levels is an important feature of a **balanced model** (see Section 12.7).

Notice also that the terminators from the higher level are not shown here: it makes no sense to have 'external entities' or 'interfaces' with the bounds of your system.

The relationship between the Level 0 (context), and Level 1 DfDs is shown explicitly in Figure 12.14: the Level 1 diagram is situated inside the Level 0 diagram. Note that in more realistic situations, there may well be further Level 2 DfDs located inside each of the three Level 1 bubbles, and so on. Note that when working on your Level 1 DfD using the CASE tool, the data flows from the context diagram will automatically be added. Similarly as you descend further into your system, flows from the higher levels will always be added automatically (see Appendix E for details).

12.4.1 Numbering the diagrams

The diagrams should all be numbered. The context diagram is considered to be DfD 0 in your system. Below this, as we've seen, you have the Level 1 DfD, which should be numbered DfD 1.

So far so good. Beyond the Level 1 DfD, the number system can get a little confusing if you don't take care. The most common convention for diagram numbering is to label the diagram (or PSpec: Section 12.5) below process 3 (for example) on the Level 1 DfD as 1-3, and so on. This numbering scheme is illustrated in Figure 12.15.

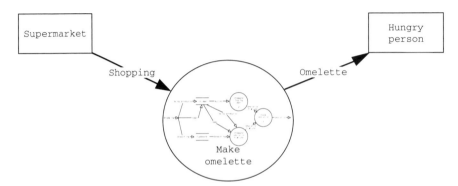

Figure 12.14 The intimate relationship between Level 0 and Level 1 DfDs in the recipe example.

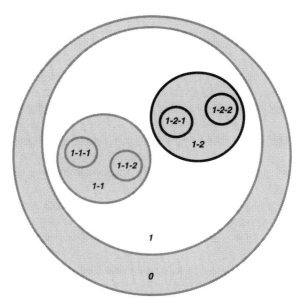

Figure 12.15 The DfD numbering system used in SADIE. Refer to text for details.

12.4.2 Drawing the initial Level 1 DfD

Many software engineers using SADIE will work from a process list, using this to draw up a Level 1 DfD. That is, they will begin by taking all the processes they have identified in the process list, and drawing a 'bubble' for each on the Level 1 DfD. This is the first stage in a 'middle out' development method.

For example, suppose we wish to continue the development of our burglar alarm control system (introduced in Section 12.2.2). We assume that discussions with our client have revealed that the context diagram in Figure 12.4 is appropriate. We further assume that these discussions have also given rise to the interface sketch shown in Figure 12.6, and to the process list given in Table 12.2.

We might start by constructing the Level 1 DfD shown in Figure 12.16. Note that it is not usually worthwhile to add flows between processes before levelling the model, a process we discuss in Section 12.4.3.

12.4.3 Levelling the Level 1 DfD

As we saw in the previous sub-section, creation of the DfD hierarchy typically begins by 'pouring' the process list onto the Level 1 diagram. This will not lead immediately to a finished product. Instead, by levelling the diagram, we try to ensure that all processes shown on a particular level of the diagram 'carry the same weight', or are 'equally important'.

Fundamentally, through levelling, we try to make sure that the basic structure of the system specification is correct, and that our process model does indeed mirror the logical relationships between the various processes to be performed by the system. Typically, this involves grouping related processes together, and moving the resulting group to a lower level in the hierarchy.

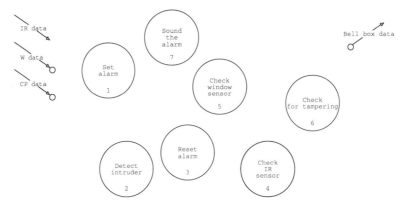

Figure 12.16 The provisional Level I DfD for a burglar alarm system.

A levelled DfD provides a better logical model of the system, and has the added bonus that it is usually much easier to read. A drawback of all DfDs with more than say 10 or 12 'bubbles' on a single level is that they can be very complex and confusing. A worthwhile side-effect of levelling is that it frequently helps to 'spread the complexity' of the model.

Levelling is fundamental to the development of an appropriate process model, but isn't an easy concept to grasp. We'll therefore try to clarify the situation by looking at two examples: the recipe system and the burglar alarm.

Example: Levelling the recipe system

We've already 'completed' the Level 1 DfD for the recipe system (Figure 12.12).

If we think about the overall structure of the system, we can see that, while there are three processes involved (Figure 12.12), the work is really carried out in two phases: a preparation phase followed by a cooking phase. The two phases are distinct, because cooking can't begin until the preparation is complete.

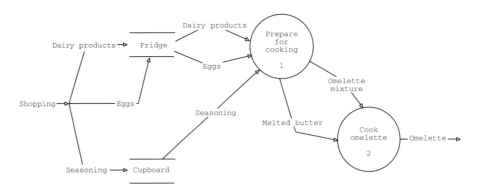

Figure 12.17 A modified Level I DfD for the recipe example.

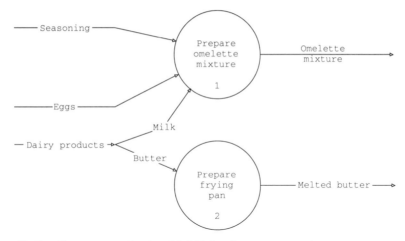

Figure 12.18 The corresponding Level 2 DfD for the recipe example.

We would usually want to make the two-phase nature of the system explicit by redrawing the DfD in the levelled form shown in Figures 12.17 and 12.18. Note that we say above that we are thinking about 'the overall structure' of the system. You might ask why we don't begin our analysis by making such decisions, rather than waiting until now to decompose the system into two main logical processes. The problem with the former 'top-down' approach is that it forces the analyst to make some of the most fundamental decisions about the structure of the project right at the start of the modelling exercise, often before a great understanding of the system has been obtained. In general, with SADIE, we use unstructured process lists and walkthroughs (see Section 12.2.5) to try and maximize understanding of the system before making such important decisions.

One of the purposes of this book is to compare and contrast the three main methods of software development in use at this time. As we shall see in later chapters, none of the three methods is perfect, and each has its own particular strengths and weaknesses. One of the perceived weaknesses of the process-oriented or structured approaches to software development is the necessity of decomposing the system at an early stage.

Example: Levelling the burglar alarm system

Returning to our discussion of levelling, we'll consider how we might level the initial Level 1 DfD from the burglar alarm study.

Here, as we consider Figure 12.16, we might conclude that the system really performs three main processes: control of the system (such as setting or resetting); detection of intruders (including polling the various sensors, and checking for tampering); and sounding the alarm (which might, according to our process list, involve contacting the police, or flashing a light).

We would normally wish to reflect this structure in the DfD, as shown in Figure 12.19. Completion of the Level 2 DfDs is left as an exercise.

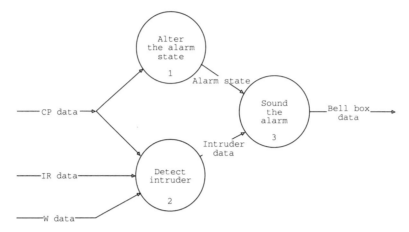

Figure 12.19 The Level I DfD for the burglar alarm after levelling.

12.5 The process specification

As we saw in Chapter 10, the bottom level DfDs in the hierarchy have associated process specifications (PSpecs), describing the operation of the corresponding bubble.

PSpecs are written in the form of notes, usually described as 'structured English'. For example, consider Figure 12.20. This process specifications begins with a description of the incoming ('Butter') and outgoing ('Melted butter') dataflows. This is followed by the PSpec name (the *same* as that of the corresponding process bubble).

(a)

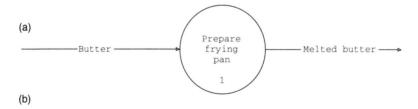

(b)

@ IN = Butter
@ OUT = Melted butter

@PSpec Prepare frying pan

Pre-condition:
    Got Butter.

Add the Butter to a frying pan. Heat the pan gently until the butter becomes Melted butter.

Post-condition:
    The frying pan is ready for use.

@

Figure 12.20 (a) Process I from the recipe example and (b) its corresponding process specification.

@ *IN = Details of new lines*
@ *INOUT = Data*

@PSPEC New record

Uses: (Data) and (Details of new lines)

This process allows the user to add a new record to the database.

@

Figure 12.21   An example of an informal PSpec.

The body of the PSpec lays out the processing to be performed. The body is bounded by a description of the pre- and post-conditions. As we saw in relation to C++ functions in Chapters 10 and 11, these define (respectively) the conditions that must apply before the process can operate, and the conditions that will apply following completion of the process.

Note that variations on these basic PSpecs are possible. It is, for example, common to have pure declarative PSpecs: that is, to have PSpecs which consist only of pre- and post-conditions. These specify what the input and output of the procedure is, rather than dictating how such results should be achieved. Where it is possible to use declarative PSpecs, these can be effective.

Finally, simple PSpecs, such as that shown in Figure 12.21, are also regularly used, and – although informal – are infinitely better than no PSpec at all.

12.6   The data dictionary

The data dictionary is the backbone of the DfD. It is important to constantly keep in mind the fact that, although we may start developing our system using an ill-defined sketch of bubbles, our aim is always to be rigorous and to have defined, in our software specification at the end of the analysis process, the precise meaning of all the terms that we have included in our system. The DfD is useful and easy for developers and users to understand: however, without the support of the data dictionary (and the PSpecs described in Section 12.5) it is merely a sketch of the required system, not the required semi-formal specification.

Definitions are entered in the dictionary in a quasi-mathematical form, called **extended BNF** (Backus–Naur format). This flexible system is usually used to represent programming languages.

The syntax of the extended Backus–Naur format is given in Table 12.1. The BNF expression can contain a mix of operators and previously defined data types. Some examples are given in Table 12.2.

BNF	Description
+	Logical AND
[|]	Logical OR
()	Component in parentheses is optional
a{ }b	Between 'a' and 'b' instances of the bracketed component (both upper and lower bounds are optional)
""	Enclosed component is a literal value
...	Implies range of values (not explicitly stated). Use with care to avoid ambiguity
\\	A textual description

Table 12.1   Components of the Backus–Naur syntax.

Data	Dictionary entry
Bolt	/ Size 31 metric bolt (brass) /
Between 2 and 5 bolts.	2 {Bolt} 5
Nut	/ Size 31 metric nut (brass) /
1 or more nuts.	1 {Nut}
Washer	/ Size 33 metric washer (steel) /
Up to 5 washers.	{Washer} 5
Mechanical assembly	[Bolt + 1 {Nut} 2 + (Washer)]
Octal digit	['0'|'1'|'2'|'3'|'4'|'5'|'6'|'7']
Hexadecimal digit	['0'|'1'|'2'|'3'|'4'|'5'|'6'|'7'|'8'|'9'|'A'|'B'|'C'|'D'|'E'|'F']
Character	['a' ... 'z'	'A' ... 'Z'	'–'	'.'	'']
Name	{Character}20

Table 12.2 Sample data dictionary entries for a factory system involving mechanical assemblies.

Remember, the aim is to be as precise as possible so that our final specification is unambiguous. In most programming situations, of course, Tables 12.1 and 12.2 will seem rather incongruous. Rather more familiar examples are given in Table 12.3.

Name	C/D/S/T	Description	Type
Program outputs	D	Request for two digits + Result of addition	–
IR Sensor	T	Model X34b infra-red sensor from Leicester Hardware Engineering.	–
Request for two digits	D	\Polite request to user to type in two single-digit numbers \	char [81]
Result of addition	D	['0'|'1'|'2'|'3'|'4'|'5'|'6'|'7'|'8'|'9'] +(['0'|'1'|'2'|'3'|'4'|'5'|'6'|'7'|'8'|'9'])	char
Two valid digits	D	['0'|'1'|'2'|'3'|'4'|'5'|'6'|'7'|'8'|'9'] , ['0'|'1'|'2'|'3'|'4'|'5'|'6'|'7'|'8'|'9']	char
User input	D	\User responses, possibly containing two valid single-digit integers \	char [81]

Table 12.3 Sample data dictionary entries for more typical programming situations.

In Table 12.3, we have a general column labelled 'C/D/S/T': this identifies the dictionary entry as a control flow, dataflow, store or terminator. Other possible entries include processes, data couples and modules; these, however, are usually less useful.

Also in Table 12.3, as in most realistic programming situations, we explicitly include the type of the data item in the dictionary. Note that this information may or may not be included by the analyst: in many situations, type information is added by the designer.

We need also to consider how stores are represented in the data dictionary. In many cases, stores contain multiple instances of simple data items. Thus you may commonly have a data item called 'Customer' flowing into (and out of) a store called 'Customers' (Figure 12.22).

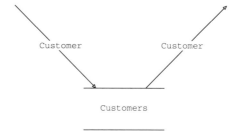

Figure 12.22 A store of customer data.

    A store will always have a corresponding data dictionary entry. As the contents of stores are collections of data flows, the same description format will be used. For example, in the case of the Customers store above, we might have the following hierarchy of entries for the store itself as follows:

```
Character  =  ['a' ... 'z' | 'A' ... 'Z' | '-' | '.' | ' ']

...

Name       =  {Character}20

...

Customer   =  [Name + Address + Phone_Number]
Customers  =  {Customer}
```

12.7   Balancing the system

An important part of the construction of the logical process model is to ensure that your final diagrams are balanced. The only good model is a balanced model; a model that is not balanced is ambiguous, and under-specified.

    In a balanced system, the following situation holds:

- Every dataflow on your DfD hierarchy will have a corresponding data dictionary entry.

- Every store on the DfD will have a corresponding dictionary entry (or cross-reference to a corresponding entity-relationship diagram).

- Every bubble on the DfD will have a corresponding lower-level DfD, *or* a corresponding PSpec.

- Every incoming flow to a bubble will be matched by an '@IN' entry in the corresponding PSpec. Similarly, outgoing flows will have matching '@OUT' entries.

- The incoming and outgoing dataflows should be mentioned in the body of the PSpec.

- Finally, the data dictionary will have been 'purged' of all entries for which there are not corresponding diagram components.

If you are doing your analysis with only paper and a pencil, expect to go through lots of trees as you develop your process model, modify it and refine it and finally attempt to balance it. Then expect to modify things again after you try (laboriously) to make sure, for example, that details of every dataflow are included in your data dictionary.

This is where CASE tools can be worth their weight in assembly language. CASE tools take many forms: a good CASE tool should make the job of performing the SADIE method both more rigorously and straightforwardly. The tool should also help you produce your documentation for the client. Most important of all, an easy-to-use CASE tool should *encourage* you to use a methodical approach to your software problem.

Naturally, the Select CASE tool satisfies all of the above requirements; we use this tool extensively throughout the remainder of this book.

12.8   Documentation

Suppose you have been asked to specify a system. You've followed all the steps in this chapter to the letter. Your DfDs are the most beautiful you've ever seen, and your CASE tool tells you that the whole system is balanced. You're finished! Using the case tool, you print out all the diagrams and clip them into a folder with your company logo on the cover. You jump in your car, rush over to your client, and deposit this 'specification', and your invoice, on the client's desk. You start day dreaming of the new Saab 9000 car you're going to buy with all this money…

Unfortunately, however, the invoice will probably never be paid. Even if you have been asked to specify (rather than design or build) the system in question, your client is unlikely to be impressed by an apparently irrelevant collection of bubble pictures. While your specification may be read by technical staff within the client company (who may be happy to read a semi-formal specification), it will almost invariably also require approval by one or more groups of members of managerial staff, who may or may not be technically qualified. Your specification therefore also needs to be supported by a textual description of the system.

In fact, it is much more likely that you will choose to relegate most if not all of your DfDs and associated diagrams to an appendix, and include a 'translation', in English (or German, Spanish, Japanese, French, and so on: delete as appropriate) in the main body of the report itself.

By way of example, the following extracts describe the burglar alarm system we have been discussing throughout this chapter.

> 'The Leicester Software Engineering (LSE) "Peace of Mind" alarm system, Model H1, is a low-cost, user-friendly intruder detection system intended for home use. Note that for business premises, use of the Leicester Software Engineering "Peace of Mind" Model B1 or B2 is recommended.
>
> …
>
> The interface to the LSE "Peace of Mind" Model H1 is a single control panel, 15 cm × 8 cm in area, 2 cm deep. The control panel contains a numeric keypad, a "set" switch, a "reset" switch and a single two-colour light-emitting diode (LED) indicating the system status.
>
> When the alarm system is in the reset (inactive) state, the System Status LED is constantly green. When the alarm is armed (set), the LED is constantly red. When the alarm is triggered or, for example, the user types an incorrect number when trying to set the alarm, the LED will flash on and off, in red, and a "bleep" will be produced by the unit once every second for a period of ten seconds, or until the "Reset" switch is depressed. If a hardware fault is detected in the H1 unit, the LED will flash alternatively in red and green, and a "bleep"

will sound twice every second. Both LED activity and sound will continue until the "Reset" switch is depressed, at which point the sound will cease, but the alternate red/green flashing will continue, until the hardware fault is rectified...'

In this case, the description would also need to include details of the hardware on which the software runs, probably in the form of circuit diagrams, along with details of the interfaces with the various sensors and siren.

12.9   Conclusions

We can conclude this chapter by summarizing in 10 steps the method we have described here for deriving a process model for your system.

(1)   *The business case*
The analyst begins by estimating the technical and economic feasibility of the project. If, for example, the project is too small to be profitable, greatly outside the experience of the available personnel, or larger than can be tackled with the available technical and human resources, then it must be rejected at this stage.

(2)   *The Context diagram*
The Context diagram is produced. Particular care is taken in the selection of appropriate terminators.

(3)   *The user interface*
Because of the impact of the system interface on all aspects of the model, it is sketched (or prototyped) at this early stage.

(4)   *The process list*
A process list is drawn up. This list is necessarily very provisional and creation of a highly polished document is not appropriate at this stage.

(5)   *The walkthrough*
A system walkthrough is performed. Where feasible, the entire development team (analysts, designers, programmers) should be involved in this process. As the walkthrough progresses, the process list, context diagram and interface sketches are modified as required.

(6)   *The Level 1 dataflow diagram*
A preliminary Level 1 DfD is sketched, on the basis of the process list.

(7)   *The DfD hierarchy*
The remainder of the DfD hierarchy is completed, and levelled as necessary.

(8)   *The PSpecs*
The process specifications are written.

(9)   *The data dictionary*
The data dictionary is completed.

(10)   *The balanced logical model*
The complete model is reviewed, checked and balanced. Any necessary supporting documentation is written.

Note that the above list should be used as a guide: that is, as a recipe rather than an algorithm. It should be modified to suit your own needs.

We apply this approach in the remaining case studies in this part of the book.

Exercises

12.1 One crucial step in the production of good omelettes is to brown the cooked omelette under a hot grill for thirty seconds just before you serve it. The aim of this exercise is to modify the recipe 'specification' given in this chapter so as to incorporate this additional requirement: in doing this, you will also gain experience in the use of the CASE tool. (If you have not already installed this software on your computer, it is recommended that you do so now, following the directions in Appendix A.)

Follow the following steps.

[1] Start by creating a new project as described in Appendix B (p.853).
[2] Create a copy of the original recipe files given in this chapter: note that use of the dataflow diagram editor is described in Appendix E (p.903).
[3] Modify your copy of the recipe specification so as to incorporate the 'grilling requirement'.
[4] Finish the project, making sure the whole system is balanced.
[5] Finally, check that your DfD hierarchy is complete, as described on p.910.

12.2 Using the CASE tool, complete the logical process model for the burglar alarm system outlined in this chapter.

12.3 Consider the Context diagrams given in Figure 12.3. In each case, using the CASE tool, draw up an appropriate Level 1 dataflow diagram.

12.4 Suppose you are given, in machine-readable form, a detailed textual description of a system required by one of your clients (for example, something like the description of the burglar alarm given in Section 12.8). How far do you think it would be possible to automatically derive a process list and preliminary Level 1 DfD from such a description?

12.5 If you have access to a computer running MS-DOS and Windows, consider a piece of software developed and running under MS-DOS. Decide how you would modify the user interface to take advantage of the Windows environment. What would the advantages, from the user's perspective, in running in Windows? What would be the disadvantages?

12.6 Repeat Exercise 12.5, but this time in reverse. That is, consider how you might effectively port a Windows program to run under MS-DOS or vanilla UNIX.

12.7 We suggested in this chapter that the three main GUI environments are the Microsoft Windows environment running on a variety of computer systems, the X-Window/Motif interface running on UNIX workstations and the Apple Macintosh interface for the Macintosh. If you have access to such systems, make a detailed comparison of the features provided by each interface. Consider that you had to port a piece of software between any two of these environments: what would be the costs and processes involved? To what extent could this process be automated? How would you deal with the fact that each of the three suppliers will update their products at regular and frequent intervals?

13 Case Study:
Loughborough Bell Foundry

13.1 Introduction

In this first 'analysis' case study, we develop a logical process model of a simple system using P-O SADIE. As we develop the model, we draw attention to the ways in which the CASE tool supports the modelling process.

The CASE tool project files for this chapter are included on the example disk: Appendix C explains how to install these project files on your computer.

13.2 Scenario

Loughborough is a small town a few miles north of Leicester. The town is notable for its technical university, and for its bell foundry. Loughborough Bell Foundry manufactures bells of a very high standard in a traditional manner. The bells, some of which weigh many tonnes, are exported all over the world.

John Chime, chief engineer at Loughborough Bell Foundry (henceforth LBF) has approached Leicester Software Engineering for help. John's call is put through to Jane. With a full order book well into the next century, John explains, LBF would like to be able to speed up the manufacturing process 'without sacrificing the quality of the bells in any way'.

One area in which LBF feel that they may be able to increase their production rate is by controlling their metal furnace more accurately. Specifically, John asks Jane to develop a system that will make regular measurements of the temperature within this furnace.

13.3 Overview of the analysis process

We outlined the ten steps necessary to analyse process-oriented systems in Chapter 12. We repeat them here for ease of reference.

(1) *The business case*
The analyst begins by estimating the technical and economic feasibility of the project. If, for example, the project is too small to be profitable, greatly outside the experience of the available personnel, or larger than can be tackled with the available technical and human resources, then it must be rejected at this stage.

(2) *The Context diagram*
      The Context diagram is produced. Particular care is taken in the selection of appropriate terminators.

(3) *The user interface*
      Because of the impact of the system interface on all aspects of the model, it is sketched (or prototyped) at this early stage.

(4) *The process list*
      A process list is drawn up. This list is necessarily very provisional, and creation of a highly polished document is not appropriate at this stage.

(5) *The walkthrough*
      A system walkthrough is performed. Where feasible, the entire development team (analysts, designers, programmers) should be involved in this process. As the walkthrough progresses, the process list, context diagram and interface sketches are modified as required.

(6) *The Level 1 dataflow diagram*
      A preliminary Level 1 DfD is sketched, on the basis of the process list.

(7) *The dataflow diagram hierarchy*
      The DfD hierarchy is completed, and levelled as necessary.

(8) *The process specifications*
      The process specifications are written.

(9) *The data dictionary*
      The data dictionary is completed.

(10) *The balanced logical model*
      The complete model is reviewed, checked and balanced. Any necessary supporting documentation is written.

Naturally, Jane follows these steps precisely.

13.4   The business case

The analyst begins by estimating the technical and economic feasibility of the project. If, for example, the project is too small to be profitable, greatly outside the experience of the available personnel, or larger than can be tackled with the available technical and human resources, then it must be rejected at this stage.

Jane arranges a meeting with John at LBF. At the meeting they discuss what is required of the system LSE is to design and deliver.

The software is to record the temperature at regular intervals, storing the results on disk and displaying them on a monitor. The display on the monitor is to be updated every half hour, showing the temperature most recently recorded along with some statistics comparing the current temperature with recent average temperatures so that the operator can determine whether or not the furnace needs to be adjusted. The system is to be used near a very high temperature furnace, in a generally hot and dirty environment. Jane realizes that an ordinary desktop computer would have a very short lifetime in such conditions, and that special-purpose hardware will be required.

After consulting Stephanie and Harry, Jane is confident that this is an assignment that LSE can handle. It is a small job, and she knows from past experience that she can estimate the work involved to a reasonable degree of accuracy. After doing some scribbling on the back of an envelope, she calculates that the job will take three person-days. Allowing an extra day for unexpected complications, and charging the company time at £250 a day, she has a basic labour cost of £1000.00.

As she estimates the labour cost, Jane has already agreed with Stephanie that it will be necessary to develop the system around a single-board PC compatible computer: this is an 'embedded' computer, and one that can be easily packaged to withstand the hostile conditions in the furnace area. It will, however, still run C++ programs developed on a conventional desktop system, a fact which will speed up the development process, reducing the overall project cost. Jane envisages a system whereby the board would be connected via a keyboard port to an appropriate temperature sensor. A high-temperature lead will then take the results from the computer to a monitor in the control area.

The basic hardware will therefore be a single-board 386 computer, which will be more than adequate for this task. With appropriate packaging and a small monochrome monitor, Jane knows that her usual hardware company can deliver one within 24 hours for £900.00. The cost of producing necessary documentation, packaging and software media she estimates at £200. After adding the usual 10% overhead for the hardware items, she offers delivery in four days for a fee of £2250, plus tax.

LBF are happy with this price, and the time scale. Contracts are drawn up and exchanged, the hardware is ordered and Jane starts work.

13.4.1 ASIDE: Avoiding demarcation disputes

In an ideal parallel universe, software engineers live an easy life. Analysts analyse, designers design, and programmers program. Sadly, in our own universe, real life is less well structured. In this case study, for example, Jane should simply describe what the system will do, without worrying about how such a goal can be achieved. This is a laudable aim, but it quickly breaks down in practice. In this example, as in most realistic situations, the software and hardware elements cannot be viewed in isolation.

The approach Jane adopts is a pragmatic one. She makes the initial contact with the client and records all the information she can about the required system. She and her colleagues then make 'design' and 'implementation' decisions before the system specification is even complete. This is not uncommon! In many realistic situations, it is impossible to specify at any useful level of detail a software system for which no details of the operating environment are known.

13.5 The Context diagram

The Context diagram is produced. Particular care is taken in the selection of appropriate terminators.

Armed with this rough idea of what the system is to do, Jane draws up a context diagram (Figure 13.1). The system is, as expected, straightforward.

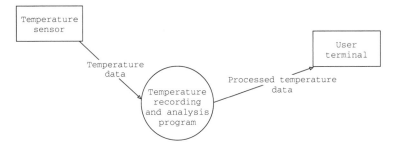

Figure 13.1 The provisional Context diagram.

13.6 The user interface

Because of the impact of the system interface on all aspects of the model, it is sketched (or prototyped) at this early stage.

The required interface will be a simple one. It involves a display of temperature and time information, in a format specified by staff at LBF. It is illustrated in Figure 13.2.

```
LSE: Furnace Temperature Monitor
Current time : 14:40
Average Temperature (Celsius):   1509
Latest Temperature (Celsius)  :  1505
     Recorded at : 14:25
Maximum Temperature (Celsius):   1530
     Recorded at : 12:15
Minimum Temperature (Celsius):   1480
     Recorded at : 08:00
```

Figure 13.2 A sketch of the user interface.

13.7 The process list

A process list is drawn up. This list is necessarily very provisional, and creation of a highly polished document is not appropriate at this stage.

Through discussions with John Chime and his staff, Jane identifies two basic processes to be performed by the system (Table 13.1).

Process name	Notes
Get temperature	Get a temperature reading from the sensor.
Analyse temperature data	Analyse the temperature data.

Table 13.1 The process list.

13.8   The walkthrough

A system walkthrough is performed. Where feasible, the entire development team (analysts, designers, programmers) should be involved in this process. As the walkthrough progresses, the process list, context diagram and interface sketches are modified as required.

In a simple example like this one, the walkthrough is straightforward and is largely concerned discussing the system with those involved.

Jane begins by having a further meeting with John Chime, during which she learns that the system is required to take temperature readings every five minutes. The basic procedure will then be to take a reading, and store the result. The stored results for the last half hour (seven readings in total) will then be analysed to find the average (mean) temperature in this period. In addition, the maximum and minimum values obtained since the system was activated will also be recorded.

As John Chime won't actually be making use of the system himself, Jane asks him if she can talk to the staff who will use the product. John agrees, and introduces Jane to Geoffrey Watts, who is the main shop floor technician at LBF. Jane explains to Geoff about the system she is developing, and shows him a copy of the interface sketches.

Geoff inspects the drawings carefully. 'It might be useful,' he concludes, returning the drawings to Jane.

'You don't sound very enthusiastic,' Jane says. 'Do you think there is any way we could improve the system, to make it more useful for you? Or do you think a different kind of display would be useful?'

'I don't think so,' says Geoff, shaking his head. 'The thing is, you see, I don't see that I'm going have much time to look at the screen, no matter what you put on it.'

'You won't?'

'No. I'm responsible for the whole of the shop floor. I've got more to do than just watch the furnace heat up – I can't sit around all day. I usually just leave the furnace for two hours every morning to heat up, and get on with clearing the floor from the previous day. Chances are I won't get to look at the screen too much.'

'I see,' says Jane. 'Would it help if we included a bell with the system? That way, you wouldn't have to look at the screen all the time, but the bell would ring when the furnace reached operating temperature, or when something was wrong?'

'Now you're talking,' Geoff smiles at her. 'If your fancy computer can do that, then it just might be worth using.'

Jane adds an audible alarm to the context diagram (Figure 13.3).

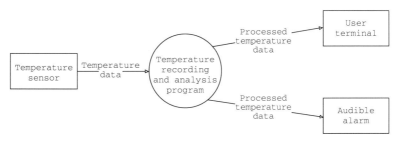

Figure 13.3   The final Context diagram.

13.9 The Level 1 dataflow diagram

A preliminary Level 1 DfD is sketched, on the basis of the process list.

Following further discussions with Mr Chime, Jane embarks upon the Level 1 DfD using the CASE tool. At first, the task looks daunting: she is faced with an almost blank screen, with only the incoming and outgoing flows visible (Figure 13.4). However, Jane perseveres, and begin to draw up a more realistic representation of the problem (Figure 13.5).

Figure 13.4 The initial appearance of the level 1 DfD.

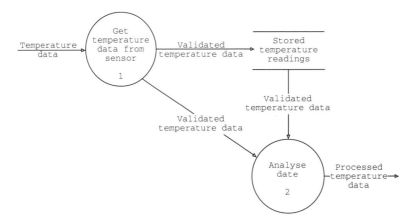

Figure 13.5 The final Level 1 DfD.

13.10 The dataflow diagram hierarchy

The DfD hierarchy is completed, and levelled as necessary.

In this example, Jane has not sufficiently defined the system with the Context diagram and Level 1 DfD. She must therefore add another layer below each of the Level 1 processes (Figures 13.6 and 13.7).

This completes the DfD hierarchy.

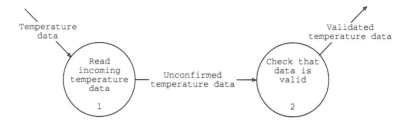

Figure 13.6 DfD 1-1.

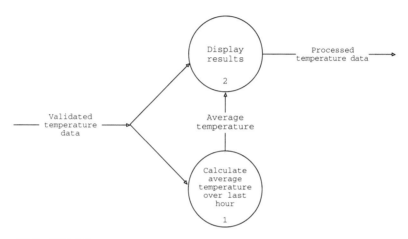

Figure 13.7 DfD 1-2.

13.11   The process specifications

The process specifications are written.

Each of the processes in the lowest-level DfDs must now be defined more carefully. Here, we will consider only PSpec 1-2-1 (Figure 13.8).

@IN = Validated temperature data
@OUT = Average temperature

@PSpec Calculate average temperature over last hour

PRE: Got valid temperature data.

The (Average temperature) is calculated by summing the (Validated temperature data) recorded during the past hour and dividing this total by the number of temperature readings made over this period.

POST: Got valid average temperature

@

Figure 13.8 PSpec 1-2-1.

13.12   The data dictionary

The data dictionary is completed.

A fragment of the draft data dictionary produced by Jane is given below. In the full specification, all data would need to be provided for all of the flows and stores.

To generate this draft data dictionary, Jane has used the reporting feature of the CASE tool to list all entries in the dictionary which contain a BNF clause. This is one of the most useful reports: details of how to generate such a report is given in Appendix B.

Project: C:\LSE\FURNACE\
Title : Loughborough Bell Foundry
Date: 1-Jan-96 Time: 17:39

Report: Item Details (Full)

This report contains an alphabetic list of SOME OF the dictionary items and their details.

Name:	Stored temperature readings
Type:	Store
BNF:	Validated temperature data
Range:	See 'Validated temperature data'

Name:	Temperature data
Type:	Discrete flow
BNF:	\Raw data from temperature sensor \
Range:	Unknown

Name:	Unconfirmed temperature data
Type:	Discrete flow
BNF:	\Temperature readings (unconfirmed)\
Range:	Unknown

Name:	Validated temperature data
Type:	Discrete flow
BNF:	+["0"|"1"|"2"|"3"|"4"|"5"|"6"|"7"|"8"|"9"]
	+["0"|"1"|"2"|"3"|"4"|"5"|"6"|"7"|"8"|"9"]
	+["0"|"1"|"2"|"3"|"4"|"5"|"6"|"7"|"8"|"9"]
Units:	Degrees Celsius
Range:	0–1999
Comment:	Char [5]?

13.13   The balanced logical model

The complete model is reviewed, checked and balanced. Any necessary supporting documentation is written.

As Jane continues to develop this project, she makes use of the CASE tool to remind her of any parts of the project that still remain unbalanced, inconsistent or incomplete.

Details of the various check facilities provided by the CASE tool are given in the appendices. Here, we give the result of a diagram consistency check on the furnace project.

Project: C:\LSE\FURNACE\
Title : Loughborough Bell Foundry
Date: 1-Jan-96 Time: 17:39

Report: Diagram Consistency checking
This report contains a consistency check of all the diagrams in the project.

Checking 0.DAT	No Errors detected, No Warnings given.
Checking 1-------D.DAT	No Errors detected, No Warnings given.
Checking 1-1----D.DAT	No Errors detected, No Warnings given.
Checking 1-1-1--P.DAT	No Errors detected, No Warnings given.
Checking 1-1-2--P.DAT	No Errors detected, No Warnings given.
Checking 1-2----D.DAT	No Errors detected, No Warnings given.
Checking 1-2-1--P.DAT	No Errors detected, No Warnings given.
Checking 1-2-2--P.DAT	No Errors detected, No Warnings given.

—— End of report ——

Suitably reassured by this 'all clear', Jane knows that her work on the bell foundry system is complete. She passes her complete set of diagrams, reports and dictionaries to Stephanie who will conduct the design process.

13.14 Conclusions

In this simple case study, we have begun to look at the ways in which SADIE methodology can be applied in more realistic situations.

In the next chapter, we shall extend the technique to allow us to model real-time systems more effectively.

14 Process-oriented analysis of inter- active systems

14.1   Introduction

Suppose we have been asked to develop a 'calculator program' for one of our clients. As part of the system specification, we have a DfD with two processes, 'Add numbers' and 'Subtract numbers' (Figure 14.1).

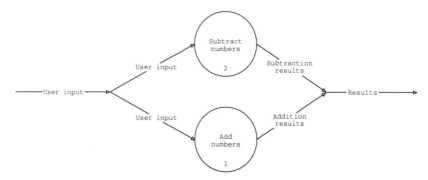

Figure 14.1   A simple DfD representation for an adding and subtracting machine.

During requirements analysis, we learn that on some days our client simply wants to add numbers, while on other days she wants only to subtract numbers. How can we redraw Figure 14.1 to represent this basic requirement?

The answer is that, with the tools we have hitherto considered, we cannot do so: we have no way of representing the fact that we do *not* want our calculator to both add *and* subtract the numbers (as Figure 14.1 implies), but that we want to *either* add *or* subtract the numbers.

Perhaps we could try and convince our client that it is a valuable 'feature' of our calculator that it always displays both the result of addition and of subtraction; even if we were able to carry this off, we still could not even specify in our logical model the order in which the addition and subtraction are carried out. Because the physical model is derived from the logical model (a procedure we will describe in Chapter 15) then there are two possible 'designs' we might end up with (Figure 14.2). Since the final program must in turn be derived from one or other of these designs, the end result of

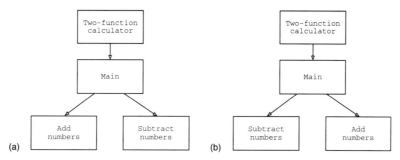

Figure 14.2 The designs for two possible adding or subtracting machine programs, each equally well represented by the ambiguous data flow diagram in Figure 14.1. (a) Module 'Main' calls first 'Add numbers' then 'Subtract numbers'. (b) Module 'Main' calls first 'Subtract numbers' then 'Add numbers'.

this ambiguous logical process model could be one of two programs, neither of which would satisfy the client's requirements (Figure 14.3).

If our original process model is unable to adequately model such a simple calculator, then we can have little confidence that it will be adequate for modelling any practical, interactive, systems. In fact, with the simple tool kit described in Chapter 12, batch systems are the only type of system we can specify.

To see how significant this is, we need to consider some important distinctions between these two system types:

● *Batch systems*
  These are 'run it, forget it, and come back in a week for the results' systems. They are used variously to print pay cheques, and for large scientific and economic simulations. Simple data gathering programs which run unattended for long periods, such as the temperature monitor in Chapter 13, may also fall into this category.

  It is no coincidence that, while large new batch systems are no longer common, their development was a widespread occupation during the 1970s when the original structured methods of software development (similar to those described in Chapter 12) were conceived.

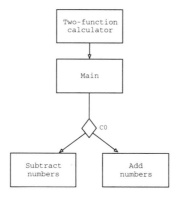

Figure 14.3 The adding machine required by the user. Condition C0 determines whether the 'Add' and/or 'Subtract' module (or neither) will be called on in any particular program run.

- *Interactive systems*

  These are systems that cannot operate without some form of control input, either from the user (through the keyboard, or some other standard input device), or perhaps from some other form of sensor. We can subdivide this category in two, as follows:

  - *Sequential flow* The basic flow of control is sequential (like the 'batch' systems), but occasionally the system will need to 'ask questions' to determine which particular sequence of actions to perform next. A good example of sequential flow in action is a menu-based system.

  - *Interrupt-driven* A system which is purely interrupt-driven does nothing until an **interrupt** is received (interrupts were discussed in Chapter 9). The key feature of such programs is not the source of the interrupts (which may arise through hardware or software), but their stochastic nature: that is, the fact that as far as your program is concerned, these events can happen at any time.

    Pure interrupt-driven programs 'sleep' until an interrupt is sensed, at which point an appropriate interrupt service routine is invoked. Upon completion of the service routine, the system then goes 'back to sleep'. Many systems which exhibit **real-time** behaviour (discussed in Section 14.3.2) are, at heart, interrupt-driven.

To enable us to model the range of interactive systems described above, we will add two further components to the SADIE toolbox in this chapter, *viz.*

- control processes, and
- state-transition diagrams (STDs).

It is important to appreciate that there is a continuous line between pure batch systems (at one extreme) and pure interrupt-driven systems (at the other). For example, systems with a graphical user interface (GUI) can be viewed as advanced menu-driven programs, typically with a very complex selection of menu options. Equally, however, from the developer's point of view, GUI-based programs are modelled as systems driven by (software) interrupts. The additional tools described in this chapter will therefore allow us to model a very wide range of programs.

We begin by considering the state-transition diagram.

14.2   State-transition diagrams

State-transition diagrams (STDs) are used to record the control information required within the real-time logical process model. The state-transition diagram is based on a finite state machine model of a computer (for example, see Gersting, 1993). Like the ideal finite state machine, the system modelled by a state-transition diagram can only ever be in one state at any particular instant of time. Once in that state, the system will generally remain there until some specified input is received.

For example, Figure 14.4 shows part of the STD that might describe a simple program. The diagram reveals that the program has two states: 'State A' and 'State B'. In general terms, a state can be considered a stable condition for a system. In Figure 14.4, the program will wait in State A indefinitely, unless some input 'Input' is received by

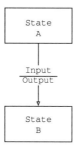

Figure 14.4 A partial state-transition diagram (STD) representation of an arbitrary (simple) system.

the program, at which point the program will move into State B. In other circumstances, states may represent periods when the control system is waiting for some process to finish. Note that details of this processing would be provided through the DfD and PSpecs: we consider links between STDs and the DfD hierarchy in Section 14.3.

During the transition between states, actions and process controls can be initiated. In Figure 14.4, the transition between State A and State B (conditional on the receipt of the Input control flow) results in the generation of the Output action.

To complete our example of a basic STD, however, we need to add an initial state. As the name suggests, this is the state which the computer enters every time the associated control process is activated. This is illustrated in Figure 14.5. The start up position (right at the top of the figure) shows the one and only 'way in' to this state-transition diagram; while there may be several possible end states, there will only be one starting position on any STD. Note that, as we see when we look at some more complex examples, there may well be more than one STD describing the operation of your program, in which case the 'start-up' state may relate to the time at which a particular *process* in your program is triggered or activated. We'll see more on this later.

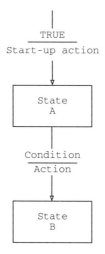

Figure 14.5 The complete STD representation of a very basic system with an implicit (single) initial state.

Movement from the initial state is given the 'condition' TRUE: in this example, this will (always) initiate 'Start-Up Action'. In your programs, Start-Up Action might well include initialization of software and/or hardware, it may simply print out a welcoming message, or it may do nothing at all.

Having initiated any initial activity, the system then moves into State A, as in the previous example, and continues from this point as before.

In a real program, the STD will, generally, be more complex with, for example, looping between states frequently carried out. Typically, having (say) triggered a process, we do not simply carry on with the program, but wait (in a state) until the process we have triggered returns a flag saying that the processing is complete, or that some error has occurred.

An example of a more realistic STD is given in Figure 14.6.

In all STDs transitions between states are **event driven**. In other words, something happens which causes the system to change from one state to another. It should be noted that not all events will necessarily cause a transition from a particular state and that any given event does not always cause a transition into the same state. There are three control flows (as opposed to dataflows) that can be associated with a particular transition. These are described and illustrated in Table 14.1.

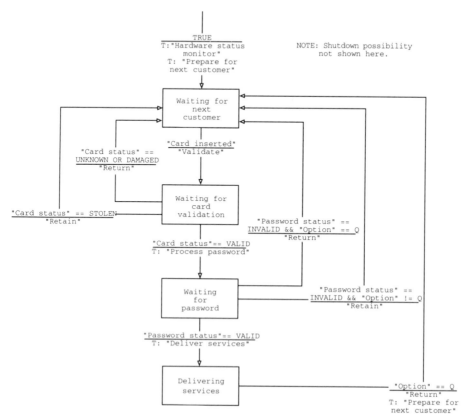

Figure 14.6 Part of the STD representation of a more realistic system.

Action	STD	Description	DfD
Trigger	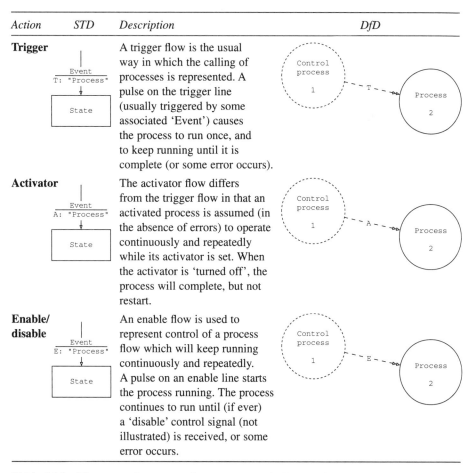	A trigger flow is the usual way in which the calling of processes is represented. A pulse on the trigger line (usually triggered by some associated 'Event') causes the process to run once, and to keep running until it is complete (or some error occurs).	
Activator		The activator flow differs from the trigger flow in that an activated process is assumed (in the absence of errors) to operate continuously and repeatedly while its activator is set. When the activator is 'turned off', the process will complete, but not restart.	
Enable/ disable		An enable flow is used to represent control of a process flow which will keep running continuously and repeatedly. A pulse on an enable line starts the process running. The process continues to run until (if ever) a 'disable' control signal (not illustrated) is received, or some error occurs.	

Table 14.1   The types of actions and process controls that may be associated with a transition on a STD. The right-hand column of the table shows the corresponding representation on the DfD: this representation is discussed in Section 14.3.

14.2.1   Example: Interrupt-driven systems

To illustrate the use of state-transition diagrams, we begin by considering how the control of interrupt-driven systems may be represented using this notation.

As we saw in Chapter 9, an interrupt can arise through a hardware failure (for example, when trying to store data on a faulty hard disk), or a software error (for example, when trying to divide by zero). Whatever the source, the impact is much the same: your program must be prepared to react 'immediately' to unpredictable events. A general STD for a pure interrupt-driven system is shown in Figure 14.7.

For example, consider that we have been asked to develop a specification for a system to control the temperature within the greenhouses of a large tomato farm.

We are told initially only that when temperature in the greenhouse 'gets too high' then the control system should activate a cooling process to cool the greenhouse. Similarly, we are told that when the temperature in the greenhouse 'gets too low' then the control system should activate a heating process to increase the temperature.

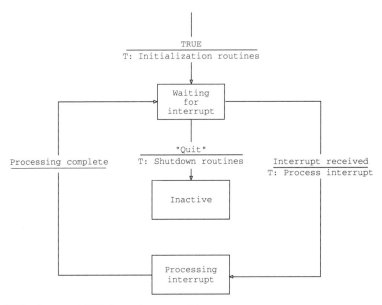

Figure 14.7 A general STD for an interrupt-driven system.

The thermostat providing information to our system has three possible states: 'Temp Too High', 'Temp OK', and 'Temp Too Low'.

We can represent the framework of our temperature control system with the simple state-transition diagram shown in Figure 14.8.

The diagram represents, succinctly, the control of our tomato greenhouse system. Each time the system is switched on it enters the idle state 'Waiting for Control Signal'. The system will remain in this state indefinitely, unless it receives either a 'Temp Too Low' control signal or a 'Temp Too High' control signal. On receipt of a 'Temp Too Low' signal, the system will enable the process 'Heating Process' and enter the 'Heating Greenhouses' state, where it will remain until a 'Temp OK' signal is received.

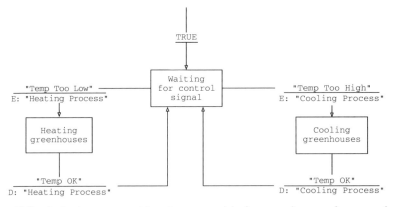

Figure 14.8 A simple state-transition diagram model of a control system for a set of tomato greenhouses.

On receipt of the 'Temp OK' signal, 'Heating Process' will be disabled, and the system will return to the 'Waiting for Control Signal' state.

Similarly, on receipt of a 'Temp Too High' signal, the system will move into state 'Cooling Greenhouses', enabling 'Cooling Process' as it does so. It will remain in this state until a 'Temp OK' signal is received, at which time the 'Cooling Process' will be disabled, and the system will move back into the state 'Waiting for Control Signal'.

14.3   Control processes

While a real-time system can be modelled using only a state-transition diagram, such a model would only provide very limited information to the system designers and programmers. For example, in Figure 14.8, the STD dictates that a 'Heating Process' is enabled in the event that a low temperature is detected in the greenhouse. However, without a DfD and PSpec to refer to, we have no information (at all) about the nature of this process.

What is required here, and for all non-trivial real-time systems, is a means of linking the STD view of the system with the data flow diagram. This link is achieved through an addition to the DfD called a **control process**.

Control processes are shown on the DfD as 'dotted' bubbles (Figure 14.9). From the control process, various control flows will be drawn, which must match with the information given on the corresponding STD. This link is made explicit in Table 14.1.

The default configuration of the CASE tool makes STDs the decomposition of control processes. The CASE tool will perform various consistency checks on STDs, see 'State-transition Diagram Checks' in the CASE tool on-line help for further information.

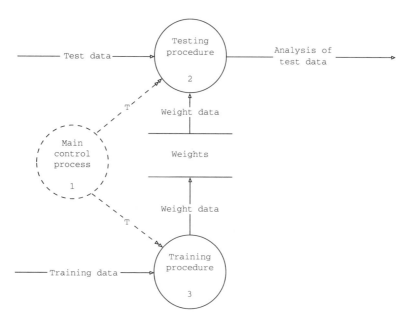

Figure 14.9   A simple DfD, with a control process (the 'dotted' bubble). The control process will have an associated (child) state-transition diagram.

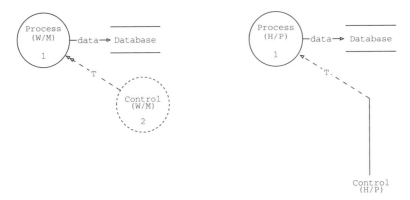

Figure 14.10 A comparison of Ward and Mellor (left) and Hatley and Pirbhai (right) notations for the same real-time DfD.

Note that the notation we use to represent control processes is based on the extended structured analysis notation for real-time systems developed by Ward and Mellor (1985). There are alternative notations for real-time DfDs, such as the notation used by Hatley and Pirbhai (1987). For example, the same diagram is shown in both notations in Figure 14.10.

You can also produce 'Hatley' DfD charts with the CASE tool, and their use is described in Appendix E. The two notations are very similar, but (in the experience of the author) the 'control bar' used in the Hatley notation can be confusing, particularly to inexperienced users; we therefore use the Ward and Mellor notation here. The type of chart you choose to use to represent your DfDs is entirely up to you.

14.3.1   Example: A machine to double numbers

To see how we make use of control processes and STDs in practice, we'll start with a simple example. Suppose the initial requirements specification for our system is as follows:

> 'Produce a program that will ask the user for a number, double the number, and display the result on the computer screen.'

Given this vague description, we might begin to develop a logical process model by producing the Context diagram shown in Figure 14.11. A possible Level 1 DfD is shown in Figure 14.12 and the STD 'under' the main control process (Figure 14.12) is given in Figure 14.13.

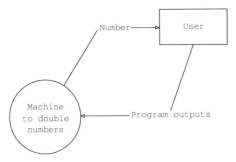

Figure 14.11   The Context diagram for the 'machine to double numbers'.

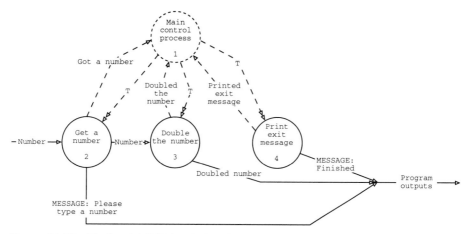

Figure 14.12 The Level 1 DfD for the 'machine to double numbers'.

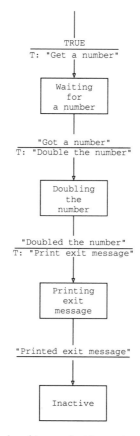

Figure 14.13 The STD for the 'machine to double numbers'.

Note that this simple example highlights the general operation of most STDs. Each process is 'called' by a trigger flow. When the process is complete, this fact is indicated by a return control flow. For example, in Figure 14.13, a trigger flow 'Double the Number' is initiated, implying the activation of the process on the same name, shown in Figure 14.12. At this point, the system is in state 'Doubling the Number'. When process 'Double the Number' is complete, it in turn initiates a return control signal 'Doubled the Number'. Receipt of this signal by the main control process causes the system to trigger the 'Print Exit Message' process.

Note that both the trigger flows and corresponding return control signals are shown both on the both on the STD and on the corresponding DfD. If these flows are *not* shown on both diagrams, then the diagrams are not balanced; this fact will be reflected in any checks you perform with the CASE tool.

14.3.2   Example: A real-time security system

We mentioned computer systems exhibiting real-time behaviour in the overview at the start of this chapter. We might define such systems as follows:

> *'Whenever a computer system is required to acquire data, emit data or interact with its environment at precise times, the system is said to be a real-time computer system.'* (Lawrence and Mauch, 1988)

Some examples of real-time software might therefore be:

- the programs that control the generation of sparks in a car electronic ignition system;
- the programs controlling the traffic lights on the street outside your house;
- the programs controlling the plane you use to fly to Paris on holiday.

Clearly, in all these instances, the software must perform precisely 'on time', or your car won't start, the traffic lights won't work correctly – and you won't reach Paris.

Real-time systems are an important class of interactive systems. In many of the examples above, the real-time systems are also embedded systems: that is, they run on special-purpose hardware built into the system they are monitoring or controlling. We consider the design and implementation of embedded systems in Chapter 15.

We look at how to specify real-time systems here. For example, consider that we have been asked to develop a security system for a large freezer complex storing frozen yoghurt. The warehouse covers an area of several square miles, and its contents are thought to be at great risk from theft. Because of the hostile (that is, very cold) conditions, the complex owners have proposed to use 'robots' rather than (human) security guards to patrol the area.

The robots will consist of a simple three-wheel trolley arrangement (Figure 14.14). These robots will follow a predefined route, marked out with white guidelines some 15 cm wide drawn throughout the factory area. The robots will be powered by 'stepper' motors, one attached to each rear wheel. Such electric motors move forward a single 'step' in response to an applied current pulse. The robot will straddle the white guidelines (Figure 14.14): where, for example, the robot reaches a curve in the guideline, one of the photoelectric sensors detects the change in light level and will adjust the appropriate stepper motor to compensate.

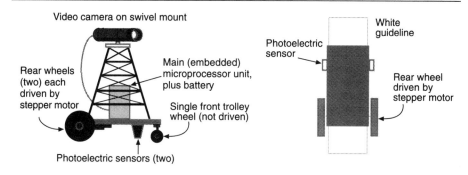

Figure 14.14 Two views of the real-time security robot system.

While touring the factory in this way, the robot will continually scan the factory area with a video camera. The images from this camera will be relayed back to a security guard by radio. If the guard sees anything suspicious, he can stop the robot, and manually control the camera. If something is amiss the guard may need to go and inspect the area more closely in person, otherwise the robot will be allowed to continue.

To specify the software for this system, we need a Context diagram (Figure 14.15).

The corresponding Level 1 DfD is shown in Figure 14.16. Note that in this figure, not untypically for such systems, we have three largely independent processes operating concurrently. Thus, the vehicle direction control is largely independent of the camera control, and of the image processing operations performed by the robot.

This is made clear on the associated STD (Figure 14.17).

Note that this system operates, again, largely as an interrupt-driven system. That is, the robot has (we presume) no way of predicting in advance when it will come across a curve in the white guide line, and be forced to make a turn. The programmer, therefore, has to ensure that the system is always in a position to react rapidly when such an event is detected.

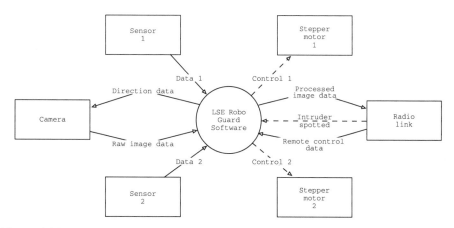

Figure 14.15 The Context diagram for the robot security system software.

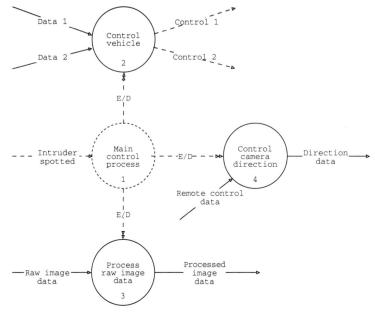

Figure 14.16 The Level I DfD for the robot security system software.

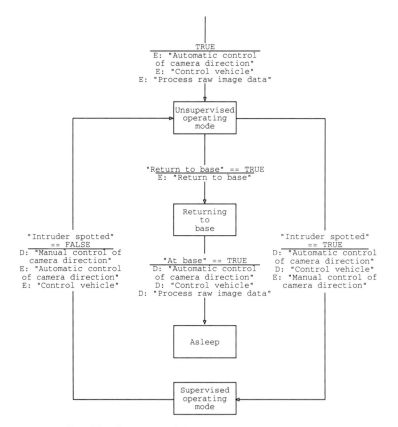

Figure 14.17 The STD (Diagram 1-1) for the robot security system software.

14.4   The impact of the user interface

Using SADIE, as we have seen, it is usual for discussions to take place with the client, involving sketches of the user interface, at the same time that the context diagram and process list are created. The specification document itself will then include these sketches or perhaps even some screen shots from an early prototype system.

Sketches of the interface may appear to be the only visible sign that the software engineer has considered the user interface, but this is misleading. The choice of interface should be considered at an early stage not simply to generate pretty screen shots, or even as part of an effort to adopt a 'user-centric' view of the system (though such an approach is generally desirable). One important reason why the interface must be considered during the development of the logical model is that such decisions may have a profound effect on the resulting system.

We'll illustrate this by considering some of the underlying differences between a menu-based program and a GUI-based program.

14.4.1   Example: Menu-driven program

As we have seen, simple programs are typically based on menus. The user is given a choice of actions to perform, makes a selection, and the program performs the required task, returning to the menu when the task is complete.

As an example of such an interface, let's return to complete the specification of the calculator described in the introduction to this chapter. We assume that discussions with the client have revealed that the required calculator will be menu-driven (Figure 14.18). The context diagram is given in Figure 14.19 and the corresponding Level 1 DfD is given in Figure 14.20. The STD is given in Figure 14.21. The overall structure of the system is clear and straightforward, with a limited number of possible options at each point in the STD.

```
MENU:
1    Add two numbers
2    Subtract two numbers
3    QUIT program.

?    :
```

Figure 14.18   A sketch of the main interface to the menu-driven calculator.

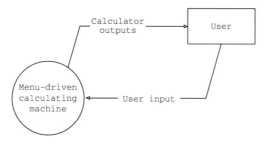

Figure 14.19   Context diagram for the calculator example.

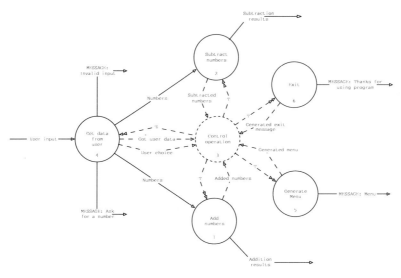

Figure 14.20 The Level I DfD for the calculator example.

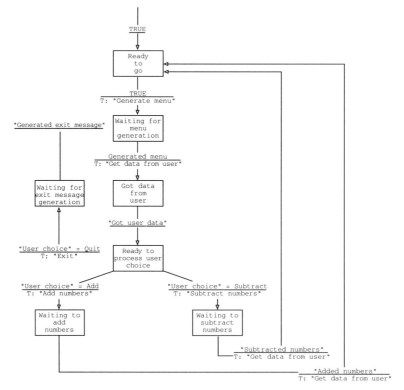

Figure 14.21 The main state-transition diagram for the calculator. The STD removes the ambiguity from the operation of the Level I DfD.

14.4.2 Example: GUI-based program

In our simple menu-driven program above, the basic flow of control was sequential. In a GUI-based system the interface tends to dominate the program structure. In such a system, the operating system communicates with your program informing it, for example, that the user has just touched a key, or that a button on the mouse has been pressed. As far as your program is concerned, these external events occur at random. Therefore, unlike the well-structured and controlled menu-driven system structure, GUI-based programs must be structured like the interrupt-driven programs we have considered in earlier examples.

Suppose, for example, that we have a more complex interface, such as that shown in Figure 14.22. In this engine control system, the sliding controls are used to control the speed of the engine, its power output and fuel supply while the engine is running. In this case, unlike the menu-driven program, the overall structure of the program is not immediately apparent, because the user may, for example, press the 'Cancel' button or move one of the sliding controls at any time during the execution of the program.

The context diagram for the above system is given in Figure 14.23. A possible Level 1 DfD for the program behind the interface shown in Figure 14.22 is given in Figure 14.24. The Level 1 DfD makes clear that, effectively, we have a collection of largely independent processes in this program. Rather than operating under the control of a central process, these are each activated by a change to some part of the user interface.

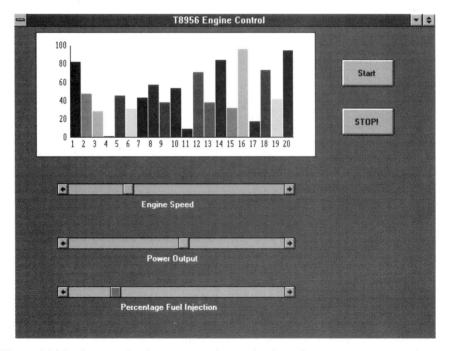

Figure 14.22 An example of a more complex graphical interface to an engine control system.

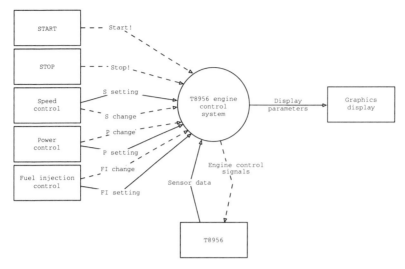

Figure 14.23 The Context diagram for the engine control program.

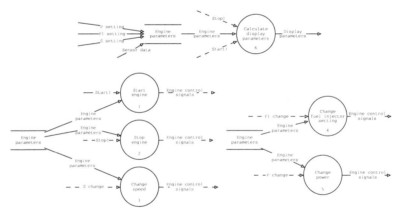

Figure 14.24 A possible Level 1 DfD for the engine control program.

Note that this structure is the basis of most GUI-based programs. In this situation, the GUI 'operating system' is proactive, rather than reactive and, for example, when the user 'presses a button' on the screen, the operating system will advise your program of this fact through (what amounts to) a software interrupt. This interrupt will frequently, as in the example here, be used to trigger a particular process, or group of processes, in your program.

14.5 Relating STDs to C++ code

As we draw to the end of the first part of the book, we're in a position to link together all the main 'high level' features of SADIE with those of the C++ programming language. As we consider state transition diagrams, it is important to understand how such diagrams are translated into C++ code.

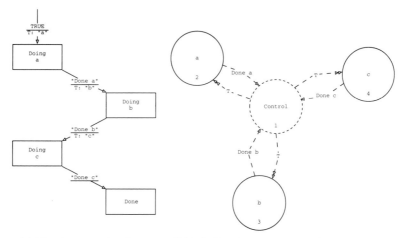

Figure 14.25   An example of a simple STD (left) and corresponding (Level I) DfD.

As an example of a simple STD, consider Figure 14.25. Here, as we have already seen, each of the process bubbles on the DfD will ultimately become functions in our C++ program. Thus, if we assume (purely for the purposes of this illustration) that the diagrams in Figure 14.25 represent the whole of our system, we expect the structure of the program itself to be something like that shown in Figure 14.26. Note that while functions a(), b() and c() are explicitly represented on the DfD (with details provided, presumably, in associated PSpecs), main() does not have a corresponding DfD representation.

```
// Comments

#include …

int main()
      {
      …
      }

int a(…)
      {
      // etc
      }

int b(…)
      {
      // etc
      }

int c(…)
      {
      // etc
      }
```

Figure 14.26   Translating from STDs to C++ code – Part I.

This is where the control process and STD come in: here, as is the general case, the `main()` function consists largely of calls to user-defined functions. In this case, the series of calls is laid out explicitly in the STD shown in Figure 14.25. Thus, in this example, the `main()` function will be as shown in Figure 14.27.

```
int main()
    {
    a();
    b();
    c();

    return 0;
    }
```

Figure 14.27   Translating from STDs to C++ code – Part 2.

It is important to note that we do not explicitly have to wait for each function to execute before continuing, as perhaps suggested by the STD. This waiting process is, in a sense, automatic in C++: for example, we cannot continue with function `c()` until `b()` is complete, and so on.

Note that, in more complicated STDs, `main()` may also include loops or selection statements. For example, Figure 14.8 might be translated into a C++ `main()` function as shown in Figure 14.28.

```
int main()
    {
    for (;;) // For ever
        {
        switch (temperature)
            {
            case "Temp Too Low":
                do
                    {
                    heating_process();
                    } while (! "Temp OK");
                break;
            case "Temp Too High":
                do
                    {
                    cooling_process();
                    } while (! "Temp OK");
            }
        }
        return 0;
    }
```

Figure 14.28   Translating the STD in Figure 14.8 into C++.

14.6   Some new guidelines

We can conclude this chapter by updating the P-O method described in Chapter 12 to deal with interactive systems.

(1) *The business case*
    The analyst begins by estimating the technical and economic feasibility of the project. If, for example, the project is too small to be profitable, greatly outside the experience of the available personnel, or larger than can be tackled with the available technical and human resources, then it must be rejected at this stage.

(2) *The Context diagram*
    The Context diagram is produced. Particular care is taken in the selection of appropriate terminators.

(3) *The user interface*
    Because of the impact of the system interface on all aspects of the model, it is sketched (or prototyped) at this early stage.

(4) *The process list*
    A process list is drawn up. This list is necessarily very provisional, and creation of a highly polished document is not appropriate at this stage.

(5) *The walkthrough*
    A system walkthrough is performed. Where feasible, the entire development team (analysts, designers, programmers) should be involved in this process. As the walkthrough progresses, the process list, context diagram and interface sketches are modified as required.

(6) *The Level 1 dataflow diagram*
    A preliminary Level 1 DfD is sketched, on the basis of the process list. It is usually inappropriate to polish this diagram, as it may change substantially when the STD is considered. For this reason, it is usual include only processes at this stage, and a bare minimum of dataflows. Note that while a Level 1 DfD is usually all that is required, on a large system you may need to go further.

(7) *The state-transition diagram*
    The state-transition diagram associated with the Level 1 DfD is produced in an iterative process involving successive modifications to both STD and DfD, as necessary. For (rare) pure 'batch' programs, where no STD is used, this stage may be omitted, while for larger systems, a network of STDs may be required.

(8) *The dataflow diagram hierarchy*
    The DfD hierarchy is completed, and levelled as necessary.

(9) *The process specifications*
    The process specifications are written.

(10) *The data dictionary*
    The data dictionary is completed.

(11) *The balanced logical model*
    The complete model is reviewed, checked and balanced. Any necessary supporting documentation is written.

As always, the above guidelines should be modified to suit your own working practices and experience.

14.7 Conclusions

In this chapter, we have extended our simple process modelling techniques to deal with interactive systems. Specifically, we have added control processes to our dataflow diagrams, and seen how the detailed operation of these processes can be modelled using state-transition diagrams. As we have seen, these extensions allow us to model a range of systems, from batch systems to interrupt-driven systems.

In Chapter 15, we go on to consider the design phase of process-oriented development projects: this provides a bridge between the logical model we have considered in this chapter, and the implementation, in C++, that we considered earlier.

Exercises

14.1 Complete the specification for the environmental control system needed on the tomato farm (Figure 14.8), by drawing up the associated DfD hierarchy, outline PSpecs and data dictionary.

14.2 Describe briefly, in words, the real-time system (hardware and software) required to provide the driver of a car with a display of instantaneous and average fuel consumption figures. Your system should provide the facility to restart the averaging process whenever the driver wishes to do so, and should allow the driver to decide whether to see the results in miles per gallon or litres per kilometre.

14.3 Use the techniques covered in this chapter to draw up a structured specification of the system described in Exercise 14.2.

14.4 Extend your specification from Exercise 14.2 to include the option of seeing either the average fuel consumption, or the expected range of the car, in miles or kilometres, (taking into account the fuel in the tank and the average fuel consumption).

14.5 Further extend your specification in Exercise 14.2 to provide the driver with the option of seeing the engine temperature, oil temperature and external air temperature. When the oil temperature goes above 120°C a visible warning should be produced. A similar warning will be issued if the engine temperature exceeds 130°C, or the expected range of the car falls below 70 miles.

14.6 Complete the specification of the robot security system described in Section 14.3.2. As you do so, consider some safety implications of the system. For example, what happens if the robot encounters an unexpected obstacle (such as a worker in the factory): incorporate some appropriate sensors to avoid injury to people who accidentally step into the robot's path.

14.7 Consider the screen shot for a simple mailing list program shown in Figure 14.29. This simple program interface allows the user to enter data into a database of customer names, to search the database for customers in a particular area (for example, find all customers in Scotland), to search the database for customers of a particular name (for example, find all customers named 'John Smith'), or to exit from the program.
Draw up a state-transition diagram representation of this program.

Figure 14.29 A very simple 'graphical' interface to a mailing list program.

14.8 Consider Figure 14.30. This is an example of the GUI for a model-based decision support system designed to help medical personnel interpret the auditory brainstem response (ABR). The ABR is measured by means of electrodes placed on the scalp and near the ears, and consists of a series of low-amplitude positive and negative potentials ('waves'), such as that visible on the

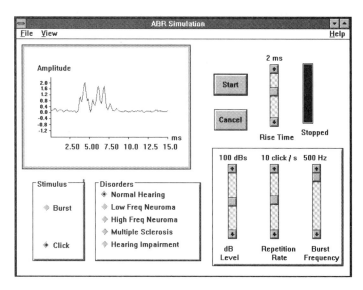

Figure 14.30 The interface to a prototype system for the simulation of auditory brainstem responses, developed by Kien Seng Wong working with the author at the University of Leicester.

Figure 14.31 An alternative graphical interface to the calculator program.

top-left display of Figure 14.30. Clinicians use the shape of ABR waves to diagnose multiple sclerosis, acoustic neuromas ('tumours' in the auditory nerve) and other nervous system diseases. We discuss decision support systems in Chapter 22.

Attempt to draw up a DfD/STD representation of this program.

14.9 Repeat the 'adding and subtracting' machine example discussed in this chapter, this time assuming that the client would like to have a greater range of functions, and a more sophisticated graphical user interface (Figure 14.31).

15 Process-oriented design

15.1 Introduction

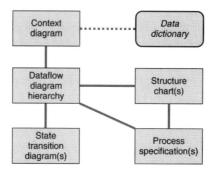

Figure 15.1 The components of the SADIE process model.

In this chapter, we examine the design phase of process-oriented systems development. Design takes place once the software requirements have been analysed and specified: that is, after the construction of the logical model of the system. Process-oriented design results in the completion of the process model of the system (Figure 15.1).

Design is conducted in six stages:

(1) *Review and refinement of the logical model*
    The specification documents are reviewed (by the design team) in order to gain an understanding of the system and to correct any flaws in the logical model.

(2) *The software and hardware architecture*
    The operating environment (hardware and/or operating system) and the basic software architecture are determined. General design decisions are made.

(3) *The preliminary physical model*
    The preliminary structure chart is derived from the logical model.

(4) *Review and refinement of the physical model*
    The provisional physical model is inspected, and issues of module coupling and cohesion are considered.

(5) *Reconciliation of the logical and physical models*
     Logical and physical models are compared and adjusted as necessary to ensure that they are fully compatible.

(6) *The test strategy*
     The overall system test strategy is drawn up.

We consider each of these stages in turn during the course of this chapter.

15.2 Review and refinement of the logical model

The physical model is built upon the logical model. This means that designer has to understand the logical model before development of the physical model can begin. Moreover, if the logical model is flawed, then the physical model, and the system itself, will reflect these flaws. For both of these reasons, it is essential that the designer should explore and, where necessary, correct the logical model before embarking upon the design.

We illustrate this process below.

15.2.1 Example: Weather monitoring system

You have been asked to complete the design of a weather monitoring system for recording humidity, wind speed and temperature simultaneously, in the Arctic circle. The individual weather sensors are already owned by the company concerned, and each has previously been used 'stand alone'. However, in order to make the whole system more reliable and efficient, your clients now want to link all three units together, and record the results on computer disk. When the disk is nearly full (which is expected to take between seven and nine days, depending on conditions), a radio message to this effect will be sent to the base camp, and a lucky volunteer will don snow shoes, and walk several miles to change the disk and the system battery. Note that, because of the volume of data and the very poor weather conditions, early tests have indicated that simply transmitting the data themselves by radio will be too unreliable.

The operating range for the sensors is given below. Provided the output of the sensors is within the ranges specified, then it should be considered valid. If it falls outside the specified ranges, or changes by more than 10% between any two consecutive readings, then they should be rejected, and the base should be informed (again by radio) that there is a problem.

The ranges are as follows:

- Temperature: −45 to +10°C
- Humidity: 0.1 to 10%
- Wind speed: 0 to 60 knots

Finally, as there have previously been sightings of yetis (abominable snowmen) in the area of the temperature sensor, your clients would like to try and observe these creatures too. The yetis only appear when the humidity is at between 3 and 4%, the temperature is below −3°C and the wind speed is between 32 and 37 knots. If such conditions occur, then your clients would like the system to send back a message to base *immediately*, so that a camera crew can be dispatched (by plane) to photograph the rare animal.

You are to design the system, and are provided with the following DfDs developed by another member of your team, plus a brief textual description as follows:

'The weather monitor will operate as described below. The system is intended to return (via radio) a single 5-digit (binary) code number every five minutes. The code will represent the overall status of the system (Table 15.1). For example, the code 01001 will signify that: the disk is OK (that is, not full), a yeti has been detected, the temperature and humidity sensors are OK, but the wind speed sensor has been shut down.'

Code	Meaning
1----	Disk nearly full
0----	Disk OK
-1---	Yeti detected
-0---	No yeti detected
--1--	Temperature sensor has been shut down
--0--	Temperature sensor functioning normally
---1-	Humidity sensor has been shut down
---0-	Humidity sensor functioning normally
----1	Wind speed sensor has been shut down
----0	Wind speed sensor functioning normally

Table 15.1 A proposed coding scheme for the weather monitoring system.

Dataflow diagrams

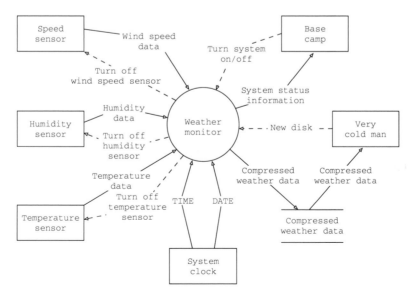

Figure 15.2 Context diagram for the weather monitoring system (note: this is a provisional version).

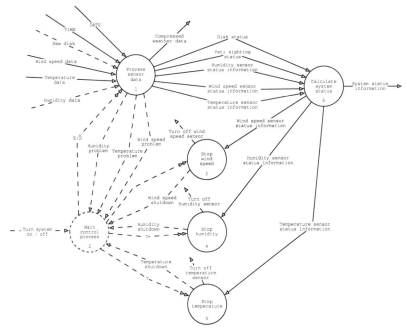

Figure 15.3 Level 1 DfD for the weather monitoring system (note: this is a provisional version).

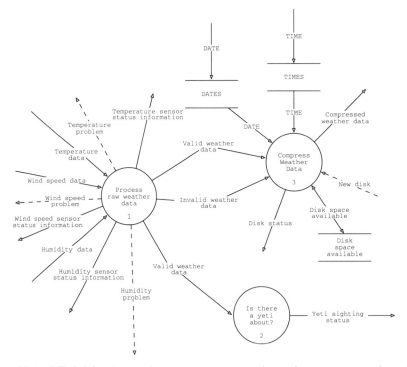

Figure 15.4 DfD 2-1 for the weather monitoring system (note: this is a provisional version).

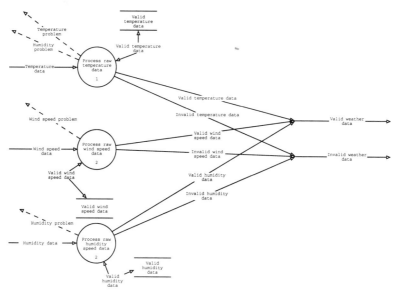

Figure 15.5 DfD 3-1 for the weather monitoring system (note: this is a provisional version).

State-transition diagram

The STD is shown in Figure 15.6.

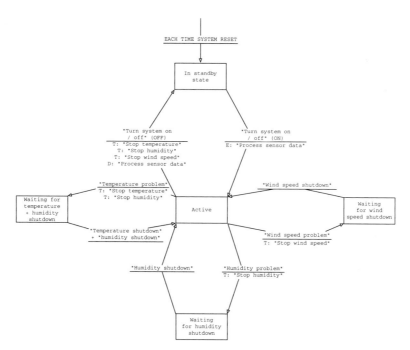

Figure 15.6 State-transition diagram for the weather monitoring system (note: this is a provisional version).

PSpecs

A selection of the relevant PSpecs is included here.

> *@IN = Wind Speed Sensor Status Information*
> *@OUT = Turn Off Wind Speed Sensor*
> *@OUT = Wind Speed Shutdown*

@PSpec Stop Wind Speed

// Disable the wind speed sensor

Pre-condition:
>   (Wind Speed Sensor Status Information) == 00001

Post-condition:
>   (Turn Off Wind Speed Sensor) = TRUE
>   (Wind Speed Shutdown) = TRUE

> @

Figure 15.7 PSpec 1-3.

> *@IN = Disk Status*
> *@IN = Yeti Sighting Status*
> *@INOUT = Humidity Sensor Status Information*
> *@INOUT = Temperature Sensor Status Information*
> *@INOUT = Wind Speed Sensor Status Information*
> *@OUT = System Status Information*

@PSpec Calculate System Status

// Calculate the overall system status

Pre-condition:
>   Valid information is available from all sources

Post-condition:
>   (System Status Information) =
>   (Disk Status)
>   && (Humidity Sensor Status Information)
>   && (Temperature Sensor Status Information)
>   && (Wind Speed Sensor Status Information)
>   && (Yeti Sighting Status)

> @

Figure 15.8 PSpec 1-6 for the weather monitoring system.

@ IN = Valid Weather Data
@ OUT = Yeti Sighting Status

@PSpec Is there a yeti about?

// See whether weather conditions are suitable for yetis

Pre-condition 1:
(−45 < (Valid Temperature Data) < −3) && (32 < (Valid Wind Data) < 37)
&& (3 < (Valid Humidity Data) < 4)

Post-condition 1:
(Yeti Sighting Status) = 01000

Pre-condition 2:
!((−45 < (Valid Temperature Data) < −3) && (32 < (Valid Wind Data) < 37)
&& (3 < (Valid Humidity Data) < 4))

Post-condition 2:
(Yeti Sighting Status) = 00000

@

Figure 15.9 PSpec 1-1-2 for the weather monitoring system.

@ IN = Temperature Data
@ INOUT = Previous Valid Temperature Data
@ OUT = Humidity Problem
@ OUT = Invalid Temperature Data
@ OUT = Temperature Problem
@ OUT = Temperature Sensor Status Information
@ OUT = Valid Temperature Data

@PSpec Process Raw Temperature Data

// Process the data from the temperature sensor

Pre-condition 1:
(Temperature Data) == "XXX" // Code for temp sensor shutdown (not
numerical)

Post-condition 1:   // Temperature sensor has been shutdown
(Temperature Sensor Status Information) = "00100"

Pre-condition 2:
(Temperature Data) is not numerical
(Temperature Data) != "XXX"

Post-condition 2:   // Seems to be a problem with the temperature sensor
(Temperature Problem) = TRUE;

Pre-condition 3:
(Temperature Data) is numerical

-45 <= (Temperature Data) <= 10
Difference between current (Temperature Data) and (Previous Valid
Temperature Data) is less than 10%
! ((Temperature Data > 0) && (Previous Valid Temperature Data < 0)) //
NOT Thaw conditions
! (Temperature Data > 5)   *// NOT temperature sensor overload*

**Post-condition 3:   // Valid temp data received: no thaw detected, no
temperature overload detected**
(Previous Valid Temperature Data) = (Valid Temperature Data);
(Valid Temperature Data) = (Temperature Data);
(Temperature Problem) = FALSE;
(Humidity Problem) = FALSE;

Pre-condition 4:
(Temperature Data) is numerical
-45 <= (Temperature Data) <= 10
Difference between current (Temperature Data) and (Previous Valid
Temperature Data) is less than 10%
(Temperature Data > 0) && (Previous Valid Temperature Data < 0)
// Thaw conditions
! (Temperature Data > 5)   *// NOT temperature sensor overload*

**Post-condition 4:   // Valid temp data received: thaw detected, no
temperature overload detected**
(Temperature Problem) = FALSE;
(Humidity Problem) = TRUE;

Pre-condition 5:
(Temperature Data) is numerical
-45 <= (Temperature Data) <= 10
Difference between current (Temperature Data) and (Previous Valid
Temperature Data) is less than 10%
(Temperature Data > 0) && (Previous Valid Temperature Data < 0)
// Thaw conditions
! (Temperature Data > 5)   *// NOT temperature sensor overload*

**Post-condition 5:   // Valid temp data received: no thaw detected, no
temperature overload detected**
(Temperature Problem) = TRUE;
(Humidity Problem) = TRUE;

Pre-condition 6:
(Temperature Data) is numerical
-45 <= (Temperature Data) <= 10
! (Difference between current (Temperature Data) and (Previous Valid
Temperature Data) is less than 10%)

Post-condition 6:   // Invalid temp data received (changing too fast)
Temperature Problem = TRUE;
Humidity Problem = TRUE;

@

Figure 15.10   PSpec 1-2-1 for the weather monitoring system.

Data dictionary

Part of the data dictionary for the system is given in Table 15.2.

Name	C/D/S/T	Description
Compressed Weather Data	S	Compressed Weather Data
Compressed Weather Data	D	\Weather Data which has been compressed\
DATE	D	\Date information from SYSTEM CLOCK every 24 hours\
DATES	S	{DATE}
Disk Status	D	{['0'|'1'] + '0000'}
Humidity Data	D	\Data from Sensor (NOT YET VALIDATED)\
Humidity Problem	C	['TRUE'|'FALSE']
Humidity Sensor	T	\LSE humidity sensor, model HEA-23b\
Humidity Sensor Status Information	D	{'000' + ['0'|'1'] + '0'}
Humidity Shutdown	C	['TRUE'|'FALSE']
Invalid Humidity Data	D	\Out of range or inappropriate data\
Turn Off Humidity Sensor	C	['TRUE'|'FALSE']
Turn System On / Off	C	['TURN SYSTEM ON'|'TURN SYSTEM OFF'|'DO NOTHING']
Valid Humidity Data	D	\0.1 to 10 %\
Valid Humidity Data	S	{Valid Humidity Data}
Valid Weather Data	D	Valid Temperature Data+Valid Wind Speed Data+Valid Humidity Data
Yeti Sighting Status	D	{'0' + ['0'|'1'] + '000'}

Table 15.2 A representative selection of entries from the data dictionary for the weather monitoring system.

Levelling the system

If you were presented with the 'logical model' given above, and asked to develop a design for the system, you would face something of a challenge. While perhaps not fundamentally flawed, the system has not been levelled. Moreover, there is very little supporting documentation, and many of the requirements are rather hazy.

To begin with, you would probably start by examining the context diagram (Figure 15.2). This appears essentially sound. The three sensors are shown as terminators, as you would expect. The 'Very Cold Man' is also shown, with the removable hard disk represented by a data store. The arrangement of the store on the context diagram with both input and output flows is unusual, but does depict quite accurately the operation of this particular system.

The presence of the 'Base Camp' terminator is more puzzling: this implies that the radio link is to be internal to the system. This fact is not reflected on the Level 1 DfD (Figure 15.3), nor apparently elsewhere in the system. The 'Base Camp' terminator would probably be more accurately entitled 'Radio link'.

Figure 15.2 is redrawn in Figure 15.11 to reflect this change, and to perform some more general tidying up.

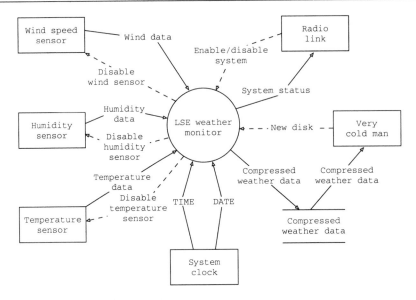

Figure 15.11   Context diagram for the levelled weather monitoring system.

The Level 1 DfD (Figure 15.3) is a cause for greater concern. Not all processes are controlled, and the three 'shut down' processes are very simple. This is redrawn in Figure 15.12 and the corresponding new DfD 1-2 is shown in Figure 15.13.

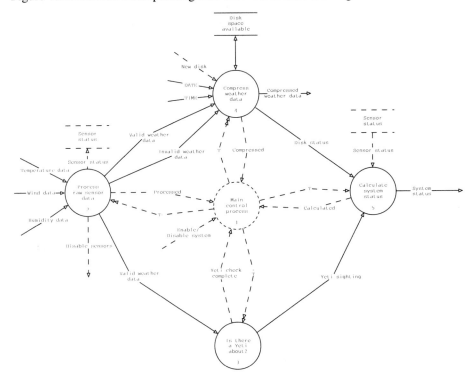

Figure 15.12   Level I DfD for the levelled weather monitoring system.

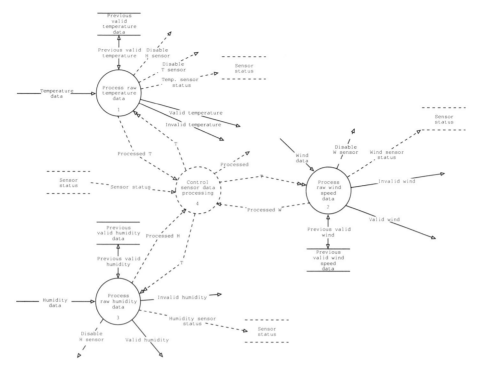

Figure 15.13 DfD 1-2 for the levelled weather monitoring system.

This completes the DfD hierarchy in the levelled system. The main STD is shown in Figure 15.14: there will also be a further STD associated with Figure 15.13 (not shown here).

The PSpecs and data dictionary in the original version are acceptable and require only minor changes: they will not be repeated here.

15.3   The software and hardware architecture

When we create the logical model of a system we are, to a first approximation, free to put aside details such as the operating system our program will work under, and the hardware upon which it will run. As we begin the design of our system, we must start to consider these and related issues much more seriously.

Here, to illustrate this process, we give examples of the design considerations that must be made when developing two important classes of system: embedded systems, and safety-critical systems. These types of system are commonly developed using the process-oriented techniques described in Part I of this book.

15.3.1 Embedded systems

Until now, we have largely assumed that you will be programming on and for a desktop computer system (Figure 15.15). This is of course not necessarily the case. As the cost of computer hardware has fallen to the point that a powerful microprocessor (such as the Motorola 68000) is available for about £2.00, it has become increasingly common to find microprocessors, coupled to a minimum of support circuitry, 'embedded' within a wide range of products, from cars to microwave ovens.

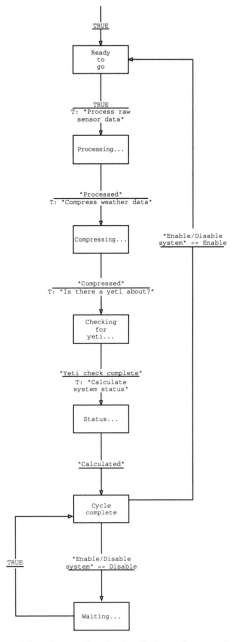

Figure 15.14 State-transition diagram for the levelled weather monitoring system.

The implementation of embedded systems is one of the most challenging aspects of software engineering, and one that crosses the narrow boundary between software engineering and electronic engineering. In this section, we begin to consider some of the particular problems facing the software engineer intent on developing software for this type of application.

Figure 15.15 A desk bound computer (left) sporting general-purpose input and output facilities (keyboard and VDU), compared with an embedded, single-board computer system which lacks any high-level I/O facilities, and doesn't even have an operating system.

System hardware

The general architecture of an embedded system is illustrated in Figure 15.16. In the simplest case, an embedded system will be required to record, at precise time intervals, the signal from some form of transducer. More generally, as in Figure 15.16, an embedded system will be required to perform both a measurement and a control function, and will be equipped with both transducers and actuators for this purpose. Note that Derenzo (1990) provides some useful practical advice on the use of general desktop computer systems for measurement and control applications.

Let's suppose that our embedded system is to be used by an environmental organization to record and automatically classify the songs of whales recorded (underwater) in the Antarctic. Our system will be encased in plastic and attached to a floating buoy. It will run on batteries for a two-year period, and will be required to send a radio broadcast to base every time it detects a whale in the vicinity.

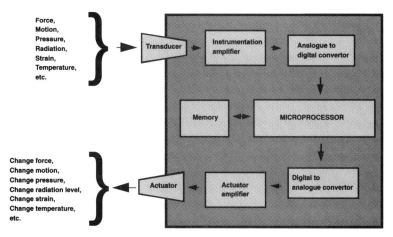

Figure 15.16 The general architecture of an embedded system.

In this case we'll need an underwater pressure **transducer** (hydrophone) to convert the fluctuations in water pressure produced by the whale song into a voltage value that can be processed by subsequent electronic circuitry; all transducers similarly convert from one physical quantity into another.

Typically, the output from any transducer will be a small (~1 mVolt) value: an instrumentation amplifier is therefore usually needed to convert this value to a range (~1 Volt) required for subsequent processing.

At this stage, however, the values are still analogue in nature and our (digital) computer can't do much with them. We therefore need to sample the sound in just the same way that ordinary compact discs (CDs) are sampled, and thereby reduce the whale song to a series of numbers (Figure 15.17).

Our sampled whale song will be passed from the A/D converter to the microprocessor for processing. Within the processor itself, we will need to have written some software to classify the song. For now, let's assume that we've managed to do this, and that our system has detected a humpback whale. We need to send the appropriate control

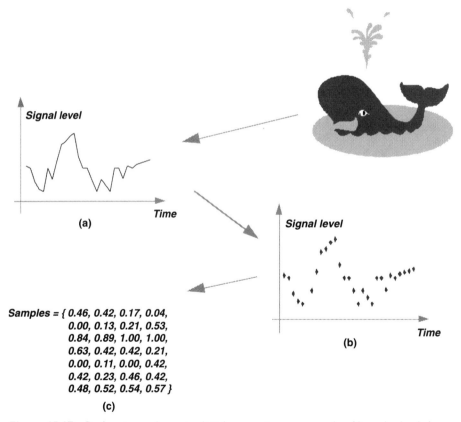

$Samples = \{ 0.46, 0.42, 0.17, 0.04,$
$0.00, 0.13, 0.21, 0.53,$
$0.84, 0.89, 1.00, 1.00,$
$0.63, 0.42, 0.42, 0.21,$
$0.00, 0.11, 0.00, 0.42,$
$0.42, 0.23, 0.46, 0.42,$
$0.48, 0.52, 0.54, 0.57 \}$

(c)

Figure 15.17 Performing analogue to digital conversion on a sample of humpback whale song. (a) The original (analogue) signal, recorded as a continuously varying voltage from an underwater microphone. (b) The sampled (quantized) version of the same signal. (c) The digital representation of the whale song to be stored on the computer.

information to our D/A converter which will convert it to analogue form. The actuator amplifier will be used (if necessary) to increase the strength of the resulting signal, and its output will control the transmission of a radio broadcast back to base.

Implementation issues

Figure 15.18 shows a typical desktop environment for a word processor program. The word processor is well protected from the underlying hardware in this situation. When it is necessary, for example, to save your latest novel on disk, the word processor asks the operating system to take care of most of this work; the operating system in turn delegates all the tricky bits to the BIOS (basic input/output system), and only the BIOS gets its hands dirty dealing with the underlying hardware.

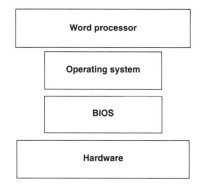

Figure 15.18   The BIOS/OS sandwich from a desk-bound computer system running some word processor software.

Unfortunately for the programmer, the environment of an embedded system is not so benign: Figure 15.19 shows the new 'sandwich' for our whale classification program. In an embedded system, such as our whale classification system, the microprocessor is generally 'naked'; that is, there is no operating system or BIOS in the conventional sense (Figure 15.20). Since both BIOS and operating system are each 'just another software layer', this does not present a fundamental problem, but it does mean the programmer has much more to do.

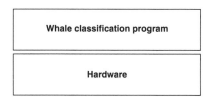

Figure 15.19   The rather thin sandwich from a microprocessor-based whale classification system.

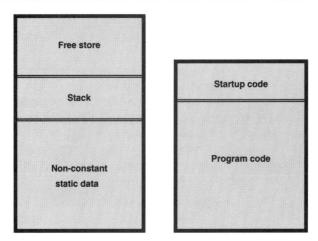

Figure 15.20 Memory structure of a simple embedded computer system.

Generally, embedded systems are single-program systems. Instead of loading programs (and, possibly, data) from disk, the program is usually stored in one fixed area of (ROM) memory, and the data to be manipulated (for example, read-write program variables) are held in different (RAM) memory areas. On development boards (and often the production version too, if the volumes aren't too great) the program will usually be stored on a form of ROM known as an EPROM: an Erasable Programmable Read Only Memory. To change the program running on the board, we usually have to change the EPROM.

Using a host computer

Let's return to our earlier example, and consider in general terms the problems we would encounter in developing the code to classify the whale song.

Assume that we have built the hardware shown in Figure 15.16. Now, suppose we want to use our favourite C++ compiler to start writing the software for this system: we immediately face some problems. Not only does our new computer system not have a disk drive from which we might load our compiler, it doesn't even have a keyboard to type on (let alone a screen to show what we've entered).

The solution is that we have to develop our code on a host computer. At the very least this means attaching an EPROM programmer to our desktop computer and, when we have finished writing the program, sending it to the EPROM programmer, blowing an EPROM, and transferring the EPROM to our embedded system. If the code doesn't work, we need to edit it on the host, blow (or re-blow) the EPROM, and so on. As each process takes (at least) several minutes, you can imagine that writing anything more than a trivial program in this manner is a non-trivial task.

Before we consider a better solution, we need to face up to some further complications. First of all, let us assume (for the moment) that the microprocessor in our host computer (say 80586) is identical to that in our embedded system. At least this means we can use the same compiler to develop our embedded system that we use for our normal programming – doesn't it?

Unfortunately, the answer is usually no. Because our embedded system doesn't usually have the operating system (or BIOS) that our desktop system has, code compiled on our desktop system won't run on our embedded system. Special compilers able to generate code for such an environment are known as ROMable compilers.

To consider why we need a different compiler, remember what happens when we run a normal program: the code is loaded into memory (by the operating system) and execution begins with the first machine code statement. With our embedded system, we may not need to load the code into memory (it's already in ROM), but we do need, somehow, to tell the microprocessor to run our program.

This is usually achieved by having the ROMable code execute every time the microprocessor is switched on. The actual execution is then initiated by a small 'harness' program, written in assembly language, that basically says to the microprocessor: 'Go to memory location 10110000 (or whatever the address is, in ROM, at which your program starts) and starting executing the code you find there'. A ROMable C++ compiler/linker will allow you to add a suitable harness to your program to allow this to happen. Cahill (1994) provides further details of this process.

Let's consider some further problems. As we noted above, it is quite likely that out host computer will use a different CPU than that used within our embedded system. The main reason for this is one of economics: while the processor in our desktop system may be state-of-the-art, it probably costs several hundreds of pounds to buy, even if purchased in bulk. By contrast, last year's microprocessor will usually cost a tenth of this amount, and will probably be more than powerful enough. In such circumstances, we often need a (ROMable) cross-compiler, that will run (say) on an 80586 but generate executable code for a 68020.

Finally, when we get tired of blowing EPROMs one hundred times a day, and inserting them in our embedded system, we can consider buying an In Circuit Emulator (ICE) package. This replaces the MPU and ROM on our board, and connects to our host computer, allowing us to compile and test programs thoroughly (and quickly) without blowing a single EPROM. Unfortunately, ICE is an expensive option: don't be surprised to find price tags of around £10 000 on a suitable system.

ASIDE: The `volatile` type specifier

There is one feature of C++ that is very relevant to our discussions of embedded system development and which we have not yet mentioned: the `volatile` type specifier.

We've already met the `const` type specifier in numerous examples. Its use is straightforward. For example, the statement:

```
const int x = 3;
```

creates a constant integer x, which cannot subsequently be modified.

When dealing with embedded systems, we often wish to deal with data transfers to and from ports, or by direct memory access (DMA). As far as C++ is concerned, we are dealing with an area of memory with contents that may be altered by external actions beyond the control of the program. Sometimes we need to make this fact explicit to the compiler.

For example, suppose our system must deal with an external sensor that writes data into a single byte of memory. As far as the C++ compiler is concerned, this area of memory is represented as an unsigned character variable called `sensor`, declared as follows:

```
const unsigned char sensor = 0;
```

If the compiler attempts to optimize this code, it may (for example) store our sensor variable in a register: in these circumstances, our sensor data will be written to a different memory area, and lost. It may in the process corrupt other parts of the program.

The volatile modifier prevents this:

```
const volatile unsigned char sensor = 0;
```

In effect, volatile tells the compiler not to optimize or alter this variable. This allows us to achieve the result we require.

If you are interested in embedded systems, then Cahill (1994) provides further useful information on this area.

15.3.2 Safety-critical systems

As we saw in Chapter 11, programs beyond some 20 000 lines in size are difficult to test exhaustively. Despite this, systems such as 'fly-by-wire' software for recent aircraft are typically more than 100 000 lines in size. A glance at these figures makes it clear that we cannot rely on testing to identify all the problems with our programs.

There are several ways we can begin to tackle this. First, and perhaps the most important, is to acknowledge the fact that our software is fallible. Such acknowledgement is a necessary precursor to taking preventative action. The next thing we need to do is to include, at the design stage, backups for every critical part of the system. Generally, such backup systems should not simply be copies of the original. This is common sense: if some combination of weather conditions causes the engines in our plane to go into reverse thrust five miles up, we want to be able to switch to a backup system that exhibits a different behaviour pattern, not one that performs in the same way.

The usual way this is achieved is by having, say, three different companies design, build and test their own version of the 'same' system. While imperfect, such an approach is generally found to be more effective than having a single company construct the entire system.

Of course, not all safety-critical systems are real-time systems. At the other end of the spectrum, for example, expert systems or decision support systems used by clinicians are also necessarily safety-critical in nature, because a wrong output can have dangerous or fatal consequences. Such systems must also therefore incorporate backups of some description. These may be implemented by using a variety of different techniques to arrive at a diagnosis, and/or by having the system explain its decision to the clinical operator. Naturally, in these circumstances, the final decision rests with the clinician, not with the machine.

15.4 The physical process model

As we saw in Figure 15.1, the physical process model consists of the logical process model, plus a structure chart. We considered the features of structure charts in Chapter 10. We'll briefly review those features below, then consider how such charts are derived from the logical process model.

15.4.1 Review of structure chart notation

We detailed the notation used to represent structure charts in Chapter 10. Figure 15.21 provides an overview of this notation for ease of reference in the following discussions.

The following notes refer to Figure 15.21:

- The module 'Program Name' is the top-level module. You can think of the 'Program' calling the main module (here called 'Main'), the equivalent of a C++ main() function.
- Module Main calls modules Module 1, Module 2 and Module 3 in order.
- The curved call arrow below 'Main' module indicates that 'Module 1', 'Module 2', and 'Module 3' may be called, in order, over and over again. This process continues until (if ever) some condition, 'C0', is satisfied: this may be, for example, until the user opts to quit, or an error occurs, or a control signal is received. Details of C0 will usually be provided in a key on, or accompanying, the diagram (you may like to refer back to Figure 10.1 for an example of this).
- The dotted call line from Module 1 to modules In Parallel 1 and In Parallel 2 means that these modules are executed *in parallel*: that is, both modules execute at the same time.

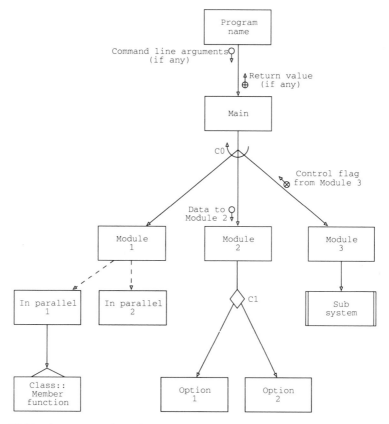

Figure 15.21 A structure chart showing the range of program features that can be represented in this notation (refer to the text for details).

- 'Module 2' can call modules 'Option 1' *or* 'Option 2', *or* neither. The particular module executed (if either) depends on the value of the condition 'C1' which – like C0 – will be detailed in a key.

- Module Sub system is parent to a further child structure chart (not shown), in exactly the same format as Figure 15.21.

- Most modules which are not subsystem modules will nonetheless still have children, in the form of process specifications (PSpecs).

- All of the modules are named.

- The module Class::Member function is used to represented a member function in the final implementation. Member functions are an essential feature of object-oriented C++ programs (see Part III).

15.4.2   Deriving preliminary structure charts

The process of translation between a logical process model and a preliminary structure chart is generally straightforward. For each (data) process on our DfD we have a corresponding module on our structure chart (SC), interconnected in a manner dictated by control constraints.

The derivation of a first-cut structure chart from the structured specification is carried out by taking the following guidelines into account:

- The hierarchy of the structure chart depends on the hierarchy of **control structures** on the DfDs, *not* on the process hierarchy.

- Where there is *no explicit* control information (that is, no control processes or STDs are included), and the specification was derived using SADIE, then the system is usually very simple and/or the flow of control is obvious. The correspondence between DfD hierarchy and preliminary structure chart should be easily determined.

- When there *is* control information, and a control process on the DfD triggers, activates or enables/disables, say, the operation of the three processes P1, P2, P3, there will be a corresponding module on the preliminary structure chart calling the modules M1, M2, M3.

- When there *is* control information, and a control process on the DfD triggers, activates or enables/disables, say, the operation of the process P4 which is not a bottom-level process, then process P4 will be translated into module M4 on the preliminary structure chart, and will call further modules in an additional (lower) layer.

Note that where a method other than SADIE was used to develop a system specification, you may find that there are no control aspects detailed. The inclusion of control information on the DfD brings forward decisions that (in early structured methods) were viewed as *design* decisions. Early consideration of control information is an important component of modern software development methods, not only because it provides an ability to model interactive systems, but more fundamentally because it bridges a gap between the three distinct 'analysis', 'design' and 'implementation' representations. As far as design is concerned, if we have made control decisions during specification, the design process becomes, in large part, a checking and polishing process.

In situations where you must work with specifications lacking control details, the process of translation between functional specification and first-cut design can prove rather more complex than the situation we will consider here. This is not a topic we will consider in detail in this book, but if you are interested, Meilir Page-Jones (1988) provides details (see especially Chapter 10: Deriving the Structure Charts for the System).

15.4.3 Example: Machine to double numbers

As usual, we illustrate the basic ideas with a simple example. Specifically, we shall produce a structure chart for the 'machine to double numbers' presented in Chapter 14.

The Level 1 DfD is particularly relevant to our discussions here and is reproduced in Figure 15.22. In this system, as in most others, we begin by translating the main control process in the DfD hierarchy into the Main module of our structure chart (Figure 15.23).

Next, we translate each of the modules on the Level 1 DfD into modules at the next level in the structure chart (Figure 15.24). The STD 'under' the main control process (Figure 15.22) is now relevant. This is reproduced in Figure 15.25. The STD confirms the timing of the calls to each module, which allows us to complete the structure chart (Figure 15.26).

Note that details of the data flow to and from modules is determined by the associated PSpecs (not shown) and data dictionary (Table 15.3).

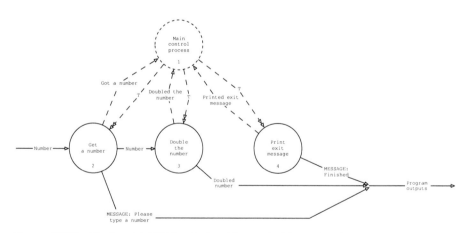

Figure 15.22   The Level 1 DfD for the 'machine to double numbers'.

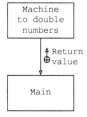

Figure 15.23   The beginnings of the structure chart for the 'machine to double numbers'.

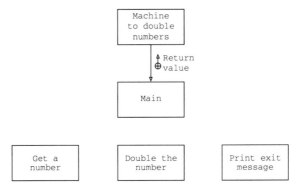

Figure 15.24 The evolving structure chart for the 'machine to double numbers'.

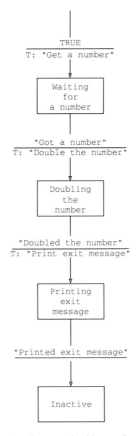

Figure 15.25 The STD for the 'machine to double numbers'.

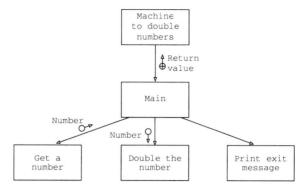

Figure 15.26 The completed structure chart for the 'machine to double numbers'.

Name	C/D/S/T	Description
Got a number	C	[TRUE | FALSE]
Number	D	Integer
MESSAGE: Finished	D	\'Finished'\
User	T	\The user of the program, interacting via keyboard and VDU\

Table 15.3 A fragment of the data dictionary for the 'machine to double numbers'.

15.4.4 Example: Weather monitoring

To give a better feel for the translation between DfD hierarchy and preliminary structure chart, we now consider a more realistic example, in the form of the levelled version of the weather monitoring system discussed in Section 15.2.1.

Construction of the preliminary structure chart begins with Figure 15.27. The necessary control information is provided by the STD associated with the 'Main control process' (Figure 15.14). We can add this information to the structure chart, giving the version shown in Figure 15.28. Finally, we can add the data flowing into and out of the modules (Figure 15.29). The preliminary structure chart is now complete.

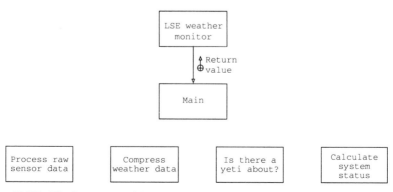

Figure 15.27 The beginnings of the physical model (structure chart) for the weather monitoring system.

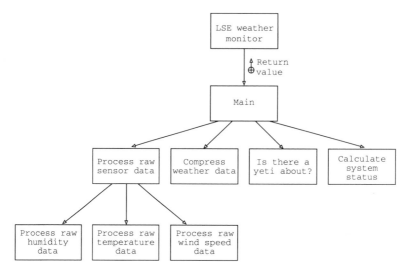

Figure 15.28 The evolving physical model (structure chart) for the weather monitoring system.

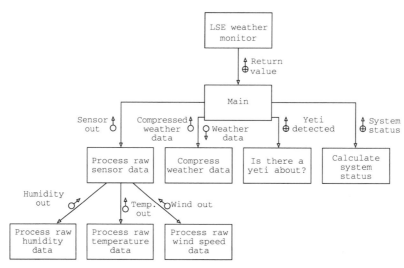

Figure 15.29 The preliminary physical model (structure chart) for the weather monitoring system.

15.5 Review and refinement of the physical model

The review and refinement of the physical model involves consideration of the preliminary structure chart to ensure that this consists of cohesive modules bound by a minimum of coupling.

Coupling is a general measure of how much modules depend on one another. We say that two modules are tightly coupled if there is a great deal of dependence between them. Loosely coupled modules have some interdependence, but the interconnections among modules are weak. Uncoupled modules have no interconnections at all. We wish to minimize the degree of coupling between modules because, as we have discussed in earlier chapters, we want to be able to alter one module (for example, improve its performance) without the effects rippling through the whole system. Similarly, if and when errors do occur, they can spread less easily (and have less impact) in loosely coupled systems.

If coupling is one side of a coin, then cohesion is the other. A module is **cohesive** if all elements of the module are directed toward, and essential for, the performance of the same single task.

We can summarize these important issues in the following familiar three-step guide:

(1) **A module should have a clearly defined task to perform.**

(2) **No module should serve more than one task.**

(3) **No single task should be split between modules.**

The main part of the review and refinement of the preliminary physical model is carried out by considering the first-cut structure chart in the light of these guidelines.

15.5.1 Example: Machine to double numbers

To further illustrate the refinement of the preliminary physical model (Figure 15.30), consider again the 'machine to double numbers' from Section 15.4.3.

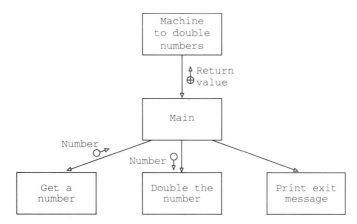

Figure 15.30 The preliminary physical model (structure chart) for the 'machine to double numbers'.

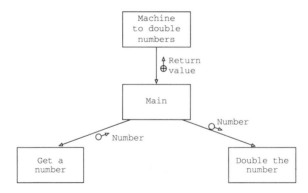

Figure 15.31 The final physical model (structure chart) for the 'machine to double numbers'.

Here, as we review this system, we would probably accept that both modules 'Get a number' and 'Double the number' have well-defined and worthwhile tasks to perform. However, we might well conclude that simply printing an exit message is a rather trivial task for a module ('Print exit message'). Instead, we might decide to display this message at the end of the 'Double the number'.

We would therefore modify the structure chart, as shown in Figure 15.31. This completes the structure chart.

15.5.2 Example: Weather monitoring

To further illustrate the refinement of the preliminary physical model, we again return to consider our weather monitoring system.

The preliminary structure chart is repeated in Figure 15.32 for ease of reference. Examining this structure chart, we can see that the bottom-level processes all serve a

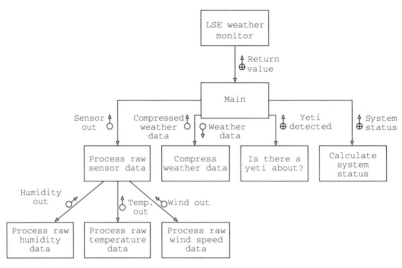

Figure 15.32 The preliminary physical model (structure chart) for the weather monitoring system.

single, well-defined and largely independent purpose. However, while each of these modules is associated with (and, in the CASE tool, linked to) an associated PSpec, there is no associated PSpec for the 'Process raw sensor data' module.

As we refine the preliminary model, we must either create a PSpec for this module, or omit this module from the final physical model. A suitable PSpec might take the form shown in Figure 15.33. As is clear from this figure, the 'Process raw sensor data module' simply calls three further modules. In such circumstances, it is usual to conclude a module has no 'clearly defined task' to perform.

@ *OUT = Sensor out*

@PSpec Process raw sensor data

Pre-condition:
 None.

 Call "Process raw humidity data"
 Call "Process raw temperature data"
 Call "Process raw wind speed data"

Post-condition:
 Got (Sensor out);

@

Figure 15.33 PSpec 1-2 for the 'Process raw sensor data' module.

We would therefore omit this module from the structure chart, replacing it with a group node (Figure 15.34). Note that this processing is not 'lost'; it will now be added to the responsibilities of the Main module, and would be reflected in a modified PSpec. This process is straightforward and is not shown here.

We also take into account the fact that this system will loop 'forever'. This completes the structure chart.

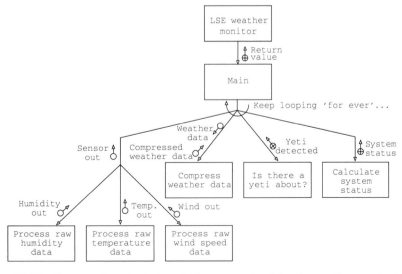

Figure 15.34 The complete physical model (structure chart) for the weather monitoring system.

15.6 Reconciling the physical and logical models

As we have seen in this chapter, the logical and physical models of a system overlap to a great extent. It is important that in this redundant system model, we do not have contradictory information. To avoid this, it is important that work on the physical model is concluded by reconciling the physical and logical system models. This involves annotating the DfD hierarchy to reflect any changes made in the refinement of the structure chart.

In addition, the designer will at this time also extend that data dictionary through the addition of data types (as discussed in Chapter 12).

15.6.1 Example: Machine to double numbers

We modified the structure chart from the 'machine to double numbers' as we reviewed the physical model for this system in Section 15.5.1. As a consequence of this, there is now a contradiction between the structure chart for the system and the corresponding DfD (both reproduced in Figure 15.35).

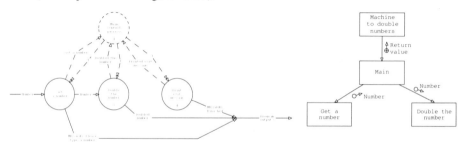

Figure 15.35 The contradiction between the three-process logical model and the two-process physical model.

We need to reconcile the two models by redrawing the DfD as shown in Figure 15.36. The data dictionary developed by the analyst would also be extended at this time to incorporate data types. For example, a fragment of an appropriate dictionary is shown in Table 15.4.

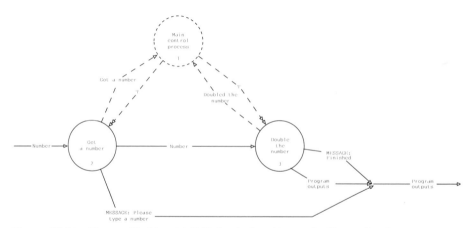

Figure 15.36 The modified Level I DfD for the 'machine to double numbers'.

Name	C/D/S/T	Description	Comment
Got a number	C	[TRUE | FALSE]	–
Number	D	Integer	int
MESSAGE: Finished	D	\'Finished'\	char [9]
User	T	\The user of the program, interacting via keyboard and VDU\	–

Table 15.4 A fragment of the data dictionary for the machine to double numbers.

15.6.2 Example: Weather monitoring

In refining the physical model of the weather monitoring system, we deleted the 'Process raw sensor data' module from the preliminary structure chart.

As in the case of the previous example, we must again make this change clear on the corresponding DfD. We could try to effect this by deleting the 'Process raw sensor data' process, but this would not be helpful. The logical model is intended to show the overall structure of the system: by omitting 'Process raw sensor data' we would, in effect, 'unlevel' the system, and obscure the system structure.

Instead, we make 'Process raw sensor data' an abstract process. This involves renaming the process with a final asterisk on the DfD, as shown in Figure 15.37. Note that abstract processes, highlighted with asterisks, are the only processes on the final DfD that will not have associated PSpecs.

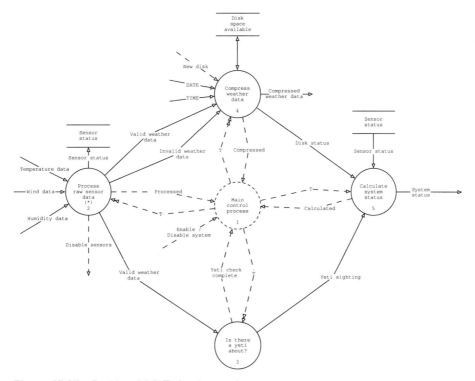

Figure 15.37 Final Level 1 DfD for the weather monitoring system.

Again, we would also extend the data dictionary to include the data types. A fragment of the modified dictionary is given in Table 15.5.

Name	C/D/S/T	Description	Comment
Compressed weather data	S	Compressed weather data	binary file
Compressed weather data	D	\Weather Data which has been compressed\	float
Disable H sensor	C	['TRUE'|'FALSE']	char
Disk status	D	{['0'|'1'] + '0000'}	char [7]
Humid. data	D	\Data from Sensor (NOT YET VALIDATED)\	short
Humidity sensor	T	\LSE humidity sensor, model HEA-23b\	–

Table 15.5 A selection of entries from the data dictionary for the weather monitoring system, after type information has been added.

15.7 The test strategy

We argued in Chapter 11 that programmers in a software team are not appropriate people to define the test strategy. Instead, the basic test plan should be drawn up by the designer before coding begins.

First of all, the test plan needs to include some general statements. For example, for module tests, software houses will typically aim to ensure that the following guidelines are adhered to:

As each module is completed, it will be tested by the programmer, as follows:

(1) White Box testing is performed by reading through the code, line by line, looking for obvious flaws. Details of the tests performed are to be included in the implementation documents and initialled by the tester.

(2) Black Box testing is performed with an individual driver program. Typically, 10% of the parameter range will be tested. Extremes of the input range of all parameters will always be tested. Details of the test performed, and of the results obtained, are to be included with the implementation documents and initialled by the tester.

An example of an appropriate module test form is given in Figure 15.38. It is the responsibility of the team manager to ensure that such forms (or their equivalents) are correctly and usefully used.

In part, the definition of tests is a direct consequence of the semi-formal development process. Because the system design will include a set of PSpecs, these (rather than the code itself) should be used by the test team to define the interface to each module. For example, consider Figure 15.39.

MODULE TEST REPORT	FT1b (function tests)
Module name	*Validate_sonar_signal( )*
Module programmer (or library name)	*Susan Armstrong*
Details of White Box testing performed	*The module implements a simple but adequate version of the Peters algorithm for sonar signal comparison. The 256 lines of code are in standard C++ throughout. The code is well structured and concisely documented.*
Module tester (BLOCK CAPITALS)	*JOHN ARMSTRONG*
Initials of tester	*JA*
Details of Black Box testing performed	*It was possible to use the standard driver function for this module, and to test 100% of the input parameter range. The tests were compared with the outputs expected from the original paper by Peters, and shown to be correct within an accuracy of 0.45%. The specification dictates a 2% accuracy requirement, so the module is deemed acceptable.*
Module tester (BLOCK CAPITALS)	*JOHN ARMSTRONG*
Initials of tester	*JA*

Figure 15.38 An example of a (completed) module test form.

```
@ IN = Disk Status
@ IN = Yeti Sighting Status
@ INOUT = Humidity Sensor Status Information
@ INOUT = Temperature Sensor Status Information
@ INOUT = Wind Speed Sensor Status Information
@ OUT = System Status Information
```

@PSpec Calculate System Status

Pre-condition:
> Valid information is available from all sources

Post-condition:
> System Status Information =
>> (Disk Status)
>> & (Humidity Sensor Status Information)
>> & (Temperature Sensor Status Information)
>> & (Wind Speed Sensor Status Information)
>> & (Yeti Sighting Status)

```
@
```

Figure 15.39 PSpec 1-6 for the original weather monitoring system.

Here the tests would verify that in the C++ function corresponding to the PSpec, an assertion (or equivalent error detection/recovery mechanism) was triggered if, for example, the function was called with a value of 'Humidity Sensor Status Information' that did not satisfy the criteria laid down in the corresponding data dictionary entry:

Name	C/D/S/T	Description
Humidity Sensor Status Information	D	{'000' + ['0'|'1'] + '0'}

In addition, the designer will frequently provide 'test tables', specifying an appropriate range of test data for each module and the corresponding outputs expected.

For example, for the 'Double the number' module in Figure 15.31, the test table might be as shown in Table 15.6.

Input	Output	Return
0	0	0
1000	2000	0
–1000	–2000	0
16383	32766	0
16384	0	–1
–16383	–32766	0
–16384	–32768	0
–16385	0	–1
20000	0	–1
–20000	0	–1

Table 15.6 Test table for the 'Double the number' module.

The selection of appropriate test data is, unfortunately, seldom a trivial exercise. In all cases zeros in the range (for example, null pointers) are good choices, as are the maximum positive and negative values of numerical variables. In more general cases, the judgement of the designer must be used.

15.8 Conclusions

In this chapter, we have explored the six stages of process-oriented design. As we have seen, these stages build on the logical process model developed during analysis, and result in a physical process model ready for implementation.

In the next chapter, we conclude our exploration of process-oriented SADIE by completing a substantial case study tying together all the material from Part I.

Exercises

15.1 Consider the logical process model of the Loughborough Bell Foundry developed in Chapter 13. From this, carry out the six stages necessary to derive a complete process model.

15.2 Building on the process model developed in Exercise 15.1, develop a prototype program for Loughborough Bell Foundry.

15.3 Draw up, in the form of a structure chart, a description of P-O SADIE.

15.4 In the exercises at the end of Chapter 14, you developed the logical model of a car computer system. In the light of the discussions on embedded systems in this chapter, outline how you would design and implement such a system.

15.5 Systems for the control of the latest generation of 'fly by wire' aircraft is an area where safety-critical software development techniques are of fundamental importance. Assume that you have been hired as a consultant to the Leicester Aircraft Corporation (LAC). Given that aircraft systems involve hundreds of thousands of lines of code, how would you suggest that LAC ensure that the aircraft they develop suffer no serious software problems?

16 Case Study: Birstall Bank

16.1 Introduction

We conclude this part of the book with a more substantial example of process-oriented system development using SADIE. The example, described below, will incorporate many of the analysis, design and implementation techniques we have discussed in previous chapters.

A complete version of this project, produced with the CASE tool, is included on the sample disk: details of how to install the project are given in Appendix C.

16.2 Scenario

The Birstall Bank was founded in 1745 by Peter Jones, and has been in the Jones family ever since. The bank has always prided itself on a personal service to its customers and, while other banks have snapped up recent technological innovations like 'hole in the wall' cash dispensers (auto teller machines: ATMs), the Birstall Bank has forsworn such gimmickry. Recently, however, the bank has found itself the subject of a hostile takeover bid, and has decided that enough is enough; it must get to grips with recent advances in technology or it will have to go out of business.

The present owner of Birstall Bank, Joseph Jones, approaches Leicester Software Engineering and asks for help.

16.3 Analysis

We outlined the eleven steps necessary to analyse process-oriented system in Chapter 14. We repeat them here for ease of reference.

(P1) *The business case*
      The analyst begins by estimating the technical and economic feasibility of the project. If, for example, the project is too small to be profitable, greatly outside the experience of the available personnel, or larger than can be tackled with the available technical and human resources, then it must be rejected at this stage.

(P2) *The Context diagram*

The Context diagram is produced. Particular care is taken in the selection of appropriate terminators.

(P3) *The user interface*

Because of the impact of the system interface on all aspects of the model, it is sketched (or prototyped) at this early stage.

(P4) *The process list*

A process list is drawn up. This list is necessarily very provisional, and creation of a highly polished document is not appropriate at this stage.

(P5) *The walkthrough*

A system walkthrough is performed. Where feasible, the entire development team (analysts, designers, programmers) should be involved in this process. As the walkthrough progresses, the process list, Context diagram and interface sketches are modified as required.

(P6) *The Level 1 dataflow diagram*

A preliminary Level 1 DfD is sketched, on the basis of the process list. It is usually inappropriate to polish this diagram, as it may change substantially when the STD is considered. For this reason, it is usual include only processes at this stage, and a bare minimum of dataflows. Note that while a Level 1 DfD is usually all that is required, on a large system you may need to go further.

(P7) *The state-transition diagram*

The state-transition diagram associated with the Level 1 DfD is produced in an iterative process involving successive modifications to both STD and DfD, as necessary. For (rare) pure 'batch' programs, where no STD is used, this stage may be omitted, while for larger systems, a network of STDs may be required.

(P8) *The dataflow diagram hierarchy*

The DfD hierarchy is completed, and levelled as necessary.

(P9) *The process specifications*

The process specifications are written.

(P10) *The data dictionary*

The data dictionary is completed.

(P11) *The balanced logical model*

The complete model is reviewed, checked and balanced. Any necessary supporting documentation is written.

16.3.1 The business case

The analyst begins by estimating the technical and economic feasibility of the project. If, for example, the project is too small to be profitable, greatly outside the experience of the available personnel, or larger than can be tackled with the available technical and human resources, then it must be rejected at this stage.

After a brief initial discussion, Jane agrees that LSE are able and willing to help Birstall Bank with their problem. Mr Jones is a little concerned that the system he requires involves a combination of hardware and software: Jane reassures him that the techniques she uses are largely implementation independent. She explains that LSE will develop a complete specification for the whole system, both hardware and software. From these specifications, Jane will sub-contract the required hardware construction work to a local electronics company, on behalf of the bank. After further discussions, Mr. Jones agrees to this.

From past experience, Jane estimates that the final prototype program will contain approximately 1000 lines of code. She knows that, on average, not more than ten lines of code will be written per day on this type of real-time project. (This may seem like a low figure but is a realistic estimate for this type of project. The figure is calculated based on the whole project duration, including planning phases, when no coding will take place.) On this basis she suggests a project duration of approximately 100 person days. She habitually allows an extra 20% for unforeseen problems. She charges the company time at £250.00 per person day, giving a total labour charge of £30 000. In addition, there will be a further charge, of not more than £5000, for agreed expenses (travel costs, consumables, and so on). In her letter tendering for the contract, Jane explains that this fee does not include final implementation of the system (hardware or software); these parts of the project will be subject to separate negotiation.

Joseph Jones haggles a little over the fee. Eventually, a price of £28 000, plus up to £4000 for receipted expenses, is settled on. A contract is drawn up, a first formal meeting is arranged, and Jane gets to work.

16.3.2 The Context diagram

The Context diagram is produced. Particular care is taken in the selection of appropriate terminators.

Jane draws up the Context diagram shown in Figure 16.1, to begin to clarify the system requirements. She discusses the diagram with Mr Jones, and he asks her to clarify the

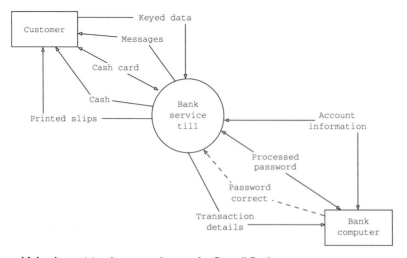

Figure 16.1 A provisional context diagram for Birstall Bank.

precise meaning of some of the dataflows, particularly the data being transmitted to and from the bank computer. 'One can't be too careful, young lady. Our customers' details must remain secure.'

By this point, Jane has done her homework: she has ascertained that each Birstall Bank customer has a bank cash card which holds their account number (encoded on the metal strip at the rear). When the card is inserted into an appropriate card reader, the account number can be read.

Jane reassures Mr Jones that the user passwords are not stored on the plastic cards. The password is stored on the bank computer and never revealed. She explains, with reference to the provisional Context diagram (Figure 16.1) that the customer types in their password. This is processed (to make sure it is the right length, and so on), and then (suitably encoded) is forwarded to the bank computer. On receipt of the encoded password, the bank computer will decode it, and will send back a control signal indicating only that the password was correct, or that it was wrong.

Jane explains that the user will only be allowed three attempts to get the password correct: if they fail to do so, then the card will be retained (Figure 16.2).

Rather than being mollified by Jane's explanation of the security system, Mr Jones seems increasingly agitated. 'Let us suppose,' he says, 'that a young gentleman travels to Birstall with the intention of partaking freely of the local ale. On passing our bank, he realizes that he has neglected to bring with him any money: he therefore decides to make a withdrawal, via our new "hole in the wall" facility.'

Mr Jones shudders visibly before continuing. 'Now, just for the sake of our conversation, let us assume that our young gentleman has a joint account and that his wife, unbeknown to him, has that very day withdrawn all the money from the account, in order to pay an overdue gas bill. Of course, under these conditions, when our young man inserts his card into your machine, requests a sum of let us say fifty pounds, he

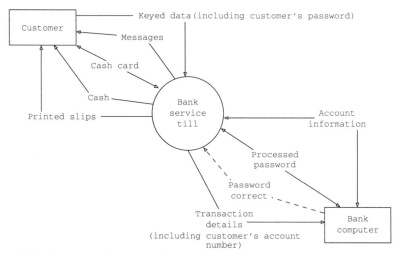

Figure 16.2 An annotated version of the provisional Context diagram, showing details of the security features included in the password entry process.

will be denied this request, being at the same time advised to make contact, as soon as practical, with his own branch to discuss the possibility of an overdraft facility.

'Now, let us further suppose that this young man is of a violent temperament. He objects to being offered advice by the machine (which he is inclined to assume is malfunctioning anyway) and responds by, shall we say, reprogramming your machine with his rather solid boots, causing it to disgorge freely of its monetary supplies all over the Birstall pavement?'

Mr Jones is clearly a little shaken by the thought of this

'I appreciate your concerns, Mr Jones,' Jane says, soothingly. 'What we need to do to avoid this problem is to check the hardware regularly. In the event that any error occurs, we will simply shut down the machine.'

Jane adds the hardware checking feature to the Context diagram (Figure 16.3). Mr Jones seems a little happier about the security implications of the system in the light of these modifications.

16.3.3 The user interface

Because of the impact of the system interface on all aspects of the model, it is sketched (or prototyped) at this early stage.

Birstall Bank require a complete solution to this problem, including the specification (and, ultimately, implementation) of both software and associated hardware. Jane's expertise lies in the field of software engineering, but she knows of a local firm (Leicester Hardware Engineering, LHE) that specializes in computer hardware. She'll be able to sub-contract the order for the relevant hardware to LHE, but in order to do so she'll need to be clear precisely what is required.

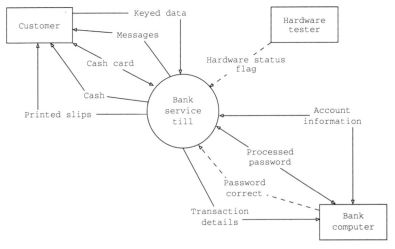

Figure 16.3 A modified Context diagram, incorporating additional features for checking the hardware status.

In this case, the hardware and software solutions to Jane's problem are clearly very closely interrelated. For instance, the user will not be presented with a standard alphanumeric keyboard in this application: therefore, normal problems (such as the user typing in a letter instead of a number in response to a prompt) simply cannot arise. Also, Jane will be able to have certain keys labelled (for instance) 'Quit' which the customer will be able to use at any time instead of having to type, say, Q U I T ↵.

Jane begins, therefore, by drawing up a crude sketch of the hardware she plans to order for the system (Figure 16.4). Jane's sketch attempts to illustrate the most important features of the ATM interface. At the heart of this there is a small monitor screen; this will provide the user with instructions in the use of the equipment. Around the screen, Jane plans to position four push softkeys. The precise function of these softkeys will vary depending where the user is in the program: for instance, in Jane's first sketch (Figure 16.4) she have drawn the screen as it will appear after the user has entered her password, and is being prompted to choose from one of four possible services, viz. delivery of cash, delivery of a printed mini-statement or balance, and ordering a cheque book. To order cash, for example, the user would press the top left of the four buttons; this would then reveal a new screen (not shown) prompting for details of the cash amount.

Jane assumes that both receipts and mini-statements, if requested, are delivered through the 'Paper Slot'.

Two other important features of the interface are the small numeric keypad, through which the user will type in her password and cash amounts, and the slot through which the card is inserted.

By using the general purpose (unlabelled) softkeys around the screen, Jane has allowed some flexibility. For instance, if the machine has run out of paper, it will still be able to offer cash (without a printed receipt), and will still be able to order a cheque book, but will not be able to provide a printed balance or a printed mini-statement. In this event, the output screen would only offer the available choices (Figure 16.5).

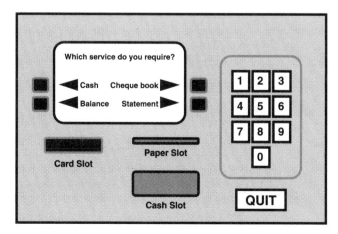

Figure 16.4 A first sketch of the developing ATM interface.

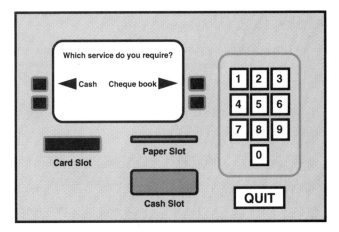

Figure 16.5 Another sketch of the first version of the ATM interface, showing the 'services' screen when there is no printer paper available.

16.3.4 The process list

A process list is drawn up. This list is necessarily very provisional, and creation of a highly polished document is not appropriate at this stage.

At this meeting, Jane discusses with Joseph Jones the problems that Birstall Bank faces. During this meeting, she draws up a list of the processes that her ATM will have to perform (Table 16.1).

Process name	Notes
Dispense cash	As far as the customer is concerned, this is the main purpose of the machine. Allows the customer to order cash from the machine. Cash will be available, in multiples of £10, up to the balance in the customer's account. Where an overdraft facility is in force, then the amount of cash available is determined by the balance available plus the overdraft limit.
Print balance	Print out a slip showing the balance of the customer's account.
Print mini-statement	Print out a 'mini-statement' detailing the last 10 transactions on the customer's account.
Order cheque book	Allow the customer to place an order for a new cheque book. The cheque book won't actually be printed by the machine, but will be sent by post within the next few days from Birstall Bank's main branch.
Get card	Prompt the customer to enter their bank card in the card reader. Read the account details from the card, if possible.
Validate card	Check with the bank computer that the customer's card has not been stolen. If it has, then retain the card. If the card is out of date, then retain the card. If the card is from a different bank or of the wrong type, eject the card. If the card is damaged, eject the card.
Enter password	Prompt the user to enter a password. Read the password.

Table 16.1 Initial process list for Birstall Bank ATM.

Process name	Notes
Validate password	Check with the bank computer that the entered password is correct. Note: security is paramount here …
Eject card	Return the card from the card reader to the customer.
Retain card	'Swallow' the customer's card. Tell the customer to contact their branch.
Check hardware	Check the hardware for damage. If any damage is detected, display an 'out of order' message. Call the engineer. Shut down the machine. Note: this is a constant process, implemented externally. An interrupt will be raised in the event of an error.
Call engineer	Contact the bank engineer.
Manual shutdown	A manual 'off' switch is provide for bank personnel (e.g. for use when replenishing the cash reserves). This will shut down the machine.
Shut down	Shut down the machine. Notify the bank computer that the machine has been shut down, indicating the cause (e.g. manual, or hardware failure).
Pre-customer system checks	Check the hardware (to be on the safe side). Check the cash and paper reserves. Display an appropriate welcome banner.

Table 16.1 *Continued.*

16.3.5 The walkthrough

A system walkthrough is performed. Where feasible, the entire development team (analysts, designers, programmers) should be involved in this process. As the walkthrough progresses, the process list, context diagram and interface sketches are modified as required.

Jane typically conducts walkthroughs at many stages of project development. Here, she simply wants to 'try out' the Birstall Bank ATM, to begin to see how it *might* perform in practice. She imagines a typical scenario as follows:

A customer approaches the ATM. At this point, the machine has already (while idle) checked its hardware condition, cash reserves (these were okay), and its reserves of printer paper (also okay).

If, for example, there was no cash AND no paper available, the initial screen would look as follows:

Welcome to Birstall Bank Cash Machine

This machine has no cash available at present:
Birstall Bank apologise for any inconvenience caused

This machine cannot print receipts at present:
Birstall Bank apologise for any inconvenience caused

Please insert your card:

If a hardware fault had been detected, the screen that greeted the virtual customer would look something like this:

> ### Welcome to Birstall Bank Cash Machine
> *This machine is not currently in service:*
> *Birstall Bank apologise for any inconvenience caused*

However, on this occasion, Jane assumes that all is well, so that the initial screen is:

> ### Welcome to Birstall Bank Cash Machine
>
> *Please insert your card:*

The virtual customer duly inserts his card. The machine responds with:

> ### Thank you

The ATM checks again that its hardware is undamaged: this check is successful, so the machine goes on to confirm that the card is a Birstall Bank card: it is, so the ATM calls the bank computer. This call confirms that the card has not been reported stolen. Having carried out these checks, the ATM is ready to continue.

> ### Please enter your password:
>
> — — — —

The customer duly types in his password: it appears on the screen, as asterisks:

> ### Please enter your password:
>
> * * * *
> — — — —

The ATM now has the customer's account number (read from the cash card) and the customer's unverified password. The password and account number are sent back to the central bank computer: if the password is incorrect, the user will be given two more attempts to get it right: if he does not, then the card will be retained in the machine (in case it is stolen, and a thief is trying to guess the number); the machine will then reset itself, and prepare for the next customer. Of course, if Birstall Bank wished to do so, they could allow users a larger or smaller number of password attempts before card confiscation.

The customer might also choose to press the 'Quit' button at this point; if he does, then his card will be returned to him, before the machine prepares for the next customer.

Jane makes a note to herself at this point to make sure that the number of password attempts is relayed to the bank computer: otherwise a thief could simply try two numbers, quit, then try a further two numbers and so on until the correct password was uncovered.

On this occasion, Jane assumes that the user types in the correct password. The next screen is as follows:

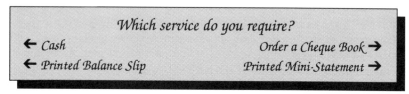

Note that if the ATM had no cash available, then the '← Cash' option would not be offered. Similarly, if there was no paper available for printing the balance or the mini-statement, then these options too would be omitted. In the event, therefore, that neither cash nor printer paper were available, then only the 'Order a Cheque Book →' option would be available.

At this point, Jane assumes that the user chooses 'Cash' (by pressing the appropriate button, adjacent to the screen, as shown in Figure 16.5). The screen then becomes:

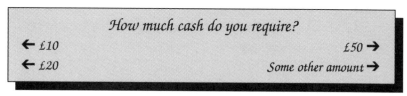

The customer strikes the button adjacent to the '£50 →' label. However, Jane assumes that from the customer's bank account details (previously copied to the ATM from the bank computer), it is clear that the customer only has £45.23 in his account. The ATM therefore responds with the following screen:

> *Sorry – the requested amount exceeds your credit limit.*
> *Please contact your branch if a higher limit is required.*

Jane considers displaying the available cash limit, but decide that this could be embarrassing for the customer (if someone is looking over their shoulder as they operate the machine, for example). If the customer requires this information it is available, discretely, through the 'Print balance' option.

Following display of this screen, the system will return to the main menu; if the user wishes to order cash again, he may do so as before.

Jane assumes that the customer perseveres. This time, however, he strikes the key adjacent to 'Some other amount →'. This produces the following screen:

> *How much cash do you require?*
> *Please enter the appropriate amount (a multiple of £10) on the keypad, then*
> *???*

Clearly, something is wrong. The customer is only permitted to order cash in multiples of £10.00 because the cash machine will contain only £10.00, £20.00, and £100.00

notes. Jane makes a note to herself at this point that the ATM needs to have an 'Enter' key adjacent to the keypads, so that the customer can indicate that he has finished entering data. Such a key is not needed for password entry (a fixed number of digits) but without it, entry of a variable cash amount would be very clumsy.

Jane therefore modifies her draft screen layout as shown in Figure 16.6, taking the opportunity to make some other features of the interface clearer. Assuming that the 'Enter' button has been added, Jane sketches the last screen again:

> *How much cash do you require?*
>
> *Please enter the appropriate amount (a multiple of £10)*
> *on the keypad, then press the 'Enter' key:*
>
> _____

Jane now assumes that her customer types in a request for £40.00. The amount requested is echoed to the screen:

> *How much cash do you require?*
>
> *Please enter the appropriate amount (a multiple of £10)*
> *on the keypad, then press the 'Enter' key:*
>
> *£40.00*

The ATM has already ascertained (Jane assumes) that the customer has sufficient reserves in his account to allow a withdrawal of this amount. The withdrawal is therefore authorized, and the following screen is displayed:

> *Would you like a receipt with this transaction?*
>
> *Yes →*
> *No →*

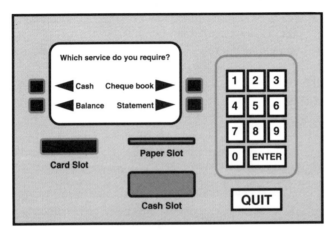

Figure 16.6   A second version of the ATM interface.

The customer is given an option here of receiving a printed receipt detailing the cash delivery (some customers are reassured by such receipts: it makes them less concerned that the machine will give them, say, £30.00 and debit their account by £300.00 ...). The ATM prints receipts (if required) and returns them to the customer along with any requested cash withdrawal.

The customer elects to have a receipt:

> *Please take your cash and receipt*

After a few seconds the next screen is displayed.

> *Would you like another service?*
>
> *Yes* →
>
> *No* →

The customer selects 'Yes':

> *Which service do you require?*
>
> *Order a Cheque Book* →
>
> ← *Printed Balance Slip*   *Printed Mini-Statement* →

To avoid the user ordering (for instance) more than one cheque book (Birstall Bank prefers that its customers only have one cheque book in operation at any particular time), or multiple mini-statements (which would use up a lot of paper) during a single transaction, the user is to be allowed to use each service only once during any single transaction.

Jane looks carefully at the previous two screens in her 'simulation'. The use of the screen-side buttons is working well and is allowing her to use the same physical switch for multiple purposes without difficulty. However, she realizes that there is no room for expansion in the present layout. Particularly, while it might be comparatively straightforward to change the software to allow the user additional options during their transaction, there are no 'spare' buttons to support such a choice. In particular, Jane considers say, offering 'cash with receipt' and 'cash without receipt' as two separate options on the main menu. This would avoid the need for an additional screen prompting the user to make this decision and, because cash delivery is a popular option, may increase the throughput of customers. Jane decides, therefore, to increase the number of screen-side buttons from four to six.

Jane also note that the use of the 'Quit' key may cause problems in its present situation. She wants to allow the user to exit the program when required; however, if an attempt was made to do so, say, while cash was being prepared for delivery, the user might expect that no delivery would take place and that no deductions would be made from the bank account: this, however, might be impossible to arrange in practice. The result would be either that the 'Quit' key appeared slow to operate, or appeared entirely inoperative.

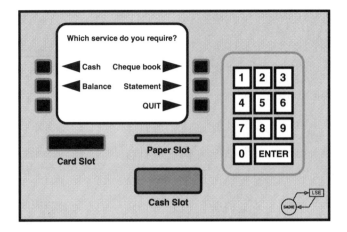

Figure 16.7 A third (and final) version of the ATM interface. The number of screen-side keys has been increased to six (cf. four), in order to increase the speed at which the current functions are executed, and to allow for possible future expansion. This change has also allowed the 'Quit' key to be incorporated into the main screen: this prevents the user from trying to exit from the system at inappropriate times.

Jane decides that the operation of the 'Quit' key would be more obvious to the user if this option was only made available at points in the program from which it was possible to exit neatly; in this event, the 'Quit' key would be better as another 'soft' key.

Jane makes the necessary changes to her draft screen layout as shown in Figure 16.7.

For her new interface, the original menu (assuming that adequate supplies of both cash and printer paper are available) would now appear as follows:

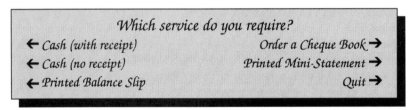

However, to our (by now rather bemused) first virtual customer, who has already had some cash dispensed, the screen now looks as follows:

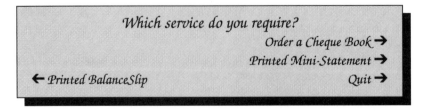

This time, Jane assumes that her customer chooses to 'Order a Cheque Book'. The resulting screen is as follows:

> *Your cheque book will be posted to you*

This screen remains for a few seconds, then is replaced by the following:

> *Which service do you require?*
>
> *Printed Mini-Statement* →
>
> *Printed Balance Slip*   *Quit* →

The remaining two operations are very similar in format.

The printed balance slip will look something like the example shown in Figure 16.8. The mini-statement gives details of the last 10 transactions on the appropriate account. For example, see Figure 16.9.

Jane assumes that her virtual customer has asked for both a balance and a mini-statement, then the main menu he is presented with will eventually be as follows:

Figure 16.8   A sample 'Balance' printout.

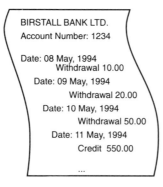

Figure 16.9   A sample 'Mini-Statement' printout.

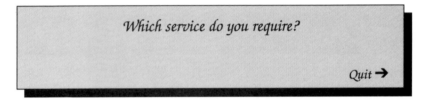

Having little option but to do so (if he wants his card back), we assume that our customer chooses 'Quit ➔'. The final screen is then as follows:

Thank you for using this service till
Please take your card

Jane assumes that, if her virtual customer hesitates for more than 60 seconds at any screen, he will be asked if he wants to continue. If he does not reply, then she will assume that he has wandered off, and she will retain his card.

Finally, assuming the customer 'quits' normally, the machine will complete some further checks, in preparation for the next customer. When these checks are complete, it will display once more the opening menu.

At this point, Jane feels she has a better understanding of the system.

Reviewing the process list at this time, Jane decides that some of the processes can be sensibly grouped together. In fact, she decides there are really five fundamental processes:

- Deliver customer services (deliver cash, print mini-statements, order cheque books and display account balance);
- Process cash card (read the customer's card; eject the card; swallow the card);
- Process password (check that the customer's password is valid, by contacting the bank computer);
- Check the machine's paper and cash supplies (can't deliver cash if the machine is empty; similarly, can't print receipts if the machine has no printer paper left);
- Check the status of the hardware (if the hardware is damaged, the machine must shut down at once).

Jane then turns her attention to the Context diagram (Figure 16.3). Clearly, she now realizes, the use of 'Customer' as a terminator is neither appropriate nor helpful. Her software will not interact with the customer 'directly' (as Figure 16.3 implies), but instead will do so via the hardware components of her system. She modifies her original Context diagram to reflect this fact (Figure 16.10).

16.3.6   The Level 1 dataflow diagram

A preliminary Level 1 DfD is sketched, on the basis of the process list. It is usually inappropriate to polish this diagram, as it may change substantially when the STD is considered. For this reason, it is usual to include only processes at this stage, and a bare minimum of dataflows. Note that while a Level 1 DfD is usually all that is required, on a large system you may need to go further.

The modified process list is reflected in the preliminary Level 1 DfD (Figure 16.11).

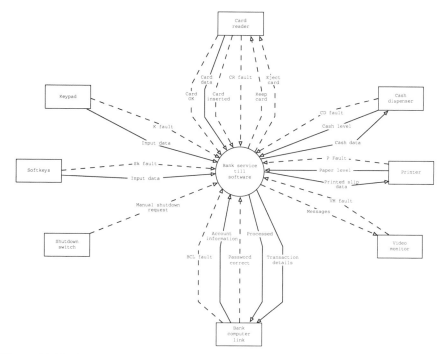

Figure 16.10   The final Context diagram.

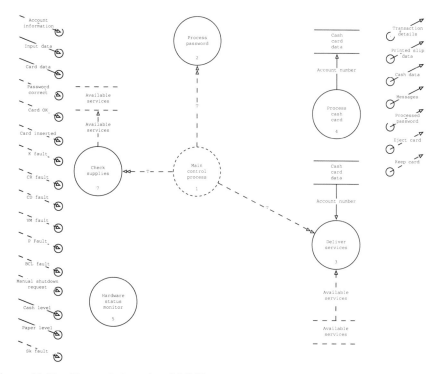

Figure 16.11   The preliminary Level I DfD.

16.3.7 The state-transition diagram

> *The state-transition diagram associated with the Level 1 DfD is produced in an iterative process involving successive modifications to both STD and DfD, as necessary. For (rare) pure 'batch' programs, where no STD is used, this stage may be omitted, while for larger systems, a network of STDs may be required.*

In this case, Jane finds that she needs a number of STDs to model. First of all, she develops the 'Main control process' STD, and simultaneously polishes the Level 1 DfD. The result of this work is shown in Figures 16.12 and 16.13.

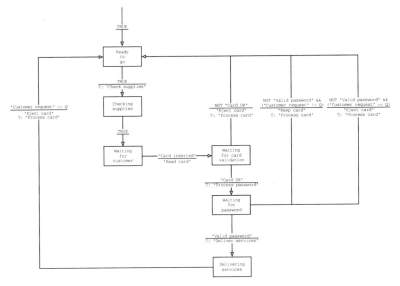

Figure 16.12 The 'Main control process' STD.

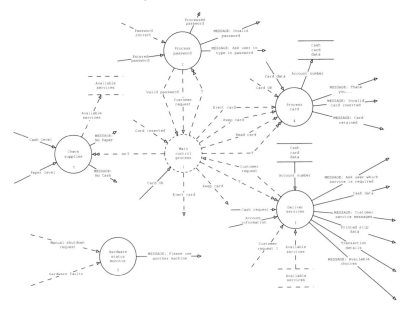

Figure 16.13 The polished Level 1 DfD.

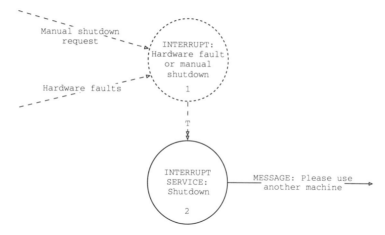

Figure 16.14 DfD 1-5.

There are several other STDs controlling the DfD hierarchy, but only the control of the hardware checking will be considered here.

Note that, as Jane has drawn Figure 16.13, the 'Hardware status monitor' process is isolated from the other processes in the system. The operation of the process is made clearer if we consider the next layer of DfDs (Figure 16.14). Here the control process 'INTERRUPT: Hardware fault or manual shutdown' forms the heart of a simple interrupt service process. The activation of the process 'INTERRUPT SERVICE: Shutdown' is in turn mediated through the STD in diagram 1-5-1, shown in Figure 16.15.

The interrupt routine provides one way of modelling the immediate disabling of the machine, no matter what state it is in at the time the fault is detected.

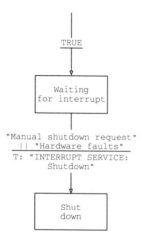

Figure 16.15 STD 1-5-1.

16.3.8 The dataflow diagram hierarchy

The DfD hierarchy is completed, and levelled as necessary.

The remainder of the DfD and STD hierarchy is developed at this stage. The results are shown in Figures 16.16 to 16.19.

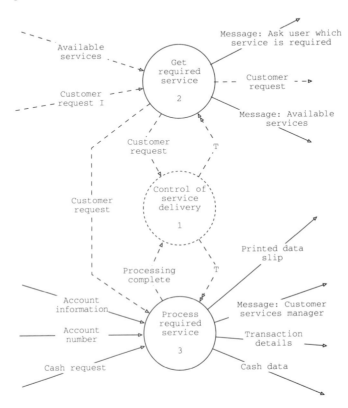

Figure 16.16 DfD 1-3.

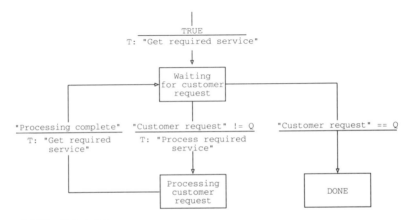

Figure 16.17 STD 1-3-1.

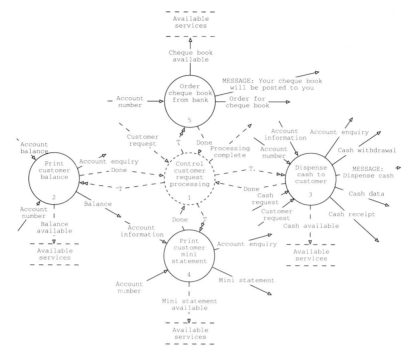

Figure 16.18   DfD 1-3-3.

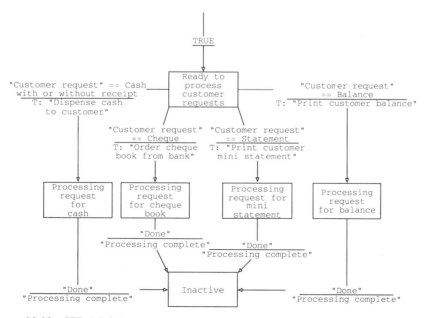

Figure 16.19   STD 1-3-3-1.

16.3.9 The process specifications

The process specifications are written.

Following the completion of the DfD hierarchy, Jane turns her attention to the process specifications. Here, we present only a representative example, PSpec 1-3-2 ('Get Required Service'). A complete set of PSpecs is included on the CD.

PSpec 1-3-2 is shown in Figure 16.20. To clarify the operation of this process, Jane includes with it a sample output screen (Figure 16.21).

@ *IN = Available services*
@ *IN = Customer request I*
@ *OUT = Customer request*
@ *OUT = MESSAGE: Ask user which service is required*
@ *OUT = MESSAGE: Available choices*

@PSpec Get required service

// Generates simple menu (containing only the available options)
// and returns a valid choice

Pre-condition:
    None

    (MESSAGE: Ask user which service is required) = "Which service do you require?"
    (MESSAGE: Available choices) = list of (Available services)
    (Customer request) = (Customer request 1)

Post-condition:
    (Customer request) is a valid choice
@

Figure 16.20   PSpec 1-3-2.

If the design of the user interface is an important component of your specification, then the use of 'screen shots' and other supporting textual and graphic material can help make the requirements for the developing product explicit to your client, and to your colleagues.

                     Which service do you require
← *Cash (with receipt*   *Order a Cheque Book* →
← *Cash (no receipt)*   *Printed Mini-Statement* →
← *Printed Balance Slip*   *Quit* →

Figure 16.21   Sample output screen generated through PSpec 1-3-2.

16.3.10 The data dictionary

The data dictionary is completed.

Finally, Jane draws up the data dictionary (Table 16.2).

Name	C/D/S/T	Description
Account balance	D	\Balance of funds available in the customer account\
Account number	D	\6 digit number uniquely identifying the customer's account\
Available services	C	(Cash available) + (Cash receipt available) + (Mini statement available) + (Cheque book available) + (Balance available)
Available services control store	CS	Unrecoverable hardware fault detected + Available services
Balance available	C	['TRUE'¦'FALSE']
Cash	D	\Cash dispensed to customer\
Cash request	D	\Cash amount requested by customer\
Cash card	D	\Customer's cash card\
Done	C	['TRUE'¦'FALSE']
Entered password	D	1{'Number'}
Hardware status flag	C	['0'¦'1']+['0'¦'1']+['0'¦'1']
MESSAGE: Your cheque book will be posted to you	D	0{'Any Valid Character'}80
Mini-statement	D	\Paper print-out of last ten transactions\
Order for cheque book	D	\Requests bank for a new cheque book\
Valid password	C	['TRUE'¦'FALSE']

Table 16.2 Selections from the data dictionary.

16.3.11 The balanced logical model

The complete model is reviewed, checked and balanced. Any necessary supporting documentation is written.

Jane reviews the model, and notes down the details of her meeting with Joseph Jones. She uses the CASE tool to check that the project is balanced, as outlined in Chapter 13 (it is).

16.4 Design

Responsibility for the design of the system passes to Stephanie. As outlined in Chapter 15, Steph has six main steps to perform, beginning where Jane finished:

(P12) *Review and refinement of the logical model*
The specification documents are reviewed (by the design team), in order to gain an understanding of the system and to correct any flaws in the logical model.

(P13) *The software and hardware architecture*
The operating environment (hardware and/or operating system) and the basic software architecture are determined. General design decisions are made.

(P14) *The preliminary physical model*
   The preliminary structure chart is derived from the logical model.

(P15) *Review and refinement of the physical model*
   The provisional physical model is inspected, and issues of module coupling and cohesion are considered.

(P16) *Reconciliation of the logical and physical models*
   Logical and physical models are compared and adjusted as necessary to ensure that they are fully compatible.

(P17) *The test strategy*
   The overall system test strategy is drawn up.

The work conducted by Steph at each stage is detailed below.

16.4.1 Review and refinement of the logical model

The specification documents are reviewed (by the programming team), in order to gain an understanding of the system and to correct any flaws in the logical model.

We assume that this review is quickly and successfully completed.

16.4.2 The software and hardware architecture

The operating environment (hardware and/or operating system) and the basic software architecture are determined. General design decisions are made.

Steph is aware that the hardware used in the final system will be decided during later negotiations with Birstall Bank staff. At present, she is required to prototype the software on a standard desktop computer.
   Her main concern is nonetheless with the hardware-based security features of the system, and in particular the way that the interrupts specified by Jane in her logical model can be made a reality in the final system.
   According to Jane's model, a manual shutdown request and (more significantly) a hardware fault will immediately cause the system to shutdown (Figure 16.22).

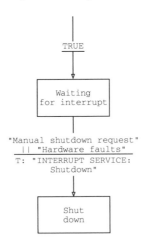

Figure 16.22   STD 1-5-1.

In practice, as Steph is only too aware, this will be difficult to achieve. In addition, because of the differences in interrupt systems between different microprocessor ranges, she knows it will be difficult for her to specify a general, portable, implementation-independent design. She is therefore forced to make a provisional decision at this early stage about the hardware upon which the final system will be implemented.

In consultation with Harry, Steph decides that the system is likely to be based around the Motorola 680×0 family of microprocessors. The 680×0 family, such as the 68000, are powerful and cost effective: importantly for Steph's application, they support a fast **vectored**, interrupt system. What this means is that a change in the voltage of one pin on the 68000 (actually, three pins, but we can ignore this added complexity) can be used to signal that a hardware fault has been detected, and a vector, given over a number of data pins, can be used to identify, if necessary, the particular device (such as the card reader or cash dispenser) that caused the error. Appropriate action can then be taken. Further details of the use of interrupts in this way are given by Lawrence and Mauch (1988).

16.4.3 The preliminary physical model

The preliminary structure chart is derived from the logical model.

For the process design itself, Steph develops the structure chart shown in Figure 16.23. The process of developing this chart is straightforward, and we won't repeat the stages involved here.

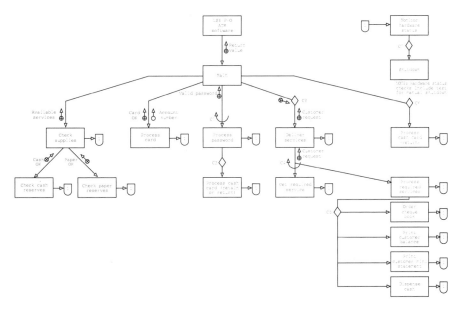

Figure 16.23 The structure chart. Conditions – C1: Keep calling 'Process password' until the user enters a valid password, the maximum number of password attempts is exceeded or the user opts to quit; C2: If the user exceeds the number of allowed password attempts, retain his or her card; C3: Only call this module if a valid card and password have been entered, and user hasn't opted to quit; C4: Keep looping until user opts to quit; C5: Call the appropriate option, depending on 'User choice'; C6: Only call this module if the card has not already been retained; C7: Only call 'Shutdown' if a hardware fault has been detected.

It is worth noting how Steph has modelled the interrupt routine in the structure chart. Here, she has assumed simply that every module, as it is called, will check for interrupts. This is a simple, but generally effective, way of modelling the required result.

16.4.4 Review and refinement of the physical model

The provisional physical model is inspected, and issues of module coupling and cohesion are considered.

Steph reviews the physical model. As she does so, she notes that the structure chart (Figure 16.23) implies incorrectly that the ATM will operate only once and then shut down. She modifies the chart to make it explicit that the program should operate in a loop until either a manual shutdown request is received, or a hardware fault occurs (Figure 16.24).

16.4.5 Reconciliation of the logical and physical models

Logical and physical models are compared and adjusted as necessary to ensure that they are fully compatible.

No modifications to either model are required.

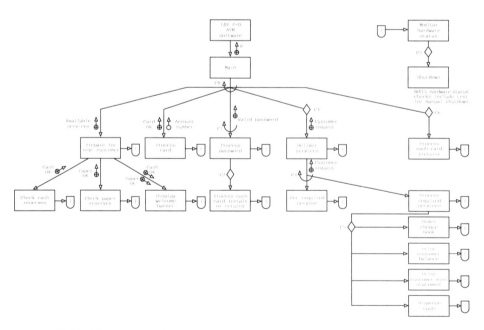

Figure 16.24 The structure chart. Conditions – C0: Keep looping until user chooses to quit; C1: Keep calling 'Process password' until the user enters a valid password, the maximum number of password attempts is exceeded or the user opts to quit; C2: If the user exceeds the number of allowed password attempts, retain his or her card; C3: Only call this module if a valid card and password have been entered, and user hasn't opted to quit; C4: Keep looping until user opts to quit; C5: Call the appropriate option, depending on 'User choice'; C6: Only call this module if the card has not already been retained; C7: Only call 'Shutdown' if a hardware fault has been detected.

16.4.6 The test strategy

The overall system test strategy is drawn up.

Steph includes the following general statement on the required test strategy:

As implementation of each module is completed, it will be tested by the programmer, as follows:

(1) *White Box testing is performed by reading through the code, line by line, looking for obvious flaws. Details of the tests performed are to be included in the implementation documents and initialled by the tester.*

(2) *Black Box testing is performed with an individual driver program. Typically, 10% of the parameter range will be tested. Extremes of the input range of all parameters will always be tested. Details of the test performed, and of the results obtained, are to be included with the implementation documents and initialled by the tester.*

As this is purely a prototype system, she considers that a set of field trials will be more generally useful than further, more specific module tests. These trials, she suggests, should first be carried out by Harry, then by herself, and then by some representatives of Birstall Bank.

Steph is still concerned about the security and reliability of the system, since this is clearly of paramount importance in this application. She notes that when the final system is assembled, it will be important to conduct a detailed series of tests.

In particular, she highlights the following:

- Buffering of data transfers to the central computer system will be an important consideration. If, for example, the cash is dispensed before this fact is notified to the central computer, then the possibility exists that an unscrupulous customer could request a large amount of cash, and – immediately afterwards – damage the dispenser. In these circumstances, it is possible that the cash obtained would not be charged to the customer's account.

- Various invasive tests will need to be performed using the final software/hardware system at all stages in the operation of the program. For example, physical blows, electrical fields, chemical solvents, water and fire attacks will all have to be considered.

- Suppose that a thief physically removes the ATM machine from its wall mounting. In doing so, it is conceivable that access to the central computer system may become possible through an exposed wiring loom. It is important to guard against this possibility.

16.5 Implementation

Responsibility for the implementation of the system passes to Harry. As outlined in Chapter 11, Harry has seven main steps to perform. These steps begin where the design phase ended:

(P18) *Review and refinement of the physical model*
The design documents are reviewed, in order to gain an understanding of the system, and to correct any flaws in the physical model.

(P19) *The system framework*

The code framework is created, using CppSpecs, based on the structure chart and the PSpecs. For some systems, a prototype hardware framework may also be required.

(P20) *The preliminary modules*

The preliminary modules are created or, preferably, recycled from a code library. In either case, the resulting function will build on the CppSpecs, and will make reference to the physical model (particularly the PSpecs and the data dictionary).

(P21) *Error detection and recovery*

The preliminary modules are extended, where necessary, through the addition of appropriate error detection and correction features.

(P22) *Module tests*

The modules are tested, by the programmers, according to the test strategy produced by the design team. Modifications are made as required.

(P23) *The prototype system*

The tested modules are assembled into a prototype system, as dictated by the structure chart(s).

(P24) *System tests and maintenance*

The complete prototype is tested again, first by the programmers and then by the test team, both working from the test strategy produced by the designers. The system is then subjected to user tests, including field tests and/or acceptance tests. The system is revised as necessary; any changes made during the testing and subsequent ongoing maintenance are recorded and reflected in the evolving process model.

16.5.1   Review and refinement of the physical model

The design documents are reviewed, in order to gain an understanding of the system and to correct any flaws in the physical model.

Harry reviews the work carried out by Steph, and finds it is of the usual high standard ...

16.5.2   The system framework

The code framework is created, using CppSpecs, based on the structure chart and the PSpecs. For some systems, a prototype hardware framework may also be required.

The code framework Harry develops is given in Program 16.1.

```
/ * * * * * * * * * * * * * * * * * * * * * * * * * * * * * * * * * * * * * * * * * * * * * * * * * * * * * *
*                                                                         *
* A Bank Service Till (ATM) Simulation (Process-Oriented)      *
*                                                                         *
* Source is:    16_01.CPP                                       *
* Created:      04 April, 1994                                  *
* Last edited:  30 June, 1995                                   *
*                                                                         *
* * * * * * * * * * * * * * * * * * * * * * * * * * * * * * * * * * * * * * * * * * * * * * * * * * * * * * /
```

```
#include <iostream.h>

// extern "C" may be necessary on some compilers
// and won't do any harm on others
extern "C"
{
#include <assert.h>
#include <stdlib.h>
#include <time.h>
}

// Maximum number of tries allowed to enter correct password
const int MAX_NUM_PASS_TRIES = 3;

// Various "flags"
const int TRUE = 1;
const int FALSE = 0;

const int OUT_OF_PAPER              = 10;
const int OUT_OF_CASH              = 11;

const int CHECK_CARD              = 12;
const int KEEP_CARD               = 13;
const int EJECT_CARD              = 14;
const int ORDER_CHEQUE_BOOK       = 15;
const int PRINT_BALANCE           = 16;
const int PRINT_MINI_STATEMENT    = 17;
const int DISPENSE_CASH           = 18;
const int QUIT                    = 19;

// Function prototypes
void Check_cash_reserves(int&);
void Check_paper_reserves(int&);
void Check_supplies(int&, int&, int&, int&);
void Deliver_services(int&, int& ,int&, int&);
void Dispense_cash_to_customer(int&);
void Get_password(int&,int&,int&);
void Get_required_service(int&, int, int, int, int);
int Hardware_fault_detected();
void Order_cheque_book_from_bank(int&);
void Print_customer_balance(int&);
void Print_customer_mini_statement(int&);
void Process_cash_card(int, int* = 0);
void Process_required_service(int, int&, int&, int&, int&);
void Shutdown(void);

/*****************************************************************
*                                                               *
* CPPSPEC: main()                                               *
*                                                               *
*****************************************************************/
int main(void)
    {
```

```
int cheque_OK,
    balance_OK,
    statement_OK,
    cash_OK;

int valid_password_entered, valid_card_entered;
int user_wants_to_quit, tries;

// Simulate (up to) one customer in queue then
// manual shut down
for (int customer = 1; customer <= 1; customer++)
    {
    // Welcome banner
    cout << "-------------------------- \n";
    cout << "PROTOTYPE BANK AUTO TELLER MACHINE\n";
    cout << "-------------------------- \n\n";

    Check_supplies(cash_OK, balance_OK,
                    statement_OK, cheque_OK);

    Process_cash_card(CHECK_CARD, &valid_card_entered);

    if (valid_card_entered)
        {
        tries = 0;
        user_wants_to_quit = FALSE;
        Get_password(valid_password_entered,
                    user_wants_to_quit, tries);

        if ((valid_password_entered)
            && (!user_wants_to_quit))
            {
            // Keep delivering services till user says quit
            // (or hardware fault)
            Deliver_services(cheque_OK, balance_OK,
                            statement_OK, cash_OK);
            Process_cash_card(EJECT_CARD);
            }
        else
            {
            // No valid password
            if (user_wants_to_quit)
                {
                // Polite ejection
                Process_cash_card(EJECT_CARD);
                }
            }
        }
    }

// Simulate manual shutdown
Shutdown();
return 0;
}
```

```
/***********************************************************
*                                                         *
* CPPSPEC:     Shutdown()                                 *
*                                                         *
* OVERVIEW:    Exit message, and exit program.            *
*                                                         *
***********************************************************/
void Shutdown(void)
    {
    cout << "Please use another machine.\n";
    cout << "*** SIMULATING MACHINE SHUTDOWN ***\n";
    exit(1);
    }

/***********************************************************
*                                                         *
* CPPSPEC:     Check_supplies()                           *
*                                                         *
* OVERVIEW:    Check cash and paper reserves &c.          *
*                                                         *
***********************************************************/
void Check_supplies(int& cash_OK_REF,
                    int& balance_OK_REF,
                    int& statement_OK_REF,
                    int& cheque_OK_REF)
    {

    cout << "Next customer please wait…\n\n";

    Check_cash_reserves(cash_OK_REF);

    int paper_level_OK; // Is paper level okay? (flag)
    Check_paper_reserves(paper_level_OK);

    // Assuming all supplies are OK
    cash_OK_REF = TRUE;
    balance_OK_REF = TRUE;
    statement_OK_REF = TRUE;
    cheque_OK_REF = TRUE;
    }

/***********************************************************
*                                                         *
* CPPSPEC:     Hardware_fault_detected()                  *
*                                                         *
* OVERVIEW:    Make sure hardware is not damaged.         *
*                                                         *
***********************************************************/
int Hardware_fault_detected()
    {
    // Assume no hardware fault.
    return 0;
    }
```

```
/*************************************************************
*                                                           *
* CPPSPEC:    Check_cash_reserves()                         *
*                                                           *
* OVERVIEW:   Check cash level.                             *
*                                                           *
*************************************************************/
void Check_cash_reserves(int& cash_OK_REF)
    {
    // Assume cash level OK
    cash_OK_REF = TRUE;
    }


/*************************************************************
*                                                           *
* CPPSPEC:    Check_paper_reserves()                        *
*                                                           *
* OVERVIEW:   Check that there is paper to print on.        *
*                                                           *
*************************************************************/
void Check_paper_reserves(int& paper_level_OK_REF)
    {
    // Assume paper level OK
    paper_level_OK_REF = TRUE;
    }


/*************************************************************
*                                                           *
* CPPSPEC:    Process_cash_card()                           *
*                                                           *
* OVERVIEW:   Validate, eject or retain cash card.          *
*                                                           *
*************************************************************/
void Process_cash_card(int required_op, int* card_OK_PTR)
    {
    /* NOTE: Process_cash_card() is a function with a
       default argument. Can call as:
       Process_cash_card(CHECK_CARD, card_OK);
       or
       Process_cash_card(KEEP_CARD);
       Process_cash_card(EJECT_CARD); */
    switch (required_op)
        {
        case CHECK_CARD:
            // Using "extra" argument
            cout << "Please insert your card.\n";
            cout << "*** SIMULATING CARD INSERTION ***\n";
            *card_OK_PTR = TRUE; // Assume card OK
            cout << "Thank you.\n\n";
            // If NOT OK call Process_cash_card(EJECT_CARD);
            break;
```

```
            case KEEP_CARD:
                cout << "Password incorrect. Card retained.\n";
                cout << "Please contact your branch.\n";
                cout << "*** SIMULATING SWALLOWING CARD ***\n\n";
                break;

            case EJECT_CARD:
                cout << "Thank you for using this machine.\n";
                cout << "*** SIMULATING EJECTING CARD ***\n\n";
                break;
        }
    }

/*************************************************************
 *                                                          *
 * CPPSPEC:    Get_password()                               *
 *                                                          *
 * OVERVIEW:   Get and validate user's password             *
 *                                                          *
 *************************************************************/
void Get_password(int& password_OK_REF,
                  int& want_to_quit_REF,
                  int& tries_REF)
    {
    int password;

    cout << "Please enter your password : ";
    cin >> password;

    cout << "*** SIMULATING CALL TO BANK COMPUTER ***\n";
    password_OK_REF = TRUE;
    cout << "*** SIMULATING CORRECT PASSWORD ***\n";
    tries_REF = 1; // Assume password correct first time
    cout << "Thank you.\n\n";

    // Assume user does not want to quit
    want_to_quit_REF = FALSE;
    }

/*************************************************************
 *                                                          *
 * CPPSPEC:    Deliver_services()                           *
 *                                                          *
 * OVERVIEW:   Ask user for reqd. service and deliver it.   *
 *                                                          *
 *************************************************************/
void Deliver_services(int& cheque_OK_REF,
                      int& balance_OK_REF,
                      int& statement_OK_REF,
                      int& cash_OK_REF)
    {
    int user_choice;

    Get_required_service(user_choice, cheque_OK_REF,
        balance_OK_REF, statement_OK_REF, cash_OK_REF);
```

```
    while (user_choice != QUIT)
        {
        Process_required_service(user_choice,
          cheque_OK_REF,
          balance_OK_REF, statement_OK_REF, cash_OK_REF);
        Get_required_service(user_choice, cheque_OK_REF,
          balance_OK_REF, statement_OK_REF, cash_OK_REF);
        }
    }

/***************************************************************
*                                                             *
* CPPSPEC:    Get_required_service()                          *
*                                                             *
* OVERVIEW:   Find out what service user requires.            *
*                                                             *
***************************************************************/
void Get_required_service(int& service_REF,
                          int   cheque_OK,
                          int   balance_OK,
                          int   statement_OK,
                          int   cash_OK)
    {
    // Ignoring cheque_OK, etc: let user order
    // as many cheque books, etc, as she likes
    cout << "Which service do you require: \n";
    cout << "Quit                - Type 1\n";
    cout << "Order cheque book   - Type 2\n";
    cout << "Print balance       - Type 3\n";
    cout << "Print statement     - Type 4\n";
    cout << "Cash                - Type 5\n";

    int service;
    do   {
         cout << "Please enter the appropriate number : ";
         cin >> service;
         } while ((service > 5) || (service < 1));
    cout << "Thank you.\n\n";
    switch (service)
        {
        case 1: service_REF = QUIT; break;
        case 2: service_REF = ORDER_CHEQUE_BOOK; break;
        case 3: service_REF = PRINT_BALANCE; break;
        case 4: service_REF = PRINT_MINI_STATEMENT; break;
        case 5: service_REF = DISPENSE_CASH; break;
        }
    }

/***************************************************************
*                                                             *
* CPPSPEC:    Process_required_service()                      *
*                                                             *
```

```
* OVERVIEW:    Perform user's requested service.              *
*                                                             *
**************************************************************/
void Process_required_service(int user_choice,
                              int& cheque_OK_REF,
                              int& balance_OK_REF,
                              int& statement_OK_REF,
                              int& cash_OK_REF)
    {
    switch (user_choice)
        {
        case ORDER_CHEQUE_BOOK:
            Order_cheque_book_from_bank(cheque_OK_REF);
        break;

        case PRINT_BALANCE:
            Print_customer_balance(balance_OK_REF);
        break;

        case PRINT_MINI_STATEMENT:
            Print_customer_mini_statement(statement_OK_REF);
        break;

        case DISPENSE_CASH:
            Dispense_cash_to_customer(cash_OK_REF);
        break;
        }
    }

/*************************************************************
*                                                           *
* CPPSPEC:    Order_cheque_book_from_bank()                  *
*                                                           *
* OVERVIEW:    Order cheque book.                           *
*                                                           *
**************************************************************/
void Order_cheque_book_from_bank(int& cheque_OK_REF)
    {
    cout << "*** SIMULATING ORDER FOR CHEQUE BOOK ***\n";
    cout << "Your cheque book will be posted to you.\n\n";
    }

/*************************************************************
*                                                           *
* CPPSPEC:    Print_customer_balance()                      *
*                                                           *
* OVERVIEW:    Print customer's balance.                    *
*                                                           *
**************************************************************/
void Print_customer_balance(int& balance_OK_REF)
    {
    cout << "Your balance is: 99.99 (*** SIMULATED ***)\n\n";
    }
```

```
/ *****************************************************************
 *                                                               *
 * CPPSPEC:      Print_customer_mini_statement()                 *
 *                                                               *
 * OVERVIEW:     Print mini statement.                           *
 *                                                               *
 *****************************************************************/
void Print_customer_mini_statement(int& statement_OK_REF)
    {
    cout << "*** SIMULATING PRINTING OF MINI STATEMENT ***";
    cout << "\nPlease take your mini statement.\n\n";
    }
/ *****************************************************************
 *                                                               *
 * CPPSPEC:      Dispense_cash_to_customer()                     *
 *                                                               *
 * OVERVIEW:     Deliver cash.                                   *
 *                                                               *
 *****************************************************************/
void Dispense_cash_to_customer(int& cash_OK_REF)
    {
    cout << "*** SIMULATING CASH DELIVERY ***\n";
    cout << "Please take your cash.\n\n";
    }
/ *****************************************************************
 *                      *** END OF PROGRAM ***                   *
 *****************************************************************/
```

Program 16.1 The code framework for the ATM software. (☺)

Harry tests the framework, and is happy that it will provide the basis for his implementation. A sample output from the framework is given below:

```
PROTOTYPE BANK AUTO TELLER MACHINE
Next customer please wait...
Please insert your card.
*** SIMULATING CARD INSERTION ***
Thank you.

Please enter your password : 9999
*** SIMULATING CALL TO BANK COMPUTER ***
*** SIMULATING CORRECT PASSWORD ***
Thank you.

Which service do you require:
Quit               - Type 1
Order cheque book  - Type 2
Print balance      - Type 3
Print statement    - Type 4
Cash               - Type 5
Please enter the appropriate number : 2
Thank you.
```

```
*** SIMULATING ORDER FOR CHEQUE BOOK ***
Your cheque book will be posted to you.

Which service do you require:
Quit                - Type 1
Order cheque book   - Type 2
Print balance       - Type 3
Print statement     - Type 4
Cash                - Type 5
Please enter the appropriate number : 3
Thank you.

Your balance is: 99.99 (*** SIMULATED ***)

Which service do you require:
Quit                - Type 1
Order cheque book   - Type 2
Print balance       - Type 3
Print statement     - Type 4
Cash                - Type 5
Please enter the appropriate number : 4
Thank you.

*** SIMULATING PRINTING OF MINI STATEMENT ***
Please take your mini statement.

Which service do you require:
Quit                - Type 1
Order cheque book   - Type 2
Print balance       - Type 3
Print statement     - Type 4
Cash                - Type 5
Please enter the appropriate number : 5
Thank you.

*** SIMULATING CASH DELIVERY ***
Please take your cash.

Which service do you require:
Quit                - Type 1
Order cheque book   - Type 2
Print balance       - Type 3
Print statement     - Type 4
Cash                - Type 5
Please enter the appropriate number : 1
Thank you.

Thank you for using this machine.
*** SIMULATING EJECTING CARD ***

Please use another machine.
*** SIMULATING MACHINE SHUTDOWN ***
```

Next, Harry begins to consider the necessary hardware framework required to support the final system. He notes that, when work on the prototype is complete, he will require a card reader, key pad and so forth, in order to be able to work on the final version of the code.

16.5.3 The preliminary modules

The preliminary modules are created or, preferably, recycled from a code library. In either case, the resulting function will build on the CppSpecs, and will make reference to the physical model (particularly the PSpecs and the data dictionary).

Harry works on all the modules in turn, building in each case from the corresponding CppSpec, and referring as he does so to the PSpecs.

For example, the PSpec given in Figure 16.20 becomes first the CppSpec `Get_required_service()` (shown in Program 16.1) and is in turn developed into the preliminary function given in Figure 16.25.

```
/ * * * * * * * * * * * * * * * * * * * * * * * * * * * * * * * * * * * * * * * * * * * * * * * * * * * * * * * *
*                                                                        *
*  FUNCTION:    Get_required_service()                                   *
*                                                                        *
*  OVERVIEW:    Find out what service user requires.                     *
*                                                                        *
*  RETURNS:     void.                                                    *
*                                                                        *
*  PRE:         No hardware faults.                                      *
*  POST:        Got valid choice.                                        *
*                                                                        *
* * * * * * * * * * * * * * * * * * * * * * * * * * * * * * * * * * * * * * * * * * * * * * * * * * * * * * * * /
void Get_required_service(int&  service_REF,
                          int    cheque_OK,
                          int    balance_OK,
                          int    statement_OK,
                          int    cash_OK)
    {
    // Pre - no hardware faults

    int service;

    cout << "Which service do you require: \n";
    cout << "Quit                        - Type 1\n";
    if (cheque_OK)
        {
        cout << "Order cheque book     - Type 2\n";
        }
    if (balance_OK)
        {
        cout << "Print balance         - Type 3\n";
        }
    if (statement_OK)
        {
        cout << "Print mini statement  - Type 4\n";
        }
    if (cash_OK)
        {
```

```
                cout << "Cash                     - Type 5\n";
                }
        do {
            cout << "Please enter the appropriate number : ";
            cin >> service;
            } while ((service > 5)
                    || (service < 1)
                    || ((service == 2) && (!cheque_OK))
                    || ((service == 3) && (!balance_OK))
                    || ((service == 4) && (!statement_OK))
                    || ((service == 5) && (!cash_OK)));

        cout << "Thank you.\n\n";

        switch (service)
            {
            case 1:
                service_REF = QUIT;
            break;

            case 2:
                service_REF = ORDER_CHEQUE_BOOK;
            break;

            case 3:
                service_REF = PRINT_CUSTOMER_BALANCE;
            break;

            case 4:
                service_REF = PRINT_CUSTOMER_MINI_STATEMENT;
            break;

            case 5:
                service_REF = DISPENSE_CASH;
            break;
            }
        // Post - got valid choice
        }
```

Figure 16.25 The preliminary function `Get_required_service()`.

16.5.4   Error detection and recovery

The preliminary modules are extended, where necessary, through the addition of appropriate error detection and correction features.

By way of example here, we extend the function in Figure 16.25 to deal with issues of error detection (Figure 16.26).

```
/***************************************************************
*                                                             *
* FUNCTION:    Get_required_service()                         *
*                                                             *
* OVERVIEW:    Find out what service user requires.           *
```

```
 *                                                              *
 * PRE:       No hardware faults.                               *
 * POST:      Got valid choice.                                 *
 *                                                              *
 * RETURNS:   void.                                             *
 *                                                              *
 **************************************************************/
void Get_required_service(int& service_REF,
                          int   cheque_OK,
                          int   balance_OK,
                          int   statement_OK,
                          int   cash_OK)
    {
    // Pre - no hardware faults
    if (Hardware_fault_detected()) { Shutdown(); }

    int service;

    cout << "Which service do you require: \n";
                        cout << "Quit                - Type 1\n";
    if (cheque_OK)      cout << "Order cheque book   - Type 2\n";
    if (balance_OK)     cout << "Print balance       - Type 3\n";
    if (statement_OK)   cout << "Print statement     - Type 4\n";
    if (cash_OK)        cout << "Cash                - Type 5\n";

    do {
        cout << "Please enter the appropriate number : ";
        cin >> service;
        } while ((service > 5)
                 || (service < 1)
                 || ((service == 2) && (!cheque_OK))
                 || ((service == 3) && (!balance_OK))
                 || ((service == 4) && (!statement_OK))
                 || ((service == 5) && (!cash_OK)));

    cout << "Thank you.\n\n";

    switch (service)
        {
        case 1: service_REF = QUIT; break;
        case 2: service_REF = ORDER_CHEQUE_BOOK; break;
        case 3: service_REF = PRINT_BALANCE; break;
        case 4: service_REF = PRINT_MINI_STATEMENT; break;
        case 5: service_REF = DISPENSE_CASH; break;
        }

    // Post - got valid choice
    assert((service_REF == QUIT) ||
           (service_REF == ORDER_CHEQUE_BOOK) ||
           (service_REF == PRINT_BALANCE) ||
           (service_REF == PRINT_MINI_STATEMENT) ||
           (service_REF == DISPENSE_CASH));
    }
```

Figure 16.26 The modified version of function `Get_required_service()`.

16.5.5 Module tests

The modules are tested, by the programmers, according to the test strategy produced by the design team. Modifications are made as required.

Harry tests each of the functions in turn, as dictated by Steph's test strategy.

By way of example, Figure 16.27 shows the test form created by Harry as function `Get_required_service()`, from Section 16.5.6, was tested. Program 16.2 was used by Harry to complete these tests.

MODULE TEST REPORT	FT1b (function tests)
Module name	*Get_required_service()*
Module programmer (or library name)	*Harry.*
Details of <u>White Box</u> testing performed	*The module was carefully inspected for errors. No problems were found.*
Module tester (BLOCK CAPITALS)	*HARRY*
Initials of tester	*HH*
Details of <u>Black Box</u> testing performed	*Black box testing used the driver program on the attached sheet (Program 16.2). The output was as shown.*
Module tester (BLOCK CAPITALS)	*HARRY*
Initials of tester	*HH*

Figure 16.27 The module test form for `Get_required_service()`.

```
/*****************************************************************
*                                                               *
* ATM Driver program                                            *
*                                                               *
* Source is:    16_02.CPP                                       *
* Created:      30 June, 1995                                   *
* Last edited:  30 June, 1995                                   *
*                                                               *
*****************************************************************/
#include <assert.h>
#include <iostream.h>
#include <stdlib.h>
#include <time.h>

// Maximum number of tries allowed to enter correct password
const int MAX_NUM_PASS_TRIES = 3;

// Various "flags"
const int TRUE = 1;
const int FALSE = 0;

const int ORDER_CHEQUE_BOOK    = 15;
const int PRINT_BALANCE        = 16;
const int PRINT_MINI_STATEMENT = 17;
```

```cpp
const int DISPENSE_CASH          = 18;
const int QUIT                   = 19;

// Function prototypes
void Get_required_service(int&, int, int, int, int);

/**************************************************************
*                                                            *
* FUNCTION:    main()                                        *
*                                                            *
**************************************************************/
int main(void)
    {
    int choice;

    cout << "DRIVER PROGRAM: Get_required_services()\n\n";

    Get_required_service(choice, 0,0,0,0);
    cout << "Choice = " << choice << "\n\n";
    Get_required_service(choice, 0,0,0,1);
    cout << "Choice = " << choice << "\n\n";
    Get_required_service(choice, 0,0,1,0);
    cout << "Choice = " << choice << "\n\n";
    Get_required_service(choice, 0,0,1,1);
    cout << "Choice = " << choice << "\n\n";
    Get_required_service(choice, 0,1,0,0);
    cout << "Choice = " << choice << "\n\n";
    Get_required_service(choice, 0,1,0,1);
    cout << "Choice = " << choice << "\n\n";
    Get_required_service(choice, 0,1,1,0);
    cout << "Choice = " << choice << "\n\n";
    Get_required_service(choice, 0,1,1,1);
    cout << "Choice = " << choice << "\n\n";
    Get_required_service(choice, 1,0,0,0);
    cout << "Choice = " << choice << "\n\n";
    Get_required_service(choice, 1,0,0,1);
    cout << "Choice = " << choice << "\n\n";
    Get_required_service(choice, 1,0,1,0);
    cout << "Choice = " << choice << "\n\n";
    Get_required_service(choice, 1,0,1,1);
    cout << "Choice = " << choice << "\n\n";
    Get_required_service(choice, 1,1,0,0);
    cout << "Choice = " << choice << "\n\n";
    Get_required_service(choice, 1,1,0,1);
    cout << "Choice = " << choice << "\n\n";
    Get_required_service(choice, 1,1,1,0);
    cout << "Choice = " << choice << "\n\n";
    Get_required_service(choice, 1,1,1,1);
    cout << "Choice = " << choice << "\n\n";

    Get_required_service(choice, 4,7,9,0);
    cout << "Choice = " << choice << "\n\n";
    Get_required_service(choice, 4,5,-1,3);
    cout << "Choice = " << choice << "\n\n";
```

```
        cout << "TEST COMPLETE";
        return 0;
        }

/****************************************************************
*                                                              *
* FUNCTION:    Get_required_service()                          *
*                                                              *
* OVERVIEW:    Find out what service user requires.            *
*                                                              *
* PRE:         No hardware faults.                             *
* POST:        Got valid choice.                               *
*                                                              *
* RETURNS:     void.                                           *
*                                                              *
****************************************************************/
void Get_required_service(int& service_REF,
                          int   cheque_OK,
                          int   balance_OK,
                          int   statement_OK,
                          int   cash_OK)
    {
    // Pre - no hardware faults
    // if (Hardware_fault_detected()) { Shutdown(); }

    int service;

    cout << "Which service do you require: \n";
                        cout << "Quit              - Type 1\n";
    if (cheque_OK)      cout << "Order cheque book - Type 2\n";
    if (balance_OK)     cout << "Print balance     - Type 3\n";
    if (statement_OK)   cout << "Print statement   - Type 4\n";
    if (cash_OK)        cout << "Cash              - Type 5\n";

    do {
        cout << "Please enter the appropriate number : ";
        cin >> service;
        } while ((service > 5)
                || (service < 1)
                || ((service == 2) && (!cheque_OK))
                || ((service == 3) && (!balance_OK))
                || ((service == 4) && (!statement_OK))
                || ((service == 5) && (!cash_OK)));

    cout << "Thank you.\n\n";

    switch (service)
        {
        case 1: service_REF = QUIT; break;
        case 2: service_REF = ORDER_CHEQUE_BOOK; break;
        case 3: service_REF = PRINT_BALANCE; break;
        case 4: service_REF = PRINT_MINI_STATEMENT; break;
        case 5: service_REF = DISPENSE_CASH; break;
        }
```

```
        // Post - got valid choice
        assert((service_REF == QUIT) ||
               (service_REF == ORDER_CHEQUE_BOOK) ||
               (service_REF == PRINT_BALANCE) ||
               (service_REF == PRINT_MINI_STATEMENT) ||
               (service_REF == DISPENSE_CASH));
      }
```

Program 16.2   Driver program for testing ATM software modules. (☺)

Program 16.2 generates the following output:

```
    DRIVER PROGRAM: Get_required_services()

    Which service do you require:
    Quit                    - Type 1
    Please enter the appropriate number : 1
    Thank you.

    Choice = 19

    Which service do you require:
    Quit                    - Type 1
    Cash                    - Type 5
    Please enter the appropriate number : 4
    Please enter the appropriate number : 1
    Thank you.

    Choice = 19

    Which service do you require:
    Quit                    - Type 1
    Print statement         - Type 4
    Please enter the appropriate number : 5
    Please enter the appropriate number : 2
    Please enter the appropriate number : 1
    Thank you.

    Choice = 19

    Which service do you require:
    Quit                    - Type 1
    Print statement         - Type 4
    Cash                    - Type 5
    Please enter the appropriate number : 1
    Thank you.

    Choice = 19

    Which service do you require:
    Quit                    - Type 1
    Print balance           - Type 3
    Please enter the appropriate number : 3
    Thank you.

    Choice = 16

    Which service do you require:
    Quit                    - Type 1
```

```
Print balance          - Type 3
Cash                   - Type 5
Please enter the appropriate number : 5
Thank you.

Choice = 18

Which service do you require:
Quit                   - Type 1
Print balance          - Type 3
Print statement        - Type 4
Please enter the appropriate number : 4
Thank you.

Choice = 17

Which service do you require:
Quit                   - Type 1
Print balance          - Type 3
Print statement        - Type 4
Cash                   - Type 5
Please enter the appropriate number : 3
Thank you.

Choice = 16

Which service do you require:
Quit                   - Type 1
Order cheque book      - Type 2
Please enter the appropriate number : 2
Thank you.

Choice = 15

Which service do you require:
Quit                   - Type 1
Order cheque book      - Type 2
Cash                   - Type 5
Please enter the appropriate number : 5
Thank you.

Choice = 18

Which service do you require:
Quit                   - Type 1
Order cheque book      - Type 2
Print statement        - Type 4
Please enter the appropriate number : 1
Thank you.

Choice = 19

Which service do you require:
Quit                   - Type 1
Order cheque book      - Type 2
Print statement        - Type 4
Cash                   - Type 5
Please enter the appropriate number : 4
Thank you.
```

```
Choice = 17

Which service do you require:
Quit                    - Type 1
Order cheque book       - Type 2
Print balance           - Type 3
Please enter the appropriate number : 3
Thank you.

Choice = 16

Which service do you require:
Quit                    - Type 1
Order cheque book       - Type 2
Print balance           - Type 3
Cash                    - Type 5
Please enter the appropriate number : 4
Please enter the appropriate number : 1
Thank you.

Choice = 19

Which service do you require:
Quit                    - Type 1
Order cheque book       - Type 2
Print balance           - Type 3
Print statement         - Type 4
Please enter the appropriate number : 4
Thank you.

Choice = 17

Which service do you require:
Quit                    - Type 1
Order cheque book       - Type 2
Print balance           - Type 3
Print statement         - Type 4
Cash                    - Type 5
Please enter the appropriate number : 4
Thank you.

Choice = 17

Which service do you require:
Quit                    - Type 1
Order cheque book       - Type 2
Print balance           - Type 3
Print statement         - Type 4
Please enter the appropriate number : 3
Thank you.

Choice = 16

Which service do you require:
Quit                    - Type 1
Order cheque book       - Type 2
Print balance           - Type 3
```

```
Print statement      - Type 4
Cash                 - Type 5
Please enter the appropriate number : 0
Please enter the appropriate number : 11
Please enter the appropriate number : 3
Thank you.

Choice = 16

TEST COMPLETE
```

As he uses the program, Harry realizes that some further error checking at the function input will be useful, to ensure that the 'available services' flags are being used correctly (Figure 16.28).

```
/****************************************************************
*                                                              *
* FUNCTION:    Get_required_service()                          *
*                                                              *
* OVERVIEW:    Find out what service user requires.            *
*                                                              *
* PRE:         No hardware faults.                             *
*              Valid list of available services                *
* POST:        Got valid choice.                               *
*                                                              *
* RETURNS:     void.                                           *
*                                                              *
****************************************************************/
void Get_required_service(int& service_REF,
                          int   cheque_OK,
                          int   balance_OK,
                          int   statement_OK,
                          int   cash_OK)
    {
    // Pre - no hardware faults
    // if (Hardware_fault_detected()) { Shutdown(); }
    // Pre - valid list of available services
    assert((cash_OK == FALSE) || (cash_OK == TRUE));
    assert((balance_OK == FALSE) || (balance_OK == TRUE));
    assert((statement_OK == FALSE) || (statement_OK == TRUE));
    assert((cheque_OK == FALSE) || (cheque_OK == TRUE));

    int service;
    cout << "Which service do you require: \n";
                        cout << "Quit             - Type 1\n";
    if (cheque_OK)      cout << "Order cheque book - Type 2\n";
    if (balance_OK)     cout << "Print balance     - Type 3\n";
    if (statement_OK)   cout << "Print statement   - Type 4\n";
    if (cash_OK)        cout << "Cash              - Type 5\n";

    do {
        cout << "Please enter the appropriate number : ";
```

```
            cin >> service;
        } while ((service > 5)
              || (service < 1)
              || ((service == 2) && (!cheque_OK))
              || ((service == 3) && (!balance_OK))
              || ((service == 4) && (!statement_OK))
              || ((service == 5) && (!cash_OK)));

    cout << "Thank you.\n\n";

    switch (service)
        {
        case 1: service_REF = QUIT; break;
        case 2: service_REF = ORDER_CHEQUE_BOOK; break;
        case 3: service_REF = PRINT_BALANCE; break;
        case 4: service_REF = PRINT_MINI_STATEMENT; break;
        case 5: service_REF = DISPENSE_CASH; break;
        }
    // Post - got valid choice
    assert((service_REF == QUIT) ||
           (service_REF == ORDER_CHEQUE_BOOK) ||
           (service_REF == PRINT_BALANCE) ||
           (service_REF == PRINT_MINI_STATEMENT) ||
           (service_REF == DISPENSE_CASH));
    }
```

Figure 16.28 The final version of function `Get_required_service()`.

16.5.6 The prototype system

The tested modules are assembled into a prototype system, as dictated by the structure chart(s).

Harry assembles the individual modules into Program 16.3.

```
/****************************************************************
 *                                                              *
 * A Bank Service Till (ATM) Simulation (Process-Oriented)      *
 *                                                              *
 * Source is:     16_03.CPP                                     *
 * Created:       04 April, 1994                                *
 * Last edited:   30 June, 1995                                 *
 *                                                              *
 ****************************************************************/
#include <assert.h>
#include <iostream.h>
#include <stdlib.h>
#include <time.h>

// Maximum number of tries allowed to enter correct password
const int MAX_NUM_PASS_TRIES = 3;

// Various "flags"
const int TRUE = 1;
```

```cpp
const int FALSE = 0;
const int OUT_OF_PAPER                 = 10;
const int OUT_OF_CASH                  = 11;

const int CHECK_CARD                   = 12;
const int KEEP_CARD                    = 13;
const int EJECT_CARD                   = 14;
const int ORDER_CHEQUE_BOOK            = 15;
const int PRINT_BALANCE                = 16;
const int PRINT_MINI_STATEMENT         = 17;
const int DISPENSE_CASH                = 18;
const int QUIT                         = 19;

// Function prototypes
void Check_cash_reserves(int&);
void Check_paper_reserves(int&);
void Check_supplies(int&, int&, int&, int&);
void Deliver_services(int&, int& ,int&, int&);
void Dispense_cash_to_customer(int&);
void Get_password(int&,int&,int&);
void Get_required_service(int&, int, int, int, int);
int Hardware_fault_detected();
void Order_cheque_book_from_bank(int&);
void Print_customer_balance(int&);
void Print_customer_mini_statement(int&);
void Process_cash_card(int, int* = 0);
void Process_required_service(int, int&, int&, int&, int&);
void Shutdown(void);

/****************************************************************
*                                                              *
* FUNCTION:     main()                                         *
*                                                              *
****************************************************************/
int main(void)
    {
    int cheque_OK,
        balance_OK,
        statement_OK,
        cash_OK;

    int valid_password_entered, valid_card_entered;
    int user_wants_to_quit, tries;

    // Set up non-repeatable random numbers for simulation
    srand((unsigned)time(NULL));

    // Simulate (up to) five customers in queue then
    // manual shut down
    for (int customer = 1; customer <= 5; customer++)
        {
        // Welcome banner
        cout << "---------------------------- \n";
        cout << "PROTOTYPE BANK AUTO TELLER MACHINE\n";
        cout << "---------------------------- \n\n";
```

```
            Check_supplies(cash_OK, balance_OK,
                          statement_OK, cheque_OK);

            Process_cash_card(CHECK_CARD, &valid_card_entered);

            if (valid_card_entered)
               {
               tries = 0;
               user_wants_to_quit = FALSE;
               Get_password(valid_password_entered,
                            user_wants_to_quit, tries);

               if ((valid_password_entered)
                  && (!user_wants_to_quit))
                  {
                  // Keep delivering services till user says quit
                  // (or hardware fault)
                  Deliver_services(cheque_OK, balance_OK,
                                   statement_OK, cash_OK);
                  Process_cash_card(EJECT_CARD);
                  }
               else
                  {
                  // No valid password
                  if (user_wants_to_quit)
                     {
                     // Polite ejection
                     Process_cash_card(EJECT_CARD);
                     }
                  }
               }
            }

      // Simulate manual shutdown
      Shutdown();
      return 0;
      }

/**************************************************************
*                                                            *
* FUNCTION:    Shutdown()                                     *
*                                                            *
* OVERVIEW:    Exit message, and exit program.               *
*                                                            *
* PRE:         None.                                         *
* POST:        None.                                         *
*                                                            *
* RETURNS:     void.                                         *
*                                                            *
**************************************************************/
void Shutdown(void)
      {
      // Pre - none
```

```
        cout << "Please use another machine.\n";
        cerr << "*** SIMULATING MACHINE SHUTDOWN ***\n";
        exit(1);

        // Post - none(!)
        }

/*************************************************************
*                                                           *
* FUNCTION:     Check_supplies()                            *
*                                                           *
* OVERVIEW:     Check cash and paper reserves &c.           *
*                                                           *
* PRE:          No hardware faults.                         *
* POST:         Got valid data.                             *
*                                                           *
* RETURNS:      void.                                       *
*                                                           *
*************************************************************/
void Check_supplies(int& cash_OK_REF,
                    int& balance_OK_REF,
                    int& statement_OK_REF,
                    int& cheque_OK_REF)

    {
    // Pre - no hardware faults
    if (Hardware_fault_detected()) { Shutdown(); }

    int paper_level_OK; // Is paper level okay? (flag)

    cout << "Next customer please wait...\n\n";

    Check_cash_reserves(cash_OK_REF);
    Check_paper_reserves(paper_level_OK);

    if (!paper_level_OK)
        {
        balance_OK_REF = FALSE;
        statement_OK_REF = FALSE;
        }
    else
        {
        // Reset these for new customer
        balance_OK_REF = TRUE;
        statement_OK_REF = TRUE;
        }
    // Reset flag for new customer (always available)
    cheque_OK_REF = TRUE;

    // Post - got valid data
    assert((cash_OK_REF == FALSE)
            || (cash_OK_REF == TRUE));
    assert((balance_OK_REF == FALSE)
            || (balance_OK_REF == TRUE));
    assert((statement_OK_REF == FALSE)
```

```
            || (statement_OK_REF == TRUE));
      assert((cheque_OK_REF == FALSE)
            || (cheque_OK_REF == TRUE));
      }
/*************************************************************
*                                                           *
* FUNCTION:    Hardware_fault_detected()                    *
*                                                           *
* OVERVIEW:    Make sure hardware is not damaged.           *
*                                                           *
* PRE:         None.                                        *
* POST:        None.                                        *
*                                                           *
* RETURNS:     TRUE (1) if fault, FALSE (0) otherwise.      *
*                                                           *
*************************************************************/
int Hardware_fault_detected()
      {
      // Pre - none
      // Simulating a hardware fault with a prob. of 1/100
      if ((rand() % 100) == 0)
          {
          cerr << "*** SIMULATING HARDWARE FAULT ***\n";
          return 1;
          }
      else
          {
          return 0;
          }
      // Post - none
      }

/*************************************************************
*                                                           *
* FUNCTION:    Check_cash_reserves()                        *
*                                                           *
* OVERVIEW:    Check cash level.                            *
*                                                           *
* PRE:         No hardware faults.                          *
* POST:        Got valid data.                              *
*                                                           *
* RETURNS:     void.                                        *
*                                                           *
*************************************************************/
void Check_cash_reserves(int& cash_OK_REF)
      {
      // Pre - no hardware faults
      if (Hardware_fault_detected()) { Shutdown(); }

      // Simulating a 1/6 chance of a cash shortage
      if ((rand() % 6)==0)
```

```
        {
        cash_OK_REF = FALSE;
        cerr << "*** SIMULATING LOW CASH LEVEL ***\n";
        }
    else
        {
        cash_OK_REF = TRUE;
        }

    // Post - got valid data
    assert((cash_OK_REF == FALSE)
        || (cash_OK_REF == TRUE));
    }

/****************************************************************
 *                                                              *
 * FUNCTION:    Check_paper_reserves()                          *
 *                                                              *
 * OVERVIEW:    Check that there is paper to print on.          *
 *                                                              *
 * PRE:         No hardware faults.                             *
 * POST:        Got valid data.                                 *
 *                                                              *
 * RETURNS:     void.                                           *
 *                                                              *
 ****************************************************************/
void Check_paper_reserves(int& paper_level_OK_REF)
    {
    // Pre - no hardware faults
    if (Hardware_fault_detected()) { Shutdown(); }

    // Simulating a 1/6 chance of a paper shortage
    if ((rand() % 6)==0)
        {
        paper_level_OK_REF = FALSE;
        cerr << "*** SIMULATING LOW PAPER LEVEL ***\n";
        }
    else
        {
        paper_level_OK_REF = TRUE;
        }

    // Post - got valid data
    assert((paper_level_OK_REF == FALSE)
        || (paper_level_OK_REF == TRUE));
    }

/****************************************************************
 *                                                              *
 * FUNCTION:    Process_cash_card()                             *
 *                                                              *
 * OVERVIEW:    Validate, eject or retain cash card.            *
 *                                                              *
```

```
 * PRE:         No hardware faults.                              *
 *              Valid operation requested.                      *
 * POST:        None.                                           *
 *                                                              *
 * RETURNS:     void.                                           *
 *                                                              *
 ****************************************************************/
void Process_cash_card(int required_op, int* card_OK_PTR)
    {
    // Pre - no hardware faults
    if (Hardware_fault_detected()) { Shutdown(); }
    // Pre - valid operation requested
    assert((required_op == CHECK_CARD) ||
           (required_op == KEEP_CARD) ||
           (required_op == EJECT_CARD));

    /* NOTE: Process_cash_card() is a function with a
       default argument. Can call as:

       Process_cash_card(CHECK_CARD, card_OK);
       or
       Process_cash_card(KEEP_CARD);
       Process_cash_card(EJECT_CARD); */

    switch (required_op)
        {
        case CHECK_CARD:
          // Using "extra" argument

          cout << "Please insert your card.\n";
          // Validate user's card
          *card_OK_PTR = (((rand() % 6) != 0)
                          ? (TRUE) : (FALSE));

          if (*card_OK_PTR)
             {
             cerr <<
             "*** SIMULATING CORRECT CARD INSERTED ***\n";
             cout << "Thank you.\n\n";
             }
          else
             {
             cerr <<
             "*** SIMULATING *INCORRECT* CARD INSERTED ***\n";
             cout << "Incorrect card.\n";
             Process_cash_card(EJECT_CARD);
             }

          break;

        case KEEP_CARD:
            cout << "Password incorrect. Card retained.\n";
            cout << "Please contact your branch.\n";
            cerr << "*** SIMULATING SWALLOWING CARD ***\n\n";
```

```
                        break;

                case EJECT_CARD:
                        cout << "Thank you for using this machine.\n";
                        cerr << "*** SIMULATING EJECTING CARD ***\n\n";

                        break;
                }

        // Post - none
        }

/*************************************************************
 *                                                           *
 * FUNCTION:    Get_password()                               *
 *                                                           *
 * OVERVIEW:    Get and validate user's password             *
 *                                                           *
 * PRE:         No hardware faults.                          *
 * POST:        Got valid data.                              *
 *                                                           *
 * RETURNS:     void.                                        *
 *                                                           *
 *************************************************************/
void Get_password(int& password_OK_REF,
                  int& want_to_quit_REF,
                  int& tries_REF)
        {
        // Pre - no hardware faults
        if (Hardware_fault_detected()) { Shutdown(); }

        int password;

        tries_REF++;
        cout << "Please enter your password"
             << "\n(or 9999 to simulate QUIT button): ";
        cin >> password;

        if (!(password == 9999))
            {
            // User did not ask to quit

            // Simulate call to bank computer
            cerr << "*** SIMULATING CALL TO BANK COMPUTER ***\n";

            // Simulating one single valid password...
            // In reality, send account number and password
            // to bank computer
            // Computer returns 'YES' or 'NO'.

            if (password == 1234)
                {
                password_OK_REF = TRUE;
                }
            else
```

```
                {
                password_OK_REF = FALSE;
                }

        if (!(password_OK_REF))
                {
            if (tries_REF < MAX_NUM_PASS_TRIES)
                {
                cout << "Password incorrect.\n";
                // Recursive call to Get_password()
                Get_password(password_OK_REF, want_to_quit_REF, tries_REF);
                }
            else
                {
                // Too many tries - could be a stolen card?
                Process_cash_card(KEEP_CARD);
                }
                }
        else
                {
            cout << "Thank you.\n\n";
                }
            }
    else
            {
            // User wants to quit
            want_to_quit_REF = TRUE;
            }
    // Post - got valid data
    assert((password_OK_REF == FALSE)
            || (password_OK_REF == TRUE));
    assert((want_to_quit_REF == FALSE)
            || (want_to_quit_REF == TRUE));
    assert(tries_REF <= MAX_NUM_PASS_TRIES);
    }
/****************************************************************
*                                                              *
* FUNCTION:    Deliver_services()                              *
*                                                              *
* OVERVIEW:    Ask user for reqd. service and deliver it.      *
*                                                              *
* PRE:         No hardware faults.                             *
*              Got valid data.                                 *
* POST:        None.                                           *
*                                                              *
* RETURNS:     void.                                           *
*                                                              *
****************************************************************/
void Deliver_services(int& cheque_OK_REF,
                      int& balance_OK_REF,
                      int& statement_OK_REF,
```

```
                         int& cash_OK_REF)
    {
    // Pre - no hardware faults
    if (Hardware_fault_detected()) { Shutdown(); }

    // Pre - got valid data
    assert((cash_OK_REF == FALSE)
           || (cash_OK_REF == TRUE));
    assert((cheque_OK_REF == FALSE)
           || (cheque_OK_REF == TRUE));
    assert((balance_OK_REF == FALSE)
           || (balance_OK_REF == TRUE));
    assert((statement_OK_REF == FALSE)
           || (statement_OK_REF == TRUE));

    int user_choice;

    Get_required_service(user_choice, cheque_OK_REF,
        balance_OK_REF, statement_OK_REF, cash_OK_REF);

    while (user_choice != QUIT)
        {
        Process_required_service(user_choice, cheque_OK_REF,
           balance_OK_REF, statement_OK_REF, cash_OK_REF);
        Get_required_service(user_choice, cheque_OK_REF,
           balance_OK_REF, statement_OK_REF, cash_OK_REF);
        }
    // Post - none
    }

/***************************************************************
*                                                             *
* FUNCTION:   Get_required_service()                          *
*                                                             *
* OVERVIEW:   Find out what service user requires.            *
*                                                             *
* PRE:        No hardware faults.                             *
* POST:       Got valid choice.                               *
*                                                             *
* RETURNS:    void.                                           *
*                                                             *
***************************************************************/
void Get_required_service(int& service_REF,
                          int  cheque_OK,
                          int  balance_OK,
                          int  statement_OK,
                          int  cash_OK)
    {
    // Pre - no hardware faults
    if (Hardware_fault_detected()) { Shutdown(); }

    int service;

    cout << "Which service do you require: \n";
                    cout << "Quit            - Type 1\n";
```

```
    if (cheque_OK)      cout << "Order cheque book  - Type 2\n";
    if (balance_OK)     cout << "Print balance      - Type 3\n";
    if (statement_OK)   cout << "Print statement    - Type 4\n";
    if (cash_OK)        cout << "Cash               - Type 5\n";

    do {
        cout << "Please enter the appropriate number : ";
        cin >> service;
        } while ((service > 5)
                || (service < 1)
                || ((service == 2) && (!cheque_OK))
                || ((service == 3) && (!balance_OK))
                || ((service == 4) && (!statement_OK))
                || ((service == 5) && (!cash_OK)));

    cout << "Thank you.\n\n";

    switch (service)
        {
        case 1: service_REF = QUIT; break;
        case 2: service_REF = ORDER_CHEQUE_BOOK; break;
        case 3: service_REF = PRINT_BALANCE; break;
        case 4: service_REF = PRINT_MINI_STATEMENT; break;
        case 5: service_REF = DISPENSE_CASH; break;
        }

    // Post - got valid choice
    assert((service_REF == QUIT) ||
            (service_REF == ORDER_CHEQUE_BOOK) ||
            (service_REF == PRINT_BALANCE) ||
            (service_REF == PRINT_MINI_STATEMENT) ||
            (service_REF == DISPENSE_CASH));
    }

/****************************************************************
*                                                              *
* FUNCTION:    Process_required_service()                      *
*                                                              *
* OVERVIEW:    Perform user's requested service.               *
*                                                              *
* PRE:         No hardware faults.                             *
*              Got valid choice of service.                    *
* POST:        None.                                           *
*                                                              *
* RETURNS:     void.                                           *
*                                                              *
****************************************************************/
void Process_required_service(int user_choice,
                              int& cheque_OK_REF,
                              int& balance_OK_REF,
                              int& statement_OK_REF,
                              int& cash_OK_REF)
    {
```

```
        // Pre - no hardware faults
        if (Hardware_fault_detected()) { Shutdown(); }

        // Pre - got valid choice
        assert((user_choice == QUIT) ||
               (user_choice == ORDER_CHEQUE_BOOK) ||
               (user_choice == PRINT_BALANCE) ||
               (user_choice == PRINT_MINI_STATEMENT) ||
               (user_choice == DISPENSE_CASH));

    switch (user_choice)
        {
        case ORDER_CHEQUE_BOOK:
            Order_cheque_book_from_bank(cheque_OK_REF);
        break;

        case PRINT_BALANCE:
            Print_customer_balance(balance_OK_REF);
        break;

        case PRINT_MINI_STATEMENT:
            Print_customer_mini_statement(statement_OK_REF);
        break;

        case DISPENSE_CASH:
            Dispense_cash_to_customer(cash_OK_REF);
        break;
        }

    // Post - none
        }

/****************************************************************
*                                                              *
* FUNCTION:    Order_cheque_book_from_bank()                    *
*                                                              *
* OVERVIEW:    Order cheque book.                              *
*                                                              *
* PRE:         No hardware faults.                             *
*              Got valid data.                                 *
* POST:        Returning valid data.                           *
*                                                              *
* RETURNS:     void.                                           *
*                                                              *
****************************************************************/
void Order_cheque_book_from_bank(int& cheque_OK_REF)
        {
        // Pre - no hardware faults
        if (Hardware_fault_detected()) { Shutdown(); }
        // Pre - got valid data
        assert((cheque_OK_REF == TRUE));
        cerr << "*** SIMULATING ORDER FOR CHEQUE BOOK ***\n";
        cout << "Your cheque book will be posted to you.\n\n";

        cheque_OK_REF = FALSE;
```

```
        // Post - returning valid data
        assert((cheque_OK_REF == FALSE));
    }


/**************************************************************
 *                                                            *
 * FUNCTION:    Print_customer_balance()                      *
 *                                                            *
 * OVERVIEW:    Print customer's balance.                     *
 *                                                            *
 * PRE:         No hardware faults.                           *
 *              Got valid data.                               *
 * POST:        Returning valid data.                         *
 *                                                            *
 * RETURNS:     void.                                         *
 *                                                            *
 **************************************************************/
void Print_customer_balance(int& balance_OK_REF)
    {
    // Pre - no hardware faults
    if (Hardware_fault_detected()) { Shutdown(); }
    // Pre - got valid data
    assert((balance_OK_REF == TRUE));

    cout << "Your balance is: 99.99 (*** SIMULATED ***)\n\n";

    balance_OK_REF = FALSE;

    // Post - returning valid data
    assert((balance_OK_REF == FALSE));
    }


/**************************************************************
 *                                                            *
 * FUNCTION:    Print_customer_mini_statement()               *
 *                                                            *
 * OVERVIEW:    Print mini statement.                         *
 *                                                            *
 * PRE:         No hardware faults.                           *
 *              Got valid data.                               *
 * POST:        Returning valid data.                         *
 *                                                            *
 * RETURNS:     void.                                         *
 *                                                            *
 **************************************************************/
void Print_customer_mini_statement(int& statement_OK_REF)
    {
    // Pre - no hardware faults
    if (Hardware_fault_detected()) { Shutdown(); }
    // Pre - got valid data
    assert((statement_OK_REF == TRUE));

    cerr << "*** SIMULATING PRINTING OF MINI STATEMENT ***";
    cout << "\nPlease take your mini statement.\n\n";
```

```
            statement_OK_REF = FALSE;

            // Post - returning valid data
            assert((statement_OK_REF == FALSE));
            }

/*************************************************************
*                                                           *
* FUNCTION:    Dispense_cash_to_customer()                  *
*                                                           *
* OVERVIEW:    Deliver cash.                                *
*                                                           *
* PRE:         No hardware faults.                          *
*              Got valid data.                              *
* POST:        Returning valid data.                        *
*                                                           *
* RETURNS:     void.                                        *
*                                                           *
*************************************************************/
void Dispense_cash_to_customer(int& cash_OK_REF)
            {
            // Pre - no hardware faults
            if (Hardware_fault_detected()) { Shutdown(); }
            // Pre - got valid data
            assert((cash_OK_REF == TRUE));

            cerr << "*** SIMULATING CASH DELIVERY ***\n";
            cout << "Please take your cash.\n\n";

            cash_OK_REF = FALSE;

            // Post - returning valid data
            assert((cash_OK_REF == FALSE));
            }

/*************************************************************
*                   *** END OF PROGRAM ***                  *
*************************************************************/
```

Program 16.3   The prototype ATM system software. (☺)

16.5.7   System tests and maintenance

The complete prototype is tested again, first by the programmers and then by the test team, both working from the test strategy produced by the designers. The system is then subjected to user tests, including field tests and /or acceptance tests. The system is revised as necessary: any changes made during the testing and subsequent ongoing maintenance are recorded and reflected in the evolving process model.

Harry checks the prototype and is happy that it performs as required. He confirms that it is matched to the physical model.

The program produces the following output on some test runs:

```
PROTOTYPE BANK AUTO TELLER MACHINE

Next customer please wait...

Please insert your card.
*** SIMULATING CORRECT CARD INSERTED ***
Thank you.

Please enter your password
(or 9999 to simulate QUIT button): 7777
*** SIMULATING CALL TO BANK COMPUTER ***
Password incorrect.
Please enter your password
(or 9999 to simulate QUIT button): 6666
*** SIMULATING CALL TO BANK COMPUTER ***
Password incorrect.
Please enter your password
(or 9999 to simulate QUIT button): 5555
*** SIMULATING CALL TO BANK COMPUTER ***
Password incorrect. Card retained.
Please contact your branch.
*** SIMULATING SWALLOWING CARD ***

PROTOTYPE BANK AUTO TELLER MACHINE

Next customer please wait...

*** SIMULATING LOW CASH LEVEL ***
*** SIMULATING HARDWARE FAULT ***
Please use another machine.
*** SIMULATING MACHINE SHUTDOWN ***
```

```
PROTOTYPE BANK AUTO TELLER MACHINE

Next customer please wait...

Please insert your card.
*** SIMULATING *INCORRECT* CARD INSERTED ***
Incorrect card.
Thank you for using this machine.
*** SIMULATING EJECTING CARD ***

PROTOTYPE BANK AUTO TELLER MACHINE

Next customer please wait...

*** SIMULATING LOW PAPER LEVEL ***
Please insert your card.
*** SIMULATING CORRECT CARD INSERTED ***
Thank you.

Please enter your password
(or 9999 to simulate QUIT button): 1234
*** SIMULATING CALL TO BANK COMPUTER ***
Thank you.

Which service do you require:
```

```
Quit                  - Type 1
Order cheque book     - Type 2
Cash                  - Type 5
Please enter the appropriate number : 2
Thank you.

*** SIMULATING ORDER FOR CHEQUE BOOK ***
Your cheque book will be posted to you.

Which service do you require:
Quit                  - Type 1
Cash                  - Type 5
Please enter the appropriate number : 5
Thank you.

*** SIMULATING CASH DELIVERY ***
Please take your cash.

Which service do you require:
Quit                  - Type 1
Please enter the appropriate number : 3
Please enter the appropriate number : 1
Thank you.

Thank you for using this machine.
*** SIMULATING EJECTING CARD ***

PROTOTYPE BANK AUTO TELLER MACHINE

Next customer please wait…
Please insert your card.
*** SIMULATING *INCORRECT* CARD INSERTED ***
Incorrect card.
Thank you for using this machine.

*** SIMULATING EJECTING CARD ***

PROTOTYPE BANK AUTO TELLER MACHINE

Next customer please wait…

*** SIMULATING LOW PAPER LEVEL ***
Please insert your card.
*** SIMULATING *INCORRECT* CARD INSERTED ***
Incorrect card.
Thank you for using this machine.
*** SIMULATING EJECTING CARD ***

PROTOTYPE BANK AUTO TELLER MACHINE

Next customer please wait…

Please insert your card.
*** SIMULATING CORRECT CARD INSERTED ***
Thank you.

Please enter your password
(or 9999 to simulate QUIT button): 1234
*** SIMULATING CALL TO BANK COMPUTER ***
```

```
Thank you.

*** SIMULATING HARDWARE FAULT ***
Please use another machine.
*** SIMULATING MACHINE SHUTDOWN ***
```

```
PROTOTYPE BANK AUTO TELLER MACHINE

Next customer please wait...

*** SIMULATING LOW CASH LEVEL ***
Please insert your card.
*** SIMULATING CORRECT CARD INSERTED ***
Thank you.

Please enter your password
(or 9999 to simulate QUIT button): 1234
*** SIMULATING CALL TO BANK COMPUTER ***
Thank you.

Which service do you require:
Quit                  - Type 1
Order cheque book     - Type 2
Print balance         - Type 3
Print statement       - Type 4
Please enter the appropriate number : 3
Thank you.

Your balance is: 99.99 (*** SIMULATED ***)

Which service do you require:
Quit                  - Type 1
Order cheque book     - Type 2
Print statement       - Type 4
Please enter the appropriate number : 4
Thank you.

*** SIMULATING PRINTING OF MINI STATEMENT ***
Please take your mini statement.

Which service do you require:
Quit                  - Type 1
Order cheque book     - Type 2
Please enter the appropriate number : 1
Thank you.

Thank you for using this machine.
*** SIMULATING EJECTING CARD ***

PROTOTYPE BANK AUTO TELLER MACHINE

Next customer please wait...

Please insert your card.
*** SIMULATING CORRECT CARD INSERTED ***
Thank you.

Please enter your password
```

```
(or 9999 to simulate QUIT button): 3333
*** SIMULATING CALL TO BANK COMPUTER ***
Password incorrect.
Please enter your password
(or 9999 to simulate QUIT button): 1235
*** SIMULATING CALL TO BANK COMPUTER ***
Password incorrect.
Please enter your password
(or 9999 to simulate QUIT button): 1234
*** SIMULATING CALL TO BANK COMPUTER ***
Thank you.

Which service do you require:
Quit                - Type 1
Order cheque book   - Type 2
Print balance       - Type 3
Print statement     - Type 4
Cash                - Type 5
Please enter the appropriate number : 5
Thank you.

*** SIMULATING HARDWARE FAULT ***
Please use another machine.
*** SIMULATING MACHINE SHUTDOWN ***
```

The system is now ready, Harry concludes, for some *real* client testing. He picks up the phone, and dials Birstall Bank …

16.6　Conclusions

In this substantial chapter, we have looked in greater depth at the application of P-O SADIE to the development of a small but nonetheless realistic real-time software system. The material in this chapter has applied much of the material in Part I of this book.

With this case study, we conclude our review of process-oriented software development. However, this isn't the end of the software engineering story; in the next few chapters, we turn our attention to the subject of information systems.

PART II
Data-oriented software development

17 Implementing isolated data in C++

17.1 Introduction

If you own a compact disc (CD) player, the value of your music collection probably greatly outweighs the cost of the equipment upon which you play the CDs. This is significant. If next year an incredible new recording system is released costing, say, £100, you are unlikely to rush out and buy such equipment if the cost of updating your existing Wagner and Springsteen recordings runs into many thousands of pounds.

In very much the same way, data drives the business environment. In previous case studies, we have considered a variety of technical computer systems, involving – for example – the monitoring of temperature in a bell foundry and the recording of weather details in the Arctic. Though there may be a lot of it, this is very **simple** data. In such circumstances, we must typically deal with a single integer or real number sampled regularly, representing the temperature of the furnace or the relative humidity. To say that such data is 'simple' is not, by any means, to belittle the processing problems involved, but to acknowledge that while the system may require efficient and complex algorithms to deal with this information in the shortest possible time, the underlying data itself can be represented very easily in any programming language. Moreover, we generally do not need to share such data widely or keep it for extended periods (Figure 17.1).

By contrast, data in a business environment covers personal data, business information and technical information. The data may not have to be typed into the computer system or sampled (via transducers) from the environment, but may in large part already be present elsewhere in the business on a PC, mini-computer or mainframe. Such data is often long-lived: for example, much business information must be kept for several years for tax purposes.

Consider a more tangible example. Suppose we wish to develop a 'mailing list' program, that is, a system to store and retrieve the names and addresses of potential customers. In many businesses, an appropriate list of customers is of great value and will be used very frequently to send out new catalogues or price lists. Such a list is likely to be kept for many years, being regularly updated and modified as required.

As programmers in a firm employing SADIE, we would expect to receive details of the required code in the form of a structure chart and process specifications. In this case, let us assume that an outline structure chart has been provided (Figure 17.2) as part of the physical model. Figure 17.2 reveals that the system is to be menu-driven.

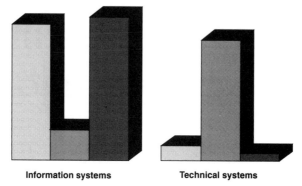

Information systems **Technical systems**

Figure 17.1 The relative complexity of data and processing requirements for information systems and technical systems. Here ▢ represents the data complexity, ▨ represents the function complexity and ▧ represents the data lifetime.

The main options are to enter records into the database, to search the existing database records for customers of a particular name, or to search for all customers in a particular geographical area. Here, as in most instances, the structure chart summarizes the required program structure in a useful manner.

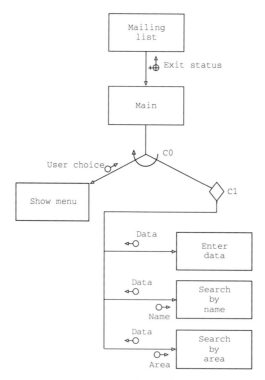

Figure 17.2 A structure chart representing the mailing list program discussed in the text. Conditions – C0: Keep calling 'Show menu' and the user's chosen function, until 'User choice' is equal to 'Quit'; C1: Call 'Enter data' or 'Search by name' or 'Search by area' depending on the value of 'User choice'.

What the structure chart does *not* do is to specify, in any way, the structure of the data that the program will be working with. Of course, we could try to say something about this data in one (or more) of the PSpecs, but this would not be logical, and might well lead to duplicate (or, worse, contradictory) data specifications appearing throughout the analysis and design documents.

We might therefore feel that the data dictionary is the appropriate place to record a data specification: this seems a more reasonable option. Yet, as the data structures grow more complex than the related processes, the software engineer is left with a suite of tools for process development (DfD, PSpec, STD, SC, and so on) and no corresponding way of developing and communicating the data requirements.

The problem is that:

*The program data and code are **separate entities**, and therefore require **separate** models.*

In this chapter, our emphasis will be on the *implementation* of isolated data: we shall consider related analysis and design issues – and the creation of a data model – in subsequent chapters.

17.2 Creating new data types with structs

A C++ struct is a collection of one or more variables, frequently of different types, grouped together under a single name: each individual variable is called a **member**, an **element** or a **field** of the struct. By contrast, an (homogeneous) array is a set of variables of a *single* data type. (Note that we will consider heterogeneous arrays in Chapter 29.)

To see why we might need to use structs, let's consider in slightly more detail the data requirements for the mailing list outlined in Section 17.1. If we were to develop a manual mailing system (using a simple card index, for example), we would probably use a single card to record the details of each customer (Figure 17.3).

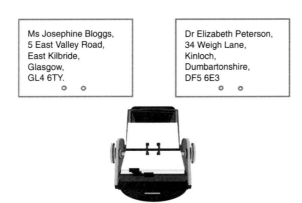

Figure 17.3 A manual version of the mailing list program.

The general format of these data is therefore:

```
< title> <firstname> <lastname>
< 1st Line of Customer's Address >
< 2nd Line of Customer's Address >
< 3rd Line of Customer's Address >
< Post code >
```

The final field, called 'post code', is the UK equivalent of what is known in the US as a 'zip code': the concept and function is universal, but UK post codes can contain letters as well as numbers.

Using C++, we can include all the information for one customer in a single user-defined `struct`, declared as follows:

```
struct sCustomer
    {
    char lastname[31];  // Customer's last name
    char firstname[31]; // Customer's first name
    char title[11];     // Customer's title
    char address1[81];  // 1st line of customer's address
    char address2[81];  // 2nd line of customer's address
    char address3[81];  // 3rd line of customer's address
    char postcode[11];  // Customer's postcode
    };
```

17.3 Creating `struct` variables

It is important to appreciate that the lines:

```
struct sCustomer
    {
    ...
    };
```

are, much like a function prototype, a declaration rather than a definition, and do not create any variables. The distinction between declarations and definitions was discussed in Chapter 3. To create a single customer variable (we'll call it `Customer`) we can do so as follows:

```
...
struct sCustomer
    {
    char lastname[31];  // customer's last name
    ...                         // ETC
    ...
    } ;
...
...
// Customer is a variable of type sCustomer
sCustomer Customer;
...
```

Typically, we shall want to store information on more than one customer. We could therefore define an array (we'll call it `Customers[]`) of (say) 10 data items of type `sCustomer`, in a natural manner, as follows:

```
...
struct sCustomer
    {
    char lastname[31];  // customer's last name
    ...                    // ETC
    ...
    } ;
...
...
sCustomer Customers[10];
```

Note that, although it is generally less useful, we could have created our array as follows:

```
// Customers[] is an array of 10 records of type sCustomer
struct sCustomer
    {
    char lastname[31];  // Customer's last name
    char firstname[31]; // Customer's first name
    char title[11];     // Customer's title
    char address1[81];  // 1st line of customer's address
    char address2[81];  // 2nd line of customer's address
    char address3[81];  // 3rd line of customer's address
    char postcode[11];  // Customer's postcode
    } Customers[10];
```

17.4   Accessing elements of `struct` variables

Generating complex user-defined data types is all very well, but if these new types are to serve any useful purpose we need to be able to access the individual elements within the variables we create.

The simplest way to access these fields is by using the **structure member operator** (the 'dot' operator). For instance, if we want to enter a customer post code (or zip code, if you prefer) into the first record of our `Customers[]` array (defined above), we could most simply use the following code fragment:

```
cout << "Enter customer postcode : ";
cin >> Customers[0].postcode;
```

Suppose, however, that you have passed a `struct`-based variable to a function using call by address: in these and similar circumstances, it is more convenient to use the second method C++ provides for accessing structure elements: the pointer operator (->).

For example, we could rewrite the code fragment above in the following equivalent form:

```
cout << "Enter customer postcode : ";
cin >> Customers->postcode;
```

To illustrate the use of both structure access operators, consider Program 17.1.

```cpp
// Playing with structs
// Source is: 17_01.CPP

#include <iostream.h>
#include <iomanip.h>

// Defining the user-defined data type number
struct sTwo_Numbers
    {
    int int_num;
    double double_num;
    };

// Use typedef - see Ch.11
typedef sTwo_Numbers* sTwo_Numbers_PTR;

int main()
    {
    // Declare two variable of sTwo_Numbers
    sTwo_Numbers Nums_A, Nums_B;

    // Nums_A_PTR is a pointer to variable Nums_A, etc...
    sTwo_Numbers_PTR Nums_A_PTR;
    sTwo_Numbers_PTR Nums_B_PTR;

    Nums_A_PTR = &Nums_A;
    Nums_B_PTR = &Nums_B;

    // Now, store some data in the user-defined variables
    // Do this using the structure pointer operator
    // and the structure member operator
    Nums_A_PTR->int_num = 1;
    Nums_A_PTR->double_num = 2.0;

    Nums_B.int_num = 3;
    Nums_B.double_num = 4.0;

    // Adjust output format
    cout << setiosflags(ios::showpoint);

    // Now, print out the stored values, again
    // using both possible structure operators
    cout << "First Structure\n";
    cout << "The int element is : "
         << Nums_A.int_num << endl;
    cout << "The double element is : "
         << (*Nums_A_PTR).double_num << endl << endl;

    cout << "Second Structure\n";
    cout << "The int element is : "
         << Nums_B_PTR->int_num << endl;
    cout << "The double element is : "
         << (*Nums_B_PTR).double_num;

    return 0;
    }
```

Program 17.1 Playing with structures. (☺)

Program 17.1 produces the following output:

```
First Structure
The int element is : 1
The double element is : 2.00000

Second Structure
The int element is : 3
The double element is : 4.00000
```

Note the equivalence of the two expressions:

```
(*Nums_A_PTR).double_num
```

and

```
Nums_A_PTR->double_num
```

The first version uses the indirection operator to de-reference the pointer, then uses the structure member operator to access the structure member double_num. The parentheses are needed because the structure member operator has a higher precedence than the indirection operator.

17.5 unions

A union is a variable that can hold, at different times, values of *different types* and sizes, with the compiler ensuring that size and alignment are maintained. *Different* kinds of data can therefore be accommodated in a *single* area of storage.

Unions use the same syntax as structures, but whereas a struct might hold an int, a double *and* a char, a union might hold an int *or* a double *or* a char.

As before, it is generally useful to use an appropriate prefix (in this case 'u') to distinguish between unions and other user-defined data structures. Program 17.2 shows a union in action.

```
// Playing with unions
// Source is: 17_02.CPP

#include <iostream.h>
#include <iomanip.h>

// User-defined data structure (union)
union uOne_Number
    {
    int     x;
    float   y;
    };

int main()
    {
    uOne_Number value;

    // Show that fields are stored in overlapping memory locations
    cout << "Address of x field : " << &value.x << endl;
    cout << "Address of y field : " << &value.y << "\n\n";
```

```
// Adjust output format
cout << setiosflags(ios::showpoint);

value.x = 100;
cout << "Put a value in the integer member "
     << "and print both members.\n"
     << "int:   " << value.x << endl
     << "float: " << value.y << endl << endl;

value.y = 100.0f;
cout << "Put a value in the float member "
     << "and print both members.\n"
     << "int:   " << value.x << endl
     << "float: " << value.y << endl << endl;

return 0;
}
```

Program 17.2   An example of a union. (☺)

Program 17.2 produces the following output:

```
Address of x field : 0x377A
Address of y field : 0x377A

Put a value in the integer member and print both members.
int:   100
float: 9.57381e-257

Put a value in the float member and print both members.
int:   0
float: 100.000
```

The first thing to note from this output is that, as expected, both fields in the union begin at the same memory address: that is, the memory locations used overlap. Thus, data placed in one field automatically 'corrupts' the other.

This example also shows that the internal representation of a float is quite different from the representation of an int. One implication of this is that you cannot, as some programmers initially assume, use a union to perform data conversions; for example, as this program illustrates, you can't store data as float and read out 'the same value' as an int.

A corollary to the above is that, if you use unions, you must make sure you keep track of the member used. One way of doing this is illustrated in Program 17.4, which is discussed below.

17.6   Creating enumerated types

C++ has another user-defined data type which we have not yet considered: the enumerated type. Enumerated simply means 'numbered'. In effect, enumerated types provide sets of integer constants which can, if used appropriately, improve code readability.

For example, we can define a new data type – we'll call it eBoolean – which takes only values FALSE (= 0) and TRUE (= 1) as follows:

```
enum eBoolean {FALSE, TRUE};
```

We can assign to an eBoolean variable only the values TRUE or FALSE: nothing else is valid.

The use of enumerated types is illustrated more clearly in Program 17.3.

```cpp
// Using enumerated types
// Source is: 17_03.CPP

#include <iostream.h>

// Defines a new data type called eMedal
enum eMedal {Bronze, Silver, Gold};

int main()
    {
    // Declare a new array (medals) of type eMedal;
    eMedal medals[4];

    // assign value of Bronze to medals[0]
    medals[0] = Bronze;        // NOT medals[0] = "Bronze"
    medals[1] = (eMedal) 1;   // Cast an int to eMedal type
    medals[2] = Gold;
    medals[3] = (eMedal) 10; // No "out of range" error...

    for (int i = 0; i <= 3; i++)
        {
        cout << (int) medals[i] << "\n"; // (int) usually needed

        switch(medals[i])
            {
            case Bronze:
                cout << "Bronze\n";
                break;
            case Silver:
                cout << "Silver\n";
                break;
            case Gold:
                cout << "Gold\n";
                break;
            default:
                cout << "Out of range!\n";
            }
        }
    return 0;
    }
```

Program 17.3 Using enumerated types. (☺)

Program 17.3 produces the following output:

```
0
Bronze
1
```

```
Silver
2
Gold
10
Out of range!
```

Program 17.3 shows that, as far as C++ is concerned, enumerated types are unique user-defined data types, with values which may be promoted to `int`, as necessary, in expressions (you may like to refer back to Figure 4.1). This means, for example, that to assign an integer value to an enumerated data type, you must use the cast operator, as shown in the line:

```
medals[1] = (eMedal) 1; // Cast an int to eMedal type
```

Note that also means that we cannot (with most compilers) simply write:

```
cout << medals[i] << "\n"; // (int) usually needed
```

but instead we must generally use a cast operator:

```
cout << (int) medals[i] << "\n";
```

Even if your compiler does allow you to omit the cast operator, you will still only display an integer on the screen: you *won't* get an output like:

```
Gold
```

To generate the 'Gold' (or 'Silver' or 'Bronze') output, you need to use a `switch` statement (or equivalent code), as in Program 17.3.

One reasonably elegant way to avoid using a `switch` statement is to encapsulate your enumerated type in a class, and overload the stream insertion operator for this class; we consider such possibilities in Part III.

Note that 'out of range' errors produced, for example, with the line:

```
medals[3] = (eMedal) 10; // No "out of range" error…
```

are not detected by the compiler. As usual, the cast operator is all-powerful.

Errors of this type will usually be detected (and won't always compile):

```
medals[3] = Blue; // Probably won't compile…
```

However, errors like this:

```
…
enum eMedal {Bronze, Silver, Gold};
enum eColours {Green, Blue};

int main()
    {
    eMedal medal = Green;
    …
```

won't (sadly) be picked up by all compilers.

In short, enumerated types can be useful, but won't change your life.

17.7   Example: A simple payroll program

Program 17.4 uses many of the features introduced in this chapter in a simple 'payroll program'. The program stores information about employees in a complex data structure called sEmployee. This structure is used throughout the program.

Note, in particular, the way in which elements of the sEmployee data structure are accessed (using call by value in the Print_Gross_Pay() function, and using call by address in the Get_Pay_Data() function). The use of call by address is, of course, simply to illustrate this feature: it would be more sensible to use call by reference in these circumstances.

```cpp
// Playing with structs, unions and enums
// Source is: 17_04.CPP

#include <iostream.h>
#include <stdlib.h>
#include <iomanip.h>

// "Data prototypes"
enum eBoolean{FALSE, TRUE};

struct sEmployee

    {
    char        surname[20];
    eBoolean    hourly_paid;
    union //   Anonymous
        {
        // Hourly-paid workers
        // Need hours worked, and rate/hour
        struct // Anonymous
            {
            int hours;
            float hourly_rate;
            } hourly;
        // Salaried workers
        // Just need monthly salary
        float monthly_salary;
        } pay;
    };

// Function prototypes
int Get_Pay_Data(sEmployee* const);
int Print_Gross_Pay(const sEmployee);

int main ()
    {
    // Local variables
    int emp_num;
    sEmployee payroll[2]; // The payroll "database"

    // Print welcome message
    cout << "Basic Payroll Program\n";
    cout << "---------------\n\n";
```

```cpp
            // Add some payroll data
            for (emp_num = 0; emp_num <= 1; emp_num++)
                {
                if (Get_Pay_Data(&payroll[emp_num]))
                    {
                    cout << "FATAL ERROR: Function Get_Pay_Data()\n";
                    exit (1);
                    }
                }

            // Print table heading
            cout << "GROSS PAY\n";
            cout << "--------\n";
            // Display the payroll data
            for (emp_num = 0; emp_num <= 1; emp_num++)
                {
                if (Print_Gross_Pay(payroll[emp_num]))
                    {
                    cout << "FATAL ERROR: Function Print_Gross_Pay()\n";
                    exit (1);
                    }
                }
            cout << "\nPay calculations complete.";

            return 0;
            }
/*****************************************************************
*                                                               *
*  FUNCTION: Get_Pay_Data                                        *
*                                                               *
*  OVERVIEW: Get pay data for specified employee.               *
*                                                               *
*****************************************************************/
int Get_Pay_Data(sEmployee* const employee_PTR)
        {
        char text_str[10];

        cout << "EMPLOYEE SURNAME : ";
        cin.getline(employee_PTR->surname,
                    sizeof(employee_PTR->surname));

        cout << "Is employee " << employee_PTR->surname << "\n";
        cout << "* Paid by the HOUR (Type 1 <RETURN>)\n";
        cout << "* Paid by SALARY (Type 0 <RETURN>)\n";
        cout << " ? : ";

        // NO error checking...
        cin.getline(text_str, sizeof(text_str));

        if (atoi(text_str))
            {
            employee_PTR->hourly_paid = TRUE;
            }
        else
```

```
            {
            employee_PTR->hourly_paid = FALSE;
            }
        if(employee_PTR->hourly_paid == TRUE)
            {
            // Hourly-paid employee
            cout << "How many hours were worked (whole number) : ";
            cin.getline(text_str, sizeof(text_str));
            employee_PTR->pay.hourly.hours = atoi(text_str);

            cout << "What is the hourly rate (££.pp) : ";
            cin.getline(text_str, sizeof(text_str));
            employee_PTR->pay.hourly.hourly_rate = (float)atof(text_str);
            }
        else
            {
            // Salaried employee
            cout << "What is the monthly salary (££.pp) : ";
            cin.getline(text_str, sizeof(text_str));
            employee_PTR->pay.monthly_salary = (float)atof(text_str);
            }
        cout << "\n";
        return 0;
        }
/*****************************************************************
*                                                               *
* FUNCTION: Print_Gross_Pay                                      *
*                                                               *
* OVERVIEW: Display gross pay for specified employee.           *
*                                                               *
*****************************************************************/
int Print_Gross_Pay(const sEmployee employee)
        {
        float gross_pay;
        if (employee.hourly_paid == TRUE)
            {
            gross_pay = employee.pay.hourly.hours
                        * employee.pay.hourly.hourly_rate;
            }
        else
            {
            gross_pay = employee.pay.monthly_salary;
            }
        cout << setiosflags(ios::fixed)
             << setprecision(2);
        cout << employee.surname << " £" << gross_pay << "\n";
        return 0;
        }
```

Program 17.4   A simple payroll program. (☺)

On a typical run, Program 17.4 generates the following output:

```
Basic Payroll Program

EMPLOYEE SURNAME : Pont
Is employee Pont
* Paid by the HOUR      (Type 1 <RETURN>)
* Paid by SALARY        (Type 0 <RETURN>)
    ? : 1
How many hours were worked (whole number) : 140
What is the hourly rate (££.pp) : 0.56

EMPLOYEE SURNAME : Dromgoole
Is employee Dromgoole
* Paid by the HOUR      (Type 1 <RETURN>)
* Paid by SALARY        (Type 0 <RETURN>)
    ? : 0
What is the monthly salary (££.pp) : 20000.01

GROSS PAY

Pont £78.40
Dromgoole £20000.01

Pay calculations complete.
```

Note the use of the anonymous data structures in Program 17.4. These could be replaced by the following (named) data structures, and the program would work as before:

```
struct sHourly
    {
    int hours;
    float hourly_rate;
    };

union uPay
    {
    // Hourly-paid workers
    // Need hours worked, and rate/hour
    sHourly hourly;
    // Salaried workers
    // Just need monthly salary
    float monthly_salary;
    };

struct sEmployee
    {
    char surname[20];
    eBoolean hourly_paid;
    uPay pay;
    };
```

Note that in the latter case sEmployee can described as an aggregate data structure, assembled from the other (user-defined) data structures, uPay and sHourly. We'll have more to say about aggregate data structures in Part III.

17.8 A rose by any other name ...

Finally, consider again our first `struct`:

```
struct sCustomer
    {
    char lastname[31];     // Customer's last name
    char firstname[31];    // Customer's first name
    char title[11];        // Customer's title
    char address1[81];     // 1st line of customer's address
    char address2[81];     // 2nd line of customer's address
    char address3[81];     // 3rd line of customer's address
    char postcode[11];     // Customer's postcode
    }
```

The name of this data structure is an abbreviation for `struct Customer`.

A list of the most important available user-defined data structures, and the prefixes used in SADIE to represent them, are given in Table 17.1.

Data structure	Prefix letter
class	c
enum	e
struct	s
union	u

Table 17.1 The prefixes used in SADIE to represent the various user-defined data structures.

Table 17.1 includes, for completeness, the `class` data structure: this is a further, very useful, user-defined data structure available to the C++ programmer; we consider this data structure throughout Part III.

Note that some programmers like to use a general postfix '_TYPE' to distinguish user-defined types from their built-in counterparts; in this notation, the `sCustomer` declaration above would have become:

```
struct Customer_TYPE
    {
    ...
    };
```

While there is nothing fundamentally wrong with the '_TYPE' notation (and it is better than no notation at all), it does not distinguish between, for example, structures and classes: as we will see in Part III, these two data structures have many features in common but also some very significant differences. In our experience, highlighting the distinctions helps prevents a number of subtle (and not so subtle) errors.

17.9 Conclusions

In this chapter, we have begun to consider the possibility of using user-defined data types in your programs. We have seen how simple `struct`, `union` and `enum` data types can be declared, and how variables of these types can be created. We will build on this material throughout the remainder of the book as we look at data-oriented and object-oriented software development techniques.

Finally, it is important to appreciate that not all software projects may be neatly characterized as either technical systems or information systems; many of the most interesting and challenging software projects require both advanced data handling *and* sophisticated real-time processing. One important class of project demonstrating such characteristics is the decision support system, discussed in Chapter 22.

Exercises

17.1 Compile the simple payroll program (Program 17.4). Run the program, ensuring that you understand how it works.

17.2 Edit Program 17.4, replacing the `union` with a `struct`. Make sure that the program still works. Compare the size of the original union-based and the new structure-based data types: which is most efficient?

17.3 Edit your solution to Exercise 17.2, replacing the function `Get_Pay_Data()` with an equivalent function using call by reference.

17.4 Using an array of four `sCustomer` variables (See Section 17.3), write a program that will satisfy the process design represented in Figure 17.4.

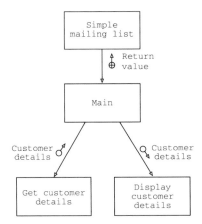

Figure 17.4 An outline process design for a simple mailing list program.

17.5 Consider the case study in Chapter 16. Edit the final program (16_03.cpp) so that it makes good use of enumerated types.

18 Dynamic memory allocation

18.1 Introduction

Arrays are useful and ubiquitous data structures in C++. Because of the simple underlying pointer representation, array access can be extremely fast, and the programmer has the option of hand-optimizing array-based code when data access times are of critical concern.

However, the arrays we have considered up until this point are inherently **static** in nature: that is, the size of the array is specified at compile-time, and cannot be increased or decreased during a program run. This often presents a problem.

Consider, for example, that we are attempting to use a static array called `stock_levels[]` to store a list of stock items in a truck assembly plant:

```
int stock_levels[1500];
```

We plan to use the array as follows. Each item used to assemble the trucks is given a stock number: for example, tyres might have stock numbers 1204 to 1230, depending on the type of truck upon which they are used. If there are 31 tyres of type 1210 in stock, we would store this information as follows:

```
stock_levels[1210] = 31;
```

We would then change the stored value when we use a tyre, or when new stock is delivered. Thus, when the factory takes delivery of 100 tyres, we simply make the following calculation:

```
stock_levels[1210] += 100;
```

Such a scheme is seductively simple, but there are many problems with this very crude data representation. One problem, relevant to our discussion here, is that while a maximum of 1500 stock items may be sufficient for a *very* small factory, stock lists usually contain many thousands of items.

Let's guess that the customer won't need more than 50 000 stock items. If we try to compile this (even using an appropriate set of compiler options), we may find that it *won't* compile because we do not have enough memory in our computer. Or, more commonly, we find that we can compile and run this program on our high-powered top-of-the-range machines but, on our customer's machines (with less memory) the program won't run.

So, how do we produce a program that runs on any machine, that stores as many items as it can within the hardware limits, and which never has to be recompiled? How do we ensure that the customer can buy our program now, for use in a small business in their garage, and keep using both the program and all the data they have amassed when they grow into a multinational in a few years' time? The answer is **dynamic memory allocation**.

We see in this chapter how the C++ programmer can produce simple dynamic arrays, arrays which set their bounds at run time rather than compile time. We then look at linked lists, a more flexible dynamic data structure that forms the heart of stack, queue and tree structures.

Note that in all cases the data structures we consider can be used either with C++'s built-in data types, or with any of user-defined data structures we considered in Chapter 17.

18.2 Simple dynamic memory allocation

To understand dynamic memory allocation, you first need to remember how memory is subdivided on the computer (Figure 18.1).

We first looked at memory issues in Chapter 7. From that discussion, recall that in a desktop environment, your running program will share memory with the operating system, and will occupy both code and data memory areas. An area of stack will also be available, and used to store temporary data, notably function parameters.

In most systems, almost all of the remaining memory is available as 'free store'. This may mean an area of several megabytes of RAM. Such memory is, with most compilers, most easily and flexibly used through dynamic memory allocation. The most useful C++ routines for accessing this large pool of memory are the unary operators `new` and `delete`.

In the simplest case, if we wanted to store an integer value in an area of free store, we could use `new` and `delete` as shown in Program 18.1. Note that, to make it as portable as possible, this program (like others in this chapter) uses no cast operator when displaying memory addresses. The result is that the program will run without alteration on your computer; however the addresses will be shown in hexadecimal

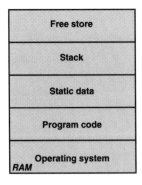

Figure 18.1 Memory organization on a simple desktop computer. Use of the area of free store is effected by dynamic memory access routines.

notation. If you are not comfortable reading 'hex', then you may like to refer back to Chapter 7, where you will find a description of the use of the (unsigned int) and (long) cast operators to display pointer addresses in decimal notation.

```cpp
// Simple dynamic memory allocation
// Source is: 18_01.CPP

#include <iostream.h>
#include <stdlib.h>
#include <string.h>

int main()
    {
    int* dynamic_int_PTR;
    float* dynamic_float_PTR;

    // Try to get some memory for an integer from free store
    if (!(dynamic_int_PTR = new int))
        {
        cerr << "*** Memory could not be allocated ***";
        exit (1);
        }
    else
        {
        cout << "Memory dynamically allocated for an integer\n"
            << "Address is : " << dynamic_int_PTR << "\n\n";
        }

    // Return memory to free store
    delete dynamic_int_PTR;
    dynamic_int_PTR = 0; // Good practice!

    // Try to get some memory for a float from free store
    if (!(dynamic_float_PTR = new float))
        {
        cerr << "*** Memory could not be allocated ***";
        exit (1);
        }
    else
        {
        cout << "Memory dynamically allocated for a float\n"
            << "Address is : " << dynamic_float_PTR << endl;
        }

    // Return memory to free store
    delete dynamic_float_PTR;
    dynamic_float_PTR = 0; // Good practice!

    return 0;
    }
```

Program 18.1 Using new and delete. (☺)

Program 18.1 produces the following output:

```
Memory dynamically allocated for an integer
Address is : 0x20d8

Memory dynamically allocated for a float
Address is : 0x20d8
```

The first point to note about Program 18.1 is that we have a corresponding `delete` operation shadowing each new operation; this is good manners and good programming practice. One of the most frustrating errors, in more sophisticated C++ programs, is 'memory leaching'. The symptoms of this problem are that your program runs happily for a while (perhaps several days), then crashes the system for no apparent reason. The root cause is often that you program is constantly borrowing small amounts from free store, and never repaying the debt. Eventually, no matter how much free store you have (and remember, some of your clients' machines will probably be less generously specified than your own), you will run out of memory.

Note also that the `delete` operation is in each case followed by an assignment operation, setting the relevant pointer variable to 0. While not completely foolproof, this is a good idea (borrowed from Horstmann, 1995). The reason for this is that performing the same delete operation twice will, at least, cause a hiccough in your free store, and at worst will crash your program. The precise results are implementation dependent, but seldom pleasant. Deleting a null pointer does nothing, so by setting your free store pointers to 0 after deletion, you can add a useful extra layer of protection to your programs.

A related point concerns the `new` operator itself. When you use `new`, *every* time you use `new`, you should check that your program has been allocated a valid area of free store. If `new` fails to find any available free store, it will return a null pointer; if you haven't checked this pointer value, and attempt to write to this area you may or may not do any immediate damage, but you'll certainly not get the result you want. Program 18.1 illustrates a reasonably elegant way of using `new` in a correct manner:

```
// Try to get some memory for an integer from free store
if (!(dynamic_int_PTR = new int))
    {
    cerr << "*** Memory could not be allocated ***";
    exit (1);
    }
else
    {
    cout << "Memory dynamically allocated for an integer\n"
         << "Address is : " << dynamic_int_PTR << "\n\n";
    }
```

Finally, note that there is no reason why we can't extend this basic technique to work with `struct`s, or other user-declared data structures. For example, given the following data declaration:

```
struct sTestResults
    {
    unsigned int test_num;      // Test number (0 - 40000)
    char         version;       // Test version (1 - 4)
```

```
      eBoolean      passed;      // TRUE or FALSE
      };
```

we could create a dynamic `sTestResults` variable, as follows:

```
if (!(dynamic_result_PTR = new sTestResults))
   {
   cerr << "*** Memory could not be allocated ***";
   exit (1);
   }
```

18.3   Dynamic arrays

Now that we know how to use `new` and `delete`, we can use these operators to build a dynamic array. An example of dynamic array allocation is given in Program 18.2.

```
// A simple dynamic array
// Source is: 18_02.CPP

#include <iostream.h>
#include <stdlib.h>

int main()
   {
   long array_size;
   int* array_PTR;

   cout << "What size of array would you like to make? ";
   cin >> array_size;

   // Must ensure value is appropriate
   if (array_size < 0)
      {
      cerr << "\n*** Inappropriate size - aborting ***\n";
      exit(1);
      }
   else
      {
      cout << "Array size : " << array_size << endl;

      // (Try to) grab some "free store" for the array
      array_PTR = new int[array_size];

      if (array_PTR == 0)
         {
         cerr << "\n*** Unable to allocate memory - aborting ***\n";
         exit(1);
         }
      else
         {
         // Initialize new array
         for (long i = 0; i < array_size; i++)
            {
            array_PTR[i] = 0;
```

```
              }
          cout << "Array created and initialized successfully.\n";

          // Return memory to free store
          delete [] array_PTR;
          array_PTR = 0;
          cout << "Array deleted.\n";
          }
      }
  return 0;
  }
```

Program 18.2   A simple dynamic array. (☺)

Program 18.2 produces the following outputs:

```
What size of array would you like to make? 7
Array size : 7
Array created and initialized successfully.
Array deleted.
```

```
What size of array would you like to make? -89
*** Inappropriate size - aborting ***
```

Note that this array is only 'semi-dynamic': that is, the size still cannot be varied at run time. In the exercises at the end of this chapter, we discuss some alternative techniques.

18.4   More complex data structures

Armed with knowledge of pointers, and the operators `new` and `delete`, we are in a position to consider some more complex data structures, such as lists, stacks, queues and trees (see Section 18.4.2).

   In particular, we focus on the linked list, the basic building-block of all of the above structures, and one which is useful in its own right.

18.4.1   Linked lists

Linked lists provide a useful facility for flexible dynamic memory allocation: this means that, quite simply, within the limits of your hardware (or possibly the compiler, if it's not a good one), you will be able to start with – say – a small memory-efficient mailing list, but add to it 'forever' should you need to.

   Consider our original (static) five-element array (Figure 18.2). If we suddenly realize that we need six elements, there's nothing we can do. However, the representation of a (singly) linked list looks something like that shown in Figure 18.3. Unlike an array, we can add (or remove) elements at will, at any point.

   Thus, linked lists are flexible; however, accessing data can be slow compared with an array. This is because an array is stored in a single block of memory and we can use pointer arithmetic to access, say, the 200th element quite rapidly. With a linked list, the list must (usually) be followed from beginning to end to find any required data type,

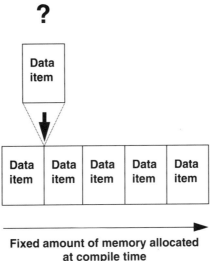

Figure 18.2 The size of a static array is fixed: it is impossible to change the number of elements at run-time.

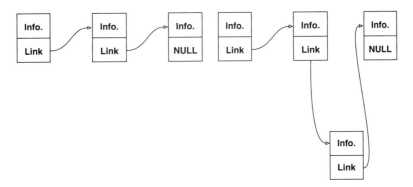

Figure 18.3 A schematic representation of a linked list. On the left is the original list, and (at the right) another element is added simply by (1) freeing an additional area of the required size *anywhere* in memory, and (2) changing the links. Note that this implies that the elements of the linked list need not be stored in a single continuous memory block, a fact which has important implications for the speed of data access.

as the location of any particular element cannot generally be simply computed. Nevertheless, this is an extremely useful type of data structure.

Links in the list are, of course, implemented through the use of pointers, as illustrated in Program 18.3.

```
// Playing with a Linked List
// Source is: 18_03.CPP

#include <iostream.h>
```

```cpp
// sElement is the SELF REFERENTIAL structure at
// the heart of the list.
struct sElement
    {
    // The actual data (just one char in this example)
    char data;
    // The ptr (link) to the next list entry
    sElement* next_PTR;
    } ;
void  Insert_element(sElement**, char);
char  Delete_element(sElement**, char);
int   Is_empty(sElement*);
void  Display_list(sElement*);
void  Help();

int main()
    {
    sElement* start_PTR = NULL;

    int choice = 0;
    char item;
    cout << "LINKED LIST DEMONSTRATION\n";
    cout << "---------------------- ";

    Display_list(start_PTR);
    Help();

    while (choice != 3)
        {
        cout << "\nInsert (1), Delete (2) or Quit (3) ? ";
        cin >> choice;

        switch (choice)
            {
            case 1:
               cout << "\nEnter a character for insertion: ";
               cin >> item;
               Insert_element(&start_PTR, item);
               Display_list(start_PTR);
               break;

            case 2:
               if (!Is_empty(start_PTR))
                  {
                  cout << "\nEnter character to be deleted: ";
                  cin >> item;

                  if (Delete_element(&start_PTR, item))
                     {
                     cout << item << " deleted.\n";
                     Display_list(start_PTR);
                     }
                  else
                     {
                     cout << item << " not found.\n\n";
```

```
                                        }
                                    }
                        else
                            {
                            cout << "List is empty.\n\n";
                            }
                        break;
                case 3:
                        cout << "\nThank you for using this program.\n";
                        break;
                default:
                        cout << "\n*** INVALID OPTION ***\n";
                        Help();
                }
            }
        return 0;
        }
/***********************************************************
*                                                         *
* FUNCTION: Help()                                        *
*                                                         *
* OVERVIEW: Tell the user how to use the program.         *
*                                                         *
***********************************************************/
void Help()
    {
    cout << "\n"
        << "Type  1 to insert an element into the list.\n"
        << "      2 to delete an element from the list.\n"
        << "      3 to QUIT.\n";
    }
/***********************************************************
*                                                         *
* FUNCTION:   Insert_element()                            *
*                                                         *
* OVERVIEW:   Insert a new element into the list          *
*.            (in alphabetical order).                    *
*                                                         *
***********************************************************/
// NOTE: E_PTR_PTR is a pointer to a pointer
void Insert_element(sElement** E_PTR_PTR, char value)
    {
    sElement* new_PTR;
    sElement* last_PTR;
    sElement* this_PTR;

    if (new_PTR = new sElement)
        {
        new_PTR->data = value;
        new_PTR->next_PTR = NULL;
```

```
                last_PTR = NULL;
                this_PTR = *E_PTR_PTR;

        while ((this_PTR != NULL) && (value > this_PTR->data))
                {
                last_PTR = this_PTR;
                this_PTR = (this_PTR)->next_PTR;
                }

        if (last_PTR == NULL)
                {
                new_PTR->next_PTR = *E_PTR_PTR;
                *E_PTR_PTR = new_PTR;
                }
        else
                {
                last_PTR->next_PTR = new_PTR;
                new_PTR->next_PTR = this_PTR;
                }
        }
    else
        {
        cout << value << " not inserted. No memory available.\n";
        }
    }

/****************************************************************
 *                                                              *
 * FUNCTION: Delete_element()                                   *
 *                                                              *
 * OVERVIEW: Deletes an element from the list.                  *
 *                                                              *
 ****************************************************************/
// NOTE: E_PTR_PTR is a pointer to a pointer
char Delete_element(sElement** E_PTR_PTR, char value)
        {
        // Compare this with the definition in Insert_element…
        sElement *last_PTR, *this_PTR, *temp_PTR;

        if (value == (*E_PTR_PTR)->data)
                {
                temp_PTR = *E_PTR_PTR;
                *E_PTR_PTR = (*E_PTR_PTR)->next_PTR;
                delete temp_PTR;
                temp_PTR = 0;
                return value;
                }
        else
                {
                last_PTR = *E_PTR_PTR;
                this_PTR = (*E_PTR_PTR)->next_PTR;

                while ((this_PTR != NULL) && (this_PTR->data != value))
                        {
```

```
                last_PTR = this_PTR;
                this_PTR = this_PTR->next_PTR;
                }
        if (this_PTR)
                {
                temp_PTR = this_PTR;
                last_PTR->next_PTR = this_PTR->next_PTR;
                delete temp_PTR;
                temp_PTR = 0;
                return value;
                }
        }
    return '\0';
    }
/*************************************************************
*                                                           *
* FUNCTION: Is_empty()                                      *
*                                                           *
* OVERVIEW: Returns 1 if the list is empty, 0 otherwise.    *
*                                                           *
*************************************************************/
int Is_empty(sElement* E_PTR)
    {
    if (E_PTR == NULL)
        {
        return 1;
        }
    else
        {
        return 0;
        }
    }

/*************************************************************
*                                                           *
* FUNCTION: Display_list()                                  *
*                                                           *
* OVERVIEW: Display all the list elements on the screen.    *
*                                                           *
*************************************************************/
void Display_list(sElement* this_PTR)
    {
    if (this_PTR == NULL)
        {
        cout    << "\nList starts at address "
                << this_PTR << endl;
        cout    << "(List is empty)\n";
        cout    << "List ends at address "
                << this_PTR << endl;
        }
```

```
        else
            {
            cout << "\nList starts at address "
                << this_PTR << endl;

            while (this_PTR != NULL)
                {
                cout << "Data " << (char) this_PTR->data << " -> ";
                cout << this_PTR->next_PTR << endl;
                this_PTR = this_PTR->next_PTR;
                }

            cout << "List ends at address "
                << this_PTR << endl;
            }
        }

/***********************************************************
*                    *** END OF PROGRAM ***                *
***********************************************************/
```

Program 18.3   A simple linked list. (☺)

The following example illustrates the basic operation of Program 18.3:

```
LINKED LIST DEMONSTRATION

List starts at address 0×0
(List is empty)
List ends at address 0×0

Type 1 to insert an element into the list.
     2 to delete an element from the list.
     3 to QUIT.

Insert (1), Delete (2) or Quit (3) ? 1

Enter a character for insertion: a

List starts at address 0×42f70edc
Data a -> 0×0
List ends at address 0×0

Insert (1), Delete (2) or Quit (3) ? 1

Enter a character for insertion: h

List starts at address 0×42f70edc
Data a -> 0×42f70fd4
Data h -> 0×0
List ends at address 0×0

Insert (1), Delete (2) or Quit (3) ? 1

Enter a character for insertion: c

List starts at address 0×42f70edc
Data a -> 0×42f710ec
Data c -> 0×42f70fd4
```

```
Data h -> 0x0
List ends at address 0x0

Insert (1), Delete (2) or Quit (3) ? 1

Enter a character for insertion: l

List starts at address 0x42f70edc
Data a -> 0x42f710ec
Data c -> 0x42f70fd4
Data h -> 0x42f71224
Data l -> 0x0
List ends at address 0x0

Insert (1), Delete (2) or Quit (3) ? 1

Enter a character for insertion: x

List starts at address 0x42f70edc
Data a -> 0x42f710ec
Data c -> 0x42f70fd4
Data h -> 0x42f71224
Data l -> 0x42f7137c
Data x -> 0x0
List ends at address 0x0

Insert (1), Delete (2) or Quit (3) ? 2

Enter character to be deleted: h
h deleted.

List starts at address 0x42f70edc
Data a -> 0x42f710ec
Data c -> 0x42f71224
Data l -> 0x42f7137c
Data x -> 0x0
List ends at address 0x0

Insert (1), Delete (2) or Quit (3) ? 2

Enter character to be deleted: b
b not found.

Insert (1), Delete (2) or Quit (3) ? 2

Enter character to be deleted: a
a deleted.

List starts at address 0x42f710ec
Data c -> 0x42f71224
Data l -> 0x42f7137c
Data x -> 0x0
List ends at address 0x0

Insert (1), Delete (2) or Quit (3) ? 3

Thank you for using this program.
```

Note that, rather than using multiple indirection, it is possible to implement this list using pointer references: this is left as an exercise.

18.4.2 Beyond linked lists

The linked list we have presented here forms the basis of many of the useful data structures in widespread commercial use.

For example, a stack is a specialized version of a linked list. New nodes are added from the stack and removed from the stack only at the top. For this reason, a stack is referred to as a **last-in first-out** (LIFO) data structure. Similarly, just as in a supermarket, in a queue the first person in a line is 'checked out' first. This is another common and useful **first-in first-out** (FIFO) data structure. We'll develop code for a stack in Chapter 26.

Whereas lists, stacks and queues are linear data structures, a tree is a non-linear, two-dimensional data structure with several useful properties. Trees are an essential component of many computer programs involving the manipulation of large amounts of data; in particular, a variety of tree known as the B-Tree (or one of its later variants) lies at the heart of most relational database programs (such as dBASE IV) – the name B-Tree stands for **Boeing tree**, the company in which the data structure was developed.

If you are intent on developing your own complex data structures in C++, or even a complete database framework, Folk and Zoellick (1992), and Budd (1994) will provide you with some useful pointers. Note that we are not suggesting that using C++ to build your own database is necessarily a practical proposition; indeed, certainly for large projects, for reasons we discuss in Chapter 20, this is very rarely a good idea.

Finally, two points should be made about the data structures we have considered in this chapter:

- Like program structures, data structures can be represented at various levels of abstraction. For example, a stack can be viewed as a conceptual model of a data structure that may be implemented as an array or as a linked list. The internal workings of such a stack are usually not defined during the analysis stage of a project.

- We have been dealing here with what might be described as 'internal' data structures. That is, data structures that are stored within the RAM of the computer. At some point, as our databases get larger, we must start to store them on disk. Such 'external' data structures introduce problems of their own, some of which we start to tackle in the next chapter.

18.5 Conclusions

In this chapter, we have looked at some more complex data structures that you may need to use in your programs. We have also looked at the ways in which some of these data structures can be implemented in a practical situation.

In the next chapter, we consider ways in which you can save your complex data on disk.

Exercises

18.1 The 'dynamic array' presented in Section 18.3 is really only semi-dynamic; while the size is set at run time, we haven't considered how to vary this size later in the program. Building on the material in Section 18.3, try to develop a true dynamic array structure.

Hint: this isn't easy using the C++ features we've looked at so far! One possibility would be to build the 'array' from a linked list. Another possible way of increasing the size of a true array structure (that is, a structure allowing fast access through pointers), is to have a function which allocates memory for the new array, copies the data from the old array into the new array, then returns the memory for the old array to free store. Obviously, if you reduce the size of an existing array, some data will be lost – but the idea is the same.

Trying to produce a dynamic array in this manner is a useful exercise, but isn't really a practical proposition. We'll look at some more flexible – and rather more elegant – ways of creating such a data structure in Part III.

18.2 The linked list program presented in this chapter is a useful simple demonstration program. However – like our simple dynamic array – it is not really representative of the type of applications for which such complex data structures are most often applied.

In this exercise, you will extend the basic linked list program. Begin by compiling the file Program 18.3. Experiment with the program while examining the source code. When you understand how the program operates, extend it so that instead of single characters, the list contains a list of ID numbers. Each ID number must be exactly seven characters long, and consist of three characters (each a capital letter, between 'A' and 'J'), followed by four digits (each between 1 and 9). Include appropriate error checking to ensure that only valid IDs are entered.

18.3 Extend your solution to Exercise 18.2 so that the list contains no duplicate ID numbers.

18.4 A doubly-linked list has connections between elements both 'up' and 'down' the list (Figure 18.4).

Such a data structure has two main advantages: (a) it can be quicker to find the elements near the bottom of the list by starting at the bottom and working up, rather than always starting at the top, and (b) the list may be more robust; if the data is corrupted, it may be easier to recover the lost information because there are two links (rather than one) to each data element.

Repeat Exercise 18.3 with doubly-linked list. (*Note*: Davies (1995) has a partial solution, in C, if you get stuck …)

18.5 Edit your solution to Exercise 18.4 so that the list is implemented using pointer references, instead of 'pointers to pointers'.

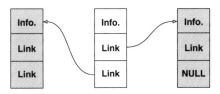

Figure 18.4 A schematic representation of a doubly-linked list.

18.6 Suppose we have a mailing list constructed from a linked list of the following user-declared data structure:

```
struct sCustomer
    {
    char lastname[31];      // Customer's last name
    char firstname[31];     // Customer's first name
    char title[11];         // Customer's title
    char address1[81];      // 1st line of customer's address
    char address2[81];      // 2nd line of customer's address
    char address3[81];      // 3rd line of customer's address
    char postcode[11];      // Customer's postcode
    };
```

We can – as we have seen in this chapter – expand or reduce the size of the mailing list as required during a program run. However, suppose we have been using the program for a while, and we decide that we need to add a new data field (specifying, say, a customer ID number). The new `struct` then takes the following form:

```
struct sCustomer2
    {
    char custID[7];         // Customer's ID number
    char lastname[31];      // Customer's last name
    char firstname[31];     // Customer's first name
    char title[11];         // Customer's title
    char address1[81];      // 1st line of customer's address
    char address2[81];      // 2nd line of customer's address
    char address3[81];      // 3rd line of customer's address
    char postcode[11];      // Customer's postcode
    };
```

How would you work around the problem? Write a program that works with a single `struct`-based variable (make it a static array of such variables, if you're feeling brave), and allows the user to add new fields or delete existing fields, as required. Assume that all the fields are character arrays, and that deleting a field destroys any associated data in the field.

Hint: One solution to this problem would be to make each sDynCust-variable a linked list of sField variables, as follows:

```
struct sDynCust
    {
    sField* FirstField;     // Ptr to start of list of cust details
    };
struct sField
    {
    char* Data;             // Pointer to the data (e.g. cust name)
    sField* NextField;      // Pointer to next field
    };
```

The list itself would be constructed as before. In a complete system, we might then opt to have a doubly-linked list of customers, each consisting of a singly-linked list of fields.

19 Saving data for posterity

19.1 Introduction

We've considered in the previous two chapters how, for example, we could use a C++ `struct` to create a new data type for storing details of components used on a truck assembly line:

```
struct sComponent
    {
    long part_num;          // Component ID number
    int  version;           // Version number
    char description[80];   // Brief description
    long stock_level;       // Number of components in stock
    };
```

We also explored various ways of assembling collections of `struct` variables into arrays and lists.

However, our vehicle component database, like many other systems, is also likely to require some form of *persistent* data; that is, data that is not lost at the end of a program run. Without such an essential feature, the whole database will have to be re-keyed every time the computer is switched off.

Generally, of course, data persistence is realized by storing data on an external storage device, such as a hard disk or magneto-optical disk during program execution, and retrieving it, possibly using a different program, at a later date.

In this chapter, we explore the topic of persistent data from a C++ perspective. We'll begin by looking at sequential file access, and then go on to look at more flexible direct access routines.

19.2 File access fundamentals

Before we consider the details of file input and output from C++, it is useful to understand a little about the underlying software and hardware.

19.2.1 The heart of the matter

A typical hard disk is shown schematically in Figure 19.1. In operation, the disk spins constantly (usually at about 3600 revolutions per minute). The disk platter itself will

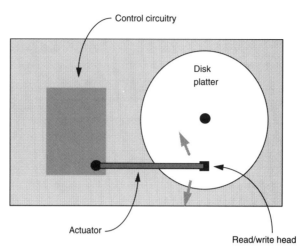

Figure 19.1 The main components of a hard disk.

usually be made of aluminium. This metal is robust but of low density, a factor of particular importance in notebook computers or in embedded data logging applications. Here a disk may be used to store weather data gathered over a period of several months: in order to save power, the platter will be stopped when the disk drive is not in use. The use of a low density aluminium platter means that the drive can be quickly brought up to operating speed when required. Since, however, aluminium cannot be magnetized, the surface must be coated with a magnetic medium.

The control electronics move the actuator, allowing the read/write head to access any part of the disk surface, as required. Note that, in reality, the disk assembly will generally have multiple platters, each with a read/write head on both top and bottom surface.

In its original raw state, the disk platter is simply a blank unstructured magnetic plate. However, a formatting operation is carried out under software control that lays down a series of tracks and sectors on the surface of the platter (Figure 19.2).

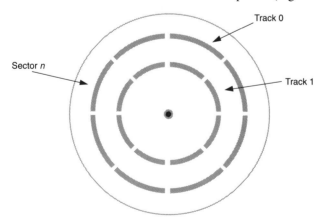

Figure 19.2 The organization of a formatted disk platter into sectors and tracks. Note that, in reality, the disk is likely to have not 2 but 80 tracks, each accommodating between about 20 and 70 sectors. Typically, a sector has a capacity of 512 bytes.

Each sector typically has a capacity of 512 bytes. Therefore, any particular byte on the disk has an address made up of a track number, a sector number and a sector position.

19.2.2 Streams in C++

Armed with a detailed knowledge of the disk in your computer, including the number of tracks, the number of sectors per track and the sector size, one can *imagine* a comparatively straightforward scheme of pointers that would allow us access any byte of disk memory in much the same way that we can directly access any byte of silicon memory. Of course, as our hard disk might have a multi-gigabyte capacity and our silicon memory is likely to be much less, we probably couldn't use exactly the same addressing scheme for disk memory, but the principles would be the same.

The problem with such a scheme is that it would be hugely implementation dependent. If you developed your code for, say, a Seagate ST3491A disk drive, suffered a disk crash and replaced your drive with a Fujitsu M2684T disk drive, you would almost certainly have to recompile all your programs. This is bad enough, but when developing applications for a client, you would need to know what kind of disk they had in their machine, and have to rely on them keeping the same hardware for the rest of the useful life of your program.

Of course, this type of problem is precisely the kind that high-level languages are intended to solve. C++ does this by insulating the programmer from the file system and providing a high-level abstract model of file access known as a *stream*.

A stream is (in its most common form) a logical interface to a 'file'. What is important to realize is that, as far as C++ is concerned, 'file' is used in a very general sense and can mean not only a disk file, but also the screen, the keyboard, or a port. As we have seen, even for disk files, the underlying format of the data may well differ according to the particular hardware installation. Streams, however, provide a consistent interface.

The programmer links a stream to a disk file using an 'open' operation; this link is broken using a 'close' operation.

19.2.3 The `iostream` class library

Back in Chapter 3, we saw that C++, in common with many other languages, does not include facilities for communicating with keyboards, screens, disks and so on, in the language itself. Instead, the (stream) input and output routines depend on the `iostream` **class library** provided with the implementation: we consider class libraries in greater detail in Part III.

As previously discussed, each source file that refers to the `iostream` I/O facilities must contain the line:

```
#include <iostream.h>
```

before the first reference to any of the facilities from this library.

19.2.4 Types of data file

Before we actually open a file, we generally need to know what kind of file it is. There are essentially two possibilities: text files and binary files.

To understand the distinction, recall that *all* data (words, numbers, code) within the computer are stored efficiently in a standard binary format. To display these data on the screen of your computer, they must usually be converted to text format. This conversion process, not surprisingly, takes time. Also, if we store the representation in text of, say, some numerical data, we generally find this representation uses much more memory (typically two to four times more) than the original binary equivalent.

For example, consider an integer. In a binary notation, the value of 32 000 can be stored in two bytes. Convert the representation to text and at least five characters, each requiring one byte of storage, are required to represent the same information.

The main reason for using text files is to allow your stored data to be accessed easily by other users, for example using a text editor or word processor program. If this isn't a requirement, then binary files, being both smaller and having faster access times, are usually a better choice.

19.2.5 Direct versus sequential access

When you've decided what kind of file to open (or create), you then have to consider how to access the data in the file: this usually involves adjusting the value of the **file position pointer** (FPP). The FPP gives the offset address of any byte of data within the file. Typically, when a file is opened, the FPP is automatically set to the beginning of the file. The FPP can subsequently take any value (in bytes) between 0 (that is, the start of the file) and the size of the file.

> *It is important to realize that – despite the similar names – the file pointer (loosely, the 'address' of the start of the file on disk) and the file position pointer are distinct and essentially unrelated entities. In particular, note that direct manipulation of the file pointer is a potentially dangerous operation not normally under the control of the programmer, while manipulation of the file position pointer is regularly carried out during file access.*

Dire warnings aside, we have two different ways of adjusting the FPP: *sequentially* or *directly*.

Sequential access is the simplest way of accessing data within a file. During sequential access, the FPP is *automatically* incremented by the program so that, for example, data items written to the file are stored in the same order that they are generated.

Direct access to files (sometimes called 'random access', largely for historical reasons) can be much faster than sequential access. Typically, direct access is used when the individual records in our file are of fixed length. The main requirement for direct access, therefore, is to be able to alter the value of the file position pointer before reading or writing to the file at any position we choose.

We will see how to perform both sequential and direct access to C++ files below.

Finally, note that – strictly – there are (usually) *two* file position pointers, one recording the position of the next write operation, and one recording the position of the next read operation. However, the simplified description given above will be adequate for our discussions here.

19.3 Opening and closing files

The fundamental file operations are the opening and closing of files. We'll see how to perform each of these basic operations in this section.

19.3.1 Opening a C++ file

The following C++ fragment opens a disk file:

```
...
fstream  file_pointer;     // A pointer to the file
...
file_pointer.open("filename", ios::out);
if (!file_pointer.good())
    {
    // The file could not be opened.
    cerr << "FATAL ERROR: Could not create file 'datafile.dat'";
    exit(1);
    }
...
```

Here the name of the file to be opened is pointed to by 'filename': this must be valid *for the particular operating system* your program will work with.

Next, file_pointer.open() returns a pointer to a data item of type fstream (a data structure holding details such as size of file, current location, access modes, and so on). Note that file_pointer.open() returns a null pointer if the specified file cannot be opened: the programmer *must* check for this and, as shown in the fragment above, take appropriate action if a null pointer is returned.

In the line:

```
file_pointer.open("filename", ios::out);
```

ios::out specifies the **access mode** of the file. In this example, the file is opened for output. This and the other possible file access modes are described in Table 19.1.

Mode	Description
ios::binary	Opens the specified field in binary mode. *Note:* this option is (at the time of writing) part of the proposed C++ standard (Rudd, 1994). This standard dictates that the default file mode is text, unless ios::binary is explicitly selected. At the time of writing, not all compilers support this keyword, and some use binary files by default.
ios::in	Opens the specified file for input (reading) only. FPP is set to the beginning of the file. *Note:* If the file does not exist or cannot be found, the default behaviour is that the open call will *not* fail: instead (if possible) a new file will be created. If this is not the behaviour you require, you'll need to use ios::nocreate, detailed below.
ios::out	Open the specified file for output (writing) only. FPP is set to the beginning of the file. *Note:* If the file already exists, the current contents will be discarded without warning!
ios::app	Open the specified file for appending: that is, open a file and set the FPP to allow data to be added to the end of the file. Creates the file if it does not exist. *Note:* all write operations must occur at the end of the file. Although the FPP can be repositioned (see later in this chapter), the FPP is always moved back to the end of the file before any write operation is carried out. Thus, using this mode stops you from overwriting existing data.
ios::ate	Set FPP to end of file.
ios::nocreate	Do not create file if it does not exist. *Note [1]:* especially relevant in conjunction with ios::in (see above). *Note [2]:* not available in ISO C++.
ios::trunc	Truncate file to zero length (i.e. discard current contents), then open.

Table 19.1 File access modes.

Note that various values from the above table can be combined. For example, the following fragment will open a binary file 'data.dat' for input and output, but not create a new file if 'data.dat' does not exist (or can't be found):

```
f_ptr.open("data.dat", ios::in | ios::out | ios::binary | ios::nocreate);
```

Note also that opening a file for input and output is *not* the same as opening a file in 'append' mode. In 'append' mode, existing data in the file cannot be overwritten: in 'read and write' mode, existing data can be overwritten *and* new data can be added.

As a general rule, you should always safeguard your data by allowing programs access only on a 'need to know' basis. That is, allow programs the minimum level of access to your data sufficient to allow correct functioning of the program.

19.3.2   Closing a C++ file

As there are limits to the number of files you can have open at any one time on any computer system (typically ~40), you should close any files you open as soon as possible, and certainly before the end of your program.

To do so, use the pointer to your file, as follows:

```
file_pointer.close();
```

Note that an ideal way to destroy the contents of a disk (or other storage device) is to pick a file pointer value at random, and close the 'associated' file. The consequences of this action vary between systems, but are almost invariably disastrous, and may involve re-formatting the whole disk ...

19.4   Sequential file access

We are now ready to perform some basic file access operations. We'll begin by looking at a simple example, then present a more useful program that allows the copying of text files. Finally, we'll consider how files can be used in conjunction with C++ functions.

19.4.1   The basics

Program 19.1 creates a text file, stores some data in the file, then retrieves it again. Note that the access here is sequential simply because we are not attempting to control the position of the file pointer. Instead, we let C++ take care of this for us automatically.

```
// Simple sequential file access with text files
// Source is: 19_01.CPP

#include <fstream.h>
#include <iostream.h>
#include <stdlib.h>

int main ()
    {
    int        Numbers[5] = {10,20,30,40,50};
    fstream    file_pointer;
    int        number, i;
```

```
    // Open the data file for writing
    file_pointer.open("datafile.dat", ios::out);
    if (!file_pointer.good())
        {
        cout << "FATAL ERROR: Could not create file 'datafile.dat'";
        exit(1);
        }
    cout << "Just opened the data file for WRITING\n";
    for (i=0; i < 5; i++)
        {
        file_pointer << Numbers[i] << endl; // Write data
        cout << "Just written : " << Numbers[i] << endl;
        }
    file_pointer.close(); // Finished writing: close the file
    // Open the file again, this time for reading
    file_pointer.open("datafile.dat", ios::in);
    if (!file_pointer.good())
        {
        cout << "FATAL ERROR: Could not open file 'datafile.dat'";
        exit(1);
        }
    cout << "\nJust opened the data file for READING\n";
    for (i=0; i < 5; i++)
        {
        file_pointer >> number; // Read data
        cout << "Just read : " << number << endl;
        }
    file_pointer.close(); // Don't forget to close the file
    return 0;
    }
```

Program 19.1   Simple sequential file access. (☺)

Program 19.1 produces the following output:

```
Just opened the data file for WRITING
Just written : 10
Just written : 20
Just written : 30
Just written : 40
Just written : 50

Just opened the data file for READING
Just read : 10
Just read : 20
Just read : 30
Just read : 40
Just read : 50
```

19.4.2 Copying text files

To illustrate a slightly more useful application of sequential access, Program 19.2 illustrates how one text file can be copied to another using this technique.

```
// Simple file copy program for text files
// Source is: 19_02.CPP

#include <iostream.h>
#include <fstream.h>

int main()
    {
    fstream orig_file_pointer, copy_file_pointer;

    orig_file_pointer.open("orig.txt", ios::in);
    copy_file_pointer.open("copy.txt", ios::out);

    if ((!orig_file_pointer) || (!copy_file_pointer))
        {
        cerr << "ERROR: Cannot open an essential file.";
        return 1; // Note use of this alternative to exit()
        }

    //Ignore white space in input
    orig_file_pointer.unsetf(ios::skipws);

    char ch;

    orig_file_pointer >> ch;

    while (!orig_file_pointer.eof()) // Keep going till end of file...
        {
        copy_file_pointer << ch;
        orig_file_pointer >> ch;
        }
    return 0;
    }
```

Program 19.2 Copying text files (cheap and cheerful version). (☺)

There are several points to note from Program 19.2. First of all, as in the simple use of the 'put to' operator with keyboard input (see Section 9.3.1), use of the 'put to' operator with files also results in the input terminating if white space is encountered. Here, by using the unsetf() function, and specifying that white space should be 'skipped', we avoid this problem. The relevant line in the code is:

```
orig_file_pointer.unsetf(ios::skipws);
```

Next, note that we don't have any way of knowing how long the file of text is when we start: it could be a shopping list or it could be a novel. We therefore use the eof() function to determine whether we are at the end of file or not. Note that use of eof() is slightly clumsy: using this simple routine, we cannot 'look ahead', instead we must read in a character, check it, and then – if it isn't the end of file character – write it to our copy file, as shown:

```
orig_file_pointer >> ch;
while (!orig_file_pointer.eof()) // Keep going till end of file...
    {
    copy_file_pointer << ch;
    orig_file_pointer >> ch;
    }
```

We can make this code slightly more elegant and flexible by making use of the peek() function. This function returns a *copy* of the next character in a stream, without removing the character from the stream. Usefully, at the end of the file, the next character will be the 'EOF' character.

Using peek(), we could rewrite the copy fragment above as follows:

```
do
    { // Keep going till end of file...
    orig_file_pointer >> ch;
    copy_file_pointer << ch;
    } while (orig_file_pointer.peek() != EOF);
```

19.4.3   On files and functions

We also, of course, need to consider the use of files and functions, including the passing of file pointers as function parameters. The process is straightforward, as illustrated by Program 19.3.

```
// Files and functions
// Source is: 19_03.CPP

#include <iostream.h>
#include <fstream.h>

// Prototype
int open_file(fstream&, char*);

int main()
    {
    fstream file_ptr;

    if (!open_file(file_ptr, "datafile.txt"))
        {
        cout << "Opened file";
        }
    else
        {
        cout << "Sorry - could not open file";
        }

    // Close the file
    file_ptr.close();

    return 0;
    }

int open_file(fstream& file_pointer_REF, char* filename_PTR)
    {
    file_pointer_REF.open(filename_PTR, ios::in);
```

```
if (!file_pointer_REF.good())
    {
    return 1;
    }
return 0;
}
```

Program 19.3 File pointers and functions. (☺)

It is important to realize that, even when you are simply planning to read from a file, you still need to pass the file pointer by reference. This is because even in reading, parts of the fstream 'object' (such as the file position pointer) will be altered. These changes need to be reflected in the calling function.

We'll provide a more realistic example of file access using C++ functions in Chapter 23.

19.5   Direct file access

Sequential access is fine if, for example, we wish to backup the entire directory structure of our hard disk onto magnetic tape. If, however, we store a large database on disk, and then want to change a particular record, we don't want to have to read in all the records in turn until we find the one we want: instead, we want to retrieve any particular record at will. Direct access gives us this ability.

19.5.1   The basics

Typically, as we have seen, when a file is opened, the file position pointer (FPP) is set to the beginning or the end of the file. During sequential access, the FPP is automatically incremented by the program so that, for example, data items written to the file are stored in the same order that they are generated. The main requirement for direct access, therefore, is to be able to alter the value of the FPP before reading or writing to the file. We can achieve this through the use of the function seekg().

For example, suppose we have a file pointer file_pointer pointing to a file containing a list of integers. If we wanted to replace the value stored for the third element of this list, we could use seekg() to adjust the FPP as follows:

```
file_pointer.seekg(2 * sizeof(int), ios::beg);
```

which sets the FPP to a position (2 * sizeof(int)) bytes relative to the position ios::beg. Here, ios::beg specifies that the calculated position is relative to the start of the file.

The use of direct file access, and seekg(), is illustrated in Program 19.4.

```
// Simple direct file access
// Source is: 19_04.CPP

#include <fstream.h>
#include <iostream.h>
```

```
int main()
    {
    char Character, characters[7] = {'a','b','c','d','e','f','g'};
    fstream file_pointer; // A pointer to the file
    file_pointer.open("datafile.dat", ios::out | ios::in);

    if (!file_pointer.good())
        {
        cout << "FATAL ERROR: Could not create file 'datafile.dat'";
        return 1;
        }

    cout << "Just opened the data file\n";

    for (int i = 0; i <= 6; i++)
        {
        file_pointer.seekg(i * sizeof(char), ios::beg);
        file_pointer << characters[i];
        cout << "Just written " << characters[i]
             << " at position " << i << endl;
        }

    file_pointer.seekg(6 * sizeof(char), ios::beg);
    file_pointer >> Character;
    cout << "\nJust read " << Character << " at position 6\n";

    file_pointer.seekg(2 * sizeof(char), ios::beg);
    file_pointer >> Character;
    cout << "Just read " << Character << " at position 2\n";

    file_pointer.seekg(5 * sizeof(char), ios::beg);
    file_pointer >> Character;
    cout << "Just read " << Character << " at position 5\n";

    file_pointer.seekg(0 * sizeof(char), ios::beg);
    file_pointer >> Character;
    cout << "Just read " << Character << " at position 0\n";

    // Finished: close the file
    file_pointer.close();

    return 0;
    }
```

Program 19.4   Simple direct access with text files. (☺)

The output from Program 19.4 using most modern compilers is as follows:

```
Just opened the data file
Just written a at position 0
Just written b at position 1
Just written c at position 2
Just written d at position 3
Just written e at position 4
Just written f at position 5
Just written g at position 6
```

```
Just read g at position 6
Just read c at position 2
Just read f at position 5
Just read a at position 0
```

The operation of Program 19.4 is straightforward.

Note, however, that where the individual data items we wish to store vary in size (for example, where we try to store integers in text format), then direct access and text files are incompatible. Program 19.5 illustrates the problem.

```cpp
// Direct file access - fails with varying length records
// Source is: 19_05.CPP

#include <fstream.h>
#include <iostream.h>

int main ()
    {
    int Number, Numbers[10] = {0,1,2,3333,4,5,600,7,8,99};
    fstream file_pointer; // A pointer to the file

    file_pointer.open("datafile.dat", ios::out | ios::in);

    if (!file_pointer.good())
        {
        cout << "FATAL ERROR: Could not create file 'datafile.dat'";
        return 1;
        }

    cout << "Just opened the data file\n";

    // "Direct" access...
    for (int i = 0; i <= 9; i++)
        {
        // This can't work!! sizeof int is not the same as the
        // (varying) size of the text equivalent.
        file_pointer.seekg(i * sizeof(int), ios::beg);
        file_pointer << Numbers[i];
        cout << "Just written " << Numbers[i]
             << " at position " << i << endl;
        }

    file_pointer.seekg(0 * sizeof(int), ios::beg);
    file_pointer >> Number;
    cout << "\nJust read " << Number << " at position 0\n";

    file_pointer.seekg(3 * sizeof(int), ios::beg);
    file_pointer >> Number;
    cout << "Just read " << Number << " at position 3\n";

    file_pointer.seekg(4 * sizeof(int), ios::beg);
    file_pointer >> Number;
    cout << "Just read " << Number << " at position 4\n";

    file_pointer.seekg(6 * sizeof(int), ios::beg);
    file_pointer >> Number;
    cout << "Just read " << Number << " at position 6\n";
```

```
    // Finished: close the file
    file_pointer.close();
    return 0;
    }
```

Program 19.5 Trying to use direct access with text files when the 'records' to be stored vary in size. (☺)

Program 19.5 generates the following output using most modern compilers:

```
Just opened the data file
Just written 0 at position 0
Just written 1 at position 1
Just written 2 at position 2
Just written 3333 at position 3
Just written 4 at position 4
Just written 5 at position 5
Just written 600 at position 6
Just written 7 at position 7
Just written 8 at position 8
Just written 99 at position 9

Just read 0 at position 0
Just read -32101 at position 3
Just read 435 at position 4
Just read 607 at position 6
```

Here, in binary notation, all integers are the same say (typically two bytes); when they have been converted to text the same two byte integers may take one byte (for example, 0) or, say, four bytes (for example, 3333). Text files are difficult to use in these circumstances.

For this reason, direct access is generally used with binary files. Program 19.6 illustrates this possibility.

```
// Simple direct file access using binary files
// Source is: 19_06.CPP
#include <fstream.h>
#include <iostream.h>
int main()
    {
    int Number, Numbers[10] = {0,1,2,3333,4,5,600,7,8,99};
    fstream file_pointer; // A pointer to the file
    file_pointer.open("datafile.dat" ios::out|ios::in|ios::binary);
    if (!file_pointer.good())
        {
        cout << "FATAL ERROR: Could not create file 'datafile.dat'";
        return 1;
        }
    cout << "Just opened the data file\n";
    // "Direct" access...
    for (int i = 0; i <= 9; i++)
```

```
        {
        file_pointer.seekg(i * sizeof(int), ios::beg);
        file_pointer.write((char*) (Numbers+i), sizeof(int));
        cout << "Just written " << Numbers[i]
             << " at position " << i << endl;
        }
    file_pointer.seekg(0 * sizeof(int), ios::beg);
    file_pointer.read((char*) &Number, sizeof(int));
    cout << "\nJust read " << Number << " at position 0\n";

    file_pointer.seekg(3 * sizeof(int), ios::beg);
    file_pointer.read((char*) &Number, sizeof(int));
    cout << "Just read " << Number << " at position 3\n";

    file_pointer.seekg(4 * sizeof(int), ios::beg);
    file_pointer.read((char*) &Number, sizeof(int));
    cout << "Just read " << Number << " at position 4\n";

    file_pointer.seekg(6 * sizeof(int), ios::beg);
    file_pointer.read((char*) &Number, sizeof(int));
    cout << "Just read " << Number << " at position 6\n";

    // Finished: close the file
    file_pointer.close();

    return 0;
    }
```

Program 19.6 Simple direct file access using binary files. (☺)

Program 19.6 produces the following output:

```
Just opened the data file
Just written 0 at position 0
Just written 1 at position 1
Just written 2 at position 2
Just written 3333 at position 3
Just written 4 at position 4
Just written 5 at position 5
Just written 600 at position 6
Just written 7 at position 7
Just written 8 at position 8
Just written 99 at position 9

Just read 0 at position 0
Just read 3333 at position 3
Just read 4 at position 4
Just read 600 at position 6
```

When comparing binary and text file output routines, it is important to appreciate that while the following code fragment will open and write to a 'text file':

```
file_pointer.open("datafile.dat", ios::out);
...
file_pointer << Numbers[i] << endl;
...
```

the following code fragment will do exactly the same (despite the explicit use of `ios::binary`):

```
file_pointer.open("datafile.dat", ios::out | ios::binary);
...
file_pointer << Numbers[i] << endl;
...
```

This happens because the use of the 'put to' operator in the output routine will (implicitly) invoke a text to binary-to-text conversion, just as happens when the same operator is used to display results on the screen.

The safest way to avoid this is to make use of `file_pointer.write()`, or equivalent, when dealing with binary files. This function performs no implicit conversion of the data, giving the required binary format. The prototype of `write()` is as follows:

```
istream& write(const unsigned char* character_buffer_PTR,
               int                  number_of_bytes);
```

We consider the return type of this function in Part III. At this time, note that `write()` takes two parameters, a pointer to a *character* buffer, and an integer specifying how many bytes (starting at the pointer address) are to be output. Note that in Program 19.6 and in many other practical cases, it is necessary to use a cast operator (`char*`) within the call to `write()` when writing from a buffer that is not defined as a character array. This is a side-effect of C++'s strong type checking; a pointer of one type will not be automatically converted to a pointer of another type.

Note finally that the corresponding `read()` function is very similar to `write()`, and has the following prototype:

```
istream& read(unsigned char* character_buffer_PTR,
              int            number_of_bytes);
```

19.5.2   Storing and retrieving `structs`

In the previous examples in this chapter, we have assumed that you will wish to maintain a disk file containing items of a simple built-in data type, such as integers. On some occasions you may wish to store user-defined types, such as the `structs` we considered in Chapter 17. This can be easily done.

For example, the following code fragment will store a single item of type `sProduct`.

```
struct sProduct
    {
    int stock_number;
    char name[30];
    int quantity;
    int price;
    int supplier_num;
    };
...
sProduct product;
...
file_pointer.write((char*) &product, sizeof(sProduct));
```

A complete example of the use of disk storage with user-defined data structures is given in Chapter 23.

19.6   Conclusions

In this chapter, we have looked at the simple file access routines provided in C++. Used in conjunction with the user-defined data structures described in Chapter 18, the features discussed here will form the heart of a range of simple information systems developed in later chapters.

Finally, we reiterate that the features discussed in this chapter are not part of the language itself, but part of the iostream **class library** provided with all C++ compilers. We consider class libraries in Part III.

Exercises

19.1   Write a C++ program that includes a function `Write_Numbers()` which will prompt the user to type in an unspecified number of floats (for example, 1.2, 2.4, 3.6) and will store the numbers in *text* file called 'nums.txt'. Note that each number should be stored on a different line in the file. Confirm using a text editor or word processor that the numbers have been stored correctly.

19.2   Write another C++ function `Read_Numbers()` to read the data from the file created in Exercise 19.1. Add this function to the program created in Exercise 19.1 so that the program calls first `Write_Numbers()`, then `Read_Numbers()`.

19.3   Modify the program created in Exercise 19.2 to work with binary files. The data should be stored in a file called 'nums.bin'. Try inspecting the resulting file with your word processor or text editor: what do you see?

19.4   Modify the program created in Exercise 19.3 so that the user can add data to an existing file of numbers. When your program is run, it should search for 'nums.bin'. If this file is not found, the program should not automatically create a new file but should offer the user the options of (a) creating a new file, or (b) exiting from the program to (for example) restore a copy of 'nums.txt' from a backup disk.

19.5   Use a text editor to generate a text file 'names.txt' containing the following names and telephone numbers:

Barbara	*123456*
Gordon	*234567*
Susan	*345678*
John	*456789*
Andrew	*567891*
Anne	*678910*

Write a program that will read in these names and allow the user to add additional names to the list, delete names from the list, and change the names or telephone numbers of people in the list. Naturally, your program should be constructed from an appropriate set of C++ functions.

19.6 Modify the program you created in Exercise 19.5 to allow the user to sort the entries in the list into alphabetical order. Make sure you just sort by name, and don't make the order of your list vary with telephone number. *Hint*: you may find the `strcmp()` library function useful.

19.7 If you have access to a technical library (on paper or on-line), see if you can find the technical specification for a common database file format appropriate for your computer: for example, the dBase file format is still widely used with PCs.

   Having found the format details, beg, steal or borrow an appropriate data file and try to write a C++ program to read the data.

19.8 In Appendix K, we outline a simple method for what is known as 'software size prediction'. The aim of this technique is to allow the software engineer to predict the number of lines of comment-free code that will be created during the course of a project, based only on information available early in the system lifecycle.

   One problem with this type of approach is that it needs to be 'fine-tuned' to match the particular coding style of the company or individual using the formula. In order to perform this fine-tuning, users need to record the number of lines of comment-free code in a range of their own projects and adjust the formula to match their particular needs.

   The aim of this exercise is to produce some software that will help gather the information needed to support such a refinement. Specifically, you are asked to write a program that will count the number of lines of comment-free code in a given C++ file.

   The program should have the simple interface illustrated below:

```
C++ Line-Counting Program

Type in the file you wish to analyse: 16_03.cpp

File '16_03.cpp' contains 455 lines of C++ code.

This calculation ignores all blank lines, and lines
containing only comments.

Do you wish to analyse another file (Y/N)? n

Finished.
```

19.9 Another problem with the simple formula for predicting lines of code discussed in Exercise 19.8 is that every programmer lays out their code differently. For example, consider the two very simple samples below:

```
for (int i = 0; i < 10; i++)   for (int i = 0; i < 10; i++)
    {                              cout << i;
    cout << i;
    }
```

   As far as a simple line-count is concerned, one sample is twice as long as the other.

   The aim of this exercise is to create a simple program that will take as an input a C++ program, and will create another file containing a copy of the program laid out according to the style guidelines given in this book. For example, in the above example, the right-hand fragment would be converted into the form on the left.

20 The relational database

20.1 Introduction

In the late 1950s, most programmers were writing in machine code, FORTRAN was beginning to emerge as a high-level programming language for technical applications, and ALGOL 60 was on the horizon. However, as far as most information system developers were concerned, these languages were next to useless, because they contained only two basic types: integers and real numbers, and appeared to give little thought to input and output features (Inglis, 1989).

What the information system programmers of the 1950s (and today) wanted were the kind of features we have looked at in the previous three chapters: explicit support for records, fields, and file processing. A world market economy and the basic rules of supply and demand meant that different suppliers were only too happy to develop such languages: however, the same free market rules meant that each new language was tied to a particular set of hardware, and was to a large extent incompatible with languages from other suppliers.

The US Department of Defense (DoD), a vast and influential user of computer systems, viewed the rash of new commercial languages with particular alarm. The DoD felt that one advantage of moving from machine code to a high-level language should be to allow programs, and programmers, to work on more than one type of computer system. FORTRAN provided just such advantages for technical program development; what was needed, the DoD argued, was a new 'information-system FORTRAN'. The DoD therefore called a meeting in Washington, out of which grew CODASYL (the Conference on Data Systems Languages) out of which, in turn, in April 1960 came the initial specification for a COmmon Business-Oriented Language (COBOL).

More than 35 years later, the split between technical systems and information systems programming is reduced but still very much evident. For that reason, some people will argue that relational databases don't belong in a book on software engineering but instead should only appear in books clearly labelled 'information systems' on the cover. As the presence of this chapter would tend to indicate, we don't agree. We hold the view that 'information system' and 'technical system' engineers can learn a lot from one another, and the emergence of a new truly common programming language (C++) is an important way of linking the two hitherto disparate programming camps. In this chapter, therefore, we provide a simple overview of business database systems, then go on to examine the essential features of database design that *all* self-respecting software engineers need to know.

20.2 Fundamentals of database systems

At the simplest level, a database is the computerized analogue of a series of filing cabinets; that is, it is a structured data repository. A database management system is merely a method of accessing this information. Thus, there are two key components of a data-based system: data (the database itself) and function (provided by the database management system).

We begin by considering the features that users of such systems have come to expect.

20.2.1 Data sharing

It is usual in a business context to have one (or more) central database(s) containing data shared by several (often many) individuals. Thus, the sales division of a company will make contents of its database available to the research division (to guide the development of popular future products), and to management. A consequence of the need for data sharing is that data must be stored in a format which a variety of different applications can access.

20.2.2 Data integration

It follows from the idea of data sharing that the same data should not be duplicated throughout the company. In a manner directly analogous to the use of functions to avoid code duplication, a fundamental aim with a database system design is to avoid duplicating data. Thus, for example, data on the names and addresses of employees will be held in one area and shared by personnel, salaries and wages, and the group sending out the company calendars once a year.

20.2.3 Data security

Users of a database must know that their data can be trusted and that is secure. Security implies both that the data won't be lost the next time lightning strikes the company's computer centre, and that 'hackers' cannot invade the system and steal, for example, sensitive business or medical records.

20.3 Why use a relational data model?

In Chapter 5, we looked at the problems of monolithic programs, like Program 20.1.

```
// Carpet Area Calculation v1.0
// Source is: 20_01.CPP
#include <iostream.h>
int main()
    {
    float width, length;
```

```
cout << "\nROOM ONE\n";
cout << "Type in width (in metres) <RETURN>: ";
cin  >> width;
cout << "Type in length (in metres) <RETURN>: ";
cin  >> length;
cout << "Area of carpet for Room 1 is: "
     << width * length << endl;

cout << "\nROOM TWO\n";
cout << "Type in width (in metres) <RETURN>: ";
cin  >> width;
cout << "Type in length (in metres) <RETURN>: ";
cin  >> length;
cout << "Area of carpet for Room 2 is: "
     << width * length << endl;

cout << "\nROOM THREE\n";
cout << "Type in width (in metres) <RETURN>: ";
cin  >> width;
cout << "Type in length (in metres) <RETURN>: ";
cin  >> length;
cout << "Area of carpet for Room 3 is: "
<< width * length << endl;

return 0;
}
```

Program 20.1   A C++ program for calculating the area of carpet required in an office v1.0. (☹)

As we saw, the solution was to use functions (Figure 20.1).

```
/*****************************************************************
*                                                               *
* FUNCTION: Calculate_Area                                      *
*                                                               *
* OVERVIEW: Calculate carpet area for one room.                 *
*                                                               *
*****************************************************************/
float Calculate_Area(int room_no)
    {
    float width, length, area;

    cout << "\nROOM " << room_no << "\n";
    cout << "Type in width (in metres) <RETURN>: ";
    cin  >> width;
    cout << "Type in length (in metres) <RETURN>: ";
    cin  >> length;

    area = width * length * 2; // Covering ceiling too.

    cout << "Area of carpet for Room " << room_no
         << " is: " << 2 * width * length << endl;

    return area;
    }
```

Figure 20.1   The `Calculate_Area()` function from the carpet solution.

An analogous problem arises in the **data domain**. Consider, for example, that you are developing a stock control system for a factory building ventilation systems. All the stock items are entered into the database, and technicians building the fans obtain the components they require from one of ten different stock distribution points. The distribution points are linked by computer to a shared central database: when the stock level of, say, Size 10 bolts falls below a pre-set level (for example, 50 units) the stock manager is automatically informed of this by the system, and a printed order for new components is automatically printed.

The information stored by the system might take the following form:

Stock #	Description	Current level	Re-order level	Supplier name	Supplier address

Note that 'Stock#' is underlined: this indicates that this field is the **primary key**. This implies that each row of the data table has a different stock number, and that we can uniquely identify any row of the table via this field.

Now, we could, as we have seen, set up a `struct` to hold all these various data items, then set up an array of such 'records' to hold the various stock items. We discuss in Section 20.6 the wisdom of using C++ for such a task, but on a more general level, we are making a (data) design decision which may not be wise.

If we consider some examples of the data we need to store in this application, then the pitfalls of this approach are revealed (Figure 20.2). From Figure 20.2 it is clear that not all of the stock items are obtained from different suppliers: in fact, there appears (from this small sample) to be a high degree of overlap.

Stock

Stock #	Description	Current Level	Re-order Level	Supplier Name	Supplier Address
1455	Size 10 bolt	30	50	Brown's	13 Slough Road, Winslow
6732	Brass washer	34	100	Littleton	34 Sutton Road, Hazleton
7852	Plastic cowling	123	5	Brown's	13 Slough Road, Winslow
8888	Manual	72	50	Littleton	34 Sutton Road, Hazleton

Figure 20.2 A 'Stock' entity.

Consider the implications of this. Suppose that the address of 'Brown's' changes. Because of the duplication of the address information throughout the table, we have not only to make many changes to the database, but we also have the potential of missing one or more of the addresses when we do the update; in that situation, the data held will be unreliable, and we won't know, for example, where to send the next 'Brown's' invoice.

This is where a **relational database** (RDB) becomes useful. In effect, at its most simple, a relational database is one containing multiple, related, tables of information. For instance, in a relational database we would probably represent the information above in two tables, as shown in Figure 20.3.

Stock

Stock #	Description	Current Level	Re-order Level	Supplier Name
1455	Size 10 bolt	30	10	Brown's
6732	Brass washer	34	100	Littleton
7852	Plastic cowling	123	5	Brown's
8888	Manual	72	50	Littleton

Supplier

Supplier Name	Supplier Address
Brown's	13 Slough Road, Winslow
Littleton	34 Sutton Road, Hazleton

Figure 20.3 A two-table version of the Stock entity.

By introducing the second linked table, we can avoid altogether the duplication of data required by the single-table approach. If we now want to find the address of the supplier of a particular component, then this becomes a two-stage process:

(1)   Look up the part number in Table One, and find the associated Supplier Name.

(2)   Look up the Supplier Name in Table Two and find the associated Supplier Address.

This is the concept at the heart of all relational database systems. We shall see how such linked tables may be implemented in Section 20.6.

Note that the term **relational** relates to the *intra*-table links between fields, not the *inter*-table links. Slightly more formally (Date, 1990):

- A **relation** corresponds to what we shall refer to as a table.
- A **tuple** (pronounced to sound like 'couple') corresponds to a row in a table.
- The **cardinality** of a table is the number of tuples.
- An **attribute** corresponds to a column in a table.
- The **degree** of a table is the number of columns.

You may see the above terms used in books and papers discussing the theory of data-bases in greater depth than is appropriate here.

20.4   Data normalization issues

When, in the above example, we split a single table in two to avoid having duplicate data in the system, we were performing a process known as **data normalization**.

There are six 'layers' of normalization, each of which builds on the previous layer. We can picture the various normal forms as an onion (Figure 20.4). As the figure attempts to illustrate, data normalization begins with first normal form (1NF); only after data is in 1NF can it be converted to 2NF, and so on. Strictly, your data is normalized as soon as it is in 1NF, after which *further* normalization occurs.

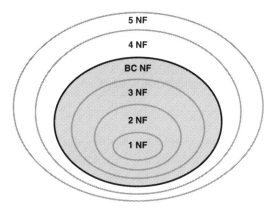

Figure 20.4 The layers of the normalization 'onion'. No system can be in, say, third normal form until it is in second normal form, and so on. Note that the fourth and fifth normal forms are generally only of theoretical interest.

Only the first three normal forms, plus an extension to third normal form (known as **Boyce–Codd normal form**: BCNF), are generally used in most commercial systems. As a consequence, data that is in BCNF is often referred to as **well-normalized data**.

As we shall see in Chapter 22, when using D-O SADIE to develop information systems, ensuring that your underlying data structures are well normalized is an important part of the design process. There are two fundamental reasons for this:

(1) Data which is not well normalized is constantly 'at risk'. For example, without meaning to, users of such data may inadvertently delete important information. More generally, data not in BCNF is liable to cause a range of update, insertion or deletion anomalies, discussed further below.

(2) In some cases, without normalization, it may be *impossible* to translate the data structure into your chosen implementation. For example, structured query language (SQL: see Section 20.6.3), a common relational database implementation language, provides only weak support for the manipulation of data not in first normal form; that is, data containing 'repeating groups'.

We discuss the various normal forms from 1NF to BCNF in Sections 20.4.1 to 20.4.3. Date (1990) provides details of 5NF and 6NF if you require it.

20.4.1 First normal form

An entity is said to be in first normal form if it contains no repeating groups.

Suppose we are trying to store a list of the orders made by a particular customer. We might want to store the customer's name (we'll make this the primary key: see Section 20.3), the customer's address, and a list of the relevant order numbers (Figure 20.5).

Here the various orders form a **repeating group**. We'll define 'repeating group' more rigorously at the end of this subsection, and see how to detect such groups in your own data. For now, we'll consider this specific example: Figure 20.5 presents us with two related problems:

Customer Orders

Customer's Name	Customer's Address	Order 1	Order 2	...	Order 10
Smith	14 Birstall Road, Leicester	123	897		563
Jones	32 Sheep Road, Hazleton	453	432		–

Figure 20.5 A table of customer data and related orders.

(1)   What do we do if there are only 2 orders for most customers, but 10 for some others? Do we pad the 'spare columns' with zeros? Surely this is a waste of space?

(2)   What do we do if, eventually, we have 11 orders for Smith? Where is the 11th order number to be stored?

As long as the number of orders for each firm is roughly the same (which may not be a reasonable assumption anyway), one solution to both problems could be to make the table small to start with, and increase the size later, as necessary. However, in most implementations, changing the dimensions of a table after the system has been loaded with data is a non-trivial task. At best, changing the table size is *very* slow (we could be talking *hours*, if the database is large; your clients won't like it ...). At worst – if, for example, you implemented your system using simple C++ `struct`s – you might (as we saw in the exercises at the end of Chapter 18) have to recompile the program every time you change the size of a table. Having users recompile your programs is even less popular than having them wait for hours every time they add a new order.

A much better solution is to add an additional table to the database, as shown in Figure 20.6. This solution works because this time when we add a new order, we only have to add a new row to the Orders table; adding rows to tables is straightforward in all implementations (and always easier than adding columns), so – assuming we have a hard disk with infinite capacity – we can have as many orders as we like. In addition, because we only add rows to the orders table when we need them, we can avoid the wasted space caused by having extra 'empty' fields stored on the disk.

Customers

Customer's Name	Customer's Address
Smith	14 Birstall Road, Leicester
Jones	32 Sheep Road, Hazleton

Orders

Customer's Name	Order
Smith	*123*
Jones	*453*
Smith	*897*
Smith	*563*
Jones	*432*

Figure 20.6 A normalized (1NF) version of the original Customer Orders table.

Finally, note that the format of our original Customer Orders table (Figure 20.5) 'looks wrong' because there are empty fields visible. In general, it is more likely that you will encounter repeating groups in the format shown in Figure 20.7. In this format, the reason for using the term 'repeating group' is clearer: such a group has multiple values for the same value of key. Here, for example, there are multiple copies of the same address for 'Smith' visible; 'Customer's Address' therefore forms a repeating group.

Customer Orders 2

Customer's Name	Customer's Address	Order #
Smith	14 Birstall Road, Leicester	*123*
Jones	32 Sheep Road, Hazleton	*453*
Smith	14 Birstall Road, Leicester	*897*
Smith	14 Birstall Road, Leicester	*563*
Jones	32 Sheep Road, Hazleton	*432*

Figure 20.7 Another version of the table of customer data and related orders (not normalized).

The general technique for eliminating repeating groups is to move the relevant fields into their own table. This implies, in this example, that the address field should be moved. As you would expect, the result of such a move is exactly the same as in the previous example (Figure 20.6).

As a rule, even if you go no further, it is generally desirable to have your data in 1NF. As always, however, there are situations when this strategy is not appropriate; we'll consider these situations in Chapter 22.

20.4.2 Second normal form

An entity is said to be in second normal form if it is in first normal form and if every attribute is functionally dependent on the whole of the combination key.

The second normal form is only of relevance where we have a combination (primary) key: that is, where a combination of two attributes must be used to access a particular row of data. We'll denote combination keys by underlining both keys.

The situation is illustrated in Figure 20.8: here, there are (at least) two suppliers called 'Brown's', and we assume that both the supplier name and the supplier town must be used to find the telephone number of a particular supplier.

Suppliers

Supplier Name	Supplier Town	Area	Telephone
Brown's	Winslow	1	345213
Littleton	Hazleton	1	674252
Brown's	Dundee	4	895632

Figure 20.8 The Suppliers table.

Because it contains no repeating groups, the table in Figure 20.8 is in 1NF; however, it is not in 2NF. This is because the area of the country in which the supplier is located depends only on the supplier town and not on the name of the supplier. This situation is known as partial functional dependency (as opposed to the full functional dependency we require).

Partial dependency can cause the following problems:

- **Deletion anomalies**
  For example, suppose Brown's of Dundee goes out of business. If we delete this row of the table, then we have also lost the information that Dundee is in area 4.

- **Insertion anomalies**
  For example, suppose we expected that in future we would have one or more suppliers in the town of 'Broughty Ferry'. We want to store the fact that this town is in (say) area 11. We could not add this information to the database, however, without also adding a 'dummy' supplier name.

- **Update anomalies**
  For example, suppose (one of the) Brown's move the head office of their firm to Glasgow. We have to change not only the name of the supplier town, but we must also remember to change the area too.

One solution is to remove 'Area' from the Suppliers entity and place it in another. The Suppliers entity is then in second normal form (Figure 20.9).

Suppliers

Supplier Name	**Supplier Town**	**Telephone**
Brown's	Winslow	345213
Littleton	Hazleton	674252
Brown's	Dundee	895632

Area

Town	**Area**
Winslow	1
Hazleton	1
Dundee	4

Figure 20.9 The new Suppliers and Area tables in 2NF.

Note that, if your data has only a primary key, you can move on immediately to translate to 3NF; normalized data with a primary key already satisfies the 2NF criteria. Instead of splitting the table in two you could, therefore, choose in these circumstances to add a new field to your table (we'll call it 'Supplier ID#': Figure 20.10). This is not necessarily a bad solution (and in some implementations you don't have the option of combination keys anyway, so you won't have much choice) but the dependency of the area field on the supplier town will still exist, and will have to be dealt with before your data can be considered well normalized.

Suppliers

Supplier ID#	Supplier Name	Supplier Town	Area	Telephone
1	Brown's	Winslow	1	345213
2	Littleton	Hazleton	1	674252
3	Brown's	Dundee	4	895632

Figure 20.10 The original Suppliers table, modified by the addition of a new (single) primary key.

20.4.3 Third normal form

An entity is said to be in third normal form if it is in second normal form and if all attributes which are not part of the key are mutually independent (that is, there are no transitive dependencies)

It is possible, even when an entity is in 2NF, to have a **transitive dependency**: that is, to have an attribute within an entity with a value dependent not only on the key, but also on another attribute. Like partial dependencies (Section 20.4.2), transitive dependencies give rise to update anomalies.

Figure 20.11 shows a 'Customer Credit' entity. This is in 2NF, because the attributes Telephone, Credit Level and Credit Rating all depend on both keys. It is not, however, in 3NF, because Credit Rating is determined simply by the Credit Level. Moving Credit Rating into a new table will leave customers in 3NF (Figure 20.12).

Customer Credit

Customer Name	Customer Town	Telephone	Credit Level	Credit Rating
Jones	Winslow	123456	9	High
Smith	Hazleton	234567	5	Medium
Jones	Dundee	345678	2	Low

Figure 20.11 The Customers table.

Customer Credit

Customer Name	Customer Town	Telephone	Credit level
Jones	Winslow	123456	9
Smith	Hazleton	234567	5
Jones	Dundee	345678	2

Credit

Credit Level	Credit Rating
9	High
5	Medium
2	Low

Figure 20.12 The 3NF version of Customer Credit.

Boyce–Codd normal form

> *An entity is said to be in Boyce–Codd normal form if it is in third normal form and every data item upon which some other data item is functionally dependent is a candidate key*

BCNF is a specialized form of 3NF.

For example, suppose we are developing a system to control the allocation of project managers to training schemes taken by new (junior) members of staff in a company. Depending on their background, junior staff members may take one or more training courses. Each course will be in a specified training area, and will be supervised by a project manager. Each project manager is a specialist in only one area, and will only work in that area. An example of a filled table is given in Figure 20.13.

Training Courses

Junior Staff Name	Training Area	Project Manager
Carey	C++	Anderson
Carey	COBOL	MacKenzie
Davis	SADIE	Johnstone
Edwards	SADIE	Johnstone
Edwards	DSS	Beavers
Peterson	Accounts	Harper
Peterson	Control	MacTavish

Figure 20.13   The Training Courses table. The candidates for combination keys (not shown) are either Junior Staff Name + Training Area or Junior Staff Name + Project Manager.

The Training Courses entity has two (equally valid) candidates for combination key: Junior Staff Name + Training Area or, Junior Staff Name + Project Manager. With either pair of combination keys, the entity is in 3NF, but there is still a potential problem. We known that each manager manages only one type of project, but the type of project managed is implicit; the fact, for example, that Beavers (only) supervises DSS training would be lost, for example, if Edwards was sacked.

We can see that there is a problem because none of the possible combination keys encompasses both Training Area and Project Manager, and these two fields together contain useful information that we wish to retain. Because this condition is not satisfied, the table is not in BCNF.

The solution is to split the Training Courses entity in two, with one (new) entity listing Junior Staff Names and Training Areas, and the other listing Training Areas and Project Managers (Figure 20.14).

Staff Areas

Junior Staff Name	Training Area
Carey	C++
Carey	COBOL
Davis	SADIE
Edwards	SADIE
Edwards	DSS
Peterson	Accounts
Peterson	Control

Area Managers

Training Area	Project Manager
C++	Anderson
COBOL	MacKenzie
SADIE	Johnstone
DSS	Beavers
Accounts	Harper
Control	MacTavish

Figure 20.14 The BCNF version of the Training Courses table.

20.5 Relationships between tables

We have considered ways in which multiple, linked, tables of information can and should be created in most realistic information systems. We have seen how normalization may result in the creation of such tables. However, we have said little about the way in which relationships between tables are established.

In general, there are three important relationships that may be formed between entities: associative relationships (the only type we will consider here), aggregation relationships (discussed in Chapter 21), and inheritance relationships (a distinguishing characteristic of object-oriented models, discussed at length in Part III).

The most general kind of associative relationship is a many-to-many relationship; the other two important relationships (one-to-one and one-to-many) are merely particular instances of this general case. We show schematically the form of these various relationships in Figure 20.15.

In looking at Figure 20.15, it may help to think of the small circles inside the grey and white ovals as fields in a database table. In such databases, one-to-many (and the equivalent many-to-one) relationships are common, while one-to-one relationships are rare.

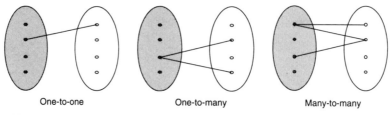

One-to-one   One-to-many   Many-to-many

Figure 20.15 Possible relationship between grey and white objects.

One-to-one and one-to-many relationships can be implemented in a straight-forward manner. Most simply (and commonly) relationships are built by storing a common data item on related records in the two tables. For example, in Figure 20.3, the relationship between the stock table and supplier table is many-to-one (Figure 20.16). The link is implemented via the Supplier Name field in the Stock table, where Supplier Name is the primary key in the Supplier table.

Stock

Stock #	Description	Current Level	Re-order Level	Supplier Name
1455	Size 10 bolt	30	10	Brown's
6732	Brass washer	34	100	Littleton
7852	Plastic cowling	123	5	Brown's
8888	Manual	72	50	Littleton

Supplier

Supplier Name	Supplier Address
Brown's	13 Slough Road, Winslow
Littleton	34 Sutton Road, Hazleton

Figure 20.16 A many-to-one relationship between Stock and Supplier tables.

Many-to-many relationships are rather more troublesome. For example, suppose we are trying to develop some software to support an international athletics meeting. We know we'll need to store a list of the competitors, and we also want to store details of the events in which they are competing. For simplicity in this example, we'll assume that only three athletes compete in each event. Figure 20.17 gives our initial choice of tables, and shows the relationship between them.

Figure 20.17 appears reasonable, until we realize that many-to-many relationships are always difficult to implement; in fact, most RDBMSs are incapable of representing many-to-many relationships directly. More generally, many-to-many relationships can be an indication of design flaws (for example, see Howe, 1989). Informally, many-to-many relationships can be viewed as a 'positive feedback loop' in your data. As you may be aware from other engineering fields, positive feedback is generally a 'Bad Thing' and, for example, a good source of explosions …

Events

Event#	Athlete1 ID	Athlete2 ID	Athlete3 ID
A	A1	A2	A4
B	A2	A4	A7
C	A1	A3	A8
D	A2	A24	A30

Athletes

Athlete ID	Name	Representing
A1	Folkard	Scotland
A2	Jones	England
A3	Fothergill	England
A4	Beynon	England
A5	Schlindwein	Brazil
A6	Gu	China
A7	Pont	Scotland
A8	Green	Wales

Figure 20.17 A many-to-many relationship between athletes and the events in which they compete.

The solution in such circumstances is to add a further table. The effect of this can be shown in general terms by redrawing the relevant part of Figure 20.15, as shown in Figure 20.18. In the case of our athletic meeting, we would add an extra table 'between' the Events table and the Athletes table, as shown in Figure 20.19.

As we shall see in Chapters 21 and 22, many-to-many relationships are likely to appear in data models developed during the analysis phase of a project; dealing with such relationships isn't complicated but is an important part of the planning process.

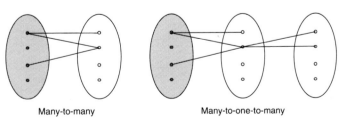

Many-to-many   Many-to-one-to-many

Figure 20.18 Converting a problematic many-to-many relationship into a many-to-one-to-many relationship.

Events

Event#	Athlete1 ID	Athlete2 ID	Athlete3 ID
A	A1	A2	A4
B	A2	A4	A7
C	A1	A3	A8
D	A2	A24	A30

Events_Athlete

Event#	Athlete ID
A	A1
A	A2
A	A4
B	A2
B	A4
B	A7
C	A1
C	A3
C	A8
D	A2
D	A24
D	A30

Athletes

Athlete ID	Name	Representing
A1	Folkard	Scotland
A2	Jones	England
A3	Fothergill	England
A4	Beynon	England
A5	Schlindwein	Brazil
A6	Gu	China
A7	Pont	Scotland
A8	Green	Wales

Figure 20.19 Resolving the many-to-many relationship between athletes and the events in which they compete.

20.6 Implementation of RDBs

We look here at ways in which linked tables might be implemented in C++. We'll then see why creating such an implementation is seldom a good idea, and look briefly at the creation of tables in SQL.

20.6.1 Using C++

Suppose as part of a system for a double-glazing company, we need to translate the tables shown in Figure 20.20 into C++. How do we do so?

Customers

Lastname	Firstname	Title	Address	Postcode
Smith	John	Dr	14 Birstall Road, Leicester	LE4 DE7
Jones	Peter	Mr	32 Sheep Road, Hazleton	HT3 DE3
Peters	Mary	Ms	24 Birstall Road, Leicester	LE4 DE7

Regions

Postcode	Area name
LE4 DE7	East Midlands
HT3 DE3	North-West Yorkshire

Figure 20.20 Two linked tables required as part of a sales system for a double-glazing company.

For a start, we need some further information. Some of this relates to the rules under which the company operates (sometimes called the 'enterprise rules' or the 'business rules'), and some of this is general knowledge about the problem space. We are told that, in the initial implementation, we shall have 50 customers, many of whom will have different postcodes; clearly, we need to allow for more customers to be added at a later date. Similarly, we learn that there are currently only three sales regions; again, we need to allow for subsequent expansion.

There are several possible implementations. For example, we might start by setting up two arrays of structs, one array for each table (Figure 20.21).

```
struct sCustomer                        struct sRegion
    {                                       {
    char last_name[21];                     char postcode[8];
    char first_name[21];                    char area_name[21];
    char title[11];                         } Regions[100];
    char address[81];
    char postcode[8];
    } Customers[100];
```

Figure 20.21 A first simple implementation of the tables given in Figure 20.20.

In this implementation, we have allowed for up to 100 customers. We could, as described in Chapter 18, use a linked list to implement the tables, rather than an array; this would improve the implementation, but would only serve to complicate the present discussion and is not considered further here.

Even with such a change, however, the solution shown in Figure 20.21 would still appear rather unsatisfactory. For one thing, we have duplicated the postcode information: while we might need only (say) a four-element Regions array, we have been forced to expand this to 100 to allow for the fact that each of our customers could have a different postcode. This seems rather inefficient. Another problem is that the data structure shows no evidence of the link between the two tables.

A solution might therefore be to link the tables, and reduce the duplication, by using pointers (Figure 20.22).

```
struct sCustomer                        struct sRegion
    {                                       {
    char last_name[21];                     char postcode[8];
    char first_name[21];                    char area_name[21];
    char title[11];                         } Regions[100];
    char address[81];
    sRegion* Region_PTR;
    } Customers[100];
```

Figure 20.22 A second implementation of the tables given in Figure 20.20.

In Figure 20.22 we have avoided the duplication of the postcode information in the two tables, and established an explicit link, through a pointer. This leads to a space saving, but still seems less than ideal, as our Regions array is still 25 times larger than it needs to be.

We could therefore try one further solution, as depicted in Figure 20.23. This solution seems generally more efficient. We've been able to reduce the size of the Regions array to 4 (cf. 100), and in the process avoided duplicating the area_name information. We could, of course, also replace the Regions array with a simpler version – either a 2-D array of characters, or a 1-D array of character pointers; we leave this as an exercise.

```
struct sCustomer                        struct sRegion
    {                                       {
    char last_name[21];                     char area_name[21];
    char first_name[21];                    } Regions[4];
    char title[11];
    char address[81];
    char postcode[8];
    sRegion* Region_PTR;
    } Customers[100];
```

Figure 20.23 A third implementation of the tables given in Figure 20.20.

However, the solution in Figure 20.23 doesn't reflect the original tables, in several ways. For one thing, in the original, we had (implicitly) a bi-directional relationship between the two entities. Thus, for example, given a postcode, we could find not only the area with which it was associated but also the details of the associated customers. We can't establish such a link simply by putting a pointer to a sCustomer struct in the sRegion struct: this would only allow us to implement a many-to-one link, and not the one-to-many link we require. We could establish such a one-to-many by implementing a linked list, as outlined in Figure 20.24.

```
struct sCustomer                          struct sRegion
    {                                         {
    char last_name[21];                       sCustomer* Customer_PTR;
    char first_name[21];                      char area_name[21];
    char title[11];                           } Regions[4];
    char address[81];
    char postcode[8];
    sRegion* Region_PTR;
    sCustomer* More_customer_PTR;
    } Customers[100];
```

Figure 20.24 A fourth implementation of the tables given in Figure 20.20.

Here, in the sRegion struct, the Customer_PTR would point to a customer with the postcode corresponding to the associated area_name. Where there were more than one customers with the same postcode, the More_customer_PTR field in the sCustomer struct would point to these, in turn, in a linked list. The associated code requirements would be quite substantial, but not impossible to achieve.

In general, while solutions three and four are in some sense 'more efficient', the original tables are best represented by the first, and most simple, solution. Since the tables represent part of the physical data model, you generally need to have a good reason not to opt for not matching your implementation to your design.

Overall, we can see that the implementation of even simple collections of linked (relational) tables in C++ is a non-trivial exercise. It is possible to do so, but we might begin to wonder if there isn't a better way …

20.6.2 Why you shouldn't use C++

In Chapters 17 to 19, we looked at C++ programming features and techniques which, in combination, would allow you to contemplate constructing your own relational database system.

The fact that many of the database management systems on the market today were developed using C/C++ is an existence proof that this language can be used to develop such systems. The fact that C was used to develop UNIX may further reassure us that C's successor is well capable of providing the degree of low-level control required. However, while it is almost always possible to implement a complete information system in C++, this approach becomes less practical as the system you are developing grows in size. Overall, while such an exercise can provide an invaluable training exercise, it is very unlikely to result in a code framework that you can exploit in 'industrial-strength' products.

This problem is less immediate if you are developing a new system from scratch, perhaps replacing an existing system based on paper rather than computer. In these circumstances, you may well be free to develop the system in any manner you choose, and you may decide to use C++ for the complete implementation, especially if you have previous experience working in this way.

However, when your system has to integrate with so-called 'legacy data' stored, perhaps, on one or more PC-based networks, mini-computer or mainframe-based systems, then a solution based *solely* on C++ becomes much less attractive. In addition, in a common networked computer environment, issues of security and data sharing become important; as we have seen, control of disk file access in C++ is an 'arms length' process, relying on the operating system to do much of the difficult work. In a networked computer environment, the programmer is forced to communicate not only with the operating system (for example, DOS), but with the network operating system (for example, Novell Netware) to take control of such issues. Naturally, such control is possible, but you have to ask yourself why you are bothering.

The only commercial justification for investing the effort and resources required to develop your own RDBMS would arise if existing 'off the shelf' products were of poor quality, were too inflexible to be linked easily to your existing software, or carried excessive royalty fees. By contrast, most modern database systems are of high quality and provide efficient data access speeds. The systems can be linked not only to C++ but also to other database systems (for example on mini- or mainframe computer systems). Royalty fees vary; however, these are rarely excessive. At the time of writing, for example, the popular Microsoft Access relational database system, aimed at PC developers, has a fixed royalty fee of a few hundred pounds, a fee which applies whether you sell one or one million copies of your product.

As a result, in a commercial setting, it is much more likely that you will choose to store your data using an existing RDBMS package, probably making use of structured query language (SQL) code (see, for example, Stanczyk, 1991; Howe, 1989). That does not mean that you should abandon C++ completely; far from it. Many of the most complex (and interesting) information system projects involve complex analysis of company data, stored in a variety of database formats. In developing such decision support systems, you may choose for example to use neural networks and/or expert systems, implemented in C++, to provide fast analysis. You are equally likely, however, to avoid reinventing the wheel and make use of third-party database access tools to help you reprieve and store the data you need to process. As we'll see in later chapters in this part of the book, D-O SADIE is equally comfortable with either strategy.

20.6.3   A thumbnail sketch of SQL

If you don't use C++ to implement your relational database, you will sooner or later encounter **Structured Query Language** (SQL) the *lingua franca* of the commercial database world. We introduce, very briefly, the features of this language in this section.

As we do so, it is important to realize that SQL is often used as an embedded language, with SQL commands used alongside, for example, C++ statements. Details of links between the two languages are, however, implementation dependent.

SQL is a 4GL

We first mentioned SQL in Chapter 3, when we discussed the various generations of programming languages; as we saw then, SQL is probably most accurately viewed as a fourth generation language (a 4GL). What this means is that the language is declarative in nature: the programmer does not specify how the program should work, but instead what the required result is.

There are three essential operations required of any relational database systems:

- table creation
- data entry
- data manipulation ('query generation')

We consider below how each of these options may be effected in SQL.

Table creation

In Section 20.6.1 we described various ways of implementing, in C++, the two linked tables given in Figure 20.20. To create tables of similar format in SQL the following commands could be entered:

```
CREATE TABLE Customers
      (last_name CHAR(20),
      first_name CHAR(20),
      title CHAR(10),
      address CHAR(80),
      postcode CHAR(7),
      PRIMARY KEY (last_name),
      FOREIGN KEY (postcode) REFERENCES Regions)

CREATE TABLE Regions
      (postcode CHAR(7),
      area_name CHAR(20),
      PRIMARY KEY (postcode))
```

Note that use of the `PRIMARY KEY` clause enforces **entity integrity**: for example, this means that the RDBMS will not allow null or duplicate values of the `last_name` field in the `Customers` table. Similarly, the `FOREIGN KEY` clause enables the RDBMS to enforce **referential integrity**. For example, here the RDBMS will ensure that any value of `postcode` entered into the `Customers` table is either null, or a primary key in the `Regions` table.

Data entry

Simple data entry may be effected using the `INSERT` command. For example,

```
INSERT INTO Regions VALUES('G83 3FG', 'Glasgow')
```

Data manipulation

Suppose we have entered the data shown in Figure 20.20 into the Customers and Regions tables defined above. We can select a single column from any table as follows:

```
SELECT Postcode FROM Regions
```

giving:

| LE4 DE7 |
| HT3 DE3 |

We can select one (or more) rows from a single table as follows:

```
SELECT * FROM Customers WHERE title = 'Dr'
```

giving:

| Smith | John | Dr | 14 Birstall Road, Leicester | LE4 DE7 |

However, the language begins to show its potential when we link tables together. For example, suppose we wished to find the surnames of any customers living in Glasgow. We would enter:

```
SELECT last_name FROM Customers, Regions
    WHERE area_name = 'Glasgow'
    AND Customers.postcode = Regions.postcode
```

giving:

| Smith |

Further information on the powerful SQL language can be found in a number of sources, including Stanczyk (1991), Date (1990), and Howe (1989).

Finally, we should point out there is a curious level of snobbery surrounding the 'correct' pronunciation of the three-letter acronym S-Q-L. Because structured query language evolved originally from a language called Sequel some software engineers are inclined to try to 'prove' their credentials by steadfastly insisting that SQL be pronounced Sequel. The sense of such an argument is that C++ should always be referred to as 'C' (or perhaps CPL if we want to be truly farcical). If you encounter people saying 'Sequel' it is your duty, as a responsible software engineer, to correct them!

20.7   Other types of database

We have considered only relational databases in this chapter: however, there are two other important alternatives: hierarchical/network databases and object-oriented databases.

In Table 20.1 we do not attempt to do more than summarize the strengths and weaknesses of each type of database. Note that we don't distinguish between the hierarchical and network databases (which have much in common). Network and hierarchical databases are discussed by Date (1990). Object-oriented databases are also discussed briefly by Date (1990), and at greater length by Hughes (1991). We consider general features of object-oriented systems in Part III.

Type of database	Main strength	Main weakness
Relational	Extremely widely used	Slower data access than equivalent network/ hierarchical database?
Network/hierarchical	Faster access than equivalent relational database?	More difficult to understand, design and use than a relational database?
Object-oriented	Easier to link with object-oriented code (see Part III)?	Few implementations yet available. Most legacy data is stored in (incompatible?) relational databases.

Table 20.1 A comparison of different database structures.

20.8 Conclusions

In what has become the standard text on database systems, Date (1990) takes about 1300 pages and two volumes to provide an introduction to the subject. His book is highly recommended; we have, of course, only begun to scratch the surface of this subject here.

It is important to realize, however, that the particular implementation used – C++, SQL or whatever – is, to a large extent, immaterial; the final construction of the database system is a relatively straightforward task, once the foundations have been laid during analysis and design – the subject of the following chapters.

Exercises

20.1 Leicester Software Engineering has been asked to develop a database system for a personnel company. The company requires the information detailed below to be stored for all applicants in its database.

- surname
- first name
- middle initials
- street address
- city
- county (state)
- postcode (zip)
- telephone area code
- telephone number
- National Insurance number (social security number)
- date of birth

- salary
- previous work experience
- names of previous employers
- names of referees
- marital status (married, single, divorced)
- names of children
- ages of children

(a) Draw up an appropriate set of tables to store this data.

(b) Place the tables in 1NF.

(c) Place the tables in 2NF.

(d) Place the tables in 3NF.

(e) Place the tables in BCNF.

20.2 As part of an order processing system, the Super Sox company have a database containing a single table of data, shown in Figure 20.25.

Everything

Order#	Order Date	Client #	Client Name	Product#	Product Description	Quantity Ordered	Product Price (per unit)
SE56	01 May	004	Colins	998	Socks X2	784	4.99
SE53	01 May	555	McKenzie	997	Socks X1	234	3.99
SE53	01 May	555	McKenzie	870	Tie B1	783	10.99
SE53	01 May	555	McKenzie	600	Tie BZ	66	11.99
SE54	08 May	879	Tain	998	Socks X2	564	4.99
SE54	08 May	879	Tain	870	Tie B1	89	10.99
SE54	08 May	879	Tain	872	Tie B2	2	14.99
SE54	08 May	879	Tain	500	Socks FG	90	4.99
SE55	10 May	879	Tain	999	Socks X3	78	5.99

Figure 20.25 The Super Sox company database (a single table).

(a) Determine a suitable primary key (which may be a combination key) for the Everything table.

(b) Super Sox say they 'have had some problems' with the database. What problems do you think they may have experienced?

(c) You are asked to re-engineer the Super Sox stock control system. Describe how, as part of this process, you would normalize Figure 20.25 to BCNF.

20.3 Create, using C++, an appropriate collection of C++ structs to implement the tables you identified in the solution to Exercise 20.2.

20.4 Write an appropriate set of C++ functions that allow a user to manipulate the data structures created in Exercise 20.3, as follows:

   (a) Write a function (or set of functions) to allow a user to add data into the data structures.

   (b) Write a function (or set of functions) to display all the data in the database relating to a particular order.

20.5 Repeat Exercise 20.4, this time using SQL.

20.6 If you have access to a technical library, investigate the various types of database described in Section 20.6.3. Are they widely used? What advantages (and disadvantages) do they have compared with the relational database model?

21 | Entity-relationship diagrams

21.1   Introduction

In the previous chapters in this part of the book, we have considered the implementation of information systems. Here, and in the remainder of Part II, the focus will be on the specification and design of a range of computer systems involving a substantial persistent data component.

In order to model the stored data required within a system, we use a slightly modified version of the **entity-relationship diagram** (ERD) originally proposed by Chen (1976). We introduce ERDs in this chapter and describe how such a diagram may be derived.

A tutorial describing how to create ERDs using the CASE tool is given in Appendix J. The integration of data models within the general framework of SADIE is discussed in Chapter 22.

21.2   Modelling general associations

Entity-relationship diagrams (ERDs) are used to model data. The notation is popular and widely used. As we saw in Chapter 20, the relational approach to data storage is currently by far the most widespread option; ERDs are particularly useful for modelling data structures that will ultimately be implemented in such databases. ERDs can also be used to develop systems implemented using network or hierarchical databases (see, for example, Batini *et al.,* 1992 for details of this process). In addition, an extended form of ERD (a *class*-relationship diagram) is an important aid to object-oriented system development (discussed in Part III).

As the above comments would tend to suggest, the ERD provides a high-level and largely implementation-independent model of data. Using ERDs you can therefore safely defer implementation decisions, and focus on analysis and design; whether you ultimately decide to build your database in C++, SQL or using an existing database package, an ERD-based model will serve you equally well.

21.2.1 Components of ERDs

ERDs model the important entities within a given system, and the ways in which these entities are inter-related. The essential components of an ERD are:

- entities,
- attributes and
- relationships

In a data model, **entities** commonly represent real-world objects, while the **relationships** between such objects model the corresponding real-world connections and interactions. In addition, each entity has an associated set of **attributes**: these represent relevant information about the real-world objects which needs to be stored in our system. So, for example, we may have a 'customer' entity in our data model, which may be related to another entity called 'order'. Relevant attributes for our customer are likely to include the name and address, while for the order itself we are likely to need to store an order number, plus a list of goods ordered.

We'll consider the translation of ERDs to database tables in Section 21.5: however, it is useful to see at this stage where we are heading. We can summarize this as follows:

> *In the systems we consider here, each entity in our final data model will become a 'table' in our final (relational) database. The attributes for each entity then represent the fields in these tables, and the relationships represent the links between tables.*

21.2.2 Example: Car parking

Let's begin by considering a simple example:

> You are asked by Scottish Boxes Ltd to set up a simple system to control the allocation of parking permits around their company headquarters in Edinburgh. Scottish Boxes have 3000 employees; each is to be provided with a self-adhesive permit, to be attached inside the windscreen of their car. Any cars not displaying such a sticker will be 'wheel clamped' by company security personnel; the clamps will only be removed on payment of a fee of £50.00.

As part of the system development, the provisional ERD shown in Figure 21.1 is developed. Note that we'll consider how one might start to produce such a figure in Section 21.4; at this stage, we are concerned mainly with understanding the notation used.

The ERD shown in Figure 21.1 is read as follows:

> 'There are two important entities in the system, employees and cars. Each employee drives one car, and no car is driven by more than one employee.'

As is customary, entities are shown as boxes and the relationships between entities are shown as diamonds. The diamond will usually contain a verb or verb phrase and the object of the resulting 'sentence' is indicated with an arrow. Thus we might have relationships labelled 'buys', 'sells', 'recommends' or 'eats' in our ERD; the entity bought, sold, recommended or eaten will be indicated with the arrow.

Figure 21.1 A provisional entity-relationship diagram modelling the data required in a car parking system.

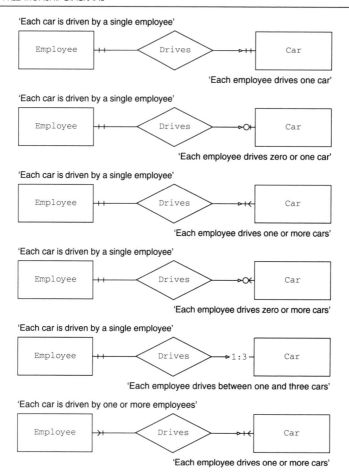

'Each car is driven by a single employee'

Employee — Drives — Car

'Each employee drives one car'

'Each car is driven by a single employee'

Employee — Drives — Car

'Each employee drives zero or one car'

'Each car is driven by a single employee'

Employee — Drives — Car

'Each employee drives one or more cars'

'Each car is driven by a single employee'

Employee — Drives — Car

'Each employee drives zero or more cars'

'Each car is driven by a single employee'

Employee — Drives — 1:3 — Car

'Each employee drives between one and three cars'

'Each car is driven by one or more employees'

Employee — Drives — Car

'Each employee drives one or more cars'

Figure 21.2 Some simple entity-relationship diagrams that might be used as part of the specification for a car parking system, along with a translation in English.

We discussed in Chapter 20 the necessity of considering the nature of the relationship between data tables. Such relationships are indicated explicitly on the data model. For example, some simple ERDs are shown in Figure 21.2.

Before we leave the car parking example, we should note that the data model in Figure 21.1 is probably rather too simple to be of very much help. We might begin to make it more useful by acknowledging that Scottish Boxes should expect to have a few visitors once in a while, and that these visitors too will need some form of permit (Figure 21.3).

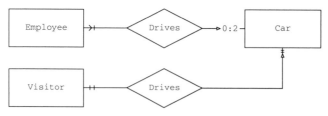

Employee — Drives — 0:2 — Car

Visitor — Drives

Figure 21.3 Making the car park data more useful.

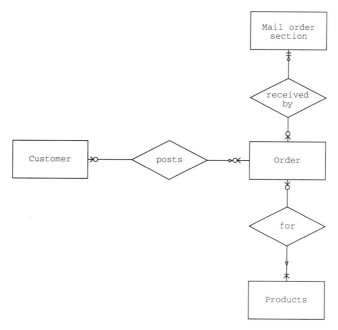

Figure 21.4 A typical example of a small ERD used to model the data required to support the order-processing part of a small business.

Note that ERDs can become more complex, as illustrated in Figure 21.4. This figure illustrates the important data features for a system dealing with the processing of orders by a small company.

The ERD is not intended to replace the DfD, or to say anything significant about the processing or control to be performed by the system. The data model says nothing about the order in which associations become relevant. Instead, the ERD simply highlights the 'entities' in the system about which we need to know. For example, in this case, we need to know the name and address of the customer. We need to know the details of the order: specifically, this will include details of the customer, and details of one or more items ordered. The items themselves may include a stock number and description, and so on. We can represent all these features of the relevant entities on attribute diagrams, described in Section 21.3.

Note that not all users of ERDs make use of directed relationships. Instead, Figure 21.1 would be represented as shown in Figure 21.5. We have found that new users find ERDs confusing and ambiguous without the direction information: Figure 21.5 could be read 'car drives employee' …

Figure 21.5 Figure 21.1 redrawn without directed relationships.

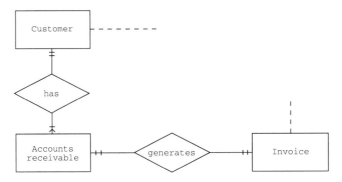

Figure 21.6 A fragment of a larger ERD, without directed relationships.

For simple examples, concern about such matters can become mere academic pedantry, but ERDs themselves only become truly useful when work with larger problems. In such situations, the ERD can become much larger and any ambiguity can be a drawback. For example, in the fragment of a larger ERD shown in Figure 21.6, we might legitimately ask whether accounts receivable gives rise to an invoice, or vice versa. Knowledge of the problem domain reduces or eliminates such ambiguity, but as a general rule we would prefer to have a notation that is as unambiguous as possible.

For the above reasons, we use directed ER representations in this text.

21.3 Using attribute diagrams

Just as DfDs are decomposed to PSpecs, ERDs too have 'child' diagrams. The main child ERD is the **attribute diagram**, discussed in this section. Another child of the general ERD, used mainly in the design phase of SADIE, is the **decomposition** diagram, which is discussed in Section 21.6.

As you would expect, we must define the details of the individual objects which are depicted on the 'top-level' ERDs. This is most often done through the use of attribute diagrams. The general form of these diagrams is illustrated in Figure 21.7.

For example, we might define the details of a firm's customers as shown in Figure 21.8.

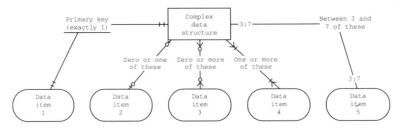

Figure 21.7 A simple entity-relationship (attribute) diagram.

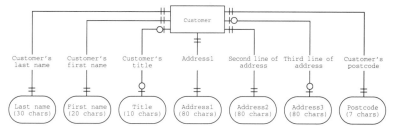

Figure 21.8 An attribute diagram representing a customer.

21.4 How to create ERDs

A basic but effective technique for uncovering candidate entities involves looking for nouns in the initial problem statement. What we are seeking to achieve is as follows:

> If there is a 'something' in the world about which your system needs to know, then that 'something' must be in your ERD.

For example, suppose we are given the following outline statement of requirements, scribbled by a systems analyst following a preliminary briefing (with nouns perceived to be relevant in italic):

> 'The UK Government *Home Office* require a new *fingerprint recognition system*. The system is to work from one or more *fingerprints* obtained from a *crime scene*. Each crime scene may produce several sets of fingerprints or none at all. The fingerprints may or may not originate from a single *suspect*. The fingerprints are to be compared with fingerprints from convicted *criminals* held by the Home Office and *police departments* throughout the country.
>
> It is expected, ultimately, that the system will be required to store more than two million fingerprints. Assuming a figure of 1 second per comparison, it could take approximately 23 days to scan this number of records. It is required that the search be completed in not more than 24 hours. To achieve this desired reduction, it is proposed that other details from the crime should also be utilized to narrow the search. This will include *geographical location*, *date* and *time* of incident, and *nature of crime*. These will be compared against stored information, again from the Home Office and police files, giving the *modus operandi*, and – where available – *alibi* information for the convicted criminals mentioned above.'

From this, we draw up a list of candidate entities:

- alibi
- crime scene
- criminal
- date
- fingerprint
- geographical location
- Home Office
- modus operandi
- nature of crime
- police department
- suspect
- time

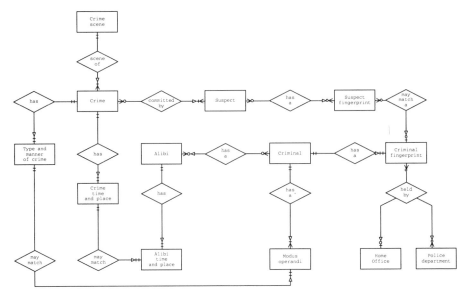

Figure 21.9 A provisional data model for the fingerprint recognition system.

From this list, in turn, a provisional data model is constructed (Figure 21.9).

After further polishing, and comparison with the corresponding process model (a method discussed in Chapter 22), this model could be translated into C++ or SQL, as required; the translation process is described in Section 21.5.

21.5 Implementing from ERDs

We considered in Chapter 20 the conversion of tables into C++ and SQL code. We were focusing at the time on 'bottom up' data modelling and saw that, in avoiding many-to-many relationships, we sometimes have to introduce an extra table into our data model.

As we see here, the use of tables to implement all relationships represented in an ERD is a straightforward approach that, while not always efficient, is always a possible solution. For example, to see how we can link ERDs to C++, let's return to reconsider our car-parking example. We assume that, as part of the system we discussed in Section 21.2.2, the programmer is presented with ERD shown in Figure 21.10. In addition, the attribute diagrams in Figure 21.11 are also provided.

As Figure 21.11 also shows, a simple way to convert this abstract data representation into C++, is to convert each attribute diagram and relationship into a `struct`. We discussed the pros and cons of this implementation, and of the use of C++ for such a task, in Chapter 20. The implementation in SQL is, as we also saw in Chapter 20, very similar.

Laying aside the choice of an implementation language, we should note that the above example deliberately presents the most general case. As we saw in Chapter 20,

Figure 21.10 A simple ERD for the car parking example.

many-to-many relationships may be represented as intermediate tables. In a real sense, all relationships are special cases of many-to-many, and therefore can be represented in this way: by representing every entity and relation in your ERD as a table (however you implement it), you will always, even in the most complex case, be able to produce a working system. However, the system may not be very efficient, in terms of memory used (because of unnecessary data duplication) or of processing speed (because of the extra 'joins' you have introduced).

We discussed in Chapter 20 ways of creating a more efficient implementation and saw that such an implementation may, except in the case of many-to-many relationships, involve two, rather than three, tables. Usually, as we will see in Chapters 22 and

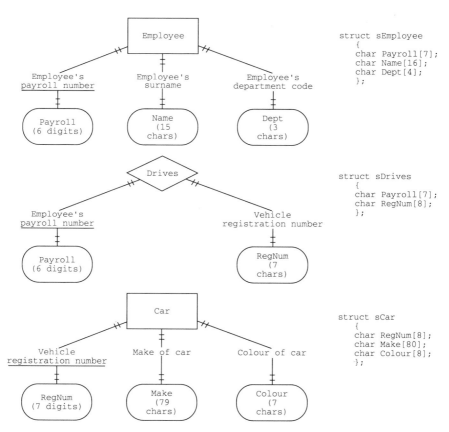

Figure 21.11 The attribute diagrams and possible C++ implementation of the ERD in Figure 21.10.

23, decisions of this nature are taken by the system designer, while the original data model will have been constructed by the analyst. As we saw in Part I, the integrity of the methodology is undermined if the logical and physical models get out of step.

To maintain the integrity of the models, we need to indicate on the ERD whether or not each relationship has been implemented as a table in the final database. The default is that a table has been used; where this is not the case, an asterisk is added to the relationship name in the ERD. For example, the attribute diagrams and C++ structs corresponding to Figure 21.12 are given in Figure 21.13.

Figure 21.12 models the situation, represented in Figure 21.13, where a 'collection' of sCar structs (say an array or a linked list) will hold the details of the vehicles, and a similar collection will hold the details of the employees. The many-to-one links between these two entities are created through the addition of a pointer field to the sCar struct.

Figure 21.12 A modified ERD for the car parking example, indicating a two-table implementation.

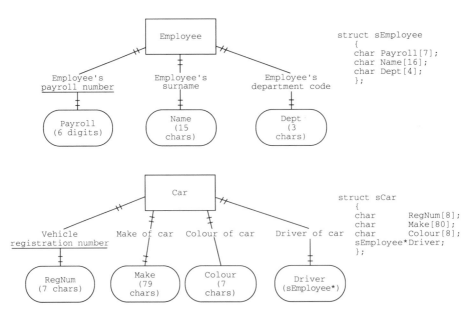

Figure 21.13 The attribute diagrams and possible C++ implementation the one-to-many relationship shown in the ERD in Figure 21.12.

One simple application of these data structures is illustrated in Program 21.1.

```cpp
// Simple car parking program
// Source is: 21_01.CPP

#include <iostream.h>
#include <stdlib.h>

// Global constants
const int EMPLOYEES = 2; // Number of employees
const int CARS = 2;      // Number of cars

const int STR_SIZE = 20; // All strings are this length...

// The data "declarations"
struct sEmployee
   {
   char Payroll[STR_SIZE];
   char Name[STR_SIZE];
   char Dept[STR_SIZE];
   };

struct sCar
   {
   char       RegNum[STR_SIZE];
   char       Make[STR_SIZE];
   char       Colour[STR_SIZE];
   sEmployee* Driver_PTR;
   };

// Function declarations
void Get_Employee_Data(sEmployee&);
void Get_Car_Data(sCar&, const sEmployee* const);
void Display_All_Data(const sCar* const);

int main()
   {
   sEmployee Employees[EMPLOYEES];  // The employees "table"
   sCar Cars[CARS];                 // The cars "table"

   cout << "Parking Program\n";
   cout << "--------------\n";

   // Add some employee data
   for (int Emp_num = 0; Emp_num < EMPLOYEES; Emp_num++)
      {
      cout << "\nPlease enter details for employee #"
           << Emp_num << "\n";

      Get_Employee_Data(Employees[Emp_num]);
      {

   // Add some car data
```

```cpp
    for (int Car_num = 0; Car_num < CARS; Car_num++)
      {
      cout << "\nPlease enter details for car #"
           << Car_num << "\n";

      Get_Car_Data(Cars[Car_num], &Employees[0]))
      }

  // Now display all data
  Display_All_Data(&Cars[0]);

  cout << "\nFinished.";
  return 0;
  }

/*************************************************************
 *                                                           *
 * FUNCTION:  Get_Employee_Data                              *
 *                                                           *
 * PURPOSE:   Get data for specified employee.               *
 *                                                           *
 *************************************************************/
void Get_Employee_Data(sEmployee& Employee_REF)
   {
   cout << "Employee surname            : ";
   cin.getline(Employee_REF.Name, STR_SIZE);

   cout << "Employee payroll number     : ";
   cin.getline(Employee_REF.Payroll, STR_SIZE);

   cout << "Employee department number   : ";
   cin.getline(Employee_REF.Dept, STR_SIZE);
   }

/*************************************************************
 *                                                           *
 * FUNCTION:  Get_Car_Data                                   *
 *                                                           *
 * PURPOSE:   Get data for specified vehicle.                *
 *                                                           *
 *************************************************************/
void Get_Car_Data(                  sCar& Car_REF,
                  const sEmployee* const EMPLOYEE_PTR)
   {
   cout << "Registration number   : ";
   cin.getline(Car_REF.RegNum, STR_SIZE);

   cout << "Make                  : ";
   cin.getline(Car_REF.Make, STR_SIZE);

   cout << "Colour                : ";
   cin.getline(Car_REF.Colour, STR_SIZE);
```

```
    cout << "\nEmployees:\n";

    for (int Emp_num = 0; Emp_num < EMPLOYEES; Emp_num++)
      {
      cout << " " << Emp_num << " "
             << (EMPLOYEE_PTR[Emp_num].Name << "\n";
      }

    char Num_Str[5];
    cout << "\nPlease enter employee number of driver : ";
    cin.getline(Num_str, sizeof(Num_str));

    Car_REF.Driver_PTR = (sEmployee*) &(EMPLOYEE_PTR[atoi(Num_str)]);
    }

/********************************************************************
*                                                                  *
* FUNCTION:   Display_All_Data                                     *
*                                                                  *
* PURPOSE:    Display full list of cars and drivers.              *
*                                                                  *
********************************************************************/
void Display_All_Data(const sCar* const CAR_PTR)
    {
    cout << "\nReg.\tMake\tColour\tDriver\n"
         << "------------------------\n";
    for (int Car = 0; Car < CARS; Car++)
      {
      cout << (CAR_PTR[Car].RegNum         << "\t"
           << (CAR_PTR[Car].Make           << "\t"
           << (CAR_PTR[Car].Colour         << "\t"
           << (CAR_PTR[Car].Driver_PTR)->Name
           << endl;
      }
    }
```

Program 21.1 Using the car-parking data structures in a simple application. (☺)

The output from Program 21.1 is as follows:

```
Parking Program

Please enter details for employee #0
Employee surname              : Pont
Employee payroll number       : 1234
Employee department number    : 56

Please enter details for employee #1
Employee surname              : Dromgoole
Employee payroll number       : 3452
Employee department number    : 67
```

```
Please enter details for car #0
Registration number          : MJP1
Make                         : Ferrari
Colour                       : Red

Employees:
                    0 Pont
                    1 Dromgoole

Please enter employee number of driver : 0

Please enter details for CAR #1
Registration number          : SKD1
Make                         : Mini
Colour                       : Maroon

Employees:
                    0 Pont
                    1 Dromgoole

Please enter employee number of driver : 1

Reg.    Make        Colour      Driver

MJP1    Ferrari     Red         Pont
SKD1    Mini        Maroon      Dromgoole

Finished.
```

21.6 Aggregation relationships

We have until now considered only general associations between entities. In some implementations (notably C++) it is possible to make direct use of an additional relationship called 'a Part of' or 'APO': that is, an aggregation relationship. In SQL, such an implementation is less elegant but still possible (see Rumbaugh *et al.,* 1991).

Suppose, for example, we have been asked to develop a simple payroll system, along the lines of that discussed in Chapter 17. The basic data model appears simple enough: each employee receives a pay cheque once a month (Figure 21.14).

However, this isn't the end of the story. As we saw in Chapter 17, we can efficiently implement this system in C++ using a `union`: that is, by storing different information depending on whether the worker is paid by salary, or by the hour. We can add this information to Figure 21.14, as shown in Figure 21.15.

Figure 21.14 The first-cut data model for a payroll system.

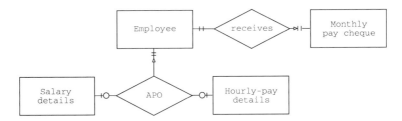

Figure 21.15   An extended data model for a payroll system, including both simple association and aggregation relationships.

Note that when diagrams get more complex it can be helpful to separate the association and aggregation relationships, by moving the aggregation details to a child (decomposition) diagram. Using such a scheme, we would represent Figure 21.15 using Figure 21.14 and Figure 21.16.

An entity subtype/supertype object type, such as that shown in Figure 21.16, consists of an entity and two sub-entities connected by a relationship. In this example, the object is `Employee`, and the sub-objects are Salaried and Hourly-Paid. The crossbar on the link to the relationship indicated that Employee is the 'parent'. The label 'E/M' within the relationship box says that the relationship is 'Exclusive and Mandatory'. That is, an Employee must include either Hourly-Paid or Salaried data. It cannot include neither and cannot include both.

The full range of possible relationships are:

- *Exclusive/mandatory*
  The entity must be one and only one of the following sub-entities.
- *Exclusive/optional*
  The entity may be one and only one of the following sub-entities.
- *Inclusive/mandatory*
  The entity must be at least one of the following sub-entities.
- *Inclusive/optional*
  The entity may be one or more of the following sub-entities.

Consider a further example. Suppose we are developing a data model to support an airport security system. We want to ensure that personnel (such as pilots, maintenance

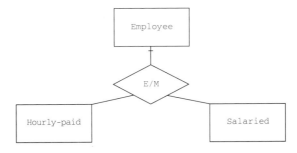

Figure 21.16   The aggregation relationship from the pay-roll system as a child of Figure 21.14.

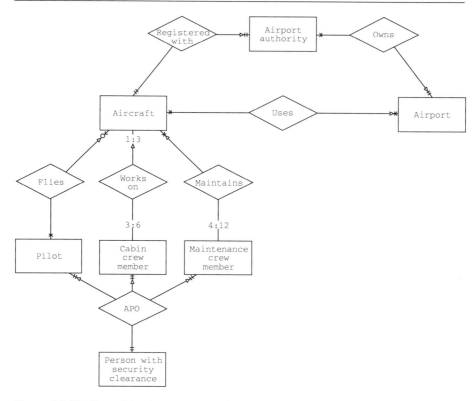

Figure 21.17 Part of the data model for an airport security system, including both association and aggregation relationships.

personnel and the cabin crew members) are able to do their jobs with the minimum of inconvenience, but at the same time only have access to parts of the airport complex which they must enter in order to perform their jobs effectively. We need a fairly detailed model of the entities in the system and their interconnections; the beginnings of such a model are sketched in Figure 21.17. Note that here we assume that all there will be common information (name, address, date of birth, National Insurance number, and so on) for all people, represented by the 'Person' entity, which is a part of each of the more specific personnel models.

Note that in Part III, when we look at inheritance, we shall consider some more powerful ways of creating similar models.

21.7   Conclusions

In this chapter we've looked at the construction of a data model, sometimes referred to as a semantic data model. The integration of such models within the general framework of SADIE is discussed in Chapter 22.

Exercises

21.1 Consider the approach suggested in Section 21.4 for finding candidate entities. Do you think it would be practical to automate this process, generating from a textual description of a problem a provisional set of entities? Consider how you might begin to tackle such a technique, using C++ to process a written description of a software problem provided in a text file.

21.2 One way of drawing up a dataflow diagram is to look first at verbs in the initial problem description. How practical would it be to extend the system in your solution to Exercise 21.1 to create a Level 1 DfD and/or a context diagram automatically, from the initial written problem statement?

21.3 Rewrite the C++ code for the car parking system in Figure 21.13 using SQL.

21.4 Draw up a set of attribute diagrams, or rough tables, corresponding to the airport security system in Figure 21.17.

21.5 Implement the data model for the payroll system given in Figure 21.14 using C++.

21.6 Consider the following problem statement for the 'Robin Hood Hotel':

'Nottingham, some 20 miles north of Leicester, is the former home of the infamous Sheriff of Nottingham, and lies in the heart of Robin Hood country. Interest in the legends and history of the area support a large tourist industry, and the newly opened Robin Hood Hotel on the outskirts of the city seeks to capitalize on this public interest.

The hotel contains five hundred rooms, three restaurants, four function suites, seven bars (including a piano bar), a swimming pool, golf course and gambling casino. On the basis of the profits from the first month since opening, annual turnover from the room sales and associated meals should be in excess of £8.9 million per annum, with an additional predicted income of £3.5 million from catered functions (wedding receptions, divorce parties, and so on).

The first month of operation in the hotel has also revealed that, in general, the management structure of the hotel is working well, with the exception of the reception desk. Here it has been necessary to employ three extra staff to keep track of the large number of guests using the various facilities. Also, on several occasions, there has been confusion over bills charged to guests with, for example, restaurant bills from the previous evening not being notified to the reception desk until after a guest has checked out, often resulting in considerable lost revenue.

The staff at the reception desk must deal with all aspects of the operation of the hotel. All check-ins and check-outs are dealt with by these staff. In addition, however, the reception staff must deal with residents who wish to use, for example, the swimming pool, the golf course, the laundry and dry-cleaning services, tours of Nottingham castle and visits to one of the many local theatres. The reception desk is also responsible for the processing invoices and information requests concerning the various function suites.

Further details of the reception desk staff duties is given below.

Check-in

The reception desk staff deal with all check-ins. Most guests already have a reservation (made usually by telephone or – less commonly – by letter, well in advance). Guests with a reservation will also have paid a deposit (minimum £50.00). The list of reserved rooms will be checked and the guest will be told their room number. The guest will be required to confirm payment details (usually a credit card number or a cash deposit) and to fill in a registration form giving name, address and car registration number. The reception desk personnel will then confirm the duration of stay in the hotel and add this information, along with the cost of the room, to the registration card, which they file. The guest will be given their room key, and – if required – a bell person may be summoned to help carry their luggage.

Guests must check out of their rooms by 11a.m., after which the rooms are cleaned. When guests arrive early in the morning, the reception desk must find out whether the reserved room is ready for use: if it is, then the guest will be able to enter the room immediately. If the room is not yet ready, it may be possible to reassign the guest to an available room. In the event that no room is available, the guest will be offered a voucher for a free cup of coffee in one of the restaurants, and may have his or her luggage stored free of charge until the room is available.

Note that each room is in a particular category (economy – 100 rooms; mid-range – 150 rooms; and business class – 250 rooms). The cost of all rooms within a particular category are the same: currently, in the introductory period, these are £70.00, £90.00 and £150.00. Each room is a double/twin room, and there is no reduction for single room occupancy. The cost of rooms does not normally include any meals, except outwith the summer period when special 'bed and breakfast' or 'bed, breakfast and dinner' packages may have been arranged. In the event that the guest has paid for such a package, a card giving details will be given to each guest, to be shown to the head waiter in the restaurant.

Where a guest does not have a reservation, then the list of available rooms will be checked to see if there is a vacancy. Though this is not publicly stated, not all rooms are always available to all guests; a small number (six, where possible) are kept in reserve for regular business guests whom, it is found, sometimes like to arrive without reservations. If no suitable vacancy can be found, then the front desk staff make efforts to find accommodation for the guest in a nearby alternative hotel. In particular, the Robin Hood has a sister hotel (the Maid Marion), also in Nottingham, and will attempt to direct guests there if possible.

Check-out

All check-outs are dealt with by the reception desk. As noted above, guests must check-out by 11 a.m. In the event that guests attempt to check-out later than 12.00 a.m. the hotel reserves the right to charge for an extra night's accommodation.

All charges for the room are entered into the guest's account on a daily basis. Guests are given a fully itemized bill listing, for example, room charges, charges for pay-as-you-view videos, telephone charges and restaurant and bar bills. Payments are usually made by credit card; payments by personal cheque are not permitted on amounts over £50.00, except by special arrangement.

Business guests who have agreed credit terms with the hotel (in advance) may charge their bill to an account.

Functions

In addition to dealing with ordinary check-ins and check-outs the reception desk will also handle enquiries and billing for various function rooms. The main business arises from business meetings (mainly during the week) and wedding receptions (at weekends). The facilities are not in the budget range, but they are of high quality and therefore already popular: the waiting time for a wedding reception, for example, is already five months.

All functions involve a similar package. The four function rooms have different capacities (100, 150, 400 and 700 people). The two largest rooms have a movable division between them; if this is drawn aside, the resulting room has capacity of 1000.

The cost of the rooms is £1.50 per person, per hour, for a minimum of three hours. The cost is calculated not on the actual number of people but on the room capacity: for example, the 100-person room costs £150.00 per hour (minimum £450.00). Catering, bar facilities, and so forth, carry additional charges: these are dealt with by the Catering Manager.

A reduction of 10% on accommodation is made on all function bookings over £5000 (including catering, and so on). On wedding receptions over £7500, free use of the Honeymoon Suite is offered.

After an event, the Catering Manager informs the reception desk of the charges due. If full or partial pre-payment has been made, then this is handed over to the reception desk.

Miscellaneous activities

Use of the golf course, swimming pool, and so on, is free for business guests. Other guests must pay, in cash, at time of booking.

Balancing accounts

On a daily basis, the hotel accountant audits the sales from the previous day. Any discrepancies between expected and received revenues is immediately investigated. Various payments (for example, credit card receipts) are processed, and banked as necessary. Invoices are posted where required.'

The Robin Hood Hotel have asked you to develop an information system to support the work of the staff on the reception desk. From this perspective:
(a)   identify the key attributes in the system;
(b)   develop an appropriate ERD;
(c)   consider how practical it would be to implement your ERD-based data model in C++;
(d)   implement the above model in SQL.

22 Data-oriented analysis and design

22.1 Introduction

To a software engineer developing an information system, particularly one involving an external database, it may appear that there is very little processing to be done. This is an illusion. Performing queries or data updates on a database generally involves a large amount of complex, and often extremely efficient, processing.

Even if you don't produce the database itself 'in-house' you will still have to write code to do *something* with the data you model; most users won't be awed by a perfect ER diagram or even some beautiful SQL. Instead, not unreasonably, they will expect the systems you develop for them to 'do something useful' with the data you have stored. This additional processing may be relatively simple, such as printing standard letters for all customers in the Edinburgh area telling them of a store opening in the vicinity. On the other hand, it may be more complicated, such as collating all available details of cancer treatment outcomes for countries within the European Union, and overlaying these on a map of the area. Whatever the system, you can be sure that *some* code will have to be written.

In this chapter, we therefore turn our attention to the use of data modelling in conjunction with the process modelling techniques we considered in Part I. In particular, we'll see how data modelling (as described in Chapter 21) is integrated into SADIE.

In outline, the problem of data modelling is conquered by splitting it into two phases, as follows:

- the analyst is responsible for determining a provisional data model;
- the designer is responsible for normalizing this data so as to make the whole system more efficient, and for ensuring that the proposed data is sufficient to ensure that all the required processing tasks can be accomplished.

It is important to realize, however, that the data model is not developed in isolation: rather, both process and data modelling are conducted 'in parallel', a procedure which, when carried out effectively, should contribute to a general understanding of the problem. Overall, the final result is the hybrid SADIE model, shown in Figure 22.1. This integrates both the process modelling and data modelling components.

We'll consider the development of appropriate hybrid models for a range of information systems in this chapter, from simple data stores to more complex decision support systems.

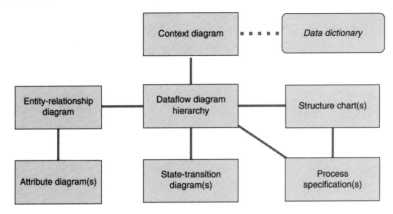

Figure 22.1 The components of the hybrid SADIE (data/process) model.

22.2 The analysis phase

As always, the analysis process will be iterative: you will start with an outline of the problem, and gradually refine this until you are happy that you have a complete understanding of the system requirements. In particular, note that data modelling activity does not (or should not) become merely an adjunct to process modelling, and vice versa. Try to exploit both of the techniques, using them to maximize your overall understanding of the problem domain.

The basic 'recipe' for the analysis phase of data-oriented SADIE is as follows:

(D1)   *The business case*
       The analyst begins by estimating the technical and economic feasibility of the project. If, for example, the project is too small to be profitable, greatly outside the experience of the available personnel, or larger than can be tackled with the available technical and human resources, then it must be rejected at this stage.

(D2)   *The Context diagram*
       The Context diagram is produced. Particular care is taken in the selection of appropriate terminators.

(D3)   *The entity diagram*
       A preliminary entity diagram is produced. This will (usually) depict only internal entities. This diagram is necessarily very provisional, and relationships are therefore usually omitted at this stage.

(D4)   *The user interface*
       Because of the impact of the system interface on all aspects of the model, it is sketched (or prototyped) at this early stage.

(D5)   *The process list*
       A process list is drawn up. This list is necessarily very provisional, and creation of a highly polished document is not appropriate at this stage.

(D6)   *The walkthrough*
A system walkthrough is performed. Where feasible, the entire development team (analysts, designers, programmers) should be involved in this process. As the walkthrough progresses, the entity diagram, process list, Context diagram and interface sketches are modified as required.

(D7)   *The Level 1 dataflow diagram*
A preliminary Level 1 DfD is sketched, on the basis of the process list. It is usually inappropriate to polish this diagram, as it may change substantially when the STD is considered. For this reason, it is usual include only processes at this stage, and a bare minimum of dataflows. Note that while a Level 1 DfD is usually all that is required, on a large system you may need to go further.

(D8)   *The state-transition diagram*
The state-transition diagram associated with the Level 1 DfD is produced in an iterative process involving successive modifications to both STD and DfD, as necessary. For (rare) pure 'batch' programs, where no STD is used, this stage may be omitted, while for larger systems, a network of STDs may be required.

(D9)   *The entity-relationship diagram*
The entity diagram (Stage D3) is extended into a first-cut ERD by adding in the relationships. A preliminary attribute set (or rough table) is produced for each entity.

(D10) *Reconciliation of the data and process models*
Checks are made to ensure that the ERD can support the DfD requirements. Either or both models are modified as required to achieve this.

(D11) *The dataflow diagram hierarchy*
The DfD hierarchy is completed, and levelled as necessary.

(D12) *The process specifications*
The process specifications are written.

(D13) *The data dictionary*
The data dictionary is completed.

(D14) *The balanced logical model*
The complete model is reviewed, checked and balanced. Any necessary supporting documentation is written.

None of the above stages are, in themselves, new; all have been considered in previous chapters. We will give a complete, substantial, example of the use of this methodology in the next chapter.

Note that when using SADIE to develop an information system in a business context, it may often be the case that there is already an existing computerized system that has proved too slow or inflexible to support the needs of the growing or changing business. It is important always to try and construct a logical model at the specification stage, representing what the system should do, putting aside preconceptions about any current physical implementation. However, the tendency in such a situation is not to create a new model, but to merely record the way in which the existing system is constructed. If you fall into this trap, you should not be surprised to find out that your model is so effective that your 'new' system performs almost as badly as the system it replaces ...

22.3 Integration of process and data models

As we have noted above, we shall focus in this chapter on the integration of the data model into the general SADIE methodology.

We can illustrate how the integrated model is represented by considering the dataflow and entity-relationship diagrams shown in Figure 22.2 as (part of) our process model, and the ERD as (part of) the data model.

In most cases, the link between the process and data models is represented by a store on the DfD. Thus, we can view the data model as a 'child' of the store on the DfD, as shown explicitly in Figure 22.3. Note that, where general control information is also required, the store is usually duplicated on the diagram, to avoid a confusing mix of data and control flow information; this procedure is illustrated in Figure 22.4.

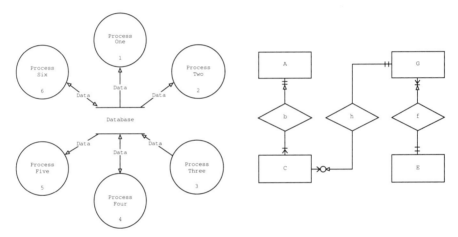

Figure 22.2 Part of the process model (left) and data model (right) for a simple information system.

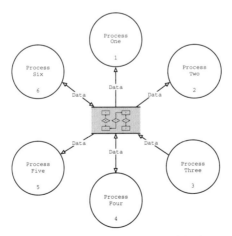

Figure 22.3 The link between the process and data models shown in Figure 22.2.

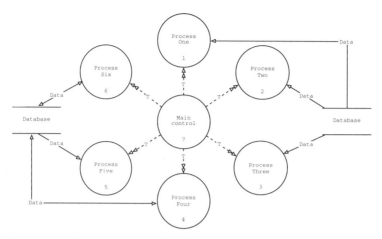

Figure 22.4 Typical form of the Level I DfD for a more substantial information system. Note that the (single) database has been duplicated to avoid confusing control and data flows at the centre of the drawing.

When using a store as a 'parent' of a data model, a question arises over the appropriate way of representing the store in the data dictionary. Clearly, there is potential for a large degree of overlap in the ERD and dictionary representations, and we could, for example, attempt to incorporate a full textual description of the relevant ERD (or ERD hierarchy) in the data dictionary. Such an approach quickly becomes impractical, however, and introduces all the usual problems associated with having 'duplicate' data entries in a system. It is more common, therefore, to simply include a cross-reference to the relevant ERDs in the data dictionary in such circumstances.

For example, consider the simple DfD shown in Figure 22.5. The corresponding data dictionary entry (BNF clause) might be:

```
data
--see XYZ.DAT
```

Finally, note that we have in a sense already considered a link between data on process and data models on every Context diagram we've presented. The 'terminators' used on such diagrams (for example, Figure 22.6) are entities, and represent models of real-world 'things' (or people) with which your system must interact.

As we shall see in Part III, it is sometimes useful to represent some of the entities (more generally, classes) in a data model as 'internal terminators' on a DfD.

Figure 22.5 A simple DfD containing a link to a data model.

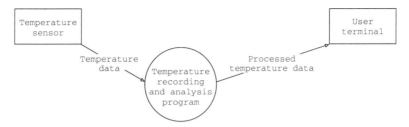

Figure 22.6 Context diagram for the bell foundry study. The terminators on the diagram are a form of data model.

22.4 Decision support systems

Thus far our discussions in this chapter have implied that the systems you develop will be either technical in nature *or* data intensive. While this may be the case in many applications, there is a large and growing demand for a breed of systems known as **decision support systems** that combine both complex data and complex processing requirements. Such systems are some of the most challenging, and interesting, systems that software engineers are called upon to produce.

There is a lot of hot air generated over the meaning of the term decision support system. Some people will argue themselves blue over fine distinctions between 'decision support systems', 'management information systems' and 'executive information systems'. The various contradictory definitions given for such systems are not generally helpful.

We shall content ourselves with the general term 'decision support system' (DSS) to describe all such systems, and any computer-based system that helps in the decision-making process. We will then subdivide the field into:

- simple decision support systems, and
- model-based decision support systems.

We define these distinct flavours of DSS below. Further details on this important field can be found in Gray (1994).

22.4.1 Simple DSSs

As we'll see in the next chapter, a stock control system that provides up-to-date inventories on demand is a crude (but useful) decision support system. We classify such systems as simple DSSs.

The characteristics of a simple DSS are:

- it contains a substantial database;
- it allows the user access to the database, usually in a controlled manner;
- it performs only quite simple processing on the underlying data.

22.4.2 Model-based DSSs

Consider that you are designing a new car. During a series of tests, you might well (a few years ago) have built a mock-up of the car and placed it in a wind tunnel to investigate the wind resistance and other features of a particular body shape. More recently, you would probably have sold your wind tunnel (if you could find a museum willing to buy it) and invested the money in a high-powered computer system. On the computer, you would simulate the car and its environment; you would do all the tests you carried out before, but without building a physical mock-up of the system in which you were interested. In such a situation, you are using a computer and mathematical model to simulate objects and events in the real world. If your model is accurate, you will be able to predict with good accuracy how a real car will perform when built. As your tests proceed, it is generally *much* cheaper and faster to ask 'what if' questions by changing your computer model than it would be to keep building new physical prototypes.

The computer simulation used by the car designer is an example of a model-based DSS. Other widely-used examples include financial models and medical models. With a good model of the economy of the country (and the world) in which we are living, an economist can ask, and get reasonable answers to, questions like: 'what will happen to unemployment in six months time if we raise interest rates to 30% tomorrow?' With the ever-better computer models of the human body under development, clinicians can begin to better predict the effects of drugs and surgery on individual patients.

The characteristics of a model-based DSS are therefore:

- it contains a substantial database;
- it allows the user access to the information in the database, usually in a controlled manner,
- it contains a mathematical or computer model of the world with which it processes the underlying data.

One final class of model-based DSS must also be mentioned: the CASE tool. Although even the most expensive and complex of such tools are still at early stages of their development, the basic model-based nature of the CASE tool is still evident. The model is, in this case, of course SADIE (or a similar methodology), and the support comes largely, at the present time, in the form of reports revealing how well the system being developed by the software engineer complies with the model requirements.

22.5 The design phase

Like the analysis process, the design process introduces no new material: the stages are all as described in previous chapters.

(D15) *Review and refinement of the logical model*
The specification documents are reviewed, in order to gain an understanding of the system, and to correct any flaws in the logical model.

(D16) *The software and hardware architecture*
The operating environment (hardware and/or operating system), and the basic software architecture are determined. General design decisions are made, including the choice of implementation for the database.

(D17) *Data design*
The data model constructed during analysis is normalized.

(D18) *The preliminary physical model*
The preliminary structure chart is derived from the logical model.

(D19) *Review and refinement of the physical model*
The provisional physical model is inspected, and issues of module coupling and cohesion are considered.

(D20) *Reconciliation of the logical and physical process models*
Logical and physical models are compared and adjusted as necessary to ensure that they are fully compatible.

(D21) *Reconciliation of the data and process models*
The process and data components of the hybrid model are checked for consistency, and adjusted as necessary.

(D22) *The test strategy*
The overall system test strategy is drawn up.

We give a complete, substantial, example of the use of this method in the next chapter.

22.6 Data normalization and speed of data access

We have argued that the process of normalization is analogous to the decomposition of monolithic program code into a nest of cohesive functions bound together by a minimum of necessary coupling. The analogy between functions and data can be taken a little further. As we have seen, use of functions carries with it a penalty: with every function call (stack) memory is used to hold the parameters, and it takes time to copy these parameters and to transfer control. Overuse of functions can therefore be counterproductive. Similarly, by normalizing your database to BCNF (or beyond) you will, as we have seen, inevitably introduce new relations. These new relations increase the complexity of database queries. Complex queries are more difficult to write, and can take longer to process. If, however, the database is not in BCNF, various anomalies (update, insertion and deletion) can arise, as we saw in Chapter 20. It's a question of swings and roundabouts …

If data access times are a major concern, then one solution is to 'throw MIPS' at the problem, and adopt a **client–server** approach, placing your (external) database on a fast server capable of performing the rapid processing you require; the performance of your 'client' program, even on a slow computer, may then improve because your user's computer will itself have less processing to perform. Renaud (1993) provides a readable introduction to client–server systems if this area is one you would like to explore further.

If using a data server isn't a practical option, or when such a server still doesn't provide speed of data access required, the software engineer may choose to take a different approach. The main processing load from a database comes from implementing the 'joins' between tables. Therefore, the software engineer may sometimes choose (or be forced) to implement a complete database as a single non-1NF table. Although such an approach is 'dangerous' in that inexperienced users, given free access to the data, may cause damage to the database, it can sometimes result in much more rapid data access.

If you are determined to 'have your cake and eat it', it is sometimes possible to have both safe data and rapid access: this can be achieved by leaving all your data in one table and ensuring data integrity by restricting the processing options provided to the user. For example, if your program gives the user only three options 'Search database', 'Add new record', 'Delete record', then you *may* be able to ensure that none of the options can, under any circumstances, cause side-effects.

One area in which the above techniques are commonly applied is in the development of decision support systems, discussed above. DS systems necessarily involve data, sometimes copious quantities of complex data. This raises a particular concern when it comes to normalization. While such a process is straightforward in 'book-sized' examples, it is a non-trivial process in real situations. Sometimes with DS applications, it is important to take a pragmatic view, and question whether the effort involved in normalizing the underlying data structures is worthwhile or appropriate.

Such decisions cannot be taken lightly: if you opt not to normalize (or fully normalize) your data, then you'll need to be able to justify this decision to your client every time this decision allows a careless user to destroy the database that you have developed.

22.7 The implementation phase

The basic 'recipe' for the implementation phase of data-oriented SADIE is as follows:

(D23) *Review and refinement of the physical model*
The design documents are reviewed, in order to gain an understanding of the system, and to correct any flaws in the physical model.

(D24) *The hardware framework*
A specialized hardware framework is created, if required.

(D25) *The data framework*
The choice of data implementation strategy is made. The data framework is created, based on the normalized data model.

(D26) *The code framework*
The code framework is created, using CppSpecs, based on the structure chart and the PSpecs.

(D27) *The preliminary modules*
The preliminary modules are created or, preferably, recycled from a code library. In either case, the resulting function will build on the CppSpecs, and will make reference to the physical model (particularly the PSpecs and the data dictionary).

(D28) *Error detection and recovery*
The preliminary modules are extended, where necessary, through the addition of appropriate error detection and correction features.

(D29) *Module tests*
The modules are tested, by the programmers, according to the test strategy produced by the design team. Modifications are made as required.

(D30) *The prototype system*
The tested modules and data framework are assembled into a prototype system, as dictated by the structure chart(s) and entity-relationship diagram(s). The system will be implemented, where appropriate, on the hardware framework.

(D31) *Data entry*
   Adequate test data is entered into the system database to allow for realistic system testing.

(D32) *System tests and maintenance*
   The complete prototype is tested again, first by the programmers, and then by the test team, both working from the test strategy produced by the designers. The system is then subjected to user tests, including field tests and/or acceptance tests. The system is revised as necessary; any changes made during the testing and subsequent ongoing maintenance are recorded and reflected in the evolving hybrid model.

We give a complete, substantial, example of the use of this method in the next chapter.

22.8 Conclusions

In this chapter we have seen how the data models described in Part II may be used in conjunction with the process modelling techniques considered in Part I, and integrated into the general system development process.

We also introduced the field of decision support, arguing that all general information system can be viewed as decision support systems. We showed that more 'intelligent' decision support requires both data and a computer or mathematical model of the system in which you are interested.

In the next chapter, we put theory into practice and describe the development of a stock control system.

Exercises

22.1 Use SADIE to design, in outline, a simple decision support system that could assist companies in finding the correct post code (zip code) for the customers on their mailing list.

22.2 Consider that you have been asked to write a system to help train passengers negotiate the railway system represented in Figure 22.7.

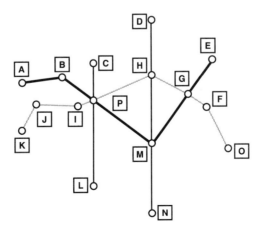

Figure 22.7 A simple railway system.

To travel, say, between station K and station D, a passenger must travel from station K to station H, then change trains and travel from station H to station D.

Each 'stop' (that is, travel between any two adjacent stations) takes 17 minutes and costs £1.10. Further, trains leave the beginning of each line (travelling in both directions) every hour, on the hour. On Sundays, special conditions apply: line maintenance is carried out on these days, and trains run more slowly, taking 25 minutes per stop.

On the basis of the above information, design and implement (in C++) a decision support system to be used by passengers to buy tickets for their journey, or simply to advise them on the route to be taken, and the train times. The system will print the tickets for the passengers, following payment by credit card.

The system should be very user-friendly, and should be able to deal with enquiries of the following form:

'I want to travel between A and K, arriving by 10.00 on Sunday morning. When do I have to leave and how much will the journey cost, please?'

'When is the first train after 21.00 on Saturday that goes from H to L?'

22.3 The task in this exercise is to design a decision support system intended to allow the user to predict the future price of shares in the stock market. The prototype system we will be concerned with here is intended to help an individual small shareholder store details of a portfolio of shares in a database. The system will allow browsing and editing of the contents of the portfolio. Much more interesting, however, the system will also provide advice to the user on the purchase or sale of particular shares.

The type of advice we require from the system will take the form of that provided by a perfect broker:

- 'I predict a rise of 100 points in the value of Share X within the next four to ten days. There are no such shares in the portfolio: I recommend immediate purchase.'
- 'I predict that the price of Share Y will fall by 10 points tomorrow. 2330 shares of this type are currently held. I would recommend sale of all such shares immediately.'
- 'I predict no significant changes in the performance of Share Z in the next 30 days. I recommend that the existing shares are maintained for this period, and that their future situation is then reviewed.'

The initial process list for our proposed system is given in Table 22.1.

Process	Process outline
Advise	Provide advice on the sale and purchase of a number of shares held in a portfolio.
Store	Keep details of the current contents of the portfolio.
Browse	Allow update and browsing of the share information.

Table 22.1 Process list.

To build such a system, we require both data and an accurate model of the economy. Let's deal with the data issue first.

The data

To predict the future value of our shares, we'll use data on past values as a guide. We could try typing in the financial data from our daily newspaper (Figure 22.8) but this wouldn't be much fun, and the data would be nearly a day old by the time we had entered it all. We need a faster solution.

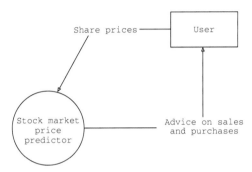

Figure 22.8 An initial Context diagram for our system.

In the UK, share price information is available over a narrow-band communication channel known as 'Teletext' broadcast along with terrestrial television pictures (one of the original – and continuing – uses of the system was to allow transmission of television subtitles for deaf individuals). By purchasing a suitable Teletext receiver for our computer, we should be able to obtain the data we require immediately. Moreover, this share data is updated approximately every 1.5 hours, so that it should be more accurate than using only the daily figures from the newspaper.

Our modified context diagram is shown in Figure 22.9.

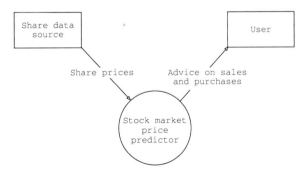

Figure 22.9 The modified Context diagram.

The Model

Now that we know we can get as much data as we like, we only need a model of the economy to work with. Such models are not all that easy to come by.

The type of prediction we want to make is sometimes referred to as time series forecasting. Specifically, our system will be attempting to predict the future value of a share price based solely on the previous values of the same item. The type of forecasting method required in such circumstances is known to statisticians as a **univariate** model.

There are various ways of performing a univariate analysis (for example, see Bowerman and O'Connell, 1987; Makridakis *et al.*, 1983) but a general neural network might be a particularly interesting and effective technique (see Lippmann, 1987 for details).

The prototype DSS

We can assemble our data and economic model as shown in Figure 22.10.

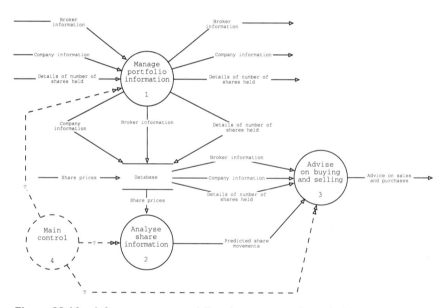

Figure 22.10 A first attempt at modelling the structure of our decision support system.

The complete analysis, design and implementation

This is where you come in. Completing the analysis, design and implementation of this system is left as an exercise.

23 Case Study: Laughing House

23.1 Introduction

In this chapter, we pull together the material from Part II, to illustrate the application of the SADIE methodology to the development of a special-purpose stock control system. The study also illustrates, more realistically than in previous studies, the contributions of the analysis, design and implementation teams to the project as it is gradually translated into a working prototype.

A complete version of this project, produced with the CASE tool, is included on the sample disk: details of how to install the project are given in Appendix C.

23.2 Scenario

According to press reports, Walter Wibble suffered years of torment at school on account of his unusual name and uncharacteristically large body size. Haunted by the laughter of his fellow pupils, and unending chants of 'Wibble Wobbles! Wibble Wobbles!', it is safe to say that Walter did not have a happy childhood. This may have induced a brief period of agoraphobia, and may in part explain why, undoubtedly intelligent as he was, Walter turned down the offer of a position on a software engineering course at the University of Cambridge, choosing instead to 'drop out'.

Six months after leaving school, after a short period of counselling which encouraged him to see all his 'problems' as 'opportunities', Walter established the Laughing House toy company in his parents' garage. Six years later, the young entrepreneur was able to squeeze himself behind the wheel of his new Lamborghini Countach ready for the drive to the opening of his hundredth toy superstore on the outskirts of Sheffield.

However, this success story does have its downside. Like many successful entrepreneurs, Walter had a loathing of paperwork. In the meteoric expansion of his business, the simple manual inventory and stock-keeping systems originally devised for a one-man, garage-based company were unable to keep up.

Driving back down the M1 motorway from Sheffield to London after the store opening, Walter didn't, unfortunately, spot the police radar tracking his car as he exceeded 150 miles per hour on the famous 'Ten Mile Straight', but he did notice a billboard advertising Leicester Software Engineering as he slowed down for the next corner. As soon as the police had finished with him, he gave Jane a call.

Jane, having recently bought a highly priced (but well-received) Wibble Wobble 'Wabbit' for her three-year-old daughter Sadie, immediately recognized Walter Wibble when he telephoned. Walter explained, succinctly, that he was looking for a stock control system to be used in his various toy superstores. His proposal was that LSE should analyse the problem and draw up a complete specification. The 'spec' would then go out to tender and different software engineering companies would be invited to bid for the contract. Naturally, Walter assured Jane, he would also welcome a bid from LSE and, while he could offer no guarantees, their knowledge of the problem, he suggests, could only be an advantage.

Jane immediately arranged a face-to-face meeting with Walter to discuss the matter at greater length.

23.3   Analysis

There are 14 steps involved in the creation of the logical hybrid model required for data-oriented development: these are repeated below for ease of reference. Remember, however, that as always these are only guidelines: you will need to adjust them to fit your own style of working.

(D1)   *The business case*
 The analyst begins by estimating the technical and economic feasibility of the project. If, for example, the project is too small to be profitable, greatly outside the experience of the available personnel, or larger than can be tackled with the available technical and human resources, then it must be rejected at this stage.

(D2)   *The Context diagram*
 The Context diagram is produced. Particular care is taken in the selection of appropriate terminators.

(D3)   *The entity diagram*
 A preliminary entity diagram is produced. This will (usually) depict only internal entities. This diagram is necessarily very provisional, and relationships are therefore usually omitted at this stage.

(D4)   *The user interface*
 Because of the impact of the system interface on all aspects of the model, it is sketched (or prototyped) at this early stage.

(D5)   *The process list*
 A process list is drawn up. This list is necessarily very provisional, and creation of a highly polished document is not appropriate at this stage.

(D6)   *The walkthrough*
 A system walkthrough is performed. Where feasible, the entire development team (analysts, designers, programmers) should be involved in this process. As the walkthrough progresses, the entity diagram, process list, Context diagram and interface sketches are modified as required.

(D7)   *The Level 1 dataflow diagram*
 A preliminary Level 1 DfD is sketched, on the basis of the process list. It is usually inappropriate to polish this diagram, as it may change substantially when the

STD is considered. For this reason, it is usual to include only processes at this stage, and a bare minimum of dataflows. Note that while a Level 1 DfD is usually all that is required, on a large system you may need to go further.

(D8) *The state-transition diagram*
The state-transition diagram associated with the Level 1 DfD is produced in an iterative process involving successive modifications to both STD and DfD, as necessary. For (rare) pure 'batch' programs, where no STD is used, this stage may be omitted, while for larger systems, a network of STDs may be required.

(D9) *The entity-relationship diagram*
The entity diagram (Stage D3) is extended into a first-cut ERD by adding in the relationships. A preliminary attribute set (or rough table) is produced for each entity.

(D10) *Reconciliation of the data and process models*
Checks are made to ensure that the ERD can support the DfD requirements. Either or both models are modified as required to achieve this.

(D11) *The dataflow diagram hierarchy*
The DfD hierarchy is completed, and levelled as necessary.

(D12) *The process specifications*
The process specifications are written.

(D13) *The data dictionary*
The data dictionary is completed.

(D14) *The balanced logical model*
The complete model is reviewed, checked and balanced. Any necessary supporting documentation is written.

Naturally, Jane – who has been instrumental in the development of SADIE – follows these steps religiously.

23.3.1 The business case

> *The analyst begins by estimating the technical and economic feasibility of the project. If, for example, the project is too small to be profitable, greatly outside the experience of the available personnel, or larger than can be tackled with the available technical and human resources, then it must be rejected at this stage.*

The situation here is a little different than that discussed in Chapter 16. In Chapter 16, the requirement was to immediately produce a prototype system; here, the client has merely requested that a specification is produced.

In these circumstances, Jane is able to estimate more easily the work involved in the project. She feels that, with the necessary meetings with representatives of Laughing House, completion of the specification can be completed within five working days. She charges the company time at £300.00 per person day, giving a total labour charge of £1500. In addition, there will be a further charge, of not more than £500, for agreed expenses (travel costs, consumables, and so on).

Walter Wibble is happy with this price, and contracts are exchanged.

23.3.2 The context diagram

The Context diagram is produced. Particular care is taken in the selection of appropriate terminators.

In discussion with Walter Wibble, Jane draws up the Context diagram (Figure 23.1). The Context diagram, Jane explains, reflects her initial understanding of the system requirements. The details of the diagram, she adds, arose from the discussions with Walter Wibble, backed up by her own experience as a software engineer.

She notes that the Context diagram is from the point of view of a single store: this, Jane feels, is appropriate for her initial analysis. However, it might also be useful, she thinks, to redraw the system from the perspective of Head Office.

Walter Wibble is not convinced. 'From your diagram, Jane, it appears that you propose to let Head Office interfere with the stock system for the individual stores, on a regular basis. Is this correct?'

'That's right,' says Jane. 'You suggested that you wanted central control of major lines: this is one efficient way of achieving that. Of course, it can easily be altered...'

'Let me explain my basic management philosophy, Jane – such as it is. I find that people only work well if you give them responsibilities. In this case, we seem to be taking much of the responsibility for the store off the shoulders of local management. That makes me uneasy.'

'I see what you mean,' Jane nods. 'What we could do is simply inform each store, by letter or fax, of changes in stock prices, and so on, leaving it up to local management to implement these changes. It's a little crude, but may be useful, as an interim or permanent measure.'

Walter agrees that this is a better solution, but he still has some misgivings. 'I'm a bit of a technophobe, I'm afraid. Till we get the system up and running I don't want to automate all the inputs from the sales tills, or from the incoming goods. Can't we just have the managers, or their personal assistants, enter this information by hand as well?'

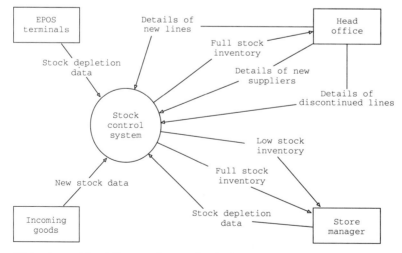

Figure 23.1 A provisional Context diagram for the Laughing House toy company.

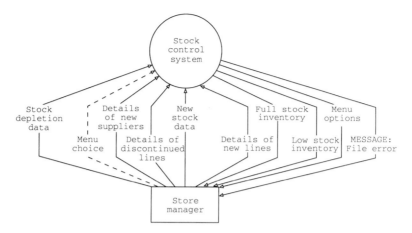

Figure 23.2   A modified Context diagram for the Laughing House toy company.

Jane smiles, and experiences a sense of *déjà vu*: she's had similar conversations on many previous occasions. 'All right, let's strip the system right down to the bare bones, and see how we get on. How does this system look?'

Jane hands over a new version of the Context diagram (Figure 23.2).

Walter Wibble looks at the diagram. 'Now the store manager does everything?'

'Yes,' says Jane, 'Nothing is automated. We'd have everything sent, on paper, to the store managers: they are responsible for all data input, and for sending any lists to head office.'

'Yes,' says Walter Wibble, 'that's precisely what I want.'

23.3.3   The entity diagram

A preliminary entity diagram is produced. This will (usually) depict only internal entities. This diagram is necessarily very provisional, and relationships are therefore usually omitted at this stage.

Jane finds that a simple **entity diagram** provides a useful first look at the data require-ments of the system. In this case, she suspects that she'll need (at least) two tables, one containing details of the products themselves (with possible attributes including 'record#', 'product name', 'supplier name', 'quantity' and 'cost'?), and another containing details of the suppliers (with, perhaps, just 'name' and 'address'?).

She draws up the preliminary ED shown in Figure 23.3.

Note that in an information system like this, with comparatively simple data requirements, it isn't usually necessary to search for nouns, and draw up a more complete data model (a process described in Chapter 21). You may wish to examine the initial requirements specification in this way, and see what kind of data model you end

Figure 23.3   The preliminary entity diagram.

up with, but the informal approach taken by Jane is more common in practice. As any model developed at this stage will be subject to thorough checking later in the project, we can afford to be less rigorous in simple cases.

If you decide to experiment with a complete data model, remember that this is also likely to include the external entities shown on the context diagram (Figure 23.1). For data-oriented development, where we are concerned with persistent data modelling, including external entities on the ERD may help you gain a better understanding of the problem space; however, such entities will probably not end up in your final list of tables. As we'll see in Part III, external entities often feature in class-relational diagrams, a central tool for object-oriented development.

23.3.4 The user interface

Because of the impact of the system interface on all aspects of the model, it is sketched (or prototyped) at this early stage.

The system will be menu-driven, and does not require a sophisticated graphical output. Jane defers details of the menu until she has considered the process list.

In common with many data-oriented systems, a central concern is with the outputs to be produced. Walter Wibble specifies that he will require inventory reports as shown in Figure 23.4. The low stock listing is to take the general form shown in Figure 23.5.

```
+ ----- + -------------- - - + ----- + ------ + ---- +
   Record #  Product  Name          Supplier   Quantity   Cost
+ ----- + -------------- - - + ----- + ------ + ---- +
   34         Wibble Wobble Wabbit   Toy X      10 000     £  9.99
   67         Wibble Wobble Whale    SuperToy    2345      £19.99
+ ----- + -------------- - - + ----- + ------ + ---- +
   The total value of the current inventory is £146776.55
```

Figure 23.4   The required format of a full inventory listing.

```
   Stock of the following items is low:
+ ----- + -------------- - - + ----- + ------ + ---- +
   Record #  Product  Name          Supplier   Quantity   Cost
+ ----- + -------------- - - + ----- + ------ + ---- +
   67         Wibble Wobble Whale    SuperToy   49         £19.99
+ ----- + -------------- - - + ----- + ------ + ---- +
```

Figure 23.5   The required format of a low stock inventory listing.

23.3.5 The process list

A process list is drawn up. This list is necessarily very provisional, and creation of a highly polished document is not appropriate at this stage.

Jane heads back to the LSE office to continue work on the system specification. Following some careful thought, and two phone calls to Walter and his staff, she believes she has identified the main set of required processes (highlighted in Table 23.1).

Process name	Notes
Display Full Inventory	Display full stock inventory (format as shown in Figure 23.4).
Display Low Stock Inventory	Display low stock inventory (format as shown in Figure 23.5).
Insert New Record	Insert a record for a new stock item. Details of information required for each stock item are given in Figure 23.4.
Delete Record	Delete the record for a discontinued line.
Update Existing Record	Change the details (e.g. quantity, price) of an existing stock item.
Update List of Suppliers	Change the list of suppliers from which Laughing House obtain their goods.

Table 23.1 Process list (main processes only).

Naturally, there will be more – probably many more – (sub) processes required to complete the system but, from her previous experience, Jane knows that such processes will arise naturally as the model of the system is refined and may be safely put to one side at this stage.

23.3.6 The walkthrough

A system walkthrough is performed. Where feasible, the entire development team (analysts, designers, programmers) should be involved in this process. As the walkthrough progresses, the entity diagram, process list, context diagram and interface sketches are modified as required.

The system Jane proposes would work as follows (please refer to Figure 23.1).

The store receives goods (by lorry) at the 'Incoming Goods' area. As, say, a box of 200 Wibble Wobble Wabbits (fluffy toy rabbits) are received, they will be entered by the stock manager into the system as a stock addition. Jane proposes that this would be carried out largely automatically by scanning a barcode label attached to the goods. At the other end of the store, as individual customers purchase (usually single) Wibble Wobble Wabbits, this fact will again be automatically recorded by the electronic point of sale (EPOS) system, this time as a stock depletion.

The up-to-the-minute stock control data is available at all times to the store manager. She can see a full inventory of the stock: this will list all the stock items, their names and value. Walter Wibble has requested that the full inventory appear in the form shown in Figure 23.4. Walter has also requested that Head Office can see copies of the full inventory from any store: this too was reflected on the original Context diagram (Figure 23.1), but does not explicitly appear on the modified version (Figure 23.2). Jane makes a note to herself that this responsibility will now fall not to her system, but to the store managers.

In addition to simply keeping an accurate record of stock levels, the system is intended to facilitate the ordering of new items before the stock in the store is completely depleted. Walter Wibble can well remember how, the previous Christmas, both of his main London stores placed urgent orders on 21 December for several thousand extra Wibble Wobble Wabbits: it simply had not been possible to meet this sudden demand and some unfortunate children were to find themselves Wabbit-less on Christmas morning. The lack of rabbit toys was reported in the press as a national tragedy: the publicity was valuable, but did not compensate for the lost sales.

To avoid such an event in future, Walter wants to be able to set a threshold of, say, 50 units: any stock items falling below this threshold are to be included on a 'Low Stock Inventory' listing, provided to the store manager only (the form of this listing is shown in Figure 23.5).

Each store holds a sub-set of the main stock list specified by Head Office. It is staff at Head Office who decide when new lines will be introduced and old lines discontinued. In addition, the same staff may change the supplier of a particular product if, say, an original supplier goes out of business or fails to produce goods of the required quality. All of these facts were reflected on the Context diagram (Figure 23.1), and may be dealt with by a future system. At present, however, Jane makes no attempt to satisfy these requirements.

Finally, Jane has to consider the prospect of shoplifting. Thefts from stores are becoming an increasing problem, Walter Wibble tells her. Jane allows for a regular manual stock check (once a week, she suggests, as a general rule: more frequently at peak times). The manual stock check is not part of the computerized system (and is not itself shown on the Context diagram); however, the results of the check are passed to the store manager who may herself need to enter stock depletion information into the system to take account of any theft.

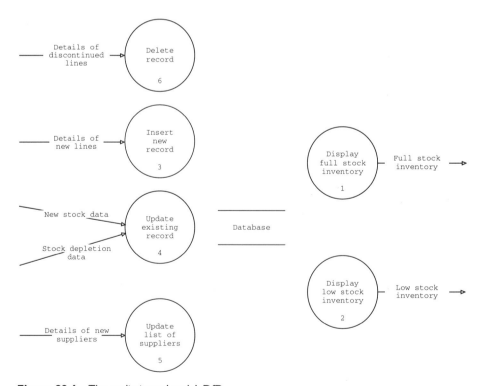

Figure 23.6 The preliminary Level I DfD.

23.3.7 The Level I dataflow diagram

Sketch a preliminary Level 1 DfD: include only processes at this stage, not flows. Usually, only a level 1 DfD is needed at this stage, but on a large system you may need to go further.

Jane draws up the preliminary Level 1 DfD shown in Figure 23.6. Note that the first-cut Level 1 DfD tends to take a similar form on all information system projects. Each of the main processes will be shown. A single database will be shown: specifically (and quite deliberately) no attempt is made to shown individual database tables on the DfD. A separate model of data and function is maintained, because this reflects the true state of affairs in the business (the functions are ephemeral, but the data goes on 'for ever').

23.3.8 The state-transition diagram

The state-transition diagram associated with the Level 1 DfD is produced in an iterative process involving successive modifications to both STD and DfD, as necessary. For (rare) pure 'batch' programs, where no STD is used, this stage may be omitted, while for larger systems, a network of STDs may be required.

As she draws up the STD, Jane begins to tidy her original Level 1 DfD representation. As she does so, she realizes that in her original DfD, and process list, she did not consider what would happen if the database system was unable to open the necessary data files. She knows she needs to correct this omission.

The modified Context diagram, Level 1 DfD and associated STD are shown in Figures 23.7, 23.8 and 23.9.

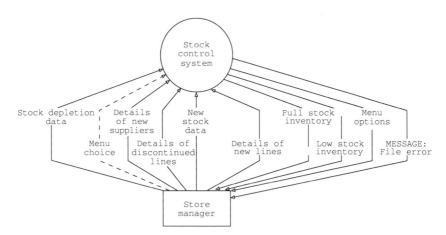

Figure 23.7 A final Context diagram for the Laughing House toy company.

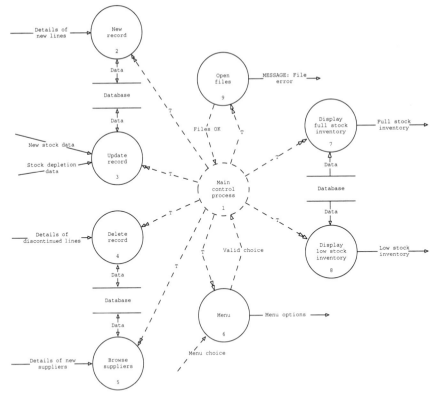

Figure 23.8 The new Level I DfD.

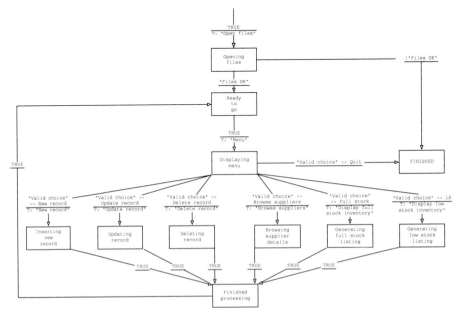

Figure 23.9 The STD for the system.

23.3.9 The ERD

The entity diagram (Stage 3) is extended into a first-cut ERD by adding in the relationships. A preliminary attribute set (or rough table) is produced for each entity.

Jane now begins to consider the database structure in more detail. She notes the fact that the product-supplier relationship is many-to-one, and includes this information in the simple ERD shown in Figure 23.10. The corresponding attribute diagrams (three) are given in Figure 23.11.

Figure 23.10 The preliminary ERD.

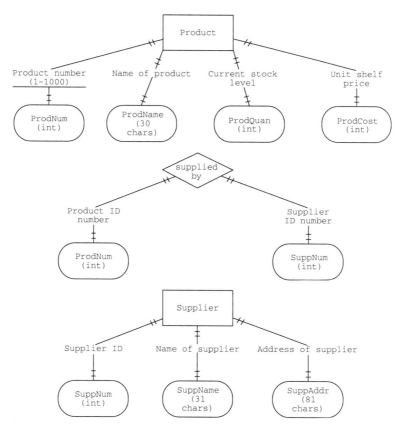

Figure 23.11 Details of the 'Product' and 'Supplier' entities, and the 'supplied by' relationship.

23.3.10   Reconciliation of the ERD and DfD models

Checks are made to ensure that the ERD can support the DfD requirements. Either or both models are modified as required to achieve this.

Jane considers each of the processes on the Level 1 DfD (Figure 23.6) in turn. In doing so, she confirms that the specified tables contain all the information required by the system.

23.3.11   The dataflow diagram hierarchy

The DfD hierarchy is completed, and levelled as necessary.

In this simple case, the DfD hierarchy has only one level, and a corresponding state-transition diagram. These have already been included above.

23.3.12   The PSpecs

The process specifications are written.

Particularly, but not exclusively, in data-oriented system development, the processing performed is very simple in nature, and an informal form of PSpec is more appropriate.

Here, we illustrate this by including some of Jane's PSpecs for this project (Figures 23.12 to 23.15).

@ IN = Details of new lines
@ INOUT = Data

@PSPEC New record

Uses: (Data) and (Details of new lines)

This process allows the user to add a new
record to the database.

@

Figure 23.12   PSpec 1-2.

@ IN = New stock data
@ IN = Stock depletion data
@ INOUT= Data

@PSPEC Update record

Uses: (Data) and (New stock data)
        and (Stock depletion data)

This process takes into account changes in
the stock level and/or the details of products
held in the database.

@

Figure 23.13   PSpec 1-3.

@ IN = Details of discontinued lines
@ INOUT = Data

@PSPEC Delete record

Uses: (Data) and (Details of discontinued lines)

This process deletes a record from the database.

Note: the process CANNOT be reversed, and assumes
that all stock levels have been depleted to zero.

@

Figure 23.14   PSpec 1-4.

@ OUT = MESSAGE: File error
@ OUT = Files OK

@PSPEC Open files

Uses: (MESSAGE: File error) and (Files OK)

Opens the various database files. If no
appropriate files are found, then offers
the user the option of creating new files.

If no files can be opened, and user does
not want to create new files, then sets
(Files OK) flag to FALSE.

@

Figure 23.15   PSpec 1-9.

23.3.13   The data dictionary

The data dictionary is completed.

Finally, Jane draws up the data dictionary (Table 23.2).

Name	C/D/S/T	Description
Data	D	\Data on stock and suppliers held in database. See related ERDs for details.\
Database	S	{Data}
Details of discontinued lines	D	\Head Office will provide this information, concerning previous product lines that have now been discontinued.\
Details of new lines	D	\Details of new products, from Head Office.\
Details of new suppliers	D	\When the suppliers of a particular product change, the information is included here.\
Files OK	C	\Control flag. TRUE is files are opened successfully, FALSE if files cannot be opened AND user opts not to create new files.\

Table 23.2   The data dictionary.

Name	C/D/S/T	Description
Full stock inventory	D	\A complete listing of all current stock items.\
Low stock inventory	D	\A listing of all stock items with a level less than (say) 50 units.\
Menu choice	C	\User input in response to menu. Not validated at this stage.\
Menu options	D	\A list of user options, supplied in the form of an on-screen menu.\
MESSAGE: File error	D	\An on-screen message advising that an essential data file cannot be opened.\
New stock data	D	\Information concerning new supplies of existing products.\
Stock depletion data	D	\Data, ultimately from EPOS terminals and from manual stock check, detailing stock reductions.\
Store Manager	T	\The manager of the particular Laughing House branch.\
Valid choice	C	\Validated response from user to menu.\

Table 23.2 *Continued.*

23.3.14 The balanced logical model

The complete model is reviewed, checked and balanced. Any necessary supporting documentation is written.

Jane reviews the components of the model one final time, then uses the CASE tool to check that the project is balanced, as outlined in Chapter 13.

23.4 Press cutting

Jane submits her proposals for the system to Laughing House Ltd. As originally agreed, adverts then appear in the press allowing other firms to submit bids for this contract. Naturally, Leicester Software Engineering also submit a tender for the design and implementation of this system.

Following LSE's submission, the following notice appears in the UK computer press.

'Leicester Software Engineering (LSE) have been awarded a contract for £500 000 to computerize all the operations of the London-based company Laughing House Ltd. The system, based on LSE's own "Support II" package, will handle stock control, planning and management information. The software will run on a DEC Alpha Server at the London head office, with ICL EPoS (electronic point of sale) tills installed initially in 12 Laughing House branches. Delivery of the system is to be completed with 12 months.'

Having been awarded the contract, Jane receives a bonus, and takes a well-earned holiday.

23.5 Design

Responsibility for the design of the stock control system passes to Stephanie.

Data-oriented design involves the creation of a physical hybrid model. The construction of this model is usually accomplished in eight stages, beginning where the analysis phase ended:

(D15) *Review and refinement of the logical model*
The specification documents are reviewed, in order to gain an understanding of the system, and to correct any flaws in the logical model.

(D16) *The software and hardware architecture*
The operating environment (hardware and/or operating system), and the basic software architecture are determined. General design decisions are made, including the choice of implementation for the database.

(D17) *Data design*
The data model constructed during analysis is normalized.

(D18) *The preliminary physical process model*
The preliminary structure chart is derived from the logical model.

(D19) *Review and refinement of the physical process model*
The provisional physical model is inspected, and issues of module coupling and cohesion are considered.

(D20) *Reconciliation of the logical and physical process models*
Logical and physical models are compared and adjusted as necessary to ensure that they are fully compatible.

(D21) *Reconciliation of the data and process models*
The process and data components of the hybrid model are checked for consistency, and adjusted as necessary.

(D22) *The test strategy*
The overall system test strategy is drawn up.

We consider these stages below.

23.5.1 Review and refinement of the logical model

The specification documents are reviewed, in order to gain an understanding of the system, and to correct any flaws in the logical model.

We assume that this review is quickly and successfully completed.

23.5.2 The software and hardware architecture

The operating environment (hardware and/or operating system), and the basic software architecture are determined. General design decisions are made, including the choice of implementation for the database.

Steph notes that this is a straightforward system, to be run (at least initially) on a desk-top computer system, without any network capabilities, and with only a single user. She decides that the system could be reasonably implemented in C++, but leaves the final decision in this matter to Harry.

23.5.3 Data design

The data model constructed during analysis is normalized.

For the data design, it is Steph's responsibility to ensure that the data used by the program is correctly normalized. In Steph's view, an information system should contain only entities normalized to BCNF, unless there are very good reasons otherwise (and she's not easily convinced).

Steph starts by inspecting the simple set of data models that Jane has produced. These, Steph concludes, are adequate: however, she translates Jane's ERD into two (rather than three) tables, deciding that the relationship 'supplied by' can safely be omitted (Figure 23.16). This results in modifications to the associated attribute diagrams (Figure 23.17).

As Steph is only too well aware, data design is an empirical science: the only way she can be sure that any design is correct is by using some real data to try out the tables. Steph rings Wibble toys and has some sample data faxed to her office. She then adds in the sample data to the two tables (Figure 23.18).

Figure 23.16 The final ERD.

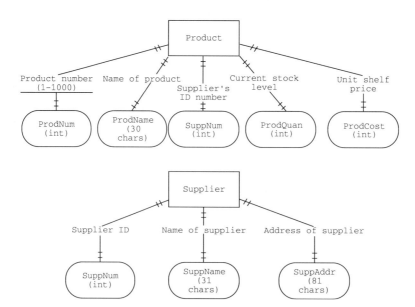

Figure 23.17 Details of the modified Product and Supplier entities.

Product

Product#	Product Name	SupplierID	Quantity	Cost
34	Wabbit	1	10000	£19.99
37	Wabbit	2	145	£39.99
38	Wabbit	1	649	£49.99
39	Wamble	2	1230	£49.99
67	Whale	3	2345	£29.99
178	Want Eater	3	2432	£39.99
567	Wallaby	1	1000	£12.99
999	Womble	2	231	£69.99

Supplier

SupplierID	Supplier	Supplier Address
1	Toy X	32 East Road
2	SuperToy	2 South Bend
3	SuperToy	15 West Road

Figure 23.18 Steph's original tables.

Steph then proceeds to convert the tables to BCNF, as described below.

Note that, for a larger system, Steph sometimes performs the normalization by sketching *determinancy* diagrams. It would be inappropriate to devote space to this technique here; Howe (1989; Chapter 6) provides a readable overview of this method which you may wish to consult.

First normal form

> *An entity is said to be in first normal form if it contains no repeating groups.*

Steph confirms that the tables in Figure 23.18 are already in 1NF.

Second normal form

> *An entity is said to be in second normal form if it is in first normal form and if every attribute is functionally dependent on the primary key.*

The second normal form is of relevance where we have a combination key: that is, where a combination of two attributes must be used to access a particular row of data. This situation does not apply to either entity: they are therefore already in 2NF.

Third normal form

> *An entity is said to be in third normal form if it is in second normal form and if all attributes which are not part of the primary key are mutually independent (that is, there are no transitive dependencies).*

As we saw in Chapter 21, it is possible, even when an entity is in 2NF, to have a transitive dependency. That is, to have an attribute within an entity with a value dependent not only on the key, but also on another attribute.

One straightforward way to achieve 3NF normalization is to examine, for every table, each pair of non-key data items. If the value of one of the first item depends on the second (or vice versa) then the data items concerned should be moved to a separate table.

In the Supplier table, there is only one non-key data item, and therefore no pairs to consider.

In the Product table, Steph needs to consider, in turn, the six possible combinations of the four non-key data items. She checks each in turn:

- *Product name* does not uniquely determine *supplier, quantity* or *cost*.
- *Supplier* does not uniquely determine *quantity* or *cost*.
- *Quantity* does not uniquely determine *cost*.

Therefore, she concludes, the tables are in 3NF.

Boyce–Codd normal form

An entity is said to be in Boyce–Codd normal form if it is in third normal form and every data item upon which some other data item is functionally dependent is a candidate key.

In the Supplier table, the address is functionally dependent on the supplier name. The supplier name is a candidate key. In the Product table, Steph notes that there is a primary key upon which every data item depends.

Steph concludes that the tables are well-normalized: they are in BCNF.

23.5.4   The preliminary physical process model

The preliminary structure chart is derived from the logical model.

For the process design, Steph develops the structure chart shown in Figure 23.19. The process of developing this chart is the same as that described in Part I: we won't discuss this further here.

As she finishes the structure charts, Steph links each of the modules to the corresponding PSpecs.

23.5.5   Review and refinement of the physical process model

The provisional physical model is inspected, and issues of module coupling and cohesion are considered.

Steph reviews the physical model, and is satisfied that, with this very simple system, no modifications are required.

23.5.6   Reconciliation of the logical and physical process models

Logical and physical models are compared and adjusted as necessary to ensure that they are fully compatible.

Steph decides that no modifications are required to either the physical or logical models.

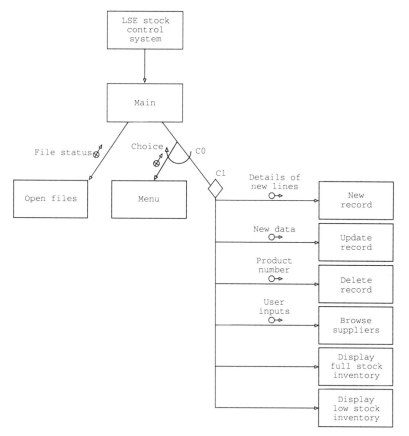

Figure 23.19 Outline structure chart for the stock control system. Conditions – C0: Keep looping until the user opts to quit. C1: Call module corresponding to 'Choice'.

23.5.7   Reconciliation of the data and process models

The process and data components of the hybrid model are checked for consistency, and adjusted as necessary.

Steph performs a mental 'walkthrough' and decides that no modifications are required to the hybrid model.

23.5.8 Test strategy

The overall system test strategy is drawn up.

Steph includes the following general statement on the required test strategy:

As implementation of each module is completed, it will be tested by the programmer, as follows:

(1)   White Box testing is performed by reading through the code, line by line, looking for obvious flaws. Details of the tests performed are to be included in the implementation documents, and initialled by the tester.

(2)   Black Box testing is performed with an individual driver program. Typically, 10% of the parameter range will be tested. Extremes of the input range of all parameters will always be tested. Details of the test performed, and of the results obtained, are to be included with the implementation documents, and initialled by the tester.

In fact, in this case, there is little in the way of module testing to perform, and Steph is more concerned that the database needs to be properly tested.

For information systems, she always aims to test first the basic modules, as outlined above, using a small set of test data. It is important that this is integrated testing, involving realistic data.

Steph always specifies that database systems need to be subsequently stress tested. **Stress testing** is a form of field trial, and involves running the system *in situ*, with a full set of data.

Sometimes, following poor design or implementation, it is found that large volumes of data can bring a new system to its knees. Changes may then, quickly, be required before the final system is shipped. Even if time is short, it is invariably easier to make changes before the system 'goes live' than it is to start tinkering with a system in active use.

For larger, multi-user systems, operating over a network, it is important to conduct the stress tests at appropriate times: during business hours, when the system is being used for normal business. If necessary, driver programs can sometimes effectively be used to simulate multiple concurrent users. Sometimes Steph finds it effective to include these tests as the final part of staff training for staff that will use the new system.

Finally, in the stock control system as in all others, Steph knows that she won't be able to switch overnight from the existing system to the new computerized version. She recommends that for a period of at least one month the existing system and the new system are operated in parallel.

23.6   Implementation

Responsibility for the implementation of the system passes to Harry. As outlined in Chapter 22, Harry has ten main steps to perform, beginning where the design phase ended:

(D23)   *Review and refinement of the physical model*
The design documents are reviewed, in order to gain an understanding of the system, and to correct any flaws in the physical model.

(D24)   *The hardware framework*
A specialized hardware framework is created, if required.

(D25)   *The data framework*
The choice of data implementation strategy is made. The data framework is created, based on the normalized data model.

(D26)   *The code framework*
The code framework is created, using CppSpecs, based on the structure chart and the PSpecs.

(D27) *The preliminary modules*
The preliminary modules are created or, preferably, recycled from a code library. In either case, the resulting function will build on the CppSpecs, and will make reference to the physical model (particularly the PSpecs and the data dictionary).

(D28) *Error detection and recovery*
The preliminary modules are extended, where necessary, through the addition of appropriate error detection and correction features.

(D29) *Module tests*
The modules are tested, by the programmers, according to the test strategy produced by the design team. Modifications are made as required.

(D30) *The prototype system*
The tested modules and data framework are assembled into a prototype system, as dictated by the structure chart(s) and entity-relationship diagram(s). The system will be implemented, where appropriate, on the hardware framework.

(D31) *Data entry*
Adequate test data is entered into the system database to allow for realistic system testing.

(D32) *System tests and maintenance*
The complete prototype is tested again, first by the programmers, and then by the test team, both working from the test strategy produced by the designers. The system is then subjected to user tests, including field tests and/or acceptance tests. The system is revised as necessary: any changes made during the testing and subsequent ongoing maintenance are recorded and reflected in the evolving hybrid model.

We consider each of these steps below.

23.6.1   Review and refinement of the physical model

The design documents are reviewed, in order to gain an understanding of the system, and to correct any flaws in the physical model.

Harry reviews the work carried out by Steph, and finds it is of the usual high standard.

23.6.2   The hardware framework

A specialized hardware framework is created, if required.

No specialized hardware is required for this project.

23.6.3   The data framework

The choice of data implementation strategy is made. The data framework is created, based on the normalized data model.

Viewing the normalized data structures, Harry realizes that he can easily put together the initial prototype system in C++; he decides to do so. If necessary, he knows, he can extend the final version quite easily to use SQL or a RDBMS.

The data implementation is straightforward. The C++ data structures are as follows:

```
struct sSupp
    {
    int    SuppNum;
    char   SuppName[30];
    char   SuppAddr[30];
    };
struct sProd
    {
    int    ProdNum;
    char   ProdName[30];
    int    ProdQuan;          //Number of items in stock
    int    ProdCost;          //Price of items - in PENCE.
    int    SuppNum;
    };
```

23.6.4   The code framework

The code framework is created, using CppSpecs, based on the structure chart and the PSpecs.

The code framework Harry develops is given in Program 23.1.

```
/*****************************************************************
*                                                               *
* A Simple (D-O) Stock Control System                           *
*                                                               *
* Source is:    23_01.CPP                                       *
* Created:      11 Dec, 1994                                    *
* Last edited:  28 Jul, 1995                                    *
*                                                               *
*****************************************************************/
#include <fstream.h>
#include <iomanip.h>
#include <iostream.h>

// extern "C" may be necessary on some compilers
// and won't do any harm on others
extern "C"
{
#include <assert.h>
#include <ctype.h>
#include <stdio.h>
#include <stdlib.h>
#include <string.h>
}

// Maximum number of different products in stock
const int MAX_STOCK = 1000;
```

```
// Maximum number of different suppliers
const int MAX_SUPPLIER = 3;

// If the stock level of a particular product falls
// below LOW_STOCK_LEVEL, an order is placed for more
const int LOW_STOCK_LEVEL = 50;

struct sSupp
    {
    int     SuppNum;
    char    SuppName[30];
    char    SuppAddr[30];
    };

struct sProd
    {
    int     ProdNum;
    char    ProdName[30];
    int     ProdQuan;         //Number of items in stock
    int     ProdCost;         //Price of items - in PENCE.
    int     SuppNum;
    };

// Function declarations
void Browse_suppliers();
void Delete_record();
void Display_all_records();
void Display_low_stock_records();
void Insert_record();
int  Menu();
void Open_files();
void Update_record();
/****************************************************************
*                                                              *
* FUNCTION:    main()                                          *
*                                                              *
****************************************************************/
int main()
    {
    cout << "Prototype Stock Control System\n";
    cout << "------------------------ \n";

    Open_files();

    int process;
    while ((process = Menu()) != 7)
        {
        switch (process)
            {
            case 1:
                Display_all_records();
                break;
            case 2:
                Display_low_stock_records();
                break;
```

```
                case 3:
                    Update_record();
                    break;
                case 4:
                    Insert_record();
                    break;
                case 5:
                    Delete_record();
                    break;
                case 6:
                    Browse_suppliers();
                }
            }
        cout << "Finished.";

        return 0;
        }

/****************************************************************
 *                                                              *
 * FUNCTION:    Menu()                                          *
 *                                                              *
 * PURPOSE:     Displays user instructions                      *
 *                                                              *
 ****************************************************************/
int Menu()
    {
    // Local variables
    int choice;
    char ip_STR[80];

    cout << "\nMENU:\n"
        << "1 List all stock items.\n"
        << "2 List items with low stock level.\n"
        << "3 Update record for a particular item.\n"
        << "4 Insert record for a new item.\n"
        << "5 Delete record for an item.\n"
        << "6 Browse supplier details.\n"
        << "7 QUIT program.\n\n"
        << "? :";

    cin.getline(ip_STR, sizeof(ip_STR));

    while ((!(sscanf(ip_STR, "%d", &choice) == 1))
        || (choice < 1) || (choice > 7))
        {
        cout << "\nOption must be in the range 1 - 7. "
            << "Please re-enter: ";
        cin.getline(ip_STR, sizeof(ip_STR));
        }

    cout << endl;

    return choice;
    }
```

```
/****************************************************************
 *                                                              *
 * FUNCTION:    Display_all_records()                           *
 *                                                              *
 * PURPOSE:     Lists all non-empty records                     *
 *                                                              *
 ****************************************************************/
void Display_all_records()
    {
    cout << "*** WILL DISPLAY ALL RECORDS ***\n";
    }
/****************************************************************
 *                                                              *
 * FUNCTION:    Display_low_stock_records()                     *
 *                                                              *
 * PURPOSE:     Lists all products with low stock levels.       *
 *                                                              *
 ****************************************************************/
void Display_low_stock_records()
    {
    cout << "*** WILL DISPLAY LOW STOCK RECORDS ***\n";
    }
/****************************************************************
 *                                                              *
 * FUNCTION:    Update_record()                                 *
 *                                                              *
 * PURPOSE:     Updates contents of a specified record.         *
 *                                                              *
 ****************************************************************/
void Update_record()
    {
    cout << "*** WILL UPDATE RECORD ***\n";
    }
/****************************************************************
 *                                                              *
 * FUNCTION:    Browse_suppliers()                              *
 *                                                              *
 * PURPOSE:     List and edit available suppliers.              *
 *                                                              *
 ****************************************************************/
void Browse_suppliers()
    {
    cout << "*** WILL ALLOW EDITING OF SUPPLIERS ***\n";
    }
/****************************************************************
 *                                                              *
 * FUNCTION:    Insert_record()                                 *
 *                                                              *
 * PURPOSE:     Allows a new record to be inserted in file.     *
 *                                                              *
 ****************************************************************/
```

```
void Insert_record()
    {
    cout << "*** WILL INSERT RECORD ***\n";
    }
/*************************************************************
 *                                                          *
 * FUNCTION:    Delete_record()                             *
 *                                                          *
 * PURPOSE:     Allows deletion of a specified record.      *
 *                                                          *
 *************************************************************/
void Delete_record()
    {
    cout << "*** WILL DELETE RECORD ***\n";
    }
/*************************************************************
 *                                                          *
 * FUNCTION:    Open_files()                                *
 *                                                          *
 * PURPOSE:     Open database.                              *
 *                                                          *
 *************************************************************/
void Open_files()
    {
    cout << "*** WILL OPEN FILES ***\n";
    }
/*************************************************************
 *                     *** END OF PROGRAM ***               *
 *************************************************************/
```

Program 23.1 The code framework. (☺)

The framework generates the following output:

```
Prototype Stock Control System

*** WILL OPEN FILES ***

MENU:
1 List all stock items.
2 List items with low stock level.
3 Update record for a particular item.
4 Insert record for a new item.
5 Delete record for an item.
6 Browse supplier details.
7 QUIT program.

? :1

*** WILL DISPLAY ALL RECORDS ***
```

```
MENU:
1 List all stock items.
2 List items with low stock level.
3 Update record for a particular item.
4 Insert record for a new item.
5 Delete record for an item.
6 Browse supplier details.
7 QUIT program.

? :2

*** WILL DISPLAY LOW STOCK RECORDS ***

MENU:
1 List all stock items.
2 List items with low stock level.
3 Update record for a particular item.
4 Insert record for a new item.
5 Delete record for an item.
6 Browse supplier details.
7 QUIT program.

? :3

*** WILL UPDATE RECORD ***

MENU:
1 List all stock items.
2 List items with low stock level.
3 Update record for a particular item.
4 Insert record for a new item.
5 Delete record for an item.
6 Browse supplier details.
7 QUIT program.

? :4

*** WILL INSERT RECORD ***

MENU:
1 List all stock items.
2 List items with low stock level.
3 Update record for a particular item.
4 Insert record for a new item.
5 Delete record for an item.
6 Browse supplier details.
7 QUIT program.

? :5

*** WILL DELETE RECORD ***

MENU:
1 List all stock items.
2 List items with low stock level.
3 Update record for a particular item.
4 Insert record for a new item.
```

```
5 Delete record for an item.
6 Browse supplier details.
7 QUIT program.

? :6

*** WILL ALLOW EDITING OF SUPPLIERS ***

MENU:
1 List all stock items.
2 List items with low stock level.
3 Update record for a particular item.
4 Insert record for a new item.
5 Delete record for an item.
6 Browse supplier details.
7 QUIT program.

? :7

Finished.
```

23.6.5   The preliminary modules

The preliminary modules are created or, preferably, recycled from a code library. In either case, the resulting function will build on the CppSpecs, and will make reference to the physical model (particularly the PSpecs and the data dictionary).

Harry works on all the modules in turn, building in each case from the corresponding CppSpec, and referring as he does so to the PSpecs.

For example, the PSpec given in Figure 23.15 becomes first the CppSpec Open_files() (shown in Program 23.1) and is in turn developed into the preliminary function given in Figure 23.20.

```
/*************************************************************
*                                                           *
* FUNCTION:    Open_files()                                 *
*                                                           *
* PURPOSE:     Open database.                               *
*                                                           *
* RETURNS:     void.                                        *
*                                                           *
*************************************************************/
void Open_files(fstream& stock_FPTR_REF,
                fstream& supp_FPTR_REF)
    {
    // Try to find an existing data file "supplier.dat" -
    supp_FPTR_REF.open("supplier.dat", ios::out | ios::in
                             | ios::nocreate | ios::binary);

    if (supp_FPTR_REF.fail())
        {
        // Can't find an existing supplier file
```

```
                cout << "\nCan't find the data file 'supplier.dat'\n";
                exit(1);
                }

        // Try to find an existing data file "stock.dat" -
        stock_FPTR_REF.open("stock.dat", ios::out | ios::in
                                  | ios::nocreate | ios::binary );

        if (stock_FPTR_REF.fail())
                {
                // Can't find an existing stock file
                cout << "\nCan't find the data file 'stock.dat'\n";
                exit(1);
                }

        }
```

Figure 23.20 The original function `Open_files()` before error detection features have been added.

23.6.6 Error detection and recovery

The preliminary modules are extended, where necessary, through the addition of appropriate error detection and correction features.

Reviewing the code, Harry notes that, in common with other information system implementations, much of the error checking must be carried out on file pointers.

For example, Figure 23.21 shows an extended version of the preliminary module in Figure 23.20, this time with the addition of error detection features.

```
    /***************************************************************
    *                                                             *
    * FUNCTION:    Open_files()                                    *
    *                                                             *
    * PURPOSE:     Open database.                                  *
    *                                                             *
    * PRE:         None.                                           *
    * POST:        Got valid file pointers.                        *
    *                                                             *
    * RETURNS:     void.                                           *
    *                                                             *
    ***************************************************************/
    void Open_files(fstream& stock_FPTR_REF,
                    fstream& supp_FPTR_REF)
        {
        // Local variable
        char ip_STR[81];

        // Try to find an existing data file "supplier.dat" -
        // if it doesn't exist (or can't find it),
        // offer user option of creating one
        supp_FPTR_REF.open("supplier.dat", ios::out | ios::in
                                  | ios::nocreate | ios::binary);
```

```
    if (supp_FPTR_REF.fail())
       {
       // Can't find an existing supplier file
       cout << "\nCan't find the data file 'supplier.dat'\n";

       // Ask user if she wants to create a new file
       cout << "\nDo you want to create a new file (Y or N): ";
       cin.getline(ip_STR, sizeof(ip_STR));

       while ((toupper(ip_STR[0]) != 'Y') &&
              (toupper(ip_STR[0]) != 'N'))
          {
          cout << "Invalid response. Enter Y or N: ";
          cin.getline(ip_STR, sizeof(ip_STR));
          }

       if (toupper(ip_STR[0]) == 'Y')
          {
          supp_FPTR_REF.clear();
          supp_FPTR_REF.open("supplier.dat", ios::out
                                    | ios::in | ios::binary);

       if (supp_FPTR_REF.fail())
          {
          cout << "\nFATAL ERROR:\n";
          cout << "File 'supplier.dat' could not be created.\n";
          cout << "Is the disk full?\n";
          exit(1);
          }

       Format_new_supplier_file(supp_FPTR_REF);
       Browse_suppliers(supp_FPTR_REF);
          }
    else
          {
          /* No supplier file exists, and user does not
             want to create a new one: no option but to QUIT */
          cout << "Please restore backup of 'supplier.dat'\n";
          cout << "Then re-run this program.\n";
          exit(1);
          }
       }
/* Try to find an existing data file "stock.dat" -
   if it doesn't exist (or can't find it),
   offer user option of creating one */
stock_FPTR_REF.open("stock.dat", ios::out | ios::in
                        | ios::nocreate | ios::binary );
if (stock_FPTR_REF.fail())
    {
    // Can't find an existing stock file
    cout << "\nCan't find the data file 'stock.dat'\n";

    // Ask user if s/he wants to create a new file
    cout << "\nDo you want to create a new file (Y or N): ";
```

```
        cin.getline(ip_STR, sizeof(ip_STR));

    while ((toupper(ip_STR[0]) != 'Y') &&
            (toupper(ip_STR[0]) != 'N'))
        {
        cout << "Invalid response. Enter Y or N: ";
        cin.getline(ip_STR, sizeof(ip_STR));
        }

    if (toupper(ip_STR[0]) == 'Y')
        {
        stock_FPTR_REF.clear();
        stock_FPTR_REF.open("stock.dat", ios::out
                                | ios::in | ios::binary);

        if (stock_FPTR_REF.fail())
            {
            cout << "\nFATAL ERROR:\n";
            cout << "File 'stock.dat' could not be created.\n";
            cout << "Is the disk full?\n";
            exit(1);
            }

        Format_new_stock_file(stock_FPTR_REF);
        Get_all_data(stock_FPTR_REF, supp_FPTR_REF);
        }
    else
        {
        /* No stock file exists, and user does not
           want to create a new one: no option but to QUIT */
        cout << "Please restore backup of 'stock.dat'\n";
        cout << "Then re-run this program.\n";
        exit(1);
        }
    }

// Post - valid file pointers
assert(stock_FPTR_REF);
assert(supp_FPTR_REF);
}
```

Figure 23.21 The modified function `Open_files()` after error detection features have been added.

23.6.7 Module tests

The modules are tested, by the programmers, according to the test strategy produced by the design team. Modifications are made as required.

The module testing process Harry employs largely involves passing null file pointers to the various modules, and ensuring that this error is detected.

Details of this process are omitted here.

23.6.8 The prototype system

The tested modules and data framework are assembled into a prototype system, as dictated by the structure chart(s) and entity-relationship diagram(s). The system will be implemented, where appropriate, on the hardware framework.

Harry assembles the tested modules into Program 23.2.

```
/***********************************************************
*                                                         *
* A Simple (D-O) Stock Control System                     *
*                                                         *
* Source is:     23_02.CPP                                *
* Created:       11 Dec, 1994                             *
* Last edited:   04 Dec, 1995                             *
*                                                         *
***********************************************************/
#include <fstream.h>
#include <iomanip.h>
#include <iostream.h>

// extern "C" may be necessary on some compilers
// and won't do any harm on others
extern "C"
{
#include <assert.h>
#include <ctype.h>
#include <stdio.h>
#include <stdlib.h>
#include <string.h>
}

// Maximum number of different products in stock
const int MAX_STOCK = 1000;

// Maximum number of different suppliers
const int MAX_SUPPLIER = 3;

// If the stock level of a particular product falls
// below LOW_STOCK_LEVEL, an order is placed for more
const int LOW_STOCK_LEVEL = 50;

struct sSupp
    {
    int     SuppNum;
    char    SuppName[30];
    char    SuppAddr[30];
    };

struct sProd
    {
    int     ProdNum;
    char    ProdName[30];
    int     ProdQuan;           //Number of items in stock
```

```
    int    ProdCost;          //Price of items - in PENCE.
    int    SuppNum;
    };

// Function declarations
int  Browse_suppliers(fstream&);
int  Choose_supplier(int&, fstream&);
void Delete_record(fstream&);
void Display_all_records(fstream&, fstream&);
void Display_low_stock_records(fstream&, fstream&);
void Display_money(const long);
void Display_record(const sProd, fstream&);
void Display_record_footer();
void Display_record_header();
void Fill_record(fstream&, fstream&, const int);
void Format_new_stock_file(fstream&);
void Format_new_supplier_file(fstream&);
void Get_all_data(fstream&,fstream&);
void Get_supplier_data(fstream&);
void Get_valid_ProdNum(int&);
void Insert_record(fstream&, fstream&);
int  Menu();
void Open_files(fstream&, fstream&);
void Type_enter_to_continue();
void Update_record(fstream&, fstream&);

/************************************************************
*                                                          *
* FUNCTION:   main()                                       *
*                                                          *
************************************************************/
int main()
    {
    // Local variables
    fstream stock_FPTR;   // File pointer: stock data file
    fstream supp_FPTR;    // File pointer: supplier data file

    cout << "Prototype Stock Control System\n";
    cout << "----------------------- \n";

    Open_files(stock_FPTR, supp_FPTR);

    int process;
    while ((process = Menu()) != 7)
        {
        switch (process)
            {
            case 1:
                Display_all_records(stock_FPTR, supp_FPTR);
                break;
            case 2:
                Display_low_stock_records(stock_FPTR, supp_FPTR);
                break;
            case 3:
```

```
                    Update_record(stock_FPTR, supp_FPTR);
                    break;
                case 4:
                    Insert_record(stock_FPTR, supp_FPTR);
                    break;
                case 5:
                    Delete_record(stock_FPTR);
                    break;
                case 6:
                    Browse_suppliers(supp_FPTR);
                    break;
                }
            }
        stock_FPTR.close();
        cout << "Finished.";
        return 0;
        }
/*************************************************************
*                                                           *
* FUNCTION:    Type_enter_to_continue()                     *
*                                                           *
* OVERVIEW:    Waits for ENTER, then returns.               *
*                                                           *
* PRE:         None.                                        *
* POST:        None.                                        *
*                                                           *
* RETURNS:     void.                                        *
*                                                           *
*************************************************************/
void Type_enter_to_continue()
    {
    // Local variable
    char ip_STR[81];

    cout << "\nType <ENTER> to continue.";
    cin.getline(ip_STR, sizeof(ip_STR));
    }
/*************************************************************
*                                                           *
* FUNCTION:    Display_record()                             *
*                                                           *
* PURPOSE:     Display (on screen) a single record.         *
*                                                           *
* PRE:         Valid file pointer.                          *
* POST:        None.                                        *
*                                                           *
* RETURNS:     void.                                        *
*                                                           *
*************************************************************/
void Display_record(const sProd Rec, fstream& supp_FPTR_REF)
```

```
    {
    // Pre - valid file pointer
    assert(supp_FPTR_REF);

    // Local variable
    sSupp temp;

    cout.setf(ios::left);
    cout << " " << setw(10) << Rec.ProdNum
         << setw(25) << Rec.ProdName;

    // Get supplier's name
    supp_FPTR_REF.seekg(Rec.SuppNum*sizeof(sSupp), ios::beg);
    supp_FPTR_REF.read((char*) &temp, sizeof(sSupp));
    cout << setw(15) << temp.SuppName;

    cout << setw(10) << Rec.ProdQuan;
    Display_money(Rec.ProdCost);
    cout << "\n";
    }
/*************************************************************
*                                                           *
* FUNCTION:    Display_record_header                        *
*                                                           *
* PURPOSE:     Display header for subsequent record(s).     *
*                                                           *
* PRE:         None.                                        *
* POST:        None.                                        *
*                                                           *
* RETURNS:     void.                                        *
*                                                           *
*************************************************************/
void Display_record_header()
    {
    cout.setf(ios::left);
    cout << "+-------+----------------"
         << "+----------+------+-----+\n";
    cout << setw(10) << " Record #"
         << setw(25) << " Product Name"
         << setw(15) << " Supplier"
         << setw(10) << " Quantity"
         << setw(8)  << " Cost" << endl;
    cout << "+-------+--------------"
         << "+----------+------+-----+\n";
    }
/*************************************************************
*                                                           *
* FUNCTION:    Display_record_footer()                      *
*                                                           *
* PURPOSE:     Display footer for previous record(s).       *
*                                                           *
* PRE:         None.                                        *
* POST:        None.                                        *
```

```
 *                                                              *
 * RETURNS:     void.                                           *
 *                                                              *
 **************************************************************/
void Display_record_footer()
    {
    cout.setf(ios::left);
    cout << "+-------+--------------- "
         << "+----------+------+-----+\n";
    }

/***************************************************************
 *                                                              *
 * FUNCTION:    Fill_record()                                   *
 *                                                              *
 * PURPOSE:     Prompt user for data (single record).          *
 *                                                              *
 * PRE:         Valid file pointers.                            *
 * POST:        None.                                           *
 *                                                              *
 * RETURNS:     void.                                           *
 *                                                              *
 **************************************************************/
void Fill_record(fstream& stock_FPTR_REF,
                 fstream& supp_FPTR_REF,
                 const int ProdNum)
    {
    // Pre - valid file pointers
    assert(stock_FPTR_REF);
    assert(supp_FPTR_REF);

    // Local variables
    char ip_STR[80];
    sProd temp;
    int SuppNumber;

    temp.ProdNum = ProdNum;

    cout << "PRODUCT NAME : ";
    // Need to use getline because of possible white space...
    cin.getline(temp.ProdName, sizeof(temp.ProdName));
    while (!temp.ProdName[0])
        {
        // User isn't able to enter blank field
        cout << "\rPRODUCT NAME : ";
        cin.getline(temp.ProdName, sizeof(temp.ProdName));
        }

    cout << "QUANTITY : ";
    cin.getline(ip_STR, sizeof(ip_STR));
    while (!ip_STR[0])
        {
        // User isn't able to enter blank field
        cout << "\rQUANTITY : ";
```

```
            cin.getline(ip_STR, sizeof(ip_STR));
            }
      temp.ProdQuan = atoi(ip_STR);

      cout << "UNIT PRICE (in pence) : ";
      cin.getline(ip_STR, sizeof(ip_STR));
      while (!ip_STR[0])
            {
            // User isn't able to enter blank field
            cout << "UNIT PRICE (in pence) : ";
            cin.getline(ip_STR, sizeof(ip_STR));
            }
      temp.ProdCost = atoi(ip_STR);

      Choose_supplier(SuppNumber, supp_FPTR_REF);
      temp.SuppNum = SuppNumber;

      stock_FPTR_REF.seekg(temp.ProdNum*sizeof(sProd),ios::beg);
      stock_FPTR_REF.write((char*) &temp, sizeof(sProd));
      }

/*****************************************************************
 *                                                               *
 * FUNCTION:    Browse_suppliers()                               *
 *                                                               *
 * PURPOSE:     List and edit available suppliers.               *
 *                                                               *
 * PRE:         Valid file pointer.                              *
 * POST:        None.                                            *
 *                                                               *
 * RETURNS:     void.                                            *
 *                                                               *
 *****************************************************************/
int Browse_suppliers(fstream& supp_FPTR_REF)
      {
      // Pre - valid file pointer
      assert(supp_FPTR_REF);

      // Local variables
      sSupp temp;
      char ip_STR[81];
      int choice;

      cout << "Current suppliers are: \n\n";

      for (int supp = 0; supp < MAX_SUPPLIER; supp++)
            {
            supp_FPTR_REF.seekg(supp*sizeof(sSupp), ios::beg);
            supp_FPTR_REF.read((char*) &temp, sizeof(sSupp));
            cout << supp << " " << setw(15) << temp.SuppName;
            cout << " " << setw(15) << temp.SuppAddr << endl;
            }
      do   {
           do
                {
```

```
                    cout << "\nType a number to edit entry, or "
                        << supp << " to QUIT ";
                    cin.getline(ip_STR, sizeof(ip_STR));
                    } while ((!ip_STR[0]));
                choice = atoi(ip_STR);
                } while ((choice < 0) || (choice > MAX_SUPPLIER));
        if (choice < MAX_SUPPLIER)
            {
            do
                {
                cout << "Enter new supplier name: ";
                cin.getline(temp.SuppName, sizeof(temp.SuppName));
                } while ((!temp.SuppName[0]));

            do
                {
                cout << "Enter new supplier SuppAddr: ";
                cin.getline(temp.SuppAddr, sizeof(temp.SuppAddr));
                } while ((!temp.SuppAddr[0]));

            temp.SuppNum = choice;
            // Update disk copy
            supp_FPTR_REF.seekg(choice*sizeof(sSupp), ios::beg);
            supp_FPTR_REF.write((char*) &temp, sizeof(sSupp));

            Browse_suppliers(supp_FPTR_REF); // Recursive call
            }
        return 0;
        }
/****************************************************************
*                                                              *
* FUNCTION:    Choose_supplier()                               *
*                                                              *
* PURPOSE:     Allow user to choose a supplier.                *
*                                                              *
* PRE:         Valid file pointer.                             *
* POST:        None.                                           *
*                                                              *
* RETURNS:     void.                                           *
*                                                              *
****************************************************************/
int Choose_supplier(int& supp_num_REF,
                    fstream& supp_FPTR_REF)
    {
    // Pre - valid file pointer
    assert(supp_FPTR_REF);

    // Local variables
    sSupp temp;
    char ip_STR[81];
    int choice;

    cout << "Available suppliers are: \n\n";
```

```
          for (int supp = 0; supp < MAX_SUPPLIER; supp++)
              {
              supp_FPTR_REF.seekg(supp*sizeof(sSupp), ios::beg);
              supp_FPTR_REF.read((char*) &temp, sizeof(sSupp));
              cout << supp << " " << setw(15) << temp.SuppName;
              cout << " " << temp.SuppAddr << endl;
              }
          do  {
              do
                  {
                  // User isn't able to enter blank field
                  cout << "\nType a number to edit entry, or "
                      << supp << " to QUIT ";
                  cin.getline(ip_STR, sizeof(ip_STR));
                  } while ((!ip_STR[0]));
              choice = atoi(ip_STR);
              } while ((choice < 0) || (choice > MAX_SUPPLIER));
          if (choice < MAX_SUPPLIER)
              {
              supp_num_REF = choice;
              }
          else
              {
              Browse_suppliers(supp_FPTR_REF);
              Choose_supplier(supp_num_REF, supp_FPTR_REF);
              }
          return 0;
          }
  /*****************************************************************
  *                                                               *
  * FUNCTION:    Format_new_stock_file()                          *
  *                                                               *
  * PURPOSE:     Fills empty data file with blank records.        *
  *                                                               *
  * PRE:         Valid file pointer.                              *
  * POST:        None.                                            *
  *                                                               *
  * RETURNS:     void.                                            *
  *                                                               *
  *****************************************************************/
  void Format_new_stock_file(fstream& stock_FPTR_REF)
          {
          // Pre - valid file pointer
          assert(stock_FPTR_REF);

          // Local variable
          sProd EmptyRecord = {0, "(BLANK)", 0, 0, 0};

          cout << "Formatting file 'stock.dat'…\n";

          for (int stock_no = 1; stock_no <= MAX_STOCK; stock_no++)
```

```
            {
            stock_FPTR_REF.seekg(stock_no*sizeof(sProd), ios::beg);
            stock_FPTR_REF.write((char*) &EmptyRecord, sizeof(sProd));
            }
        cout << "Format complete. \n"
            << MAX_STOCK << " blank records created.\n";
        }

/****************************************************************
*                                                              *
* FUNCTION:    Format_new_supplier_file()                      *
*                                                              *
* PURPOSE:     Fills empty data file with blank records.       *
*                                                              *
* PRE:         Valid file pointer.                             *
* POST:        None.                                           *
*                                                              *
* RETURNS:     void.                                           *
*                                                              *
****************************************************************/
void Format_new_supplier_file(fstream& supp_FPTR_REF)
        {
        // Pre - valid file pointer
        assert(supp_FPTR_REF);

        // Local variable
        sSupp EmptyRecord = {0, "(EMPTY)", "(EMPTY)"};

        cout << "Formatting file 'supplier.dat'…\n";

        for (int supp = 0; supp < MAX_SUPPLIER; supp++)
            {
            supp_FPTR_REF.seekg(supp*sizeof(sSupp), ios::beg);
            supp_FPTR_REF.write((char*) &EmptyRecord, sizeof(sSupp));
            }
        cout << "Format complete. \n"
            << MAX_SUPPLIER << " blank records created.\n";
        }

/****************************************************************
*                                                              *
* FUNCTION:    Get_all_data()                                  *
*                                                              *
* PURPOSE:     Allows data entry into newly-created file.      *
*                                                              *
* PRE:         Valid file pointers.                            *
* POST:        None.                                           *
*                                                              *
* RETURNS:     void.                                           *
*                                                              *
****************************************************************/
void Get_all_data(fstream& stock_FPTR_REF,
                  fstream& supp_FPTR_REF)
```

```
        {
        // Pre - valid file pointers
        assert(stock_FPTR_REF);
        assert(supp_FPTR_REF);

        // Local variables
        sProd temp;
        int stock_no;

        cout << "\nPlease supply stock information, as follows:";

        Get_valid_ProdNum(stock_no);

        while (stock_no != -1)
            {
            /* User doesn't want to quit
               Check whether requested product entry exists */
            stock_FPTR_REF.seekg(stock_no*sizeof(sProd), ios::beg);
            stock_FPTR_REF.read((char*) &temp, sizeof(sProd));

            if (!temp.ProdNum)
                {
                Fill_record(stock_FPTR_REF, supp_FPTR_REF, stock_no);
                }
            else
                {
                // Requested product entry DOES already exist
                cout << "Prod number : " << temp.ProdNum << "\n";
                cout << "A product with the specified stock number ";
                cout << "already exists.\n";
                }

            Get_valid_ProdNum(stock_no);
            }
        }

/*****************************************************************
*                                                               *
* FUNCTION:    Menu()                                           *
*                                                               *
* PURPOSE:     Displays user instructions                      *
*                                                               *
* PRE:         None.                                            *
* POST:        None.                                            *
*                                                               *
* RETURNS:     void.                                            *
*                                                               *
*****************************************************************/
int Menu()
    {
    // Local variables
    int choice;
    char ip_STR[80];

    cout << "\nMENU:\n"
         << "1 List all stock items.\n"
```

```
                    << "2 List items with low stock level.\n"
                    << "3 Update record for a particular item.\n"
                    << "4 Insert record for a new item.\n"
                    << "5 Delete record for an item.\n"
                    << "6 Browse supplier details.\n"
                    << "7 QUIT program.\n\n"
                    << "? :";

         cin.getline(ip_STR, sizeof(ip_STR));

         while ((!(sscanf(ip_STR, "%d", &choice) == 1))
                || (choice < 1) || (choice > 7))
              {
              cout << "\nOption must be in the range 1 - 7. "
                    << "Please re-enter: ";
              cin.getline(ip_STR, sizeof(ip_STR));
              }

         cout << endl;

         return choice;
         }

/************************************************************
*                                                          *
* FUNCTION:    Display_all_records()                       *
*                                                          *
* PURPOSE:     Lists all non-empty records                 *
*                                                          *
* PRE:         Valid file pointers.                        *
* POST:        None.                                       *
*                                                          *
* RETURNS:     void.                                       *
*                                                          *
************************************************************/
void Display_all_records(fstream& stock_FPTR_REF,
                         fstream& supp_FPTR_REF)
         {
         // Pre - valid file pointers
         assert(stock_FPTR_REF);
         assert(supp_FPTR_REF);

         // Local variables
         sProd temp;
         int number_of_stock_records = 0;
         long total_value = 0; // Total stock value (in pence)

         for (int stock_no =1; stock_no <= MAX_STOCK; stock_no++)
              {
              stock_FPTR_REF.seekg(stock_no*sizeof(sProd), ios::beg);
              stock_FPTR_REF.read((char*) &temp, sizeof(sProd));

              if (temp.ProdNum)
                   {
                   number_of_stock_records++;
```

```
                if (number_of_stock_records == 1)
                    {
                    Display_record_header();
                    }
                total_value += (long) temp.ProdQuan * temp.ProdCost;
                Display_record(temp, supp_FPTR_REF);
                }
            }
        if (number_of_stock_records == 0)
            {
            cout << "The stock inventory is empty. \n";
            }
        else
            {
            Display_record_footer();
            cout << "\nThe total value of the inventory is ";
            Display_money(total_value);
            cout << endl;
            }
        Type_enter_to_continue();
        }
/*************************************************************
*                                                           *
* FUNCTION:    Get_valid_ProdNum()                          *
*                                                           *
* PURPOSE:     Prompt user for a valid stock number.        *
*                                                           *
* PRE:         None.                                        *
* POST:        stock_no_REF is valid.                       *
*                                                           *
* RETURNS:     void.                                        *
*                                                           *
*************************************************************/
void Get_valid_ProdNum(int& stock_no_REF)
    {
    // Local variable
    char ip_STR[81];
    cout << "\nType a stock number (1-"
        << MAX_STOCK << "), or -1 to end input): ";
    cin.getline(ip_STR, sizeof(ip_STR));
    while ((!(sscanf(ip_STR, "%d", &stock_no_REF) == 1))
            || (stock_no_REF < -1)
            || (stock_no_REF > MAX_STOCK)
            || (stock_no_REF == 0))
        {
        cout << "\nStock number must be in range 1 - "
            << MAX_STOCK << ". Please re-enter: ";
        cin.getline(ip_STR, sizeof(ip_STR));
        }
```

```
        // Post - stock number is valid
        assert ((stock_no_REF > -2)
                && (stock_no_REF <= MAX_STOCK));
    }

/*****************************************************************
 *                                                               *
 * FUNCTION:    Display_money()                                  *
 *                                                               *
 * PURPOSE:     Display (pounds.pence) amount in pence.          *
 *                                                               *
 * PRE:         None.                                            *
 * POST:        None.                                            *
 *                                                               *
 * RETURNS:     void.                                            *
 *                                                               *
 *****************************************************************/
void Display_money(const long money)
    {
    cout << "£" << money / ((long) 100)
         << ".";

    int pence = (int)(money % ((long) 100));
    //Make sure "pence" output is displayed correctly
    //E.g. 123.07 cf. 123.7 (which would be ambiguous)
    if (pence < 10)
        {
        //Display initial 0
        cout << "0" << pence << endl;
        }
    else
        {
        cout << pence;
        }
    }

/*****************************************************************
 *                                                               *
 * FUNCTION:    Display_low_stock_records()                      *
 *                                                               *
 * PURPOSE:     Lists all products with low stock levels.        *
 *                                                               *
 * PRE:         Valid file pointers.                             *
 * POST:        None.                                            *
 *                                                               *
 * RETURNS:     void.                                            *
 *                                                               *
 *****************************************************************/
void Display_low_stock_records(fstream& stock_FPTR_REF,
                               fstream& supp_FPTR_REF)
    {
    // Pre - valid file pointers
```

```
            assert(stock_FPTR_REF);
            assert(supp_FPTR_REF);

            // Local variables
            sProd temp;
            int number_of_stock_records = 0;
            int number_of_low_stock_records = 0;

            for (int stock_no = 1; stock_no <= MAX_STOCK; stock_no++)
                {
                stock_FPTR_REF.seekg(stock_no*sizeof(sProd), ios::beg);
                stock_FPTR_REF.read((char*) &temp, sizeof(sProd));

                if (temp.ProdNum)
                    {
                    number_of_stock_records++;

                    if (temp.ProdQuan < LOW_STOCK_LEVEL)
                        {
                        number_of_low_stock_records++;

                        if (number_of_low_stock_records == 1)
                            {
                            cout << "Stock of these products is low: \n\n";
                            Display_record_header();
                            }
                        Display_record(temp, supp_FPTR_REF);
                        }
                    }
                }
        if (number_of_stock_records == 0)
            {
            cout << "The stock inventory is empty. \n";
            }
        else
            {
            if (number_of_low_stock_records == 0)
                {
                cout << "All stock levels are >= "
                    << LOW_STOCK_LEVEL << " units. \n";
                }
            else
                {
                Display_record_footer();
                }
            }
        Type_enter_to_continue();
        }

/****************************************************************
*                                                              *
* FUNCTION:    Update_record()                                 *
*                                                              *
* PURPOSE:     Updates contents of a specified record.         *
```

```
 *                                                                    *
 * PRE:          Valid file pointers.                                 *
 * POST:         None.                                                *
 *                                                                    *
 * RETURNS:      void.                                                *
 *                                                                    *
 *********************************************************************/
void Update_record(fstream& stock_FPTR_REF,
                   fstream& supp_FPTR_REF)
    {
    // Pre - valid file pointers
    assert(stock_FPTR_REF);
    assert(supp_FPTR_REF);

    // Local variables
    sProd temp;
    int stock_no;
    char ip_STR[30];

    Get_valid_ProdNum(stock_no);

    if (stock_no != -1) // -1 => quit
        {
        stock_FPTR_REF.seekg(stock_no*sizeof(sProd), ios::beg);
        stock_FPTR_REF.read((char*) &temp, sizeof(sProd));

        if (temp.ProdNum)
            {
            Display_record_header();
            Display_record(temp, supp_FPTR_REF);

            cout << "New NAME (or <ENTER> to leave unchanged) : ";
            cin.getline(ip_STR, sizeof(ip_STR));

            if (*ip_STR)
                {
                // input was NOT blank, therefore update entry
                strcpy(temp.ProdName, ip_STR);
                }

            cout << "New QUANTITY (or <ENTER> to leave unchanged) : ";
            cin.getline(ip_STR, sizeof(ip_STR));

            if (*ip_STR)
                {
                // input was NOT blank, therefore update entry
                temp.ProdQuan = atoi(ip_STR);
                }

            cout << "New PRICE (or <ENTER> to leave unchanged) : ";
            cin.getline(ip_STR, sizeof(ip_STR));

            if (*ip_STR)
                {
                // input was NOT blank, therefore update entry
                temp.ProdCost = atoi(ip_STR);
                }
```

```
                  stock_FPTR_REF.seekg(temp.ProdNum*sizeof(sProd),ios::beg);
                  stock_FPTR_REF.write((char*) &temp, sizeof(sProd));

                  Display_record_header();
                  Display_record(temp, supp_FPTR_REF);
                  }
            else
                  {
                  cout << "Cannot update. The record is empty.\n";
                  }
            }

      Type_enter_to_continue();
      }

/****************************************************************
 *                                                              *
 * FUNCTION:    Insert_record()                                 *
 *                                                              *
 * PURPOSE:     Allows a new record to be inserted in file.     *
 *                                                              *
 * PRE:         Valid file pointers.                            *
 * POST:        None.                                           *
 *                                                              *
 * RETURNS:     void.                                           *
 *                                                              *
 ****************************************************************/
void Insert_record(fstream& stock_FPTR_REF,
                   fstream& supp_FPTR_REF)
      {
      // Pre - valid file pointers
      assert(stock_FPTR_REF);
      assert(supp_FPTR_REF);

      // Local variables
      sProd temp;
      int stock_no;

      Get_valid_ProdNum(stock_no);

      stock_FPTR_REF.seekg(stock_no*sizeof(sProd), ios::beg);
      stock_FPTR_REF.read((char*) &temp, sizeof(sProd));

      if (!temp.ProdNum)
            {
            Fill_record(stock_FPTR_REF, supp_FPTR_REF, stock_no);
            }
      else
            {
            cout << "A product with the specified stock number ";
            cout << "already exists.\n";
            }

      Type_enter_to_continue();
      }
```

```
/******************************************************************
 *                                                                *
 * FUNCTION:    Delete_record()                                   *
 *                                                                *
 * PURPOSE:     Allows deletion of a specified record.            *
 *                                                                *
 * PRE:         Valid file pointer.                               *
 * POST:        None.                                             *
 *                                                                *
 * RETURNS:     void.                                             *
 *                                                                *
 ******************************************************************/
void Delete_record(fstream& stock_FPTR_REF)
    {
    // Pre - valid file pointer
    assert(stock_FPTR_REF);
    // Local variables
    sProd EmptyRecord = {0, "(EMPTY)", 0, 0}, temp;

    int stock_no;

    Get_valid_ProdNum(stock_no);

    if (stock_no != -1)
        {
        stock_FPTR_REF.seekg(stock_no*sizeof(sProd), ios::beg);
        stock_FPTR_REF.read((char*) &temp, sizeof(sProd));

        if (temp.ProdNum)
            {
            stock_FPTR_REF.seekg(stock_no*sizeof(sProd), ios::beg);
            stock_FPTR_REF.write((char*) &EmptyRecord, sizeof(sProd));
            cout << "Record deleted.\n";
            }
        else
            {
            cout << "Cannot delete. The record is empty.\n";
            }
        }

    Type_enter_to_continue();
    }
/******************************************************************
 *                                                                *
 * FUNCTION:    Open_files()                                      *
 *                                                                *
 * PURPOSE:     Open database.                                    *
 *                                                                *
 * PRE:         None.                                             *
 * POST:        Got valid file pointers.                          *
 *                                                                *
 * RETURNS:     void.                                             *
 *                                                                *
 ******************************************************************/
```

```
void Open_files(fstream& stock_FPTR_REF,
                fstream& supp_FPTR_REF)
    {
    // Local variable
    char ip_STR[81];

    // Try to find an existing data file "supplier.dat" -
    // if it doesn't exist (or can't find it),
    // offer user option of creating one
    supp_FPTR_REF.open("supplier.dat", ios::out | ios::in
                                 | ios::nocreate | ios::binary);
    if (supp_FPTR_REF.fail())
        {
        // Can't find an existing supplier file
        cout << "\nCan't find the data file 'supplier.dat'\n";

        // Ask user if s/he wants to create a new file
        cout << "\nDo you want to create a new file (Y or N): ";
        cin.getline(ip_STR, sizeof(ip_STR));
    while ((toupper(ip_STR[0]) != 'Y') &&
           (toupper(ip_STR[0]) != 'N'))
        {
        cout << "Invalid response. Enter Y or N: ";
        cin.getline(ip_STR, sizeof(ip_STR));
        }
    if (toupper(ip_STR[0]) == 'Y')
        {
        supp_FPTR_REF.clear();
        supp_FPTR_REF.open("supplier.dat", ios::out
                                 | ios::in | ios::binary);

        if (supp_FPTR_REF.fail())
            {
            cout << "\nFATAL ERROR:\n";
            cout << "File 'supplier.dat' could not be created.\n";
            cout << "Is the disk full?\n";
            exit(1);
            }

        Format_new_supplier_file(supp_FPTR_REF);
        Browse_suppliers(supp_FPTR_REF);
        }
    else
        {
        /* No supplier file exists, and user does not
           want to create a new one: no option but to QUIT */
        cout << "Please restore backup of 'supplier.dat'\n";
        cout << "Then re-run this program.\n";
        exit(1);
        }
    }
/* Try to find an existing data file "stock.dat" -
   if it doesn't exist (or can't find it),
```

```
            offer user option of creating one */
   stock_FPTR_REF.open("stock.dat", ios::out | ios::in
                              | ios::nocreate | ios::binary );
   if (stock_FPTR_REF.fail())
       {
       // Can't find an existing stock file
       cout << "\nCan't find the data file 'stock.dat'\n";

       // Ask user if s/he wants to create a new file
       cout << "\nDo you want to create a new file (Y or N): ";
       cin.getline(ip_STR, sizeof(ip_STR));

       while ((toupper(ip_STR[0]) != 'Y') &&
              (toupper(ip_STR[0]) != 'N'))
           {
           cout << "Invalid response. Enter Y or N: ";
           cin.getline(ip_STR, sizeof(ip_STR));
           }
       if (toupper(ip_STR[0]) == 'Y')
           {
           stock_FPTR_REF.clear();
           stock_FPTR_REF.open("stock.dat", ios::out
                                      | ios::in | ios::binary);
           if (stock_FPTR_REF.fail())
               {
               cout << "\nFATAL ERROR:\n";
               cout << "File 'stock.dat' could not be created.\n";
               cout << "Is the disk full?\n";
               exit(1);
               }
           Format_new_stock_file(stock_FPTR_REF);
           Get_all_data(stock_FPTR_REF, supp_FPTR_REF);
           }
       else
           {
           /* No stock file exists, and user does not
           want to create a new one: no option but to QUIT */
           cout << "Please restore backup of 'stock.dat'\n";
           cout << "Then re-run this program.\n";
           exit(1);
           }
       }
   // Post - valid file pointers
   assert(stock_FPTR_REF);
   assert(supp_FPTR_REF);
   }

/********************************************************
*    ***                 END OF PROGRAM ***            *
********************************************************/
```

Program 23.2 The prototype stock control system. (☺)

23.6.9 Data entry

Adequate test data is entered into the system database to allow for realistic system testing.

Harry makes contact with Walter Wibble, and borrows a substantial quantity of data, on paper, with which to test his system. He employs his usual secretary, James, to enter the data into the prototype system ready for testing.

23.6.10 System tests and maintenance

The complete prototype is tested again, first by the programmers, and then by the test team, both working from the test strategy produced by the designers. The system is then subjected to user tests, including field tests and/or acceptance tests. The system is revised as necessary: any changes made during the testing and subsequent ongoing maintenance are recorded and reflected in the evolving hybrid model.

The various module tests, integration tests, and stress tests outlined by Steph are performed on the system. As the final stage of this testing, some user trials are performed, giving rise to the outputs shown below.

```
Prototype Stock Control System

Can't find the data file 'supplier.dat'

Do you want to create a new file (Y or N): y
Formatting file 'supplier.dat'…
Format complete.
3 blank records created.
Current suppliers are:

0      (EMPTY)           (EMPTY)
1      (EMPTY)           (EMPTY)
2      (EMPTY)           (EMPTY)

Type a number to edit entry, or 3 to QUIT 0
Enter new supplier name: SuperToy
Enter new supplier SuppAddr: 13 Hill Road
Current suppliers are:

0      SuperToy      13 Hill Road
1      (EMPTY)           (EMPTY)
2      (EMPTY)           (EMPTY)

Type a number to edit entry, or 3 to QUIT 1
Enter new supplier name: TeddyBare
Enter new supplier SuppAddr: 674 West St.
Current suppliers are:

0      SuperToy      13 Hill Road
1      TeddyBare      674 West St.
2      (EMPTY)           (EMPTY)

Type a number to edit entry, or 3 to QUIT 2
Enter new supplier name: Cheapo
```

```
Enter new supplier SuppAddr: 34 Cheapside
Current suppliers are:

0      SuperToy      13 Hill Road
1      TeddyBare     674 West St.
2        Cheapo      34 Cheapside

Type a number to edit entry, or 3 to QUIT 3

Can't find the data file 'stock.dat'

Do you want to create a new file (Y or N): y
Formatting file 'stock.dat'…
Format complete.
1000 blank records created.

Please supply stock information, as follows:
Type a stock number (1-1000), or -1 to end input): 1
PRODUCT NAME  : Wibble Wobble Whale
QUANTITY      : 1000
UNIT PRICE (in pence)   : 3458
Available suppliers are :

0      SuperToy      13 Hill Road
1      TeddyBare     674 West St.
2        Cheapo      34 Cheapside

Type a number to edit entry, or 3 to QUIT 0

Type a stock number (1-1000), or -1 to end input): 345
PRODUCT NAME  : Teddy bear
QUANTITY      : 1234
UNIT PRICE (in pence)   : 8976
Available suppliers are :

0      SuperToy      13 Hill Road
1      TeddyBare     674 West St.
2        Cheapo      34 Cheapside

Type a number to edit entry, or 3 to QUIT 2

Type a stock number (1-1000), or -1 to end input): 899
PRODUCT NAME  : Video Game
QUANTITY      : 2341
UNIT PRICE (in pence)   : 6789
Available suppliers are :

0      SuperToy      13 Hill Road
1      TeddyBare     674 West St.
2        Cheapo      34 Cheapside

Type a number to edit entry, or 3 to QUIT 0

Type a stock number (1-1000), or -1 to end input): -1

MENU:
1 List all stock items.
2 List items with low stock level.
3 Update record for a particular item.
4 Insert record for a new item.
```

```
5 Delete record for an item.
6 Browse supplier details.
7 QUIT program.

? :7

Finished.
```

```
Prototype Stock Control System

MENU:

1 List all stock items.
2 List items with low stock level.
3 Update record for a particular item.
4 Insert record for a new item.
5 Delete record for an item.
6 Browse supplier details.
7 QUIT program.

? :1

+------+---------------+--------+-------+-----+
 Record #  Product Name         Supplier   Quantity  Cost
+------+---------------+--------+-------+-----+
   1         Wibble Wobble Whale  SuperToy   1000       £34.58
   345       Teddy bear           Cheapo     1234       £89.76
   899       Video Game           SuperToy   2341       £67.89

+------+---------------+--------+-------+-----+
The total value of the inventory is £304274.33

Type <ENTER> to continue.

MENU:
1 List all stock items.
2 List items with low stock level.
3 Update record for a particular item.
4 Insert record for a new item.
5 Delete record for an item.
6 Browse supplier details.
7 QUIT program.

? :2

All stock levels are >= 50 units.

Type <ENTER> to continue.

MENU:
1 List all stock items.
2 List items with low stock level.
3 Update record for a particular item.
4 Insert record for a new item.
5 Delete record for an item.
6 Browse supplier details.
7 QUIT program.

? :3
```

```
Type a stock number (1-1000), or -1 to end input): 899
+-------+----------------+-------+-------+-----+
 Record #  Product Name        Supplier  Quantity  Cost
+-------+----------------+-------+-------+-----+
 899        Video Game          SuperToy  2341      £67.89
New NAME (or <ENTER> to leave unchanged)    :
New QUANTITY (or <ENTER> to leave unchanged) : 45
New PRICE (or <ENTER> to leave unchanged)    :
+-------+----------------+-------+-------+-----+
 Record #  Product Name        Supplier  Quantity  Cost
+-------+----------------+-------+-------+-----+
 899        Video Game          SuperToy  45        £67.89
Type <ENTER> to continue.
MENU:
1 List all stock items.
2 List items with low stock level.
3 Update record for a particular item.
4 Insert record for a new item.
5 Delete record for an item.
6 Browse supplier details.
7 QUIT program.

? :2
Stock of these products is low:
+-------+----------------+-------+-------+-----+
 Record #  Product Name        Supplier  Quantity  Cost
+-------+----------------+-------+-------+-----+
 899        Video Game          SuperToy  45        £67.89
+-------+----------------+-------+-------+-----+
Type <ENTER> to continue.
MENU:
1 List all stock items.
2 List items with low stock level.
3 Update record for a particular item.
4 Insert record for a new item.
5 Delete record for an item.
6 Browse supplier details.
7 QUIT program.

? :1
+-------+----------------+-------+-------+-----+
 Record #  Product Name        Supplier  Quantity  Cost
+-------+----------------+-------+-------+-----+
 1          Wibble Wobble Whale SuperToy  1000      £34.58
 345        Teddy bear          Cheapo    1234      £89.76
 899        Video Game          SuperToy  45        £67.89
+-------+----------------+-------+-------+-----+
The total value of the inventory is £148398.89
Type <ENTER> to continue.
```

```
MENU:
1 List all stock items.
2 List items with low stock level.
3 Update record for a particular item.
4 Insert record for a new item.
5 Delete record for an item.
6 Browse supplier details.
7 QUIT program.

? :5

Type a stock number (1-1000), or -1 to end input): 1
Record deleted.

Type <ENTER> to continue.

MENU:
1 List all stock items.
2 List items with low stock level.
3 Update record for a particular item.
4 Insert record for a new item.
5 Delete record for an item.
6 Browse supplier details.
7 QUIT program.

? :6

Current suppliers are:
0      SuperToy      13 Hill Road
1      TeddyBare     674 West St.
2        Cheapo      34 Cheapside
Type a number to edit entry, or 3 to QUIT 0
Enter new supplier name: XToy
Enter new supplier SuppAddr: 13-14 Hill Road
Current suppliers are:
0          XToy 13-14 Hill Road
1      TeddyBare      674 West St.
2        Cheapo       34 Cheapside
Type a number to edit entry, or 3 to QUIT 3

MENU:
1 List all stock items.
2 List items with low stock level.
3 Update record for a particular item.
4 Insert record for a new item.
5 Delete record for an item.
6 Browse supplier details.
7 QUIT program.

? :1

+-------+----------------+--------+--------+-----+
  Record #  Product Name      Supplier  Quantity  Cost
+-------+----------------+--------+--------+-----+
  345       Teddy bear        Cheapo    1234      £89.76
  899       Video Game        XToy        45      £67.89
+-------+----------------+--------+--------+-----+
```

```
The total value of the inventory is £113818.89
Type <ENTER> to continue.
MENU:
1 List all stock items.
2 List items with low stock level.
3 Update record for a particular item.
4 Insert record for a new item.
5 Delete record for an item.
6 Browse supplier details.
7 QUIT program.

? :7
Finished.
```

Harry is happy that the system is ready for the clients.

Before finishing, however, he has to update the various pieces of documentation. In particular, the structure chart developed by Steph no longer represents the system he has constructed. He therefore develops a modified structure chart along with associated 'PSpecs' (these are omitted here).

23.7　Conclusions

To conclude our exploration of data-oriented software development, we have considered here a substantial case study, showing how the SADIE methodology may be applied effectively to the development of information systems.

In Part III, we go on to consider how the data models we have considered here may be extended to become not only a means of modelling persistent data, but a powerful way of representing new, fully integrated, data types.

PART III
Object-oriented software development

24 Why we need objects

24.1 Introduction

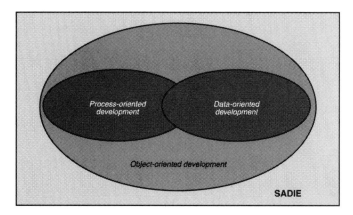

Figure 24.1 The three software development approaches supported by the 'Simple Analysis, Design & Implementation' (SADIE) methodology discussed in this book. As we will see in Part III, object-oriented techniques build on the P-O and D-O approaches discussed in Part I and Part II.

In Part I, we looked in detail at a process-oriented approach to software development (Figure 24.1). This approach, the most widely used of the semi-formal approaches at the time of writing, generally proves effective and easy to learn. As we saw, the process-oriented approach was particularly suitable for the development of technical systems. In Part II, we extended the process-oriented approach to deal with information systems and hybrid systems: in these circumstances, data dominated the problem domain and, we argued, it was appropriate that a data-oriented solution be adopted (Figure 24.1). Again, the result was a flexible, extensible and widely-used approach to software development.

To date, therefore, we seem to have 'covered all the bases', providing well-tested development strategies for the various types of software product identified in the Introduction: technical, information, and hybrid systems. So, if the process-oriented and data-oriented approaches were so good, why do we need a further technique? Why do we need to add objects and classes?

The aim of this chapter, and of the remainder of this book, is to begin to provide an answer to these questions.

24.2 A thought experiment revisited

We opened this book with a rather strange thought experiment, asking you to imagine that you had the task of remembering numbers dictated over the radio. The idea was that the numbers would be dictated one day and you would have to recall them a week later.

As our first sideways look at the limitations of process-oriented software development methods, consider the thought experiment one final time. One solution to this problem would be to call all your friends around to your house, and ask them each to remember – say – half a dozen numbers for you. This might not be such a bad solution, and it would certainly succeed in breaking down the original problem into bite-sized chunks.

However, what happens when the problem gets larger, and the numbers just keep pouring out of the radio? Let's assume you are fortunate enough to have lots of good friends, all willing to take part in this odd experiment. You still have the problem of keeping track of the order in which your friends have heard the numbers (so that you can eventually relay them back in the correct sequence). As the list of numbers grows larger, eventually there will come a time when you lose track of what is going on: for example, was Joe at position 313 in the list, or position 323? And was that Joe Smith or Joe Anderson?

When you try to follow a process-oriented (P-O) or data-oriented (D-O) software development strategy, you experience a similar problem to that encountered in this latest version of the thought experiment. When the resulting process design can be represented by the structure chart shown in Figure 24.2, such an approach is very effective. By the time your structure chart looks like Figure 24.3, the complexity of the corresponding dataflow model will be considerable, and you are likely to be beginning to experience many of the same problems that occur with (much smaller) monolithic programs. That is, it becomes difficult to keep track of so many functions, and to remember how they relate and interact.

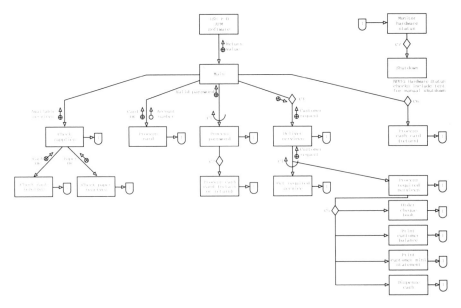

Figure 24.2 The outline P-O design (structure chart) for a small system.

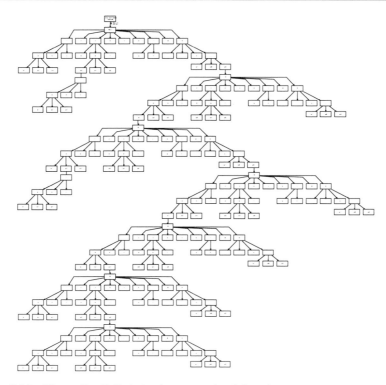

Figure 24.3 The outline P-O design (structure chart) for a larger system.

We can consider the implications of Figure 24.3 in a more quantitative manner. It is generally estimated that, using P-O/D-O techniques, the average software team might expect to produce and maintain programs up to 50 000 or perhaps 100 000 lines in size. To put this figure in perspective, none of the example programs in this book is more than 1000 lines long. A program of even 50 000 lines is clearly a substantial program; these days, however, it may not be substantial enough. As users' requirements and expectations of software systems grow, it is inevitable that the size of programs are growing too, beyond even our 100 000 line limit: indeed, as we saw in the Introduction, the software controlling the US space shuttle consists of some 3 000 000 lines of code.

In an ideal world, what we'd like to be able to do is reduce the complexity of the system represented by the structure chart in Figure 24.3 to the level shown in Figure 24.2, while at the same time not reducing the functionality of our program *or* the level of detail provided by our design. On the surface, such a translation appears to fly in the face of good programming practice. The structure chart represents the functions in our program, with (approximately) one module on the structure chart to every program function. The only way we could reduce the size of the structure chart and maintain the same functionality would be by increasing the size of the functions we use, and this would contradict all the guidelines concerning cohesion we have seen in earlier parts of this book, as well as increasing the chances of errors occurring in any particular function.

As we'll see in Chapter 31, structure charts are an important component of O-O designs, and – though the notation used to represent such charts is extended slightly to represent the new O-O features – the overall size of the structure chart remains largely unchanged. There is, nonetheless, a way we can produce 'larger functions' without sacrificing the cohesiveness of our design. This is by achieved by grouping related functions, and data, together into a new program structures called an **object**. Because objects may contain, on average, perhaps five or ten functions, we have the *potential* of reducing the complexity of our system by almost the same factor.

The tying together of data and functions in this way is usually referred to as **encapsulation**, for reasons we'll come to shortly, and is the first of three distinguishing characteristics of true object-oriented systems, *viz.*

- encapsulation
- polymorphism
- inheritance

We consider the meaning of each of these terms below. Before we do so, however, note that – despite the introduction to the topic given here – classes are not only relevant when we are developing large programs. As we will see in the remainder of this chapter, and throughout the remainder of Part III, classes can be used, often to good effect, in programs of any size.

24.3 Encapsulation

Encapsulation is something that programmers do to data in object-oriented programs. The term refers to the way in which objects are created by wrapping up data inside collections of functions.

The mechanism of encapsulation becomes particularly powerful because we can render our data private to the object in which it is contained; private data is known to, and accessible only by, another component of the same object. Thus, private data is protected from 'outside interference' by parts of the program that exist outside the object boundaries. By contrast, public parts of an object may be accessed by other parts of the program. Typically, the public parts of an object (often, but not exclusively, functions) are used to provide a carefully controlled interface to the private parts of the object (often, but not exclusively, data). In this way, it is claimed, an object-oriented approach leads to systems with lower coupling and higher cohesion (Somerville, 1996).

24.3.1 A C++ example

An appreciation of encapsulation is fundamental to effective object-oriented software development. However, before we further consider this idea, we'll try to avoid the discussion becoming unduly abstract by looking at a 'real' example of a C++ class and object (Program 24.1).

```
// A first simple class and object example
// Source is: 24_01.CPP
#include <iostream.h>
class cFirst_Class
    {
    public:
        // Public member functions
```

```
        void Set_Num(const int); // Mutator member function
        void Show_Num() const;    // Accessor member function
    private:
        // Private data
        int _Num;
    };
// Member functions
// Note use of scope resolution operator

// Mutator member function
void cFirst_Class::Set_Num(const int NUMBER)
    {
    _Num = NUMBER;
    }

// Accessor member function (note const)
// N.B. Cannot change private data
void cFirst_Class::Show_Num() const
    {
    cout << "Number is " << _Num;
    }

int main()
    {
    // Create an object of type cFirst_Class
    cFirst_Class Object;

    // Call the Set_Num() mutator function
    Object.Set_Num(9);

    // Call the Show_Num() accessor function
    Object.Show_Num();

    return 0;
    }
```

Program 24.1 A first simple class and object. (☺)

Program 24.1 produces the following output:

```
Number is 9
```

Dissecting Program 24.1

Like most O-O programs, Program 24.1 is built around a *class*, in this case called cFirst_Class:

```
class cFirst_Class
    {
    public:
        // Public member functions
        void Set_Num(const int);       // Mutator member function
        void Show_Num() const;         // Accessor member function
    private:
```

```
                // Private data
                int _Num;
        };
```

Three points should be immediately emphasized:

- The class format is very similar to that of the `structs` we considered in Part II (in fact, `struct` is a subset of `class`). For example, we have (under a label `private`, which we will consider in due course) a data item, called _Num, forming one component in our user-defined composite data type.
- The major difference between a class and a `struct` (as usually used) is that a class has closely associated with it a set of member functions (implementing a set of methods). In this case, the member functions are `Set_Num()` and `Show_Num()`: the prototypes for these functions are placed within the class definition.
- A class, from the programmer's perspective, is simply a new kind of user-defined data type. As we will see, the major difference between the user-defined types we considered in Part II, and the types we will consider in the remainder of this book, is that classes are *integrated* data types: unlike (most) `struct`-based variables, class-based variables can be made to behave in precisely the same way as variables created from one of C++'s built-in types.

To understand Program 24.1, we first need to emphasize the distinction between *objects* and *classes*. To do so, consider the following code fragment:

```
{
int        sum;
float      average;
    ...
    ...
}
```

Here, of course, `int` and `float` are data types, while `sum` and `average` are instances of these types. Similarly, *classes* are user-defined data types, and *objects* are instances of these types. To put this another way, objects are class variables.

Thus, in Program 24.1, we create an object of type `cFirstClass` as follows:

```
// Create an object of type cFirst_Class
cFirst_Class Object;
```

Of course, we've seen some user-defined data types before, in Part II. However, as the rest of this chapter will begin to make clear, class-based data types are much more powerful and flexible than the simpler types discussed previously.

Encapsulating private data behind a public interface

To begin to see why encapsulation is useful, we can add a line to the main function in Program 24.1, as follows:

```
cout << Object._Num << endl;
```

If we do this, the compiler will generate an error along the following lines:

```
...cannot access private member declared in class 'cFirst_Class'
```

The key to understanding this error message is to note the labels in the class definition:

```
class cFirst_Class
    {
    public:
        // Public member functions
        void Set_Num(const int);      // Mutator member function
        void Show_Num() const;        // Accessor member function
    private:
        // Private data
        int _Num;
    };
```

Because _Num appears beneath a 'private:' label it is *private* data, and not accessible to 'the outside world'. It is conventional, as we first noted in Chapter 3, to indicate that a variable (or function) is private by preceding the name of the variable with an underscore.

Clearly, therefore, we need to have some way of manipulating the _Num variable; we can (only) do so via a **member function**. Provided this is a public member function (that is, it appears under a 'public:' label) then we can manipulate our private variables, as required. Note that we'll consider some important situations where even member functions cannot alter our private data in the next section.

One of the implications of this encapsulation mechanism is that our private data are protected from outside interference. This is a useful feature, but the real impact of this superficially minor change is to change the way we think about creating software: we discuss this further below.

24.3.2 Accessors and mutators

We need to highlight one further important feature about our first simple class, and that is the nature of the member functions. As we have seen, the encapsulation process at the heart of object-oriented software development means that we almost always rely on member functions to gain access to the data in our programs. As we have seen in earlier parts of this book, a fundamental concern in software development is to maintain the integrity of the program data: in Part I, for example, we emphasized the importance of using call by value as a default, and only resorting to call by reference or call by address when it was essential to do so.

A similar concern arises in connection with object-oriented programming, but the solution is slightly different. When working with objects, we generally divide member functions into two groups:

- **Accessor (member) functions:** Accessor functions merely access or reveal the values of hidden data members: they do not change the values. The const modifier is used to enforce this (as described below).

- **Mutator (member) functions:** Mutator functions are able to 'mutate' or change the private data members of their associated class. Mutator functions are therefore inherently more 'dangerous' and need to be written (and used) with care.

In cFirst_Class, the mutator member function Set_Num() is, as we've already seen, able to manipulate the private data member _Num. This is clearly essential behaviour for this member function, and it is appropriately implemented.

As the comments (and behaviour) suggest, Show_Num() is an accessor member function. Not only does this member function not have to alter the private data values, it is unable to do so. For example, if we try to modify the definition of Show_Num() as follows:

```
void cFirst_Class::Show_Num() const
    {
    cout << "Number is " << _Num;
    _Num = 9;  // CAN'T!!!
    }
```

then the program will not compile.

This behaviour arises, of course, because of the const modifier. Note that const cannot be used in this way with the 'ordinary' functions we considered in Parts I and II.

This use of const is powerful, and effective. Even if we try to use a reference return value to change the value of _Num, we won't be able to do so. Thus, this code will not compile:

```
class cSecond_Class2
    {
    public:
        int& Access_Num() const;  // Accessor member function?
    private:
        int _Num;
    };

int& cSecond_Class::Access_Num() const
    {
    return _Num;  // CAN'T!!!
    }
```

Finally, note that the use of the 'external' const modifier does not remove the need for 'constant call by value' (or 'constant call by reference') when passing information to an accessor function, as in the Multiply_Num() member function below:

```
class cThird_Class
    {
    public:
        void Set_Num(const int);            // Mutator member function
        void Multiply_Num(const int) const; // Accessor member function
    private:
        int _Num;
    };
```

Identification of accessor and mutator functions is an important part of object-oriented software development; we'll see many more examples of this style of coding in later chapters.

24.3.3   Abstract data types

As we've seen, classes can be viewed from a programming perspective simply as a flexible form of user-defined data structure. The use of O-O techniques as an engineering method, however, more commonly requires the production of what are usually called **abstract data types** (ADTs). Here the term 'abstract' is used to mean that (unlike integers or floating point numbers, for example) the ADTs have no physical reality at the heart of the computer system. In fact, to the programmer, ADTs are not abstract at all; instead, these types are, in some sense, models of the problem domain in which the programmer is working. Thus the programmer might create data types called cCustomer, cRadar_unit and cMoney to help in a range of programming tasks.

To get a feeling for the way the use of ADTs, and an object-oriented view of the world, influence the software development process, we'll turn now to look in outline at a more realistic example. Consider that you wish to develop an object-oriented solution to the simple weather monitoring system we discussed in Chapter 15.

The context diagram for the system is reproduced in Figure 24.4. Suppose that we had built such a weather monitoring system, using a process-oriented development strategy. Now, further suppose that the company manufacturing the particular temperature sensor we were using has goes out of business. Or, alternatively, suppose that we are asked to adapt our system for use at the equator, and require to measure a rather different range of temperatures. In either case, we would be obliged to go through the code and locate all lines related to our original temperature sensor, modifying them as necessary. Of course, an experienced software engineer should take care during the specification and design of the system to minimize the impact caused by such subsequent changes but, in the real world, portability is often one of the first system characteristics to suffer as deadlines start to bite.

Using the ideas of encapsulation and ADTs discussed above allows us to find an elegant solution to the problem, effectively 'building in' portability as a side-effect of the software development process. By taking an object-oriented approach to this problem, we would create a 'model' of a temperature sensor in our code, as shown in the following class definition:

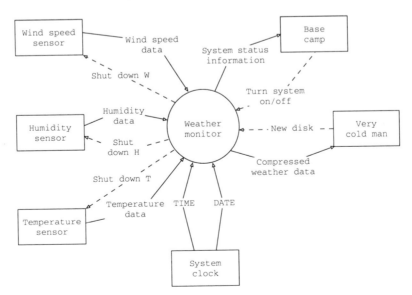

Figure 24.4   Context diagram for the weather monitoring system.

```
class cTemperature_Sensor
    {
    public:
        void turn_off();    // Turn off sensor
        void show();        // Show current temp
    private:
        int _temperature;   // Temperature
        eBool _status;      // Status of sensor
    };
```

In developing this class, note (from Figure 24.4) that the system must interact with the temperature sensor in two ways: to read data, and to turn the sensor off. The first thing that the cTemperature_Sensor class does is to turn these two actions into member functions. Importantly, these two functions are now firmly linked together: if there are any changes to the temperature sensor, we know we only have to modify the code in this area. Secondly, we have the temperature (data) details hidden inside the class. We may be able to use direct memory access (DMA) to transfer the data from the sensor to this area of memory, and simply read out the result (see Cahill, 1994, for details of this process). Alternatively, we may need to connect the sensor to a port and communicate with this port to capture the temperature reading. Either way, the relevant code will be encapsulated within the cTemperature_Sensor class.

When used in this way, object-oriented techniques can make it easier to recycle our code in new projects. We'll see some further advantages of the O-O approach to this problem in Section 24.4.

24.3.4 Developing simulations

We developed an outline abstract data type representing a temperature sensor in the weather monitoring system in Section 24.3.3. We can take this modelling process a stage further and actually use C++ to develop **simulations** of real world processes.

This process is significant in part because one of Stroustrup's inspirations in creating C++ was the programming language Simula, a language originally developed to allow the creation of such simulations. For example, in Chapter 18 of an interesting book, Horstmann (1995) describes the simulation of customers joining a queue in a bank. Similarly, Stroustrup (1991) himself outlines the use of C++ for modelling traffic flow in a city. The use of objects and classes in this way can help new programmers to begin to see the world from an object-oriented perspective.

Suppose, for example, we wished to develop a simulation such as that proposed by Stroustrup. We might start by thinking about one important class of vehicles, the car (Figure 24.5). This car model emphasizes that, as far as the average user is concerned, the various *methods* – 'Steer', 'Change gear', 'Brake' – are all they are concerned about. They don't wish to know anything about the engine or other mechanics (at least until something goes wrong ...). These methods therefore form a useful interface, separating the user from the underlying complexity of the engine, electronics and mechanics that power and control the car. This interface allows the user to communicate with and control the underlying 'data' and 'processes' in a useful way.

Of course, if we have a car class, then we can create individual objects of this class (Figure 24.6). We can also see, in a straightforward way, how we might go about

Car class

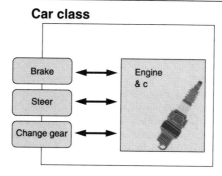

Figure 24.5 A schematic representation of a car class.

constructing such a simulation in C++. For example, a simple car class compatible with Figure 24.6 could be defined as follows:

```
class cCar
    {
    public:
        // Public member function declarations
        void brake();              // Reduce speed
        void steer(const int);     // Turn car
        void change_gear(const int); // Change gear
    private:
        // Private data
        int _speed;                // Speed
        int _gear;                 // Gear position
        int _steering;             // Steering wheel angle
    };
```

Following such a class definition, having written the appropriate member functions, we could create a car object with the line:

```
cCar Volvo_480ES;   // Create a Volvo car
```

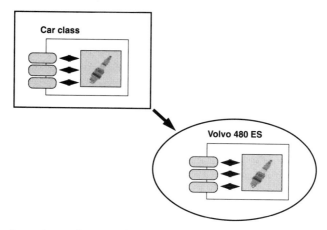

Figure 24.6 A car class and a particular car object.

We could continue the simulation example, and attempt to build a simulation of traffic flow. To do so, however, we would probably need to make use of both the polymorphism and inheritance mechanisms we discuss below.

24.4   Polymorphism

We have already met polymorphism in previous chapters. As we saw, the name has Greek origins and means 'many forms'. In the context of OOP, polymorphism is useful because it allows a single name to specify a general class of actions.

To a limited extent, almost all programming languages support polymorphism. When we write:

```
{
int      sum;
float    average;
    ...

    ...
sum = 7 + 3;
    ...
average = 99.99f + 22.1f;
}
```

the computer will, generally, take quite different actions (at a hardware level) to add two integer values (7 + 3) and to perform the 'same' addition operation on floating-point values (99.99f + 22.1f). As programmers, we view the actions in the same way, and we are happy to let the compiler sort out the most appropriate (different) action to be performed in each case.

In C++, polymorphism (or overloading) can be applied to both functions (as we have seen) and to **operators**. Operator overloading is very important, because it allows the user-defined types created by the programmer to be fully integrated into the C++ language. We investigate the overloading of operators in some detail in the following chapters. However, to whet your appetite, we'll present a simple data structure for a mailing list, encapsulate it in a new class and overload the insertion and extraction operators to give us easy ways of getting data into our new database (Program 24.2).

```
// A Fragment of a Mailing List Program
// Demonstrating classes and operator overloading
// Source is: 24_02.CPP

#include <iostream.h>
#include <stdlib.h>

// Maximum size of the "database"
const int MAX_LIST_SIZE = 3;

// The ADT cCustomer
class cCustomer
    {
    public:
```

```
        friend istream &operator>> (istream&, cCustomer&);
        friend ostream &operator<< (ostream&, const cCustomer&);
    private:
        char _lastname[81];  // Customer's last name
        char _firstname[81]; // Customer's first name
        char _title[81];     // Customer's title
        char _address1[81];  // 1st line of customer's addr
        char _address2[81];  // 2nd line of customer's addr
        char _address3[81];  // 3rd line of customer's addr
        char _postcode[81];  // Customer's postcode
    };

/***********************************************************
*                                                         *
* OPERATOR    FUNCTION: >>                                 *
*                                                         *
* PURPOSE:    Overload ">>" operator.                     *
*                                                         *
***********************************************************/
istream &operator>> (istream& input, cCustomer& Cust)
    {
    cout << "Enter customer's last name : ";
    input.getline(Cust._lastname, 80);

    cout << "Customer's first name : ";
    input.getline(Cust._firstname, 80);

    cout << "Customer's title (e.g. Ms Mr) : ";
    input.getline(Cust._title, 80);

    cout << "First line of customer's address : ";
    input.getline(Cust._address1, 80);

    cout << "Second line of customer's address : ";
    input.getline(Cust._address2, 80);

    cout << "Third line of customer's address : ";
    input.getline(Cust._address3, 80);

    cout << "Customer's postcode : ";
    input.getline(Cust._postcode, 80);
    cout << endl;

    return input;
    }

/***********************************************************
*                                                         *
* OPERATOR    FUNCTION: <<                                 *
*                                                         *
* PURPOSE:    Overload "<<" operator.                     *
*                                                         *
***********************************************************/
ostream &operator<< (ostream& output, const cCustomer& Cust)
    {
```

```
       output << Cust._title << " ";
       output << Cust._firstname << " ";
       output << Cust._lastname << endl;
       output << Cust._address1 << endl;
       output << Cust._address2 << endl;
       output << Cust._address3 << endl;
       output << Cust._postcode << "\n\n";

       return output;
       }
// Ordinary function prototype
int menu(int&);

int main ()
    {
    cCustomer cust[MAX_LIST_SIZE]; // Array of objects
    int list_size = 0; // Size of the list

    int choice;

    cout << "OBJECT-BASED MAILING LIST\n";
    cout << "------------------------ \n\n";

    do {
       if (menu(choice))
          {
          cerr << "FATAL ERROR in function menu()";
          exit(1);
          }
       else
          {
          switch(choice)
             {
             case 1: // Enter new name
                if (list_size <= (MAX_LIST_SIZE-1))
                   {
                   cin >> cust[list_size]; // Note !!
                   list_size++;
                   }
                else
                   {
                   cout << "Sorry - the database is full\n\n";
                   }
                break;

             case 2: // Display (all) names
                if (list_size)
                   {
                   for (int c = 0; c < list_size; c++)
                      {
                      cout << cust[c]; // Note !!
                      }
                   }
                else
                   {
```

```
                    cout << "Sorry - database is empty\n\n";
                    }
              }
          }
      } while(choice != 3);
  cout << "Finished.";
  return 0;
  }
/****************************************************************
*                                                              *
* FUNCTION:   menu                                             *
*                                                              *
* PURPOSE:    Offer user options and return a selection.       *
*                                                              *
****************************************************************/
int menu(int& choice)
    {
    char text_str[81];

    cout << " 1. Enter New Data\n";
    cout << " 2. Display All Data\n";
    cout << " 3. Quit\n\n";
    do
        {
        cout << "? : ";
        cin.getline(text_str, 80);
        choice = text_str[0] - '0';
        } while((choice < 1) || (choice > 3));

    return 0;
    }
```

Program 24.2 Prototype mailing list program. (☺)

Typical output from Program 24.2 is as follows:

```
OBJECT-BASED MAILING LIST

 1. Enter New Data
 2. Display All Data
 3. Quit

? : 1
Enter customer's last name         : Smith
Customer's first name              : Peter
Customer's title (e.g. Ms Mr)      : Prof.
First line of customer's address : Computer Training (UK) Ltd
Second line of customer's address: PO Box 34352
Third line of customer's address : Birmingham
Customer's postcode                : BN4 HJ6

 1. Enter New Data
```

```
   2. Display All Data
   3. Quit

?  :  2
Prof. Peter Smith
Computer Training (UK) Ltd
PO Box 34352
Birmingham
BN4 HJ6

   1. Enter New Data
   2. Display All Data
   3. Quit

?  :  3
Finished.
```

This program deserves careful study. First of all, let's look at the advantages we have obtained from the object-based approach. At first glance, these appear quite trivial, but that is simply a tribute to the power of the method!

For example, in the lines:

```
cCustomer cust[MAX_LIST_SIZE]; // Array of objects
...
cin >> cust[list_size];
```

we are applying exactly the same operator used were we to type, for example:

```
int a[MAX_LIST_SIZE]; // Array of ints
...
cin >> a[list_size];
```

yet, in the first case, we are dealing with a complex, user-defined data structure, and in the second case we are dealing with a (comparatively) very simple built-in data type. What we have achieved is to reduce – as far as 'the end programmer' is concerned – the complexity of the system. That is, by overloading the 'get from' operator, we have succeeded in making the 'same' operation ('get some data from user') operate in the same manner, despite the necessary detailed differences in the implementation.

Of course, exactly the same can be said about the line:

```
cout << cust[c];
```

which displays the contents of a database record on the screen. In particular, it is informative to compare the results of this overloaded operator with the output from the following code fragment (adapted from Program 17.3):

```
...
// Defines a new data type called eMedal
enum eMedal {Bronze, Silver, Gold};

int main()
     {
     // Declare a new array (medals) of type eMedal;
     eMedal medals[4];

     cout << (int) medals[i] << endl;
     ...
```

In the case of enumerated types (and simple `struct-` or `union`-based variables, as generally used) the input and output of information is less than elegant, and can make complex programs less easy to write. Similarly, other operations (like addition and subtraction) become very straightforward and 'natural' using objects; we provide details of all these mechanisms in Chapter 27.

Finally, note that both the function overloading we have previously considered and the related operator overloading involve compile-time polymorphism: that is, the version of an overloaded function or operator called at a particular point in your program is determined by the compiler and 'hard wired' into the object code of your executable program. There is, however, one other type of polymorphism that we have not yet considered: run-time polymorphism. Here, the particular version of an overloaded function used is determined only when your program runs: that is, at run-time. As we will see, C++ also supports run-time polymorphism; this adds significantly to the power of the language.

24.5   Inheritance

We can start by approaching the concept of inheritance from a familiar perspective. Consider Figure 24.7. The figure shows a jumbled collection of animals. As Charles Darwin was one of the first to record, however, there is order in this apparent chaos (Figure 24.8).

Figure 24.7   A jumbled collection of animals.

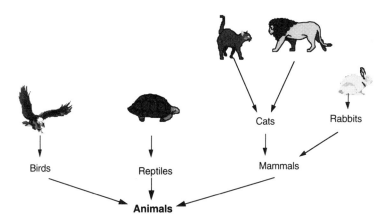

Figure 24.8   A rough taxonomy of 'animals'.

This taxonomy provides a structure to the system. In a sense, we can think of this as the equivalent to normalizing a single large table of information or as the equivalent, in data terms, of restructuring a monolithic program into a set of cohesive functions. Either way, it implies adding some *structure* to the system we are developing, and this, as we've seen throughout this book, is usually 'A Good Thing'.

24.5.1 A less abstract example

To begin to see how inheritance may be used in a practical software development environment, let's consider the weather monitoring system again. We saw in Section 24.3.2 how we could bundle up all the functions and data related to a temperature sensor together into a class. However, we also need a wind sensor and a humidity sensor in the system. We might therefore begin by drawing up a provisional class diagram showing the various classes we plan to have in the final system (Figure 24.9). The class diagram doesn't, obviously, say very much at this stage, but we'll come back to it later. For now, we'll focus on the C++ code used in this system. The new classes we'll use are shown in Figure 24.10.

Figure 24.9 A provisional class diagram for the object-oriented version of the weather monitoring system.

```
class cTemperature_Sensor
    {
    public:
        void turn_off();  // Turn off sensor
        void show();      // Show current temperature
    private:
        int _temperature; // Temperature
        eBool _status;    // Status of sensor (i.e. on or off)
    };
```

```
class cHumidity_Sensor
    {
    public:
        void turn_off();  // Turn off sensor
        void show();      // Show current humidity
    private:
        int _humidity;    // Humidity
        eBool _status;    // Status of sensor (i.e. on or off)
    };
```

```
class cWind_Speed_Sensor
    {
    public:
```

```
            void turn_off();     // Turn off sensor
            void show();         // Show current wind speed
        private:
            int _wind_speed;     // Wind speed
            eBool _status;       // Status of sensor (i.e. on or off)
        };
```

Figure 24.10 C++ code to implement three new sensor classes.

As you look at the code, you may perhaps feel a sense of *déjà vu*.

Compare this with an example of process-oriented code (Program 24.3).

```
// Carpet Area Calculation v1.0
// Source is: 24_03.CPP

#include <iostream.h>

int main()
    {
    float width, length;
    cout  << "\nROOM ONE\n";
    cout  << "Type in width (in metres) <RETURN>: ";
    cin   >> width;
    cout  << "Type in length (in metres) <RETURN>: ";
    cin   >> length;
    cout  << "Area of carpet for Room 1 is: "
          << width * length << endl;

    cout  << "\nROOM TWO\n";
    cout  << "Type in width (in metres) <RETURN>: ";
    cin   >> width;
    cout  << "Type in length (in metres) <RETURN>: ";
    cin   >> length;
    cout  << "Area of carpet for Room 2 is: "
          << width * length << endl;

    cout  << "\nROOM THREE\n";
    cout  << "Type in width (in metres) <RETURN>: ";
    cin   >> width;
    cout  << "Type in length (in metres) <RETURN>: ";
    cin   >> length;
    cout  << "Area of carpet for Room 3 is: "
          << width * length << endl;

    return 0;
    }
```

Program 24.3 A C++ program for calculating the area of carpet required in an office v1.0. (☹)

As we have seen in earlier chapters, the best way around the code problem illustrated in Program 24.3 is to collect all the common processing together in a single function, and call this function three times.

As far as the C++ classes in the weather monitoring system are concerned, we can do a conceptually similar thing. Consider the new version of the class relationship

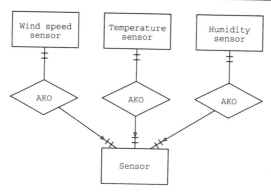

Figure 24.11 A partial class relationship diagram for the object-oriented version of the weather monitoring system. The AKO relationship means A Kind Of, and indicates that – for example – the Humidity Sensor is a kind of (basic) sensor: that is, the Humidity Sensor inherits code from the Sensor class.

diagram, shown in Figure 24.11. What this indicates is that we intend to have a (base) class 'Sensor', which may have a number of general 'behaviour patterns' useful for all sensors; for example, referring back to Figure 24.1, we know that in this particular example the sensors we need can all be shut down, and all provide data. We might therefore make these operations features of our base class, and inherit these behaviours in each of our Wind Speed Sensor, Temperature Sensor and Humidity Sensor classes.

We consider inheritance mechanisms in greater depth in Chapter 29.

24.6   Classes for courses

We can end this introductory chapter by acknowledging that classes take different forms, and serve different purposes. More generally still, classes fit into a spectrum of data types that are used in C++ programming.

Table 24.1 summarizes the position. We consider further examples of these various data types, and the details of their implementation, in later chapters.

Data type	Comments	C++ example
Base type	One of the built-in types in the language. C++ supports two basic sets of types: integer types, and floating-point types. The language also supports modified types, including pointers and characters. Together, these are all classified as base types.	`int`

Simple data type	A simple data type (SDT) can be classified as a user-defined data type that must be handled differently from a base type. Notable examples are enumerated types and (most	`struct sHourly`
		`{`
		`int hours;`
		`float hourly_rate;`
		`};`

Table 24.1 A comparison of the different kinds of data types used in C++ programs.

struct-based types and union-based types. These are all created by the programmer but, in general, cannot be manipulated (for example, they cannot be added together using the + operator) in the same way as the base types.

Integrated data type   Integrated data types (IDTs) are class-based variables. They can be (if necessary) created so that they are as convenient to use as the base types: for example, they employ operator overloading to allow use of the stream insertion operator in the same way that this operator is used with integers. Usually this category will include mainly basic, general-purpose program components, such as arrays, linked lists, stacks, string classes, and so on.

```
template <class Type, int Size>
class cArray
{
  public:
    cArray();
    cArray(const cArray&);
    ~cArray();
    Type& operator[](int);
    int size() const;
  private:
    Type* _start_PTR;
    int _size;
};
```

Abstract data type   Abstract data types (ADTs) are a special kind of integrated data type. Instances of these types (that is, objects) model an object in the real world in code. Thus, we might have a customer ADT, or a keyboard ADT.

```
class cHumidity_Sensor
{
  public:
    void turn_off();
    void show();
  private:
    int _humidity;
    eBool _status;
};
```

Table 24.1   *Continued.*

24.7   Conclusions

Object-oriented methods require, as we began to see in this chapter, a new way of thinking about a problem, and, hence, a new way of implementing a solution. Change is always a concern. At the mention of objects, many software engineers become uncomfortable, worried that their past experience and skills – the very things that make them employable – are being relegated to history books. Similarly, project managers are concerned by the growing interest in objects, worried that the use of objects may require a substantial investment in retraining staff. Managers are also concerned that if they don't immediately adopt object-oriented techniques, they may lose ground to their competitors, and that if – on the other hand – the claimed advantages for object-oriented techniques prove ultimately unfounded, any investment in retraining, or the use of objects on substantial projects, may prove to have been a very costly mistake.

There are no easy answers to such concerns, except perhaps to repeat that there is no 'right' way to develop software; in many substantial modern projects, a mixture of the three basic approaches described in this book will be adopted. In addition, even if the whole world were to decide unanimously that, from tomorrow, all new projects were to be constructed solely using object-oriented techniques, then the necessary legislation could not act retrospectively: that is to say, legacy software systems would retain their process- or data-oriented nature, and would still have to be maintained. Perhaps the only, rather trite, advice that can be given both to software engineers and their managers is: objects are here to stay, and you can't afford to ignore them, but neither should you put all your eggs in one object-oriented basket.

Finally, while acknowledging that objects introduce some new ways of thinking, it is also important to appreciate that object-oriented programming builds on techniques we have hitherto discussed, notably functions and data structures. In addition, object-oriented software development uses many of the same notations and methods used in process-oriented and data-oriented software development. In a nutshell, we can say that object-oriented methods do the following for the C++ user:

- They provide a way of linking functions and `structs` together into classes.
- They allow a new inheritance relationship to be used between class-derived variables that was unavailable for `struct`-derived variables.

If you are familiar with process-oriented and data-oriented software development methods then, when you start 'moving to objects', the territory will be new but you'll be stepping into a different country, not onto a different planet.

Exercises

24.1 Explore Program 24.1, and ensure you understand how the program operates.

24.2 Add a new member function (`double_num()`) to `cFirstClass` (Program 24.1) that doubles the private data member _Num. Modify the program to make use of this new member function.

24.3 Add another new member function (`get_num()`) to `cFirstClass` in Program 24.1, that will return (using the return statement) the value of the private data member _Num. Again, modify the program to make use of this new member function.

24.4 Try to write an equivalent `struct` and (ordinary) function code to emulate `cFirstClass` (Program 24.1).

24.5 Thinking purely in terms of the speed of your programs, do you think forcing the user to access all data through a function call is 'A Good Thing'? Explain your answer.

24.6 Explore the operation of the mailing list program (Program 24.2). Try to understand the basic structure of the program: note that we return to consider the details of operator overloading in later chapters.

25 Encapsulation

25.1 Introduction

As we saw in Chapter 24, encapsulation is the foundation upon which object-oriented software development is built. In this chapter, we'll explore the mechanisms C++ provides to support the encapsulation process in much greater depth.

The early parts of the chapter are devoted to the topics of constructor and destructor functions. We then examine error handling in object-oriented programs, and conclude with a more realistic example to integrate and illustrate the material from this chapter.

25.2 Constructor functions

Typically, when we have complex data types, we wish to initialize the data at the start of the program. Sometimes we wish to simply initialize all data to the same value (typically 0), while on other occasions we may wish to use a more complex initialization routine involving dynamic memory allocation. To perform such tasks, C++ provides **constructor functions**.

Constructor functions play a central role in the manufacture of new data types. We consider how to write and use such functions in this section, and build on this material in the remainder of this chapter.

25.2.1 First example

We begin by considering a simple class with a constructor function (Program 25.1).

```
// A class example using a constructor
// Source is: 25_01.CPP

#include <iostream.h>

class cClass
    {
    public:
            cClass(); // The constructor function
        void Show_Num() const;
    private:
```

```
            int _Num;
     };
// Member functions
cClass::cClass()
     {
     cout << "Constructing a cClass object" << endl;
     _Num = 9999;
     }
void cClass::Show_Num() const
     {
     cout << "Number is " << _Num;
     }
int main()
     {
     // Create an object of type cClass
     cClass Object;
     // Call the show member function
     Object.Show_Num();

     return 0;
     }
```

Program 25.I Using constructor functions. (☺)

Program 25.1 produces the following output:

```
Constructing a cClass object
Number is 9999
```

The first thing to note from Program 25.1 is that the constructor function must have the same name as the class 'for which it constructs'; thus, here, the constructor function is called `cClass()`.

The next thing to note is that the constructor function is never *explicitly* called: that is, there is no function call:

```
Object.cClass();
```

In fact, if there was such a call, then the program would *not* compile.

Instead, the constructor function is only (usually) called implicitly, automatically, every time we create an instance of the associated class. Thus, the call to the constructor function is generated by the line:

```
cClass Object;
```

If we changed `main()` to the following:

```
int main()
     {
     cClass 01,02,03;
     return 0;
     }
```

then the output would become:

```
Constructing a cClass object
Constructing a cClass object
Constructing a cClass object
```

Finally, note that the constructor function cannot return a value (not even void). This makes sense. We never explicitly call the function, and having a return value could make all object definitions both clumsy and different from the definition of base types. In addition, as we see towards the end of this chapter, return values are generally not used for error detection or error correction in member functions. The reasons for this, along with alternative error-detection techniques, will be discussed in Section 25.7.

25.2.2 Constructor functions with parameters

Note that constructor functions can also take parameters; we demonstrate this in Program 25.2.

```
// A class example using a constructor with parameters
// Source is: 25_02.CPP
#include <iostream.h>
class cClass
    {
    public:
            cClass(const int); // Constructor with parameter
        void Show_Num() const;
    private:
        int _Num;
    };
cClass::cClass(const int NUMBER)
    {
    cout << "Constructing a cClass object (" << NUMBER << ")" << endl;
    _Num = NUMBER;
    }
void cClass::Show_Num() const
    {
    cout << "Number is " << _Num << endl;
    }
int main()
    {
    // Create 2 objects of type cClass
    cClass Object1(999); // 'Explicit' constructor function call
    cClass Object2 = 111; // 'Implicit' constructor function call

    // Display the private data for each object
    Object1.Show_Num();
    Object2.Show_Num();

    return 0;
    }
```

Program 25.2 Demonstrating constructor functions with parameters. (☺)

Program 25.2 produces the following output:

```
Constructing a cClass object (999)
Constructing a cClass object (111)
Number is 999
Number is 111
```

Note the two different ways in which the parameter is passed to the objects at the time they are created:

```
cClass Object1(999); // 'Explicit' constructor function call
cClass Object2 = 111; // 'Implicit' constructor function call
```

In the 'implicit' case we can supply only a **single** parameter: if the constructor requires two or more parameters, the explicit constructor call form must be used.

Note also that if we modify the class so as to give the constructor a **default value**:

```
class cClass
    {
    public:
            cClass(const int = 0); // Constructor with parameter
        void Show_Num() const;
    private:
        int _Num;
    };
```

then we can create two objects of this class as follows:

```
// Create 2 objects of type cClass
cClass Object1;
cClass Object2 = 111;
```

Note that we do not need brackets in the first case: in fact, if you do type

```
cClass Object1();
```

then (in this case) the program will not compile.

25.2.3 Overloading constructor functions

Just like ordinary functions, we can overload constructor functions; in fact, as we will see in Section 25.2.4, it is usually very important that we do so.

Overloaded constructors are illustrated in Program 25.3.

```
// A class example using an overloaded constructor
// Source is: 25_03.CPP
#include <iostream.h>
class cClass
    {
    public:
            cClass();           // Default constructor
            cClass(const int); // Overloaded constructor
        void Show_Num() const;
```

```
    private:
        int _Num;
    };

// Member functions
cClass::cClass()
    {
    cout << "Constructing a cClass object (default)" << endl;
    _Num = 9999;
    }

cClass::cClass(const int NUMBER)
    {
    cout << "Constructing a cClass object (" << number << ")" << endl;
    _Num = number;
    }

void cClass::Show_Num() const
    {
    cout << "Number is " << _Num << endl;
    }

int main()
    {
    // Create 2 objects of type cClass
    cClass Object1;
    cClass Object2(3);

    // Display the private data for each object
    Object1.Show_Num();
    Object2.Show_Num();

    return 0;
    }
```

Program 25.3 A class example using an overloaded constructor. (☺)

Program 25.3 produces the following output:

```
Constructing a cClass object (default)
Constructing a cClass object (3)
Number is 9999
Number is 3
```

Here, with the statements:

```
cClass Object1;
cClass Object2(3);
```

we can call the overloaded constructor functions, passing no parameters and a single parameter respectively. Note that constructors which take no parameters, as in the first case here, are usually known as **default constructors**.

We see further important uses for overloaded constructor functions when we consider arrays of objects in the next subsection, and copy constructors in Section 25.4.3.

25.2.4 Problem with arrays

Creating an array of objects is generally straightforward. Program 25.4 shows a simple case.

```
// Arrays and constructors - v1.0
// Source is: 25_04.CPP

#include <iostream.h>

class cClass
    {
    public:
            cClass(const int = 999); // The (default) constructor
        void Show_Num() const;
    private:
        int _Num;
    };

cClass::cClass(const int NUMBER)
    {
    cout << "Constructing a cClass object (" << number << ") " << endl;
    _Num = NUMBER;
    }

void cClass::Show_Num() const
    {
    cout << "Number is " << _Num << endl;
    }

int main()
    {
    // Create an array of FOUR objects of type cClass
    cClass Object[4] = {10,20,30}; // Explicitly init THREE elements

    Object[2].Show_Num(); // Display explicitly initialised element
    Object[3].Show_Num(); // Display default initialised element

    return 0;
    }
```

Program 25.4 Building arrays. (☺)

Program 25.4 produces the following output:

```
Constructing a cClass object (10)
Constructing a cClass object (20)
Constructing a cClass object (30)
Constructing a cClass object (999)
Number is 30
Number is 999
```

Here, the array is created in 'the normal way':

```
// Create an array of four objects of type cClass
cClass Object[4] = {10,20,30}; // Explicity init. THREE elements
```

As expected, the constructor function is called four times. In the first three constructor calls, the initial values provided (10, 20, 30) are used: in the fourth case, the default value (999) is used.

What happens, however, if the constructor requires a parameter? Suppose, for example, our class looks like this:

```
class cClass
    {
    public:
            cClass(const int); // Constructor requires parameter
        void Show_Num() const;
    private:
        int _Num;
    };
```

Do we declare our array like this:

```
// Create an array of objects (constructor with parameters)
cClass Object[4](0); // Won't work!!!
```

or like this:

```
// Create an array of objects (constructor with parameters)
cClass Object(0)[4]; // Won't work!!!
```

In fact, neither will work, and we have no way of creating an array of such objects without providing an initial value for **every** element: this is clearly impractical for large arrays.

The bottom line is as follows:

*Only instances of classes with a **default** constructor (that is, a constructor taking no parameters) can be conveniently used in arrays. All well-designed classes should therefore include such a constructor.*

25.3   Being destructive

Constructor functions are designed to facilitate the process of object creation and initialization; **destructor functions** are designed to clean up after we have finished with our objects.

At their most useful, destructor (and constructor) functions are usually associated with dynamic memory allocation. By making appropriate use of constructors and destructors, we can encapsulate the details of our dynamically allocated data types within our objects.

Program 25.5 illustrates the approach.

```
// A class example using a destructor
// Source is: 25_05.CPP
#include <iostream.h>
#include <stdlib.h>
class cDynamic
    {
    public:
            cDynamic(const int = 0); // Constructor
```

```
                    ~cDynamic();            // Destructor
               void show() const;
          private:
               int* _num_PTR;
          };

    cDynamic::cDynamic(const int NUMBER)
          {
          cout << "Constructing a cDynamic object (" <<NUMBER << ")" << endl;
          _num_PTR = new int;

          if (_num_PTR == 0)
             {
             cerr << "Unable to allocate memory - aborting program\n";
             exit(1);
             }
          else
             {
             *_num_PTR = NUMBER;
             }
          }
    cDynamic::~cDynamic()
          {
          cout << "Destructing a cDynamic object\n";
          delete _num_PTR;
          _num_PTR = 0;
          }
    void cDynamic::show() const
          {
          cout << "number is " << *_num_PTR << endl;
          }
    int main()
          {
          cDynamic Object1, Object2(3);
          // Display the private data for each object
          Object1.show();
          Object2.show();

          // NOTE - destructor is never (apparently) called...
          return 0;
          }
```

Program 25.5 A class example using a destructor. (☺)

Program 25.5 produces the following output:

```
Constructing a cDynamic object (0)
Constructing a cDynamic object (3)
number is 0
number is 3
Destructing a cDynamic object
Destructing a cDynamic object
```

It is important to note, as shown by Program 25.5, that the destructor function is not explicitly called by the programmer; this call is carried out implicitly when the object goes out of scope.

In this case, going out of scope means that the program is at an end; of course, this will not always be the case. If we add an artificial program block to our code (as first discussed in Chapter 6):

```
int main()
    {
    cout << "Entering main()" << endl;
    cDynamic Object1;

    // Program block
        {
        cout << "Entering block" << endl;
        cDynamic Object1;
        cout << "Leaving block" << endl;
        }

    cout << "Leaving main()" << endl;
    return 0;
    }
```

then the output reveals that the 'within block' objects are 'destructed' as soon as they are out of scope:

```
Entering main()
Constructing a cDynamic object (default)
Entering block
Constructing a cDynamic object (default)
Leaving block
Destructing a cDynamic object
Leaving main()
Destructing a cDynamic object
```

25.4 Functions, objects and copies

As we shall see in Chapter 31, 'pure' object-oriented languages, like Smalltalk, do not provide support for ordinary functions – all the functions must be member functions. We can often adopt a similar philosophy in our C++ programs; however, there are times – for example, we create associative relationships between classes (see Chapter 26) – that it is impossible to fully embrace this approach. In these circumstances, our class-derived data structures will be used in programs along with ordinary functions; clearly, we need to be able to make the classes and functions 'talk to' one another.

New C++ programmers are sometimes surprised to realize that objects can be passed to function arguments just as easily as other data types. To do so, you simply need to declare the function's parameter as a class type, and then use an appropriate object of the class as an argument when calling the function.

However, there are a few pitfalls awaiting the unwary. As we see below, you need a good understanding of constructor and destructor functions to avoid unexpected hiccoughs in your code when mixing objects and ordinary functions.

25.4.1 Passing objects by reference

We begin (for reasons that will become clear) by looking at passing objects to functions by reference; this is illustrated in Program 25.6.

```
// Passing objects to functions by reference
// Source is: 25_06.CPP
#include <iostream.h>
class cClass
    {
    public:
            cClass() { cout << "Construct!" << endl; }
            ~cClass() { cout << "Destruct!" << endl; }
        void set(const int);
        void show() const;
    private:
        int _num;
    };
void cClass::set(const int NUMBER)
    {
    _num = NUMBER;
    }
void cClass::show() const
    {
    cout << "number is " << _num << endl;
    }
int Ordinary_Function(cClass&);
int main()
    {
    cClass Object;
    Object.set(9);
    Object.show();
    Ordinary_Function(Object);
    Object.show();
    return 0;
    }
int Ordinary_Function(cClass& FunctionObject_REF)
    {
    cout << "Just entered function\n";
    FunctionObject_REF.set(30);
    FunctionObject_REF.show();
    cout << "Just about to leave function\n";
    return 0;
    }
```

Program 25.6 A simple class passed to a function by reference. (☺)

Program 25.6 produces the following output:

```
Construct!
number is 9
Just entered function
number is 30
Just about to leave function
number is 30
Destruct!
```

The operation of this program is straightforward and hold no surprises: the object is passed by reference to the function, and the value assigned to the private data member remains in force in `main()`.

25.4.2   Passing objects by value

As with other data types, objects are passed to functions by value (unless you specify otherwise). Program 25.7 gives an example of an object passed to a function by value.

```cpp
// Passing objects to functions by value
// Source is: 25_07.CPP

#include <iostream.h>

class cClass
    {
    public:
                cClass() { cout << "Construct!" << endl; }
                ~cClass() { cout << "Destruct!" << endl; }
        void set(const int);
        void show() const;
    private:
        int _num;
    };
void cClass::set(const int NUMBER)
    {
    _num = NUMBER;
    }
void cClass::show() const
    {
    cout << "number is " << _num << endl;
    }
int Ordinary_Function(cClass);

int main()
    {
    cClass Object;

    Object.set(9);
    Object.show();

    Ordinary_Function(Object);
```

```
        Object.show();
        return 0;
        }

   int Ordinary_Function(cClass FunctionObject)
        {
        cout << "Just entered function\n";

        FunctionObject.set(30);
        FunctionObject.show();

        cout << "Just about to leave function\n";
        return 0;
        }
```

Program 25.7 A simple class, this time passed to a function by value. (☹)

Program 25.7 produces the following output:

```
    Construct!
    number is 9
    Just entered function
    number is 30
    Just about to leave function
    Destruct!
    number is 9
    Destruct!
```

Looking at the output from Program 25.7 highlights an important point: when we pass an object to a function, we pass a copy of the object, not the original. Since a new object must thus be created, we might expect the constructor function to be called. As the example above illustrates, this does not happen. (You may like to compare this output with the output from Program 25.6).

If you consider what is happening in this situation, then this makes sense. A constructor function is intended (and usually does) initialize the associated object; in many cases, this could mean – for example – assigning all data value to zero. When passing an object to a function, we want the *current* values of any data elements to be available within the function, not the initial values: calling the constructor function would usually be disastrous.

By contrast, note that our function call (or, more accurately, returning from the function call) does call the destructor function. This is, usually, a good idea, since it can 'tidy up' after the copy of our object is no longer required. Note, however, that care must be taken with some destructor functions, particularly those dealing with dynamic memory allocation. Here, if the copy of the data frees up the memory allocated for the *original* object, then the original may be damaged (and is effectively rendered useless) by the function call.

There are two solutions to this problem. The object can be passed to the function by reference, as we saw in Section 25.4.1. More generally, we can use a copy constructor (described in 25.4.3). We illustrate the second possibility in Section 25.5, after we have considered some other problems that occur during simultaneous copying and construction.

25.4.3 More problems with copied objects

The copying problems we have highlighted above in the context of function calls don't simply apply to functions: they are much more widespread. Consider Program 25.8.

```cpp
// More problems with copied objects
// Source is: 25_08.CPP
#include <iostream.h>
#include <stdlib.h>
class cDynamic
    {
    public:
                cDynamic(const int = 0); // Constructor
                ~cDynamic();                // Destructor
            int  show() const;
            void set(const int);
        private:
            int* _num_PTR;
    };
cDynamic::cDynamic(const int NUMBER)
    {
    cout << "\n*** Constructing a cDynamic object ("
        << NUMBER << ") ***\n\n";
    _num_PTR = new int;
    if (_num_PTR == 0)
        {
        cerr << "Unable to allocate memory - aborting program\n";
        exit(1);
        }
    else
        {
        *_num_PTR = NUMBER;
        }
    }
cDynamic::~cDynamic()
    {
    cout << "\n*** Destructing a cDynamic object ***\n\n";
    delete _num_PTR;
    _num_PTR = 0;
    }
int cDynamic::show() const
    {
    return *_num_PTR;
    }
void cDynamic::set(const int I)
    {
    *_num_PTR = I;
    }
int  main()
    {
```

```
cDynamic Object1(9);
// Anonymous block
    {
    cDynamic Object2 = Object1; // Copy object 1??

    cout << "Object1 : " << Object1.show();

    cout << "\n\nSetting Object2 private data to 4\n";
    Object2.set(4);

    cout << "Object2 : " << Object2.show() << endl;
    }
cout << "Object1 : " << Object1.show() << endl;
return 0;
}
```

Program 25.8   A class example using a destructor – v2.0. (☹)

Program 25.8 produces the following output:

```
*** Constructing a cDynamic object (9) ***

Object1 : 9

Setting Object2 private data to 4
Object2 : 4

*** Destructing a cDynamic object ***

Object1 : 772

*** Destructing a cDynamic object ***
```

Although this example is rather contrived, it does illustrate a key point. In Program 25.8 the line:

```
cDynamic Object2 = Object1; // Copy object 1??
```

does *not* invoke the cDynamic class constructor function: instead, both objects share an area of (free store) memory. The destruction of Object2 as it passes out of scope *does*, however, invoke the corresponding destructor, hereby returning the block of memory (still occupied by Object1) to the free store. This means that Object1 is rendered useless as a side-effect of Object2 going out of scope.

We'll see a general and flexible solution to this problem in the next section.

25.5   Copy constructors

In the last section we saw that, in situations where we need to simultaneously 'construct' a new object, and at the same time copy the (data) members from an existing object, a constructor function is *not* invoked. As we have discussed, this may well lead to disastrous side effects if the class contains a destructor (which is used to return memory to free store).

Of course, we could work around this problem. For a start, we could lay down a company coding guideline specifying that O-O programs should use only call by reference (and constant call by reference) and should never use call by value. However, even if we could come up with a complete set of 'rules' to cover these situations, this would seem to be a rather unsatisfactory solution. Generally, we wish to avoid having to 'think differently' when we use class-based variables: we wish to be able to use such variables in the *same* way that instances (variables) of the built-in types are used.

In fact, there is an elegant solution that will allow us to solve all the problems from Section 25.4: the solution is known as a *copy constructor*. Copy constructors are special constructor functions which are invoked *only* during simultaneous copy and construction operations.

For example, consider Program 25.9.

```cpp
// A class example using a copy constructor
// Source is: 25_09.CPP
#include <iostream.h>
#include <stdlib.h>
class cDynamic
    {
    public:
                cDynamic(const int = 0);   // Default constructor
                cDynamic(const cDynamic&); // Copy constructor
                ~cDynamic();               // Destructor
        int   Show_Num() const;
        void Set_Num(const int);
    private:
        int* _Num_PTR;
    };
cDynamic::cDynamic(const int NUMBER)
    {
    cout << "*** Constructing a cDynamic object ("
        << NUMBER << ") ***\n";
    _Num_PTR = new int;
    if (_Num_PTR == 0)
        {
        cerr << "Unable to allocate memory - aborting program\n";
        exit(1);
        }
    else
        {
        *_Num_PTR = NUMBER;
        }
    }
cDynamic::cDynamic(const cDynamic& 0_REF)
    {
    cout << "*** Copy constructing a cDynamic object ***\n";
    _Num_PTR = new int;
    if (_Num_PTR == 0)
        {
        cerr << "Unable to allocate memory - aborting program\n";
        exit(1);
        }
    else
```

```
                {
                *_Num_PTR = *(O_REF._Num_PTR);
                }
            }
    cDynamic::~cDynamic()
            {
            cout << "*** Destructing a cDynamic object ***\n";
            delete _Num_PTR;
            _Num_PTR = 0;
            }
    int cDynamic::Show_Num() const
            {
            return *_Num_PTR;
            }
    void cDynamic::Set_Num(const int I)
            {
            *_Num_PTR = I;
            }
    // Ordinary function prototype
    int Ordinary_Function(cDynamic);
    int main()
            {
            // Create a cDynamic object
            cout << "About to create new object\n";
            cDynamic one;
            one.Set_Num(1); // Set value of private data
            // Create new object
            cout << "\nAbout to create new (copy) object\n";
            cDynamic two(one); // Explicit call of copy constructor
            // Create new object
            cout << "\nAbout to create new (copy) object\n";
            cDynamic three = two; // Implicit call of copy constructor
            cout << "\nAbout to call Ordinary_Function() by value\n";
            Ordinary_Function(two);
            cout << "\nAbout to try ordinary object copy…\n";
            three = one;
            cout << "\nAbout to leave main()\n";
            return 0;
            }
    int Ordinary_Function(cDynamic FunctionObject)
            {
            cout << "Just entered ordinary function\n";
            FunctionObject.Set_Num(30);
            FunctionObject.Show_Num();
            cout << "Just about to leave ordinary function\n";
            return 0;
            }
```

Program 25.9 Solving (most) problems with constructor functions. (~☺)

The output from Program 25.9 is as follows:

```
About to create new object
*** Constructing a cDynamic object (0) ***

About to create new (copy) object
*** Copy constructing a cDynamic object ***

About to create new (copy) object
*** Copy constructing a cDynamic object ***

About to call Ordinary_Function() by value
*** Copy constructing a cDynamic object ***
Just entered ordinary function
Just about to leave ordinary function
*** Destructing a cDynamic object ***

About to try ordinary object copy...

About to leave main()
*** Destructing a cDynamic object ***
*** Destructing a cDynamic object ***
*** Destructing a cDynamic object ***
```

In Program 25.9 the copy constructor takes the following form:

```
cDynamic::cDynamic(const cDynamic& O_REF)
    {
    cout << "*** Copy constructing a cDynamic object ***\n";
    _Num_PTR = new int;
    if (_Num_PTR == 0)
        {
        cerr << "Unable to allocate memory - aborting program\n";
        exit(1);
        }
    else
        {
        *_Num_PTR = *(O_REF._Num_PTR);
        }
    }
```

First of all, it is important to note that there is nothing very unusual about copy constructors: they are simply a useful example of the general overloaded constructor functions we first considered in Section 25.2.3. These functions are called whenever an cDynamic object is simultaneously created and the values of its hidden data members copied from an existing cDynamic object.

Thus, while the lines:

```
// Create a couple of cDynamic objects
cout << "About to create two new objects\n";
cDynamic one, two;
```

call the ordinary constructor functions (as before), the copy constructor is called (explicitly) with the lines:

```
// Create new object
cout << "\nAbout to create new (copy) object\n";
cDynamic two(one); // Explicit call of copy constructor
```

The copy constructor is used here in exactly the same way as other constructor functions. Similarly, as we required, the following function call (by value) also invokes the copy constructor:

```
cout << "\nAbout to call Ordinary_Function() by value\n";
Ordinary_Function(two);
```

Less obvious is the fact that the following lines also invoke the copy constructor:

```
// Create new object
cout << "\nAbout to create new (copy) object\n";
cDynamic three = two; // Implicit call of copy constructor
```

Here, as we have seen, use of the copy constructor is necessary, and the language is designed to meet this requirement.

Finally, note that our class is still not complete. For example, while we can write:

```
cDynamic three = two;
```

we cannot write the 'equivalent' version:

```
cDynamic three;
three = two;
```

In this last fragment, the first line will invoke an ordinary constructor function (as required); however, the second line requires an **overloaded assignment operator** in order to operate correctly. When such an operator is not included in the class, no constructor is invoked. For example, see the output from Program 25.9 in response to the lines:

```
cout << "\nAbout to try ordinary object copy…\n";
three = one;
```

Thus, in most well-designed classes, we require both a copy constructor function, and an overloaded assignment operator: we'll consider various overloaded operators in Chapter 27.

25.6 Example: A new array type

As we have seen on numerous occasions, C++ has a primitive array representation, based on pointers. This array representation is very efficient and flexible: however, it is also error-prone. A particularly common "out of bounds" error arises because it is easy for the programmer to, say, declare an array with 20 elements:

```
int Array[20];
```

then subsequently try to access array element 21:

```
Array[20] = 5; // This is element 21!
```

We therefore use the O-O features we have considered so far to develop a new, better, array data type. To make this data type useful, we make extensive use of the constructor and destructor functions we've been exploring in this chapter.

Program 25.10 shows the array class in operation.

```cpp
// A new dynamic array data type
// Source is: 25_10.CPP

#include <iostream.h>
#include <stdlib.h>

class cIntArray
    {
    public:
                cIntArray(const int=1);       // Constructor
                cIntArray(const cIntArray&);  // Copy constructor
                ~cIntArray();                 // Destructor
        int&  Access(const int);
        int   Get_Size() const;
    private:
        int*  _Start_PTR;
        int   _Size;
    };

cIntArray::cIntArray(const int SIZE)
    {
    cout << " Using normal constructor\n";
    _Size = SIZE;

    if (_Size < 1)
        {
        cerr << "\n*** Array size " << _Size << " can't be created. ***\n";
        exit(1);
        }
    else
        {
        _Start_PTR = new int[_Size];

        if ( _Start_PTR == 0)
            {
            cerr << "\n*** Unable to allocate memory - aborting ***\n"
            exit(1);
            }
        else
            {
            // Initialize new array
            for (int i = 0; i < _Size; i++)
                {
                _Start_PTR[i] = 0;
                }
            }
        }
    }
```

```cpp
// Copy constructor
cIntArray::cIntArray(const cIntArray& A)
    {
    cout << " Using copy constructor\n";
    _Size = A._Size;
    // Memory is allocated for the copy
    _Start_PTR = new int[A._Size];
    if(! _Start_PTR)
      {
      cout << "ERROR!";
      exit(1);
      }
    for (int i = 0; i < A._Size; i++)
      {
      _Start_PTR[i] = A._Start_PTR[i];
      }
    }
cIntArray::~cIntArray()
    {
    cout << " Using destructor\n";
    delete [] _Start_PTR;
    _Start_PTR = 0;
    }
int& cIntArray::Access(const int I)
    {
    if ((I < 0) || (I >= _Size))
      {
      cerr << "\n*** Array out of bounds error ***\n";
      exit(1);
      }
    return (_Start_PTR[I]);
    }
int cIntArray::Get_Size() const
    {
    return (_Size);
    }
// Prototype
int display_array(cIntArray);
int main()
    {
    // Create a couple of arrays
    cout << "About to create two new arrays\n";
    cIntArray one(4), two(3);
    one.Access(1) = 2; // Set values of some elements
    two.Access(2) = 999;
    // Create new array
    cout << "About to create new (copy) array\n";
    cIntArray three = one;
```

```
        cout << "About to call display_array()\n";
        display_array(one);
        cout << "About to call display_array()\n";
        display_array(three);

        cout << "About to leave main()\n";
        return 0;
        }
    int display_array(cIntArray ArrayObject)
        {
        cout << "Just entered display_array()\n";

        for (int i = 0; i < ArrayObject.Get_Size(); i++)
          {
          cout << " Element " << i << " = "
              << ArrayObject.Access(i) << endl;
          }

        cout << "Just leaving display_array()\n";
        return 0;
        }
```

Program 25.10 A new array class with copy constructor. (☺)

Program 25.10 produces the following output:

```
    About to create two new arrays
       Using normal constructor
       Using normal constructor
    About to create new (copy) array
       Using copy constructor
    About to call display_array()
       Using copy constructor
    Just entered display_array()
       Element 0 = 0
       Element 1 = 2
       Element 2 = 0
       Element 3 = 0
    Just leaving display_array()
       Using destructor
    About to call display_array()
       Using copy constructor
    Just entered display_array()
       Element 0 = 0
       Element 1 = 2
       Element 2 = 0
       Element 3 = 0
    Just leaving display_array()
       Using destructor
    About to leave main()
       Using destructor
       Using destructor
       Using destructor
```

This class operates as required. Naturally, if we wished to use it in a practical situation, we would remove the various 'Using ...' messages.

Having made such a change, we could immediately make use of the improved array type in our programs, without difficulty. However, there would be a time penalty in doing so, mainly due to the function call overheads associated with the class. We illustrate this, and the integration of classes into existing programs, in Program 25.11. Note that the intention in this program is not to illustrate the copying operation, but instead simply to make heavy use of each type of array.

```cpp
// Copying simple arrays and class-based arrays
// Compares the speed of each technique.
// Source is: 25_11.CPP

#include <iostream.h>
#include <time.h>
#include <stdlib.h>

class cIntArray
    {
    public:
                cIntArray(const int = 1);      // Constructor
                cIntArray(const cIntArray&);   // Copy constructor
                ~cIntArray();                  // Destructor
        int&  Access(const int);
        int   Get_Size() const;
    private:
        int*  _Start_PTR;
        int   _Size;
    };

cIntArray::cIntArray(const int SIZE)
    {
    _Size = SIZE;
    if (_Size < 1)
        {
        cerr << "\n*** Array size " << _Size << " can't be created. ***\n";
        exit(1);
        }
    else
        {
        _Start_PTR = new int[_Size];
        if ( _Start_PTR == 0)
            {
            cerr << "\n*** Unable to allocate memory - aborting ***\n";
            exit(1);
            }
        else
            {
            // Initialize new array
            for (int i = 0; i < _Size; i++)
                {
```

```
                          _Start_PTR[i] = 0;
                          }
                      }
                  }
              }
    // Copy constructor
    cIntArray::cIntArray(const cIntArray& A)
          {
          _Size = A._Size;

          // Memory is allocated for the copy
          _Start_PTR = new int[A._Size];

          if(! _Start_PTR)
              {
              cout << "ERROR!";
              exit(1);
              }

          for (int i = 0; i < A._Size; i++)
              {
              _Start_PTR[i] = A._Start_PTR[i];
              }
          }

    cIntArray::~cIntArray()
          {
          cout <<"Using destructor\n";
          delete [] _Start_PTR;
          _Start_PTR = 0;
          }

    int& cIntArray::Access(const int I)
          {
          if ((I < 0) || (I >= _Size))
              {
              cerr << "\n*** Array out of bounds error ***\n";
              exit(1);
              }

          return (_Start_PTR[I]);
          }

    int cInteArray::Get_Size() const
          {
          return (_Size);
          }

    int main()
          {
          const int   DIM = 1000;
          const long  NUM_PASSES = 100000;

          int   Orig[DIM] = {0};
          int   Copy[DIM];
          cIntArray Orig2(DIM); // IDT Arrays
          cIntArray Copy2(DIM);
```

```
double    elapsed_time;
time_t    start_time, stop_time; // time_t is defined in time.h

cout << "Starting first calculation - please wait…\n";

// METHOD ONE
start_time = time(NULL);

for (long pass = 0; pass <= NUM_PASSES; pass++)
    {
    for (int i = 0; i < DIM; i++)
        {
        Copy[i] = Orig[i];
        }
    }

stop_time = time(NULL);
elapsed_time = difftime(stop_time, start_time);
cout << "Using normal arrays, time (in seconds) : "
     << elapsed_time << endl;

cout << "Starting second calculation - please wait…\n";

// METHOD TWO
start_time = time(NULL);

for (pass = 0; pass <= NUM_PASSES; pass++)
    {
    for (int i = 0; i < DIM; i++)
        {
        Copy2.Access(i) = Orig2.Access(i);
        }
    }

stop_time = time(NULL);
elapsed_time = difftime(stop_time, start_time);
cout << "Using class-based arrays, time (in seconds) : "
     << elapsed_time << endl;

return 0;
}
```

Program 25.11   Copying normal arrays and class-based arrays. (☺)

The output from Program 25.11 is as follows:

```
Starting first calculation - please wait…
Using normal arrays, time (in seconds) : 16
Starting second calculation - please wait…
Using class-based arrays, time (in seconds) : 74
```

The results vary considerably depending on the compiler and computer used, but the relative differences in performance remain largely fixed. The above output was produced using a Microsoft Visual C++ compiler (v5.0), and was executed on a PC with an Intel Pentuim 100 processor. In the above case, a 'no optimization' option was selected. If full optimization is selected (optimizing for maximum speed), the following results are obtained:

```
Starting first calculation - please wait...
Using normal arrays, time (in seconds) : 7
Starting second calculation - please wait...
Using class-based arrays, time (in seconds) : 12
```

This change results in a dramatic performance improvement: overall, the class-based array is now half as fast (as opposed to 4 times slower) than the ordinary array. (You may like to consider why the ordinary array version speeds up; this has little to do with array itself, and more to do with the associated loops).

Nonetheless, it is clear from the results is that, regardless of the particular compiler options used, the user-defined array carries a speed overhead compared with the ordinary array. Whether such an overhead is significant or not depends on your particular application. If speed of execution is of paramount importance then, with some further tinkering, you may be able to speed up this particular implementation; however, the fact that access to the safe array *requires* a (member) function call is often unavoidable – this call takes time. Even if the access function is placed in line, it still (necessarily) takes time to perform the bounds checking that is our new array's *raison d'être*.

One solution might be to try and allow bounds checking during development (via assertions), and to disable this checking in the final version. Program 25.12 illustrates this approach in action.

```cpp
// Copying simple arrays and class-based arrays
// Compares the speed of each technique.
// Source is: 25_12.CPP

// Fast version with inline Access function & assertions

#define NDEBUG // Switch off assertions

#include <assert.h>
#include <iostream.h>
#include <time.h>
#include <stdlib.h>

class cIntArray
    {
    public:
                        cIntArray(const int = 1);
                        cIntArray(const cIntArray&);
                        ~cIntArray();
        inline int& Access(const int);
                int   Get_Size() const;
    private:
        int* _Start_PTR;
        int  _Size;
    };

cIntArray::cIntArray(const int SIZE)
    {
    _Size = SIZE;
```

```cpp
        if (_Size < 1)
           {
           cerr << "\n*** Array size " << _Size << " can't be created. ***\n";
           exit(1);
           }
        else
           {
           _Start_PTR = new int[_Size];

           if (_Start_PTR == 0)
              {
              cerr << "\n*** Unable to allocate memory - aborting ***\n";
              exit(1);
              }
           else
              {
              // Initialize new array
              for (int i = 0; i < _Size; i++)
                 {
                 _Start_PTR[i] = 0;
                 }
              }
           }
        }

// Copy constructor
cIntArray::cIntArray(const cIntArray& A)
     {
     _Size = A._Size;

     // Memory is allocated for the copy
     _Start_PTR = new int[A._Size];

     if(! _Start_PTR)
       {
       cout << "ERROR!";
       exit(1);
       }

     for (int i = 0; i < A._Size; i++)
        {
        _Start_PTR[i] = A._Start_PTR[i];
        }
     }

cIntArray::~cIntArray()
     {
     delete [] _Start_PTR;
     _Start_PTR = 0;
     }

int& cIntArray::Access(const int I)
     {
     // Precond (bounds checking)
     assert ((I >= 0) && (I < _Size));
```

```
            return (_Start_PTR[I]);
            }
    int cIntArray::Get_Size() const
            {
            return (_Size);
            }
    int main()
            {
            const int   DIM = 1000;
            const long NUM_PASSES = 100000;
            int     Orig[DIM] = {0};
            int     Copy[DIM];
            cIntArray Orig2(DIM); // IDT Arrays
            cIntArray Copy2(DIM);
            double    elapsed_time;
            time_t    start_time, stop_time; // time_t is defined in time.h
            cout << "Starting first calculation - please wait...\n";
            // METHOD ONE
            start_time = time(NULL);
            for (long pass = 0; pass <= NUM_PASSES; pass++)
                {
                for (int i = 0; i < DIM; i++)
                    {
                    Copy[i] = Orig[i];
                    }
                }
            stop_time = time(NULL);
            elapsed_time = difftime(stop_time, start_time);
            cout << "Using normal arrays, time (in seconds) : "
                << elapsed_time << endl;
            cout << "Starting second calculation - please wait...\n";
            // METHOD TWO
            start_time = time(NULL);
            for (pass = 0; pass <= NUM_PASSES; pass++)
                {
                for (int i = 0; i < DIM; i++)
                    {
                    Copy2.Access(i) = Orig2.Access(i);
                    }
                }
            stop_time = time(NULL);
            elapsed_time = difftime(stop_time, start_time);
            cout << "Using class-based arrays, time (in seconds) : "
                << elapsed_time << endl;
            return 0;
            }
```

Program 25.12 Another version of the class-based (IDT) array, this time using assertions for bounds checking. (☺)

Program 25.12 generates the following results, fully optimized, with assertions enabled:

```
Starting first calculation - please wait…
Using normal arrays, time (in seconds) : 7
Starting second calculation - please wait…
Using class-based arrays, time (in seconds) : 12
```

With assertions disabled (in the 'shipping' version), the results are as follows:

```
Starting first calculation - please wait…
Using normal arrays, time (in seconds) : 7
Starting second calculation - please wait…
Using class-based arrays, time (in seconds) : 7
```

As these results reveal, the use of assertions in these circumstances can provide a useful speed saving. In general, it is not practical to 'in line' all member functions, because the resulting executable code would be very large (see pages 191-193). As a result, most 0-0 programs run more slowly than P-0 programs with the same functionality: Stroustrup (1994) suggests that an object-oriented C++ application is likely to run 25% slower than the equivalent application implemented in FORTRAN.

Remember, however, that the particular numbers in this example are not representative of most realistic programs, because (even when arrays are used) the programs will also tend to perform other tasks too. In real programs, therefore, any speed problems will be considerably diluted.

We expand upon this simple data structure in Section 25.7 and extend it further in Chapter 28.

25.7 Dealing with errors

As you will recall, dealing with errors in a process-oriented program could often usefully be accomplished by making use of the return value from the function, as illustrated in Program 25.13.

```
// Program to find the sum of the squares of two numbers
// This time with error detection & recovery
// Source is: 25_13.CPP

#include <iostream.h>
#include <limits.h>

// Function declaration
int Sum_of_Squares5(const int, const int, int&);

int main()
    {
    int Num_1;
    int Num_2;
    int Result;
    do
        {
        cout << "Type first number : ";
```

```
              cin >> Num_1;
              cout << "Type second number : ";
              cin >> Num_2;
              } while (Sum_of_Squares5(Num_1, Num_2, Result));
        return 0;
        }
/************************************************************
* FUNCTION:   Sum_of_Squares5                              *
*                                                          *
* OVERVIEW:   To calculate the sum of the squares          *
*             of A and B (both integers) returning the     *
*             result via reference variable sum_REF        *
*                                                          *
* RETURNS:    0 on normal completion.                      *
*             1 if numbers too large (sum_REF =0)          *
************************************************************/
int Sum_of_Squares5(const int A, const int B, int& sum_REF)
        {
        float test = ((float) A * A) + ((float) B * B);

        if (test > INT_MAX)
            {
            // Numbers too large: can't represent result as int
            cerr << "\n*** Numbers too large! ***\n\n";
            sum_REF = 0;
            return 1;
            }
        else
            {
            sum_REF = (int) test;
            cout << "Sum of squares is : " << sum_REF;
            return 0;
            }
        }
```

Program 25.13 The sum of squares program, using error detection and recovery. (☺)

Program 25.13 generates the following outputs on two sample runs:

```
Type first number : 10
Type second number : 10
Sum of squares is : 200
```

```
Type first number : 1000
Type second number : 1000
*** Numbers too large! ***
Type first number : 100
Type second number : 100
Sum of squares is : 20000
```

As we have seen, while this approach is not universally appropriate, it can prove effective in many process- and data-oriented programs.

When it comes to object-oriented programs, however, a different approach is usually required, and return values from (member) functions are seldom used to code errors. In these circumstances, C++ programmers tend to use a new error handling mechanism, **exception handling**, allowing the management of run-time errors. Unlike the `assert()` macro, the exception handling mechanism is specifically designed to allow (limited) error recovery rather than simple error detection. In addition, while assertions are usually disabled in the final version of a product, exception handling will be employed at all stages of product development – including the version used by the customer.

Exception handling relies on three new keywords: `try`, `catch` and `throw`. In general, the program statements you want to control are contained in what is known as a `try` block. If an error occurs in the `try` block, it is thrown (using `throw`), to a `catch` statement, where it is processed.

This rather vague outline of exception handling is illustrated in Program 25.14.

```cpp
// Program to illustrate exception handling.
// Source is: 25_14.CPP

#include <iostream.h>
#include <string.h>
#include <ctype.h>

int main ()
    {
    char name[80], * ch;
    int age;

    // The user is asked to input the name and age of an
    // employee - exceptions are generated and the program
    // exits if the name or age is not sensible.

    cout << "What is the employee's name? ";
    cin.getline(name, 80);

    cout << "How old are they? ";
    cin >> age;

    try
        {
        if (age < 16) throw -1;
        if (age > 60) throw 1;
        if (strlen(name) == 0) throw 's';
        ch = name;
        while (*ch != '\0')
            {
            if (!isalpha(*ch) && (*ch != ' ')) throw *ch;
            ch++;
            }
        }

    // An integer exception will be thrown if the age input
    // is less than 16 or greater than 60.
    catch (int i)
        {
```

```
            if (i == -1)
                {
                cout << "You are too young to work for us." << endl;
                }
            if (i == 1)
                {
                cout << "You are too old to work for us." << endl;
                }
            // Quit the program.
            return 1;
            }

        catch (char c)
            {
            if (c == 's')
                {
                cout << "No name entered." << endl;
                }
            else
                {
                cout << "Non-alphabetical character " << c
                    << " found." << endl;
                }
            return 1;
            }

        // The program will only reach this point if no exceptions have
        // been found.

        cout << "Employee " << name << " is " << age << " years old" << endl;

        return 0;
        }
```

Program 25.14 Using exceptions. (☺)

Program 25.14 generates the following outputs:

```
What is the employee's name? John
How old are they? 12
You are too young to work for us.
```

```
What is the employee's name? Peter Jones
How old are they? 43
Employee Peter Jones is 43 years old
```

```
What is the employee's name? M.J.Pont
How old are they? 25
Non-alphabetical character . found.
```

Program 25.14 illustrates some of the fundamental technical features of exception handling. In addition, note the following:

- Exception handling is an 'all or nothing' situation: if your program throws an exception that isn't caught, then (by default) your program will be aborted. This may be just the type of behaviour you are trying to avoid.

- If your program uses a class library, then you may need to catch exceptions thrown by this library even if you don't generate exceptions in your own code.

- If you want to catch *all* exceptions, then use `catch(...)`, with the ellipsis (three dots) in the brackets.

Note that exceptions were not an invention of Stroustrup: they've been used in other languages (notably Ada: see Watt *et al.*, 1987) over several years. The general rationale for this approach is that normal processing in a program should be planned, and coded, separately from 'abnormal' or error processing.

In an object-oriented program, however, the approach has an additional signifi-cance. When an error occurs in an ordinary C++ function, one with 'a clearly defined task to perform', then the response to this error may be comparatively straightforward to calculate. For example, if the function `Control_radar_dish_rotation()` returns an error code, it may be a good idea to immediately stop the radar dish rotating any further. Similarly, if the function `Open_database_files()` returns an error, then it may be appropriate to ask the user if the files are stored in a different directory.

However, if the member function of a dynamic array class returns an error, what should be done? Accessing an array may be carried out in any part of a program, and the appropriate response to this error may vary depending on where and when this call originates. For example, suppose your program is creating a dynamic array variable at the start of a program run. In these circumstances, it may be appropriate simply to abort the program, after warning the user to free up some memory (perhaps by closing another active application). However, if the user has already spent two hours typing data into the system before this dynamic array error is detected, then shutting down your program will not be acceptable, however polite the error message may be.

One way of viewing this problem is to consider that the building-blocks of object-oriented programs are classes, not functions: it is therefore more appropriate to consider error handling mechanisms at the level of the *class*, rather than at the level of the function.

As a more realistic example of exception handling, Program 25.15 shows our dynamic array (from earlier in this chapter) with some added exception handling mechanisms, more appropriate for this type of application. Note also the addition of the **private member function** to handle all memory allocation requests.

```
// A new dynamic array data type this time with exceptions
// Note also the appropriate use of a private member function
// Source is: 25_15.CPP
#include <iostream.h>
#include <stdlib.h>
/***************************************************************
****************************************************************
*                                                             *
*  CLASS:      cIntArray                                       *
*                                                             *
*  EXCEPT:     Throws 1 (int) on error                        *
*                                                             *
****************************************************************
****************************************************************
```

```cpp
class cIntArray
    {
    public:
            cIntArray(const int);            // Constructor
            cIntArray(const cIntArray&);     // Copy constructor
            ~cIntArray();                    // Destructor
        int& Access(const int);
        int  Get_Size() const;

    private:
        void New_Memory(); // Group memory handling here

        int* _Start_PTR;
        int _Size;
    };

cIntArray::cIntArray(const int SIZE)
    {
    if (SIZE < 1)
        {
        cerr << "\n*** Array size " << size << " can't be created. ***\n";
        throw 1;
        }
    else
        {
        _Size = SIZE;

        New_Memory(); // Grab memory from free store
        // Initialize new array
        for (int i = 0; i < _Size; i++)
            {
            _Start_PTR[i] = 0;
            }
        }
    }

// Copy constructor
cIntArray::cIntArray(const cIntArray& A)
    {
    _Size = A._Size;

    // Memory is allocated for the copy
    New_Memory();

    // Copy 'old' data to 'new' array
    for (int i = 0; i < _Size; i++)
        {
        _Start_PTR[i] = A._Start_PTR[i];
        }
    }

cIntArray::~cIntArray()
    {
    delete []   _Start_PTR;
    _Start_PTR = 0;
    }
```

```
int& cIntArray::Access(const int I)
    {
    if ((I<0) || (I>= _Size))
        {
        throw 1;
        }
    return ( _Start_PTR[I]);
    }
int cIntArray::Get_Size() const
    {
    return ( _Size);
    }
void cIntArray::New_Memory()
    {
    _Start_PTR = new int[_Size];
    if (!_Start_PTR)
        {
        throw 1;   // Out of memory...
        }
    }
int main()
    {
    try
        {
        // Create an array
        cIntArray one(100);
        one.Access(1) = 1;    // Set values of some elements
        one.Access(99) = 99;
        cout << "Position 1  : " << one.Access(1) << endl;
        cout << "Position 99 : " << one.Access(99) << endl;
        cout << "Position 100 : " << one.Access(100) << endl;
        cout << "Position 7  : " << one.Access(7) << endl;
        }
    catch (...)
        {
        cout << "\n*** An exception has occurred ***";
        return 1;
        }
    return 0;
    }
```

Program 25.15 An array class with exceptions. (☺)

Program 25.15 produces the following output:

```
Position 1   : 1
Position 99  : 99
*** An exception has occurred ***
```

Note that the choice and use of exceptions is a complex process, and requires careful and detailed investigation. We'll see some further examples of this approach to error handling in Chapter 32.

25.8 Guidelines

We can sum up the material in this chapter (and Chapter 24) in the form of some guidelines for developing good classes:

(1)   Like process-oriented and data-oriented software systems, object-oriented systems should be developed with the aim of safeguarding your data as much as possible.

(2)   All the classes in your program should be well encapsulated, with no 'leaks'; your data should always be private (or protected: see Chapter 29), and your member functions should (generally) provide a carefully controlled public interface to these data.

(3)   Private member functions are 'A Good Thing' and can be useful.

(4)   Think of your member functions as accessors or mutators: use (`const`) accessor functions wherever possible.

(5)   Just like ordinary functions, member functions should use call by value (or constant call by reference) whenever possible, and only resort to call by reference, or call by address, when absolutely necessary.

(6)   Always provide a default constructor, or users of your code won't be able to create arrays of your objects.

(7)   If your class involves dynamic memory allocation, or involves a destructor for any other reason, make sure you provide a copy constructor.

(8)   When thinking of errors (and you should be), focus primarily on errors that may affect the class, rather than errors associated with individual member functions.

We build on these guidelines in subsequent chapters.

25.9 Conclusions

In this chapter, we have begun to see some of the benefits of working with objects. We have seen how constructor and destructor functions can be used to make integrated data types useful, particularly when such types involve dynamic memory allocation. We have also seen that a different error detection and correction strategy is usually required in object-oriented programs.

Exercises

25.1   Write a program that passes a `cDynamic` object (Program 25.5) to a function, and changes the value of the object so that this change remains in effect in the calling function.

25.2 Program 25.16 gives an example of an object returned from a function.

```cpp
// Returning an object from a function
// Source is: 25_16.CPP
#include <iostream.h>
class cClass
    {
    public:
            cClass() { cout << "Construct!" << endl; }
            ~cClass() { cout << "Destruct!" << endl; }
        void Set_Num(const int);
        void Show_Num () const;
    private:
        int _Num;
    };
void cClass::Set_Num(const int NUMBER)
    {
    _Num = NUMBER;
    }
void cClass::Show_Num() const
    {
    cout << "number is " << _Num << endl;
    }
cClass Ordinary_Function(cClass);
int main()
    {
    cClass Object;

    Object.Set_Num(9);
    Object.Show_Num();

    (Ordinary_Function(Object)).Show_Num();

    Object.Show_Num();

    return 0;
    }
cClass Ordinary_Function(cClass FunctionObject)
    {
    cout << "Just entered function\n";

    FunctionObject.Set_Num(30);
    FunctionObject.Show_Num();

    cout << "Just about to leave function\n";
    return FunctionObject;
    }
```

Program 25.16 Returning an object from a function. (☺)

Program 25.16 produces the following output:

```
Construct!
number is 9
Just entered function
number is 30
Just about to leave function
Destruct!
number is 30
Destruct!
number is 9
Destruct!
```

As can be seen from the output of Program 25.16, the constructor is not called during the return process; the destructor, however, is called.

Explain why this behaviour is necessary and appropriate. Suggest circumstances in which such behaviour might cause problems.

25.3 Create a class (cMoney) that stores the values, in pounds and pence (both integers) of certain objects. Using member functions, allow the user to modify and display (with appropriate formatting) the values of the private data members. Make appropriate use of exception handling in your class.

25.4 Write a function Add_Money(). Use it to add the values of two cMoney objects (created above) and return the result (as an object) to the calling program. Display the result of the addition from the main program.

25.5 Investigate what happens to Program 25.10 when the copy constructor is omitted.

25.6 If you are familiar with the concept of complex numbers, implement a complex number data type.

25.7 Implement a 2-D version of the array class presented in this chapter. The class should include appropriate exception handling routines.

25.8 We have commented repeatedly on the primitive string data type available in C++. Implement a String data type, based on the 1-D array class discussed in this chapter. Create two strings, called str1 and str2 of this type, and display their contents via the ordinary function Display_String(). The main() function in your final program should appear as follows:

```
int main()
    {
    StringType str1("Hello"), str2("World");

    Display_String(str1);
    Display_String(str2);

    return 0;
    }
```

25.9 Consider the stock control program developed in the case study in Chapter 23. If you were asked to develop an object-oriented version of this program, describe (in general terms) how you think exceptions could be used to minimize loss of data in the event of a hardware error.

26 A first look at class relationships

26.1 Introduction

The majority of our programs to date have contained only a single user-defined class. In a sense, this is akin to writing a process-oriented program using only a single function. In realistic programming situations, tens or hundreds of classes are commonly used. In isolation, however, these classes are still not useful; to make our object-oriented systems productive, we need to establish relationships between classes.

As we see over the next few chapters, there are three fundamental relationships: **aggregation**, **association** and **inheritance**. Here we consider aggregation and association relationships. We consider inheritance in Chapter 29.

Finally, we need to consider the relationship between objects of the same class; we'll conclude this chapter by examining this important topic.

26.2 Aggregations (APO relationships)

Just as functions are the building-blocks of process-oriented programs, classes are the building blocks of object-oriented programs. The simplest way in which these blocks can be joined together is in an aggregation relationship. In such relationships, one class becomes 'A Part Of' another: for this reason, aggregations are often referred to as APO relationships.

In this section, we begin to consider APO relationships.

26.2.1 APO relationships in data-oriented programs

We've already met APO relationships in Part II. For example, consider the `struct`- and `union`-based data structure at the heart of the payroll program presented in Chapter 17 (Program 17.4). As we saw, this data structure can be created either in an 'anonymous' form, or alternatively (and more explicit) in this form:

```
struct sHourly          union uPay              struct sEmployee
  {                       {                       {
  int   hours;            sHourly hourly;         char     surname[20]
  float hourly_rate;      float monthly_salary;   eBoolean hourly_paid;
  };                      };                      uPay     pay;
                                                  };
```

In this explicit form, as we observed in Chapter 17, sEmployee is an aggregate data structure, assembled from the other (user-defined) data structure, uPay and sHourly.

26.2.2 APO relationships in object-oriented programs

APO relationships in object-oriented programs are not significantly different to those seen in data-oriented programs. To illustrate this, Program 26.1 shows an alternative version of the payroll program from Chapter 17 (Program 17.4), this time implemented using classes.

```
// Demonstrating APO relationships
// Source is: 26_01.CPP

#include <iostream.h>
#include <stdlib.h>
#include <iomanip.h>

enum eBoolean{FALSE, TRUE};

class cPay
    {
    public:
        int& hours(){return _pay._hourly._hours;}
        float& hourly_rate(){return _pay._hourly._hourly_rate;}
        float& monthly_salary(){return _pay._monthly_salary;}
    private:
        union // Anonymous
            {
            // Hourly-paid workers
            // Need hours worked, and rate/hour
            struct // Anonymous
                {
                int   _hours;
                float _hourly_rate;
                } _hourly;
            // Salaried workers
            // Just need monthly salary
            float _monthly_salary;
            } _pay;
    };

class cEmployee
    {
    public:
        void Get_pay_data();
        void Print_gross_pay();
    private:
        char      _surname[20];
        eBoolean  _hourly_paid;
        cPay      _pay; // cPay is APO cEmployee
    };

void cEmployee::Get_pay_data()
    {
    char text_str[10];
```

```
    cout << "EMPLOYEE SURNAME : ";
    cin.getline(_surname, sizeof(_surname));

    cout << "Is employee " << _surname << "\n";
    cout << "* Paid by the HOUR (Type 1 <RETURN>)\n";
    cout << "* Paid by SALARY (Type 0 <RETURN>)\n";
    cout << " ? : ";

    // NO error checking…
    cin.getline(text_str, sizeof(text_str));

    if (atoi(text_str))
        {
        _hourly_paid = TRUE;
        }
    else
        {
        hourly_paid = FALSE;
        }

    if(_hourly_paid == TRUE)
        {
        // Hourly-paid employee
        cout << "How many _hours were worked (whole number) : ";
        cin.getline(text_str, sizeof(text_str));
        _pay.hours() = atoi(text_str);

        cout << "What is the hourly rate (ff.pp) : ";
        cin.getline(text_str, sizeof(text_str));
        _pay.hourly_rate() = (float)atof(text_str);
        }
    else
        {
        // Salaried employee
        cout << "What is the monthly salary (ff.pp) : ";
        cin.getline(text_str, sizeof(text_str));
        _pay.monthly_salary() = (float)atof(text_str);
        }
    cout << "\n";
    }

void cEmployee::Print_gross_pay()
    {
    float gross_pay;

    if (_hourly_paid == TRUE)
        {
        gross_pay = _pay.hours() * _pay.hourly_rate();
        }
    else
        {
        gross_pay = _pay.monthly_salary();
        }

    cout << setiosflags(ios::fixed)
```

```
                 << setprecision(2);
         cout << _surname << " £" << gross_pay << "\n";
         }

  int main ()
     {
     int      emp_num;
     cEmployee    payroll[2]; // The payroll "database"

     cout << "Basic Payroll Program\n";
     cout << "--------------- \n\n";

     for (emp_num = 0; emp_num <= 1; emp_num++)
         {
         payroll[emp_num].Get_pay_data();
         }

     cout << "GROSS PAY\n";
     cout << "-------- \n";
     for (emp_num = 0; emp_num <= 1; emp_num++)
         {
         payroll[emp_num].Print_gross_pay();
         }

     cout << "\nPay calculations complete.";

     return 0;
     }
```

Program 26.1   A simple payroll program, this time implemented using classes. (☺)

On a typical run, Program 26.1 generates the following output:

```
Basic Payroll Program

EMPLOYEE SURNAME : Pont
Is employee Pont
* Paid by the HOUR (Type 1 <RETURN>)
* Paid by SALARY (Type 0 <RETURN>)
   ? : 1
How many _hours were worked (whole number) : 150
What is the hourly rate (££.pp) : 0.67

EMPLOYEE SURNAME : Dromgoole
Is employee Dromgoole
* Paid by the HOUR (Type 1 <RETURN>)
* Paid by SALARY (Type 0 <RETURN>)
   ? : 0
What is the monthly salary (££.pp) : 22000.99

GROSS PAY

Pont £100.50
Dromgoole £22000.99

Pay calculations complete.
```

Aggregation relationships are generally straightforward to implement. In this case, the cPay class is simply a part of cEmployee. As the output reveals, the program operates much as the previous version.

We look at ways of identifying APO relationships during the planning phase of projects in Chapter 30.

26.2.3 Initializing member objects

Aggregation relationships are generally straightforward to implement. However, care must be taken when you need to initialize a member object in your class. When you do so, one (or more) of the following conditions must be met:

- The member object's class has no constructor;
- The member object's class has an accessible default constructor;
- The aggregate class's constructor performs an explicit initialization of the contained object.

The first possibility was illustrated in Program 26.1, where the cPay class had no constructor. This, like the second of the three possibilities listed above, is straightforward to implement. We illustrate the third possibility in the code fragment below:

```
class cPoint
    {
    public:
        // No default constructor...
        cPoint(int x, int y) {_x = x; _y = y;}
    private:
        int _x, _y;
    };
class cLine
    {
    public:
        cLine(int, int, int, int);
    private:
        cPoint _Start, _Finish;
    };
// Constructor for cLine.
// Must *explicitly* initialize the component objects
cLine::cLine(int x1, int y1, int x2, int y2)
    : _Start(x1, y1), _Finish(x2, y2)
    {
    }
```

26.3 Associations (NTKA relationships)

The idea of private data tucked away safely inside a class is theoretically comfortable. However, this ideal cannot always be achieved: sometimes, for example, you'll want to be able give a class access to the private members of a different classes. In doing so, you are setting up an **association** between two classes.

An alternative way of viewing this is that associations are relationships which result when one class 'needs to know about' the (private) details of another class. Associations are sometimes therefore referred to as NTKA relationships. Commonly (but not exclusively) NTKA relationships are established using a feature of C++ known as `friend` functions.

In most circumstances, relying on `friend` functions means 'breaking the rules' and circumventing the safeguards that C++ provides to keep your private data private: in this way, `friend` functions are analogous to `goto` statements in process-oriented programs (see Chapter 4). However, like `goto` statements, it can, occasionally, be very useful to have `friend` functions in your code.

We'll consider some examples in this section.

26.3.1 Simple use of `friend` functions

We'll begin with a simple example (Program 26.2).

```
// Simple use of friend functions
// Source is: 26_02.CPP
#include <iostream.h>
class cClass
    {
    public:
                void set(int);      // Member function
        friend void show(cClass); // Friend function
    private:
            int _num;
    };
void cClass::set(int number)
    {
    _num = number;
    }
int main()
    {
    cClass Object;

    Object.set(2001);

    // Call the show friend function
    show(Object);

    return 0;
    }
// Friend (ordinary) function definition
// NB: no scope resolution operator &c
// NB: no mention of "friend" here
void show(cClass Object)
    {
    cout << "Using friend function, number is " << Object._num;
    }
```

Program 26.2 Introducing `friend` functions. (☺)

Program 26.2 produces the following output:

```
Using friend function, number is 2001
```

To highlight the differences between the use of `friend` functions and member functions, consider the equivalent operation carried out using member functions. In the case of member functions, `show()` would be declared as follows:

```
class cClass

    public:
    // Public member function declarations
    void show() const;

    ...
```

and called as follows:

```
// Call the show member function
Object.show();
```

without any function arguments.

Three important points should be highlighted:

- The `friend` function is defined like an ordinary function. It is not a member function and may not be qualified by an object name.

- A `friend` function is called just like the ordinary functions we discussed in Part I.

- In this simple case, there is no relationship established between classes: only one class is involved.

26.3.2 Implementing NTKA relationships between classes

We can (and frequently do) use `friend` functions to implement relationships ('need to know about', or association, relationships) between classes. There are two general ways in which this can be achieved:

- A single ordinary function can be made a `friend` of two different classes.

- A member function in one class can be a `friend` function of another class: in this way, one class is given access to the private data members of a second class.

Program 26.3 gives an example of this first case.

```
// Another use of friend functions
// Here friend is an ordinary function linking two classes
// Source is: 26_03.CPP

#include <iostream.h>

class cClass2; // Forward reference

class cClass1
    {
    public:
            void set(int);
        friend void show(cClass1,cClass2);
```

```
    private:
        int _num;
    };
void cClass1::set(int number)
    {
    _num = number;
    }
class cClass2
    {
    public:
                void set(int);
        friend void show(cClass1, cClass2);
    private:
        int _num;
    };
void cClass2::set(int number)
    {
    _num = number;
    }
int main()
    {
    cClass1 01;
    cClass2 02;

    01.set(2001);
    02.set(1999);

    // Call the show friend function
    show(01,02);

    return 0;
    }
// Friend (ordinary) function definition
void show(cClass1 x, cClass2 y)
    {
    cout << "Friendly sum is " << x._num + y._num;
    }
```

Program 26.3 Linking functions with a mutual friend. (☺)

The output from Program 26.3 is as follows:

```
Friendly sum is 4000
```

Note that here we require a forward reference – that is, with the line:

```
class cClass2; // Forward reference
```

we tell the compiler (in effect) 'there's a class called cClass2 used in this program: I'll give you the details later'. This is necessary because we need to refer to cClass2 in the cClass1 declaration (and vice versa).

Program 26.4 shows a similar case, but in this case one class is made the friend of another class. This grants the friend class access to the private data members of the befriending class.

```cpp
// Another use of friend functions
// Here friend is a member function
// linking two classes
// Source is: 26_04.CPP
#include <iostream.h>
class cClass2; // Forward reference
class cClass1
    {
    public:
                void set(int);
            friend class cClass2;
        private:
            int _num;
        };
void cClass1::set(int number)
    {
    _num = number;
    }
class cClass2
    {
    public:
            void set(int);
            void show(cClass1);
        private:
            int _num;
        };
void cClass2::set(int number)
    {
    _num = number;
    }
void cClass2::show(cClass1 x)
    {
    cout << "Friendly sum is " << x._num + _num;
    }
int main()
    {
    cClass1 01;
    cClass2 02;
    01.set(2001);
    02.set(1999);
    // Call the show friend function
    02.show(01);
    return 0;
    }
```

Program 26.4 Linking functions with a mutual friend (v2.0). (☺)

The output from Program 26.4 is as follows:

```
Friendly sum is 4000
```

Two points should be made regarding C++ `friend` functions:

- Friendship is not a reversible operation. For example, suppose Class A is a friend of Class B. This does *not* (automatically) mean that Class B is a friend of Class A.

- Friendship is not transferable. For example, suppose Class B is a friend of Class A, and Class C is a friend of Class B. This does *not* (automatically) mean that Class C is a friend of Class A.

We have more to say about NTKA relationships in later chapters.

26.4 Relationships between objects

As you make use of class-based variables, you need to understand that such variables have much in common. Just as links between classes form the glue that binds the program together, the relationships between instances of the *same* class can also be important.

26.4.1 Class-based access

Consider what happens when we create two instances of a simple class (Program 26.5).

```cpp
// A simple class and object example revisited
// Source is: 26_05.CPP
#include <iostream.h>
class cClass
    {
    public:
        void set(int number);
        void show() const;
        void copy(cClass);
    private:
        int _num;
    };
void cClass::copy(cClass 0)
    {
    _num = 0._num; // Note that this IS correct!
    }
void cClass::set(int number)
    {
    _num = number;
    }
void cClass::show() const
    {
    cout << "number is " << _num << endl;
    }
```

```
int main()
    {
    cClass 01,02;

    01.set(111);
    01.show();

    02.set(222);
    02.show();

    02.copy(01);
    02.show();

    return 0;
    }
```

Program 26.5 A first simple class and object revisited. (☺)

Program 26.5 produces the following output:

```
number is 111
number is 222
number is 111
```

What this insignificant output implies (correctly) is that any instance of a class has access not only, of course, to its own private members, but also to private members of *other instances of the same class*. The class-based nature of access privileges in C++ is an important feature of the language, and one that is, for example, not shared by Smalltalk.

26.4.2 Static data members

In Program 26.5, while all objects of type cClass had access to the private data members of other instances of this class, each object still had its own set of encapsulated data. Sometimes, however, this is not what we require.

Consider, for example, Program 26.6.

```
// Static data members
// Source is: 26_06.CPP

#include <iostream.h>

class cStaticClass
    {
    public:
        void set(int number);
        void show() const;
    private:
        static int _num;
    };

// Need a separate *definition*
// Note: _num isn't global...
int cStaticClass::_num;

void cStaticClass::set(int number)
```

```
    {
    _num = number;
    }
void cStaticClass::show() const
    {
    cout << "number is " << _num << endl;
    }
int main()
    {
    cStaticClass 01,02,03,04;

    01.show();
    02.show();
    03.show();
    04.show();

    02.set(999);

    01.show();
    02.show();
    03.show();
    04.show();

    return 0;
    }
```

Program 26.6   Using static data members. (☺)

Program 26.6 produces the following output:

```
number is 0
number is 0
number is 0
number is 0
number is 999
number is 999
number is 999
number is 999
```

The first four lines of this output reveal only that static data members are initialized to
0; the remaining four lines reveal that changing the value of the data member in one
object has an impact on *all other objects of that class*. This is because all the objects
share the same (static) variable.

In effect, we have created a 'class global' variable: it is visible to all objects of
that class but not (if it is a private data member) to objects outside the class. This type
of behaviour can be useful in some kinds of error detection scheme.

Note that to create our static data member, we had to include the static modifier
in the class declaration; we also had to include a separate definition of this variable outside the class. The implication is that this static data member will exist for the duration
of the program, even if no instance of class cStaticClass is defined.

We illustrate this last point in Program 26.7.

```
// Static data members 2.0
// Source is: 26_07.CPP

#include <iostream.h>

class cStaticClass2
    {
    public:
        static int _num; // Public data…
    };

int cStaticClass2::_num;

int main()
    {
    // No cStaticClass objects…

    cout << cStaticClass2::_num << endl;
    cStaticClass2::_num = 999;
    cout << cStaticClass2::_num << endl;

    return 0;
    }
```

Program 26.7   More on static data members. (☹)

The output from Program 26.7 is as follows:

```
0
999
```

Program 26.7 only works because the static data member is declared public. Program 26.7 is intended to illustrate only the mechanism underlying static data members; it is difficult to think of a practical use for such variables outwith the class context.

Finally, note that it is also possible to have static member functions: these are rather specialized and won't be considered here (see Stroustrup, 1991, for details).

26.5   Conclusions

The process of object-oriented software development can be split into three overlapping phases:

- determine which classes you require in your programs;
- identify the links between classes;
- implement the linked classes.

In this chapter, we have begun to consider the links between classes, and between instances of a single class. We build on this material throughout the remainder of Part III.

Exercises

26.1 Modify the class `cIntArray` from Chapter 25 so that it can hold a string: call
the new class `cString`. Thus, rework the payroll program (Program 26.1) so
that the main class is as follows:

```
class cEmployee2
    {
    public:
        cEmployee2();
        void Get_Pay_Data();
        void Print_Gross_Pay();
    private:
        cString(25)   _Name;
        eBoolean      _Hourly_paid;
        cPay          _Pay;
    };
```

26.2 Translate the following data types into appropriate C++ classes. Hence develop
an object-based version of the car-parking program in Chapter 21.

```
struct sEmployee
    {
    char  Payroll[STR_SIZE];
    char  Name[STR_SIZE];
    char  Dept[STR_SIZE];
    };
struct sCar
    {
    char        RegNum[STR_SIZE];
    char        Make[STR_SIZE];
    char        Colour[STR_SIZE];
    sEmployee*  Drives_PTR;
    };
```

26.3 Consider the features of class-based access discussed in Section 26.4.1. Hence,
modify the `cIntSafeArray` introduced in Program 25.15 so that it has a
member function `copy()` that allows the contents of one array to be copied to
another. *Note:* consider how you will handle the case where the programmer
tries to copy two arrays of different sizes. You *may* feel it is appropriate to use
an exception handling routine in these circumstances.

26.4 You have been asked to consider the provision of fire-fighting facilities in
London. In particular, you are to develop a simulation of London traffic that
will enable the city Planning Department to determine where the fire stations
should be situated so as to minimize the time taken to reach a fire.

Suppose, as one small part of the simulation, you have decided to create a
fire appliance class (`cFireAppliance`) and a road class (`cRoad`).
Unfortunately, not all London roads are wide enough for larger fire appliances
to drive through: `cFireAppliance` will therefore include details of the size of
the fire appliance, and `cRoad` will include details of the width of the road.
Create first attempts at the `cRoad` and `cFireAppliance` classes, and a suitable
friend function (`Is_Wide_Enough()`) that will allow you to determine whether
a particular fire appliance can travel down a specified road.

27 Polymorphism

27.1 Introduction

Polymorphism is the mechanism that allows creators of classes to make instances of these classes behave in the same way as the base types. Thus, using polymorphism, we can perform operations like those illustrated in the following code fragment:

```
...
cMyClass object1, object2, object3;
...
object1 += object2;
...
cout << object3;
...
```

In the above case, we have exploited C++'s support for polymorphism and overloaded the operators += and <<, enabling us to treat the instances of cMyClass in the same manner as we would, for example, treat integers.

This behaviour is not simply an 'emergent property' of the object-oriented programming process: that is, you have to explicitly code such capabilities in your classes. For this reason, Program 27.1 will not compile.

```
// Automatic operator overloading?
// NOTE: WILL NOT COMPILE!!!
// Source is: 27_01.CPP

#include <iostream.h>

class cMyClass
    {
    public:
        void Set_Num(const int);
    private:
        int _Num;
    };

void cMyClass::Set_Num(const int NUMBER)
    {
```

```
        _Num = NUMBER;
        }
    int main()
        {
        cMyClass Object1, Object2, Object3;
        Object1 += Object2;      // Illegal operation!
        Object3.Set_Num(3);
        cout << Object1 << endl; // Illegal operation!
        cout << Object3 << endl; // Illegal operation!
        return 0;
        }
```

Program 27.1 Polymorphism isn't automatic: operators (here += and <<) must be explicitly overloaded to work with instances of your own classes. (☹)

In this case, the operators += and << 'don't know what to do' with instances of cMyClass, because the programmer has not provided this information. If you attempt to compile this program, you'll be met with a string of errors along the lines of 'illegal operation'.

In this chapter, we examine how the necessary information can be provided to allow operator overloading to take place. As we'll see, some of the results are cosmetic, in the sense that (for example) overloading the stream extraction operator may allow you to display information on the screen in a neat way, but you could have achieved the same result with an appropriate member function. However, the use of overloaded operators does allow us to spread the complexity of a complex program, and can make such programs much easier to understand, debug and maintain. In addition, there are some operators (notably the assignment operator, =) that must generally be overloaded for new classes if we wish our code to be reliable (see Section 27.4).

Before we can begin to consider polymorphism, we first need to consider the this pointer.

27.2 The this pointer

There is one important feature of C++ programs incorporating objects and member functions that we have not yet considered: the this pointer. The this pointer is automatically passed to any member function when it is called; this is a *pointer to the object that generates the call*. Note that only member functions are passed a this pointer: ordinary functions (and friend functions, discussed in Chapter 26) are *not* passed such a pointer.

For example, consider Program 27.2.

```
// A simple class example revisited
// Source is: 27_02.CPP
#include <iostream.h>
class cClass
    {
```

```
        public:
            void Set_Num(const int);
            void Show_Num() const;
        private:
            int _Num;
        };
// Member functions
// Note use of scope resolution operator
void cClass::Set_Num(const int NUMBER)
        {
        _Num = NUMBER;
        }
void cClass::Show_Num() const
        {
        cout << "Number is " << _Num << "\tAddress "
            << "of object is " << (int) this << endl;
        }
int main()
        {
        cClass Objects[4];

        // Call the show member function
        Objects[0].Show_Num();
        Objects[1].Show_Num();
        Objects[2].Show_Num();
        Objects[3].Show_Num();

        return 0;
        }
```

Program 27.2 Demonstrating the `this` pointer. (☺)

Program 27.2 produces the following output:

```
Number is 14847 Address of object is 13546
Number is 13563 Address of object is 13548
Number is 122   Address of object is 13550
Number is 14839 Address of object is 13552
```

As usual, use of the `(unsigned int)` cast operator with pointer addresses is not completely portable (see Chapter 7 for details).

Note the addresses themselves: these differ by two bytes. As we have generated an array of objects, we know that these objects are stored in consecutive memory locations. Thus, each of these objects are two bytes in size; this corresponds (on the machine the program was compiled on) to the size of an integer. These results reveal that only the data fields of our object are repeated in memory. Thus, when we create an object, we do not repeat the code for the member functions and the data: only one copy of each member function will be stored per *class*, elsewhere in memory.

We consider some rather more useful applications for the `this` pointer as we look at operator overloading.

27.3 Overloading binary operators

Program 27.3 shows the basic cMoney class we will build on in this chapter to illustrate the process of operator overloading.

```cpp
// A simple money class
// Source is: 27_03.CPP

#include <iostream.h>

class cMoney
    {
    public:
            cMoney(const int = 0, const int = 0);
        void Show() const;
    private:
        int _Pounds, _Pence;
    };

cMoney::cMoney(const int PO, const int PE)
    {
    _Pounds = PO;
    _Pence = PE;
    }

void cMoney::Show() const
    {
    if (_Pence < 10)
        {
        cout << "£" << _Pounds << ".0" << _Pence;
        }
    else
        {
        cout << "£" << _Pounds << "." << _Pence;
        }
    }

int main()
    {
    cMoney cash(1,03);
    cash.Show();
    return 0;
    }
```

Program 27.3 A simple money class. (☺)

The output from Program 27.3 is as follows:

```
£1.03
```

27.3.1 Overloading the + operator

What we wish to be able to do is, for example, create three money objects, as follows:

```
    cMoney cash1(1,03), cash2(10,03), cash3;
```

then add two of them together in a natural way, as follows:

```
    cash3 = cash1 + cash2;
```

Program 27.4 shows how this can be achieved.

```
// A simple money class
// with overloaded + operator
// Source is: 27_04.CPP
#include <iostream.h>
class cMoney
    {
    public:
                cMoney(const int = 0, const int = 0);
        void    Show() const;
        cMoney operator+(const cMoney&) const;
    private:
        int    _Pounds, _Pence;
    };
cMoney::cMoney(const int PO, const int PE)
    {
    _Pounds = PO;
    _Pence = PE;
    }
void cMoney::Show() const
    {
    if (_Pence < 10)
        {
        cout << "£" << _Pounds << ".0" << _Pence << endl;
        }
    else
        {
        cout << "£" << _Pounds << "." << _Pence << endl;
        }
    }
// Overload + relative to cMoney class
cMoney cMoney::operator+(const cMoney& R_OP) const
    {
    cMoney Sum;

    Sum._Pounds = this->_Pounds + R_OP._Pounds;
    Sum._Pence =*this->_Pence + R_OP._Pence;

    while (Sum._Pence > 99)
        {
        Sum._Pence-=100;
        Sum._Pounds+=1;
        }

    return Sum;
    }
```

```
int main()
    {
    cMoney cash1(1,33), cash2(2,90), cash3, cash4;

    // Explicit call of operator+ function
    cash3 = cash1.operator+(cash2);
    cash3.Show();

    // Implicit call of operator+ function
    cash3 = cash1 + cash2;
    cash3.Show();

    // Can add more than two objects...
    cash4 = cash1 + cash2 + cash3;
    cash4.Show();

    // Can also do this (if you want to...)
    (cash4 + cash4).Show();

    return 0;
    }
```

Program 27.4   Adding an overloaded + operator to the simple money class. (☺)

Program 27.4 produces the following output:

```
£4.23
£4.23
£8.46
£16.92
```

Let's consider what is happening here. First of all, as before, we are creating some cMoney objects with the line:

```
cMoney cash1(1,33), cash2(2,90), cash3, cash4;
```

We are then, in a logical way, able to add together the values of cash1 and cash2 and assigning the result to cash3, which we then display in the usual way:

```
cash3 = cash1 + cash2;
cash3.Show();
```

This makes use of our new overloaded + operator, and assigns the result of the addition operation (itself an object) to cash3. Note that, in fact, we have not overloaded the assignment operator, yet this assignment still works correctly in this case. We consider the implications of this in Section 27.3.2.

Having seen the result of the operator overloading, let's consider how this result is achieved. The first thing to note is that operator overloading resembles function overloading: it is in fact simply a form of function overloading.

The overloaded operator function is as follows:

```
// Overload + relative to cMoney class
cMoney cMoney::operator+(const cMoney& R_OP) const
    {
    cMoney Sum;
```

```
Sum._Pounds = this->_Pounds + R_OP._Pounds;
Sum._Pence = this->_Pence + R_OP._Pence;
while (Sum._Pence > 99)
    {
    Sum._Pence-=100;
    Sum._Pounds+=1;
    }
return Sum;
}
```

For new C++ programmers, the most confusing part of operator functions can be that, apparently, this *binary* operator has only a single formal parameter rather than two:

```
cMoney cMoney::operator+(const cMoney& R_OP) const
    {
    cMoney Sum;

    ...

    return Sum;
    }
```

Where, then, does the other parameter come from? The answer is that – like all member functions – function operators have access to the `this` pointer (discussed in Section 27.2) and that we are therefore able (implicitly) to access both operands.

The way the operator function operates is clearer in the explicit call:

```
// Explicit call of operator+ function
cash3 = cash1.operator+(cash2);
cash3.Show();
```

Though this type of explicit call is not commonly used, it does serve to illustrate the way that data is transferred to the function. As the above fragment makes clear, **the left operand** (here `cash1`) **is the object that generates the operator function call:** it is this operand that is passed implicitly to the function.

When overloading binary operators, you need to remember:

When a binary operator is overloaded, the left operand is passed implicitly to the function (via the `this` *pointer) and the right operand is passed as an argument.*

Thus, when we write:

```
cash3 = cash1 + cash2;
```

the communication illustrated in Figure 27.1 takes place.

Because of this implicit transfer of the left operand, we can in fact write the operator function as follows:

```
// Overload + relative to cMoney class
cMoney cMoney::operator+(const cMoney& R_OP) const
    {
    cMoney Sum;

    Sum._Pounds = _Pounds + R_OP._Pounds;
    Sum._Pence = _Pence + R_OP._Pence;
```

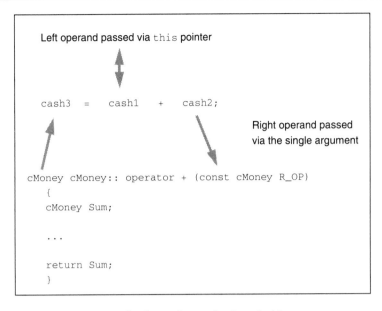

Figure 27.1 Information transfer during the overloading of a binary operator.

```
while (Sum._Pence > 99)
    {
    Sum._Pence-=100;
    Sum._Pounds+=1;
    }

return Sum;
    }
```

Here _Pounds is *conceptually* equivalent to obj1._Pounds, where obj1 is the name of the left operand. Of course _Pounds is *exactly* equivalent to this->_Pounds, as used in the previous version of the function. Sometimes, explicitly including this in your code makes the program easier to understand.

The next thing to note is that we return an object from the function, this object itself being of type cMoney. This is essential to the correct operation of the operator, and also has the side effect that we can enter lines like this:

```
(cash1 + cash2).Show();
```

Here we add cash1 and cash2 again, this time directly calling the Show() member function with the object returned by the operator function.

27.3.2   Overloading the − and = operators

We extend the money class to include an overloaded subtraction operator and an over-loaded assignment operator (Program 27.5).

```cpp
// A simple money class
// with overloaded +,- and = operators
// Source is: 27_05.CPP

#include <iostream.h>

class cMoney
    {
    public:
                cMoney(const int = 0, const int = 0);
        void    Show() const;
        cMoney operator+(const cMoney&) const;
        cMoney operator-(const cMoney&) const;
        cMoney operator=(const cMoney&);
    private:
        int     _Pounds, _Pence;
    };

cMoney::cMoney(const int PO, const int PE)
    {
    _Pounds = PO;
    _Pence = PE;
    }

void cMoney::Show() const
    {
    if (_Pence < 10)
        {
        cout << "£" << _Pounds << ".0" << _Pence << endl;
        }
    else
        {
        cout << "£" << _Pounds << "." << _Pence << endl;
        }
    }

// Overload + relative to cMoney class
cMoney cMoney::operator+(const cMoney& R_OP) const
    {
    cMoney Sum;

    Sum._Pounds = this->_Pounds + R_OP._Pounds;
    Sum._Pence = this->_Pence + R_OP._Pence;

    while (Sum._Pence > 99)
        {
        Sum._Pence-=100;
        Sum._Pounds+=1;
        }

    return Sum;
    }

// Overload - relative to cMoney class
cMoney cMoney::operator-(const cMoney& R_OP) const
```

```
    {
    cMoney Diff;

    Diff._Pounds = this->_Pounds - R_OP._Pounds;
    Diff._Pence = this->_Pence - R_OP._Pence;

    if (Diff._Pence < 0)
        {
        Diff._Pence+=100;
        Diff._Pounds-=1;
        }

    return Diff;
    }

// Overload = relative to cMoney class
cMoney cMoney::operator=(const cMoney& R_OP)
    {
    this->_Pounds = R_OP._Pounds;
    this->_Pence = R_OP._Pence;

    return *this;
    }

int main()
    {
    cMoney cash1(1,33), cash2(2,90), cash3;

    cash3 = cash1 + cash2;
    cash3.Show();

    cash3 = cash2 - cash1;
    cash3.Show();

    cash3 = cash2 = cash1;
    cash1.Show();
    cash2.Show();
    cash3.Show();

    return 0;
    }
```

Program 27.5 The money class, this time with overloaded +, − and = operators. (☺)

Program 27.5 generates the following output:

```
£4.23
£1.57
£1.33
£1.33
£1.33
```

In Program 27.5 the use of the overloaded + and − operators is much as before: note, however, that the overloaded assignment operator is a little different. The reason for this is as follows. When we write:

```
var1 + var2;
```

for any data types, we don't expect either `var1` or `var2` to be changed by the addition operation. Thus, when we are overloading the addition (or subtraction) operators, we generally wish to create a new, temporary, variable (of an appropriate type) within the operator function and return this temporary copy to the calling function. As a consequence of this, we have been able to use the `const` modifier in these cases, thereby treating the overloaded operators as a form of accessor function.

On the other hand, when we write:

```
var1 = var2;
```

we do, of course, expect the value of `var1` to be changed by the assignment operation. As we have seen, when using operator overloading, the left operand is passed via the `this` pointer. If, as here, we wish to change the value of the left operand due to the operation of the operator function, then we can effect this by changing the contents of the memory location pointed to by `this`, as in the example here:

```
// Overload = relative to cMoney class
cMoney cMoney::operator=(const cMoney& R_OP)
    {
    this->_Pounds = R_OP._Pounds;
    this)->_Pence = R_OP._Pence;

    return *this;
    }
```

As in this case above, we could have achieved the same result, and Program 27.5 would still have worked, if we had implemented our overloaded assignment operator as follows:

```
// Overload = relative to cMoney class
void cMoney::operator=(const cMoney& R_OP)
    {
    this->_Pounds = R_OP._Pounds;
    this->_Pence = R_OP._Pence;
    }
```

However, by explicitly returning the contents of `this`, we are able to write expressions of the form:

```
cash3 = cash2 = cash1;
```

and

```
if (cash3 = cash2)
    {
    ...
```

Such expressions are valid for the built-in types; we therefore wish to allow our user-defined types to behave in the same way.

Note that, by default, when the assignment operator is applied to an object, a bit-wise copy of the object on the right is placed in the object on the left: in many circumstances – such as this example – you will achieve *nothing* by providing your own imple-mentation of this operation. However, in cases where dynamic memory allocation takes place, it is useful (often essential) to provide your own overloaded assignment operator. A useful 'rule of thumb': if your class has a destructor, you need to overload the assignment operator.

27.3.3   Overloading relational and logical operators

To end our first look at the overloading of binary operators, note that the relational and logical operators (>, &&, | |, ==, etc.) can also be overloaded in a straightforward manner. In this case, however, you will usually want to return TRUE or FALSE values.
Program 27.6 illustrates the overloading of == operators.

```
// A simple money class
// with overloaded == operator
// Source is: 27_06.CPP

#include <iostream.h>

class cMoney
    {
    public:
        cMoney(const int = 0, const int = 0);
        void Show();
        int   operator==(const cMoney&);
    private:
        int   _Pounds, _Pence;
    };

cMoney::cMoney(const int PO, const int PE)
    {
    _Pounds = PO;
    _Pence = PE;
    }
void cMoney::Show()
    {
    if (_Pence < 10)
        {
        cout << "£" << _Pounds << ".0" << _Pence;
        }
    else
        {
        cout << "£" << _Pounds << "." << _Pence;
        }
    }
// Overload == relative to cMoney class
int cMoney::operator==(const cMoney& R_OP)
    {
    if ((this->_Pounds == R_OP._Pounds)&&(this->_Pence == R_OP._Pence))
        {
        return 1;
        }
```

```
        else
            {
            return 0;
            }
        }
    int main()
        {
        cMoney cash1(1,33), cash2(2,90), cash3(1,33);
        cash1.Show();
        if (cash1 == cash2)
            {
            cout << " is the same as ";
            }
        else
            {
            cout << " is NOT the same as ";
            }
        cash2.Show();
        cout << endl;
        cash1.Show();
        if (cash1 == cash3)
            {
            cout << " is the same as ";
            }
        else
            {
            cout << " is NOT the same as ";
            }
        cash3.Show();
        cout << endl;
        return 0;
        }
```

Program 27.6 The money class again, this time with overloaded && and == operators. (☺)

The output from Program 27.6 is as follows:

```
£1.33 is NOT the same as £2.90
£1.33 is the same as £1.33
```

27.4 Copy Constructors vs. Assignment

In Chapter 25, we introduced copy constructors. Here, we have looked at overloaded assignment operators. It is important to appreciate that a well-designed class will generally define both. Where the class involves dynamic memory allocation (and many do), it is *essential* to define both operations.

Program 27.7 illustrates that even in a very simple program, both copy constructors and overloaded assignment operators will be invoked.

```cpp
// A simple money class with copy constructor and overloaded = operator
// Source is: 27_07.CPP
#include <iostream.h>
class cMoney
    {
    public:
                cMoney(const int = 0, const int = 0);
                cMoney(cMoney&);
        void    Show() const;
        void    operator=(const cMoney&);
    private:
        int     _Pounds, _Pence;
    };
cMoney::cMoney(const int PO, const int PE)
    {
    cout << "*** Ordinary constructor ***\n";
    _Pounds = PO;
    _Pence = PE;
    }
cMoney::cMoney(cMoney& R_OP)
    {
    cout << "*** Copy constructor ***\n";
    _Pounds = R_OP._Pounds;
    _Pence = R_OP._Pence;
    }
void cMoney::Show() const
    {
    if (_Pence < 10)
        {
        cout << "£" << _Pounds << ".0" << _Pence << endl;
        }
    else
        {
        cout << "£" << _Pounds << "." << _Pence << endl;
        }
    }
// Overload = relative to cMoney class (simple version)
void cMoney::operator=(const cMoney& R_OP)
    {
    cout << "*** Overloaded assignment operator ***\n";
    _Pounds = R_OP._Pounds;
    _Pence = R_OP._Pence;
    }
int main()
    {
    cout << "cMoney cash1(1,33);\n";
    cMoney cash1(1,33);
    cout << "\ncMoney cash2 = cash1\n";
    cMoney cash2 = cash1;
```

```
        cout << "\ncash1 = cash2;\n";
        cash1 = cash2;
        return 0;
        }
```

Program 27.7 Illustrating the need for both copy constructors and overloaded assignment operators. (☺)

The output from Program 27.7 is as follows:

```
    cMoney cash1(1,33);
    *** Ordinary constructor ***

    cMoney cash2 = cash1
    *** Copy constructor ***

    cash1 = cash2;
    *** Overloaded assignment operator ***
```

Note that there are subtle differences between writing, for example:

```
    cMoney cash2 = cash1;
```

and:

```
    cMoney cash2;
    cash2 = cash1;
```

Note also the very simple nature of the overloaded assignment operator. It is left as an exercise to explore what happens when the overloaded operator in Program 27.7 is replaced with the similar operator from Program 27.5.

27.5   Overloading unary operators

When you understand how binary operator overloading works, the overloading of unary operators is straightforward. As we have seen, when you overload a binary operator with a member operator function, the left operand is passed implicitly to the function; in the case of overloaded unary operators, this means that the member operator function does not need to have any parameters.

In Program 27.8 we illustrate a range of overloaded unary operators.

```
    // A simple money class with
    // overloaded unary and binary operators
    // Source is: 27_08.CPP

    #include <iostream.h>

    class cMoney
        {
        public:
```

```cpp
        cMoney(const int = 0, const int = 0);
        void Show() const;
        cMoney operator-(const cMoney&) const; // Binary version
        cMoney operator-();                     // Unary version
        cMoney operator+(const cMoney&) const; // Binary version
        cMoney operator++();                    // Prefix
        cMoney operator++(int);                 // Postfix
        int operator>(const cMoney&) const;
    private:
        int _Pounds, _Pence;
    };

cMoney::cMoney(const int PO, const int PE)
    {
    _Pounds = PO;
    _Pence = PE;
    }

void cMoney::Show() const
    {
    if (_Pounds < 0)
        {
        cout << "-£" << -_Pounds;
        }
    else
        {
        cout << "£" << _Pounds;
        }

    if (_Pence < 10)
        {
        cout << ".0" << _Pence << endl;
        }
    else
        {
        cout << "." << _Pence << endl;
        }
    }

// Overload binary - relative to cMoney class
cMoney cMoney::operator-(const cMoney& R_OP) const
    {
    cMoney Diff;

    Diff._Pounds = this->_Pounds - R_OP._Pounds;
    Diff._Pence = this->_Pence - R_OP._Pence;

    if (Diff._Pence < 0)
        {
        Diff._Pence+=100;
        Diff._Pounds-=1;
        }

    return Diff;
    }
```

```
// Overload unary - relative to cMoney class
cMoney cMoney::operator-()
    {
    this->_Pounds = -this->_Pounds;
    return *this;
    }
// Overload binary + relative to cMoney class
cMoney cMoney::operator+(const cMoney& R_OP) const
    {
    cMoney Sum;

    Sum._Pounds = this->_Pounds + R_OP._Pounds;
    Sum._Pence = this->_Pence + R_OP._Pence;

    if (Sum._Pence > 99)
        {
        Sum._Pence-=100;
        Sum._Pounds+=1;
        }

    return sum;
    }
// Overload unary prefix ++ relative to cMoney class
cMoney cMoney::operator++()
    {
    ++(this->_Pounds);
    ++(this->_Pence);

    if (this->_Pence > 99)
        {
        this->_Pence-=100;
        this->_Pounds+=1;
        }

    return *this;
    }
// Overload unary postfix ++ relative to cMoney class
cMoney cMoney::operator++(int /* DUMMY PARAMETER */)
    {
    cMoney Return_value = *this;

    (this->_Pounds)++;
    (this->_Pence)++;

    if (this->_Pence > 99)
        {
        this->_Pence-=100;
        this->_Pounds+=1;
        }

    return Return_value;
    }
int cMoney::operator>(const cMoney& R_OP) const
    {
    if (((this->_Pounds > R_OP._Pounds)
```

```
            || ((this->_Pounds == R_OP._Pounds)
            && (this->_Pence > R_OP._Pence))))
            {
            return 1;
            }
        else
            {
            return 0;
            }
        }
int main()
    {
    cMoney cash1(1,01), cash2(2,00), cash3;
    cash3 = cash1;
    cout << "cash3 = ";
    cash3.Show();
    cout << "cash2 = ";
    cash2.Show();
    if (cash3++ > cash2)
        {
        cout << "cash3++ > cash2\n";
        }
    else
        {
        cout << "cash3++ <= cash2\n";
        }
    cout << "cash3 = ";
    cash3.Show();
    cout << "cash2 = ";
    cash2.Show();
    cout << endl;
    cash3 = cash1;
    cout << "cash3 = ";
    cash3.Show();
    cout << "cash2 = ";
    cash2.Show();
    if (++cash3 > cash2)
        {
        cout << "++cash3 > cash2\n";
        }
    else
        {
         cout << "++cash3 <= cash2\n";
        }
    cout << "cash3 = ";
    cash3.Show();
    cout << "cash2 = ";
    cash2.Show();
    cout << endl;
```

```
cash3 = cash1;
cout << "cash3 = ";
cash3.Show();
cout << "-cash3 = ";
(-cash3).Show();

return 0;
}
```

Program 27.8   Overloading unary operators. (☺)

Program 27.8 gives the following output:

```
cash3 = £1.01
cash2 = £2.00
cash3++ <= cash2
cash3 = £2.02
cash2 = £2.00

cash3 = £1.01
cash2 = £2.00
++cash3 > cash2
cash3 = £2.02
cash2 = £2.00

cash3 = £1.01
-cash3 = -£1.01
```

The operation of these operators is straightforward, with the exception of the unary ++ operator. As you will recall, the ++ operator may be applied as a prefix or postfix operator. Implementing such facilities in overloaded operators is possible if, as this example shows, a little fiddly.

First of all, note that for the prefix operator, the function is as expected. For the postfix operator, however, a slightly more complicated coding is required:

```
// Overload unary postfix ++ relative to cMoney class
cMoney cMoney::operator++(int /* DUMMY PARAMETER */)
    {
    cMoney return_value = *this;

    this->_Pounds++;
    this->_Pence++;

    if (this->_Pence > 99)
        {
        this->._Pence-=100;
        this->_Pounds+=1;
        }

    return Return_value;
    }
```

First of all, to distinguish between the two cases, a dummy integer parameter is included in the postfix function. This anonymous parameter will not be used by the function; it is merely used (internally) by the compiler to distinguish between the prefix and postfix cases. In short, the dummy parameter is a C++ 'feature' or – most honestly – a language patch. Early compilers provided no way of distinguishing between the prefix and postfix operators; this is how modern compilers make the distinction.

Within the body of the function, note that we make an initial copy of the current contents of the `this` pointer. We then change the value of the `this` pointer to perform the postincrement, but return the 'old' contents of `this`. The result is that the change in value (in this case, the increment) is only apparent the next time the program 'looks at' the operand: this is precisely what we require.

27.6   Using `friend` functions for operator overloading

In most circumstances we can overload an operator relative to a class by using a friend (operator) function rather than member (operator) function. This is possible because, as we saw in Chapter 26, functions granted the status of 'friend' have access to the private elements of a class.

In general, friend functions weaken a class by making it 'less well encapsulated': therefore, where it is possible to do so, using member functions for operator overloading is the preferred technique. However, there are two main occasions when you **need** to use a `friend` function:

● when you mix certain combinations of objects and built-in types, and

● when you overload the insertion (>>) and extraction (<<) operators.

We consider each of these possibilities in turn below.

27.6.1   Mixing objects and built-in types

Using an overloaded binary member operator, we can easily create operators that allow us to write code as follows:

```
cMoney Cash1
… Cash1 * 10;
```

However, if we try to do the following;

```
cMoney Cash1
… 10 * Cash1;
```

then we are in difficulty: this is because, as we have seen, the left operand in a binary operation generates the member function call. To make this operation work we would therefore need to create an appropriate member function for the `int` 'class' (rather than the `cMoney` class): modifying the built-in types (like `int`) is something which we cannot do.

We could always try to write our programs to avoid the second scenario, but this may not always be practical. In addition, this approach leads to the programmer having to 'think differently' about built-in and user-defined types and, as we have seen, we generally wish to avoid such a demarcation.

The use of friend functions offers a reasonably elegant solution. For example, Program 27.9 uses the `friend` keyword to overload the * operator, allowing integers to be multiplied with one of the built-in types 'in either direction'.

```cpp
// A simple money class with overloaded * operators
// implemented as friend functions
// Source is: 27_09.CPP

#include <iostream.h>

class cMoney
    {
    public:
                cMoney(const int = 0, const int = 0);
                    void Show();
                cMoney operator*(const int) const;      // obj * int
            friend cMoney operator*(const int, const cMoney); // int* obj
    private:
        int _Pounds, _Pence;
    };

cMoney::cMoney(const int PO, const int PE)
    {
    _Pounds = PO;
    _Pence = PE;
    }

void cMoney::Show()
    {
    if (_Pence < 10)
        {
        cout << "£" << _Pounds << ".0" << _Pence << endl;
        }
    else
        {
        cout << "£" << _Pounds << "." << _Pence << endl;
        }
    }

// cMoney * int
cMoney cMoney::operator*(const int INTEGER) const
    {
    cMoney Product;

    Product._Pounds = this->_Pounds * INTEGER;
    Product._Pence = this->_Pence * INTEGER;

    while (Product._Pence > 99)
        {
        Product._Pence-=100;
        Product._Pounds+=1;
        }

    return Product;
    }
```

```
    // int * cMoney
    cMoney operator*(const int INTEGER, const cMoney OBJ)
        {
        cMoney Product;

        Product._Pounds = OBJ._Pounds * INTEGER;
        Product._Pence = OBJ._Pence * INTEGER;

        while (Product._Pence > 99)
            {
            Product._Pence-=100;
            Product._Pounds+=1;
            }

        return Product;
        }
int main()
        {
        cMoney cash1(1,33), cash2;

        cash2 = cash1 * 10;
        cash2.Show();

        cash2 = 10 * cash1;
        cash2.Show();

        return 0;
        }
```

Program 27.9   Operator overloading using friend functions. (☺)

The output from Program 27.9 is as follows:

```
    £13.30
    £13.30
```

Note that, to allow the addition to occur 'in either direction' it is necessary to overload the operator twice, once using a friend function, and once without. We could, of course, use a friend function in each case, but we would generally wish to restrict the use of friend functions to cases where they **must** be used.

27.6.2   Overloading insertion and extraction operators

The main situation in which friend functions are used for operator overloading is when we wish to overload the insertion and extraction operators. This is a useful process that can add to the readability and extensibility of your programs.

What we aim to do is avoid the rather clumsy use of member functions, as in (from Program 27.9):

```
    cash2.Show();
```

instead, allowing the programmer to write:

```
    cout << cash2;
```

So, why can't we just overload the stream insertion (or extraction operator) by making it a member operator function for the appropriate class? The problem is similar to that highlighted in Section 27.6.1 when we wanted to mix objects and built-in types. Then we saw that there was a problem if a variable of a built-in type formed the left operand. In the case of overloaded stream operators, the left operand is a **stream**. Because we are unable to modify the classes in the `stream` class library, we have to resort to using a `friend` function.

Program 27.10 illustrates how this can be achieved.

```cpp
// A simple cMoney Class with overloaded << and >> operators
// Source is: 27_10.CPP
#include <iostream.h>
class cMoney
    {
    public:
                            cMoney(const int = 0, const int = 0);
                    cMoney operator+(const cMoney&) const;
                    cMoney operator-(const cMoney&) const;
            friend ostream& operator<<(ostream&, const cMoney&);
            friend istream& operator>>(istream&, cMoney&);
    private:
            int _Pounds, _Pence;
    };
cMoney::cMoney(const int PO, const int PE)
    {
    _Pounds = PO;
    _Pence = PE;
    }
// Overload + relative to cMoney class
cMoney cMoney::operator+(const cMoney& R_OP) const
    {
    cMoney Sum;
    Sum._Pounds = this->_Pounds + R_OP._Pounds;
    Sum._Pence = this->_Pence + R_OP._Pence;

    while (Sum._Pence > 99)
        {
        Sum._Pence-=100;
        Sum._Pounds+=1;
        }
    return Sum;
    }
// Overload - relative to cMoney class
cMoney cMoney::operator-(const cMoney& R_OP) const
    {
    cMoney Diff;
    Diff._Pounds = this->_Pounds - R_OP._Pounds;
    Diff._Pence = this->_Pence - R_OP._Pence;
    if (Diff._Pence < 0)
        {
        Diff._Pence+=100;
```

```
                   Diff._Pounds-=1;
                   }
              return Diff;
              }
       ostream& operator<<(ostream& stream, const cMoney& R_OP)
              {
              if (R_OP._Pounds < 0)
                   {
                   stream << "-£" << -R_OP._Pounds;
                   }
              else
                   {
                   stream << "£" << R_OP._Pounds;
                   }
              if (R_OP._Pence < 10)
                   {
                   stream << ".0" << R_OP._Pence;
                   }
              else
                   {
                   stream << "." << R_OP._Pence;
                   }
              return stream;
              }
       istream& operator>>(istream& stream, cMoney& R_op)
              {
              cout << "Please enter cash amount \n";
              cout << " Pounds : ";
              stream >> R_op._Pounds;
              cout << " Pence : ";
              stream >> R_op._Pence;
              cout << "Thank you.\n\n";
              return stream;
              }
       int main()
              {
              cMoney cash1, cash2, cash3;
              cin >> cash1;
              cin >> cash2;
              cash3 = cash1 + cash2;
              cout << "Result of " << cash1 << " + " << cash2 << " = "
                   << cash3 << endl;
              cash3 = cash1 - cash2;
              cout << "Result of " << cash1 << " - " << cash2 << " = "
                   << cash3 << endl;
              return 0;
              }
```

Program 27.10 Operator overloading using friend functions: insertion and extraction operators. (☺)

One particular advantage gained by making use of the insertion and extraction operators in C++ programs (as opposed, say, to the use of `printf()` and `scanf()` discussed in Chapter 9) is that the functions can be overloaded, and that such overloading then naturally extends from the use of screen output to the use of disk files.

For example, replacing the function `main()` from Program 27.10 with the code below allows us (in a transparent manner involving no changes to the rest of the code) to store the data on disk:

```
int main()
    {
    fstream file_pointer;
    file_pointer.open("money.dat", ios::out);
    if (!file_pointer.good())
        {
        // The file could not be opened.
        cerr << "FATAL ERROR: Could not create file 'money.dat'";
        exit(1);
        }
    cMoney cash1, cash2, cash3;
    cin >> cash1;
    cin >> cash2;
    cash3 = cash1 + cash2;
    cout << "Result of " << cash1 << " + " << cash2 << " = "
            << cash3 << endl;
    file_pointer << "Result of " << cash1 << " + " << cash2 << " = "
                << cash3 << endl;
    cash3 = cash1 - cash2;
    cout << "Result of " << cash1 << " - " << cash2 << " = "
            << cash3 << endl;
    file_pointer << "Result of " << cash1 << " + " << cash2 << " = "
                << cash3 << endl;
    file_pointer.close();
    return 0;
    }
```

Including these lines in the program leads, as expected, to the simultaneous generation of screen output and a text file with the following contents:

```
Result of £4.03 + £2.10 = £6.13
Result of £4.03 - £2.10 = £1.93
```

27.7 **Guidelines**

We are now in a position to add some further guidelines for developing good classes:

(1) Overload operators with care. C++ opposes no *semantic* restrictions on the programmer, and you are free to make the + operator display 'hello, Mum' on the screen every time it is used. Naturally, you should limit the use of overloaded operators to appropriate cases, and implement only appropriate behaviour.

(2) Don't try to be 'cute' when overloading operators. For example, creating a cCustomer class (containing name and address fields) and overloading + to represent marriage so that (Paul Jones of 23 Hill Road) + (Mary Smith of 45 West St) becomes (Paul and Mary Smith, 45 West St) is an example of cute programming, and generally should be avoided.

(3) If your class involves dynamic memory allocation (or, if for some other reason you have provided a destructor), you will *need* to overload the assignment operator.

27.8   Conclusions

We have seen in this chapter how to overload the various operators used throughout C++ programs. By making judicious use of operator overloading, you are able – as we have seen – to seamlessly integrate your own abstract data types into the C++ language: in effect, you are able to extend and customize the language to suit your particular application area. We have also seen that where the type of the left argument is either not a class, or a class which we are unable to modify (for example, in a class library), then it is necessary to use friend functions to overload the operators.

Finally, please note that in the '\27' directory on the CD, you will find a final version of the cMoney class which incorporates all the features discussed in this chapter.

Exercises

27.1 Using a suitable implementation of the cMoney abstract data type, write a C++ program that will prompt the user to type in the salaries for 10 company employees, and will calculate the total company pay bill.

27.2 Consider the cMoney class again: suppose, given a money object representing an annual salary, we wish to calculate the amount of tax to be paid. Let's assume that the tax threshold (that is, the amount of money you must earn before you pay any tax) is £1000.00, and that the tax paid on any money above £1000.00 is 20%. It would be useful to be able to write something like this:

```
cMoney salary(30000,00), tax;
tax = salary.find_tax(1000,20);
```

Edit the cMoney class to provide the required features.

27.3 Integrate your extended cMoney class (from Exercise 27.2) into the salary program in Exercise 27.1, allowing the user to calculate the total wages bill for the company, along with the total tax bill due to the government.

27.4 Rewrite Program 27.8, this time storing the 'pounds' and 'pence' private data in free store (that is, rewrite the class so that it uses dynamic memory allocation). As far as the user is concerned, the class should operate in an identical way.

27.5 Look back at Program 17.3. Rewrite the program in such a way that the programmer can omit the switch statement, and instead simply type:

```
cout << medal;
```

This should give an output similar to the following:

```
Gold
```

28 Generic programming

28.1   Introduction

Polymorphism, which we considered in Chapter 27, can be viewed as a subset of the much larger field of generic programming (GP). The aim with GP is to create data structures and/or code modules which can be used with data of 'any' type.

We introduce the field of GP in this chapter, and consider both generic functions and generic classes.

28.2   Generic functions

A generic function describes processing that may be performed on data of different types. This is possible because a generic function has, as one parameter, the **type** of data upon which it will operate. Some people like to refer to this mechanism as **parametric polymorphism**.

For example, suppose we wish to copy the contents of one array to another. This process is a good candidate for a generic function because we know that – regardless of whether we have (say) an array of integers, an array of floating-point numbers, or an array of characters – the basic processing required to perform the function will always be the same.

Program 28.1 begins to illustrate the generic approach in action.

```
// A simple generic function
// Source is: 28_01.CPP
#include <iostream.h>
// Declaration of Copy()
template <typename TYPE>
void Copy (Type* const, const TYPE* const, const int);
int main()
    {
    int  Int1[5]  = {99,99,99,99,99};
    int  Int2[5]  = {1,2,3,4,5};
    char Char1[6]  = "XXXXX";
    char Char2[6]  = "Hello";
    cout << "Before copying :\n";
```

```
        for (int p = 0; p < 5; ++p)
            {
            cout << Int1[p] << " ";
            }
        cout << endl;

        cout << Char1 << endl << endl;

        Copy(Int1,Int2,5);    // Copy int arrays
        Copy(Char1,Char2,5); // Copy char arrays

        cout << "After copying :\n";
        for (p = 0; p < 5; ++p)
            {
            cout << Int1[p] << " ";
            }
        cout << endl;

        cout << Char1 << endl;

        return 0;
        }
// The generic function Copy()
template <typename TYPE>
void Copy (TYPE* const TO_PTR, const TYPE* const FROM_PTR, const int SIZE)
        {
        for (int Element = 0; Element < SIZE; Element++)
            {
            To_PTR[Element] = FROM_PTR[Element];
            }
        }
```

Program 28.1   A simple generic (template) function in action. (☺)

The output from Program 28.1 is as follows:

```
    Before copying :
    99 99 99 99 99
    XXXXX

    After copying :
    1 2 3 4 5
    Hello
```

To understand how this output arises, we need to consider the declaration of Copy():

```
    template <typename TYPE>
    void Copy (TYPE* const, const TYPE* const, const int);
```

This declaration introduces two new C++ keywords: template and typename. Here, template is used to indicate that we are declaring a generic (or template) function. The keyword typename indicates that the (read-only) *variable* Type is to be used to identify the *type of data* upon which the particular version of Copy() will operate. The compiler will generate the correct code for the particular version(s) of Copy() used in any program in which we use Copy(), replacing Type with the appropriate type name (such as `int` or `char`). The final feature of the declaration is `void`, which is simply the return type of `Copy()`.

We can achieve many of the same results using pre-processor macros (see Chapter 8) instead of generic functions. However, using macros, no type checking will be performed, raising the prospect that we can produce some subtle and difficult to detect errors in our programs. We can illustrate the type-checking process by trying to use `Copy()` to copy elements from an array of floats into an integer array, as follows:

```
int main()
    {
    int Ints[5] = {99,99,99,99,99};
    float Floats[5] = {0.0f};

    cout << "Before copying :\n";
    for (int p = 0; p < 5; ++p)
        {
        cout << Floats[p] << " ";
        }
    cout << endl;

    // Try to copy float array to int array...
    Copy(Ints, Floats, 5);

    cout << "After copying :\n";
    for (p = 0; p < 5; ++p)
        {
        cout << Floats[p] << " ";
        }
    cout << endl;

    return 0;
    }
```

Here the compiler will complain that there no version of `Copy()` has been declared that allows a mixture of `int*` and `float*` types. Note that a macro would not generally detect such an error.

Where necessary, we can also create generic functions which operate with data of more than one type: this possibility is illustrated in Program 28.2.

```
// A simple generic function
// Source is: 28_02.CPP

#include <iostream.h>

// Declaration of Copy() - v2.0
template <typename T1, typename T2>
void Copy (T1* const, const T2* const, const int);

int main()
    {
    int    Ints[5] = {99,99,99,99,99};
    float Floats[5] = {0.0f};

    cout << "Before copying :\n";
    for (int p = 0; p < 5; ++p)
        {
```

```
                    cout << Floats[p] << " ";
                    }
            cout << endl;

            // Try to copy int array to float array...
            Copy(Floats, Ints, 5);

            cout << "After copying :\n";
            for (p = 0; p < 5; ++p)
                    {
                    cout << Floats[p] << " ";
                     }
            cout << endl;

            return 0;
            }
    // The generic function Copy() - v2.0
    template <typename T1, typename T2>
    void Copy (T1* const To_PTR, const T2* const FROM_PTR, const int SIZE)
            {
            for (int Element = 0; Element < SIZE; ++Element)
                    {
                    To_PTR[Element] = FROM_PTR[Element];
                    }
            }
```

Program 28.2 Another generic function ((☺))

The output from Program 28.2 is as follows:

```
Before copying :
0  0  0  0  0
After copying :
99 99 99 99 99
```

Here, we explicitly state that Copy() may work with arrays of two different types, by including a list of the types (T1, T2) in the function declaration and definition.

Note that we can use a mixture of generic functions and overloaded functions in the same program. When we do so, there is the possibility that more than one function will match the specification. The particular function called is selected, as follows:

(1)   If there is an exact match with an ordinary function (which may or may not be overloaded), then the compiler will use this function;

(2)   If condition 1 is not satisfied, then the compiler will try to find an exact match with a template function;

(3)   If neither of the above conditions are satisfied, then the compiler will use the usual type promotion rules to find a match with an ordinary function (which, again, may or may not be an overloaded function). Note that the compiler will *not* use type promotion rules to try to match template functions.

Some of these possibilities are illustrated in Program 28.3.

```cpp
// Mixing generic functions and ordinary functions
// Source is: 28_03.CPP

#include <iostream.h>

// Declaration of generic Copy()
template <typename TYPE>
void Copy (TYPE* const, const TYPE* const, const int SIZE);

// Declaration of ordinary function Copy()
void Copy(int* const, const char* const, const int);

int main()
    {
    int Int1[5]  =  {99,99,99,99,99};
    int Int2[5]  =  {1,2,3,4,5};

    char Char1[6]  =  "XXXXX";
    char Char2[6]  =  "Hello";

    cout << "Before copying :\n";
    for (int p = 0; p < 5; ++p)
        {
        cout << Int1[p] << " ";
        }
    cout << endl;

    cout << Char1 << endl << endl;

    Copy(Char1, Char2, 5); // Copy char arrays with generic fn.
    Copy(Int1, Char2, 5);  // Copy char to int with ordinary fn.

    cout << "\nAfter copying :\n";
    for (p = 0; p < 5; ++p)
        {
        cout << Int1[p] << " ";
        }
    cout << endl;

    cout << Char1 << endl;

    return 0;
    }

// The generic function Copy()
template <typename TYPE>
void Copy (TYPE* const To_PTR, const TYPE* const FROM_PTR, const int SIZE)
    {
    for (int Element = 0; Element < SIZE; Element++)
        {
        To_PTR[Element]  =  FROM_PTR[Element];
        }
    cout << "I'm a generic function!\n";
    }

// The definition of ordinary function Copy()
void Copy(int* const i_PTR, const char* const C_PTR, const int SIZE)
```

```
        {
    for (int Element = 0; Element < SIZE; ++Element)
        {
        i_PTR[Element] = C_PTR[Element];
        }
    cout << "I'm an ordinary function!\n";
    }
```

Program 28.3 Mixing generic functions and overloaded functions. (☺)

The output from Program 28.3 is as follows:

```
Before copying :
99 99 99 99 99
XXXXX

I'm a generic function!
I'm an ordinary function!

After copying :
71 101 108 108 111
Hello
```

By combining generic and overloaded functions, it is possible to write a small number of, say, sorting functions that are able to deal with an enormous range of different data types in a consistent manner. For example, it is possible to write an alternative version of the standard library function `qsort()` that is easier to use.

Finally, it is important to realize that in all of the above cases, we are discussing selections made between different functions at compile time: this is sometimes called *early binding*. We will consider ways in which similar selections can be made at run-time (that is, *late binding*) in Chapter 29.

28.3 Generic classes

C++ also provides a facility for creating generic classes. These allow the programmer to create a class that defines the various algorithms to be performed, but allows the type of data to be manipulated to be specified when objects of that class are created.

We illustrate the use of generic classes by creating a very simple generic stack class. We then create two stack objects, one for handling characters, one for handling integers (Program 28.4).

```
// A simple generic stack class
// Source is: 28_04.CPP

#include <iostream.h>

// Crude way of setting stack size...
// Compare this with Program 28_06
const int SIZE = 3;

// The generic stack class
template <typename TYPE>
```

```
class cStack
    {
    public:
            cStack() { _Top = 0; } // Constructor
        void Push(const TYPE);      // Push onto stack
        TYPE Pop();                 // Pop from stack
    private:
        TYPE _Data[SIZE];          // The data
        int  _Top;                 // Index of top of stack
    };
// Push function
template <typename TYPE>
void cStack<TYPE>::Push(const TYPE OBJ)
    {
    if (_Top == SIZE)
        {
        cout << "Sorry, can't push - the stack is full\n";
        }
    else
        {
        cout << "Pushed " << OBJ << " onto the stack.\n";
        _Data[_Top] = OBJ;
         _Top++;
        }
    }

// Pop function
template <typename TYPE>
Type cStack<TYPE>::Pop()
    {
    if (_Top == 0)
        {
        cout << "Sorry, can't pop - the stack is empty\n";
        return 0; // Empty stack - return 0
        }
    else
        {
        _Top--;
        cout << "Popped " << _Data[_Top] << " from the stack.\n";
        return _Data[_Top];
        }
    }
int main()
    {
    cout << "Creating a character stack..." << endl;
    cStack<char> Char_stack;

    Char_stack.Push('a');
    Char_stack.Push('b');
    Char_stack.Push('c');
    Char_stack.Push('d');
```

```
Char_stack.Pop();
Char_stack.Pop();
Char_stack.Pop();
Char_stack.Pop();
cout << endl;

cout << "Creating an integer stack..." << endl;
cStack<int> Int_stack;

Int_stack.Push(1);
Int_stack.Push(20);
Int_stack.Push(300);
Int_stack.Push(4000);

Int_stack.Pop();
Int_stack.Pop();
Int_stack.Pop();
Int_stack.Pop();

return 0;
}
```

Program 28.4   Using templates to implement a simple generic stack. (☺)

Program 28.4 generates the following output:

```
Creating a character stack...
Pushed a onto the stack.
Pushed b onto the stack.
Pushed c onto the stack.
Sorry, can't push – the stack is full
Popped c from the stack.
Popped b from the stack.
Popped a from the stack.
Sorry, can't pop – the stack is empty

Creating an interger stack...
Pushed 1 onto the stack.
Pushed 20 onto the stack.
Pushed 300 onto the stack.
Sorry, can't push – the stack is full
Popped 300 from the stack.
Popped 20 from the stack.
Popped 1 from the stack.
Sorry, can't pop – the stack is empty
```

Program 28.5 shows an example of more general use. Here we take the simple integer array class introduced in Chapter 25, and translate it into a generic array. At the same time, we tidy this class by incorporating an overloaded [] operator. We now also use assertions to perform the bounds checking, allowing us to speed up the final version of the code.

   No initialization of the array is performed; in most cases, we assume that the array will be used with classes that 'already know how to initialize themselves'. This is generally good generic programming practice. Where built-in types are used, as with ordinary automatic arrays, it is left to the user of the class to perform any required initialization.

Note also that Program 28.5 incorporates a template with two parameters, the second parameter being used to specify the size of the array. This feature can add to the flexibility of your generic classes.

Finally, note how easy and 'natural' it is to use this new array, and in particular how the 2-D array is produced.

```cpp
// A new generic dynamic array data type
// Source is: 28_05.CPP

#include <iostream.h>
#include <stdlib.h>
#include <assert.h>

template <typename TYPE, int SIZE>
class cGenericArray
    {
    public:
      // Construction and destruction
      cGenericArray();                         // Default constructor
      cGenericArray(const cGenericArray&);     // Copy constructor
      ~cGenericArray();                        // Destructor

      // General member functions
      TYPE& operator[](const int); // Overload [] operator
      int   Get_Size() const;

    private:
        void   New_Memory(); // Place common memory handling here

        TYPE* _Start_PTR;
        int   _Size;
    };

template <typename TYPE, int SIZE>
cGenericArray<TYPE,SIZE>::cGenericArray()
    {
    assert(SIZE > 0); // Precond

    _Size = SIZE;

    New_Memory();   // Grab memory from free store
    }

// Copy constructor
template <typename TYPE, int SIZE>
cGenericArray<TYPE,SIZE>::cGenericArray(const cGenericArray<Type,Size>& A)
    {
    _Size = A._Size;

    New_Memory(); // Memory is allocated for the copy
    for (int i = 0; i < _Size; i++)
      {
      _Start_PTR[i] = A._Start_PTR[i];
      }
    }
```

```cpp
template <typename TYPE, int SIZE>
cGenericArray<TYPE,SIZE>::~cGenericArray()
    {
    delete [] _Start_PTR;
     _Start_PTR = 0;
    }

template <typename TYPE, int SIZE>
Type& cGenericArray<TYPE, SIZE>::operator[](const int I)
    {
    assert((I >=0) && (I <_Size)); // Precond

    return (_Start_PTR[I]);
    }

template <typename TYPE, int SIZE>
int cGenericArray<TYPE,SIZE>::Get_Size() const
    {
    return (_Size);
    }

template <typename TYPE, int SIZE>
void cGenericArray<TYPE,SIZE>::New_Memory()
    {
    _Start_PTR = new TYPE[_Size];

    if(!_Start_PTR)
        {
        throw 1;  // Out of memory...
        }
    }

int main()
    {
    try
        {
        // Create a couple of integer arrays
        cout << "About to create two new integer arrays\n";
        cGenericArray<int,4> one, two;

        one[3] = 0;     // Set values of some elements
        two[2] = 999;

        cout << one[3] << endl;
        cout << two[2] << endl;

        // Create new integer array
        cout << "About to create new (copy) integer array\n";
        cGenericArray<int,4> three = one;
        cout << three[3] << endl;

        // Create a 2-D array
        cout << "About to create 2-D array\n";
        cGenericArray<cGenericArray<int,3>,3> four;

        four[1][1] = 3;
        cout << four[1][1];
        }
```

```
      catch (...)
         {
         cout << "An error has occurred..." << endl;
         return 1;
         }
      return 0;
      }
```

Program 28.5 A generic array. Note that this creates an array with any number of dimensions, as illustrated. (☺)

The output from Program 28.5 is as follows:

```
About to create two new integer arrays
0
999
About to create new (copy) integer array
0
About to create 2-D array
3
```

Finally, rather than creating our template array from free store, we can do so (more simply) from the stack. Program 28.6 illustrates this possibility.

```
// A new generic dynamic array data type
// This time stored in stack area
// Source is: 28_06.CPP

#include <iostream.h>
#include <stdlib.h>
#include <assert.h>

template <typename TYPE, int SIZE>
class cGenericArray
    {
    public:
                cGenericArray();
        TYPE& operator[](const int); // Overload [] operator
        int   Get_Size() const;
    private:
        TYPE _Start_PTR[SIZE];  // Array in stack
        int  _Size;
    };

template <typename TYPE, int SIZE>
cGenericArray<TYPE,SIZE>::cGenericArray()
    {
    assert(SIZE > 0); // Precond

    _Size = SIZE;
    }

template <typename TYPE, int SIZE>
TYPE& cGenericArray<TYPE, SIZE>::operator[](const int I)
```

```
        {
        assert((I >=0) && (I <_Size)); // Precond

        return (_Start_PTR[I]);
        }

template <typename TYPE, int SIZE>
int cGenericArray<TYPE,SIZE>::Get_Size() const
        {
        return (_Size);
        }

int main()
        {
        // Create a couple of integer arrays
        cout << "About to create two new integer arrays\n";
        cGenericArray<int,4> one, two;

        one[3] = 0;      // Set values of some elements
        two[2] = 999;

        cout << one[3] << endl;
        cout << two[2] << endl;

        // Create new integer array
        cout << "About to create new (copy) integer array\n";
        cGenericArray<int,4> three = one;
        cout << three[3] << endl;

        // Create a 2-D array
        cout << "About to create 2-D array\n";
        cGenericArray<cGenericArray<int,3>,3> four;

        four[1][1] = 3;
        cout << four[1][1];

        return 0;
        }
```

Program 28.6   Another generic array. This time the array is stored in the stack. (☺)

The output from Program 28.6 is as follows:

```
About to create two new integer arrays
0
999
About to create new (copy) integer array
0
About to create 2-D array
3
```

Note that here we do not need a destructor and hence do not need a copy constructor or overloaded assignment operator.

28.4 Guidelines

We are now in a position to add a further guideline for developing good object-oriented programs:

(1) Treat generic classes (and functions) with caution. Don't try to provide appropriate initializations for all possible types of data; where possible, let the objects passed to your generic class perform their own initializations.

28.5 Conclusions

Generic programming is clearly related to the subject of object-oriented programming, but is, in reality, a large field in its own right. The Standard Template Library (STL), which looks at the time of writing as though it will become part of ISO C++, includes a wide variety of generic classes and functions for use in C++ programs. If your compiler does not support the STL, Nelson (1995) provides readable introduction to this area: his book also includes a copy of the library on disk. The fact that Nelson's book is approximately the same size as this one gives some indication of the size of this new library, and of the importance of generic programming to future implementations of the C++ language.

Exercises

28.1 Write a generic function (`Swap()`) that allows you to swap any two elements in an array of characters, integers or floating-point numbers.

28.2 Use your `Swap()` function from Exercise 28.1 to create a program that will allow you to sort an array of integers, characters or floating-point numbers into ascending order. That is, the array of elements {5,3,4,1,2,0} will become {0,1,2,3,4,5}.

28.3 Create a new version of the generic stack class, where the size of the stack is passed as one of the (template) parameters.

28.4 Referring to the example in Section 28.3, extend the generic array with two new member functions called `shrink()` and `grow()`. These should allow you to vary the dimensions of an array after it has been created. Are these new functions compatible with arrays of more than one dimension?

28.5 Create a 3-D generic array of long doubles. Compare the speed of this array with a conventional array, with and without bounds checking enabled.

28.6 Compare the speed of the generic arrays stored in the stack area and in the free store area. Explain any differences you observe.

28.7 Consider the class `cStack` presented in this chapter (Program 28.4). Create a new version of this class which is **fully dynamic**: that is, increase the size of the stack when new elements are added, and reduce the size of the stack when elements are removed.

As the use of the `new` operator can be quite time-consuming, you may find your stack is more efficient if you always increase the size in blocks of (say) 10 elements at a time, and only reduce the size of the stack when you have more than (say) twenty free elements. Implement both a 'buffered' stack and a simple dynamic stack and compare the performance of the two implementations with the 'static' version in this chapter.

29 Inheritance

29.1 Introduction

Inheritance is important. One of the major advantages of an O-O approach is claimed
to be software reuse, made possible through the mechanisms of inheritance built into
the C++ language, and provided on a practical level for the developer by the purchase
or production of class libraries. Class libraries, in turn, are based on inheritance.

We devote the whole of this chapter to this important topic.

29.2 Single inheritance

C++ allows you to derive new classes from existing classes using a process called
inheritance. The class from which the derived class is adapted is called the base class
(Figure 29.1).

Figure 29.1 A representation of single inheritance using a class-relationship diagram (CRD).
Here 'AKO' is an acronym for 'a kind of', which underlines one way of thinking of the
inheritance relationship. CRDs are discussed in detail in Chapter 30.

29.2.1 Example

We begin with a simple example (Program 29.1).

```
// A first look at inheritance
// Source is: 29_01.CPP

#include <iostream.h>

class cBase_Class
    {
    public:
```

```
        void set_b(int x) { _b = x ;}
        void show_b() const { cout << _b << endl; }
private:
        int _b;
};

class cDerived_Class : public cBase_Class
    {
    public:
        void set_d(int y) { _d = y;}
        void show_d() const { cout << _d << endl; }
    private:
        int _d;
    };

int main()
    {
    cDerived_Class object;

    object.set_b(10);
    object.set_d(20);

    object.show_b() const;
    object.show_d() const;

    return 0;
    }
```

Program 29.1   A first look at C++ inheritance. (☺)

Program 29.1 generates the following output:

```
10
20
```

To see what this insignificant-looking output actually means, note that the program deals only with an object of the derived type, not of the base type. Despite this, we use member functions from the base type, and access data 'in the base type' as if we were dealing with a class in the form shown in Figure 29.2.

```
class cCombined_Class
    {
    public:
        void set_d(int y) { _d = y;}
        void show_d() const { cout << _d << endl; }
        void set_b(int x) { _b = x ;}
        void show_b() const { cout << _b << endl; }
    private:
        int _d;
        int _b;
    };
```

Figure 29.2   An initial simplified approximation of the 'combined class' resulting from Program 29.1.

By using inheritance in your programs, you can, as here, start with simple data building blocks (analogous to function building blocks) and assemble them into 'virtual' data structures that match your precise requirements.

One final important point: no modifications to the source code of the base class are required to make use of inheritance. This means that you can inherit from a base class (perhaps one in a class library) even if you do not have access to the source code for the base class. Of course, you will still need to have some information about the base class, and you will need a pre-compiled version of the code in these circumstances.

29.2.2 Using `protected` data members

The simple example of inheritance given in Program 29.1 is all very well, but as soon as we begin to modify our derived class we start to experience problems. For example, suppose we assume that our derived class examined in Section 29.2.1 does take the form shown in Figure 29.2. We should then be able to modify our derived class as follows:

```
class cDerived_Class : public cBase_Class
    {
    public:
        void set_d(int y) { _d = y;}
        void show_db() const { cout << _b << endl; } // Can't !!!
    private:
        int _d;
    };
```

Here we are trying, in a derived class member function (`show_db()`), to access one of `private` data members from the base class. This we are unable to do: a derived class *never* has access to the `private` members of a base class. Because of this, our new combined class in Figure 29.2 is perhaps better represented as shown in Figure 29.3.

```
class cCombined_Class
    {
    public:
        void set_d(int y) { _d = y;}
        void show_d() const { cout << _d << endl; }
        void set_b(int x) { _b = x ;}
        void show_b() const { cout << _b << endl; }
    private:
        int _d;
    very_private:
        int _b;
    };
```

Figure 29.3 A more accurate representation of the 'combined class' resulting from Program 29.1. Note that `very_private` is not a keyword: it is merely used to emphasize that the derived class does not have access to the `private` data members inherited from the base class.

As Figure 29.3 emphasizes, `private` data from the base class is *very private* in the derived class, and not directly accessible. If you need access to a `private` base class member, you could make this member `public`, but this would seem to undo all the ideas about encapsulation of `private` data that lie at the heart of many of our previous discussions.

The solution is to make use of the `protected` access specifier. This is equivalent to the `private` specifier, with the single notable exception that `protected` members of a base class are accessible to members of derived classes. To the rest of your program, `pro-tected` members are as inaccessible as `private` members. Incidentally, `protected` data members are still usually represented using names preceded with a single underscore.

Program 29.2 shows the protected access specifier in action.

```
// Another look at inheritance
// Source is: 29_02.CPP

#include <iostream.h>

class cBase_Class
    {
    public:
        void set_b(int x) { _b = x ;}
        void show_b() const { cout << _b << endl; }
    protected:
        int _b;
    };

class cDerived_Class : public cBase_Class
    {
    public:
        void set_db(int y) { _b = y;}
        void show_d() const { cout << _d << endl; }
        void show_db() { cout << _b << endl; }
    private:
        int _d;
    };

int main()
    {
    cDerived_Class object;

    object.set_db(20);

    object.show_db();

    return 0;
    }
```

Program 29.2 Using the `protected` access specifier. (☺)

The output from Program 29.2 is as follows:

```
20
```

Another way in which we can retain the `private` access, and consequent data security, is by editing Program 29.2 to give the version shown in Program 29.3.

```
// Another look at inheritance
// Source is: 29_03.CPP

#include <iostream.h>
```

```
class cBase_Class
    {
    public:
        void set_b(int x) {_b = x ;}
        void show_b() const {cout << _b << endl;}
    private:
        int _b;
    };
class cDerived_Class : public cBase_Class
    {
    public:
        void set_d(int y) {_d = y;}
        void set_bd(int z) {set_b(z);}
        void show_d() const {cout << _d << endl;}
        void show_bd() const {show_b();}
    private:
        int _d;
    };
int main()
    {
    cDerived_Class object;
    object.set_bd(10);
    object.set_d(20);

    object.show_bd();
    object.show_d();
    return 0;
    }
```

Program 29.3 Solving problems with inheritance. (☺)

The output from Program 29.3 is as follows:

```
10
20
```

Note that in Program 29.3, within the `set_bd()` function, the (public) member function `set_b()` from the base class can be accessed: this is permissible because `set_b()` is a `public` member of the derived class.

29.2.3 `Public`, `protected` and `private` **inheritance**

All our previous examples have used public inheritance, and we have glossed over the fact that inheritance itself may take three forms: public, and (rather less usefully) protected or private.

The type of (single) inheritance required is specified as follows:

```
class derived_class_name : <type of inheritance> base_class_name
    {
    ...
    }
```

For example, *protected* inheritance can be specified like this:

```
class d_c : protected b_c
    {
    ...
    }
```

We summarize what happens to public, protected and private members of the base class during the various forms of inheritance in Table 29.1.

	Public inheritance	*Protected inheritance*	*Private inheritance*
Public element in base class	public	protected	private
Protected element in base class	protected	protected	private
Private element in base class	very private	very private	very private

Table 29.1 How inheritance affects members of the base class. The table shows that, for example, a `protected` element in the base class will become a `protected` element in the derived class, if a `protected` inheritance is used. If a `private` inheritance is used, then the same element will become a very `private` member of the derived class.

Table 29.1 attempts to make clear that, whatever type of inheritance is used, private elements in the base are inaccessible in the derived class. Note that 'very' is not a keyword: it is used simply to emphasize that private elements of the base class do *not* become private members of the derived class.

It is important to appreciate that only public inheritance is 'true inheritance', and that the use of protected or private 'inheritance' results in a relationship more like aggregation (see Chapter 26). Protected and private 'inheritance' can cause great confusion, and are best avoided.

29.2.4 Why you should avoid protected data

Inheritance is important, and `private` data cannot be (directly) accessed in a derived class. However, protected data is also (apparently) encapsulated data, and can be directly accessed. The obvious conclusion is that we should never use `private` data again, and instead always use `protected` data.

This is a common argument, but a seriously flawed one. As a general rule, you should *avoid* using `protected` data, unless absolutely necessary. The reason for this is that, if you have `protected` data in a base class, then this data can only ever be altered by changing all derived classes. This is usually not a practical proposition and goes against what we are trying to achieve with encapsulation. What we want to be able to do is make local changes to the internal workings of a class (for example, to make it faster) while leaving users of the class able to use the new class without altering their own code.

In the following fragment, for example, suppose we were using the `private` data member _b to keep a count of users a particular database; at some point, we may decide that the integer data value used is too short for our purposes, and we might wish to change the type of this data to (say) unsigned int or long int. This, however, would be almost impossible, because to make such a change, we would also have to track down and change all the associated derived classes that assume this data member is an int.

```
class cBase_Class
    {
    public:
        void set_b(int x) { _b = x ;}
        void show_b() const { cout << _b << endl; }
    protected:
        int _b; // Can't alter type!!!
    };
class cDerived_Class : private cBase_Class
    {
    public:
        void set_db() { _d = _b; } // Relies on protected data!!!
        void show_d() const { cout << _d << endl; }
    private:
        int _d;
    };
```

On the other hand, in this second fragment, the programmer is free to alter the base class:

```
class cBase_Class
    {
    public:
        void set_b(int x) { _b = x ;}
        void get_b() const { return (int) _b; }
    private:
        int _b; // Altering this to long won't impact on derived class
    };
class cDerived_Class : private cBase_Class
    {
    public:
        void set_db() { _d = get_b(); }
        void show_d() const { cout << _d << endl; }
    private:
        int _d;
    };
```

Although this is a rather contrived example, the point should be clear. The 'bottom-up' nature of software development with classes leaves the programmer with additional responsibilities.

29.2.5 Overriding functions

We have considered that, as far as the programmer is concerned, simple inheritance offers a way of linking classes together to form conglomerate classes. While this is an attractive and useful technique, we need to be able to deal with several side-effects of this approach; here we consider possible conflicts that may arise when members of base and derived classes are of the same name (and type).

For example, consider Program 29.4.

```
// Name conflicts?
// Source is: 29_04.CPP
#include <iostream.h>
class cBase_Class
    {
    public:
        void get(int x) { _b = x ;}
        void show_b() const { cout << _b << endl; }
    private:
        int _b;
    };
class cDerived_Class : public cBase_Class
    {
    public:
        void get(int y) { _d = y;}
        void show_d() const { cout << _d << endl; }
    private:
        int _d;
    };
int main()
    {
    cDerived_Class object;
    object.get(10); // Which one?
    object.cBase_Class::get(10); // This works...
    object.cDerived_Class::get(10); // This works too...
    cout << "show (base) : ";
    object.show_b();
    cout << "show (derived) : ";
    object.show_d();
    return 0;
    }
```

Program 29.4 Overriding base class functions with equivalent versions from the derived class. (☺)

Program 29.4 generates the following output:

```
show (base)    : 10
show (derived)   : 10
```

Here, by default, the get() member function in the derived class *overrides* the function of the same name in the base class: the base class member function is not called:

```
object.get(10); // Derived class func overrides base class func
```

The normal rules of overloaded functions also apply here: that is, functions can be overloaded but must differ by more than just the type of their return value (see Chapter 8). Note also that we can use the scope resolution operator explicitly to access either version.

We reconsider some of the issues raised here when we consider virtual functions in Section 29.4.

29.2.6 Constructors and destructors

Suppose we inherit from a base class with constructor and destructor functions, and the derived class also has such functions; how are the various functions called (and in what order?).

Program 29.5 begins to provide an answer.

```
// Inheritance with constructors and destructors.
// Source is: 29_05.CPP
#include <iostream.h>
class cBase_Class
    {
    public:
            cBase_Class() { cout << "Cons base object\n"; }
            ~cBase_Class() { cout << "Dest base object\n"; }
        void set_b(int x) { _b = x ;}
        void show_b() const { cout << _b << endl; }
    private:
        int _b;
    };
class cDerived_Class : public cBase_Class
    {
    public:
            cDerived_Class() { cout << "Cons derived object\n"; }
            ~cDerived_Class() { cout << "Dest derived object\n"; }
        void set_d(int y) { _d = y;}
        void show_d() const { cout << _d << endl; }
    private:
        int _d;
    };
int main()
    {
    cDerived_Class object;
    return 0;
    }
```

Program 29.5 Inheritance with constructors and destructors. (☺)

Program 29.5 generates the following output:

```
Cons base object
Cons derived object
Dest derived object
Dest base object
```

As is apparent from this example, during the construction process, the base class constructor is called first, followed by the derived class constructor. During the destruction process, the opposite occurs: the derived object is 'destructed' first, followed by the base object.

So far, so good; you may legitimately ask, however, what happens when either the base class or derived class, or both, have constructor functions with parameters?

Let's first see how to pass a parameter to the constructor function for the derived class (Program 29.6).

```cpp
// Inheritance with constructors and destructors: passing arguments
// Source is: 29_06.CPP

#include <iostream.h>

class cBase_Class
    {
    public:
            cBase_Class() { cout << "Cons b object\n"; }
            ~cBase_Class() { cout << "Dest b object\n"; }
        void set_b(int x) { _b = x ; }
        void show_b() const { cout << _b << endl; }
    private:
        int _b;
    };

class cDerived_Class : public cBase_Class
    {
    public:
            cDerived_Class(int x) { cout << "Cons d object "<< x << endl; }
            ~cDerived_Class() { cout << "Dest d object\n"; }
        void set_d(int y) { _d = y;}
        void show_d() const { cout << _d << endl; }
    private:
        int _d;
    };

int main()
    {
    cDerived_Class object(3);

    return 0;
    }
```

Program 29.6   Constructors and destructors with arguments. (☺)

Program 29.6 generates the following output:

```
Cons base object
Cons derived object 3
Dest derived object
Dest base object
```

In many cases, the base and derived class constructor functions will require different arguments. We deal with this common situation by passing all required arguments to the derived class, then having the derived class constructor function pass any necessary arguments to the base class.

Program 29.7 illustrates this process in action.

```
// Inheritance with constructors and destructors: passing args v2.0
// Source is: 29_07.CPP
#include <iostream.h>
class cBase_Class
    {
    public:
        cBase_Class(char ch) { cout << "Cons b " << ch << endl; }
        ~cBase_Class() { cout << "Dest b\n"; }
    };
class cDerived_Class : public cBase_Class
    {
    public:
        cDerived_Class(int x, char ch) : cBase_Class(ch)
            { cout << "Cons d " << x << endl; }
        ~cDerived_Class() { cout << "Dest d\n"; }
    };
int main()
    {
    cDerived_Class object(3,'A');
    return 0;
    }
```

Program 29.7 Another look at constructors and destructors with arguments. (☺)

Program 29.7 generates the following output:

```
Cons b A
Cons d 3
Dest d
Dest b
```

Note that in Program 29.7 the derived class constructor simply ignores the character argument and passes it on to the base class constructor.

29.2.7 The next generation

Using inheritance, we are not restricted to a single generation. We can use a derived class as the base class of another inheritance relationship. For example, in Program 29.8 we have a base class, we derive a class from this, and derive another class from the derived class.

```
// Simple "multiple" inheritance
// Source is: 29_08.CPP
```

```
#include <iostream.h>

class cBase_Class
    {
    public:
        cBase_Class() { cout << "Cons base object\n"; }
        ~cBase_Class() { cout << "Dest base object\n"; }
    };

class cDerived_Class1 : public cBase_Class
    {
    public:
        cDerived_Class1() { cout << "Cons derived1 object\n"; }
        ~cDerived_Class1() { cout << "Dest derived1 object\n"; }
    };

class cDerived_Class2 : public cDerived_Class1
    {
    public:
        cDerived_Class2() { cout << "Cons derived2 object\n"; }
        ~cDerived_Class2() { cout << "Dest derived2 object\n"; }
    };

int main()
    {
    cDerived_Class2 object;

    return 0;
    }
```

Program 29.8   Simple 'multiple' inheritance. (☺)

Program 29.8 generates the following output:

```
Cons base object
Cons derived1 object
Cons derived2 object
Dest derived2 object
Dest derived1 object
Dest base object
```

The operation of Program 29.8 is straightforward. In this case, the class hierarchy is as shown in Figure 29.4.

Figure 29.4   A CRD representation of simple 'multiple' inheritance.

29.3 Multiple inheritance

We have hitherto considered only single inheritance. As you would expect, multiple inheritance is more flexible: this allows us to derive a new class from more than one base class. We can illustrate the underlying idea with an example. Suppose we feel there is a gap in the market for a new type of pet cat (Figure 29.5). Here, we wish to inherit basic 'pet' properties (essentially friendly, likes to sit on your knee and purr), and mix them with the larger size property of the lion, to generate a new breed of larger (but still, we hope, friendly) 'SuperCat'.

A more general representation of this type of inheritance relationship is given in the class-relationship diagram in Figure 29.6.

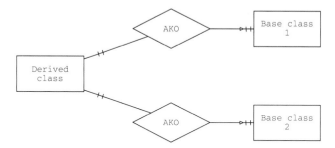

(inherits basic pet cat characteristics)

(inherits larger size)

SuperCat

Figure 29.5 Engineering a 'SuperCat'.

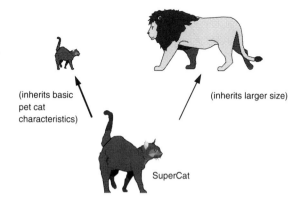

Figure 29.6 A CRD representation of general multiple inheritance.

Program 29.9 translates Figure 29.6 into C++.

```
// Multiple inheritance
// Source is: 29_09.CPP
#include <iostream.h>
class cBase_Class1
    {
    public:
            cBase_Class1() { cout << "Cons base1 object\n"; }
            ~cBase_Class1() { cout << "Dest base1 object\n"; }
```

```
            void set_b1(int x) { _prot_data_b1 = x ;}
            void show_b1() const { cout << _prot_data_b1 << endl;}
        protected:
            int _prot_data_b1;
        };
    class cBase_Class2
        {
        public:
                cBase_Class2() { cout << "Cons base2 object\n"; }
                ~cBase_Class2() { cout << "Dest base2 object\n"; }
            void set_b2(int x) { _prot_data_b2 = x;}
            void show_b2() const { cout << _prot_data_b2 << endl;}
        protected:
            int _prot_data_b2;
        };
    class cDerived_Class : public cBase_Class2, public cBase_Class1
        {
        public:
                cDerived_Class() { cout << "Cons derived object\n";}
                ~cDerived_Class() { cout << "Dest derived object\n";}
            void set_d(int y) { _d = y;}
            void show_d() const { cout << _d << endl;}
            void show_db1() const { cout << _prot_data_b1 << endl;}
            void show_db2() const { cout << _prot_data_b2 << endl;}
        private:
            int _d;
        };
    int main()
        {
        cDerived_Class object;

        object.set_b1(4);
        object.set_b2(6);
        object.set_d(8);

        object.show_d();
        object.show_db1();
        object.show_db2();

        return 0;
        }
```

Program 29.9 Multiple inheritance. (☺)

Program 29.9 generates the following output:

```
Cons base2 object
Cons base1 object
Cons derived object
8
4
```

```
6
Dest derived object
Dest base1 object
Dest base2 object
```

Note that Program 29.9 is little different in concept from our previous single inheritance examples, and that the details of Table 29.1 still apply. Here, we list the classes from which we wish to create our derived class, and provide a separate access specifier for each one:

```
class cDerived_Class : public cBase_Class2, public cBase_Class1
```

The order in which the constructors are called is dictated by this line. If we make alterations, as follows:

```
class cDerived_Class : public cBase_Class1, public cBase_Class2
```

then the output would become:

```
Cons base1 object
Cons base2 object
Cons derived object
8
4
6
Dest derived object
Dest base2 object
Dest base1 object
```

Note that we can use (say) public inheritance with one class and protected inheritance with another. This allows the programmer to develop a range of different derived classes from a simple collection of base classes.

29.3.1 Inheriting more than one copy of a base class

Multiple inheritance begins to become more interesting when we have a hierarchy like that shown in Figure 29.7.

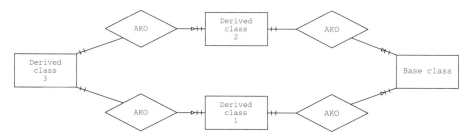

Figure 29.7 Problems can arise when multiple base classes are directly inherited by a derived class.

Program 29.10 illustrates the possibility shown in Figure 29.7.

```
// Attempted multiple inheritance… (WON'T COMPILE)
// Source is: 29_10.CPP

#include <iostream.h>

class cBase_Class
    {
    public:
        int a; // Public data!!!
            cBase_Class() { cout << "Constructing base object\n"; }
            ~cBase_Class() { cout << "Destructing base object\n"; }
        };

class cDerived_Class1 : public cBase_Class
    {
    public:
        int b;
            cDerived_Class1() { cout << "Constructing derived1 object\n"; }
            ~cDerived_Class1() { cout << "Destructing derived1 object\n"; }
        };

class cDerived_Class2 : public cBase_Class
    {
    public:
        int c;
            cDerived_Class2() { cout << "Constructing derived2 object\n"; }
            ~cDerived_Class2() { cout << "Destructing derived2 object\n"; }
        };

class cDerived_Class3 : public cDerived_Class1, public
cDerived_Class2
    {
    public:
        int sum() const { return a + b + c; } // WON'T COMPILE!!!
            cDerived_Class3() { cout << "Constructing derived1 object\n"; }
            ~cDerived_Class3() { cout << "Destructing derived1 object\n"; }
        };

int main()
    {
    cDerived_Class3 object;

    object.a = 2; // WON'T COMPILE: Which a???
    object.b = 4;
    object.c = 6;

    cout << "\nSum is " << object.sum() << "\n\n";

    return 0;
    }
```

Program 29.10 Problems with multiple inheritance. (☹)

Program 29.10 will not compile. The problem arises because, in derived class 3, we inherit – indirectly – two copies of the base class. In such circumstances, the compiler has no way of knowing which class any member function call refers to; in Program 29.10 any reference to the integer variable a through a cDerived_Class3 object could refer either to the a inherited from the top branch in Figure 29.7 or equally to the a from the lower branch.

Program 29.11 is a version of Program 29.10 that does compile.

```cpp
// Multiple inheritance with
// virtual base classes
// Source is: 29_11.CPP

#include <iostream.h>

class cBase_Class
    {
    public:
        int a; // Public data!!!
            cBase_Class() { cout << "Constructing base object\n"; }
            ~cBase_Class() { cout << "Destructing base object\n"; }
    };

class cDerived_Class1 : virtual public cBase_Class
    {
    public:
        int b;
            cDerived_Class1() { cout << "Constructing derived1 object\n"; }
            ~cDerived_Class1() { cout << "Destructing derived1 object\n"; }
    };

class cDerived_Class2 : virtual public cBase_Class
    {
    public:
        int c;
            cDerived_Class2() { cout << "Constructing derived2 object\n"; }
            ~cDerived_Class2() { cout << "Destructing derived2 object\n"; }
    };

class cDerived_Class3 : public cDerived_Class1,
                        public cDerived_Class2
    {
    public:
        int sum() const { return a + b + c; }
            cDerived_Class3() { cout << "Constructing derived3 object\n"; }
            ~cDerived_Class3() { cout << "Destructing derived3 object\n"; }
    };

int main()
    {
    cDerived_Class3 object;

    object.a = 2; // virtual base class keyword disambiguates this
    object.b = 4;
    object.c = 6;

    cout << "\nSum is " << object.sum() << "\n\n";

    return 0;
    }
```

Program 29.11 Problems with multiple inheritance solved using virtual base classes. (☺)

Program 29.11 generates the following output:

```
Constructing base object
Constructing derived1 object
Constructing derived2 object
Constructing derived1 object

Sum is 12

Destructing derived1 object
Destructing derived2 object
Destructing derived1 object
Destructing base object
```

In Program 29.11 we have resolved the problems in Program 29.11 using the `virtual` keyword, as in the line:

```
class cDerived_Class1 : virtual public cBase_Class
```

In most circumstances, `virtual` will do nothing; however, if the program attempts to include (through multiple inheritance) more than one copy of `cBase_Class` in any derived class, the use of `virtual` will ensure that only a single copy is inherited.

29.4   Virtual functions, pointers and polymorphism

We have already met polymorphism in several previous chapters, when we considered function and operator overloading. Both function and operator overloading involve compile-time polymorphism: that is, the particular version of an overloaded function or operator called at a particular point in your program is determined by the compiler and 'hard wired' into the object code of your executable program.

There is, however, one other type of polymorphism that we have not yet considered: run-time polymorphism. Here, the particular version of an overloaded function used is determined only when your program runs: that is, at run-time. Run-time polymorphism (also known as late-binding or dynamic-binding) is important in larger programs because it adds to the flexibility to the language.

Run-time polymorphism in C++ is provided through the use of **virtual functions**; at its most simple, a virtual function is a member function declared within a base class and redefined by a derived class. The power of virtual functions arises in turn through the use of pointers.

29.4.1   Pointers and inheritance

When using pointers with C++ classes, you need to be aware that a base class pointer may also be used to point to any class derived from this base class. The implications of this apparently minor new language feature are far-reaching, because we now have a situation where a variable has two types: a static type (the 'usual' type) and a dynamic type.

When using pointers in this way, bear the following in mind:

- Pointer arithmetic won't usually work with derived objects, which are likely to be a different size than the base class.

- Using a pointer to a derived object, you can access only those members of the derived object that were inherited from the base.

- While a base pointer can point to a derived object without a type mismatch, the reverse operation can't be carried out. Use of a cast operator to circumvent such restrictions is possible, but dangerous (and *not* recommended).

To take advantage of these new features, we need to use virtual functions, as illustrated in Program 29.12.

```
// Playing with virtual functions
// Source is: 29_12.CPP

#include <iostream.h>

class cBase_Class
    {
    public:
                    cBase_Class(int i = 999) {_b = i;}
            // virtual needed here
            virtual void show() const {cout << "_b = " << _b << endl;}

    private:
            int _b;
    };

class cDerived_Class : public cBase_Class
    {
    public:
            cDerived_Class(char c = 'D') {_d = c;}
            void show() const {cout << "_d = " << _d << endl;}

    private:
            char _d;
    };

int main()
    {
    cBase_Class base_object;
    cDerived_Class derived_object;

    cBase_Class* base_PTR;        // Pointer variable

    base_PTR = &base_object;      // Points to object of BASE class
    cout << "Calling the cBase_Class show()\n";
    base_PTR->show();

    base_PTR = &derived_object;   // Points to object of DERIVED class
    cout << "\nCalling the cDerived_Class show()\n";
    base_PTR->show();

    return 0;
    }
```

Program 29.12 Playing with virtual functions. (☺)

Program 29.12 generates the following output:

```
Calling the cBase_Class show()
_b = 999
Calling the cDerived_Class show()
_d = D
```

Note the use of the pointer operator ->, as in the line:

```
base_PTR->show();
```

The operation of this program differs significantly from Program 29.4 discussed earlier. Unlike the previous version, we now have (easy) access to *both* member functions, without using the scope resolution operator.

If the `virtual` keyword is omitted from `cBase_Class`, then the binding will be *static*: that is, it will occur at compile time. As a result, only the base class member function will be accessible. In these circumstances, the output becomes:

```
Calling the cBase_Class show()
_b = 999
Calling the cDerived_Class show()
_b = 999
```

29.4.2 Essentials of run-time polymorphism

Program 29.12 illustrates the use of pointers, but conceals the power of virtual functions. Program 29.13 illustrates that the use of virtual functions does indeed allow run-time polymorphism.

```
// Playing with virtual functions - run-time polymorphism
// Source is: 29_13.CPP
#include <iostream.h>
class cBase_Class
    {
    public:
                    cBase_Class(int i = 999){_b = i;}
        virtual void show() const {cout<< "_b = " << _b << endl;}
    private:
        int _b;
    };
class cDerived_Class : public cBase_Class
    {
    public:
                cDerived_Class(char c = 'D') {_d = c;}
        void show() const {cout << "_d = " << _d << endl;}
    private:
        char _d;
    };
int main()
    {
```

```
    cBase_Class base_object;
    cDerived_Class derived_object;

    int type;
    cBase_Class* general_PTR;

    cout << "Type 0 (base) or 1 (derived) :";
    cin >> type;

    if (type)
        {
        general_PTR = &derived_object;
        }
    else
        {
        general_PTR = &base_object;
        }

    general_PTR->show();

    return 0;
    }
```

Program 29.13   Achieving run-time polymorphism with virtual functions. (☺)

Program 29.13 generates the following outputs:

```
Type 0 (base) or 1 (derived) :0
_b = 999
```

```
Type 0 (base) or 1 (derived) :1
_d = D
```

Program 29.13 operates as follows. The user elects to use either the base or derived class version of show(). As we saw in Program 29.12, the user has access to both member functions, because of the use of the virtual keyword.

It is important to appreciate that the particular function called with the line

```
    general_PTR->show();
```

is determined at run-time, not at compile time. In effect, in this way, we have created a more flexible, and easier to use, function pointer (as originally discussed in Chapter 7).

If the virtual keyword is omitted, then the program will use early (compile-time) binding, and not late (run-time) binding. As a result, only one version of the show() function will be accessible.

29.4.3   Exploiting run-time polymorphism

The 'toy' examples above don't really convey why C++ programmers find dynamic binding such an important addition to the C++ language. In fact, one of the most common uses for dynamic binding is to fill container classes (such as arrays and queues) with *heterogeneous* collections of objects. That is to say, by exploiting dynamic binding, programmers are able to take even simple arrays and fill them with objects of different (dynamic) types. Naturally, in this case, the *static* type of all the objects in the array must be the same: therefore *dynamic* binding must be used.

As an example, Program 29.14 creates a heterogeneous array of objects of two 'different' types. The end result is the framework for a simple CASE tool.

```cpp
// A simple example of run-time polymorphism
// Source is: 29_14.cpp
#include <iostream.h>
class cSymbol
    {
    public:
        virtual void Draw() { cout << "Draw nothing here..." << endl; }
    };
class cTerminator : public cSymbol
    {
    public:
        void Draw() { cout << "Draw terminator here" << endl; }
    };
class cProcess : public cSymbol
    {
    public:
        void Draw() { cout << "Draw process here" << endl; }
    };
int main()
    {
    cSymbol* SymbolArray[10];
    int choice;
    for (int index = 0; index < 10; index++)
        {
        cout << "Type 1 for Term, 2 for Proc :   ";
        cin >> choice;
        switch(choice)
            {
            case 1:
                SymbolArray[index] = new cTerminator;
                break;
            case 2:
                SymbolArray[index] = new cProcess;
                break;
            }
        }
    for (index = 0; index < 10; index++)
        {
        SymbolArray[index]->Draw();
        }
    return 0;
    }
```

Program 29.14 Using dynamic binding to create a heterogeneous array. Note that in this simple example, the delete operator is not used: this would not be sensible in a real application. (☺)

Program 29.14 generates the following output:

```
Type 1 for Term, 2 for Proc :  2
Type 1 for Term, 2 for Proc :  2
Type 1 for Term, 2 for Proc :  1
Type 1 for Term, 2 for Proc :  2
Type 1 for Term, 2 for Proc :  1
Type 1 for Term, 2 for Proc :  1
Type 1 for Term, 2 for Proc :  1
Type 1 for Term, 2 for Proc :  2
Type 1 for Term, 2 for Proc :  1
Type 1 for Term, 2 for Proc :  2
Draw process here
Draw process here
Draw terminator here
Draw process here
Draw terminator here
Draw terminator here
Draw terminator here
Draw process here
Draw terminator here
Draw process here
```

Although this is a simple example, the technique extends easily: for example, the exercises at the end of this chapter will involve using the generic array from earlier chapters as a container class for a heterogeneous collection of objects.

29.4.4   A question of speed

Having 'discovered' dynamic binding, some programmers are inclined to apply it whenever possible in their programs; this is seldom a good idea. Dynamic binding is powerful, and useful. It is also *very* slow compared to static binding.

For example, consider Program 29.15.

```cpp
// Timing implications of dynamic binding...
// Source is: 29_15.CPP
#include <iostream.h>
#include <time.h>
class cBase_Class
    {
    public:
                     cBase_Class(int i = 999){_b = i;}
         virtual void set() {_b = 10;}
    private:
         int _b;
    };
class cDerived_Class : public cBase_Class
    {
    public:
              cDerived_Class(int i = 999) {_d = i;}
         void set() {_d = 10;}
    private:
```

```
            int _d;
        };
    int main()
        {
        cBase_Class b1;
        cDerived_Class d1;
        cBase_Class* base_PTR;
        const long NUM_PASSES = 10000000;
        double      elapsed_time;
        time_t      start_time, stop_time; // time_t is defined in time.h
        cout << "Starting calculation - please wait...\n";
        start_time = time(NULL);
        for (long i = 0; i <= NUM_PASSES; i++)
            {
            base_PTR = &b1;
            base_PTR->set();
            base_PTR = &d1;
            base_PTR->set();
            }
        stop_time = time(NULL);
        elapsed_time = difftime(stop_time, start_time);
        cout << "Elapsed time (in seconds) : " << elapsed_time << endl;
        return 0;
        }
```

Program 29.15 Timing dynamic binding. (☺)

Program 29.15 generates the following output:

```
    Starting calculation - please wait...
    Elapsed time (in seconds) : 45
```

The above example illustrates dynamic binding; if we modify Program 29.15 so that the virtual keyword is removed from the base class (and hence resort to static binding) then the output becomes:

```
    Starting calculation - please wait...
    Elapsed time (in seconds) : 30
```

In both cases the code (compiled on a Watcom v10.0 compiler, run on a Dell 486 DX2 66 PC) uses 'maximum speed' optimization. Note that the difference in speed is very significant (some 50% slower in the dynamic binding case). As always, the precise figures must be treated with caution; however, the difference in performance is real.

29.5 Pure virtual functions

We saw in Section 29.2.5 that it is sometimes necessary or desirable to be able to override functions derived in a base class. In particular cases, you may wish to *force* programmers to override the base class function; this is achieved using pure virtual functions.

Pure virtual functions, when used with care, can be a useful feature of class libraries. For example, suppose you had a library of mathematical classes, and you wished to specify that all classes in the library must provide addition and subtraction operations. However, because of the range of possible classes in the library, you have no way of writing appropriate generic functions (or generic classes) to deal with all possible eventualities. You can, however, create a 'manual' generic base class by using pure virtual functions. This is done by specifying appropriate pure virtual (operator?) functions in a common library base class, from which all classes in the library are derived. All programmers developing for the library are then encouraged to provide appropriate member functions in all the classes they produce for the library.

Naturally, pure virtual functions should be used sparingly. It is one thing to provide written guidelines concerning good programming style; to *impose* a particular style of programming through the use of pure virtual functions can place other programmers in your team in a straitjacket, and can make your classes awkward and cumbersome for others to use.

Note also that classes including pure virtual functions are incomplete data types – no objects of such classes can be created; they are generally known, therefore, as *abstract classes*.

To make a virtual function pure is straightforward: you simply include '= 0' after the function prototype in the base class. Program 29.16 shows pure virtual functions in action.

```cpp
// Playing with pure virtual functions
// Source is: 29_16.CPP
#include <iostream.h>
class cSymbol
    {
    public:
        virtual void Draw() = 0;   // Pure virtual function
    };
class cTerminator : public cSymbol
    {
    public:
        void Draw() { cout << "Draw terminator here" << endl; }
    };
class cProcess : public cSymbol
    {
    public:
        void Draw() { cout << "Draw process here" << endl; }
    };
int main()
    {
    cSymbol* SymbolArray[10];
    int choice;
    for (int index = 0; index < 10; index++)
        {
        cout << "Type 1 for Term, 2 for Proc :   ";
        cin >> choice;
        switch(choice)
            {
            case 1:
                SymbolArray[index] = new cTerminator;
                break;
            case 2:
```

```
                    SymbolArray[index]  =  new cProcess;
                    break;
                }
            }
        for (index = 0; index < 10; index++)
            {
            SymbolArray[index]->Draw();
            }
        return 0;
        }
```

Program 29.16 Playing with pure virtual functions. The output is the same as that produced by Program 29.15. (☺)

In this example, if the programmer did not redefine the `Draw()` function in the derived classes, the code would not compile.

29.6   Guidelines

We are now in a position to complete our guidelines for developing good classes. As this is the last 'programming' chapter, we'll repeat all the previous guidelines too:

(1)   Like process-oriented and data-oriented software systems, object-oriented systems should be developed with the aim of safeguarding your data as much as possible.

(2)   All the classes in your program should be well encapsulated, with no 'leaks'; your data should always be private (or, where necessary, `protected`: see Guideline 6), and your member functions should (generally) provide a carefully controlled public interface to these data.

(3)   Think of your member functions as accessors or mutators: use `const` accessor functions wherever possible.

(4)   Just like ordinary functions, member functions should use call by value (or `const` call by reference) whenever possible, and only resort to call by reference, or call by address, when absolutely necessary.

(5)   `Private` (or `protected`) member functions are 'A Good Thing' and can be useful; one example of such use is given in Guideline 11.

(6)   Use `protected` *data* only where essential. As all derived classes are able to directly interact with such data, making changes at a future date will be difficult (if not impossible), because you have no way of knowing which derived classes will need to be edited in these circumstances. In effect, classes with `protected` data have 'leaks' in their encapsulation.

(7)   Always provide a default constructor, otherwise users of your code won't be able to create arrays of your objects, or create simple 'APO' relationships.

(8)   If your class involves dynamic memory allocation (or if you have provided a destructor for some other reason), make sure you provide a copy constructor.

(9)   Overload operators with care. C++ opposes no semantic restrictions on the programmer, and you are free to make the + operator display 'hello, Mum' on the screen every time it is used! Naturally, you should limit the use of overloaded operators to appropriate cases, and implement only appropriate behaviour.

(10) Don't try to be 'cute' when overloading operators. For example, creating a `cCustomer` class (containing name and address fields) and overloading + to represent marriage so that (Paul Jones of 23 Hill Road) + (Mary Smith of 45 West St) becomes (Paul and Mary Smith, 45 West St) is an example of cute programming, and should be avoided.

(11) If your class involves dynamic memory allocation (or, again, if you have provided a destructor for some other reason), you will need to overload the assignment operator (*as well as* providing a copy constructor).

Note that the constructor, overloaded assignment operator and copy constructor will often share common code. It's often possible (and a good idea) to create a `private` or `protected` member function to perform the shared operations.

(12) Treat generic classes (and functions) with caution. Don't try to provide appropriate initializations for all possible types of data; where possible, let the objects passed to your generic class perform their own initializations.

(13) Inheritance is useful: indeed, it's a distinguishing characteristic of object-oriented programs. However, don't forget the aggregation ('a part of') and association ('need to know about') relationships considered in earlier chapters.

We'll say more about the high-level decisions involved in choosing an appropriate relationship in the remainder of Part III.

(14) Treat multiple inheritance with great caution. Consider carefully whether you need to add this extra level of complexity to your code.

(15) Get to know the features of dynamic binding, but use it only where necessary. Dynamic binding can have an impact on the speed of your programs if used excessively.

(16) When you create abstract classes, do so with caution. Users of such classes won't thank you for imposing arbitrary rules concerning the member functions they must include in their derived classes.

(17) When thinking of exceptions, focus primarily on errors that may affect the class, rather than those associated with individual member functions. Exceptions should be thrown only as a last resort, in the event of a catastrophic and unpredictable error (for example, hard disk failure). Don't throw exceptions when return values will do the job; ignoring a return value won't harm your program, but failing to trap an exception will cause an abrupt (and usually unpopular) termination.

(18) Errors occur, and they are not always the fault of the software engineer; it is, however, the responsibility of the engineer to have an appropriate error detection and correction harness in place. Focus always on trying to minimize the impact of errors and – in a worst-case scenario – trying to keep the system up and running (for example) till all buffers are flushed to disk. Imagine you are programming a control system for a telephone exchange. To lose one call in the event of an error is not good, but probably acceptable; shutting down the whole exchange must be avoided at all costs.

29.7 Conclusions

With this chapter, we conclude our overview of the object-oriented programming features provided by the C++ language. We have seen here how both single and multiple inheritance can be implemented in C++.

The material in this chapter should begin to provide a flavour of the techniques used to develop object-oriented C++ programs. While, for example, process-oriented software development involved working in a top-down direction, decomposing an original problem into functions, object-oriented development places more emphasis on bottom-up development. This approach rests on the ability to start with smaller classes and, in part through the inheritance mechanisms we have discussed here, customize and combine these classes to produce larger and more useful code modules.

We consider this development process in more depth in the remaining chapters in Part III.

Exercises

29.1 Explore the operation of Program 29.1. Satisfy yourself that you understand how it works. What happens if `protected` (rather than `public`) inheritance is used?

29.2 Suggest a programming situation in which `private` inheritance might be useful?

29.3 Extend Program 29.9 so that there is a further generation of classes derived, using single inheritance, from `cDerived_Class`.

29.4 Add another generation to Program 29.13, and allow the user to access a version of `show()` from any of the generations.

29.5 Extend Program 29.1 to replace the `show_b()` and `show_d()` member functions with their insertion operator equivalents.

29.6 Edit Program 29.13 so that the `virtual` keyword is eliminated. Explain why this minor change has the impact it does. If you have access to a disassembler, inspect assembly language versions of each program. What differences can you detect?

29.7 Using the generic stack class from Chapter 28, implement a heterogeneous stack.

29.8 A firm of architects requires a program that allows clients to 'design their own homes or office buildings' on a computer screen. Your company has been employed to develop some appropriate software, and your boss has suggested that the program should contain (at least) four classes: `cRoom`, `cBuilding`, `cHouse` and `cOffice`. Your boss further suggests that `cRoom` will be 'a part of' `cBuilding`. `cHouse` and `cOffice` will then be 'a kind of' `cBuilding`. Do you agree with these suggestions? Try to create an appropriate set of classes that could be useful in this application, and write a test program to demonstrate that your classes work as required.

29.9 In the exercises in Chapter 26, we considered the provision of fire-fighting facilities in London. In particular, we began to develop a simulation of London traffic intended to enable the city Planning Department to determine where the fire stations should be situated so as to mimimize the time taken to reach a fire. Consider this problem again, in the light of the material on inheritance discussed in this chapter. What classes do you need in this program, and how will they be related? How will you use NTKA, APO and AKO relationships between classes?

Consider that the traffic of interest in the simulations consists of cars, taxis, buses, lorries, bicycles, motor bikes. Each is likely to have different properties (such as average speed, size, number of wheels, etc.). Implement some appropriate classes, and write a test program to confirm that they operate as required.

30 Class-relationship diagrams

30.1 Introduction

In Part III, we've been exploring the object-oriented features of the C++ programming language. In particular, we have begun to look at the way in which object-oriented extensions, added to the base C language by Stroustrup (1991), allow the programmer to add new data types to the language and fully integrate these so that they become indistinguishable from the simple built-in types.

We've seen in Parts I and II how process models (built using tools such as the dataflow diagram) and data models (built largely from entity-relationship diagrams) contribute to the software engineering process. In order to model the classes required within a system, and the connections between them, we use an extended version of the entity-relationship diagram (ERD), originally discussed in Chapter 21; the extended diagram is, perhaps not surprisingly, called a **class-relationship diagram** (CRD).

We introduce CRDs in this chapter. A tutorial describing how to create such diagrams using the CASE tool is given in Appendix J. The integration of class models within the general framework of SADIE is discussed in Chapter 31.

30.2 Entities vs classes

Classes are, in O-O parlance, 'a kind of' entity: that is, in a real sense, classes have evolved from entities. There are, however, several fundamental distinctions between an entity and a class:

- An entity is a 'data only' data type; it has no member functions. The data are `public` data.

- A class is a data type consisting of both data and member functions. In general, data are `private` (encapsulated), while member functions are `public`. Access to the data is (usually) only possible via member functions.

- An entity supports two kinds of relationship with another entity: associations and aggregations.

- A class supports three kinds of relationship with another class: associations, aggregations and inheritance.

- An entity is a 'simple data type' (see Table 24.1); an instance of such a type must be used by the programmer in a fundamentally different way than an instance of a base type.
- A class is an 'integrated data type'; an instance of such a type may be used by the programmer in a manner identical to an instance of a base type.
- An instance of an entity is (usually) a persistent data item.
- An instance of a class is not (usually) a persistent data item.
- An entity can be viewed as a crude model of a real world object, and a good model of a database table.
- A class can be viewed as a good model of a real world object, and a crude model of a database table.

We need to keep these differences in mind as we develop class-relationship diagrams.

30.3   Class-relationship diagrams

When you use classes in your system development, it is helpful to have an appropriate set of diagrams to represent the details of, and relationships between them. The notation used in SADIE to represent such classes is described in this section.

30.3.1   Representing the relationships between classes and between objects and classes

As we noted above, the two fundamental relationships supported by entities are aggregation and association. These two forms of possible relationship are shown in Figure 30.1 as they might appear in an analysis document. We can represent Figure 30.1 in C++ as shown in Figure 30.2.

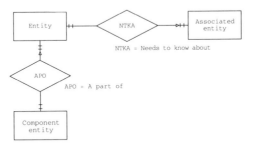

Figure 30.1   The two fundamental relationships between entities.

```
// Demonstration of entity relationships
// sComponent_Entity is a part (APO) of sEntity
struct sComponent_Entity
    {
    int num0;
    int num1;
    };
```

```
// Data in cAssoc_Entity are public and therefore visible to
// sEntity struct-variables
struct sAssoc_Entity
    {
    int num2;
    };
// NTKA is (usually) implemented via a pointer
// APO is (usually) implemented directly
struct sEntity
    {
    int                  num3;
    sComponent_Entity CE;
    sAssoc_Entity*    AE_PTR;
    };
```

Figure 30.2   An implementation, in C++, of the entities represented in Figure 30.1.

By contrast, there are three fundamental relationships between classes and between objects and classes: inheritance, aggregation and association. All three relationships are illustrated schematically in Figure 30.3. We can represent Figure 30.3 in C++ as shown in Figure 30.4.

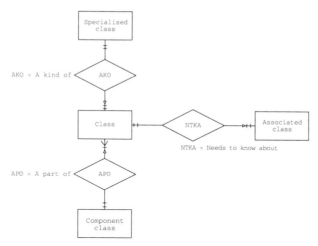

Figure 30.3   The three fundamental relationships between classes and between objects and classes.

```
// Demonstration of class relationships
// cComp is a part (APO) of cClass
class cComp
    {
    public:
        Set(int number) {_p = number;};
    private:
        int _p;
    };
```

```
// cAssoc is an associated class
// Private data in cAssoc are visible to cClass objects
// NOTE: Our association is "one way" (directed)
class cAssoc
    {
    public:
        Set(int number) {_a = number;};
    // Here, we make *all* memb funcs friends of cClass
    // You can be more selective, as appropriate
    friend class cClass;
    private:
        int _a;
    };
// cClass needs to know about (NTKA) cAssoc
// cComponent is a part of cClass
class cClass
    {
    public:
        Set1(int number) {_c = number;};
        // Access to (public) members of component class only
        Set2(int number) {_Comp.Set(number);};
        // Access to public and private parts of assoc class
        Set3(int number) {_Assoc_PTR->_a = number;};
    private:
        int    _c;
        cComp  _Comp;       // _Comp is part of cClass
        cAssoc* _Assoc_PTR; // Assoc object is not part of cClass
    };
// cSpecialised is a kind of (AKO) cClass
class cSpecialised : public cClass
    {
    public:
        Set(int number) {_e = number;};
    private:
        int _e;
    };
```

Figure 30.4 An implementation, in C++, of the classes represented in Figure 30.3.

Note that in Figure 30.3 the various flows may be labelled, if this helps communicate the meaning of the diagrams. However, the notation used is not intrinsically important; we consider some alternative ways of representing the relationships in Figure 30.3 in Section 30.3.3.

30.3.2   Representing class features

In addition to representing the relationships between classes, it is useful to have a way of representing the data and member functions of a given class. Figure 30.5 shows the simple representation used in SADIE. Note that there are three areas in the figure, representing private, protected and public data and/or functions.

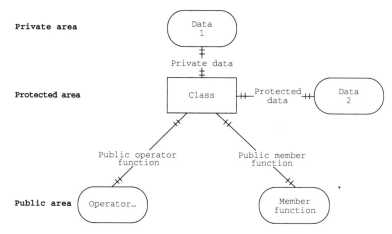

Figure 30.5   Representing a class in an attribute diagram.

We can represent the above features in C++ as shown in Figure 30.6.

```
/*********************************************************
 *                                                       *
 * CLASS:   cClass                                       *
 *                                                       *
 *********************************************************/
class cClass
    {
    public:
        ... operator...(...);
        ... Member_Function();
    protected:
        ... _Data2;
    private:
        ... _Data1;
    };
```

Figure 30.6   An implementation, in C++, of the classes represented in Figure 30.5.

Note that, compared with our previous attribute diagrams from our D-O techniques (such as that shown in Figure 30.7), this diagram is 'upside down'. This emphasizes the significant difference between the struct and class implementations of the two, apparently overlapping, 'data' structures.

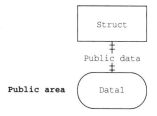

Figure 30.7   A C++ struct represented in a class diagram.

30.3.3 Alternative notations

There are a range of different notations used to represent class-relationship diagrams. For example, Figure 30.8 repeats the CRD given in Figure 30.3, this time using the notation used by Rumbaugh *et al.* (1991) in their Object Modelling Technique (OMT), and in the notation used by Booch (1994). The particular notation used is largely unimportant, although it is probably sensible to stick to a single notation on a particular project.

We use a simple form of CRD which is well-supported by a range of inexpensive CASE tools. If you have other CASE tools available, you will find it straightforward to use either of the notations shown in Figure 30.8 (or a different notation) in conjunction with the methodology described in this book.

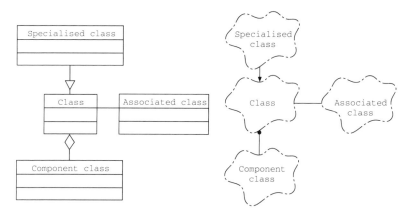

Figure 30.8 The class-relationship diagram from Figure 30.3 redrawn [left] using the OMT notation described by Rumbaugh *et al.* (1991), and [right] using the Booch (1994) notation.

30.4 Identifying appropriate classes

Early in the life of an object-oriented system development, the software engineer has to find some appropriate classes and/or objects with which to model the problem domain. When O-O methods were just beginning to gain in popularity, this was not considered a major problem. Shlaer and Mellor (1988) claim that 'Identifying objects is pretty easy to do'. Meyer (1988) has also memorably claimed: 'The objects are just there for the picking' ...to which Coad and Yourdon (1991) later replied succinctly: 'Nuts!'

Most engineers would probably agree with Coad and Yourdon: finding *appropriate* classes is a non-trivial activity. In this section we'll look at some of the alternatives.

30.4.1 A lesson from Smalltalk

We first mentioned the object-oriented programming language Smalltalk in Chapter 3. While C++, as we've seen, is a hybrid programming language, supporting process-oriented, data-oriented and object-oriented development, Smalltalk is a pure (or at least purer) object-oriented programming language. Coad and Yourdon (1991) argue that experience with Smalltalk can help make software engineers think in an object-oriented manner; this is good advice.

However, without rushing out and buying a Smalltalk environment, we can immediately gain a few insights into pure O-O programming style simply by considering two pertinent features of this language:

(1)   In Smalltalk, everything is an object. For example, an integer variable is an object.

(2)   There are no 'ordinary' or 'stand-alone' functions: that is, all Smalltalk functions are the equivalent of C++ member functions, and are associated with an object.

Clearly, we can't achieve this ideal in C++ even if we wished to because, for example, all C++ programs must contain a stand-alone `main()` function.

However, the above points do suggest that when we are beginning to draw up a class list, the first thing we should start to consider is that our system itself will be one of the main classes in our preliminary class list.

30.4.2   Deriving a class model from the problem statement

The most basic technique for uncovering candidate classes, it is generally agreed, involves looking for nouns in the initial problem statement (for example, see Abbott, 1983). This is, of course, exactly the same technique we used to derive our data models in Part II; as we'll see, however, we apply the same basic approach in some slightly different ways when trying to draw up a class diagram.

For example, given the following very brief description of a simple calculator program:

'The **calculator** will read two **numbers** from the **keypad**, add them together and display the **result** on the **computer screen**.'

we might start by considering the classes/objects shown in Figure 30.9.

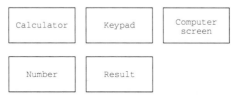

Figure 30.9   Some candidate classes for a calculator example.

Next, we need to review these classes. 'Calculator', 'Keypad' and 'Computer Screen' seem the most promising of the group. If we assume for our purposes here that the program is to add integers, then both 'Number' and 'Result' will be 'integer objects', rather than classes in their own right.

Our initial class diagram then looks as shown in Figure 30.10.

Figure 30.10   The initial class diagram for a calculator example.

30.4.3 Forming relationships

Having determined an initial class diagram, we need to determine the relationships between classes. Naturally, at this stage the class model is still in a state of flux, and it is seldom wise to grow too attached to any particular class; as you draw in the relationships, your understanding of the system under development should increase, and you are likely to modify the initial class list.

As far as relationships are concerned, as we've seen, there are essentially three possibilities: APO (aggregation) relationships, NTKA (association) relationships and AKO (inheritance) relationships. These fall naturally into two groups, **NTKA relationships** and **AxO relationships**. The following observations may help you choose an appropriate relationship:

- NTKA relationships are formed, in general, between classes of different kinds: a bank needing to know the address of a customer in order to authorize a loan, or a doctor needing to know the blood type of a patient before prescribing a particular treatment.

- AxO relationships are, by contrast, between classes which are, in some sense, more similar. A keypad may be part of a desktop calculator, and a scientific calculator may be a kind of desktop calculator (with a few additional buttons and functions).

- AxO and NTKA relationships can usually be distinguished comparatively easily. Unless you are an old hand at the O-O game, it is sometimes less obvious is whether a particular AxO relationship is 'part' or 'kind' in nature. In particular: 'Multiple inheritance is often confused with aggregation' (Booch, 1994, p.130).

- APO and AKO may be distinguished according to the following rules:

  – APO relationships means aggregation. According to Rumbaugh *et al.* (1991, p. 57): 'Aggregation is a strong form of association in which an aggregate object is made of components.'

  – AKO relationships mean inheritance. If in doubt, if you can't swear to the presence of an 'is a' relationship then don't use AKO; use the simpler APO.

Our calculator example from above is, of course, rather simple. Here, the computer screen and keyboard are both 'a part of' the calculator system (Figure 30.11).

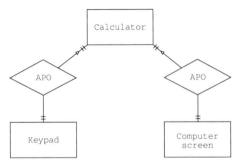

Figure 30.11   The class-relationship diagram for the simple calculator.

30.5 Conclusions

In this brief chapter, we have begun to look at the subject of class-relationship diagrams. As we will see in Chapter 31, CRDs are an important component of O-O SADIE, but they are not on their own sufficient to represent the data, process and control aspects of the system. To complete the object model, we need to take another look at structure charts.

Exercises

30.1 In Chapter 24, we illustrated our introduction to object-oriented software development by describing, in outline, a weather monitoring system for the Arctic. Complete the class-relationship diagram (CRD) for this system, highlighting any areas of ambiguity. Develop, as far as possible, a first prototype of this system in C++ (simulate all the sensor inputs via the keyboard in your prototype).

30.2 Given the following problem statement, draw up an appropriate CRD:

'As part of a prototype system for monitoring the core temperature in the Happyfield nuclear reactor, English Nuclear Ltd require a software product that works as follows. A technician will use a remotely controlled temperature sensor to record the temperature of the reactor core (in degrees Celsius) and a long-range laser measurement sensor to record the length of a sample reactor control rod (in metres). These values will be typed in to a computer terminal at five-minute intervals. The computer will store the values and display them in an appropriate format on the screen. In addition, as each temperature is typed in, the program will calculate the minimum and maximum permissible control rod lengths, according to the following equations:

Minimum length = $T^3 - 456T^2 - 321T$
Maximum length = $2T^3 - 456T^2 - 321T$

Note that here, T is *average* temperature reading recorded over the last hour, in degrees Celsius.

If the current length of the sample control rod exceeds the safety thresholds specified by these equations, then the program should issue a suitable warning; otherwise, the program should issue an 'OK' message.'

30.3 In Chapter 29 (Exercise 29.8) we considered a software system to support a firm of architects who wished to allow their clients the opportunity to actively participate in the design of their new home or office building. Draw up a CRD for this system. Highlight any areas of ambiguity.

30.4 Consider the stock control system discussed in the case study in Chapter 23. Represent this system using a CRD. Compare and contrast the CRD-based software model with the original data-oriented model.

30.5 In the exercises in Chapters 26 and 29, we considered a software system for simulating the flow of traffic in the streets of London. Draw up a CRD to describe this system.

30.6 If you have access to a technical library, look up some books on Smalltalk. Investigate how you could implement Figure 30.3 in this language.
    Note: the Free Software Foundation distribute an excellent version of (GNU) Smalltalk which is freely available: if you have access to the Internet, you may find it informative to get hold of a copy of this language and explore its features.

31 | **Object-oriented SADIE**

31.1   Introduction

In order to compare and contrast process-oriented and data-oriented software development, we have introduced the Simple Analysis, Design & Implementation methodology (SADIE), hitherto consisting of two overlapping methods, namely process-oriented (P-O) SADIE and data-oriented (D-O) SADIE. In this chapter, we describe the final, object-oriented (O-O) component of SADIE.

We discuss the issues involved in semi-formal object-oriented software development and present a step-by-step 'recipe' to facilitate the process.

31.2   Why CRDs are not enough

The material in this chapter uses the notation for the class-relationship diagram presented in Chapter 30; however, CRDs, on their own, do not form complete object models.

In a sense, CRDs are analogous to the simple dataflow diagrams used in 'traditional' process-oriented (structured) methods of software development we first introduced in Chapter 12. We soon found it necessary to add control processes to our basic dataflow diagrams, and to represent the detailed operation of these processes using state-transition diagrams. These extensions, described in Chapter 14, allowed us to model a much wider range of systems, from batch systems to interrupt-driven systems.

However, the implications of the addition of control modelling capabilities to the SADIE tool kit extend much further, and relate directly to our discussions here. To explain why this is so, recall that our first logical process models focused on only two aspects of the system in which we are interested:

- *Process*: what does it do?
- *Data:* what does it do it to?

However, as we saw in Chapter 14, we need to be able to add a further feature to this list:

- *Control:* when does it do it?

Thus, we began to view our software systems from three perspectives: process, data and control. These features of the problem aren't simply relevant for a process-oriented model, they are relevant for *any* model, because they represent the fundamental operations at the heart of a computer, and we are ultimately constrained in what our programs can do, not only by the capacity and power of the particular computer model we use but also by the very nature of *all* computers.

What we have seen through the course of this book is that all of our modelling techniques necessarily involve these three views of a system, but place the emphasis differently. Thus, in a process-oriented model, we might rate the important system features in this order:

(1)   *Process:* what does it do?

(2)   *Control:* when does it do it?

(3)   *Data:* what does it do it to?

By contrast, for a data-oriented model, we might rate the system features as follows:

(1)   *Data:* what does it do it to?

(2)   *Process:* what does it do?

(3)   *Control:* when does it do it?

Finally, for an object-oriented model, we might rate the system features as follows

(1)   *Process and Data:* What does it do, and what to?

(2)   *Control:* when does it do it?

In this case, the process and data models are combined and considered to be equally important, and the necessary control information is provided through an extended form of structure chart.

31.3   Building the object model

With simple process-oriented software development, there are clear divisions between analysis, design and implementation, with a separate 'notation' – dataflow diagram (and so on), structure charts (and so on) and C++ – used at each stage.

A division between design and implementation is necessary, we have previously argued, if we are to avoid 'hacking'. However, we have progressively seen this division reduced in size. For example, as we added control information to our dataflow diagram, we had to make decisions during analysis which, in early process-oriented methods, would have been considered part of the system design. Similarly, as we considered data-oriented development, the roles of analyst and designer in the production of the essential (isolated) data structures were even less clear-cut, with the same notation being used for both analysis and design.

This progressive blurring of the distinction between analysis and design is even more apparent in O-O approaches, because:

> *In an O-O approach, we try to model the world in software. The distinctions between* what *a system does,* how *it does it, and the system (software) itself begin to fade away as we start to 'think in objects'. In effect, objects encapsulate both 'what' and 'how' decisions.*

Thus, with O-O SADIE, we do not have a separate analysis and design component in our development. Instead, both analysis and design may legitimately be conducted using the same notation; this 'blurring' of the distinction between analysis and design is seen by some O-O users as a significant advantage of this approach (for example, see Eliëns, 1994, p.19).

31.4   The components of the object model

The object model (Figure 31.1) uses the class-relationship diagram presented in Chapter 30 along with various modelling tools (structure chart, process specification, context diagram, data dictionary) from earlier chapters. We outline how these components are used in this section.

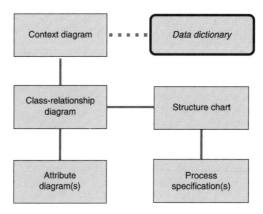

Figure 31.1   The components of the SADIE object model.

To illustrate our discussions, we'll apply O-O techniques to a traditional D-O problem: the development of a specialized 'mailing list' program; the scenario is given below. As a general rule, object-oriented techniques may be used for any software development project which previously may have used either process-oriented or data-oriented techniques. In the next chapter, we'll develop a complete O-O solution to compare with the original (process-oriented) bank ATM system in Chapter 16.

Note that simply because O-O techniques may be used does not mean that they should always be used: when we have considered the two examples mentioned above, we'll be in a position (in Chapter 33) to consider the case for and against each of the three approaches we have discussed during the course of this book.

31.4.1   Scenario

Leicester Software Engineering have been approached by Pete Cool of Cool Talkers Ltd. Cool Talkers specializes in telephone sales, and (they claim) can sell *anything* over the phone. In particular, at the present time, they specialize in last-minute holiday sales, offering potential customers substantial discounts on remaining seats on packages offered by Happy Holidays Ltd.

The package holidays include flights via London's Gatwick airport to (and from) the destination, hotel accommodation and meals for the two-week duration of the holiday. Usually, the Happy Holidays company charters a plane, and books hotel rooms in bulk at a reduced price: their packages are usually offered at competitive prices. However, if the chartered plane has empty seats, then Happy Holidays risks losing money. Two weeks before the departure date Happy Holidays therefore sell any remaining holiday places to Cool Talkers at a 60% reduction. Cool Talkers then have two weeks to sell these holidays (at half price) before the flights leave. Clearly, the more quickly they can sell, the better chance they have of being successful.

Pete Cool founded his company in the early 1980s, and has since seen business grow very steadily from a one-man operation in 1982 to a company employing nearly 200 people in 1996. At the heart of the business, and jealously safeguarded, is the company database system. This includes names, personal details (credit rating, salary, interests) and, of course, telephone numbers for over four million households in the UK. It is this information, all gathered legally over the years, that the company thrives on.

Because of the heavy reliance on information and information processing, Pete Cool employs an experienced team of software engineers. When, for example, a contract to sell cars is taken on, it is the responsibility of this team to produce an appropriate list of people to call. In this case, it would probably not be very successful trying to sell to people above the age of about 75, those on very low incomes, or those who have purchased a car in the last year.

Recently, after a near disaster with late production of a telephone list for a double glazing contract, the head of the computing section, Paul Gray, has been considering ways in which the reliability of the code produced by the software team might be improved. In particular, he would like to explore the potential of object-oriented methods to upgrade their present software system.

Paul Gray therefore asks Jane and her colleagues to prepare a simple demonstration mailing list program for them, using object-oriented techniques.

We outline a solution to this problem in this section.

31.4.2 The Context diagram

We've used Context diagrams in both process-oriented and data-oriented software development, and considered this diagram to be part of our process model. Of course, it is really no such thing: the Context diagram is really a hybrid, representing classes (which of course encompasses entities) and dataflows (for example, Figure 31.2).

Because of their hybrid nature, Context diagrams are no less useful for object-oriented development, and we shall continue to use them as our first project diagrams.

Cool Talkers example

Liaising with Paul Gray, it is immediately clear to Jane that, unusually, the requirements for the system are to be largely her own decision.

'The only important thing,' says Paul Gray at the end of their conversation, 'is that the system works. We want to be able to compare the object model you produce with the data- and process-oriented models we usually use. We want to see if this object-oriented stuff is worth the retraining costs, or if it's all just hype.'

Jane is happy to comply, and begins by drawing up the Context diagram (Figure 31.3).

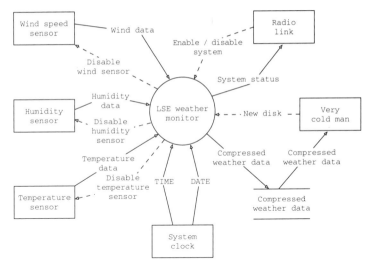

Figure 31.2 Context diagram for a weather monitoring system.

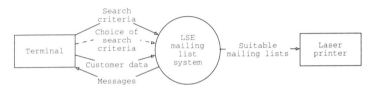

Figure 31.3 Context diagram for the O-O mailing list.

31.4.3 The class-relationship diagram

Class-relationship diagrams (Figure 31.4) are of course an essential tool for object-oriented software development. These diagrams were discussed at length in Chapter 30, and won't be further considered here.

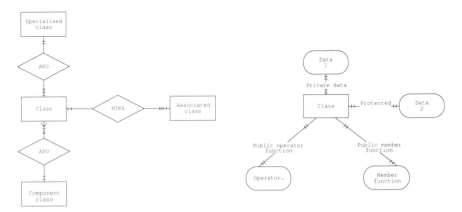

Figure 31.4 A general class-relationship diagram, and associated attribute diagram.

Cool Talkers example

Jane begins to think about the class-relationship diagram for Cool Talkers. The central class, she decides, will be a customer class: this will be, in effect, an 'entity' wrapped in a class, with overloaded operators to make the input and output of data a straight-forward process. In addition, she will need some kind of container class: a collection of customer objects, forming the database itself. This container class will have a number of member functions for searching the database and storing the data.

To help her think about the problem, Jane draws up a process list (Table 31.1). The class diagram itself is shown in Figure 31.5.

Process name	Notes
Menu	Offer user list of options
Enter	Allow user to enter information into the database
Name search	Search the database for a customer by name
Area search	Search the database for a particular company by area
All search	List all customers in the database
Quit	Close the programming, closing files as appropriate

Table 31.1 Process list for the mailing list.

Figure 31.5 The class-relationship diagram.

The attribute diagrams corresponding to Figure 31.5 are given in Figure 31.6 and Figure 31.7.

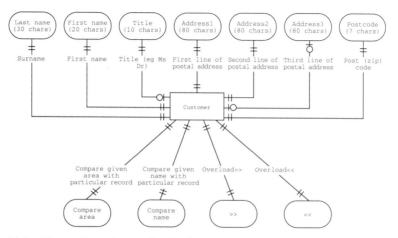

Figure 31.6 The attribute diagram for the Customer class.

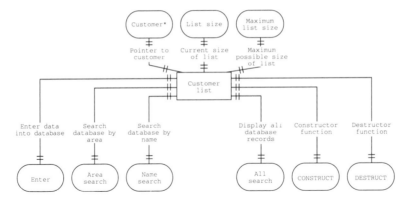

Figure 31.7 The attribute diagram for the Cust List class.

31.4.4 The structure chart

As we saw in Section 31.2, we need to have a way of representing control information in our object models. Structure charts (for example, Figure 31.8) provide a familiar way of representing this information in a concise manner. In addition, structure charts are sufficiently flexible to allow us to model not only 'pure' object-oriented programs (such as might be developed using Smalltalk), but also hybrid programs (of a kind that can be implemented in C++). Note that an alternative to structure charts is discussed in Appendix K.

Figure 31.8 shows the type of structure chart we have considered in previous chapters. The modules on the chart would be associated with PSpecs and would, of course, become ordinary (as opposed to member) functions in a C++ implementation.

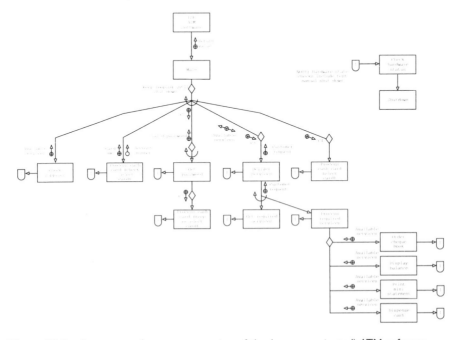

Figure 31.8 A structure chart representation of the (process-oriented) ATM software.

Suppose, however, we have the CRD representation of a system shown in Figure 31.4. One possible (partial) structure chart representation of this system is given in Figure 31.9. Note that the operation of the structure chart is precisely as before: the only difference is that we use 'contained' boxes to represent member functions. More generally, of course, we can expect our structure charts to become more complex (Figure 31.10).

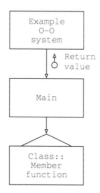

Figure 31.9 A partial structure chart representation of the CRD shown in Figure 31.4.

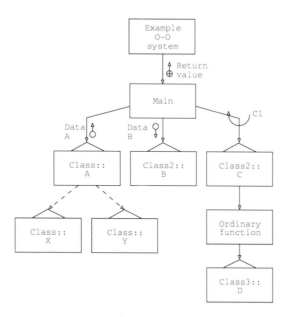

Figure 31.10 A more representative structure chart for an object-oriented system.

Cool Talkers example

Jane draws up the structure chart for Cool Talkers (Figure 31.11).

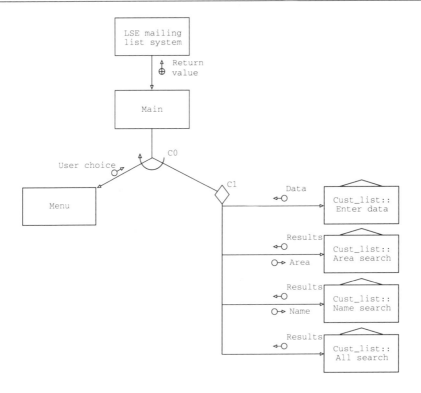

Figure 31.11 The structure chart.

31.4.5 The PSpecs

The operation of both member functions and ordinary functions in an object-oriented system is described using PSpecs. These take the same form as in previous examples.

Cool Talkers example

The PSpecs are the same as previous examples and are omitted here.

31.4.6 The data dictionary

As with the PSpecs, the data dictionary takes the same form in an object model that it did in previous examples. See Table 32.2 in the next chapter.

Cool Talkers example

The dictionary is the same as previous examples and is omitted here.

31.5 Implementing the object model

As we first saw in Chapter 11, the implementation process is an non-trivial exercise. Even when you have successfully developed the object model, there is still considerable work to be done in creating the final code.

We'll consider this process in the section, linking the material from here and the previous chapter with the material on programming from earlier in Part III.

31.5.1 Program structure

As we saw in Chapter 11, a valuable feature of the C++ programming language, and one which facilitates the rapid development of large programs, is the ability to arrange a single program in multiple source files, and to combine all these files into a single project.

When following a process-oriented approach, it is likely that your project will comprise at least some of the following files:

- `project.mak` The project file. This will contain (in an implementation dependent format) details of all the files in the project, and the links between them. Note that the name of this file varies: typically it will have the filename extension '.mak', '.prj' or '.wpj'.

- `project.h` The header file. This is likely to contain function declarations and details of read-only variables, etc.

- `project1.cpp, project2.cpp` The source files. These will include definitions of the various C++ functions. The function `main()` will usually be in a file alone: other functions may be pre-compiled, and stored in library files (see below).

- `project.lib`, etc.   Library files. These pre-compiled files contain object code for C++ functions that your program will use. This object code needs to be linked with other files in the project.

Note that with data-oriented programs, it is usual to include declarations of the user-defined data structures (typically, `struct`-based data structures) in (one or more) header files.

With object-oriented C++ programs, there is unfortunately less general agreement on the 'division of labour' between the various files in the project. Typically, the structure and file names used are as given below:

- `project.mak` The project file. It takes the same form as those used with process- and data-oriented projects.

- `project.h` The header file. This will usually be similar to header files in process- and data-oriented projects. Note that some programmers place class prototypes in such header files, while placing the definitions of the member functions in files with extension '.cpp'.

- `project1.hpp, project2.hpp`, etc   Typically, such files will contain member function definitions, but some programmers include class prototypes in these files as well.

  Note that the '.hpp' extension is usually reserved for source files: when such files are pre-compiled (and, for example, provided as part of a class library), the extension '.lib' is typically used.

- `project.cpp` This will typically contain the `main()` function for the project.

Whether the structure used precisely matches the above layout or not, the aim should always be to draw a distinction between the implementation of, and the interface to, the classes used in the system. To this end, we recommend that – where large numbers of classes are used – the following structure is followed with object-oriented C++ programs:

- `project.mak` The project file. The format of this file will depend on the compiler you use.

- `project.h` The header file. This, as for process- and data-oriented programs, should be used for (ordinary) function prototypes, and declarations of read-only variables. *Don't* put class prototypes in here!

- `project.cpp` Put the `main()` function for the project in a file of its own. Give this file the same name as the project.

- `project1.h`, `project2.h`, etc. These are 'interface' files: use them for class prototypes. Don't try to put one prototype per file – group related classes in the same file.

- `project1.cpp`, `project2.cpp`, etc. These are 'implementation' files. If you have three class prototypes in a file, put the corresponding member function definitions in an implementation file with the same name, but a different extension.

- `project1.lib`, `project2.lib`, etc. Library files represent pre-compiled versions of '.h' and '.cpp' files. If you compile (for example) the files 'project1.hpp' and 'project1.cpp', the resulting library should be called 'project1.lib'.

31.5.2 Translating class diagrams into C++

Object-oriented software development techniques support three kinds of relationship between components: associations, aggregations and inheritance. We considered briefly some ways of implementing these relationships in Chapters 26 and 30; here we explore the implementation of these relationships in more depth.

Inheritance (AKO)

We considered the implementation of inheritance relationships in Chapter 29. We saw then that there are essentially two possibilities: single inheritance and multiple inheritance. What we did not consider was if, and when, multiple inheritance should be used.

You should be aware that multiple inheritance is the subject of some controversy in the O-O community. This is because the technique is seen to have two central disadvantages:

- It can greatly increase the complexity of a class hierarchy, making the code difficult to implement correctly and difficult for users of the (source) code (that is, other programmers) to understand.

- It is (or can be) conceptually untidy. Inheritance models 'a kind of' relationship; how, it is argued, can one object be a kind of two different (base) objects? This situation becomes even more (conceptually) confusing when we consider multiple inheritance from the same base class. How can a derived object be two different kinds of objects at the same time?

The bottom line is: use multiple inheritance with care. These issues are discussed in greater depth by Cargill (1992), Jacobson *et al.* (1993) and Horstmann (1995).

Aggregations (APO)

Aggregations are APO (A Part Of) relationships. One possibility is illustrated in Figure 31.12. This example is taken from the mailing list program we discussed earlier.

```
const int STRG_SZ = 81; // Size of character arrays…
/*****************************************************************
 *****************************************************************
 *                                                               *
 * CLASS:     cCustomer                                          *
 *                                                               *
 *****************************************************************
 ****************************************************************/
class cCustomer
    {
    public:
        friend istream &operator>> (istream&, cCustomer&);
        friend ostream &operator<< (ostream&, const cCustomer&);

        int Compare_Name(char*) const;
        int Compare_Area(char*) const;

    private:
        char _lastname[STRG_SZ];    // Last name
        char _firstname[STRG_SZ];   // First name
        char _title[STRG_SZ];       // Title
        char _address1[STRG_SZ];    // 1st line of address
        char _address2[STRG_SZ];    // 2nd line of address
        char _address3[STRG_SZ];    // 3rd line of address
        char _postcode[STRG_SZ];    // Postcode
    };
/*****************************************************************
 *****************************************************************
 *                                                               *
 * CLASS:     cCustomer_List                                     *
 *                                                               *
 *****************************************************************
 ****************************************************************/
class cCustomer_List
    {
    public:
        cCustomer_List();   // Constructor
        ~cCustomer_List();  // Destructor
    void Enter();
    void Name_Search() const;
    void Area_Search() const;
    void All_Search()  const;

    private:
        int         _max_list_size;
        cCustomer*  _List_PTR;
        int         _list_size;
    };
```

Figure 31.12 The class structure from the mailing list program, illustrating aggregation.

It is important to note that, in Figure 31.12, the APO relationship is implemented via a pointer; this is sometimes viewed immediately (and erroneously) as an association relationship, because the cCustomer object pointed to has (implicitly) 'a life of its own', or an 'independent' existence. Here, however, we must use pointers, along with dynamic memory allocation, to create an array of cCustomer objects in free store. The cCustomer array will never be accessed outwith the cCustomer_List class, and the relationship is one of aggregation. Finally, note that the complete code for this program is given at the end of this chapter.

Associations (NTKA)

Associations are 'need to know about' relationships. One possibility is illustrated in Program 31.1.

```cpp
// Demonstration of association relationships - v1.0
// Source is: 31_01.CPP

#include <iostream.h>

class cClass; // forward reference

// cAssoc is an associated class
class cAssoc
    {
    public:
            cAssoc() {_a = 999;};
        void Set(int number) {_a = number;};
        void Show() const {cout << _a << endl;};

        // Here, we make cClass a friend
        friend class cClass;

    private:
        int _a;
    };

// cClass needs to know about (NTKA) cAssoc
class cClass
    {
    public:
            cClass(cAssoc*);
        void Set(int number) {_c = number;};
        void Show() const {cout << _c << endl;};

        // Access to private parts of assoc class...
        void Link() {_c = _Assoc_Object_PTR->_a;};

    private:
        int _c;
        cAssoc* _Assoc_Object_PTR;
    };

cClass::cClass(cAssoc* A_PTR)
    {
    _c = 0;
    _Assoc_Object_PTR = A_PTR;
    }
```

```
int main()
    {
    cAssoc AssocObject;
    cClass Object(&AssocObject);

    Object.Show();
    AssocObject.Show();
    Object.Link(); // Link via friend (member) function

    Object.Show();
    AssocObject.Show();

    return 0;
    }
```

Program 31.1   One way of implementing associations. (☺)

The output from Program 31.1 is as follows:

```
0
999
999
999
```

Note there are several ways in which associations can be implemented. As we saw in Part II, for example, it was always possible to implement many-to-one relationships between two tables through the use of an additional table. In the case of associations between classes, the equivalent link can be established by using an ordinary `friend` function. This general solution is illustrated in Program 31.2.

```
// Demonstration of association relationships - v2.0
// Source is: 31_01.CPP

#include <iostream.h>

class cClass; // forward reference

// cAssoc is an associated class
class cAssoc
    {
    public:
            cAssoc() {_a = 999;};
        void Set(int number) { _a = number;};
        void Show() const {cout << _a << endl;};

        // Here, we make (ordinary) function Link() a friend
        friend void Link(cClass&, cAssoc&);
    private:
        int _a;
    };

// cClass needs to know about (NTKA) cAssoc
// Note: the link is now external...
class cClass
    {
```

```
        public:
                cClass() {_c = 0;};
            void Set(int number) {_c = number;};
            void Show() const {cout << _c << endl;};

            // Here, we make (ordinary) function Link() a friend
            friend void Link(cClass&, cAssoc&);
        private:
            int _c;
    };

// Declaration of Assoc()
void Link(cClass&, cAssoc&);

int main()
    {
    cAssoc AssocObject;
    cClass Object;

    Object.Show();
    AssocObject.Show();

    Link(Object, AssocObject);   // Link via ordinary function

    Object.Show();
    AssocObject.Show();

    return 0;
    }

void Link(cClass& c, cAssoc& a)
    {
    c._c = a._a;
    }
```

Program 31.2 Another way of implementing associations ((☺))

The output from Program 31.2 is (again) as follows:

```
0
999
999
999
```

The key points to note about associations are as follows:

- An associated object has an independent existence: that is, it is used elsewhere in the program. If the 'associated' object is not used elsewhere, then the relationship may be better represented as aggregation.

- There are numerous ways to implement associations. Use an implementation that is as simple as possible, without leaving your data vulnerable. Under this rule, for example, the friend member function solution (Program 31.1) would usually be chosen over the equivalent ordinary function version (Program 31.2).

A recent discussion of the implementation of associations in C++ is given by Hope (1995).

31.6 Testing object-oriented systems

We have presented in earlier chapters general guidelines for testing process-oriented systems. These are repeated below:

As each module is completed, it will be tested by the programmer, as follows:

(1)   White Box testing is performed by reading through the code, line by line, looking for obvious flaws. Details of the tests performed are to be included in the implementation documents and initialled by the tester.

(2)   Black Box testing is performed with an individual driver program. Typically, 10% of the parameter range will be tested. Extremes of the input range of all parameters will always be tested. Details of the test performed, and of the results obtained, are to be included with the implementation documents and initialled by the tester.

These guidelines apply equally well to the testing of class-based (member) functions. However, object-oriented systems also introduce some further testing headaches.

First of all, testing should be carried out on a 'by class' basis, testing all member functions first by inspection, and then using an appropriate driver program as each class is completed. This is straightforward, and largely self-explanatory.

However, two new problems arise as a direct consequence of the O-O approach, and need to be considered at this stage:

- A member function that works perfectly well in a base class may not work correctly in a derived class. One obvious way in which this may occur is if, during single- or multiple-inheritance, the base class member function is overridden by a new member function in the derived class. More subtly, it may also occur, for example, if the data members in the base class have different values than those in the derived class, resulting in different pattern of behaviour from the member function (for example see Eliëns, 1994; Graham, 1994).

   This implies that system testing, where modules are used 'in context' becomes even more important for object-oriented systems; this provides the necessary top-down testing of the system.

   At the module testing stage, only White Box testing and knowledge of the code in question can begin to address these potential problems. This means that the implementer of the class is likely to have to be involved in testing the class; as we have discussed in previous chapters, this is not an ideal scenario.

- The widespread use of polymorphism in object-oriented systems, and in particular of late binding (run-time polymorphism) can make it difficult if not impossible to consider all possible ways in which a class may ultimately be used, making it harder to define the limits of the test strategy and therefore to ensure that testing is complete (for example see Jacobson *et al.,* 1993).

Overall, this means that code from class libraries must not be reused without retesting. In addition, it suggests that reuse of code where the source is not available (for example, where pre-compiled code libraries have been purchased) may be more difficult than is sometimes implied by promoters of an object-oriented approach.

Testing of object-oriented systems is an important topic, but one which has not yet attracted the attention it deserves. This is perhaps best illustrated by the paucity of material presented by two of the main proponents of O-O techniques (Booch, 1994; Rumbaugh *et al.,* 1991) to the topic of testing. Of this, Booch's contribution (Booch, 1994) consists of half a page of general discussion on unit testing vs system testing, while Rumbaugh *et al.* (1994) suggest that: 'Both testing and maintenance are simplified by an object-oriented approach, but the traditional methods used in these phases are not significantly altered' (p.144).

We do not claim to have provided here any solutions to the problems of testing in object-oriented systems. We merely highlight the fact that this is an area where further work will be required as object-oriented methods grow more mature.

31.7   A recipe for success

We conclude this chapter with a final recipe for object-oriented software development. As with all the recipes in this book, it should be adjusted to taste.

(O1)   *The business case*
The software engineer begins by estimating the technical and economic feasibility of the project. If, for example, the project is too small to be profitable, greatly outside the experience of the available personnel, or larger than can be tackled with the available technical and human resources, then it must be rejected at this stage.

(O2)   *The Context diagram*
The Context diagram is produced. The operating environment (hardware and/or operating system), and the basic software architecture are considered.

(O3)   *The class diagram*
A preliminary class diagram is produced.

(O4)   *The user interface*
Because of the impact of the system interface on all aspects of the model, it is sketched (or prototyped) at this early stage.

(O5)   *The process list*
A process list is drawn up. This list is necessarily very provisional, and creation of a highly polished document is not appropriate at this stage.

(O6)   *The walkthrough*
A system walkthrough is performed. Where feasible, the entire development team (analysts, designers, programmers) should be involved in this process. As the walkthrough progresses, the class diagram, process list, context diagram and interface sketches are modified as required.

(O7)   *The class-relationship diagram*
The class diagram (Stage 3) is extended into a first-cut CRD by adding in the relationships.

(O8)   *The attribute diagrams*
A preliminary attribute set is produced for each class.

(O9)   *The preliminary structure chart*
The preliminary structure chart is created.

(O10) *The process specifications*
The process specifications are written.

(O11) *The data dictionary*
The data dictionary is completed.

(O12) *The test strategy*
The overall system test strategy is drawn up. Testing is conducted on a class-by-class basis.

(O13) *The balanced object model*
The complete object model is reviewed, checked and balanced. Any necessary supporting documentation is written.

At this stage, the responsibility for the project passes to the programming team.

(O14) *Review and refinement of the object model*
The object model is reviewed by the programmer, in order to gain an understanding of the system, and to correct any flaws.

(O15) *The system framework*
The code framework is created, using CppSpecs, based on the class diagram, the structure chart and the PSpecs. For some systems, a prototype hardware framework may also be required.

(O16) *The preliminary modules*
The preliminary modules are created or, preferably, recycled from class and/or function libraries.

(O17) *Error detection and recovery*
The preliminary modules are extended, where necessary, through the addition of appropriate error detection and correction features.

(O18) *Module tests*
The modules are tested, by the programmers, according to the test strategy produced by the planning team. Modifications are made as required.

(O19) *The prototype system*
The tested modules are assembled into a prototype system, as dictated by the CRD and the structure chart(s).

(O20) *System tests and maintenance*
The complete prototype is tested again, first by the programmers and then by the test team, both working from the test strategy produced by the designers. The system is then subjected to user tests, including field tests and/or acceptance tests. The system is revised as necessary; any changes made during the testing and subsequent ongoing maintenance are recorded and reflected in the evolving object model.

31.8 Conclusions

We've described a third, and final, method of software development in this chapter, based on the object model. We've described the components of this new model, and illustrated how it may be used.

In the next chapter, we'll apply the software development 'recipe' presented in this chapter to a more substantial problem.

31.9   Appendix: Source code for mailing list

A complete source listing for the mailing list program described in this chapter is given below.

```
/***********************************************************
 *                                                         *
 * A Simple (object-based) Mailing List Program            *
 *                                                         *
 * Source is:    31_03.CPP                                 *
 * Created:      11 December, 1994                         *
 * Last edited:  25 July, 1995                             *
 *                                                         *
 ***********************************************************/

#include <assert.h>
#include <fstream.h>
#include <iostream.h>
#include <stdlib.h>
#include <string.h>

const int STRG_SZ = 81;    // Size of character arrays…

/***********************************************************
 ***********************************************************
 *                                                         *
 * CLASS:        cCustomer                                 *
 *                                                         *
 ***********************************************************
 ***********************************************************/
class cCustomer
    {
    public:
        friend istream &operator>> (istream&, cCustomer&);
        friend ostream &operator<< (ostream&, const cCustomer&);

        int Compare_Name(char*) const;
        int Compare_Area(char*) const;

    private:
        char _lastname[STRG_SZ];   // Last name
        char _firstname[STRG_SZ];  // First name
        char _title[STRG_SZ];      // Title
        char _address1[STRG_SZ];   // 1st line of address
        char _address2[STRG_SZ];   // 2nd line of address
        char _address3[STRG_SZ];   // 3rd line of address
        char _postcode[STRG_SZ];   // Postcode
    };

/***********************************************************
 *                                                         *
 * O FUNCTION:   >>                                        *
 *                                                         *
```

```
* CLASS:        cCustomer                                          *
*                                                                  *
* PURPOSE:      Overload ">>" operator.                            *
*                                                                  *
* RETURNS:      istream&                                           *
*                                                                  *
******************************************************************/
istream& operator>> (istream& input,
                     cCustomer& cust_REF)
    {
    cout << "Enter last name (ENTER to quit)        : ";
    input.getline(cust_REF._lastname, STRG_SZ)      ;

    if(!(cust_REF._lastname[0] == '\0'))
       { // User didn't just hit <ENTER> - so continue
       cout << "First name                          : ";
       input.getline(cust_REF._firstname, STRG_SZ)  ;

       cout << "Title (e.g. Ms Mr)                  : ";
       input.getline(cust_REF._title, STRG_SZ)      ;

       cout << "First line of address               : ";
       input.getline(cust_REF._address1, STRG_SZ)   ;

       cout << "Second line of address              : ";
       input.getline(cust_REF._address2, STRG_SZ)   ;

       cout << "Third line of address               : ";
       input.getline(cust_REF._address3, STRG_SZ)   ;

       cout << "Post (zip) code                     : ";
       input.getline(cust_REF._postcode, STRG_SZ)   ;
       }

    return input;
    }

/*****************************************************************
*                                                                *
* O FUNCTION:  <<                                                *
*                                                                *
* CLASS:        cCustomer                                        *
*                                                                *
* PURPOSE:      Overload "<<" operator.                          *
*                                                                *
* RETURNS:      ostream&                                         *
*                                                                *
******************************************************************/
ostream& operator<< (ostream& output,
                     const cCustomer& cust_REF)
    {
    output << cust_REF._title     << ' ';
    output << cust_REF._firstname << ' ';
    output << cust_REF._lastname  << '\n';
    output << cust_REF._address1  << '\n';
    output << cust_REF._address2  << '\n';
    output << cust_REF._address3  << '\n';
    output << cust_REF._postcode;
```

```
              return output;
              }
/**************************************************************
 *                                                            *
 * A FUNCTION:   Compare_Name()                               *
 *                                                            *
 * CLASS:        cCustomer                                    *
 *                                                            *
 * PURPOSE:      Compare given named and private data field   *
 *                                                            *
 * PRE:          None.                                        *
 * POST:         None.                                        *
 *                                                            *
 * RETURNS:      0 (int) if a match is found.                 *
 *                                                            *
 **************************************************************/
int cCustomer::Compare_Name(char* name_PTR) const
     {
     return strcmp(name_PTR, _lastname);
     }
/**************************************************************
 *                                                            *
 * A FUNCTION:   Compare_Area()                               *
 *                                                            *
 * CLASS:        cCustomer                                    *
 *                                                            *
 * PURPOSE:      Compare given area and private data field.   *
 *                                                            *
 * PRE:          None.                                        *
 * POST:         None.                                        *
 *                                                            *
 * RETURNS:      0 (int) if a match is found.                 *
 *                                                            *
 **************************************************************/
int cCustomer::Compare_Area(char* Area_PTR) const
     {
     /* In the UK, a postcode consists of 2 groups of 3
      * letters and numbers: for example, "LE1 7RH". Only the
      * first two letters of the first group are used in this
      * comparison. These two letters (e.g. LE for Leicester,
      * DD for Dundee) give a sufficiently accurate area check
      * for our purposes.
      *
      * If you live outside the UK, apply an appropriate rule
      * for your own situation. */
     return strncmp(Area_PTR, _postcode, 2);
     }
/**************************************************************
 **************************************************************
 *                                                            *
 * CLASS:        cCustomer_List                               *
 *                                                            *
 **************************************************************
 **************************************************************/
```

```
class cCustomer_List
    {
    public:
            cCustomer_List();    // Constructor
            ~cCustomer_List();   // Destructor
        void Enter();
        void Name_Search()    const;
        void Area_Search()    const;
        void All_Search()     const;
    private:
        int         _max_list_size;
        cCustomer*  _List_PTR;
        int         _list_size;
    };
/*****************************************************************
*                                                               *
* C FUNCTION:    cCustomer_List()                               *
*                                                               *
* CLASS:         cCustomer_List                                 *
*                                                               *
* PURPOSE:       Load the customer file from disk into          *
*                a dynamically-created array.                   *
*                                                               *
* PRE:           None.                                          *
* POST:          Detailed below.                                *
*                                                               *
* RETURNS:       void.                                          *
*                                                               *
*****************************************************************/
cCustomer_List::cCustomer_List()
    {
    // No pre-conditions

    fstream file_ptr;
    _list_size = 0;
    _max_list_size = 0;

    // Try to open a data file on disk
    file_ptr.open("mail.dat",
                ios::in | ios::nocreate | ios::binary);
    if (file_ptr.fail())
        {
        // Couldn't find an existing data file
        cout << "WARNING:    Can't find file 'mail.dat'\n";
        cout << "            A new file will be created.\n\n";
        }
    else
        {
        cout << "File 'mail.dat' opened successfully.\n";

        // Opened the existing data file successfully.
        // The first entry gives the number of records
        file_ptr.read((char*) &_list_size, sizeof(_list_size));

        cout  << "The file presently contains "
              << _list_size << " records.\n";
        }
```

```
    /* Memory for the database is to be allocated
     * dynamically. Try to grab enough memory for the data
     * on disk (if any), plus 10 new records.    */
    _max_list_size = _list_size + 10;

    _List_PTR = new cCustomer[_max_list_size];

    if (_List_PTR == NULL)
        {
        cout << "Sufficient memory could not be allocated.";
        exit(1);
        }
    else
        {
        cout  << "Memory allocated for "
              << _max_list_size << " records.\n\n";

        if (!file_ptr.fail())
            {
            // Read the records from disk (if poss)
            file_ptr.read((char*) _List_PTR,
                _list_size*sizeof(cCustomer));

            if (file_ptr.fail())
                {
                cout << "A disk error was detected\n";
                exit(1);
                }

            file_ptr.close();
            }
        }
    // Post-conditions
    assert(_list_size >= 0);
    assert(_max_list_size >= 0);

    // end of function cCustomer_List()
    }
/*********************************************************
*                                                       *
* D FUNCTION:    ~cCustomer_List()                      *
*                                                       *
* CLASS:         cCustomer_List                         *
*                                                       *
* PURPOSE:       Save the customer data on disk.        *
*                Return memory to free store.           *
*                                                       *
* PRE:           Detailed below.                        *
* POST:          None.                                  *
*                                                       *
* RETURNS:       void.                                  *
*                                                       *
*********************************************************/
cCustomer_List::~cCustomer_List()
    {
    // Pre-conditions
    assert(_List_PTR != NULL);
    assert(_list_size >= 0);
```

```
        fstream file_ptr;
        file_ptr.open("mail.dat", ios::out | ios::binary);
        if (file_ptr.fail())
            {
            cout << "ERROR: Cannot create data file 'mail.dat'\n";
            }
        else
            {
            cout << "List size is " << _list_size << endl;
            // Write the file header first (see Load_Data())
            file_ptr.write((char*) &_list_size, sizeof(_list_size));
            //Now write the array of data
            file_ptr.write((char*) _List_PTR,
                        _list_size*sizeof(cCustomer));
            file_ptr.close();
            cout << "Data saved successfully.\n";
            }
        // No post-conditions
        }
/******************************************************************
*                                                                *
* M FUNCTION:   Enter()                                          *
*                                                                *
* CLASS:        cCustomer_List                                   *
*                                                                *
* PURPOSE:      Enter records into database.                     *
*                                                                *
* PRE:          Detailed below.                                  *
* POST:         Detailed below.                                  *
*                                                                *
* RETURNS:      void.                                            *
*                                                                *
******************************************************************/
void cCustomer_List::Enter()
    {
    // Pre-conditions
    assert(_List_PTR != NULL);
    assert(_list_size >= 0);
    assert(_list_size <= _max_list_size);
    char answer[STRG_SZ];
    do
        {
        cin >> _List_PTR[_list_size];
        if (_List_PTR[_list_size].Compare_Name('\0'))
            {
            _list_size++; // Only increment count if new data added
            }
        if (_list_size <= _max_list_size)
            {
            cout << "Do you want to enter further names? ";
            cin.getline(answer, STRG_SZ);
```

```
            }
        else
            {
            // List is full - set answer to 'n' to
            // force termination of the loop.
            cout << "Sorry - list is full.\n";
            answer[0] = 'n';
            }
        } while (answer[0] != 'n');
    // Post-conditions
    assert(_list_size >= 0);
    assert(_list_size <= _max_list_size);
    }

/**************************************************************
*                                                            *
* A FUNCTION:   Name_Search()                                *
*                                                            *
* CLASS:        cCustomer_List                               *
*                                                            *
* PURPOSE:      Search by customer name.                     *
*                                                            *
* PRE:          Detailed below.                              *
* POST:         None.                                        *
*                                                            *
* RETURNS:      void.                                        *
*                                                            *
**************************************************************/
void cCustomer_List::Name_Search() const
    {
    // Pre-conditions
    assert(_List_PTR != NULL);
    assert(_list_size >= 0);

    char name[STRG_SZ];
    int i, found;

    cout << "Last Name: ";
    cin.getline(name, STRG_SZ);

    found = 0;

    for(i=0; i<_list_size; i++)
        {
        if(!_List_PTR[i].Compare_Name(name))
            {
            cout << _List_PTR[i];
            found = 1;
            cout << "\n";
            }
        }

    if(!found)
        {
        cout << "No customers of that name found\n";
        }

    // No Post-condition checks
    }
```

```
/ * * * * * * * * * * * * * * * * * * * * * * * * * * * * * * * * * * * * * * * * * * * * * * * * * * * *
 *                                                                              *
 * A FUNCTION:    Area_Search()                                                 *
 *                                                                              *
 * CLASS:         cCustomer_List                                                *
 *                                                                              *
 * PURPOSE:       Search for customer by postcode.                             *
 *                                                                              *
 * PRE:           Detailed below.                                              *
 * POST:          None.                                                         *
 *                                                                              *
 * RETURNS:       void.                                                         *
 *                                                                              *
 * * * * * * * * * * * * * * * * * * * * * * * * * * * * * * * * * * * * * * * * * * * * * * * * * * * * /
void cCustomer_List::Area_Search() const
    {
    // Pre-conditions
    assert(_List_PTR != NULL);
    assert(_list_size >= 0);

    char area[STRG_SZ];
    int i, found;

    cout << "Postcode: ";
    cin.getline(area, STRG_SZ);

    found = 0;

    for(i=0; i<_list_size; i++)
        {
        if(!_List_PTR[i].Compare_Area(area))
          {
          cout << _List_PTR[i];
          found = 1;
          cout << "\n";
          }
        }

    if(!found)
        {
        cout << "No customers found in the area specified\n";
        }

    // No Post-condition checks
    }
/ * * * * * * * * * * * * * * * * * * * * * * * * * * * * * * * * * * * * * * * * * * * * * * * * * * * *
 *                                                                              *
 * A FUNCTION:    All_Search()                                                  *
 *                                                                              *
 * CLASS:         cCustomer_List                                                *
 *                                                                              *
 * PURPOSE:       Display all database records.                                *
 *                                                                              *
 * PRE:           Detailed below.                                              *
 * POST:          None.                                                         *
 *                                                                              *
 * RETURNS:       void.                                                         *
 *                                                                              *
 * * * * * * * * * * * * * * * * * * * * * * * * * * * * * * * * * * * * * * * * * * * * * * * * * * * * /
```

```cpp
void cCustomer_List::All_Search() const
    {
    // Pre-conditions
    assert(_List_PTR != NULL);
    assert(_list_size >= 0);

    int i, found;

    found = 0;

    for(i=0; i<_list_size; i++)
        {
        cout << _List_PTR[i];
        found = 1;
        cout << "\n";
        }

    if(!found)
        {
        cout << "The list is empty.\n";
        }
    // No Post-condition checks
    }

// Ordinary function prototypes
int Menu();

int main()
    {
    cout << "PROTOTYPE MAILING LIST PROGRAM (O-O version)\n";
    cout << "---------------------------------- \n\n";

    cCustomer_List The_List;
    int choice;

    do
        {
        choice = Menu();

        switch(choice)
            {
            case 1: // Enter names
                The_List.Enter();
                break;
            case 2: // Search by customer name
                The_List.Name_Search();
                break;
            case 3: // Search by postcode
                The_List.Area_Search();
                break;
            case 4: // "Search" for *all* records
                The_List.All_Search();
            }

        } while(choice!=5);

    cout << "Finished.";

    return 0;
    }
```

```
/*************************************************************
*                                                           *
* FUNCTION:     Menu()                                       *
*                                                           *
* PURPOSE:      Tell user options and return valid choice.   *
*                                                           *
* PRE:          None.                                        *
* POST:         None.                                        *
*                                                           *
* RETURNS:      User choice (int).                           *
*                                                           *
*************************************************************/
int Menu()
    {
    int i;
    char text_str[STRG_SZ];

    cout << "\n 1. Enter New Data\n";
    cout << " 2. Search Database by Customer Name\n";
    cout << " 3. Search Database by Region\n";
    cout << " 4. Display all data\n";
    cout << " 5. Quit\n\n";
    do
        {
        cout << "? : ";
        cin.getline(text_str, STRG_SZ);
        i = text_str[0] - '0';
        } while((i<1) || (i>5));

    return i;
    }
/*************************************************************
*                     *** END OF PROGRAM ***                *
*************************************************************/
```

Exercises

31.1 Given the problem statement in Exercise 30.1 draw up an appropriate *object* model.

31.2 Following the implementation guidelines given in Section 31.5.1, split the object-oriented mailing list program (see Section 31.10) over multiple source files.

31.3 Working from your multiple-source version of the mailing list program, make the ordinary function `Menu()` a member function of the `cCust_List` class.

31.4 Following a serious lightning strike at the LSE office, all that Jane has left from a P-O/D-O model of the mailing list system are the diagrams given in Figures 31.13 and 31.14. Complete the physical model of this system (correcting it as necessary), and compare the result with the O-O version. Which is better, and why?

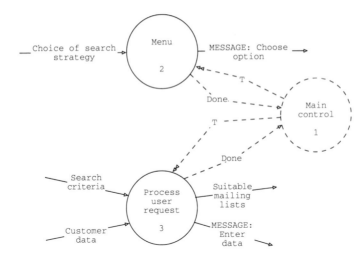

Figure 31.13 The Level I DfD.

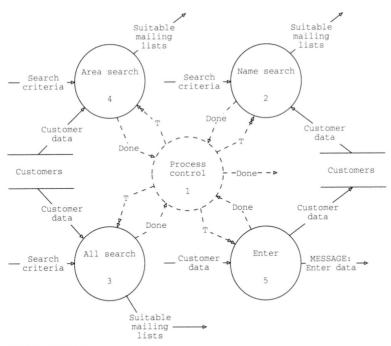

Figure 31.14 DfD 1-3.

32 Case Study: Birstall Bank revisited

32.1 Introduction

In this chapter, we conclude Part III with a more substantial case study. Here we look once again at the auto-teller machine for Birstall Bank, and develop a novel, fully object-oriented solution to this problem.

A complete version of this project, produced with the CASE tool, is included on the sample CD: details of how to install the project are given in Appendix C.

32.2 Scenario

Late in the summer of 1995, Jane was saddened to read in the Birstall Post newspaper about the death of Joseph Jones, the owner of Birstall Bank, at the age of 78. Jane and Stephanie attended the funeral, along with a great many current and former customers from the bank, as well as a number of friends and relations.

Some three weeks after the funeral, Jane had a call from a Mr Joe Jones; he introduced himself as Joseph's grandson. Joe explained that he had inherited his grandfather's business, and had been going through the bank records. He discovered in doing so that Leicester Software Engineering had developed the auto teller machines (ATMs) that were used in all the bank's branches. Joe said he was been very impressed by the bank ATMs, and would like to discuss with Jane a further project. A meeting was arranged for the following week at Birstall Bank.

At the meeting, the new manager immediately got down to business. 'I won't beat about the bush, Ms Macleod. My accountant and I have been through the books with a fine-toothed comb. While our present financial position is very healthy, the medium-term outlook is much less rosy. The bottom line is that a very small bank like this cannot hope to survive in the present economic climate: our only plausible future is in amalgamation with one of our larger competitors.'

Jane nods, 'I see, but I'm not ... '

Joe Jones holds up his hand, and continues. 'To ensure the best deal for our shareholders, including myself and my family, I would like to raise the profile of the bank over the next 12 months, with a view to raising the share price and encouraging a takeover.'

'I appreciate you being so candid with me, Mr Jones,' says Jane, finally getting an opportunity to speak, 'however, I'm not completely clear how Leicester Software Engineering can help you with this?'

'I believe we can help each other, Ms Macleod. As you will be aware, my grandfather's insistence on using a local company to develop an ATM machine rather than simply purchasing a suitable device "off the shelf" from one of the major suppliers caused some interest in the trade press, not least because most observers initially thought he was making a very foolish and expensive decision. They changed their minds, however, when they saw your finished product. I believe your system has a better security record than any other on the market, and that you've had some enquiries now about developing similar systems for several of the larger banks?'

Jane nods. 'The ATM system we developed for your grandfather has since proved very popular.'

'I can believe that – and that's why, Ms Macleod, I'd like to go one stage further. As I mentioned, I wish to encourage a takeover of the bank – at a suitable price, of course. I therefore plan to raise the bank's profile over the next two years through a process of technological innovation. By that I mean that I want to have Birstall Bank ATM outlets running, as usual, in all bank branches. In addition, inside the branches, I want to have further ATMs, with a wider range of facilities, such as paying in cash, and adjusting standing orders. These extended ATMs will be available to all customers; a charge will be made, however, for dealing with counter staff directly. In addition, as far as possible, I want to have a Birstall Bank ATM available through the televisions in the homes of our customers; this will allow them to see their account balance, and details of recent transactions.'

Joe pauses, then adds: 'Could you do this for me?'

Jane thinks quickly: what Joe Jones appears to describing is a range of large software-rich systems. The need for easy portability across a very wide range of environments, Jane realizes, would suggest an object-oriented implementation.

Before she has a chance to speak, Joe Jones says: 'The changes I am proposing will attract considerable publicity for the bank, and I daresay for yourself and your company too. What do you say?'

Jane knows Joe Jones is right. 'I think you have some interesting ideas, Mr Jones, and I believe we can do what you require. But I will need some further details.'

'Naturally,' says Joe Jones, nodding sagely.

32.2 Developing the object model

As we have discussed, there are no distinct analysis and design phases: there is simply an evolving object model. We outlined the 13 steps necessary to construct such a model in Chapter 31. We repeat them here for ease of reference.

(O1) *The business case*

The software engineer begins by estimating the technical and economic feasibility of the project. If, for example, the project is too small to be profitable, greatly outside the experience of the available personnel, or larger than can be tackled with the available technical and human resources, then it must be rejected at this stage.

(O2) *The Context diagram*

The Context diagram is produced. The operating environment (hardware and/or operating system), and the basic software architecture are considered.

(O3) *The class diagram*
A preliminary class diagram is produced.

(O4) *The user interface*
Because of the impact of the system interface on all aspects of the model, it is sketched (or prototyped) at this early stage.

(O5) *The process list*
A process list is drawn up. This list is necessarily very provisional, and creation of a highly polished document is not appropriate at this stage.

(O6) *The walkthrough*
A system walkthrough is performed. Where feasible, the entire development team (analysts, designers, programmers) should be involved in this process. As the walkthrough progresses, the class diagram, process list, context diagram and interface sketches are modified as required.

(O7) *The class-relationship diagram*
The class diagram (Stage 3) is extended into a first-cut CRD by adding in the relationships.

(O8) *The attribute diagrams*
A preliminary attribute set is produced for each class.

(O9) *The preliminary structure chart*
The preliminary structure chart is created.

(O10) *The process specifications*
The process specifications are written.

(O11) *The data dictionary*
The data dictionary is completed.

(O12) *The test strategy*
The overall system test strategy is drawn up. Testing is conducted on a class-by-class basis.

(O13) *The balanced object model*
The complete object model is reviewed, checked and balanced. Any necessary supporting documentation is written.

Jane, with some help from Stephanie, follows these steps religiously.

32.3.1   The business case

The software engineer begins by estimating the technical and economic feasibility of the project. If, for example, the project is too small to be profitable, greatly outside the experience of the available personnel, or larger than can be tackled with the available technical and human resources, then it must be rejected at this stage.

Jane agrees with Joe Jones that she will begin this project by developing a new proto-type of the existing ATM software. This object-oriented version, she explains, will be more easily adapted to cope with the very wide range of environments that Birstall Bank now wish to consider.

She agrees with Joe Jones an all-in price of £10 000 for the development of the new prototype.

32.3.2 The Context diagram

> **The Context diagram is produced. The operating environment (hardware and/or operating system), and the basic software architecture are considered.**

Jane begins by developing the Context diagram for new object-oriented version of the previous process-oriented system. This is, of course, largely the same as the previous version (Figure 32.1).

Because of the lack of a division between the analysis and design phases of the O-O planning process, Jane usually finds it useful to review the operating environment and basic software architecture requirements at this stage. Typically, Stephanie would be asked to consider whether the system under development would be required to operate on, say, a mainframe, desktop, mini or embedded system. Steph would also consider the likely operating system (if any), and consider any hardware constraints, such the type of processor to be used, and whether a parallel implementation would be required.

In this particular case, the hardware will (in the initial prototype) be the same as that used in the previous P-O system. More generally, the operating environment is known only to be very varied.

Steph agrees with Jane that the need for a very high degree of portability makes the selection of an object-oriented solution appropriate.

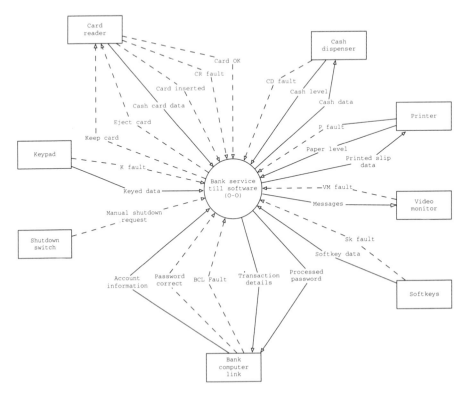

Figure 32.1   The Context diagram for the O-O ATM system.

32.3.3   The class diagram

A preliminary class diagram is produced.

Jane finds that there are two useful 'rules of thumb' when it comes to drawing up the initial class diagram:

- Look for nouns in the problem statement. Each noun becomes a provisional class.
- Include the terminators from your context diagram in your provisional class diagram. This is particularly important if the terminators are hardware components, but generally useful anyway.

The provisional class diagram that Jane produces is given in Figure 32.2.

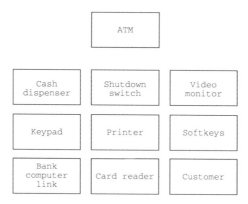

Figure 32.2   The class diagram.

32.3.4   The user interface

Because of the impact of the system interface on all aspects of the model, it is sketched (or prototyped) at this early stage.

In this case, Jane has already determined the interface requirements (for the basic O-O system) from her previous study (Figure 32.3).

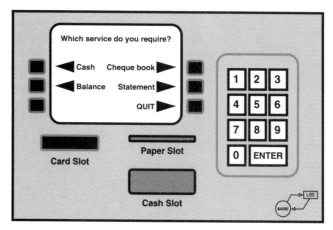

Figure 32.3   The interface to the standard (O-O) ATM.

32.3.5 The process list

> **A process list is drawn up. This list is necessarily very provisional, and creation of a highly polished document is not appropriate at this stage.**

Again, the process list is the same as the previous version (Table 32.1).

Process name	Notes
Dispense cash	As far as the customer is concerned, this is the main purpose of the machine. Allow the customer to order cash from the machine. Cash will be available, in multiples of £10, up to the balance in the customer's account. Where an overdraft facility is in force, then the amount of cash available is determined by the balance available plus the overdraft limit.
Print balance	Print out a slip showing the balance of the customer's account.
Print mini statement	Print out a 'mini statement' detailing the last ten transactions on the customer's account.
Order cheque book	Allow the customer to place an order for a new cheque book. The cheque book won't actually be printed by the machine, but will be sent by post within the next few days.
Get card	Prompt the customer to enter their bank card in the card reader. Read the account details from the card, if possible. If the card is out of date, then retain the card. If the card is from a different bank or of the wrong type, eject the card. If the card is damaged, eject the card.
Validate card	Check with the bank computer that the customer's card has not been stolen. If it has, then retain the card.
Enter password	Prompt the user to enter a password. Read the password.
Validate password	Check with the bank computer that the entered password is correct. Note: security is paramount here ...
Eject card	Return the card from the card reader to the customer.
Retain card	'Swallow' the customer's card. Tell the customer to contact their branch.
Check hardware	Check the hardware for damage. If any damage is detected, display an 'out of order' message. Call the engineer. Shut down the machine. Note: this is a constant process, implemented externally. An interrupt will be raised in the event of an error.
Call engineer	Contact the bank engineer.
Manual shutdown	A manual 'off' switch is provide for bank personnel (e.g. for use when replenishing the cash reserves). This will shut down the machine.
Shut down	Shut down the machine. Notify the bank computer that the machine has been shut down, indicating the cause (e.g. manual, or hardware failure).
Pre-customer system checks	Check the hardware (to be on the safe side). Check the cash and paper reserves. Display an appropriate welcome banner.

Table 32.1 Initial process list for Birstall Bank ATM.

32.3.6 The walkthrough

A system walkthrough is performed. Where feasible, the entire development team (analysts, designers, programmers) should be involved in this process. As the walkthrough progresses, the class diagram, process list, context diagram and interface sketches are modified as required.

The walkthrough is performed primarily to gain an understanding of the system. Jane already understands the requirements for this system; a further walkthrough is therefore unnecessary.

32.3.7 The CRD

The class diagram (Stage 3) is extended into a first-cut CRD by adding in the relationships. A preliminary attribute diagram is produced for each class.

Jane finds that there are three useful 'rules of thumb' when it comes to drawing up the class-relationship diagram:

- Try to consider what the program is assembled from. What are the building blocks? Use the process list to help you clarify this.
- Don't be afraid to draw a DfD, if this helps.
- Try making the system under construction the main class. Consider how the other provisional classes can be assembled to contribute to this main class.

In this case, Jane initially assumes, there will be two main classes: 'ATM' and 'Customer' (Figure 32.4). The various hardware 'simulation' classes will be component parts of the ATM (Figure 32.5).

As she looks at Figure 32.5, Jane realizes that the 'Customer' and 'Bank computer link' classes are really one and the same: both classes encapsulate details about the customer, and the customer's account. She decides that she can safely omit the 'Customer' class.

Figure 32.4 The nascent class relationship diagram (CRD) for the ATM system (incomplete).

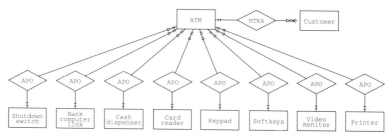

Figure 32.5 The evolving class relationship diagram (CRD) for the ATM system.

At the same time, Jane decides that the 'Shutdown switch' class really has very little to do: she decides to try and implement Shutdown() as a method (member function) in the 'ATM' class (we'll see details of this below).

The CRD resulting from these changes is shown in Figure 32.6.

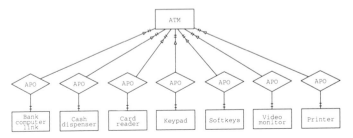

Figure 32.6 The evolving class relationship diagram (CRD) for the ATM system after removal of the 'Customer' class and 'Shutdown switch' class.

Next, Jane focuses on the relationships between the various hardware components. She realizes that the 'Printer' and 'Video monitor' classes will have much in common: both will display simple information, either on the screen or on paper. She decides to try and exploit this common behaviour by deriving both classes from a common base class.

In addition, Jane knows from her experience with the previous ATM software (and common sense) that the softkeys around the outside of the monitor, and the monitor itself, are closely related: for example, before displaying a prompt on the screen, the programmer needs to know how many softkeys there are. Jane therefore opts to combine the 'Softkeys' class and the 'Video monitor' class into a new softkey monitor class.

These changes are reflected in the final version of the CRD (Figure 32.7).

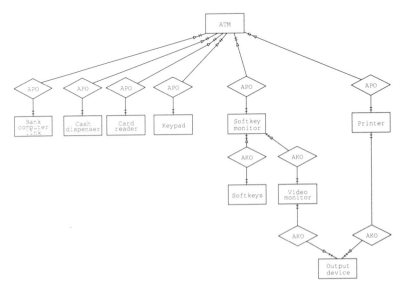

Figure 32.7 The final class relationship diagram (CRD) for the ATM system.

32.3.8 The attribute diagrams

A preliminary attribute set is produced for each class.

The attribute diagrams are shown in Figures 32.8 to 32.17.

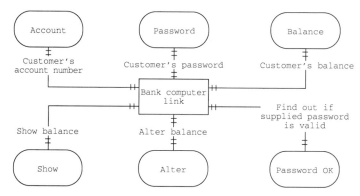

Figure 32.8 The provisional attribute diagram for the 'Bank computer link' class. *Note:* the class contains details of only a single customer in this prototype: a collection of customers (possibly via a linked list of objects of class 'Customer'?) would be needed in a complete implementation.

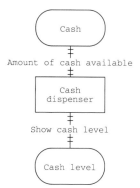

Figure 32.9 The provisional attribute diagram for the 'Cash dispenser' class.

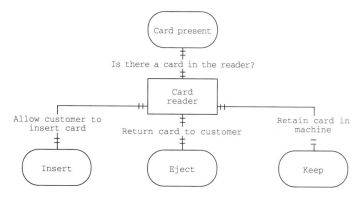

Figure 32.10 The provisional attribute diagram for the 'Card reader' class.

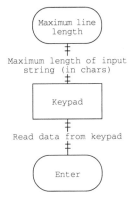

Figure 32.11 The provisional attribute diagram for the 'Keypad' class.

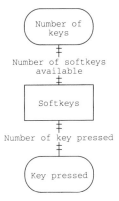

Figure 32.12 The provisional attribute diagram for the 'Softkeys' class.

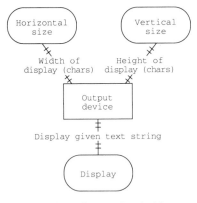

Figure 32.13 The provisional attribute diagram for the 'Output device' class.

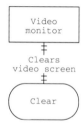

Figure 32.14 The provisional attribute diagram for the 'Video monitor' class.

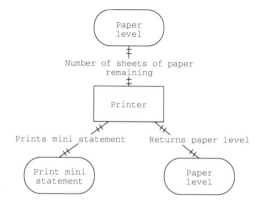

Figure 32.15 The provisional attribute diagram for the 'Printer' class.

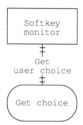

Figure 32.16 The provisional attribute diagram for the 'Softkey monitor' class.

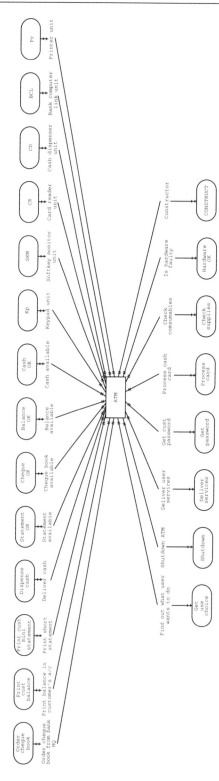

Figure 32.17 The provisional attribute diagram for the 'ATM' class.

32.3.9 The preliminary structure chart

The preliminary structure chart is created.

The preliminary structure chart Jane develops is shown in Figure 32.18. Note that this is only an outline structure chart showing the operation of the ATM class; further detail can be added, if necessary, showing the contributions of the other classes to the operation of the program.

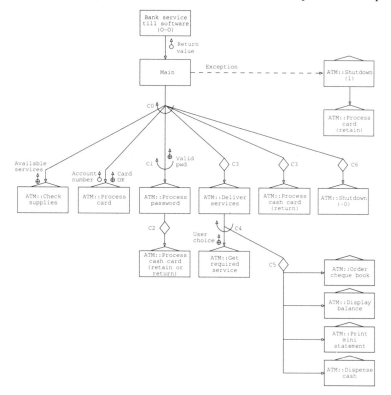

Figure 32.18 The structure chart. Conditions – C0: Keep looping until user chooses to quit; C1: Keep calling 'Process password' until the user enters valid password, the maximum number of password attempts is exceeded or the user opts to quit; C2: If the user exceeds the number of allowed password attempts, retain their card; C3: Only call this module if the user hasn't opted to quit; C4: Keep looping until user opts to quit; C5: Call the appropriate option, depending on 'User choice'; C6: Only call this module if a manual shutdown request has been received.

32.3.10 The PSpecs

The process specifications are written.

The PSpecs used in this case are similar to those used in previous (P-O and D-O) studies. We omit them here. Note, however, that in this project the final 'PSpecs' take the form of 'CppSpecs': a complete set is included on the CD-ROM.

32.3.11 The data dictionary

The data dictionary is completed.

Finally, Jane draws up the data dictionary (Table 32.2).

Name	Type	Description
ATM	Class	\The main class. See Figure 32.17 for details\
Account number	Dataflow	\6 digit number uniquely identifying the customer's account\
Available services	Control Flow	(Cash available) + (Cash receipt available) + (Mini statement available) + (Cheque book available) + (Balance available)
Available services control store	Control Store	Unrecoverable hardware fault detected + Available services
Balance available	Control flow	["TRUE"|"FALSE"]
Bank Computer Link	Class	\The interface with the bank computer. See the attribute diagram AT_BCL.DAT for details.\
Cash	Dataflow	\Cash dispensed to customer\
Cash request	Dataflow	\Cash amount requested by customer\
Cash Card	Dataflow	\Customer's cash card\
Done	Dataflow	["TRUE"|"FALSE"]
Entered password	Dataflow	1{"Number"}
Hardware status flag	Dataflow	["0"|"1"]+["0"|"1"]+["0"|"1"]
MESSAGE: Your cheque book will be posted to you	Dataflow	0{"Any Valid Character"}80
Mini statement	Dataflow	\Paper print-out of last ten transactions\
Printer	Class	\The Printer class. See Figure 32.15 for details\
Valid password	Control Flow	["TRUE"|"FALSE"]

Table 32.2 Selections from the data dictionary.

32.3.12 The test strategy

The overall system test strategy is drawn up. Testing is conducted on a class-by-class basis.

Jane provides the following general guidelines for subsequent testing of the system:

As each ordinary function is completed, it will be tested by the programmer, as follows:

(1) White Box testing is performed by reading through the function, line by line, looking for obvious flaws. Details of the tests performed are to be included in the implementation documents and initialled by the tester.

(2) Black Box testing is performed with an individual driver program. Typically, 10% of the parameter range will be tested. Extremes of the input range of all parameters will always be tested. Details of the test performed, and of the results obtained, are to be included with the implementation documents, and initialled by the tester.

As each class is completed, each member function will be tested by the programmer, as follows:

(1)   White Box testing is performed by reading through the function, line by line, looking for obvious flaws. Details of the tests performed are to be included in the implementation documents and initialled by the tester.

Where inheritance is involved, and source code is available, particular care must be taken to ensure that no side-effects are being introduced.

(2)   Black Box testing is performed with an individual driver program. Typically, 10% of the parameter range will be tested. Extremes of the input range of all parameters will always be tested. Details of the test performed, and of the results obtained, are to be included with the implementation documents and initialled by the tester.

Where inheritance is employed, particular care will be taken to test the member functions of the derived class in context.

32.3.13   The balanced object model

The complete object model is reviewed, checked and balanced. Any necessary supporting documentation is written.

We assume this stage is completed without difficulty.

32.4   Implementation of the class model

Responsibility for the implementation of the system passes to Harry. As outlined in Chapter 31, Harry has seven main steps to perform, as outlined below:

(O14) *Review and refinement of the object model*
The object model is reviewed by the programmer, in order to gain an understanding of the system, and to correct any flaws.

(O15) *The system framework*
The code framework is created, using CppSpecs, based on the class diagram, the structure chart and the PSpecs. For some systems, a prototype hardware framework may also be required.

(O16) *The preliminary modules*
The preliminary modules are created or, preferably, recycled from class and/or function libraries.

(O17) *Error detection and recovery*
The preliminary modules are extended, where necessary, through the addition of appropriate error detection and correction features.

(O18) *Module tests*
The modules are tested, by the programmers, according to the test strategy produced by the planning team. Modifications are made as required.

(O19) *The prototype system*
The tested modules are assembled into a prototype system, as dictated by the CRD and the structure chart(s).

(O20) *System tests and maintenance*

The complete prototype is tested again, first by the programmers, and then by the test team, both working from the test strategy produced by the designers. The system is then subjected to user tests, including field tests and/or acceptance tests. The system is revised as necessary; any changes made during the testing and subsequent ongoing maintenance are recorded and reflected in the evolving object model.

32.4.1 Review and refinement of the object model

The object model is reviewed by the programmer, in order to gain an understanding of the system, and to correct any flaws.

We assume that this review is quickly and successfully completed.

32.4.2 The system framework

The code framework is created, using class CppSpecs, based on the class diagram (including attribute diagrams), the structure chart and the PSpecs. For some systems, a prototype hardware framework may also be required.

The code framework Harry develops is given in Program 32.1. Note that this framework is based on the outline structure chart, and includes only the ATM class at this time. Nonetheless, it provides a useful skeleton around which the rest of the program can be constructed.

```
/*****************************************************************
*                                                               *
* A Bank Service Till (ATM) Framework (O-O version)             *
*                                                               *
* Source is:    32_01.CPP                                       *
* Created:      07 December, 1994                               *
* Last edited:  02 January, 1995                                *
*                                                               *
*****************************************************************/
#include <iostream.h>
#include <stdlib.h>

// Maximum number of tries allowed to enter correct password
const int MAX_NUM_PASS_TRIES = 3;

// Various "flags"
enum eBool {FALSE, TRUE};
enum eProcess {CHECK_CARD = 12, KEEP_CARD, EJECT_CARD};

/*****************************************************************
*****************************************************************
*                                                               *
* CLASS:        cATM                                            *
*                                                               *
*****************************************************************
*****************************************************************/
```

```
class cATM
    {
    public:
                cATM();
        eBool   Hardware_OK();
        void    Check_supplies();
        void    Process_card(eProcess, int* = 0, int* = 0);
        void    Get_password(int&, int&, int);
        void    Deliver_services();
        void    Shutdown();
        int     Get_user_choice();
    private:
        void    _Order_cheque_book_from_bank();
        void    _Print_customer_balance();
        void    _Print_customer_mini_statement();
        void    _Dispense_cash_to_customer();

        eBool   _cheque_OK;
        eBool   _balance_OK;
        eBool   _statement_OK;
        eBool   _cash_OK;
    };
/*************************************************************
*                                                           *
* C FUNCTION:  cATM()                                       *
*                                                           *
* CLASS:       cATM                                         *
*                                                           *
*************************************************************/
cATM::cATM()
    {
    cout << "*** CONSTRUCTOR: cATM ***\n";
    }
/*************************************************************
*                                                           *
* M FUNCTION:  Hardware_OK()                                *
*                                                           *
* CLASS:       cATM                                         *
*                                                           *
* OVERVIEW:    Polls hardware to determine system status.   *
*                                                           *
*************************************************************/
eBool cATM::Hardware_OK()
    {
    cout << "*** cATM: WILL CHECK HARDWARE STATUS ***\n";

    // Say hardware is OK
    return TRUE;
    }
/*************************************************************
*                                                           *
* M FUNCTION:  Check_supplies()                             *
```

```
*                                                              *
* CLASS:        cATM                                           *
*                                                              *
* OVERVIEW:     Checks supplies of paper and cash.             *
*                                                              *
**************************************************************/
void cATM::Check_supplies()
    {
    cout << "*** cATM: WILL CHECK SUPPLIES ***\n";

    // Dummy values
    _cheque_OK = TRUE;
    _balance_OK = TRUE;
    _cash_OK = TRUE;
    _statement_OK = TRUE;
    }
/**************************************************************
*                                                              *
* M FUNCTION:   Process_card()                                 *
*                                                              *
* CLASS:        cATM                                           *
*                                                              *
* OVERVIEW:     Check, keep or eject cash card (simulated)     *
*                                                              *
**************************************************************/
void cATM::Process_card(eProcess    required_op,
                        int*        acc_PTR,
                        int*        card_OK_PTR)
    {
    /* NOTE: Process_card() is a function with a
       default argument. Can call as:

       Process_card(CHECK_CARD, card_OK);
       or
       Process_card(KEEP_CARD);
       Process_card(EJECT_CARD); */

    switch (required_op)
        {
        case CHECK_CARD:
          // Using "extra" argument
          cout << "Please insert your card.\n";
          cout << "*** SIMULATING INSERTION OF CORRECT CARD ***\n";
          // Card assumed OK
          cout << "Thank you.\n\n";
          *card_OK_PTR = TRUE;

          break;

        case KEEP_CARD:
          cout << "Your card has been retained. ";
          cout << "Please contact your branch.\n\n";
          cout << "*** SIMULATING CARD RETAINED ***\n";
          break;
```

```
           case EJECT_CARD:
             cout << "Please take your card.\n\n";
             cout << "*** SIMULATING RETURN OF CARD ***\n";
             break;
           }
       }
/***************************************************************
*                                                             *
* M FUNCTION:   Get_password()                                *
*                                                             *
* CLASS:        cATM                                          *
*                                                             *
* OVERVIEW:     Get password, and check it via BCL            *
*                                                             *
***************************************************************/
void cATM::Get_password(int& password_OK_REF,
                        int& tries_REF,
                        int account_no)
    {
    int password;
    tries_REF++;
    cout << "Please enter your password : ";
    cin >> password;
    if (password == 1234)
        {
        cout << "*** PASSWORD IS CORRECT ***\n";
        password_OK_REF = TRUE;
        }
    else
        {
        password_OK_REF = FALSE;
        }
    if (!(password_OK_REF))
        {
        if (tries_REF < MAX_NUM_PASS_TRIES)
            {
            cerr << "Your password was incorrect.\n";
            // Recursive call to Get_password()
            Get_password(password_OK_REF, tries_REF, account_no);
            }
        else
            {
            // Too many tries - could be a stolen card?
            Process_card(KEEP_CARD);
            }
        }
    }
/***************************************************************
*                                                             *
* M FUNCTION:   Deliver_services()                            *
```

```
*                                                             *
* CLASS:        cATM                                          *
*                                                             *
* OVERVIEW:     Deliver required customer services            *
*                                                             *
*************************************************************/
void cATM::Deliver_services()
    {
    int user_choice;
    do {
        user_choice = Get_user_choice();
        switch (user_choice)
            { // If "Quit" then do nothing...
            case 1:
               _Order_cheque_book_from_bank();
            break;
            case 2:
               _Print_customer_balance();
            break;
            case 3:
               _Print_customer_mini_statement();
            break;
            case 4:
               _Dispense_cash_to_customer();
            break;
            }
        } while (user_choice != 0); // 0 is assumed quit
    }
/*************************************************************
*                                                             *
* M FUNCTION:  Get_user_choice()                              *
*                                                             *
* CLASS:        cATM                                          *
*                                                             *
* OVERVIEW:     Find out what user wants to do                *
*                                                             *
*************************************************************/
int cATM::Get_user_choice()
    {
    int service;
    cout << "\nAvailable options are: \n";
    cout << " 0. QUIT\n";
    if (_cheque_OK == TRUE)    cout << " 1. Cheque book\n";
    if (_balance_OK == TRUE)   cout << " 2. Balance\n";
    if (_statement_OK == TRUE) cout << " 3. Statement\n";
    if (_cash_OK == TRUE)      cout << " 4. Cash\n";
    cout << "\nPlease enter choice : ";
    // No checking yet...
    cin >> service;
```

```
      return service;
      }

/*****************************************************************
*                                                               *
* M FUNCTION:   _Order_cheque_book_from_bank()                  *
*                                                               *
* CLASS:        cATM                                            *
*                                                               *
* OVERVIEW:     Order cheque book from bank.                    *
*                                                               *
*****************************************************************/
void cATM::_Order_cheque_book_from_bank()
      {
      cout << "\n*** SIMULATING ORDER FOR CHEQUE BOOK ***\n";
      cout << "Your cheque book will be posted to you.\n";

      _cheque_OK = FALSE;
      }

/*****************************************************************
*                                                               *
* M FUNCTION:   _Print_customer_balance()                       *
*                                                               *
* CLASS:        cATM                                            *
*                                                               *
* OVERVIEW:     Print customer balance.                         *
*                                                               *
*****************************************************************/
void cATM::_Print_customer_balance()
      {
      cout << "\n*** SIMULATED BALANCE ***\n";
      cout << "Your balance is: £99.99\n";

      _balance_OK = FALSE;
      }

/*****************************************************************
*                                                               *
* M FUNCTION:   _Print_customer_mini_statement()                *
*                                                               *
* CLASS:        cATM                                            *
*                                                               *
* OVERVIEW:     Print customer mini statement                   *
*                                                               *
*****************************************************************/
void cATM::_Print_customer_mini_statement()
      {
      cout << "\n*** SIMULATED MINI STATEMENT ***\n";
      cout << "Please take your mini statement.\n";

      _statement_OK = FALSE;
      }
```

```
/**************************************************************
 *                                                            *
 * M FUNCTION:   _Dispense_cash_to_customer()                 *
 *                                                            *
 * CLASS:        cATM                                         *
 *                                                            *
 * OVERVIEW:     Dispense cash to customer                    *
 *                                                            *
 **************************************************************/
void cATM::_Dispense_cash_to_customer()
    {
    cout << "\n*** SIMULATED CASH DELIVERY ***\n";
    cout << "Please take your cash.\n";

    _cash_OK = FALSE;
    }

/**************************************************************
 *                                                            *
 * M FUNCTION:   Shutdown()                                   *
 *                                                            *
 * CLASS:        cATM                                         *
 *                                                            *
 * OVERVIEW:     Shut down cash machine.                      *
 *                                                            *
 **************************************************************/
void cATM::Shutdown()
    {
    cout << "\nPlease use another machine.\n";
    cout << "*** SIMULATING MACHINE SHUTDOWN ***\n";

    exit(1);
    }

/**************************************************************
 **************************************************************/
int main()
    {
    cATM cash_machine;
    int acc;
    int valid_card_entered;
    int tries, valid_password_entered;
    int user_wants_to_quit;

    // Simulate two customers in queue then manual shut down
    for (int customer = 1; customer <= 2; customer++)
        {
        cout << "\n--------------------------- \n";
        cout << "PROTOTYPE BANK AUTO TELLER MACHINE\n";
        cout << "--------------------------- \n\n";

        cash_machine.Check_supplies();

        cash_machine.Process_card(CHECK_CARD, &acc,
                                  &valid_card_entered);
```

```
            if (valid_card_entered)
               {
               tries = 0;
               user_wants_to_quit = FALSE;

               cash_machine.Get_password(valid_password_entered,
                                           tries,acc);

               if (valid_password_entered)
                  {
                  // Keep delivering services till user
                  // says quit (or hardware fault)
                  cash_machine.Deliver_services();
                  cash_machine.Process_card(EJECT_CARD);
                  }
               }
            }
      // Simulate manual shutdown
      cash_machine.Shutdown();

      return 0;
      }
```

Program 32.1 The code framework. As in most cases, this includes only the main ('system') class, in this case cATM. (☺)

The framework generates the following output:

```
*** CONSTRUCTOR: cATM ***

PROTOTYPE BANK AUTO TELLER MACHINE

*** cATM: WILL CHECK SUPPLIES ***
Please insert your card.
*** SIMULATING INSERTION OF CORRECT CARD ***
Thank you.

Please enter your password : 1234
*** PASSWORD IS CORRECT ***

Available options are:
 0. QUIT
 1. Cheque book
 2. Balance
 3. Statement
 4. Cash

Please enter choice : 1

*** SIMULATING ORDER FOR CHEQUE BOOK ***
Your cheque book will be posted to you.

Available options are:
 0. QUIT
 2. Balance
 3. Statement
 4. Cash
```

```
Please enter choice : 2

*** SIMULATED BALANCE ***
Your balance is: £99.99

Available options are:
 0. QUIT
 3. Statement
 4. Cash

Please enter choice : 3

*** SIMULATED MINI STATEMENT ***
Please take your mini statement.

Available options are:
 0. QUIT
 4. Cash

Please enter choice : 4

*** SIMULATED CASH DELIVERY ***
Please take your cash.

Available options are:
 0. QUIT

Please enter choice : 0
Please take your card.
*** SIMULATING RETURN OF CARD ***


PROTOTYPE BANK AUTO TELLER MACHINE

*** cATM: WILL CHECK SUPPLIES ***
Please insert your card.
*** SIMULATING INSERTION OF CORRECT CARD ***
Thank you.

Please enter your password : 123
Your password was incorrect.
Please enter your password : 456
Your password was incorrect.
Please enter your password : 897
Your card has been retained. Please contact your branch.

*** SIMULATING CARD RETAINED ***

Please use another machine.
*** SIMULATING MACHINE SHUTDOWN ***
```

32.4.3 The preliminary classes

The preliminary classes are created or, preferably, recycled from class and/or function libraries.

Harry works on all the classes in turn, referring as he does so to the attribute diagrams and PSpecs. For example, the attribute diagram given in Figure 32.8 is developed into the preliminary class given in Figure 32.19.

```
/*******************************************************
 *******************************************************
 *                                                     *
 * CLASS:        cBank_Computer_Link                   *
 *                                                     *
 *******************************************************
 ******************************************************/
class cBank_Computer_Link
     {
     public:
               cBank_Computer_Link();
          eBool Password_OK(int, int) const;
          void  Alter(int x) {_balance+=x;}
          int   Show() const {return _balance;}
     private:
          // Simulating only one single valid password
          // and account combination...
          int    _account;
          int    _password;
          int    _balance;
     };
/*******************************************************
 *                                                     *
 * C FUNCTION:   cBank_Computer_Link()                 *
 *                                                     *
 * CLASS:        cBank_Computer_Link                   *
 *                                                     *
 * OVERVIEW:     Initiates connection with bank computer. *
 *                                                     *
 ******************************************************/
cBank_Computer_Link::cBank_Computer_Link()
     {
     // In this prototype version, this constructor
     // simply provides basic information on one account.
     _password = 1234;
     _account = 4321;
     _balance = 70;
     }
/*******************************************************
 *                                                     *
 * A FUNCTION:   Password_OK()                         *
 *                                                     *
 * CLASS:        cBank_Computer_Link                   *
 *                                                     *
 * OVERVIEW:     Passes password to bank computer.     *
 *                                                     *
 * RETURNS:      TRUE (eBool) if password correct,     *
 *               FALSE otherwise.                      *
 *                                                     *
 ******************************************************/
```

```
eBool cBank_Computer_Link::Password_OK(int pass, int acc) const
    {
    // Simulate call to bank computer
    cerr << "\n*** SIMULATING CALL TO BANK COMPUTER ***\n";
    // Simulating one single valid password
    // and account combination...
    if ((pass == _password) && (acc == _account))
        {
        cerr << "*** PASSWORD CORRECT ***\n";
        return TRUE;
        }
    else
        {
        cerr << "*** PASSWORD *NOT* CORRECT ***\n\n";
        return FALSE;
        }
    }
```

Figure 32.19 The preliminary class `cBank_Computer_Link` before error detection and correction features have been added.

32.4.4 Error detection and recovery

The preliminary classes are extended, where necessary, through the addition of appropriate error detection and correction features.

As we have discussed in previous chapters, error detection and recovery must be considered both at a member function level, and at a class level. This error harness will take the form both of aids to developers who reuse your classes (often in the form of assertions) and more general error handling strategies, aimed at recovering from minor errors, and shutting down the system as gracefully as possible in the face of irrecoverable errors.

The provisional attribute diagrams (see Section 32.3.8) imply that all hardware checks will be performed by the ATM class itself; this, Harry concludes, is not an appropriate approach. He knows that the overall security of the system depends on the provision of a robust error detection strategy that will 'constantly' monitor the state of each of the individual hardware components, and shut down the whole system if a component develops a fault. This requires, in Harry's view, an error *detection* strategy that operates at the level of the individual class simulating each hardware component. Errors detected at this level will then generate an exception (Harry opts simply to throw integer exceptions) which will be detected and dealt with at a *system* level. In short, Harry's motto is: 'Detect errors locally, deal with them globally'.

As an example, consider how the class `cBank_Computer_Link` from Figure 32.19 is extended with an error harness based on exceptions (Figure 32.20).

```
/************************************************************
 ************************************************************
 *                                                          *
 * CLASS:        cBank_Computer_Link                        *
 *                                                          *
 ************************************************************
 ***********************************************************/
```

```
class cBank_Computer_Link
    {
    public:
                cBank_Computer_Link();
        eBool   Password_OK(int, int) const;
        eBool   Faulty() const;
        void    Alter(int x) {_balance+=x;}
        int     Show() const {return _balance;}

    private:
        // Simulating only one single valid password
        // and account combination...
        int     _account;
        int     _password;
        int     _balance;
    };
```

```
/**************************************************************
 *                                                            *
 * C FUNCTION:   cBank_Computer_Link()                        *
 *                                                            *
 * CLASS:        cBank_Computer_Link                          *
 *                                                            *
 * OVERVIEW:     Initiates connection with bank computer.     *
 *                                                            *
 * PRE:          None.                                        *
 * POST:         None.                                        *
 *                                                            *
 **************************************************************/
cBank_Computer_Link::cBank_Computer_Link()
    {
    // In this prototype version, this constructor
    // simply provides basic information on one account.
    _password   = 1234;
    _account    = 4321;
    _balance    = 70;
    }
```

```
/**************************************************************
 *                                                            *
 * A FUNCTION:   Password_OK()                                *
 *                                                            *
 * CLASS:        cBank_Computer_Link                          *
 *                                                            *
 * OVERVIEW:     Passes password to bank computer.            *
 *                                                            *
 * PRE:          Hardware not faulty.                         *
 * POST:         Got valid response.                          *
 *                                                            *
 * RETURNS:      TRUE (eBool) if password correct,            *
 *               FALSE otherwise.                             *
 *                                                            *
 **************************************************************/
```

```
eBool cBank_Computer_Link::Password_OK(int pass, int acc) const
    {
    // Pre - the hardware is OK
    if (Faulty()) {throw 1;}
    // Simulate call to bank computer
    cerr << "\n*** SIMULATING CALL TO BANK COMPUTER ***\n";
    // Simulating one single valid password
    // and account combination...
    if ((pass == _password) && (acc == _account))
        {
        cerr << "*** PASSWORD CORRECT ***\n";
        return TRUE;
        }
    else
        {
        cerr << "*** PASSWORD *NOT* CORRECT ***\n\n";
        return FALSE;
        }
    }
/*****************************************************************
*                                                               *
* A FUNCTION:   Faulty()                                         *
*                                                               *
* CLASS:        cBank_Computer_Link                             *
*                                                               *
* OVERVIEW:     Detects hardware fault.                          *
*                                                               *
* PRE:          None.                                            *
* POST:         None.                                            *
*                                                               *
* RETURNS:      TRUE if fault detected, FALSE otherwise.         *
*                                                               *
*****************************************************************/
eBool cBank_Computer_Link::Faulty() const
    {
    if ((rand() % 100) == 0)
        {
        cerr << "*** SIMULATING BANK COMP LINK FAULT ***\n";
        return TRUE;
        }
    else
        {
        return FALSE;
        }
    }
```

Figure 32.20   The class cBank_Computer_Link after error detection and correction features have been added. See text for details.

In Figure 32.20, Faulty() is a new member function for detecting errors in the bank link. In the (software only) prototype, detection of hardware errors must, necessarily, be simulated; in the final system, this member function would be responsible for performing an appropriate error detection strategy, possibly by polling a number of hardware interrupt lines.

A similar approach is adopted in all other classes: the details of this, and of the framework used to 'catch' the exceptions, are given in the extended versions of the attribute diagrams in Figures 32.21 to 32.29.

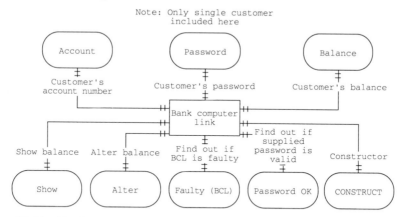

Figure 32.21 The final attribute diagram for the 'Bank computer link' class.

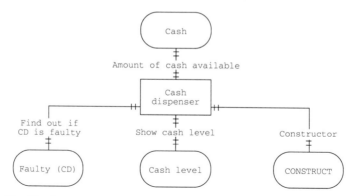

Figure 32.22 The final attribute diagram for the 'Cash dispenser' class.

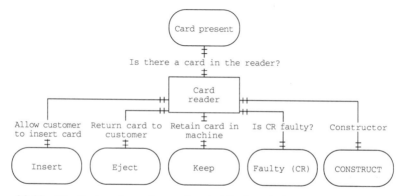

Figure 32.23 The final attribute diagram for the 'Card reader' class.

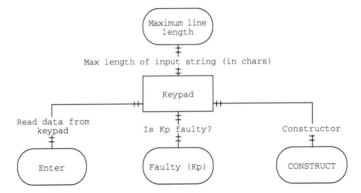

Figure 32.24 The final attribute diagram for the 'Keypad' class.

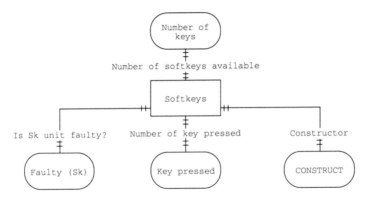

Figure 32.25 The final attribute diagram for the 'Softkeys' class.

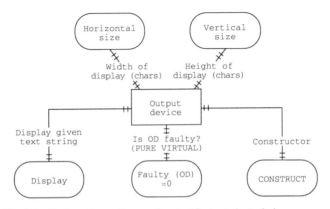

Figure 32.26 The final attribute diagram for the 'Output device' class.

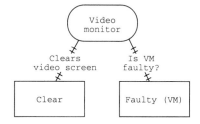

Figure 32.27 The final attribute diagram for the 'Video monitor' class.

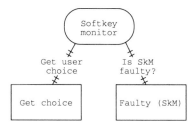

Figure 32.28 The final attribute diagram for the 'Softkey monitor' class.

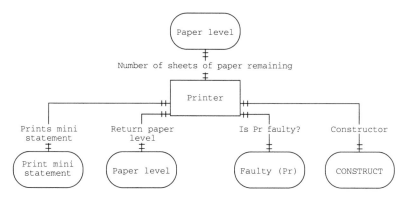

Figure 32.29 The final attribute diagram for the 'Printer' class.

32.4.5 Class tests

The classes are tested, by the programmers, according to the test strategy produced by the planning team. Modifications are made as required.

Harry performs the required tests, as detailed in Section 32.3.12.

32.4.6 The prototype system

The tested classes are assembled into a prototype system, as dictated by the CRD and the structure chart(s).

Harry assembles the tested classes into the implementation given in Program 32.2.

```
/**************************************************************
*                                                            *
* A Bank Service Till (ATM) Simulation (O-O version)         *
*                                                            *
* Source is:    32_02.CPP                                    *
* Created:      20 December, 1994                            *
* Last edited:  01 August, 1995                              *
*                                                            *
**************************************************************/
#include <iostream.h>

// extern "C" may be necessary on some compilers
// and won't do any harm on others
extern "C"
{
#include <assert.h>
#include <stdio.h>
#include <stdlib.h>
#include <string.h>
#include <time.h>
}

// Width of monitor (in columns)
const int MON_SIZE = 30;

// Number of softkeys on monitor:
const int NUM_SOFT_KEYS = 6;

// Maximum number of tries allowed to enter correct password
const int MAX_NUM_PASS_TRIES    = 3;

// Various "flags"
enum eBool {FALSE, TRUE};
enum eProcess {CHECK_CARD = 12, KEEP_CARD, EJECT_CARD};

/**************************************************************
**************************************************************
*                                                            *
* CLASS:      cBank_Computer_Link                            *
*                                                            *
* EXCEPT:     Throws 1 (int) on hardware error.              *
*                                                            *
**************************************************************
**************************************************************/
class cBank_Computer_Link
    {
    public:
                cBank_Computer_Link();
        eBool   Password_OK(int, int) const;
        eBool   Faulty() const;
        void    Alter(int x) {_balance+=x;}
        int     Show() const {return _balance;}

    private:
    // Simulating only one single valid password
```

```
      // and account combination...
      int    _account;
      int    _password;
      int    _balance;
      };
/****************************************************************
*                                                              *
* C FUNCTION:   cBank_Computer_Link()                          *
*                                                              *
* CLASS:        cBank_Computer_Link                            *
*                                                              *
* OVERVIEW:     Initiates connection with bank computer.       *
*                                                              *
* PRE:          None.                                          *
* POST:         None.                                          *
*                                                              *
****************************************************************/
cBank_Computer_Link::cBank_Computer_Link()
      {
      // In this prototype version, this constructor
      // simply provides basic information on one account.
      _password  = 1234;
      _account   = 4321;
      _balance   = 70;
      }
/****************************************************************
*                                                              *
* A FUNCTION:   Password_OK()                                  *
*                                                              *
* CLASS:        cBank_Computer_Link                            *
*                                                              *
* OVERVIEW:     Passes password to bank computer.              *
*                                                              *
* PRE:          Hardware not faulty.                           *
* POST:         Got valid response.                            *
*                                                              *
* RETURNS:      TRUE (eBool) if password correct,              *
*               FALSE otherwise.                               *
*                                                              *
****************************************************************/
eBool cBank_Computer_Link::Password_OK(int pass, int acc) const
      {
      // Pre - the hardware is OK
      if (Faulty()) {throw 1;}

      // Simulate call to bank computer
      cerr << "\n*** SIMULATING CALL TO BANK COMPUTER ***\n";
      // Simulating one single valid password
      // and account combination...
      if ((pass == _password) && (acc == _account))
          {
```

```
            cerr << "*** PASSWORD CORRECT ***\n";
            return TRUE;
            }
        else
            {
            cerr << "*** PASSWORD *NOT* CORRECT ***\n\n";
            return FALSE;
            }
        }

/****************************************************************
*                                                              *
* A FUNCTION:   Faulty()                                       *
*                                                              *
* CLASS:        cBank_Computer_Link                           *
*                                                              *
* OVERVIEW:     Detects hardware fault.                       *
*                                                              *
* PRE:          None.                                          *
* POST:         None.                                          *
*                                                              *
* RETURNS:      TRUE if fault detected, FALSE otherwise.      *
*                                                              *
****************************************************************/
eBool cBank_Computer_Link::Faulty() const
    {
    if ((rand() % 1000) == 0)
        {
        cerr << "*** SIMULATING BANK COMP LINK FAULT ***\n";
        return TRUE;
        }
    else
        {
        return FALSE;
        }
    }

/****************************************************************
****************************************************************
*                                                              *
* CLASS:        cCard_Reader                                   *
*                                                              *
* EXCEPT:       Throws 1 (int) on hardware error.             *
*                                                              *
****************************************************************
****************************************************************/
class cCard_Reader
    {
    public:
                    cCard_Reader(eBool = FALSE);
        eBool       Insert(int&);
        void        Eject();
```

```
        void    Keep();
        eBool   Faulty() const;
    private:
        eBool _card_present;
    };

/*************************************************************
*                                                           *
* C FUNCTION:   cCard_Reader()                              *
*                                                           *
* CLASS:        cCard_Reader                                *
*                                                           *
* PRE:          None.                                       *
* POST:         None.                                       *
*                                                           *
*************************************************************/
cCard_Reader::cCard_Reader(eBool card)
    {
    _card_present = card;
    }

/*************************************************************
*                                                           *
* M FUNCTION:   Insert()                                    *
*                                                           *
* CLASS:        cCard_Reader                                *
*                                                           *
* OVERVIEW:     Simulates insertion and reading of card.    *
*                                                           *
* PRE:          Hardware not faulty.                        *
* POST:         None.                                       *
*                                                           *
* RETURNS:      TRUE if card readable, FALSE otherwise.     *
*                                                           *
*************************************************************/
eBool cCard_Reader::Insert(int& acc_REF)
    {
    // Pre - the hardware is OK

    if (Faulty()) {throw 1;}

    if (_card_present)
        {
        cerr << "*** THERE IS ALREADY A CARD IN THE MACHINE ***\n";
        }
    else
        {
        cerr << "*** SIMULATING INSERTION OF CARD ***\n";
        _card_present = TRUE;

        cerr << "*** SIMULATING READING A/C NUMBER ***\n";
        acc_REF = 4321;
        }
```

```
        if ((rand() % 10) == 0)
            {
            cerr << "*** SIMULATING UNREADABLE CARD ***\n";
            return FALSE;
            }
        else
            {
            return TRUE;
            }
        }
/**************************************************************
 *                                                            *
 * M FUNCTION:   Eject()                                      *
 *                                                            *
 * CLASS:        cCard_Reader                                 *
 *                                                            *
 * OVERVIEW:     Ejects card from machine (simulated)         *
 *                                                            *
 * PRE:          Hardware not faulty.                         *
 * POST:         None.                                        *
 *                                                            *
 * RETURNS:      void.                                        *
 *                                                            *
 **************************************************************/
void cCard_Reader::Eject()
        {
        // Pre - the hardware is OK
        if (Faulty()) {throw 1;}
        if (!_card_present)
            {
            cerr << "*** THERE IS NO CARD IN THE MACHINE ***\n";
            }
        else
            {
            cerr << "*** SIMULATING EJECTION OF CARD ***\n";
            _card_present = FALSE;
            }
        }
/**************************************************************
 *                                                            *
 * M FUNCTION:   Keep()                                       *
 *                                                            *
 * CLASS:        cCard_Reader                                 *
 *                                                            *
 * OVERVIEW:     Simulates retention of card by card reader   *
 *                                                            *
 * PRE:          Hardware not faulty.                         *
 * POST:         None.                                        *
 *                                                            *
 * RETURNS:      void.                                        *
 *                                                            *
 **************************************************************/
```

```
void cCard_Reader::Keep()
    {
    // Pre - the hardware is OK
    if (Faulty()) {throw 1;}

    if (!_card_present)
        {
        cerr << "*** THERE IS NO CARD IN THE MACHINE ***\n";
        }
    else
        {
        cerr << "*** SIMULATING RETENTION OF CARD ***\n";
        _card_present = FALSE;
        }
    }

/****************************************************************
*                                                              *
* A FUNCTION:   Faulty()                                        *
*                                                              *
* CLASS:        cCard_Reader                                   *
*                                                              *
* OVERVIEW:     Detects hardware fault.                        *
*                                                              *
* PRE:          None.                                          *
* POST:         None.                                          *
*                                                              *
* RETURNS:      TRUE if fault detected, FALSE otherwise.       *
*                                                              *
****************************************************************/
eBool cCard_Reader::Faulty() const
    {
    if ((rand() % 1000) == 0)
        {
        cerr << "*** SIMULATING CARD READER FAULT ***\n";
        return TRUE;
        }
    else
        {
        return FALSE;
        }
    }

/****************************************************************
****************************************************************
*                                                              *
* CLASS:        cKeypad                                        *
*                                                              *
* EXCEPT:       Throws 1 (int) on hardware error.             *
*                                                              *
****************************************************************
****************************************************************/
class cKeypad
    {
```

```
    public:
                    cKeypad(int = 81);
            int     Enter() const;
            eBool   Faulty() const;

    private:
            int     _max_line_length;
    };
/*****************************~*****************************
*                                                        *
* C FUNCTION:   cKeypad()                                *
*                                                        *
* CLASS:        cKeypad                                  *
*                                                        *
* OVERVIEW:     Configures the keypad.                   *
*                                                        *
* PRE:          None.                                    *
* POST:         None.                                    *
*                                                        *
***********************************************************/
cKeypad::cKeypad(int length)
    {
    _max_line_length = length; // Sets max input line length
    }
/*********************************************************
*                                                        *
* A FUNCTION:   Enter()                                  *
*                                                        *
* CLASS:        cKeypad                                  *
*                                                        *
* OVERVIEW:     Simulates entry of data on keypad.       *
*                                                        *
* PRE:          Hardware not faulty.                     *
* POST:         None.                                    *
*                                                        *
* RETURNS:      TRUE if fault detected, FALSE otherwise. *
*                                                        *
***********************************************************/
int cKeypad::Enter() const
    {
    // Pre - the hardware is OK
    if (Faulty()) {throw 1;}

    char tmp[81];

    cin.getline(tmp, 81);

    return atoi(tmp);
    }
/*********************************************************
*                                                        *
* A FUNCTION:   Faulty()                                 *
*                                                        *
```

```
*  CLASS:         cKeypad                                              *
*                                                                     *
*  OVERVIEW:      Detects hardware fault.                             *
*                                                                     *
*  PRE:           None.                                               *
*  POST:          None.                                               *
*                                                                     *
*  RETURNS:       TRUE if fault detected, FALSE otherwise.            *
*                                                                     *
**********************************************************************/
eBool cKeypad::Faulty() const
    {
    if ((rand() % 800) == 0)
        {
        cerr << "*** SIMULATING KEYPAD FAULT ***\n";
        return TRUE;
        }
    else
        {
        return FALSE;
        }
    }
/********************************************************************
********************************************************************
*                                                                     *
*  CLASS:         cSoftKeys                                            *
*                                                                     *
*  EXCEPT:        Throws 1 (int) on hardware error.                   *
*                                                                     *
********************************************************************
********************************************************************/
class cSoftKeys
    {
    public:
                cSoftKeys(const int = NUM_SOFT_KEYS);
        int     Key_pressed() const;
        eBool   Faulty() const;

    protected:
        int _num_keys;
    };
/********************************************************************
*                                                                     *
*  C FUNCTION:    cSoftKeys                                            *
*                                                                     *
*  CLASS:         cSoftKeys                                            *
*                                                                     *
*  PRE:           None.                                               *
*  POST:          None.                                               *
*                                                                     *
**********************************************************************/
```

```
cSoftKeys::cSoftKeys(const int keys)
    {
    _num_keys = keys;
    }
/****************************************************************
*                                                              *
* A FUNCTION:   Key_pressed()                                  *
*                                                              *
* CLASS:        cSoftKey                                       *
*                                                              *
* OVERVIEW:     Returns number of softkey pressed              *
*                                                              *
* PRE:          Hardware not faulty.                           *
* POST:         None.                                          *
*                                                              *
* RETURNS:      Key number.                                    *
*                                                              *
*****************************************************************/
int cSoftKeys::Key_pressed() const
    {
    // Pre - the hardware is OK
    if (Faulty()) {throw 1;}
    char ip_STR[81]; // Input string buffer
    int key_number;
    cin.getline(ip_STR,sizeof(ip_STR));
    key_number = atoi(ip_STR);
    return key_number;
    }
/****************************************************************
*                                                              *
* A FUNCTION:   Faulty()                                       *
*                                                              *
* CLASS:        cSoftKeys                                      *
*                                                              *
* OVERVIEW:     Detects hardware fault.                        *
*                                                              *
* PRE:          None.                                          *
* POST:         None.                                          *
*                                                              *
* RETURNS:      TRUE if fault detected, FALSE otherwise.       *
*                                                              *
*****************************************************************/
eBool cSoftKeys::Faulty() const
    {
    if ((rand() % 1000) == 0)
        {
        cerr << "*** SIMULATING SOFTKEY FAULT ***\n";
        return TRUE;
        }
    else
```

```
        {
        return FALSE;
        }
    }

/****************************************************************
 ****************************************************************
 *                                                              *
 * CLASS:        cCash_Dispenser                                *
 *                                                              *
 * EXCEPT:       Throws 1 (int) on hardware error.              *
 *                                                              *
 ****************************************************************
 ****************************************************************/
class cCash_Dispenser
    {
    public:
                    cCash_Dispenser(const int=1000);
            int     cash_level() const {return _cash;}
            eBool   Faulty() const;
    private:
            int     _cash; // Amount of cash available
    };

/****************************************************************
 *                                                              *
 * C FUNCTION:   cCash_Dispenser()                              *
 *                                                              *
 * CLASS:        cCash_Dispenser                                *
 *                                                              *
 * PRE:          None.                                          *
 * POST:         None.                                          *
 *                                                              *
 ****************************************************************/
cCash_Dispenser::cCash_Dispenser(const int initial_cash)
    {
    _cash = initial_cash;
    }

/****************************************************************
 *                                                              *
 * A FUNCTION:   Faulty()                                       *
 *                                                              *
 * CLASS:        cCash_Dispenser                                *
 *                                                              *
 * OVERVIEW:     Detects hardware fault.                        *
 *                                                              *
 * PRE:          None.                                          *
 * POST:         None.                                          *
 *                                                              *
 * RETURNS:      TRUE if fault detected, FALSE otherwise.       *
 *                                                              *
 ****************************************************************/
```

```
eBool cCash_Dispenser::Faulty() const
    {
    if ((rand() % 100) == 0)
        {
        cerr << "*** SIMULATING CASH DISPENSER FAULT ***\n";
        return TRUE;
        }
    else
        {
        return FALSE;
        }
    }
/****************************************************************
 ****************************************************************
 *                                                              *
 * CLASS:        cOutput_Device                                 *
 *                                                              *
 * EXCEPT:       Throws 1 (int) on hardware error.              *
 *                                                              *
 ****************************************************************
 ****************************************************************/
class cOutput_Device
    {
    public:
                cOutput_Device(const int = 50, const int = 10);
        void    Display(char*) const;
        virtual eBool Faulty() const = 0; // Pure virtual
    private:
        int  _h_size;
        int  _v_size;
    };
/****************************************************************
 *                                                              *
 * C FUNCTION:  cOutput()                                       *
 *                                                              *
 * CLASS:       cOutput_Device                                  *
 *                                                              *
 * OVERVIEW:    Configures output device.                       *
 *                                                              *
 * PRE:         None.                                           *
 * POST:        None.                                           *
 *                                                              *
 ****************************************************************/
cOutput_Device::cOutput_Device(const int horiz,
                               const int vert)
    {
    // _h_size is horizontal size, in columns, of device
    _h_size = horiz;
    // _v_size is number of rows that can be displayed
    _v_size = vert;
    }
```

```
/*************************************************************
 *                                                           *
 * M FUNCTION:  Display()                                    *
 *                                                           *
 * CLASS:       cOutput_Device                               *
 *                                                           *
 * OVERVIEW:    Displays given message on output device.     *
 *                                                           *
 * PRE:         string_PTR != 0                              *
 *              Hardware not faulty.                         *
 * POST:        None.                                        *
 *                                                           *
 * RETURNS:     void.                                        *
 *                                                           *
 *************************************************************/
void cOutput_Device::Display(char* string_PTR) const
    {
    // Pre - the hardware is OK
    if (Faulty()) {throw 1;}
    // pre - string is not null
    assert(string_PTR != 0);

    // To change the display size requires only
    // local changes here.
    char temp_str[80];
    strncpy(temp_str, string_PTR, _h_size);
    cout << temp_str;
    }
/*************************************************************
 *************************************************************
 *                                                           *
 * CLASS:       cVideo_Monitor                               *
 *                                                           *
 * EXCEPT:      Throws 1 (int) on hardware error.            *
 *                                                           *
 *************************************************************
 *************************************************************/
class cVideo_Monitor : virtual public cOutput_Device
    {
    public:
        void Clear() const;
        eBool Faulty() const;

    private:
    };
/*************************************************************
 *                                                           *
 * A FUNCTION:  Clear()                                      *
 *                                                           *
 * CLASS:       cVideo_Monitor                               *
 *                                                           *
 * OVERVIEW:    Clears video monitor display.                *
```

```
*                                                              *
* PRE:          Hardware not faulty.                           *
* POST:         None.                                          *
*                                                              *
* RETURNS:      void.                                          *
*                                                              *
**************************************************************/
void cVideo_Monitor::Clear() const
     {
     // Pre - the hardware is OK
     if (Faulty()) {throw 1;}

     // Print a number of blank lines to clear the
     // display: crude but (almost) universally effective

     // NOTE: disabled here to make book example clearer
     for (int line = 1; line <= 0; line++)
        {
        Display("\n");
        }
     }


/*************************************************************
*                                                              *
* A FUNCTION:   Faulty()                                       *
*                                                              *
* CLASS:        cVideo_Monitor                                 *
*                                                              *
* OVERVIEW:     Detects hardware fault.                        *
*                                                              *
* PRE:          None.                                          *
* POST:         None.                                          *
*                                                              *
* RETURNS:      TRUE if fault detected, FALSE otherwise.       *
*                                                              *
**************************************************************/
eBool cVideo_Monitor::Faulty() const
     {
     if ((rand() % 10000) == 0)
        {
        cerr << "*** SIMULATING VIDEO MONITOR FAULT ***\n";
        return TRUE;
        }
     else
        {
        return FALSE;
        }
     }


/*************************************************************
**************************************************************
*                                                              *
* CLASS:        cPrinter                                       *
*                                                              *
```

```
* EXCEPT:       Throws 1 (int) on hardware error.           *
*                                                            *
**************************************************************
*************************************************************/
class cPrinter : virtual public cOutput_Device
    {
    public:
                cPrinter(int = 10);
        void    Print_Mini();
        int     Paper_Level() const {return _Paper_level;}
        eBool   Faulty() const;
    private:
        int     _Paper_level;
    };

/*************************************************************
*                                                            *
* C FUNCTION:  cPrinter()                                    *
*                                                            *
* CLASS:       cPrinter                                      *
*                                                            *
* PRE:         None.                                         *
* POST:        None.                                         *
*                                                            *
*************************************************************/
cPrinter::cPrinter(int p)
    {
    // Number of initial sheets of paper
    _Paper_level = p;
    }

/*************************************************************
*                                                            *
* M FUNCTION:  Print_Mini()                                  *
*                                                            *
* CLASS:       cPrinter                                      *
*                                                            *
* OVERVIEW:    Generates mini statement (simulated)          *
*                                                            *
* PRE:         Hardware not faulty.                          *
* POST:        None.                                         *
*                                                            *
* RETURNS:     void.                                         *
*                                                            *
*************************************************************/
void cPrinter::Print_Mini()
    {
    // Pre - the hardware is OK
    if (Faulty()) {throw 1;}

    cout << "*************************************\n";
    cout << "*     SIMULATED MINI STATEMENT      *\n";
    cout << "*************************************\n";
```

```
        cout << "\n\t£10\n\t£20\n\t£30\n\t£40\n";
        cout << "************************************\n";
        _Paper_level--;
        }
/****************************************************************
 *                                                              *
 * A FUNCTION:   Faulty()                                       *
 *                                                              *
 * CLASS:        cPrinter                                       *
 *                                                              *
 * OVERVIEW:     Detects hardware fault.                        *
 *                                                              *
 * PRE:          None.                                          *
 * POST:         None.                                          *
 *                                                              *
 * RETURNS:      TRUE if fault detected, FALSE otherwise.       *
 *                                                              *
 ****************************************************************/
eBool cPrinter::Faulty() const
        {
        if ((rand() % 500) == 0)
            {
            cerr << "*** SIMULATING PRINTER FAULT ***\n";
            return TRUE;
            }
        else
            {
            return FALSE;
            }
        }
/****************************************************************
 ****************************************************************
 *                                                              *
 * CLASS:        cSoftKeyMonitor                                *
 *                                                              *
 * EXCEPT:       Throws 1 (int) on hardware error.              *
 *                                                              *
 ****************************************************************
 ****************************************************************/
class cSoftKeyMonitor : public cSoftKeys,
                        public cVideo_Monitor
        {
        public:
            int    Get_choice(char two_d[][MON_SIZE]) const;
            eBool  Faulty() const;
        };
/****************************************************************
 *                                                              *
 * A FUNCTION:   Get_choice()                                   *
 *                                                              *
```

```
 *  CLASS:         cSoftKeyMonitor                                    *
 *                                                                    *
 *  OVERVIEW:      Get user choice of service.                        *
 *                                                                    *
 *  PRE:           Hardware not faulty.                               *
 *  POST:          None.                                              *
 *                                                                    *
 *  RETURNS:       void.                                              *
 *                                                                    *
 **********************************************************************/
int cSoftKeyMonitor::Get_choice(char two_d[][MON_SIZE]) const
    {
    // Pre - the hardware is OK
    if (Faulty()) {throw 1;}

    int key;
    int key_OK;
    int valid_entry[NUM_SOFT_KEYS];

    Display("\nAvailable options: \n");

    for (int x = 0; x < _num_keys; x++)
        {
        valid_entry[x] = 0; // Default

        if (two_d[x][0] != 'X')
            {
            Display(&two_d[x][0]);
            Display("\n");
            valid_entry[x] = 1;
            }
        }

    do
        {
        cerr << "Please enter the appropriate number : ";
        key = Key_pressed();

        // Determine if key choice is valid
        if ((key >= 0) && (key < _num_keys))
            {
            key_OK = valid_entry[key];
            }
        else
            {
            key_OK = 0;
            }
        } while (!key_OK);

    Display("Thank you.\n\n");

    return key;
    }

/**********************************************************************
 *                                                                    *
 *  A FUNCTION:  Faulty()                                             *
```

```
*                                                              *
* CLASS:         cSoftKeyMonitor                               *
*                                                              *
* OVERVIEW:      Detects hardware fault.                       *
*                                                              *
* PRE:           None.                                         *
* POST:          None.                                         *
*                                                              *
* RETURNS:       TRUE if fault detected, FALSE otherwise.      *
*                                                              *
***************************************************************/
eBool cSoftKeyMonitor::Faulty() const
    {
    if (cSoftKeys::Faulty() || cVideo_Monitor::Faulty())
        {
        cerr << "*** SIMULATING SOFTKEY MONITOR FAULT ***\n";
        return TRUE;
        }
    else
        {
        return FALSE;
        }
    }

/***************************************************************
****************************************************************
*                                                              *
* CLASS:         cATM                                          *
*                                                              *
* EXCEPT:        Throws 1 (int) on hardware error              *
*                                                              *
****************************************************************
***************************************************************/
class cATM
    {
    public:
        eBool   Hardware_OK();
        void    Check_supplies();
        void    Process_card(eProcess, int* = 0, int* = 0);
        void    Get_password(int&, int&, int);
        void    Deliver_services();
        void    Shutdown(int);
        int     Get_user_choice();

    private:
        void    _Order_cheque_book_from_bank();
        void    _Print_customer_balance();
        void    _Print_customer_mini_statement();
        void    _Dispense_cash_to_customer();

        eBool   _cheque_OK;
        eBool   _balance_OK;
        eBool   _statement_OK;
```

```
            eBool    _cash_OK;

            cKeypad                  _Kp;
            cSoftKeyMonitor          _SKM;
            cCard_Reader             _CR;
            cCash_Dispenser          _CD;
            cBank_Computer_Link      _BCL;
            cPrinter                 _Pr;
        };


/****************************************************************
 *                                                              *
 * M FUNCTION:  Hardware_OK()                                   *
 *                                                              *
 * CLASS:       cATM                                            *
 *                                                              *
 * OVERVIEW:    Polls hardware to determine system status.      *
 *                                                              *
 * PRE:         None.                                           *
 * POST:        None.                                           *
 *                                                              *
 * RETURNS:     void.                                           *
 *                                                              *
 ****************************************************************/
eBool cATM::Hardware_OK()
    {
    // Check all hardware
    if (_Kp.Faulty() || _SKM.Faulty() || _CR.Faulty() ||
      _CD.Faulty() || _BCL.Faulty() || _Pr.Faulty())
        {
        return FALSE;
        }
    else
        {
        return TRUE;
        }
    }


/****************************************************************
 *                                                              *
 * M FUNCTION:  Check_supplies()                                *
 *                                                              *
 * CLASS:       cATM                                            *
 *                                                              *
 * OVERVIEW:    Checks supplies of paper and cash.              *
 *                                                              *
 * PRE:         All hardware working normally                   *
 * POST:        None.                                           *
 *                                                              *
 * RETURNS:     void.                                           *
 *                                                              *
 ****************************************************************/
```

```
void cATM::Check_supplies()
    {
    // Do full check of all hardware before new customer
    // uses the machine
    if (!Hardware_OK()) {throw 1;}

    _SKM.Clear();
    _SKM.Display("Next customer please wait...\n\n");

    // Reset for new customer
    _cheque_OK = TRUE;

    if (_CD.cash_level() > 0)
        {
        // Reset these for new customer
        _balance_OK = TRUE;
        _cash_OK = TRUE;
        }
    else
        {
        _balance_OK = FALSE;
        _cash_OK = FALSE;
        }

    if (_Pr.Paper_Level() > 0)
        {
        // Reset these for new customer
        _balance_OK = TRUE;
        _statement_OK = TRUE;
        }
    else
        {
        _balance_OK = FALSE;
        _statement_OK = FALSE;
        }
    }

/**************************************************************
*                                                            *
* M FUNCTION:   Process_card()                               *
*                                                            *
* CLASS:        cATM                                         *
*                                                            *
* OVERVIEW:     Check, keep or eject cash card (simulated)   *
*                                                            *
* PRE:          None.                                        *
* POST:         None.                                        *
*                                                            *
* RETURNS:      void.                                        *
*                                                            *
**************************************************************/
void cATM::Process_card(eProcess    required_op,
                        int*        acc_PTR,
                        int*        card_OK_PTR)
```

```
    {
    /* NOTE: Process_card() is a function with a
       default argument. Can call as:
       Process_card(CHECK_CARD, card_OK);
       or
       Process_card(KEEP_CARD);
       Process_card(EJECT_CARD); */
    switch (required_op)
        {
        case CHECK_CARD:
            // Using "extra" argument
            _SKM.Clear();
            _SKM.Display("Please insert your card.\n\n");
            if (_CR.Insert(*acc_PTR))
                { // Valid card inserted
                _SKM.Display("\nThank you.\n\n");
                *card_OK_PTR = TRUE;
                }
            else
                {
                _SKM.Display("Sorry - your card is unreadable.\n\n");
                _CR.Eject();
                *card_OK_PTR = FALSE;
                }
            break;

        case KEEP_CARD:
            _SKM.Display("Your card has been retained. ");
            _SKM.Display("Please contact your branch.\n\n");
            _CR.Keep();
            break;

        case EJECT_CARD:
            _SKM.Display("Please take your card.\n\n");
            _CR.Eject();
            break;
        }
    }
/*****************************************************************
 *                                                               *
 * M FUNCTION:  Get_password()                                   *
 *                                                               *
 * CLASS:       cATM                                             *
 *                                                               *
 * OVERVIEW:    Get password, and check it via BCL               *
 *                                                               *
 * PRE:         None.                                            *
 * POST:        None.                                            *
 *                                                               *
 * RETURNS:     void.                                            *
 *                                                               *
 *****************************************************************/
```

```
void cATM::Get_password(int& password_OK_REF,
                        int& tries_REF,
                        int account_no)
    {
    int password;

    tries_REF++;
    _SKM.Display("Please enter your password on the keypad : ");
    password = _Kp.Enter();
    if (_BCL.Password_OK(password, account_no))
        {
        password_OK_REF = TRUE;
        }
    else
        {
        password_OK_REF = FALSE;
        }
    if (!(password_OK_REF))
        {
        if (tries_REF < MAX_NUM_PASS_TRIES)
            {
            cerr << "Your password was incorrect.\n";
            // Recursive call to Get_password()
            Get_password(password_OK_REF, tries_REF, account_no);
            }
        else
            {
            // Too many tries - could be a stolen card?
            Process_card(KEEP_CARD);
            }
        }
    }

/******************************************************************
 *                                                                *
 * M FUNCTION:  Deliver_services()                                *
 *                                                                *
 * CLASS:       cATM                                              *
 *                                                                *
 * OVERVIEW:    Deliver required customer services                *
 *                                                                *
 * PRE:         None.                                             *
 * POST:        None.                                             *
 *                                                                *
 * RETURNS:     void.                                             *
 *                                                                *
 ******************************************************************/
void cATM::Deliver_services()
    {
    int user_choice;
    do {
        user_choice = Get_user_choice();
```

```
        switch (user_choice)
            { // If "Quit" then do nothing...
            case 1:
                _Order_cheque_book_from_bank();
            break;

            case 2:
                _Print_customer_balance();
            break;

            case 3:
                _Print_customer_mini_statement();
            break;

            case 4:
                _Dispense_cash_to_customer();
            break;
            }
        } while (user_choice != 0); // 0 is assumed quit
    }

/****************************************************************
 *                                                              *
 * M FUNCTION:   Get_user_choice()                              *
 *                                                              *
 * CLASS:        cATM                                           *
 *                                                              *
 * OVERVIEW:     Find out what user wants to do                 *
 *                                                              *
 * PRE:          None.                                          *
 * POST:         None.                                          *
 *                                                              *
 * RETURNS:      void.                                          *
 *                                                              *
 ****************************************************************/
int cATM::Get_user_choice()
    {
    int service;

    char options[NUM_SOFT_KEYS][MON_SIZE] = {{" 0. Quit"},
                                             {"X"},
                                             {"X"},
                                             {"X"},
                                             {"X"},
                                             {"X"}};

    if (_cheque_OK == TRUE)    strcpy(options[1], " 1. Cheque book");
    if (_balance_OK == TRUE)   strcpy(options[2], " 2. Balance");
    if (_statement_OK == TRUE) strcpy(options[3], " 3. Statement");
    if (_cash_OK == TRUE)      strcpy(options[4], " 4. Cash");

    service = _SKM.Get_choice(options);

    return service;
    }
```

```
/************************************************************
*                                                          *
* M FUNCTION:    _Order_cheque_book_from_bank()            *
*                                                          *
* CLASS:         cATM                                      *
*                                                          *
* OVERVIEW:      Order cheque book from bank.              *
*                                                          *
* PRE:           None.                                     *
* POST:          None.                                     *
*                                                          *
* RETURNS:       void.                                     *
*                                                          *
************************************************************/
void cATM::_Order_cheque_book_from_bank()
    {
    cerr << "*** SIMULATING ORDER FOR CHEQUE BOOK ***\n\n";
    _SKM.Display("Your cheque book will be posted to you.\n");

    _cheque_OK = FALSE;
    }


/************************************************************
*                                                          *
* M FUNCTION:    _Print_customer_balance()                 *
*                                                          *
* CLASS:         cATM                                      *
*                                                          *
* OVERVIEW:      Print customer balance.                   *
*                                                          *
* PRE:           None.                                     *
* POST:          None.                                     *
*                                                          *
* RETURNS:       void.                                     *
*                                                          *
************************************************************/
void cATM::_Print_customer_balance()
    {
    char tmp[12];

    // String conversion
    sprintf(tmp, "%d", _BCL.Show());

    _Pr.Display("Your balance is: £");
    _Pr.Display(tmp);
    _Pr.Display("\n");

    _balance_OK = FALSE;
    }


/************************************************************
*                                                          *
* M FUNCTION:    _Print_customer_mini_statement()          *
*                                                          *
* CLASS:         cATM                                      *
```

```
*                                                               *
* OVERVIEW:     Print customer mini statement                   *
*                                                               *
* PRE:          None.                                           *
* POST:         None.                                           *
*                                                               *
* RETURNS:      void.                                           *
*                                                               *
***************************************************************/
void cATM::_Print_customer_mini_statement()
    {
    _Pr.Print_Mini();
    _SKM.Display("\nPlease take your mini statement.\n");
    _statement_OK = FALSE;
    }
/***************************************************************
*                                                               *
* M FUNCTION:   _Dispense_cash_to_customer()                    *
*                                                               *
* CLASS:        cATM                                            *
*                                                               *
* OVERVIEW:     Dispense cash to customer                       *
*                                                               *
* PRE:          None.                                           *
* POST:         None.                                           *
*                                                               *
* RETURNS:      void.                                           *
*                                                               *
***************************************************************/
void cATM::_Dispense_cash_to_customer()
    {
    int service, request;
    char options[NUM_SOFT_KEYS][MON_SIZE] = {{" 0. QUIT"},
                                             {" 1. £10"},
                                             {" 2. £20"},
                                             {" 3. £50"},
                                             {" 4. £100"},
                                    {"5. Some other amount"}};
    service = _SKM.Get_choice(options);
    switch (service)
        {
        case 0:
            request = 0;
        break;
        case 1:
            request = 10;
        break;
        case 2:
            request = 20;
        break;
```

```
        case 3:
            request = 50;
        break;
        case 4:
            request = 100;
        break;
        case 5:
            request = -1;
        break;
        }
    if (request > 0)
        {
        if (request <= _BCL.Show())
            {
            _BCL.Alter(-request);

            cerr << "*** SIMULATING CASH DELIVERY ***\n\n";
            _SKM.Display("Please take your cash.\n");
            _cash_OK = FALSE;
            }
        else
            {
            _SKM.Display("Sorry - the requested amount ");
            _SKM.Display("exceeds your credit limit.\n");
            }
        }
    else
        {
        if (request < 0)
            {
            _SKM.Display("How much cash do you require? ");
            request = _Kp.Enter();
            if (request % 10 != 0) // Only multiples of £10…
                {
                _SKM.Display("Sorry - must be multiple of £10\n");
                }
            else
                {
                if (request <= _BCL.Show())
                    {
                    _BCL.Alter(-request);

                    cerr << "*** SIMULATING CASH DELIVERY ***\n\n";
                    _SKM.Display("Please take your cash.\n");
                    _cash_OK = FALSE;
                    }
                else
                    {
                    _SKM.Display("Sorry - the requested amount ");
                    _SKM.Display("exceeds your credit limit. ");
                    }
```

```
                             }
                         }
                     }
                 }
/* * * * * * * * * * * * * * * * * * * * * * * * * * * * * * * * * * * * * * * * * * * *
*                                                                            *
*  M FUNCTION:    Shutdown()                                                 *
*                                                                            *
*  CLASS:         cATM                                                       *
*                                                                            *
*  OVERVIEW:      Shut down cash machine.                                    *
*                                                                            *
*  PRE:           None.                                                      *
*  POST:          None.                                                      *
*                                                                            *
*  RETURNS:       void.                                                      *
*                                                                            *
* * * * * * * * * * * * * * * * * * * * * * * * * * * * * * * * * * * * * * * * * * * */
void cATM::Shutdown(int level)
    {
    if (level)
        {
        _SKM.Display("A hardware error has been detected.\n\n");
        cerr << "*** SIMULATING EMERGENCY SHUTDOWN ***\n";
        }
    else
        {
        _SKM.Display("Please use another machine.\n\n");
        cerr << "*** SIMULATING ORDINARY MACHINE SHUTDOWN ***\n";
        }
    exit(1);
    }
/* * * * * * * * * * * * * * * * * * * * * * * * * * * * * * * * * * * * * * * * * * * *
* * * * * * * * * * * * * * * * * * * * * * * * * * * * * * * * * * * * * * * * * * * */
int main()
    {
    cATM cash_machine;
    int acc;
    int valid_card_entered;
    int tries, valid_password_entered;
    int user_wants_to_quit;

    // Set up non-repeatable random numbers for simulation
    srand((unsigned)time(NULL));

    try
        {
        // Simulate (up to) five customers in queue
        // then manual shut down
        for (int customer = 1; customer <= 5; customer++)
            {
```

```
cout << "\n-------------------------- \n";
cout << "PROTOTYPE BANK AUTO TELLER MACHINE\n";
cout << "-------------------------- \n\n";

cash_machine.Check_supplies();

cash_machine.Process_card(CHECK_CARD, &acc,
                          &valid_card_entered);

if (valid_card_entered)
   {
   tries = 0;
   user_wants_to_quit = FALSE;
   cash_machine.Get_password(valid_password_entered,
                          tries,acc);
   if (valid_password_entered)
      {
      // Keep delivering services till user
      // says quit (or hardware fault)
      cash_machine.Deliver_services();
      cash_machine.Process_card(EJECT_CARD);
      }
   }

// Simulate manual shutdown
cash_machine.Shutdown(0);
} // End of try block
// Deal with hardware or other errors
catch (...)
   {
   cash_machine.Shutdown(1);
   try
      {
      // Keep card: customer may have caused fault...
      cash_machine.Process_card(KEEP_CARD);
      exit(1);
      }
   catch(...)
      {
      exit(1);
      }
   }
return 0;
}
```

Program 32.2 The prototype O-O ATM system. (☺)

32.4.7 System tests and maintenance

The complete prototype is tested again, first by the programmers, and then by the test team, both working from the test strategy produced by the designers. Particular attention must be paid to system components

involving inheritance. The system is then subjected to user tests, including field tests and/or acceptance tests. The system is revised as necessary; any changes made during the testing and subsequent ongoing maintenance are recorded and reflected in the evolving object model.

During this stage of the project, Harry completes his usual system test strategy, as specified by Jane.

During these and subsequent tests, Harry's first concern is with the reliability of the system. In embedded systems such as the ATM, such reliability figures depend (of course) not only on the nature of the software, but also on the choice of hardware components. Harry therefore uses figures from the manufacturer of each of the possible hardware components that might be used in the final system to determine how likely it is that any component will fail. If, for example, a particular card reader is likely to fail (that is, break down) once every 30 000 operations, Harry can incorporate this figure in the Faulty() member function for the corresponding cCard_Reader class. With a complete set of such figures for each of the hardware components, he can simulate the complete ATM system, and determine (in the absence of outside factors, such as vandalism, at this stage) how reliable the final system is likely to be. This allows him to select between a variety of different hardware components so as to maximize the reliability of the final system.

During some of this system testing, the program produces the following output:

```
PROTOTYPE BANK AUTO TELLER MACHINE

Next customer please wait...

Please insert your card.

*** SIMULATING INSERTION OF CARD ***
*** SIMULATING READING A/C NUMBER ***

Thank you.

Please enter your password on the keypad : 1234

*** SIMULATING CALL TO BANK COMPUTER ***
*** PASSWORD CORRECT ***

Available options:
 0. Quit
 1. Cheque book
 2. Balance
 3. Statement
 4. Cash
Please enter the appropriate number : 2
Thank you.

Your balance is: £70

Available options:
 0. Quit
 1. Cheque book
 3. Statement
 4. Cash
Please enter the appropriate number : 4
Thank you.
```

```
Available options:
 0. QUIT
 1. £10
 2. £20
 3. £50
 4. £100
 5. Some other amount
Please enter the appropriate number : 3
Thank you.

*** SIMULATING CASH DELIVERY ***

Please take your cash.

Available options:
 0. Quit
 1. Cheque book
 3. Statement
Please enter the appropriate number : 0
Thank you.

Please take your card.

*** SIMULATING EJECTION OF CARD ***


PROTOTYPE BANK AUTO TELLER MACHINE

Next customer please wait…

Please insert your card.

*** SIMULATING INSERTION OF CARD ***
*** SIMULATING READING A/C NUMBER ***

Thank you.

Please enter your password on the keypad : 123

*** SIMULATING CALL TO BANK COMPUTER ***
*** PASSWORD *NOT* CORRECT ***

Your password was incorrect.
Please enter your password on the keypad : 12

*** SIMULATING CALL TO BANK COMPUTER ***
*** PASSWORD *NOT* CORRECT ***

Your password was incorrect.
Please enter your password on the keypad : 1235

*** SIMULATING CALL TO BANK COMPUTER ***
*** PASSWORD *NOT* CORRECT ***

Your card has been retained. Please contact your branch.

*** SIMULATING RETENTION OF CARD ***


PROTOTYPE BANK AUTO TELLER MACHINE

Next customer please wait…

Please insert your card.
```

```
*** SIMULATING INSERTION OF CARD ***
*** SIMULATING READING A/C NUMBER ***

Thank you.

Please enter your password on the keypad : 1234

*** SIMULATING CALL TO BANK COMPUTER ***
*** PASSWORD CORRECT ***

Available options:
 0. Quit
 1. Cheque book
 2. Balance
 3. Statement
 4. Cash
Please enter the appropriate number : 2

Thank you.

Your balance is: £20

Available options:
 0. Quit
 1. Cheque book
 3. Statement
 4. Cash
Please enter the appropriate number : 4
Thank you.

Available options:
 0. QUIT
 1. £10
 2. £20
 3. £50
 4. £100
 5. Some other amount
Please enter the appropriate number : 4
Thank you.

Sorry - the requested amount exceeds your credit limit.

Available options:
 0. Quit
 1. Cheque book
 3. Statement
 4. Cash
Please enter the appropriate number : 0
Thank you.

Please take your card.

*** SIMULATING EJECTION OF CARD ***


PROTOTYPE BANK AUTO TELLER MACHINE

Next customer please wait...

Please insert your card.
```

```
*** SIMULATING INSERTION OF CARD ***
*** SIMULATING READING A/C NUMBER ***
```

Thank you.

Please enter your password on the keypad : 1234

```
*** SIMULATING CALL TO BANK COMPUTER ***
*** PASSWORD CORRECT ***
```

Available options:
 0. Quit
 1. Cheque book
 2. Balance
 3. Statement
 4. Cash
Please enter the appropriate number : 3
Thank you.

```
***********************************
*      SIMULATED MINI STATEMENT      *
***********************************
```
     £10
     £20
     £30
     £40
```
***********************************
```

Please take your mini statement.

Available options:
 0. Quit
 1. Cheque book
 2. Balance
 4. Cash
Please enter the appropriate number : 1
Thank you.

```
*** SIMULATING ORDER FOR CHEQUE BOOK ***
```

Your cheque book will be posted to you.

Available options:
 0. Quit
 2. Balance
 4. Cash
Please enter the appropriate number : 0
Thank you.

Please take your card.

```
*** SIMULATING EJECTION OF CARD ***
```

PROTOTYPE BANK AUTO TELLER MACHINE

Next customer please wait…

Please insert your card.

```
*** SIMULATING INSERTION OF CARD ***
```

```
*** SIMULATING READING A/C NUMBER ***
*** SIMULATING UNREADABLE CARD ***
Sorry - your card is unreadable.

*** SIMULATING EJECTION OF CARD ***
Please use another machine.

*** SIMULATING ORDINARY MACHINE SHUTDOWN ***
```

In addition, of course, the system must also be secure. Harry therefore discusses with the hardware manufacturers, and staff at Leicester Hardware Engineering, ways of ensuring that the security of the system is maintained.

On completion of these discussions, the final system (software and hardware) is assembled, and subjected to long-term user tests.

32.5 Key features of this case study

There are some important points illustrated in this case study which are worth highlighting.

- Note how the cATM class is constructed in C++: the code (like the physical machine itself) is assembled from recognizable components – card readers, printers, etc. – in a logical manner. There are clear correlations between the simple CRD, the final code, **and** the 'real world':

```
class cATM
    {
        ...

        cKeypad                 _Kp;
        cSoftKeyMonitor         _SKM;
        cCard_Reader            _CR;
        cCash_Dispenser         _CD;
        cBank_Computer_Link     _BCL;
        cPrinter                _Pr;
    };
```

- Note the use of private member functions in the cATM class: these are a generally useful form of 'encapsulated function'. Don't forget that, if we wanted to use cATM as a base class (or expected to do so) it would be important to make these protected (rather than private) functions.

- Note the use of multiple inheritance:

```
class cSoftKeyMonitor :  public cSoftKeys,
                         public cVideo_Monitor
    {
        ...
    };
```

This use of multiple inheritance is valid (although you may wish to consider other alternative implementations), because the classes involved are disjoint (that is, they have nothing on common).

- Note the appropriate use of the pure virtual function:

```
class cOutput_Device
    {
    ...
    virtual eBool Faulty() const = 0; // Pure virtual
    ...
    };
```

- Perhaps the most important thing to note is that the end result is 'more than a simulation'. True, the program simply *emulates* an ATM machine in its present form, but it is clear how this code could be ported to work (for example) as an embedded system.

    For example, consider how information is displayed on the 'softkey monitor'. First of all, note that this information is *not* displayed by writing:

```
cout << "Next customer please wait...\n\n";
```

Instead, the user of the cATM class calls the Clear() and Display() member functions for the monitor object:

```
_SKM.Clear();
_SKM.Display("Next customer please wait...\n\n");
```

Similar encapsulation is carried out for the printer hardware:

```
_Pr.Display("Your balance is: £");
```

The end result is that the implementation-dependent features of the monitor and printer are firmly encapsulated in the related classes. This means that the prototype code listed here can be ported to any appropriate hardware without altering the structure of the program in any way, but simply by modifying a small number of member functions in the appropriate hardware-related classes.

32.6   Conclusions

To conclude our exploration of object-oriented software development, we have considered in this chapter a substantial case study, and illustrated how the O-O SADIE methodology may be applied effectively to the development of a more realistic technical system.

    This brings us to the end of Part III. In Chapter 33 we conclude the book by reviewing the material we have discussed, and providing a final comparison of process-oriented, data-oriented and object-oriented software development.

Conclusions

33 Ending at the beginning

33.1 Introduction

During the course of this book, we've presented a software engineering methodology called Simple Analysis, Design & Implementation (SADIE). By doing so we have been able to compare and contrast the three fundamental approaches to software development in widespread use at the time of writing. We've shown, we hope convincingly, that C++ can be effectively used to develop substantial and reliable software using any of the three approaches, and that CASE technology can help in this process.

In this final chapter, we address the question of how one should go about choosing an appropriate method for use in a specific software project. We conclude by providing some suggestions for further reading.

33.2 Which method should you use?

An obvious question following from the discussions throughout this book is 'which method should I use?' Unfortunately, there is no easy answer to this.

Process-oriented methods are very widely used for developing technical systems. However, object-oriented techniques are also appropriate in such situations. In general terms, code developed using a process-oriented approach may run more efficiently (that is, faster) than the equivalent code developed in an object-oriented manner. Such factors may or may not be important for your particular project.

Process-oriented designs can be implemented easily in, for example, C++, C or FORTRAN, whereas it is more difficult to implement object-oriented designs in languages without full O-O support. If there are restrictions in the choice of implementation language, this may be significant.

A summary of some important strengths and weaknesses of O-O and P-O techniques for technical system development are given in Table 33.1.

	Strengths	Weaknesses
P-O	Well known	Reliable code size limit ~100 000 lines
	Widely used	Top-down nature makes reuse of code more difficult
	Supported by a range of programming languages	Division between physical and logical models
	Generate efficient code	
O-O	Reliable code size limit ~1 000 000 lines	Not well known: staff (re-)training costs may be high
	Bottom up nature facilitates code reuse	Not widely used
	Division between physical and logical models is small	Restricted range of programming languages available
		Code may run more slowly than P-O equivalent

Table 33.1 A comparison of the strengths and weaknesses of P-O and O-O methods for the development of technical software.

The development of information systems raises further questions. At the present time, the vast majority of business data is stored on relational database systems which are usually most effectively designed and accessed using data-oriented development techniques. Ultimately, as object-oriented database systems are developed and become more widespread, O-O approaches may become appropriate for the development of information systems; time will tell. Similarly, hybrid systems are usually currently developed using a data-oriented approach. However, if you are developing from scratch, and have no legacy (relational) data to deal with, then it may be appropriate to consider using an object-oriented database. This may be particularly true if your data is complex, or graphical in nature.

A summary of some important strengths and weaknesses of O-O and D-O techniques for information system and hybrid system development are given in Table 33.2.

	Strengths	Weaknesses
D-O	Well known	Division between data and process models
	Widely used	
	Supported by all relational database systems	
	Most legacy data is in this format	
O-O	Support for inheritance	Not widely used
	May allow development of a new range of powerful database systems (e.g. for CAD)	Very few O-O databases currently on the market
		Link to RDB systems not transparent

Table 33.2 A comparison of the strengths and weaknesses of D-O and O-O methods for the development of information and hybrid technical/information software.

33.3 Varying and mixing the recipes

In Parts I, II and III we have presented (respectively) guidelines for software development using process-, data- and object-oriented development. As we have stated repeatedly, these guidelines are intended to be used as 'recipes', not 'algorithms': that is, it is to be expected that – as you grow more experienced in one or more of the development techniques – you will expand some of the stages, and concatenate others.

As we conclude this book, it is important to emphasize again that currently there are not (and never will be) any 'right answers' when it comes to software engineering. Software development is a creative process: you need to find – or produce for yourself – a method which is sufficiently rigorous and controlled to give you repeatable results, and one with which you feel comfortable. Any method (or methodology) you use should encourage 'good practice' without becoming a straitjacket to your creativity.

Numerous variations on the recipes presented here are, of course, possible. To give one example, a variation of the process-oriented system development recipe might combine features of P-O and O-O development. This new recipe might reduce the division between 'analysis' and 'design' phases of the project by omitting STDs (and control processes) completely, and providing control information solely through the structure chart. The main features of such a process model would then simply be the Context diagram, the DfD (without control information), the SC and the PSpecs.

33.4 Beyond SADIE

The SADIE methodology described in this book is a simplified version of an 'industrial-strength' software development methodology known as 'Integrated Software Engineering' (ISE). ISE, like SADIE, supports P-O, D-O and O-O development. However, ISE also provides support for agent-oriented (A-O) software development, a technique which can be used effectively, for example, to develop applications for the World Wide Web (using C++ or the Java programming language) as well as for other forms of multi-threaded system development. In all four system types (P-O, D-O, O-O and A-O), ISE provides additional support for key economic issues, such as software size prediction.

Further information about the ISE methodology is provided in Appendix K.

33.5 Conclusions

This is the end of the book, and yet we've scarcely scratched the surface of the field of software engineering. Overall, we hope we've demonstrated that the problems facing the engineer are complex and multi-faceted; while a methodology can help, it can never be a replacement for intelligence, creativity or experience. In short, software engineering involves an enormous number of questions, and no single answer or recipe-style solution will ever be possible.

What we have sought to provide with this book is a foundation for further study and practical experience in what is one of the most challenging – and exciting – areas of modern engineering. If you want to pursue any of the topics here in greater depth, then the bibliography in Chapter 34 may prove useful.

34 Bibliography

This chapter contains a collected list of books and papers either directly referenced in the text, or of related interest.

Abbott, R. J. (1983). Program design by informal English descriptions. *Comm. ACM.*, **26**(11), 882–94

Andrews, D. and Ince, D. (1991). *Practical Formal Methods with VDM*. London: McGraw-Hill

Apple Corporation (1993). *Macintosh Human Interface Guidelines*. Reading MA: Addison-Wesley

Bass, L. and Coutaz, J. (1991). *Developing Software for the User Interface*. Reading MA: Addison-Wesley

Batini, C., Ceri, S. and Navanthe, S. B. (1992). *Conceptual Database Design: An Entity-relationship Approach*. Redwood City CA: Benjamin Cummings

Beizer, B. (1990). *Software Testing Techniques*. Van Nostrand Reinhold

Berlage, T. (1991). *OSF/Motif Concepts and Programming*. Wokingham: Addison-Wesley

Boehm, B. W. (1991). *Software Engineering Economics*. Englewood Cliffs NJ: Prentice-Hall

Booch, G. (1994). *Object-Oriented Analysis and Design*. Redwood City CA: Benjamin Cummings

Bowerman, B. L. and O'Connell, R. T. (1987). *Time Series Forecasting: Unified Concepts and Computer Implementation*. Boston MA: Duxbury Press

Brooks, F. P. (1975). *The Mythical Man-Month: Essays on Software Engineering*. Reading MA: Addison-Wesley

Brumbaugh, D. E. (1994*). Object-Oriented Development: Building CASE Tools with C++*. New York: John Wiley

Bruno, G. (1995). *Model-Based Software Engineering*. London: Chapman & Hall

Budd, T. A. (1994). *Class Data Structures in C++*. Reading MA: Addison-Wesley

Cahill, S.J. (1994). *C for the Microprocessor Engineer*. New York: Prentice-Hall

Cardelli, L. and Wegner, P. (1985). On understanding types, data abstraction, and polymorphism. *ACM Computing Surveys*, **17**(4), 471–522

Cargill, T. (1992). *C++ Programming Style*. Reading MA: Addison-Wesley

Chen, P. P. (1976). The entity-relationship model: towards a unified view of data. *ACM Transactions on Database Systems*. **1**(1), 9–36

Clifton, H. D. and Sutcliffe, A. G. (1994). *Business Information Systems* 5th edn. London: Prentice-Hall

Coad, P. and Yourdon, E. (1991). *Object-Oriented Analysis* 2nd edn. Englewood Cliffs NJ: Yourdon Press

Dahl, O. J., Dijkstra, E. W. and Hoare, C. A. R. (1972). *Structured Programming*. Academic Press

Date, C. J. (1990). *An Introduction to Database Systems* 5th edn. Reading MA: Addison-Wesley

Davies, P. (1995). *The Indispensable Guide to C*. Wokingham: Addison-Wesley

DeMarco, T. (1979). *Structured Analysis and System Specification*. Englewood Cliffs NJ: Prentice-Hall

Derenzo, S. E. (1990). *Interfacing: A Laboratory Approach Using the Microprocessor for Instrumentation. Data Analysis and Control*. Englewood Cliffs NJ: Prentice-Hall

Dijkstra, E. W. (1973). *A Discipline of Programming*. Englewood Cliffs NJ: Prentice-Hall

Dixon, R. L. (1992). *Winning with CASE* 2nd edn. New York: McGraw-Hill

Eliëns, A. (1994). *Principles of Object-Oriented Software Development*. Wokingham: Addison-Wesley

Folk, M. J. and Zoellick, B. (1992). *File Structures* 2nd edn. Reading MA: Addison-Wesley

Friedman, F. L. and Koffman, E. B. (1994*). Problem Solving, Abstraction and Design Using C++*. Reading MA: Addison-Wesley

Galitz, W. O. (1985). *Handbook of Screen Format Design* 2nd edn. Wellesley Hills, MA: QED Information Sciences, Inc.

Gersting, J. L. (1993). *Mathematical Structures for Computer Science* 3rd edn. W.H. Freeman & Company

Goldsmith, S. (1993). *A Practical Guide to Real-Time Systems Development*. New York: Prentice-Hall

Graham, I. (1994). *Object-Oriented Methods* 2nd edn. Wokingham: Addison-Wesley

Gray, P. (1994). *Decision Support and Executive Information Systems*. London: Prentice-Hall

Hatley, D. J. and Pirbhai, I. A. (1987). *Strategies for Real-Time System Specification*. New York: Dorset House

Hayes, I. (1993). *Specification Case Studies* 2nd edn. London: Prentice-Hall

Henry, S. and Kafura, D. (1981). Software structure metrics based on information flow. *IEEE Trans. Software Engineering*, **7**(5), 510–18

Hollicker, C. (1991). *Software Review and Audit Handbook*. John Wiley

Hope, W. (1995). Seamless, but open to interpretation. *EXE Magazine*, **10**(1), 47–54

Horstmann, C. S. (1995). *Mastering Object-Oriented Design in C++*. New York: John Wiley

Howden, W. E. (1982). Weak mutation testing and the completeness of test cases. *IEEE Trans. on Software Engineering*, **8**(4), 371–79

Howe, D. R. (1989). *Data Analysis for Database Design* 2nd edn. London: Edward Arnold

Hughes, J. G. (1991). *Object-Oriented Databases*. New York: Prentice-Hall

Ince, D. (1991). *Object-Oriented Software Engineering with C++*. Maidenhead: McGraw-Hill

Inglis, J. (1989). *COBOL 85 for Programmers*. Chichester: John Wiley

Jacobson, I. Christerson, M., Jonsson, P. and Övergaard, G. (1993). *Object-Oriented Software Engineering* (revised printing). Wokingham: Addison-Wesley

Lawrence, P. D. and Mauch, K. (1988). *Real-Time Microcomputer System Design: An Introduction*. New York: McGraw-Hill

Lippmann, P. (1987). An introduction to computing with neural networks. *Acoustics, Speech and Signal Processing*, Institute of Electrical and Electronic Engineers (USA), April

Macguire, S. (1993). *Writing Solid Code*. Redmond WA: Microsoft Press

Macguire, S. (1994). *Debugging the Development Process*. Redmond WA: Microsoft Press

Makridakis, S., Wheelwright, S. C. and McGee. V. E. (1983). *Forecasting: Methods and Applications*. New York: John Wiley

McCabe, T. J. (1976). A software complexity measure. *IEEE Trans. Software Engineering*, **2**(6), 308–20

McConnell, S. (1993). *Code Complete*. Redmond WA: Microsoft Press

Meyer, B. (1988). *Object-Oriented Software Construction*. Englewood Cliffs NJ: Prentice-Hall

Microsoft Corporation (1992). *The Windows™ Interface: An Application Design Guide*. Redmond WA: Microsoft Press

Myers, G. (1979). *The Art of Software Testing*. New York: John Wiley

Nelson, M. (1995). *C++ Programmer's Guide to the Standard Template Library*. Foster City CA: IDG Books

Norris, M., Rigby, P. and Payne, M. (1993). *The Healthy Software Project: A Guide to Successful Development and Management*. Chichester: John Wiley

Page-Jones, M. (1988). *The Practical Guide to Structured Systems Design* 2nd edn. Englewood Cliffs NJ: Prentice-Hall

Perry, D. E. and Kaiser, G. E. (1990). Adequate testing and object-oriented programming. *Journal of Object-Oriented Programming*, **3**(5), 13–19

Petrowski, H. (1985). *To Engineer is Human*. New York: St. Martin's Press

Pfleeger, S. L. (1987). *Software Engineering: The Production of Quality Software*. Macmillan

Plauger, P. J. (1992). *The Standard C Library*. Englewood Cliffs NJ: Prentice-Hall

Pont, M. J. (1997) An integrated method for software size estimation, University of Leicester, Department of Engineering, Technical Report 97-1, January 1997. [Available electronically over the WWW via the address given at the end of the Preface.]

Pont, M. J. and Damper, R. I. (1991). A computational model of afferent neural processing from the cochlea to dorsal acoustic stria. *Journal of the Acoustical Society of America*, **89**, 1213–28

Pont, M. J. and Moreale, E. (1996) Towards a Practical Methodology for Agent-Oriented Software Engineering with C++ and Java, University of Leicester, Department of Engineering, Technical Report 96-33, December 1996. [A copy is provided on the CD included with this book.]

Pont, M. J. and Wong, K. S. (1994) Computer Simulation of Auditory Evoked Responses: A Pilot Study. *Proceedings of the Institute of Acoustics,* **16**: 147–54.

Press, W. H., Teulolsky, S. A., Vettering, W. T. and Flannery, B. P. (1992*). Numerical Recipes in C: The Art of Scientific Computing*. Cambridge: Cambridge University Press

Pressman. R. (1992). *Software Engineering: A Practitioner's Approach* 3rd edn. New York: McGraw-Hill

Ralston, A. and Meek, C. L. (1976). *Encyclopaedia of Computer Science*. Petrocelli/Charter

Renaud, P. E. (1993). *Introduction to Client/Server Systems*. New York: John Wiley

Rudd, A. (1994). *C++ Complete: A Reference and Tutorial to the Proposed C++ Standard*. New York: John Wiley

Rumbaugh, J., Blaha, M., Premerlani, W., Eddy, F. and Lorensen, W. (1991). *Object-Oriented Modeling and Design*. Englewood Cliffs NJ: Prentice-Hall

Sewell, D. R. and Pont, M. J. (forthcoming) An object-oriented model of the transtympanic membrane, *British Journal of Audiology.*

Shlaer, S. and Mellor, S. J. (1988*). Object-Oriented Systems Analysis: Modelling the World in Data*. Englewood Cliffs NJ: Prentice-Hall

Sommerville, I. (1996). *Software Engineering* 5th edn. Wokingham: Addison-Wesley

Stanczyk, S. (1991). *Programming in SQL*. London: Pitman Publishing

Stroustrup, B. (1991). *The C++ Programming Language* 2nd edn. Reading MA: Addison-Wesley

Stroustrup, B. (1994). *The Design of C++*. Stanford CA: University Video Communications. Recorded 2 March 1994

Ward, P. T. and Mellor, S. J. (1985). *Structured Development for Real-Time Systems*. Englewood Cliffs NJ: Prentice-Hall

Watt, D. A., Wichmann, B. A. and Findlay, W. (1987). *ADA Language and Methodology*. New York: Prentice-Hall

Yourdon, E. N. (1985). *Structured Walkthroughs* 3rd edn. Englewood Cliffs NJ: Prentice-Hall

Yourdon, E. N. (1989). *Modern Structured Analysis*. Englewood Cliffs NJ: Prentice-Hall

Yourdon, E. N. and Constantine, L. L. (1978). *Structured Design*. Englewood Cliffs NJ: Prentice-Hall

Appendices

APPENDIX A

CASE tool:

Installation

A.1 Introduction

This appendix describes how to install the Select CASE tool. You will need to carry out the installation process described here before you can use the tool, or complete any of the tutorials from later appendices.

A.2 About SELECT Yourdon

SELECT Yourdon has been designed by SELECT Software Tools Ltd as a computer-aided software engineering (CASE) tool which allows software engineering to be carried out using the Yourdon or Simple Analysis, Design & Implementation (SADIE) methodologies.

SELECT Yourdon features the following:

- method support for Yourdon
- method support for SADIE
- Ward-Mellor and Hatley real time extensions
- intuitive Windows interface
- integrated data dictionary
- rules-based consistency checking
- supports the following techniques:
  - dataflow diagrams
  - class-relationship diagrams
  - process specifications
  - process lists
  - state transition diagrams
  - entity-relationship diagrams
  - structure charts

A.3 Operational requirements

A.3.1 Software requirements

- Microsoft Windows 3.1 or above.
- (MS-DOS 5.0 or above.)
- *Configuration*
  The FILES parameter in CONFIG.SYS must read at least 40. If the CONFIG.SYS file needs editing you will have to re-boot your PC before the new file settings are recognized.

A.3.2 Hardware requirements

- *Computer*
  IBM PC or close compatible
  80386 processor (sx or dx)
- *Memory*
  3Mb of RAM
  3Mb hard disk space
- *Graphics*
  VGA (that is: 640 × 480, 16 colours)
- *CD-ROM drive*
  Any CD-ROM supported by Windows
- *Printer*
  Any printer supported by Windows
- *Mouse*
  Any mouse supported by Windows

A.4 Directory and file structure

A.4.1 Directory names

When you install SELECT Yourdon you will create four types of directory:

(1) C:\SELECT The **root directory** for all of the SELECT Yourdon files. This directory can be used as the **work directory**; if so it will contain files such as check files, plot files and any generated reports.

(2) C:\SELECT\WINEXE The **executable file directory**, it contains all SELECT Yourdon executable files as well as the help and configuration files.

(3) C:\SELECT\SYSTEM The **system data directory**. The database files are used to record inter-project links and Licence details.

(4) C:\SELECT\SYSTEM\PROJECT The **project directory** contains all the diagram definitions, data dictionary and all shared files for an individual project.

Installation also sets up a directory for the tutorial project: \SELECT\SYSTEM\EXAMPLE\
    Note that, in the example, the directory structure is shown in Drive C:

A.4.2 Project file names

The file names in C:\SELECT\SYSTEM\PROJECT are as follows:

    Generated, shared, database files: *.DBF
    Diagram database files: *.DAT

(These files are only valid when used in conjunction with the shared database files.)
    Template file for the dictionary format TEMPLATE.TXT

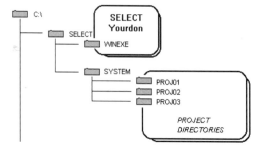

Directory structure.

A.5 Installation

Before you start, make sure that your equipment matches the list in Operational Requirements.

A.5.1 Installation procedure

Open the Windows *Program Manager* and put the CD supplied with this book into your CD-ROM drive (drive D:).

> From the *Program Manager* menu bar
> Select **File**, then
> Choose **Run** and
> See the *Run* dialog box.

> In the *Run* box
> Type the *letter of your CD-ROM drive*
> Followed by the directory \CASETOOL\SELECT\
> Followed by the word SETUP

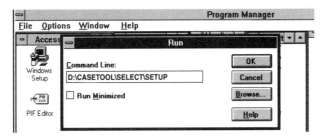

Run box.

For example,

> Type: D:\CASETOOL\SELECT\SETUP

Then choose *OK* and wait, while the initializing process is carried out.

> The *SELECT Setup Program* window comes on-screen

> Choose *Continue* and
> Keep going.

(You may also choose *Exit* at any time during the setup, and cancel the process.)

Welcome message.

See a reminder that you will have to add your licence number at a later stage

> Choose *Continue* and
> Keep going.

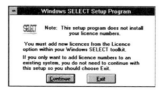

Reminder: Add licences later.

You will be asked two questions during this stage of the setup:

- The path name of the directory where you want to place the program files; the default setting is:

  C:\SELECT\WINEXE

  Choose **_Continue_** to accept
  (Or choose **_Exit_** to quit.)

System directory path.

- The path name of the directory where you want to place the system data files; the default setting is:

  C:\SELECT\SYSTEM

  Choose **_Continue_** to accept
  (Or choose **_Exit_** to quit.)

Program directory path.

The setup process will also create an example directory, in the system directory, to hold the tutorial example:

  C:\SELECT\SYSTEM\EXAMPLE

A.5.2 End Setup

A message will come on-screen to remind you of the directories that have been created.

  Choose **_Continue_** if you are happy with the settings;
  choose **_Restart_** to make changes, or
  choose **_Exit_** to abandon the setup process.

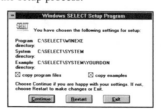

Directories Setup.

Now wait.

Watch the display that shows you how fast the system is being loaded.

System loading message.

See a message to tell you that the tool has been loaded successfully.

Installation complete.

Choose *Have Fun*

The installation will be complete.

A.5.3   Icon

When the installation is complete you will see the following on your screen:

- The *Program Manager – [Select Case Tool]* window has been created on the Windows *Program Manager*.
- The SELECT Yourdon *Icon* appears on the *Program Manager*.

Select Case Tool program group

Select program group.

A.6   Entering the licence numbers

Open the Microsoft Windows *Program Manager* and double-click on the SELECT Yourdon icon. The opening window will come on-screen.

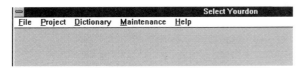

Menu bar on the opening window.

A.6.1   Opening window

The first screen you see has no diagram on it and, depending on the way your Microsoft Windows is set up, you may see a patterned background.

In the opening window you can carry out various project maintenance tasks; from the window you will also choose the project you want to open.

A.6.2 Enter the licence

Before you use the tool for the first time, you must enter the licence number that was supplied with your copy of the software. You will find your licence numbers written inside the cover of this book.

Select **Maintenance** menu and
Choose **Licences** option.

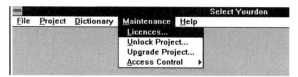

Maintenance menu.

See the *Licences* dialog box
Type the *licence number*

Type the LETTERS in capitals, and separate each block of characters with a hyphen (-); for example:
A22A-2A22-A22A-2A22

Licences box.

Choose *Add*
See the number printed in the dialog box
Make sure that the correct number is shown as an *Installed Licence*.

Choose *Exit*
See the active SELECT Yourdon screen.

You can read more about licences in the on-line help.

QUICK HELP – *ENTER LICENCE NUMBER*

Find the SELECT Yourdon icon on the *Program Manager*
    double-click the mouse on SELECT Yourdon icon
    in **Maintenance** menu, choose   **Licences**
    in the *Licences* box, type   Licence Number
    choose   *Add*
    choose   *Exit*
    see   active SELECT Yourdon screen

A.7 Conclusions

Your copy of the CASE tool is now fully installed. If you have not used a Select CASE tool before, you may find it useful to work through some of the tutorials in the following chapters to become familiar with the operation of the system.

CASE tool:

Managing a project

B.1   Introduction

The information in this appendix describes some basic features of project management using the Select CASE tool, such as opening projects, creating new projects and creating backup copies.

B.2   Opening an existing project

B.2.1   Project

A project is a set of interrelated diagrams and associated data dictionary descriptions. Every project will have its own database which is found in a unique **project directory**.

You may associate a project with any number of subsidiary projects. The inter-project links which connect the projects are kept in the **system directory**.

B.2.2   Open

Once you have begun work on a project you will want to return to it frequently. Use the **File** menu **Open** option to see a file in an existing project.

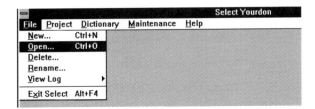

Select: File menu, Open.

The first time you run the tool it will, as a default, show the Example Project which was installed with the system.

B.2.3   View Example project

Open the **File** menu and choose **Open**. The *Diagram File Selector* box will come on-screen.

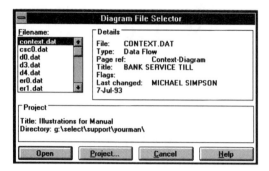

Diagram File Selector box.

Because SELECT Yourdon comes with a ready-made Example project, you can use the **Open** command straight away and access the example project without creating any files yourself.

> Select CONTEXT.DAT
> Choose **Open**

See the CONTEXT.DAT diagram on-screen.

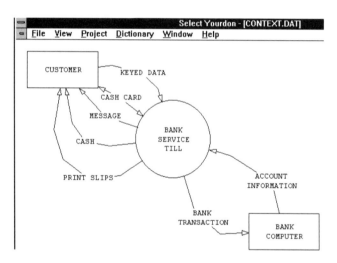

Example Project CONTEXT.DAT.

Turn to Appendix D to read about the Example Project.

B.2.4 Exit

To quit SELECT Yourdon at any time:

> Select **File** menu
> Choose **Exit** Select

This will clear the diagram from the screen and take you back to the Windows *Program Manager*.

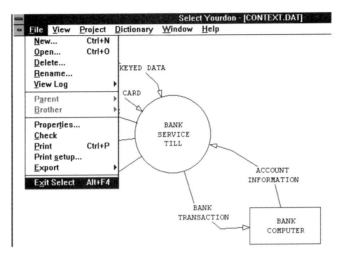

Exit option.

B.2.5   Crash

If you shut down SELECT Yourdon accidentally, or if your system has a crash, you will see a warning message when you next try to open the tool from *the Program Manager*.

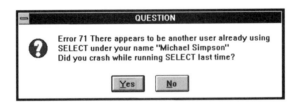

Did you crash?

In the *Question* box
Choose *Yes*

The tool will load normally.

B.2.6   Unlock

If the system crashes while you are working with a multi-user version of SELECT Yourdon, you may find that, after you have started the tool, you cannot open the files.

In the SELECT Yourdon opening window
Select **Maintenance**
Choose **Unlock Project**

This will unlock any files that became locked accidentally.

QUICK HELP – START TUTORIAL

Find the SELECT Yourdon icon on the **Program Manager**
        double-click the mouse on   SELECT Yourdon icon
        see on-screen   active Yourdon
        from **File** menu, choose   **Open**
        see **Diagram File Selector** listing   **Project**
               Details
               Filename
Read Part 2, Tutorial
        select a **File name**, eg.   CONTEXT.DAT
        choose   **OK**
        see   active SELECT Yourdon screen
        Continue with Tutorial

B.3   The diagram screen

This illustration shows what the Example project looks like when it is loaded onto the screen.

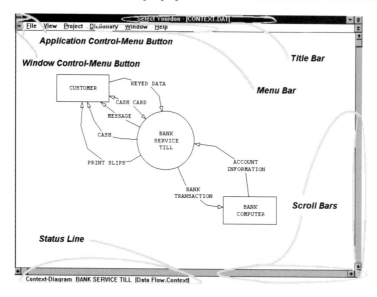

Parts of the window.

Check that you are familiar with the name and purpose of the parts of the Windows environment; these names will be used throughout the help messages screens and these appendices.

B.3.1   Title bar

The top line of the screen, it contains:

- *Application and File Names*
  Printed in the middle of the bar.

- *Application Control-Menu Button*
  On the left of the bar, click the button to see the Application Control menu.

- *Maximum/Minimum Buttons*
  On the right of the bar, choose up (↑) to restore the application window to full size; choose down (↓) to reduce the window in size or turn it into an icon.

B.3.2 Menu bar

The second line of the screen, it contains:

- *Drop-down Menu Names*
  Select a name and see the relevant drop-down menu.

- *Window Control Menu Button*
  On the left of the bar, click the button to see the Window Control menu.

- *Maximum/Minimum Buttons*
  On the right of the bar, choose up (↑) to restore the project window to full size; choose down (↓) to reduce the window in size or turn it into an icon.

B.3.3 Scroll bars

Found at the left and bottom margins of the screen:

- *Vertical*
  Moving bar at the right margin, drag the button to scroll up or down.

- *Horizontal*
  Moving bar at the bottom margin, drag the button to pan right or left.

B.3.4 Status line

This is the single line at the bottom of the screen; it displays a brief help message about what is happening in the window. If a file, menu or option is selected, the status line will describe what it is used for.

B.4 Starting a new project

Before you create new files in your own project, you must set up the project itself.

> Select the **Project** menu and choose **New**. The *Project Directory* box will come on-screen, type in the path and directory name where you want to hold your project data files.

(Read Directory Structure & Project Files for more information about creating directories).

> The *Title* box will come on-screen, type the title and choose *OK*.
> You have now set up a project and you can go to the **File** menu and start a new file.

The tutorial in Appendix D will give you practice in starting a new project and opening new files.

QUICK HELP – START NEW PROJECT
Find the SELECT Yourdon icon on the *Program Manager*
      double-click the mouse on   SELECT Yourdon icon
      see on-screen   active SELECT Yourdon screen
1 Create Directory:
      from **Project** menu, choose   **New**
      see box   *Project Directory*
      type   *Path and Directory name*
      answer *Question*, if Yes choose   *OK*
      in *Title* box, type   *Title*
      choose   *OK*
2 Create Diagram File:
      from **File** menu, choose   **New**
      in *Create New Diagram*, type   *Type of Diagram*
      in *Filename*, type   *filename*
      choose   *Create*
Start work on your new project.

B.5   Inter-project links

B.5.1   About inter-project links

A large project can consist of many smaller sub-projects, each of which will use a separate directory. This gives the following advantages:

- The system can reuse an existing component, such as a library routine, that is used within several projects.

- The tool has less information to deal with during a session; this leads to improved performance.

An inter-project link is similar to a normal parent/child decomposition, except that the child diagram will be found in a different project.

You need to know if inter-project links exist in a project before you run a backup or restore procedure. See Backup Inter-Project links.

B.6   Managing project files

SELECT Yourdon has a number of options to let you carry out file management procedures. You should use SELECT Yourdon options whenever possible.

You must always close a project and go to the SELECT Yourdon opening window before you carry out any file management.

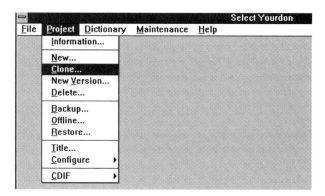

Project menu.

B.6.1   Cloning projects

The Clone procedure allows you to make an exact copy of an existing project and put it in a directory of your own choice.

> *When you move to the Tutorial, you may wish to clone the Example project and work on your own version so as to practise developing a project as much as you like.*

At the opening screen
Select the **Project** menu and
Choose the **Clone** option.

See the **Project Selector** box on-screen and
Choose the project you want to clone.

Then choose **Clone**.

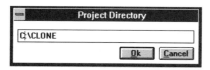

Project Selector box.

See a question asking if you want to continue the **C**lone procedure and reminding you that inter-project links will not be copied.

Choose *Yes*, and continue.

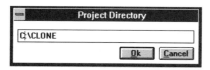

Continue clone procedure?

See a *Project Directory* box on-screen.
Type the *path* and *directory* where you want to place the copy project.

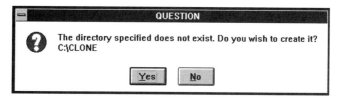

Destination directory.

If you specify a new directory the system will create it for you.

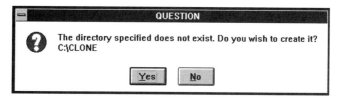

Question: Create new directory?

See the *Title Box* on-screen, type in a *title* for the copy project.

Title box.

See a confirmation message that a cloned copy of the project has been created.

Choose **OK**

See the screen go clear.

QUICK HELP – CLONE A PROJECT

Start SELECT Yourdon but do not open any projects
in **Project** menu select   **Clone**
from **Project Selector** box, select   *Project to clone*
choose   **Clone**
confirm that you want to continue
choose   **Yes**
in **Project Directory** box, type   *Name of new directory*
in **Title** box, type   *Title of new project*
see confirmation, choose   **OK**

A cloned copy of the original project has been created in the directory
you chose.

B.6.2 New Version

Use the **Project** menu **New Version** option to create a baselined copy of a project with an automatically up-dated version number.

The purpose and procedure of new version is similar to that described for **Clone**, you will
need to decide which form of copy is suitable for you.

The version number is added to the titles of the projects after the new version has been
created, you will see the title in the **Project** panel of the **Diagram File Selector** box.

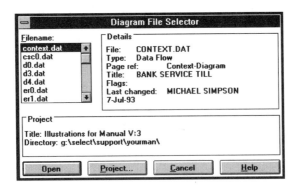

Title of project with version number.

The version numbering procedure is as follows:

ORIGINAL PROJECT	NEW VERSION
myproject	–
each project is given a version number	
When a new version is created	
myproject V:0	myproject V:1

QUICK HELP – CREATE NEW VERSION

Start SELECT Yourdon but do not open any projects

    In **Project** menu, select   **New Version**
    from **Project Selector** box, select   *project for New Version*
    choose   **New Version**
    confirm that you want to continue
    choose   **Yes**
    in **Project Directory** box, type   *name of new directory*
    see confirmation message, choose   **OK**

A New Version of the project is created with a version number that is 1 number higher than the previous version.

B.6.3 Backup

You may need to make a backup for good housekeeping practice or if you want to establish a base you can return to after entering temporary data

    At the opening screen
    Select the **Project** menu and
    Choose the **Backup** option
    See the **Project Selector** box on-screen

    Select the Project you want to back up
    Choose **Backup**

See a directory box **Save files into which directory**

    Type in the *path* and *name* of an existing directory or
    specify a new directory (which the system will create for you).
    Choose **OK**.

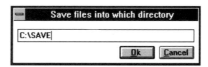

Destination Directory box.

You will see a question asking if you wish to continue. If you back up to an existing directory you will over-write any files that are already in the directory.

If you want to continue

    Choose *Yes*

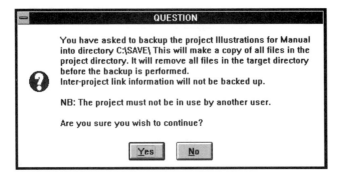

Continue backup procedure?

If you have created any inter-project links you must back up the System Directory (where the inter-project links are kept) as well as the Project Directory.

When you see a confirmation message that the project has been backed up

Choose **OK**

See the screen go clear.

Message: Upgrade before opening.

Summary A backup copy of the project has been created and the current version is still available for further development.

B.6.4 Restore projects

If you want to restore a project to the same directory it was saved from, you follow a similar procedure to the one you used for **Backup**.

At the opening screen
Select the **Project** menu and
Choose the **Restore** option

See a directory box *Enter directory where backup is stored*.

Type in the *path* and *name* (for example: C:\SAVE\) and
Choose *OK*.

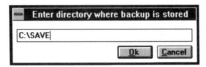

Backup Source Directory.

See a question which asks if you want to restore the project to the same directory it came from.

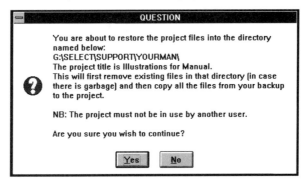

┌──┐
│ ⊟   **QUESTION**   │
├──┤
│   You are about to restore the project files into the directory │
│   named below: │
│   G:\SELECT\SUPPORT\YOURMAN\   │
│   The project title is Illustrations for Manual. │
│   This will first remove existing files in that directory (in case │
│   ❓   there is garbage) and then copy all the files from your backup │
│   to the project.   │
│   │
│   NB: The project must not be in use by another user. │
│   │
│   Are you sure you wish to continue?   │
│   │
│   ┌──────┐   ┌──────┐   │
│   │ Yes │   │ No │   │
│   └──────┘   └──────┘   │
└──┘

Continue Restore Procedure?

If you want to continue
> Choose *Yes*

See the confirmation message that the project has been restored.
> Choose *OK* and

See the screen go clear.

┌──────────────────────────────────────┐
│ ⊟   **INFO**   │
├──────────────────────────────────────┤
│   │
│   ℹ️   Project Restore - completed ok │
│   │
│   ┌──────┐   │
│   │ OK │   │
│   └──────┘   │
└──────────────────────────────────────┘

Restore completed.

Summary Any files that were in the destination directory (such as another version of the project) have been overwritten with a copy of the restored backup version. The backup source files will remain in their directory.

B.6.5 Backup inter-project links

If you know that inter-project links have been used to connect common data used in different projects, you *must* copy or backup the *entire* system directory and project directory if the links are to be preserved. You will need to use the DOS command **COPY** or **BACKUP** to do this.

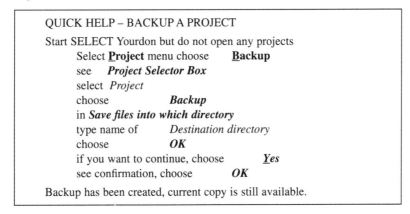

┌──┐
│   QUICK HELP – BACKUP A PROJECT   │
│   Start SELECT Yourdon but do not open any projects   │
│   Select **Project** menu choose   **Backup**   │
│   see   *Project Selector Box*   │
│   select *Project*   │
│   choose   *Backup*   │
│   in *Save files into which directory*   │
│   type name of   *Destination directory*   │
│   choose   *OK*   │
│   if you want to continue, choose   *Yes*   │
│   see confirmation, choose   *OK*   │
│   Backup has been created, current copy is still available. │
└──┘

> QUICK HELP – RESTORE A PROJECT
>
> Start SELECT Yourdon but do not open any projects
>> In **Project** menu, select **Restore**
>> see
> ***Enter directory where backup is stored,***
>>> type name of   Backup directory
>>> press **OK**
>>> if you want to continue, press   *Yes*
>>> see confirmation, press   **OK**
>> Current copy has been overwritten with the backup version.

B.6.6 Offline a project

You can use the **Offline** option to delete a project from its current directory and save it to another directory (usually, for archive purposes, on another drive). This single option combines the procedures of backup and delete.

> At the opening screen
> Select the **Project** menu and
> Choose the **Offline** option

Refer to the instructions for Backup.

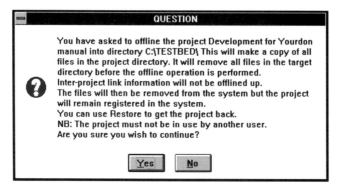

QUESTION

You have asked to offline the project Development for Yourdon manual into directory C:\TESTBED\ This will make a copy of all files in the project directory. It will remove all files in the target directory before the offline operation is performed.
Inter-project link information will not be offlined up.
The files will then be removed from the system but the project will remain registered in the system.
You can use Restore to get the project back.
NB: The project must not be in use by another user.
Are you sure you wish to continue?

Yes   No

Continue offline procedure?

When you see a confirmation message that the project has been off-lined

> Choose **OK** and

See the screen go clear.

Summary   The project files have all been removed from the current directory, but the directory name will remain on the drive so that the tool can automatically restore an off-lined copy to its original site.

B.6.7 Delete a project

You must use the SELECT Yourdon **Delete** option if you need to delete a project.

> At the opening screen
> Select the **Project** menu and
> Choose the **Delete** option

See a *Project Selector Box* on-screen
Scroll through the directories or titles and
Select the project you want to delete
Choose **Delete**.

Delete will erase all traces of a project from the system database.

*If you were to use a DOS command instead of using **Delete** you would leave traces of the project behind in the database, and these might corrupt your data if the project was subsequently restored.*

QUICK HELP – DELETE A PROJECT

Start SELECT Yourdon screen, but do not open any projects
         in **Project** menu select   **Delete**
         see   *Project Selector Box*
         select *Project*, choose   **Delete**
         if you want to continue, choose   *Yes*
         or abandon **Delete**, choose   *No*

B.6.8   Rename a file

Use this option if you need to change the file name of an existing diagram in a project.

At the opening screen
Select the **File** menu and
Choose the **Rename** option

A *Diagram File Selector* box will come on-screen.

Select the *file name* you want to change and
Choose **Rename**.

To continue, Choose *Yes*

See a *Filename* dialog box on-screen

Type in the new *filename* and extension, then
Choose *OK*.

Do not attempt to use an MS-DOS command to change a filename, it would not rename all the appropriate components.

QUICK HELP – RENAME A FILE

Open SELECT Yourdon, close the diagram you want to rename
         in **File** menu, choose   **Rename**
         see   *Diagram File Selector* box
         select   *Old Filename*,
         choose   *Rename*
         to continue, choose *Yes*
         in *Filename* box, type   *New Filename*
         choose   *OK*

Return to renamed diagram.

B.6.9   Title

You may wish to change the title of a project after it has been created, for example it would be necessary to give a cloned copy a distinguishing name.

At the opening screen
Select the **Project** menu and
Choose the **Title** option

See the *Project Selector* box

Select the project to which you want to give a new title and
Choose *Title*.

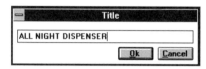

Title box.

See the Title box on-screen
In the *Title* box, type the *new title*,
(For example: ALL NIGHT DISPENSER)
Choose *OK*

The project has been retitled.

B.7 Access control

You can control access to a project through a personal password.

You will manage access control through the **Maintenance** menu **Access Control** option and its cascading **User** menu.

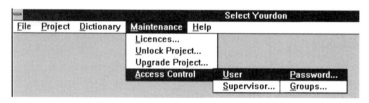

Access Control menus.

The default value of your password is null, but you may change this to give yourself an operational password.

If you have created an operational password the tool will ask you to enter the word immediately after you have selected the SELECT Yourdon icon from *the Program Manager*; you will need to enter the password again when the tool opening window comes on-screen.

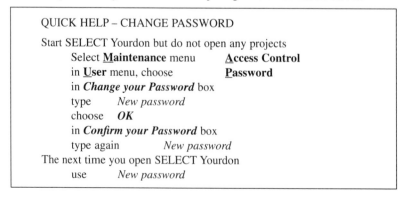

QUICK HELP – CHANGE PASSWORD

Start SELECT Yourdon but do not open any projects
    Select **Maintenance** menu   **Access Control**
    in **User** menu, choose   **Password**
    in *Change your Password* box
    type   *New password*
    choose   *OK*
    in *Confirm your Password* box
    type again   *New password*
The next time you open SELECT Yourdon
    use   *New password*

When you type a password in a box, the letters do not appear, instead they are represented by stars (*).

QUICK HELP – USE PASSWORD

In the **Program Manager**, choose   SELECT Yourdon icon
in **Select User Password** box, type   *your password*
wait, while SELECT Yourdon is loaded
in **Select User Password** box
type again   *your password*

Now run SELECT Yourdon

B.8   Conclusions

This chapter has provided an overview of some basic features of the Select CASE tool. We'll consider how to install the sample (case study) files in Appendix C.

CASE tool:

Installing the sample projects

C.1 Introduction

There are four sample projects included on the CD:

- Loughborough Bell Foundry (process-oriented)
- Birstall Bank (process-oriented)
- Laughing House (data-oriented)
- Birstall Bank (object-oriented)

These are copies of the projects included in Chapters 13, 16, 23 and 32 respectively. Details of how to use these projects are given below.

C.2 Installing the samples

The four projects described above are 'backed up' on the disk, in the directories:

```
D:\CASETOOL\EXAMPLES\CHAP_13
D:\CASETOOL\EXAMPLES\CHAP_16
D:\CASETOOL\EXAMPLES\CHAP_23
D:\CASETOOL\EXAMPLES\CHAP_32
```

To install these projects, you need to follow the procedure detailed below four times (once for each project). As you do so, by default, the files will be restored into the directories on the C: drive listed below.

```
C:\SELECT\PONT\CHAP_13
C:\SELECT\PONT\CHAP_16
C:\SELECT\PONT\CHAP_23
C:\SELECT\PONT\CHAP_32
```

You can change the specified drive and location used during the installation process if you wish to do so.

The procedure is as follows:

At the opening screen
Select the **Project** menu and
Choose the **Restore** option

See a directory box *Enter directory where backup is stored.*

Type in the *path* and *name* (for example: D:\CASETOOL\EXAMPLES\CHAP_13) and Choose *OK*.

Backup Source Directory.

See a question which asks if you want to restore the project to the same directory it came from.

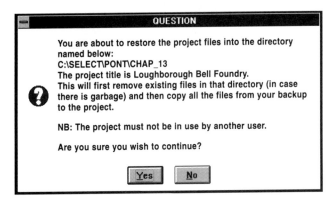

Continue Restore procedure?

If you want to continue

Choose *Yes*

See the confirmation message that the project has been restored.

Choose *OK* and

See the screen go clear.

Restore completed.

Summary   Any files that were in the destination directory (such as another version of the project) have been overwritten with a copy of the restored backup version. The backup source files will remain in their directory.

C.3   Conclusions

This short appendix has outlined how to install the sample projects, and the standard SADIE project.

By using the standard project, you will find that the CASE tool better supports the SADIE methods for process-oriented, data-oriented and object-oriented development.

CASE tutorial:

General

Introduction

D.1 Introduction

This general introductory tutorial has been structured so that the exercises will give you progressive experience of the main operations you can carry out with the CASE tool.

You will open a ready-made example project ('Cash Dispenser'), manipulate it, add to it and take from it, and then close it down. The tutorial will go on to explain how you set up a new project and populate it with your own data.

When you are familiar with the fundamental operations you can go on to work with your own projects, or complete the more detailed tutorials given in the rest of the appendices.

You will find it useful to familiarize yourself with the material in Appendix B before you begin this tutorial.

D.2 Basic instructions

In this tutorial some instructions will be repeated many times. The Microsoft Windows terminology is used to describe the following basic procedures.

D.2.1 Mouse

- *Click*
  To press and release the left mouse button once, quickly.
- *Double-click*
  To click the mouse button twice in rapid succession.
- *Drag*
  To hold down the left mouse button while you move the mouse.
- *Point*
  To move the mouse until the mouse pointer on the screen rests on the area you have chosen.

D.2.2 Choose

The phrase *to choose an item* is used to mean that you carry out an action on the item.

You will often be asked to choose an option from a menu. The procedure is the same in each case and it is described here, using the **File** menu **Open** option:

> At the SELECT Yourdon opening window
> Point to the **File** menu and
> Click the mouse

You will see the drop-down **File** menu appear.

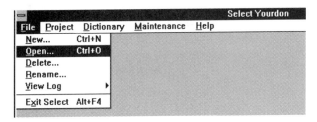

File menu on the opening screen.

In the **File** menu
Point to the **Open** option and

Click the mouse
See *Diagram File Selector* dialog box.

Summary You have *chosen* the **File** menu **Open** option in order to bring the *Diagram File Selector* dialog box on-screen.

D.2.3 Diagram File Selector

The *Diagram File Selector* is used in many parts of the SELECT Yourdon system; it is a box that shows the names and details of all the files in a project, and it allows you to open a file or to move to another project.

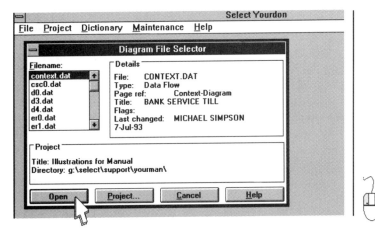

Diagram File Selector.

The *Diagram File Selector* will, by default, show details of the last project that was open. When a tool is used for the first time, the data is taken from the example project (the Cash Dispenser project).

In the *Diagram File Selector* box there are three panels of information: *Filename, Details* and *Project*.

- *Filename panel*
  This panel shows a list of all the files in the project directory.

- *Details panel*
  You can read the following information about the file name you have selected:

- **File**

  The file name, for example CONTEXT.DAT.

- **Type**

  The type of diagram, for example Dataflow.

- **Page Ref**

  An optional means of indexing a diagram, sometimes used in a large project.

- **Title**

  Written name of the diagram, for example Bank Service Till. The name is derived from the project name unless changed.

- **Flags**

  These may be:

  IN-USE – showing that the diagram is open, or
  INCONSISTENT – showing that the diagram has not been checked for errors
  If there are no flags, it means that the project has satisfied a consistency check.

- **Last Changed**

  The name of the last person to work on the diagram, and the date it happened.

  If you have not recorded your name in your computer system the message will read: UNKNOWN USER.

- *Project panel*

  Each project is known by its title and its directory pathname; check in the ***Project*** panel that your Example Project has been loaded, you should see:

  Title: CASH DISPENSER
  Directory: C:\SELECT\WINEXE\EXAMPLE\

  *If you find that the Example Project has **NOT** been loaded, refer to the quick-help instructions, Change Project.*

D.2.4 Select file name

The phrase to *select an item* means that you mark an item before carrying out an action on the item.

You will often be asked to select a file name from a list box in the ***Diagram File Selector***. The procedure is the same in each case and it is described here, using the file name CONTEXT.DAT:

In the ***Diagram File Selector*** list box
Point to the file name CONTEXT.DAT and
Click the mouse
See the name CONTEXT.DAT highlighted

Summary   This means that you have *selected* the file named CONTEXT.DAT and whatever subsequent command you give (for example, choose ***Open***, or choose ***Delete***), it will be performed on that file.

D.3 Working with a diagram

In this section you can work through a series of exercises and practise managing the Cash Dispenser project diagrams on-screen.

You will use some or all the techniques with all the SELECT Yourdon diagram types, so it is worth spending the time to make yourself familiar with the working techniques before you start to develop your own project.

Later in the appendices there will be reference to the techniques you have practised here; so, if you find you do not know what to do, you will need to turn back to these pages.

D.4 Opening and closing an existing diagram

The starting point for this exercise is the SELECT Yourdon opening window, the blank screen you see as soon as you have started the tool from the Windows *Program Manager*.

In summary, you will:

- view SELECT Yourdon Opening Screen

- use *Diagram File Selector* to choose a file

- view diagram on-screen

- close diagram and return to Opening Screen

D.4.1 Open diagram

In the tutorials you will often be asked to open a diagram file. The procedure is the same in each case and it is described fully here, using the diagram file CONTEXT.DAT:

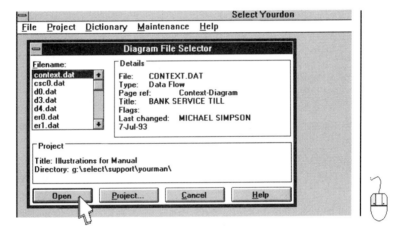

Open file – CONTEXT.DAT.

At the opening window
Choose **File** menu **Open**

In the *Diagram File Selector*
Select file CONTEXT.DAT
Find the *Open* button (at the foot of the *Diagram File Selector*)
Choose *Open*.

See the CONTEXT.DAT diagram on-screen in a new window.

D.4.2 Examine diagram

Make yourself familiar with the appearance of a SELECT Yourdon diagram in a Windows setting.

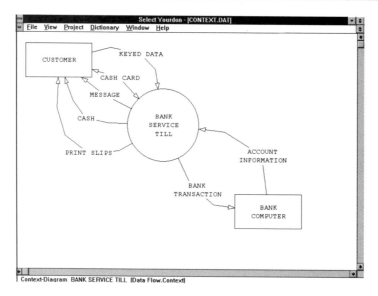

Dataflow diagram.

D.4.3   Close diagram

You may close a file without closing the tool, this will bring you back to the opening window. You will need to do this:

- when you have finished working on a diagram, but have not finished using the tool;
- when you need to carry out certain management procedures (such as clone and delete);
- when you need to use the Maintenance menu, which is only available at the opening window.

Find the **Window Control Menu Button**, this is the box on the left of the Menu Bar that has a white hyphen (-) inside it. (Do not confuse the Window Control with the Application Control Menu Button, which is found on the Title Bar.)

> Point to the **Window Control Menu Button** and
> Click the mouse

See the **Window Control** menu drop down.

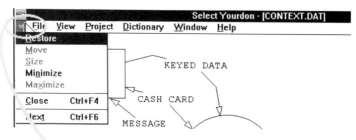

Window Control-Menu Button

Window Control menu.

In the **Window Control** menu
Choose **Close**

See the diagram clear from the screen. If no other diagrams are open, you will see the plain background of the opening screen.

D.4.4   Shortcut keys

File menu:

Open, press   <CTRL>+<O>
Exit
(Exit SELECT Yourdon), press   <ALT>+<F4>

Window Control menu:

This does not have a mnemonic letter
To open the menu, press   <ALT>+<->
Close, press   <CTRL>+<F4>

QUICK HELP – *OPEN EXISTING DIAGRAM*

See on-screen the active SELECT Yourdon application
        from **File** menu, choose   **Open**
        see   *Diagram File Selector*
        select a *file name*   OBJECT.DAT
        choose   *OPEN*
see OBJECT.DAT diagram on-screen.

QUICK HELP – *CLOSE DIAGRAM*

While the diagram is on-screen
        open   **Window Control** menu,
        choose   **Close**
see opening window on-screen.

D.5   Switching between diagrams

A **project** is a set of interrelated diagrams. When you are working on a project it may be convenient to have more than one diagram open at a time and, with SELECT Yourdon, you can either view the diagrams on the same screen or switch between the diagrams using one of the Windows techniques.

In summary, you will:

- open two diagrams and tile the display
- open many diagrams and cascade the display
- switch between two windows
- close all windows.

Start this exercise with one diagram open, then open more diagrams and practise switching between them.

D.5.1   Open two diagrams

Open CONTEXT.DAT and
See the Bank Service Till dataflow diagram on-screen

Choose **File** menu **Open**
Select D3.DAT
Choose *Open*

See the D3.DAT file, the Process Required Service dataflow diagram, on-screen.

Note that the CONTEXT.DAT diagram is obscured by D3.DAT and, although you cannot see the first diagram any more, the tool regards both diagrams as open.

Shortcut key

Open, press   <CTRL>+<O>

D.5.2   Window menu

Open the **Window** menu to see a list of the files you have opened, then choose a menu option to view the files.

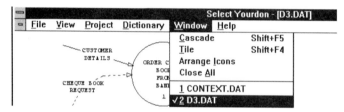

Window menu.

Open D3.DAT and
See Process Required Service dataflow diagram on-screen
Choose the **Window** menu

See that two file names are listed, and that there is a tick (✔) against D3.DAT, this shows that the file has been enabled.

If you click on an open diagram you will enable it. You may have many files open on-screen, but you can only work on the one that is enabled.

Shortcut key

From the **Window** menu list of files
Type *index number*

Display the file you have chosen.

D.5.3   Tile

The most convenient way of viewing two diagrams at the same time is to tile them.

Open D3.DAT and
See Process Required Service data-flow diagram on-screen
Choose the **Window** menu

Choose **Tile**

See the screen divide into two windows, each window showing part of a diagram and displaying a title bar with a filename.

Click anywhere on the D3.DAT window

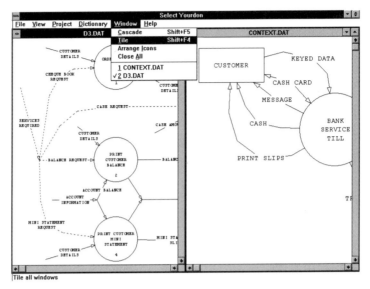

D3.DAT and CONTEXT.DAT tiled, D3.DAT is enabled.

Note that the D3.DAT title bar is shaded, this is to indicate that the window is enabled and you can work on it.

> Click anywhere on the CONTEXT.DAT window

Note that now the CONTEXT.DAT title bar is shaded, and the bar on D3.DAT has cleared. This shows that the CONTEXT.DAT diagram is now enabled.

Shortcut keys

Tile, press	<SHIFT>+<F4>
Switch between open diagrams, either press	<SHIFT>+<TAB>
or go to **Next**, press	<CTRL>+<F6>

D.5.4 Close a diagram

In order to save space on your screen (and on your PC's memory) you will want to close a diagram when you have stopped working with it.

> Open CONTEXT.DAT and D3.DAT
> Tile the diagrams and select D3.DAT

> Open the **Window Control** menu on D3.DAT
> Choose **Close**

See D3.DAT diagram has cleared from the screen leaving CONTEXT.DAT open on its own (the topic of re-sizing a diagram will be covered in View and Print a Diagram).

Shortcut key

> Close a diagram, press   <CTRL>+<F4>

D.5.5 Open many diagrams

You have practised viewing two diagrams at the same time; but the system will permit you to open up to 10 diagrams at the same time.

Remember that you may exhaust the Windows memory if you open too many files at once.

Open CONTEXT.DAT

Then open these files in succession:
D3.DAT
ER1.DAT
P1.DAT
SC0.DAT

To find some of these files you will need to use the scroll bar on the drop-down file list.

See SC0.DAT Control Transaction Jackson structure on-screen

Select **Window** menu

Check the list of files that you have opened.
See the diagram file SC0.DAT on-screen.

Shortcut key
Open, press   <CTRL>+<O>

D.5.6   Cascade

The most convenient way of viewing all the diagrams that are open is to use the Cascade option.

Open five files, the last one being SC0.DAT
See SC0.DAT on-screen
Select **Window** menu
Choose **Cascade**

See all five diagrams cascaded across the screen.

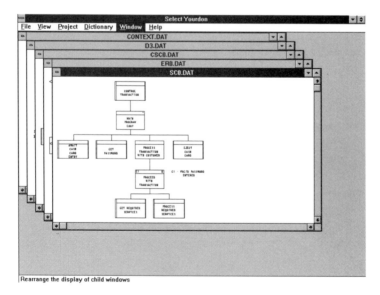

Five cascaded diagrams.

You can select any diagram to enable it, for example:

Click on the title bar of CONTEXT.DAT

The CONTEXT.DAT diagram will come to the front of the cascade, it is enabled and you can work on it

If you want to choose any other file you can either click on the title bar (if you can see it) or you can choose **Cascade** again and make your selection from the display.

Shortcut key

Cascade, press	<SHIFT>+<F5>
Switch between open diagrams,	
either press	<SHIFT>+<TAB>
or go to **Next**, press	<CTRL>+<F6>

D.5.7   Close All

If you want to return to the SELECT Yourdon opening window (for example, if you want to carry out system maintenance) you can close all the diagrams.

See a cascade display of files
Select **Window** menu
Choose **Close All**

All the diagrams will clear from the screen and you will see the SELECT Yourdon opening window.

QUICK HELP – *SWITCH BETWEEN DIAGRAMS*

With one file open on-screen
    from **File** menu, choose   **Open**
    select   *file name*
    choose   ***Open***
    see on-screen   *file name* diagram
Repeat the **Open** procedure for all the files you want to see
    from **Window** menu, choose   **Cascade**
    See Title Bars of all open files
    click on *file name*
    See on-screen selected *file name* diagram

QUICK HELP – *CLOSE ALL DIAGRAMS*
With one or many diagrams on-screen
    from **Window** menu, choose   **Close All**
See the opening SELECT Yourdon window

D.6   Navigating between diagrams

SELECT Yourdon allows you to create a hierarchy of diagrams. The tutorials will explain how you create a single Context diagram in a project. The descendant of a Context diagram is a Primary dataflow diagram. Primary dataflow diagrams can be decomposed to Secondary dataflow diagrams.

Each descendant diagram may be opened from the Diagram File Selector (as has been explained), or you may find it convenient to move backwards and forwards between parent and child.

D.6.1   Go to Child diagram

In this example you will move from the Context diagram CONTEXT.DAT to the Primary dataflow diagram D0.DAT.

Open the Context dataflow diagram CONTEXT.DAT
Click on Context Node BANK SERVICE TILL
From menu, select **Child**
Choose **Go** to

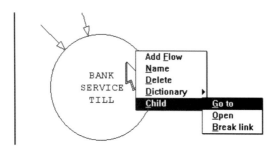

Child, Go To option.

See the child:

Primary dataflow diagram D0.DAT on-screen.

D.6.2   Return to parent

When you open a child diagram by choosing **Go to**, the parent diagram is closed when the child diagram is opened.

With D0.DAT on-screen
In **File** menu
Select **Parent**
Choose **Go** to

The child diagram will close and you will see CONTEXT.DAT on-screen.

D.6.3   Open child diagram

If, instead of choosing **Go** to, you chose **Open** you would open the child diagram as the second window in the SELECT Yourdon tool.

D.7   Viewing a diagram

In this exercise you will look at a diagram through different magnifications.

D.7.1   View a diagram

When you create a diagram, the SELECT Yourdon virtual screen behaves as if you are using a single limitless page and the tool allows you to go on adding objects in any direction.

The options of the **View** menu let you look at all or part of a diagram in as much detail as you want.

D.7.2   Zoom out

Zoom out reduces the size of the image on-screen.

Open CONTEXT.DAT
Select **View** menu
Choose **Zoom out**.

See the diagram shrink in size and retreat towards the top left corner of the screen.

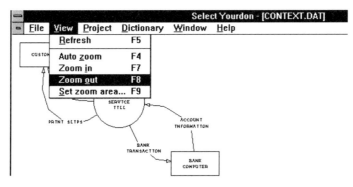

View Menu.

You can repeat **Zoom out** as often as necessary to create more space, use the extra space to place new objects when you add them to the diagram.

Keep the zoomed-out diagram on-screen for the next part of the exercise.

Shortcut key

Zoom out, press   <F8>

D.7.3   Increase margins

Zoom **out** always sets the diagram in the top left corner of the screen and you may need to make more space at the top or the left of the diagram. Do this by increasing the margins.

Look at the zoomed-out diagram CONTEXT.DAT and
Prepare to increase the top margin

Click once on the **UP arrow** on the vertical scroll bar

See a message

... Do you want to increase the margin?

Choose **Yes**.

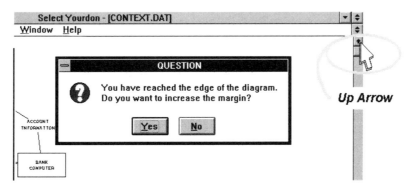

Use the up arrow – increase the top margin.

See the top margin increase by half the depth of the screen.

You can move the left margin in a similar way if you click on the **LEFT arrow** of the horizontal scroll bar.

Keep the zoomed-out diagram on-screen for the next part of the exercise.

D.7.4 Auto zoom

Use **Auto zoom** to display the diagram at optimum size whenever you have added objects to, or taken them away from, the edge of a diagram.

When you have increased the top margin you will notice that much of the diagram has dropped out of sight; use **Auto zoom** to bring the diagram back on-screen.

> Look at the zoomed-out diagram CONTEXT.DAT
> Select **View** menu
> Choose **Auto zoom**

See the diagram return, filling the screen as far as its size will permit.

Shortcut key

> Auto zoom, press   <F4>

D.7.5 Zoom In

As a diagram becomes bigger it becomes more difficult to read the details of the text. You may **Zoom in** to see part of the diagram in more detail.

Before you start this part of the exercise, reduce the size of the diagram on-screen.

> See the reduced diagram CONTEXT.DAT
> Select **View** menu, and
> Choose **Zoom out** repeatedly, until
> CONTEXT.DAT is too small to read comfortably.
>
> Choose **Zoom in**
> Note that this has the opposite effect to **Zoom out**
>
> Choose **Zoom in** repeatedly, until
> CONTEXT.DAT has gone back to its original size.

Note that **Zoom in** always aligns the diagram with the top left corner of the screen, you can use the vertical and horizontal scroll bars to scroll down or across to the area you want to view.

Shortcut key

> Zoom in, press   <F7>

D.7.6 Set zoom area

Instead of using **Zoom in** to enlarge a diagram step-by-step, you may define an area of the diagram that you want to enlarge, and zoom in to it in one step.

Before you start this part of the exercise, reduce the size of the diagram on-screen.

> See the reduced diagram CONTEXT.DAT
> Select **View** menu, and
> Choose **Set zoom area**.

The mouse pointer changes from an arrow to a cross, use this to draw a 'rubber band' round the area you want to enlarge (the zoom area).

> Place the mouse cross on the top left corner of the zoom area
> Drag the mouse down
> Bring the mouse cross to the bottom right corner of the zoom area
>
> When the dotted line surrounds the zoom area
> Release the left mouse button.

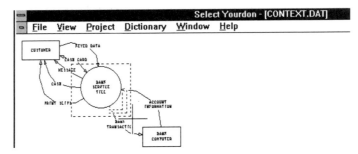

Draw box around Set-zoom area.

See the zoom area enlarged on-screen.

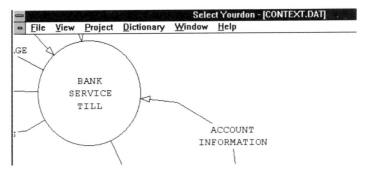

Diagram area – Zoomed-out.

If you need to cancel the effect of zooming:

Choose **Auto zoom**

Restore CONTEXT.DAT diagram to its optimum size.

Shortcut key

Set zoom area, press   \<F9>

D.7.7 Refresh

When you have zoomed in and out you may find that the diagram has become faint, or that some of the features have been damaged. You can redraw the diagram with the **Refresh** option.

View the file CONTEXT.DAT and
Select **View** menu
Choose **Zoom in**, then **Zoom out**
Select **View** menu
Choose **Refresh**

See the diagram has been redrawn.

Shortcut key

Refresh, press   \<F5>

D.7.8 Saving

The diagram is saved automatically whenever it is altered, you do not have to carry out any other operation. This means that you cannot cancel a move once you have released the mouse button.

If you are undertaking any empirical trials you should make a backup of your project before you make the trial alterations. If, subsequently, you want to abandon your trials you will be able to go back to an reliable, saved, version.

```
QUICK HELP – VIEW A DIAGRAM

Zoom Out to create space round a diagram
        Use <F8>

Zoom In to magnify part of a diagram
        Use <F7>

Auto Zoom to view a diagram at its optimum size
        Use <F4>

Set Zoom area for selective enlargement
        Use <F9>

Refresh a diagram
        Use <F5>
```

D.8   Printing

You can use SELECT Yourdon to print a copy of a diagram at any stage of its development. You can also use the Windows Clipboard to export the image of a diagram to another package, to a word processor, for example.

The default setting of the tool will print the whole diagram, however large it may be, on one sheet of paper. If you choose portrait format, the diagram will be scaled to fit the shorter side of the printing paper. Choose landscape format if you want a greater degree of enlargement.

You have the option of setting the tool to print a single diagram over 1, 2, 4, 8 or 16 sheets of A4 paper. The mosaic option (the multi-page option) is useful when you want to reproduce a particularly large and detailed diagram.

D.8.1   Set up printer

Before you start printing, make sure that your printer is on-line and check that the **Print Setup** matches your requirements.

> Open the diagram CONTEXT.DAT
> Select **File** menu
> Choose **Print Setup**

See the Windows **Print Setup** dialog box and check that the details match your requirements:

Detail option	Example
Printer	Default (HP LaserJet 4)
Page Orientation	Portrait
Paper Size	A4
Paper Source	Default (Paper cassette)

Options, normally accept **Defaults**

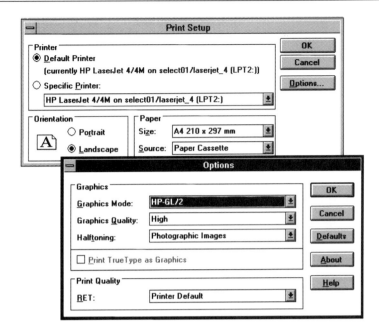

Print Setup box and Options box.

D.8.2 Single-page printing

With CONTEXT.DAT on-screen
Select **File** menu
Choose **Print**

See the SELECT Yourdon *Print* dialog box on-screen:

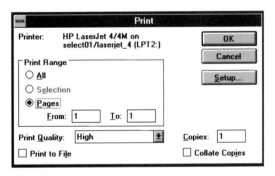

Print box, Page 1 to 1.

Check the default setting:

Pages	selected
From	1
To	1

Copies   1
Print to File   disabled

When you are satisfied with the print settings

Choose *OK*

See *Printing* message and wait, or

Choose *Cancel* to abandon printing.

This will make a single copy of the diagram print, on a single sheet of A4 paper. Change the number of copies, if you need more, and refer to the section Mosaic Printing to see how to print in greater magnification.

The printout will be over-printed to show:

- diagram type and title
- diagram directory and file name
- page number of the printout.

D.8.3   Mosaic printing

This means printing one diagram across many sheets of paper. In the following example you will print the diagram on 4 sheets, but the tool gives you the options of printing across 1, 2, 4, 8 or 16 sheets.

With CONTEXT.DAT on-screen
Select **File** menu
Choose **Print**

See the SELECT Yourdon *Print* dialog box on-screen.
Change the settings to the following:

Pages   selected
From   1
To   4
Copies   1
Print to File   disabled

When you are satisfied with the print settings

Choose *OK*

See *Printing* message and wait, or

Choose *Cancel* to abandon printing.

This will make a single copy of the diagram print, spread over four sheets of A4 paper. Change the number of copies, if you need more copies; refer to Single-Page Printing if you want the print on only one sheet.

The printout has been over-printed to show:

- diagram type and title
- diagram directory and file name
- page number of the printout.

QUICK HELP – *PRINT A DIAGRAM*

Put the Printer on-line
  While the diagram is on-screen:
  from *File* menu, choose   *Print*
  in *Print* box, select   **Pages** from 1 to 1

> choose **OK**
> wait, then collect: single-page print
> Surrounded with a border and stamped with Diagram File details.

D.8.4   Print to file

If you do not have a printer currently available (or if you are using a Postscript or HPGL printer) you may print your diagram to a file.

> With CONTEXT.DAT on-screen
> Select **File** menu
> Choose **Print**

See the SELECT Yourdon *Print* dialog box on-screen and check the print settings.
> When you are satisfied with the print settings

> Select the *Print to File* check box.
> Choose *OK*

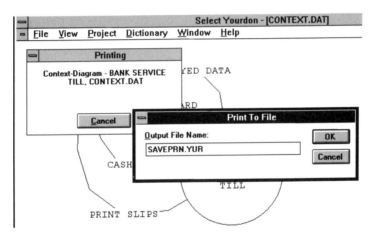

Print-to-File box.

You will see the *Print To File* dialog box

> Type the *Output File Name*
> Choose *OK*

You have created a file in your work directory which can be printed out when a suitable printer is available.

D.9   Exporting diagrams

Instead of printing a diagram through the tool you can transfer a diagram to another package; for example, you may want to paste or embed the diagram into a word processor file.

D.9.1   Clipboard

Use Windows **Clipboard** to paste a graphics file of the diagram into a text document.

> With CONTEXT.DAT on-screen
> Select **File** menu

Select **Export**
Choose **Clipboard**

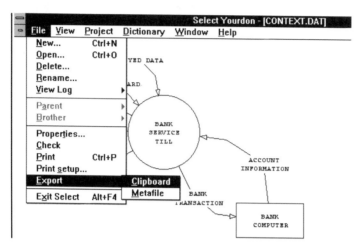

Export to Clipboard.

Open a text document (for example in Windows Write) and
Decide where you want to insert a SELECT Yourdon diagram.
In your Write document

Click the cursor at the point where you want the picture to appear
Select **Edit**
Choose **Paste**

See the diagram pasted into your text document.

D.9.2 Metafile

Create a Windows Metafile that you can include in another Windows package. When the file is
generated it will automatically be saved in your work directory.

With CONTEXT.DAT on-screen
Select **File** menu
Select **Export**
Choose **Metafile**

Use the Windows file manager to verify that the file CONTEXT.WMF has been saved in your
work directory; for example:

```
C:\SELECT\PROJ1\CONTEXT.WMF
```

D.9.3 Embed a metafile

Read the documentation which came with your own word processor and see how to manage a
metafile. This example shows the procedure for adding a Windows metafile to a Word for
Windows document.
In SELECT Yourdon

Create a metafile, for example CONTEXT.WMF.

In Word for Windows

Open a new document, for example REPORT01.DOC
Place the insertion point where you want the illustration to appear.

In Word **Insert** menu
Choose **Picture**

In Word *Picture* file manager
Select CONTEXT.WMF
Choose *OK*

See the metafile illustration drawn in the Word document.

D.9.4   Revise a metafile

SELECT Yourdon will, by default, give a metafile the same name as the diagram file (with the extension .WMF). This means that, if you run the export procedure again, after you have modified the Yourdon design, the metafile in your work directory will be revised.

You can then update the illustration in your word processor.
In SELECT Yourdon

Revise and alter CONTEXT.DAT
Create a new metafile called, by default, CONTEXT.WMF

In Word for Windows
Open the existing document REPORT01.DOC
Select the metafile image of the earlier CONTEXT.WMF

In Word **Insert** menu
Choose **Picture**

In Word *Picture* file manager
Select CONTEXT.WMF
Choose *OK*

See the original metafile illustration re-drawn with the new image.

D.10   Manipulating diagrams

In the following exercises you will practise moving parts of the diagram about the screen. Before you start you may take the following precautions:

- Make a clone copy of the example project to create a new project (for example, called TESTBED). Then you can manipulate the TESTBED project as much as you like, leaving the example project untouched.
- Make a print of the screen before you start to make any changes. Then you can refer to the print at the end of the exercise and move the parts of the diagram back to their original positions.

The exercises use the dataflow diagram CONTEXT.DAT to give you experience of moving, adding and deleting objects and flows. These are important techniques for you to master, but they are not techniques that are needed in all diagram structures (you will find, for example, that Jackson structures are not manipulated in quite the same way as Yourdon structures).

Later in the tutorial, as each diagram structure is explained, you will see references to the techniques you practised in this section.

- add objects
- delete objects
- move objects   .
- move an object outside the margins
- cancel a move in mid-procedure
- move a flow

- move a waypoint
- cancel a waypoint
- use free format text

D.11 Moving an object

When you add an object to a diagram, the tool places it at the point where the mouse pointer was standing when you entered the name of the new object. You may need to change the location of the object as you develop the diagram.

The distinction between the different types of object will be described in the relevant tutorial exercise.

The objects you will move in this exercise are a node and a terminator.

Click on an	object
Look at	status line
See the object's	name and description.

D.11.1 Move a node

Open CONTEXT.DAT

Print a copy of the diagram, you will need it later in this exercise.

Point to the inside of the node BANK SERVICE TILL
Hold down the left mouse button, and
Drag BANK SERVICE TILL to the top right corner of the screen.

Note that, while you are moving the object, the name is blanked out and the mouse pointer changes from an arrow to a cross.

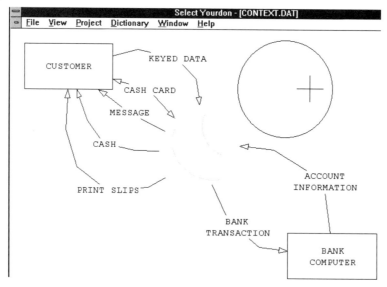

Move an object, step 1.

When the object is in its new position
Release the left mouse button.

See the name of BANK SERVICE TILL appear again.

Note that the flows from the terminators CUSTOMER and BANK COMPUTER have stretched so that they remains attached to the node. (In a later set of exercises you will practise moving and aligning flows.)

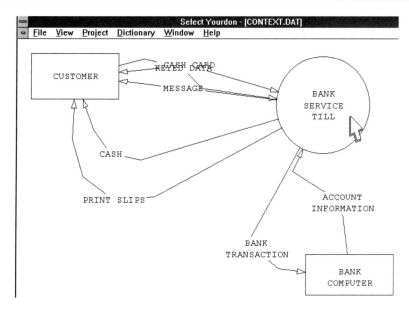

Move an object, step 2.

Keep this diagram on-screen as the starting point of the next part of the exercise.

D.11.2 Move beyond the margins

When you are developing a diagram you may need to extend it beyond the margins of the original screen.

> Open CONTEXT.DAT
> Note that the node bank service till is at the top right corner
> Click on the UP arrow of the vertical scroll bar

See the question:

>   Do you want to increase the margin?
> Choose *Yes*

The top margin will increase.

> Move the terminator CUSTOMER
> To the middle of the empty part of the screen

You are only looking at part of the newly arranged diagram; if you want to see the whole of the diagram on-screen:

> Select **View**
> Choose **Auto zoom**

Note that the size of the drawing has been reduced to accommodate the deeper view you see on-screen.

> Keep this diagram on-screen as the starting point of the next part of the exercise (Cancel Changes).

D.11.3 Cancel a move in mid-procedure

You can cancel a move in mid-procedure so long as you have not released the left mouse button.

Open CONTEXT.DAT
Point to the node BANK SERVICE TILL
Hold down the left mouse button, and
Drag the node towards the bottom left corner of the screen
Continue to hold down the left button and, at the same time,
Press the right mouse button.

See the node jump back to its original position and note that the mouse pointer has become an arrow again.

D.11.4 Cancel changes

If you want to cancel all the changes you have made on a diagram, you must either revert to a backup you made earlier or redraw it by moving the objects back to their original positions.

For this reason you will find it helpful to make a print of a diagram before you make any significant changes.

Open CONTEXT.DAT
(Check that this is the version you have just modified)

Refer to the print of CONTEXT.DAT that you took at the start of the exercise.

Move the terminator CUSTOMER and
The node BANK SERVICE TILL
Back to their original positions

Note that the diagram has become small and is aligned to one side of the screen

Select **View**
Choose **Auto zoom**

See the diagram redrawn to its original size and centred in the middle of the screen.

D.12 Moving a flow

A flow is the link between two objects. The start is called the source; the end is called the destination.

You may need to move a flow on an existing diagram if you have rearranged the layout. You will need to move a flow on a new diagram when you arrange the layout for the first time.

There are different types of flow and each one will be described as you encounter it later in the tutorial. If you want to know the type of a particular flow:

Click on a flow
Look at status line
See the flow's name and description.

In this exercise you will move a flow and practise adding and deleting waypoints.

D.12.1 About waypoints

A waypoint is a point through which a flow passes. A waypoint is usually a bend in a flow but, whenever a name is shown on the diagram, there is also a waypoint beneath the flow name. You create a waypoint when you put the mouse pointer on a part of a flow and then drag it to another position.

D.12.2 Move flow end

You may need to move a flow from one terminator to another. In this exercise you will move the flow message from the terminator customer to the terminator bank computer.

Open CONTEXT.DAT
Double click anywhere on the flow MESSAGE
See a pop-up menu
Choose **Move**

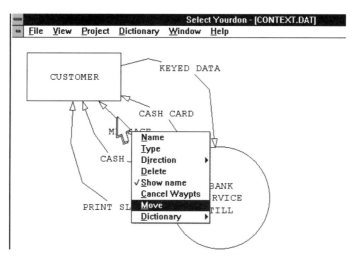

Move menu.

Click inside the object attached to the end of the flow that you want to move.

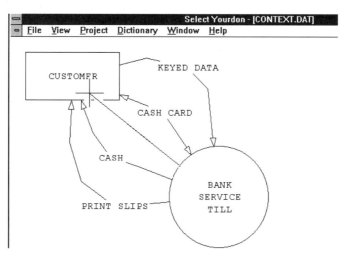

Click on flow end.

The flow breaks away from the terminator CUSTOMER and ends instead at the mouse cross.

Move the mouse cross and put it
Inside the terminator BANK COMPUTER
Click once inside BANK COMPUTER

The flow MESSAGE is now drawn as a straight line from BANK SERVICE TILL to BANK COMPUTER.

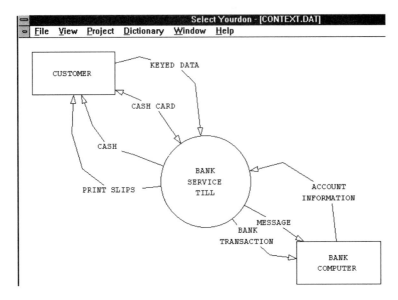

Flow MESSAGE at a new site.

D.12.3   Move a waypoint

You may need to move a waypoint in order to improve the layout of the diagram. Sometimes, when two or more flows are created between the same objects, the flows will lie on top of each other; when this happens you must bend the flows so that they can be distinguished from each other.

In this exercise you will bend the flow MESSAGE so that it runs alongside the flow BANK TRANSACTION.

> Open CONTEXT.DAT
> Point to the word MESSAGE on the flow
> (There is always a waypoint underneath a name)
> Hold down the left mouse button
> Drag the waypoint downwards to a new location
> When you have realigned the flow
> Release the mouse button.

See the waypoint redrawn in its new position.

> Point to part of the flow between
> MESSAGE and BANK SERVICE TILL
> Hold down the left mouse button
> Drag the waypoint downwards to a new location
> When you have realigned the flow
> Release the mouse button.

You have created a new waypoint where the flow bends.

> Point to part of the flow between
> MESSAGE and BANK COMPUTER
> Hold down the left mouse button
> Drag the waypoint downwards to a new location
> When you have realigned the flow
> Release the mouse button.

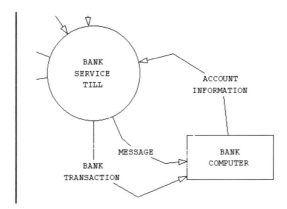

Move a Waypoint.

The flow MESSAGE now has three waypoints and it follows the same sort of course as the flow BANK TRANSACTION.

D.12.4   Cancel a waypoint

> Open CONTEXT.DAT
> Look at the flow MESSAGE that you have just aligned
> Point to a waypoint that you have just created
> Hold down the left mouse button (to select the waypoint)
> At the same time, click the right mouse button.

See the waypoint disappear.

D.12.5   Cancel all waypoints

> Open CONTEXT.DAT
> Click on any part of the flow MESSAGE
> See a pop-up menu
> Choose **Cancel Waypts**

All the waypoints will disappear and the flow will become a straight line.

D.12.6   Show and hide name

A flow will always have a name, but you may choose whether you want to show it on the diagram or not.

> Open CONTEXT.DAT
> Click on the flow ACCOUNT INFORMATION
> From the menu, choose ✔ **Show Name**

The name will disappear from the diagram

> Click again on the flow ACCOUNT INFORMATION
> From the menu, choose **Show Name**

The name will show on the diagram again.

D.12.7   Change direction

You may change the direction of a flow on a diagram after it has been drawn.

> Open CONTEXT.DAT
> Click on the flow ACCOUNT INFORMATION

This flow is shown as an input to BANK SERVICE TILL

> From the menu, select **Direction**
> Choose **Change**

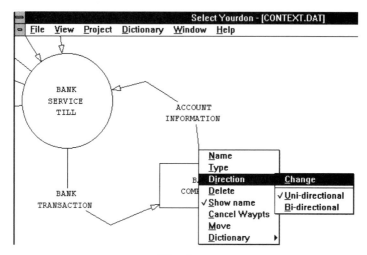

Direction menu.

The flow has been reversed and now shows as an output from BANK SERVICE TILL.
　　When the flow is created it will be uni-directional; you may need to change the nature of the flow.

> Open CONTEXT.DAT
> Click on the flow ACCOUNT INFORMATION

This flow is a uni-directional output from BANK SERVICE TILL.

> From the menu, select **Direction**
> Choose **Bi-directional**

The flow is shown with an arrow pointing from each end.

> Click on the flow ACCOUNT INFORMATION

> From the menu, select **Direction**
> Choose **Bi-directional**

> From the menu, select **Direction**
> Choose **Change**

The flow is shown as a uni-directional input to BANK SERVICE TILL.

D.12.8　Tidy the diagram

- Before you leave these exercises, move the flow MESSAGE so that it runs again from the node BANK SERVICE TILL to the terminator CUSTOMER.
- If the lines of the diagram appear to be damaged, press <F5> to refresh the screen.

D.12.9　Group move

When you are developing a diagram you may want to move a group of objects and flows at the same time. To do this, follow the Group Move procedure.
　　In Group Move you will draw a 'rubber band' around all the objects you want to move; this will look like a dotted rectangle on the screen and you will be able to move the rectangle and its contents to another part of the screen.

Open CONTEXT.DAT

Prepare to move the node BANK SERVICE TILL, the terminator CUSTOMER and the connecting flows, from the top of the diagram to the bottom of the diagram.

First of all press <F8> to zoom out and give yourself more room on the screen to carry out the manoeuvres.

Click on a point on the empty screen above the
Top left corner of the terminator CUSTOMER
Hold down the left mouse button
A dotted rectangle will extend from the corner where you clicked
Draw the rectangle out from its bottom right corner
Until the 'rubber band' encloses
CUSTOMER and BANK SERVICE TILL
Release the left mouse button.

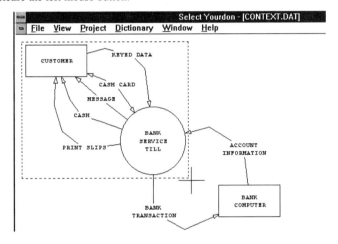

Group Move, step 1.

Move the mouse.

See a second dotted rectangle move in response to the mouse.

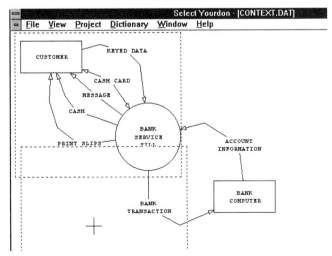

Group Move, step 2.

Move this second rectangle to the new site for the group
Press the left mouse button

Note that the dotted rectangles have disappeared and the objects CUSTOMER and BANK SER-
VICE TILL are in their new position.

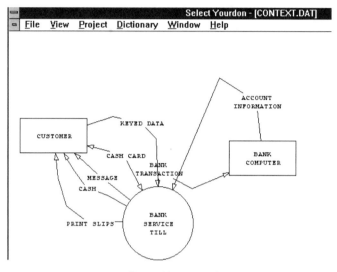

Group Move, step 3.

See that the flows from the group are still attached to the objects that did not move. You will need
to delete the waypoints and realign the flows that look untidy.

> QUICK HELP – MOVE AN OBJECT
>
> When there is an object on-screen
>
> > Put mouse pointer inside   object
> > hold down   left mouse button
> > drag object to   new site
> > release   mouse button

> QUICK HELP – CANCEL WAYPOINTS
>
> When there is a diagram on-screen
>
> > Put mouse pointer on   Flow
> > Click once to see pop-up menu
> > select option   **Cancel Waypoints**
> > add new   Waypoints
>
> See the Flow re-drawn.

D.13 Adding and deleting objects

SELECT Yourdon allows you to use the diagrams to add and delete objects, flows and text.

D.13.1   Add object

An object may be a node, terminator or a store and, for this exercise, you will practise adding a terminator (called ROUTINE OVERHAUL).

> Open CONTEXT.DAT
> Click on the empty space above BANK SERVICE TILL
> From the menu, choose **Terminator**

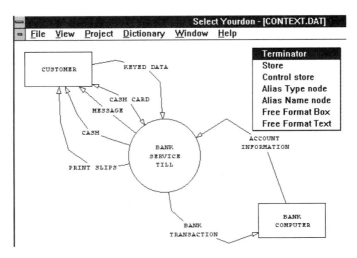

Terminator menu.

> In the **Enter Name** box
> Type ROUTINE OVERHAUL

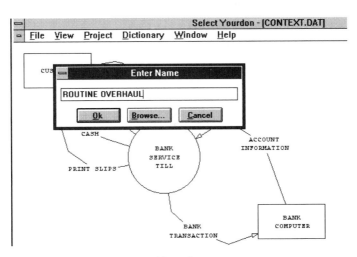

Name box.

> Choose **OK**

See a new terminator, ROUTINE OVERHAUL, drawn in the empty space. If necessary, move the new terminator to a more convenient site.

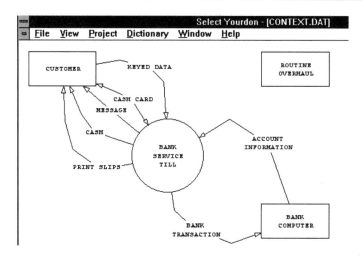

New terminator.

D.13.2   Add flow

After you have created a new object, you will need to link it to the diagram with a flow.

    Open CONTEXT.DAT
    Click on BANK SERVICE TILL
    From the menu, choose **Add Flow**

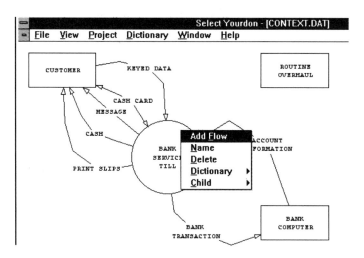

Add Flow menu.

The cursor changes from a pointer to a cross, and a flow is drawn out from the source (BANK SERVICE TILL) to the cursor.

    Click on ROUTINE OVERHAUL

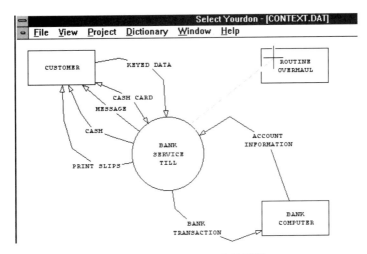

Click on ROUTINE OVERHAUL.

Choose from the list one of the flow type options that are permitted by the rules of the method you are using.

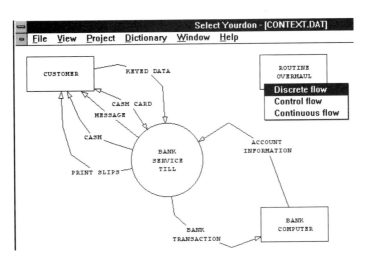

Flow menu.

If you have selected a destination that is not permitted by the method, you will see an error message telling you to try a different destination.

From the menu choose **Discrete Flow**
In the *Name Box*, type VOLUME OF TRANSACTIONS

See a uni-directional discrete flow, VOLUME OF TRANSACTIONS, drawn from BANK SERVICE TILL to ROUTINE OVERHAUL.

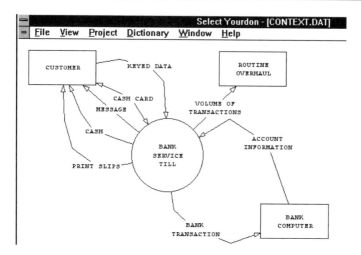

New flow appears.

Now that you have created a flow you can amend its properties:

- **Type**
  Control or continuous.
- **Direction**
  Uni-directional or bi-directional.
  Change direction.
- **Show Name**
  Show name or conceal name.
- **Move**
  Move the flow.

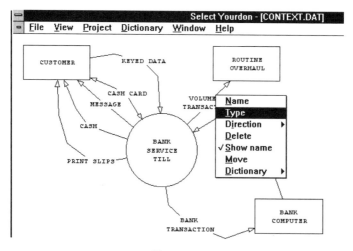

Type menu.

D.13.3 Delete flow

Open CONTEXT.DAT
Click on the flow VOLUME OF TRANSACTIONS
From the menu, choose **Delete**

Answer the confirmation message:
You do want to delete VOLUME OF TRANSACTIONS
Choose *Yes*

The flow is removed from the diagram. But the information about the flow remains listed in the dictionary, with 'u' in front of it to indicate that the data is 'unused'.

D.13.4 Delete object

Open CONTEXT.DAT
Click on the terminator ROUTINE OVERHAUL
From the menu, choose **Delete**

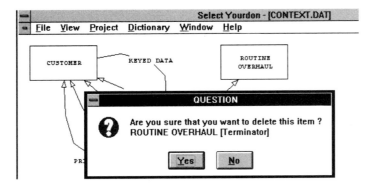

Confirmation Question: Delete?

Answer the confirmation message:
You do want to delete ROUTINE OVERHAUL
Choose *Yes*

The object is removed from the diagram. (But the information about the terminator remains listed in the dictionary.)

D.13.5 Add through dictionary

It is possible to have data listed in the dictionary which is unused in the diagram. This data may be a listing that is left over after an item has been deleted, or it may be an item that you have used to populate the dictionary.
(Populating the dictionary will be described in the Dictionary section.)

Open CONTEXT.DAT
Click on the empty space above BANK SERVICE TILL
From the menu, choose **Terminator**

In the *Enter Name* box
Choose *Browse*

See the *Dictionary Item Selector* box, scroll through the list to find an item you want to use

Click on, for example:
```
    'u'    Terminator    Routine Overhaul
```
Choose *Select*

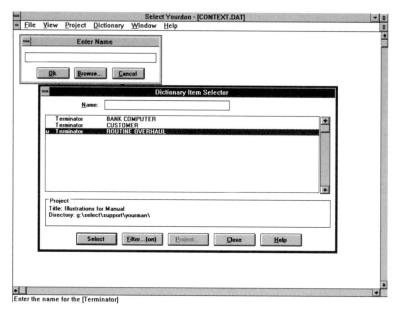

Browse for a name.

See ROUTINE OVERHAUL appear in the ***Enter Name*** box
Choose ***OK***

See a new terminator, ROUTINE OVERHAUL, drawn in the empty space. If necessary, move the new terminator to a more convenient site.

You can use the dictionary Browse option to search for, and use, the names of any items which have been listed in the dictionary.

Now delete the terminator ROUTINE OVERHAUL.

D.13.6   Free format text

You may add a block of text (up to 50 characters at a time) to the diagram.

Open CONTEXT.DAT
Click on the empty space above BANK SERVICE TILL
From the menu, choose **Free format text**
In the ***Enter Name*** box

Type a comment, for example
```
Special Project X
```
Choose ***OK***

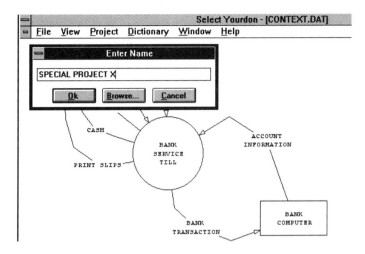

Type text in box.

See the line of text printed in the space on the diagram.

D.13.7 Edit text

Open CONTEXT.DAT
Click on the line of free format text

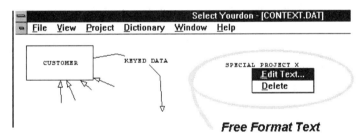

Text menu.

From the menu, choose **Edit Text**
In the *Free Format Text* box
Type your *revisions*
Choose *OK*

See the revised text on screen.

D.13.8 Free format box

You may want to mark a part of your diagram for reference purposes. SELECT Yourdon allows you to draw a rectangle on the screen.

The free format box does not have a significance in any method, it is for display purposes only.

Open CONTEXT.DAT
Click in empty space
From the menu, choose **Free Format Box**

See a dotted rectangle drawn in the empty space. You can move one corner of this box so that it marks the corner of the free format box you want to create.

Click on the edge of the box
From the menu, choose **Move**

The lines become solid and the box moves in response to the cursor.

Move the box to a new position
Click once to anchor the box
Point to another corner of the box
Hold down the cursor and drag the corner
Until the box covers the area you want to mark

Click on the edge of the box
From the menu, choose **Solid Line**

See the box drawn with a solid line instead of a dotted line.

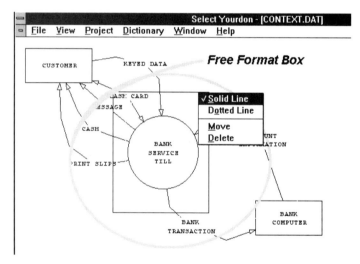

Free format box.

D.13.9   Delete box

Click on the edge of the box
From the menu, choose **Delete**

The box will disappear.

D.14   Conclusions

When you have explored the general features of the CASE tool introduced in this chapter, you are ready to start work on your own projects, or to conduct one of the more specific diagram tutorials given in the remaining appendices.

CASE tutorial:

Dataflow diagrams

E.1 Introduction

In the following exercises you will use the dataflow diagram (DfD) editor of the CASE tool.

The exercises assume that you have installed the CASE tool as described in Appendix A, and are familiar with the basic operation of the software; the best way to gain such experience is to complete the general tutorial (Appendix D) before you attempt the exercises in this appendix.

The tutorial will use the sample project 'Bank Service Till' which will, by default, have been installed in the directory `c:\select\system\example`. You need to open this project before continuing.

E.2 Basic operations

The DfD editor is a context-sensitive working environment. This means that when you click on an object (or in free space) a pop-up menu of relevant options will appear on a diagram.

The nodes that the project rules allow you to use are listed in a pop-up menu when you click in open space.

The following illustration shows you what happens when you click in open space in the Context diagram CONTEXT.DAT in the sample project.

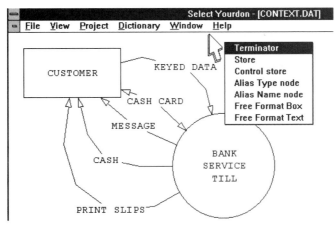

Node types.

E.2.1 Add a node

In this exercise you will add a node to the Level 0 DfD diagram.

> Open the diagram D0.DAT
> Click in the open space on the right side of the diagram above PROCESS REQUIRED SERVICES.

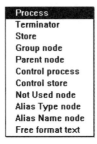

Process menu.

> From the menu, choose **Process**
> In *Enter Name*, type RECORD TRANSACTION DETAILS

Enter Name box.

See the new Process box added to the diagram.

All processes on the diagram will be numbered automatically starting from 1. You can renumber an individual process by clicking on the process and selecting **Renumber**.

E.2.2 Add flow

In this exercise you will add a discrete flow in the D0.DAT diagram.

The flow will be added to the process RECORD TRANSACTION DETAILS which you created in the previous exercise.

> Open the diagram D0.DAT
>
> Click on PROCESS REQUIRED SERVICES
> From the menu select **Add Flow**

See a cross-hair cursor attached to a flow.

Add Flow menu.

> Drag the cross hair cursor to RECORD TRANSACTION DETAILS.
> When the cursor is on record transaction details, click the left mouse button to place the flow end in the box.

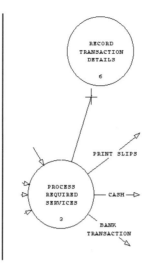

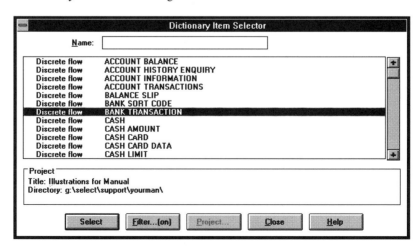

Drag a flow into position.

A pop-up menu will be displayed offering the choice of creating different flows.

> From the menu, choose **Discrete flow**
> In *Enter Name*, type TRANSACTION DETAILS
> Choose *OK*

See the flow TRANSACTION DETAILS appear on the diagram.

E.2.3 Add flow from the dictionary

In this exercise you will add a flow that is already being used in the Data Dictionary.

> Move the flow TRANSACTION DETAILS to one side, by inserting a waypoint.

Follow the same procedure for inserting a flow between the two processes as described in the previous exercise (Add a Flow).

> When you see *Enter Name* dialog box
> Choose *Browse* before you enter any text.

See the *Dictionary Item Selector* dialog box.

Dictionary item selector.

Find BANK TRANSACTION.

Refer to WORKING WITH THE DATA DICTIONARY for more information.

Select BANK TRANSACTION
Choose *Select*.

See the ***Enter Name*** dialog box shows BANK TRANSACTION.

Click on *OK*

The diagram will be redrawn with the new flow added.

E.2.4 Rename a node or a flow

You can rename a node or a flow either on the diagram or through the dictionary.

When you rename on the diagram you have the option of renaming the occurrence of the node or flow that you are working on, or you can carry out a global rename of all occurrences of the node or flow within the project.

When you rename through the Data Dictionary the changes are global, that is, *all* occurrences of the name within the project are changed.

In this example we rename a node and a flow from within the diagram; we shall carry out an individual rename of a node and then carry out a global rename of a flow.

E.2.5 Single rename a node

In this exercise you will use the diagram to change the name of GET PASSWORD to OBTAIN PASSWORD

Open D0.DAT
Click on GET PASSWORD
From the menu, choose **Name**

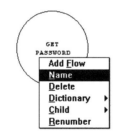

Name menu.

In the ***Enter Name*** dialog box
Erase GET PASSWORD
Type OBTAIN PASSWORD
Choose *OK*.

You can also use the ***Browse*** option to put a name in the ***Enter Name*** dialog box; the ***Dictionary Item Selector*** will offer you all the process entries in the Data Dictionary.

E.2.6 Global rename a flow

In this exercise you will carry out a global rename and change the name MESSAGE to MESSAGES.

Open D0.DAT
Click on MESSAGE
From the menu, choose **Name**

In the *Enter Name* dialog box
Erase MESSAGE
Type MESSAGES
Choose *OK*.

You can also use the *Browse* option to put a name in the *Enter Name* dialog box; the *Dictionary Item Selector* dialog box will offer you all the discrete flow entries in the Data Dictionary.

The *Question* box asks you if you want to make a single name change (**No**) or carry out a global change (**Yes**).

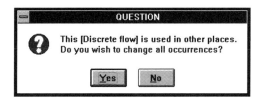

Change all occurrences.

Choose **Yes**

All the discrete flows with the same name within the project will be renamed.

E.2.7 Change the type of a flow

The type of flow can be changed without changing the Data Dictionary description.
In this exercise you will change the discrete flow CASH into a continuous flow.

Open D0.DAT
Click on the flow CASH
From the menu, select **Type**
Choose **Continuous**

Change type of flow.

See the flow will be changed from a discrete flow (single arrow) to a continuous flow (double arrow).

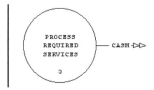

Continuous flow.

E.3 Creating a child DfD

You can move through the DfD hierarchy using the parent to child linking that is set up when the diagrams are created.

E.3.1 Move to child diagram

Open the context diagram, CONTEXT.DAT
Click on BANK SERVICE TILL
From the menu, select **Child**
Choose **Open**

See the child diagram D0.DAT on-screen.

E.3.2 Create child DfD

During the development of a project, a hierarchy of DfDs is created using the parent to child structure. In this exercise you will create a child DfD of the RECORD TRANSACTION DETAILS process box from within the D0.DAT diagram.

Open D0.DAT
Click on RECORD TRANSACTION DETAILS
From the menu, select **Child**
Choose **Open**

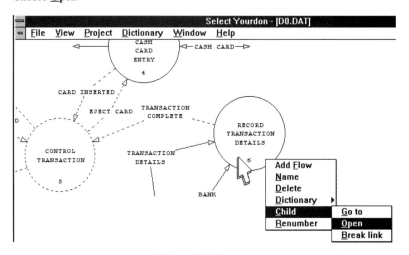

Select child diagram.

See a *Question* dialog box which gives two options for creating a new child diagram.

Create child diagram.

- **New**
  Allows you to create a new diagram, the tool will automatically generate the input and output flows.

- **Existing**

    Allows you to make a link with a diagram that has already been created.

    Choose **New**

See *Create New Diagram* box.

    Type D4 as *Filename*
    Select DATA FLOW as *Type of diagram*
    Choose *Create*

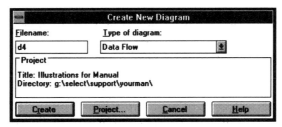

Create New Diagram box.

The child diagram D4.DAT will be generated with the relevant input and output flows created and attached to a group node.

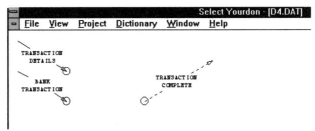

New child DfD.

*Do not delete the **D4.DAT** diagram, you will need it for a later exercise.*

E.3.3   Develop the diagram

Now you can add new processes (and stores, and so on) and connect the input/output flows to them by clicking on the flow and choosing **Move** from the menu.

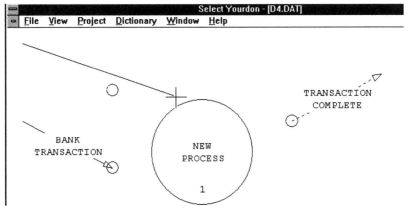

Develop a child diagram.

E.4   Checking a DfD

The check report will tell you if the diagram is consistent with the rules of the method and with the construction of its parent.

You run a check on an open diagram by selecting **File** and choosing **Check**. The check report will come on-screen and you can print it or save it according to your requirements.

E.4.1   Flows

The input and output flows on a diagram must be consistent with its parent in the following details:

- name
- type
- direction of flow

When a group flow appears in a decomposed form on a child diagram, the BNF (Backus–Naur Format) clause will be checked for consistency.

E.4.2   Process interface

Processes must have both:

- inputs
- outputs

E.4.3   Store balancing

Each store must be given a BNF clause to specify the content of the store terms of flows.

Input and output flows on the diagram must be consistent with the BNF definition of the store.

If stores appear on more than one diagram, a full store-balancing can be carried out when you use the report generator.

E.4.4   Check report

When a diagram has failed a check the failures are reported as **errors** or **warnings**.

- **Errors**
  Inconsistencies that you must correct before the project balances.
- **Warnings**
  Less serious than errors and may not require attention before the project balances.

If the diagram as not been checked, or it has failed a check, you will see a star (*) on the status line at the bottom of the diagram.

If the diagram is still inconsistent when you open it again from the SELECT Yourdon opening window, you will see the inconsistent flag in the *Diagram File Selector*.

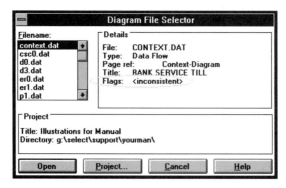

Diagram File Selector.

E.4.5 Check a consistent DfD

In this exercise you will carry out a check of the Context diagram.

> Open CONTEXT.DAT
> Select **File**
> Choose **Check**

The check operation will be carried out.

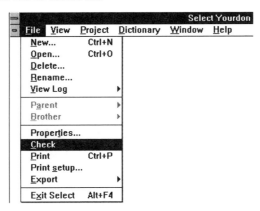

Choose the Check option.

When the check operation has been completed *the Preview of diagram consistency checks* dialog box will show the check report. In this example there were no errors detected or warnings given.

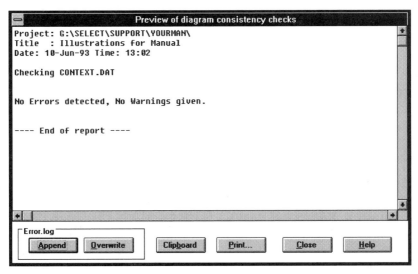

Preview of diagram consistency checks.

The buttons at the foot the *Preview of diagram consistency checks* dialog box gives you the choice of:

- **Append**
  Attaches the newly generated error log to the end of the current ERROR.LOG file which is saved in your work directory.

- **O**verwrite

  Overwrites the current ERROR.LOG file with details of the newly generated report.

- **Clip**board

  Saves the ERROR.LOG to the Windows Clipboard.

- **P**rint

  Sends the ERROR.LOG file to your printer.

E.4.6 View log

You can view the ERROR.LOG at any time.

> Select **File** menu
> Select **View Log**
> Choose **Errors**

The latest ERROR.LOG generated will be displayed.

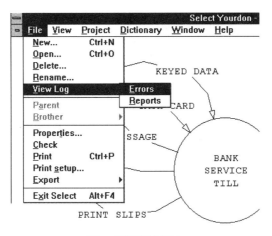

View ERROR.LOG.

E.5 Dataflow decomposition

Group flows are dataflows (discrete, control, or continuous) that divide or merge as they cross a diagram.

The exact definition of a group flow is contained in the Data Dictionary and not on the diagram. The definitions are entered into the Data Dictionary in a BNF (Backus–Naur Format) clause.

In this exercise you will decompose the discrete flow transaction details that you added to the D0.DAT diagram in the Add a Flow part of the tutorial.

You will decompose the flow two ways:

- using a Group flow
- using Parent nodes

E.5.1 Create BNF clause

The discrete flow TRANSACTION DETAILS will be split into two separate sub-discrete flows called DATE OF TRANSACTION and TRANSACTION TYPE. The new sub-flows will need to be defined as a BNF statements in the Data Dictionary.

Open D0.DAT
Click on the flow TRANSACTION DETAILS

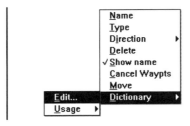

Dictionary Edit option.

From the menu, select **Dictionary**
Choose **Edit**

See the ***Discrete Flow Editor – [TRANSACTION DETAILS]*** dialog box.

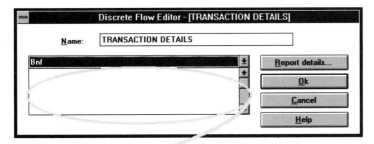

Template text box

Discrete Flow Editor.

In the template text box
Type DATE OF TRANSACTION + TRANSACTION TYPE
Choose *OK*

See the **BNF checking** dialog box.

Add both flows as **Discrete flows** to the Data Dictionary.

E.5.2   BNF syntax

Refer to the on-line Help to see examples of BNF syntax.

E.5.3   Use group node

When the child diagram is created the flows are automatically inserted in the child diagram. The input and output flows start and end with group nodes

Open D4.DAT
Add a process called TRANSACTION DETAILS RECORDED

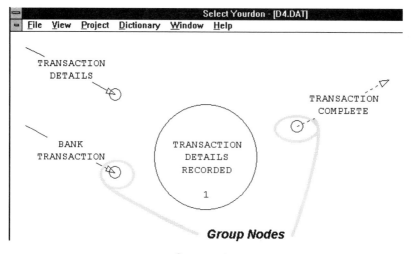

Group nodes.

Click on the group node on the end of TRANSACTION DETAILS
From the menu, select **Add Flow**
Drag the flow and connect it to TRANSACTION DETAILS RECORDED

From the menu, choose **Discrete Flow**
In the *Enter Name* box, choose *Browse*

In the *Dictionary Item Selector*
Select DATE OF TRANSACTION
Choose *Select*

See the *Enter Name* dialog box, showing DATE OF TRANSACTION

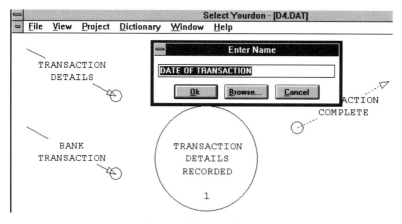

Name of discrete flow.

Choose *OK*

See the diagram redrawn with the new sub-flow added. Move the new flow to one side by inserting a waypoint.

Repeat the procedure, and
Add a second sub-flow (TRANSACTION TYPE)
Between TRANSACTION DETAILS and
TRANSACTION DETAILS RECORDED

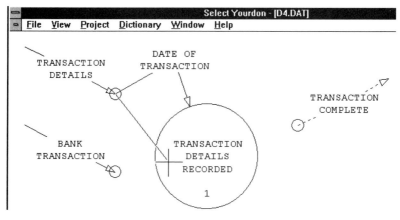

Add second sub-flow.

Connect the input flow BANK TRANSACTION and
Output flow TRANSACTION COMPLETE
To the process TRANSACTION DETAILS RECORDED.

You can **Move** the flows to make the diagram clearer.

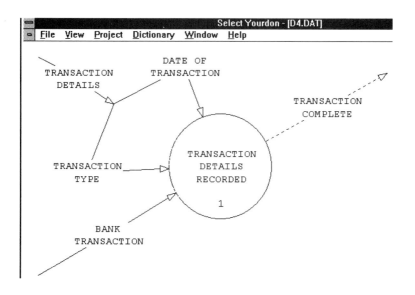

All flows connected.

Carry out a **Check** of the diagram to ensure that the parent to child links balance.

E.5.4   Use parent nodes

If you have carried out the previous exercise (Use Group Node) you must now delete the flows TRANSACTION DETAILS, DATE OF TRANSACTION, and TRANSACTION TYPE from D4.DAT.

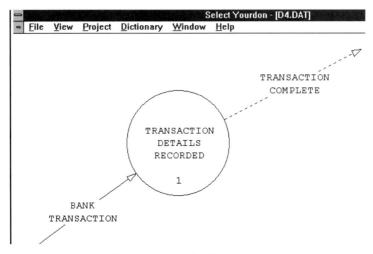

Opening diagram for this exercise.

In D4.DAT
Click in space to the left of TRANSACTION DETAILS RECORDED
From the menu, choose **Parent Node**

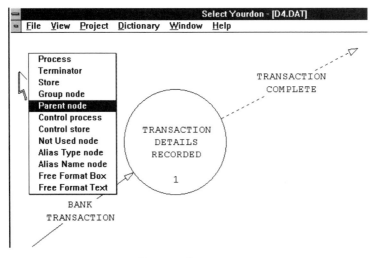

Parent node option.

A small box is created, this will become the parent node of the new flow.

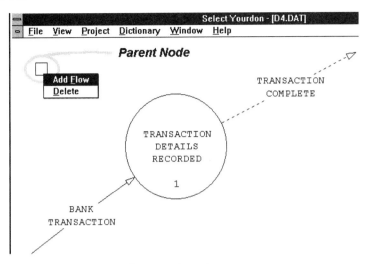

Parent node, and menu.

Click inside the parent node
Choose **Add Flow**
Drag the flow and connect it to TRANSACTION DETAILS RECORDED

From the menu, choose **Discrete flow**
In *Enter Name* choose *Browse*
In the *Dictionary Item Selector*
Select DATE OF TRANSACTION.
Choose *OK*

See the diagram redrawn with the new discrete flow added.
    Repeat the procedure, and add the discrete-flow TRANSACTION TYPE to D4.DAT.

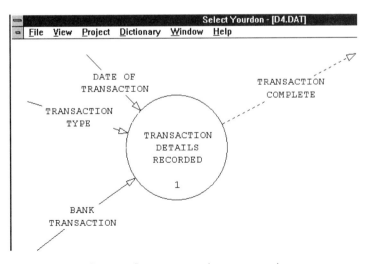

Discrete flows connected to parent nodes.

Carry out a **Check** of the diagram to ensure that the parent to child links balance.

E.6   The Context diagram

The Context diagram shows the information which flows between the system and the external entities. The Context diagram consists of a single process node (context node), terminators, and information flows.

E.6.1   Open new project

In the following exercise you will begin a new system model by creating a new Context diagram in a new project.

> Create a new project called, for example, NEWPROJ.

E.6.2   Create Context diagram

> From SELECT Yourdon opening window
> Select **File** menu
> Choose **New**

See the *Create New Diagram* dialog box.

> Choose *Project*

See the *Project Selector* dialog box.

> Select NEWPROJ from the drop-down list
> Choose *Switch to*

Make NEWPROJ your default project.

See *Create New Diagram* box.

> Type CONTEXT as *Filename*
> Select DATA FLOW as *Type of diagram*
> Choose *Create*

Create New Diagram box.

See a *Question* dialog box asking you if you want to make the diagram the Context diagram for the project.

DfD Question box.

> Choose *Yes*

The context node (with the default name TBD) will be created in a new diagram.

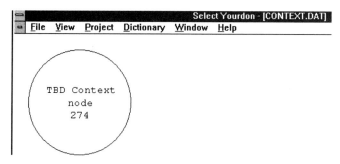

Start of Context diagram.

Click on the node TBD
From the menu, choose **Name**
In *Enter Name*, type the name of the new context node.

You can now develop this diagram and create a new DfD hierarchy below it by using the parent–child links.

E.7   Hatley DfDs

Hatley is the name commonly given to the Hatley/Pirbhai Structured Method. This method was developed in the mid-1980s by Derek Hatley and Imiatz Pirbhai, and embodies ideas from Yourdon, and Ward and Mellor.

The differences between Yourdon and Hatley are on the whole very subtle. Hatley does not utilize the various control triggers of Ward and Mellor and the symbology used to denote control specifications differ (control processes in Yourdon and CSpec Bar in Hatley).

The method covers the practices of structured analysis and structured design using dataflow diagrams, structure charts, state-transition diagrams, entity-relationship diagrams, and a data dictionary.

If you wish to use the Hatley variant of dataflow diagrams, select Data Flow (Hatley) as the diagram type when you create the context diagram, or the first dataflow diagram.

E.8   Conclusions

The exercises in this chapter have introduced the DfD editor. This is a fundamental feature of the process-oriented and data-oriented software development techniques discussed in Parts I and II.

F

CASE tutorial:

Data dictionary

F.1 Introduction

Every project created with the CASE tool will have an associated Data Dictionary. Any item you add to a project diagram will automatically be recorded in the Data Dictionary.

This tutorial will describe how to work with the most commonly used elements of the dictionary. There will be references to the dictionary throughout the rest of the tutorial chapters, so you may find it useful to refer back to these pages from time to time.

The exercises assume that you have installed the CASE tool as described in Appendix A, and are familiar with the basic operation of the software; the best way to gain such experience is to complete the general tutorial (Appendix D) before you attempt the exercises in this chapter.

The tutorial will use the sample project 'Bank Service Till' which will, by default, have been installed in the directory `c:\select\system\example`. You need to open this project before continuing.

F.2 Browsing the Data Dictionary

The **Dictionary** option **Browse** allows you to search the dictionary for an item. When you find the item you can **Edit** the information and check the **Usage** of the item on the diagrams.

For example, in the sample project:

Open CONTEXT.DAT
Open **Dictionary** menu
Select **Browse** option

Or use shortcut key   <CTRL> + <B>

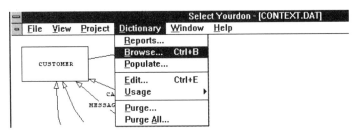

Dictionary menu.

See the **Dictionary Item Selector** box on-screen.

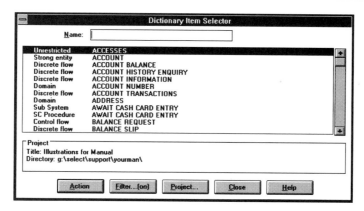

Dictionary menu.

F.2.1 Search

You can browse through the Data Dictionary in two ways:

- **Scroll bar**

  The scroll bar is on the right side of the dialog box. Use the up and down arrows on the bar to scroll one *entry* at a time.

  To scroll a *page* at a time, click in the scroll bar between the arrow and centre button.

  To go to the *top* or *bottom* of the Data Dictionary list, move the central button to the top or bottom of the scroll bar.

- **Alphabetical Search**

  Type the first letter of the item name that you want to find in the **Name** box. The list box will show the first item that starts with that letter. The more letters of a name that you type, the more specific the search will be.

F.2.2 Action

When you have selected a data item you can **Edit** it or check its **Usage** on the diagrams.

Select the discrete flow CASH

Choose *Action*

See a drop-down menu (the options **Edit** and **Usage** are described later in this section).

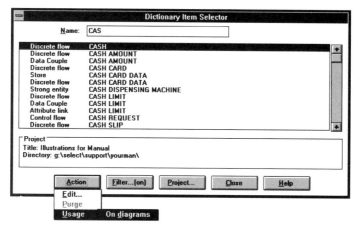

Action: Drop-down menus.

F.3 Type Filter

You can use a Type Filter to make your search for an item in the browse list easier.

> In *Dictionary Item Selector*
> Choose *Filter*

See the *Types Filter* box.

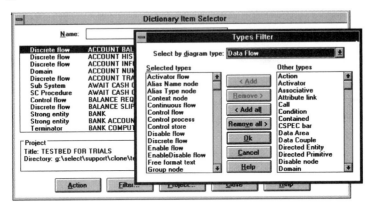

Types Filter box.

There are three lists in this box.

- **Selected Types**
  A list of all the types that will be included in your browse selection.
- **Other Types**
  A selection list of the names of all the other types used in the tool.
- **Select by Diagram Type**
  Choose a diagram type and add to **Selected Types** all the types that are supported by that diagram.

There is a range of command buttons in the box, these allow you to add and delete the names of types to the **Selected Types** list.

> Choose *Remove all*

See the **Selected Types** list is empty, all the types have been moved to the **Other Types** list.

F.3.1 Add

> In the **Other Types** list
> Select CONTEXT NODE
> Choose *Add*

The name Context Node is moved into the **Selected Types** list.

> Use *Add all* to add all the titles from the **Other Types** list.

F.3.2 Remove

> In the **Selected Types** list
> Select CONTEXT NODE
> Choose *Remove*

The name Context Node is moved into the **Other Types** list.

> Use *Remove all* to remove all the titles from the **Selected Types** list.

F.3.3 Select by Diagram Type

> In **Select by Diagram Type**
> Click on the down arrow

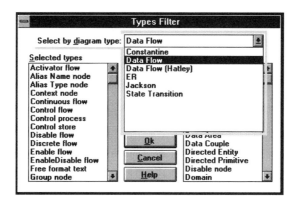

Select by Diagram Type.

From the list of diagrams
Choose DATA FLOW

All the types that are permitted in Data Flow diagrams are listed in *Selected Types*.

Now return to the *Dictionary Item Selector*.

Press *OK*

See that the *Dictionary Item Selector* only contains items which are listed as *Selected Types* (in this case, all the types supported by Data Flow diagrams).

F.4   Edit

Any object that has been created in a project will have a Dictionary entry. You can use the **Edit** option to access this dictionary through an appropriate dialog.

In the *Dictionary Item Selector*
Select the discrete flow CASH
Press *Action* button
From menu, choose **Edit**

See the *Discrete Flow Editor [Cash]* on-screen.

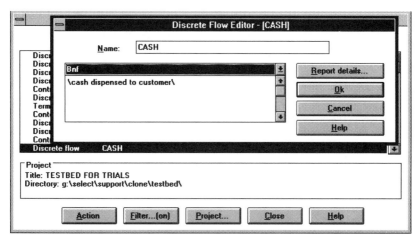

Discrete Flow Editor.

F.4.1 Editor

The Editor consists of:

- **Name panel**
  The box where the item is shown.

- **Command buttons**
  These allow you to save or cancel any changes.
  > If you choose ***Report details***
  > See a ***Preview of item report details*** on-screen.
  > (Reports are described later in this section)

- **Option list**
  In this example the line will show BNF.
  > Click on the scroll arrow
  > See an option list of the features of a Discrete Flow.

  Select an option and write or edit a description.

- **Text panel**
  In this panel (beneath the option) you can type or edit a description of the option you have selected.

  In this example the description of the BNF reads:

  ```
  cash dispensed to customer
  ```

  You can cut and paste text from the text panel of one option to the text panel of another option.

Use the shortcut keys:

Cut	\<CTRL> + \<X>
Copy	\<CTRL> + \<C>
Paste	\<CTRL> + \<V>

F.4.2 Purpose

The different uses of the editor will be described at the relevant point in the tutorial.

F.5 Usage

An object in the Data Dictionary may be used in one or more of the project diagrams.

The **Usage** option allows you to create and display a list of all the diagrams where a particular object is used. You can generate a list of the diagrams and open them.

> In the ***Dictionary Item Selector***
> Select the discrete flow CASH
> Press ***Action*** button
> From menu, select **Usage**
> Choose **On diagrams**

See a list of diagrams where the item is used.

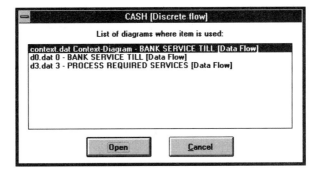

List of diagrams where item is used.

Select D3.DAT
Press *Open*

See the diagram D3.DAT on screen, the discrete flow CASH is used in this diagram as well as in the CONTEXT.DAT diagram where you began your search.

F.6   Purge

All items are placed in the Data Dictionary when they are first created. While you develop a project you may delete one of these objects from the diagram but, because it might be needed in another diagram in the project, SELECT Yourdon will not delete the entry from the data dictionary at that time.

When you review the contents of your Data Dictionary you may remove any unwanted entries; use the options **Purge** or **Purge All**.

Open CONTEXT.DAT
In **Dictionary** menu
Select **Purge**

See a *Dictionary Item Selector* box with a list of any unreferenced items. The letter 'u' at the start of the line confirms that these items are unreferenced.

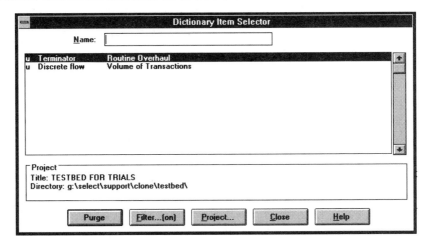

List of items to purge.

Select terminator ROUTINE OVERHAUL
Press *Purge*

ROUTINE OVERHAUL will disappear from the list and you can go on to purge another item, or press *Close* to return to the diagram.

F.6.1 Purge all

This is an option to carry out a purge of all unwanted Data Dictionary items across the whole project.

The **Purge All** option should be used with care because an item may have been added to the dictionary with the intention of linking to the diagram at a later occasion.

Open CONTEXT.DAT
In **Dictionary** menu
Select **Purge All**

See a *Project Selector* box, and check that you have specified the project which you want to purge.

Choose *Purge All*

See a message asking you to confirm that you want to carry out the purge.

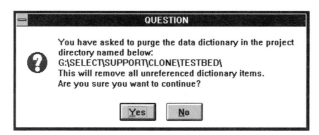

Confirmation – Purge All.

Choose *Yes*

The names of the unreferenced items will be flashed on the status line as they are purged from the dictionary.

After the purge you will be sent back to the diagram.

F.7 Populate

New items placed on a diagram will automatically be entered into the Data Dictionary.

Items can also be entered directly into the Data Dictionary by the user. This is known as 'populating the dictionary'.

If the item is to appear on the diagram you can add it later. First draw the symbol, and then add the name through the Dictionary browser.

Open CONTEXT.DAT
From the **Dictionary** menu
Choose **Populate**

See a *Project Selector* box and check that you are working on the correct project.

Choose **Populate**

See the *Add New Items into Dictionary* dialog box.

Add New Items into Dictionary.

> From the *Type* list
> Select STORE
> Choose *Add*

The *Store Editor* dialog box will come on-screen.

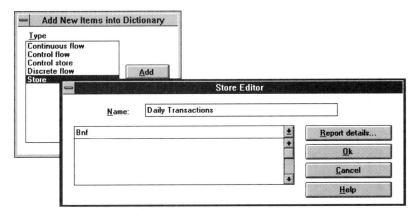

Store Editor.

> In the *Name* box
> Type DAILY TRANSACTIONS
> Choose *OK*

See a confirmation message telling you that the item has been successfully added to the dictionary.

> Choose *OK*

F.7.1 Purpose

The *Item Editors* will be described fully at the relevant point in the tutorial; but note that, whenever possible, you should add the dictionary definitions at the same time that you add the item to the dictionary.

F.8 Reports

Reports are text files based on the contents of the Data Dictionary. When you have generated a report you can view it on-screen, add it to your REPORT.LOG, put it in the clipboard or print it out.

> Open CONTEXT.DAT
> In **Dictionary** menu

Select **Reports**

See the *Report Generator* on-screen.

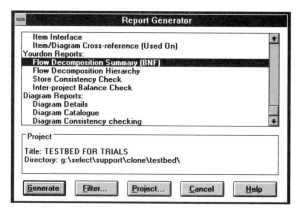

Report Generator.

This is a drop-down list of titles of all the reports that can be generated. To help you view the range, the titles are indented under group headings.

You move through the list by using the scroll bar or the filter.

In the *Report Generator*
Select FLOW DECOMPOSITION SUMMARY (BNF)
Choose *Generate*

See *Preview of Report* window, you can scroll through the report on-screen or you can save it to the REPORT.LOG file.

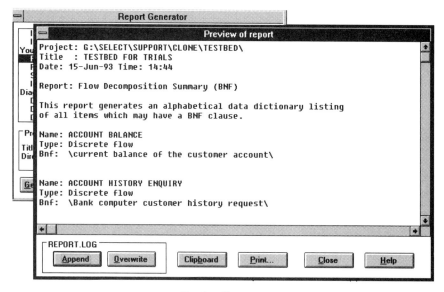

Preview Report.

- **REPORT.LOG**
  In this panel you can choose *Append* to add the report to the REPORT.LOG file or choose *Overwrite* to write over any material that is in the log.

The REPORT.LOG file is always written to your work directory.

- **Clipboard**
  Choose *Clipboard* and copy the report into the Windows **Clipboard** so it can be loaded into another Windows-supported application, such as a word processor.
- **Print**
  Choose *Print* and print out a copy of the report.

When you have finished *viewing, transferring* or *printing* the report:

Choose *Close*.

F.8.1 Filter reports

In the same way that you filter the list of items for a dictionary browse, you can filter the items that are run through the *Report Generator*.

In the *Report Generator*
Choose **Filter ... [on]**
In the *Types Filter* box
Add STORE to *Selected Types* list

See that STORE is the only type selected

Choose *OK*
In the *Report Generator*
Select FLOW DECOMPOSITION SUMMARY (BNF)
Choose *Generate*

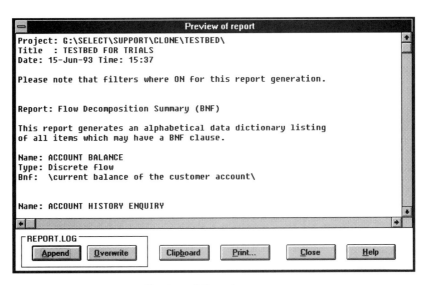

Preview of filtered reports.

View a report similar to the one you have just generated but showing information that only refers to Stores.

F.8.2 Multiple selection

Instead of running each report on its own, you can select a number of reports at the same time so that they are generated together.

- **Select one report**
  Click the report name

- **Select a number of different reports**
  Click the first name
  Hold down <CTRL>
  Click on each other name in turn.

- **Select a block of reports**
  Click the first name in the block
  Hold down <SHIFT>
  Click the last name in the block.

F.9   Conclusions

The exercises in this appendix have introduced the data dictionary editor. This is a fundamental feature of all the software development techniques discussed in the book.

G

CASE tutorial:

Process specifications

This tutorial explores the creation and editing of process specifications (PSpecs) using the CASE tool.

The exercises assume that you have installed the CASE tool as described in Appendix A, and are familiar with the basic operation of the software; the best way to gain such experience is to complete the general tutorial (Appendix D) before you attempt the exercises in this chapter.

The tutorial will use the sample project 'Bank Service Till' which will, by default, have been installed in the directory `c:\select\system\example`. You need to open this project before continuing.

G.1   Opening an existing PSpec

A PSpec consists of two sections: a header (I/O specification) and a body (processing description). All dataflows listed in the header must be referenced in the body. The process is usually defined using Structured English or a similar syntax.

You can open an existing PSpec in the sample project as follows:

Open diagram D3.DAT
Click on the process box ORDER CHEQUE BOOK FROM BANK
From the menu, select **Child**
Choose **Open**

See the PSpec P31.DAT (ORDER CHEQUE BOOK FROM BANK)

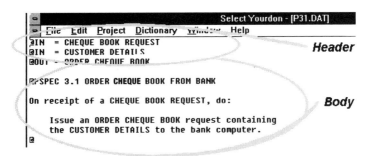

Existing process specification.

G.1.1 Header

The following statement types are in the header:

- *flowname*
  Indicates a flow into the process

G.1.2 Body

The following statement types are in the body:

> @*PSPEC file title*
> Marks the start of the body section

The file title is copied by the system from the name of the parent diagram. You may use Structured English (or some other appropriate notation) to describe the required processing.

> @
> Marks the end of the body section and of the PSPEC

Close file D3.DAT

G.1.3 Delete a PSpec

> From SELECT Yourdon opening window
> Select **File** menu
> Choose **Delete**

> In the *Diagram File Selector* box.
> Select file P31.DAT
> Choose **Delete**

> Choose **Yes**

The PSpec file is deleted.

G.2 Creating a new PSpec

> Open D3.DAT
> Click on the process ORDER CHEQUE BOOK FROM BANK
> From the menu, select **Child**
> Select **Open**
> Choose **New**

Create New Diagram box.

> In *Create New Diagram* dialog box
> Type P31 as *Filename*
> Select PSpec as the *Type of diagram*
> Choose *Create*

See the PSpec P31.DAT on-screen, the statements in it have been generated by the system.

```
┌─────────────────────────────────────────────────────────┐
│ ─                       Select Yourdon - [P31.DAT]        │
│ ─│ File  Edit  Project  Dictionary  Window  Help          │
│ @IN  = CHEQUE BOOK REQUEST                                │
│ @IN  = CUSTOMER DETAILS                                   │
│ @OUT = ORDER CHEQUE BOOK                                  │
│                                                           │
│ @PSPEC ORDER CHEQUE BOOK FROM BANK                        │
│ -- CHEQUE BOOK REQUEST                                    │
│ -- CUSTOMER DETAILS                                       │
│ -- ORDER CHEQUE BOOK                                      │
│ @                                                         │
```

New process specification.

G.2.1   Edit the body

The Open P32.DAT
At the line – CHEQUE BOOK REQUEST
Delete the sign –
Type:

On receipt of a CHEQUE BOOK REQUEST, do:

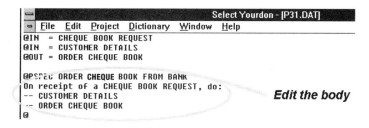

```
┌─────────────────────────────────────────────────────────┐
│ ─                       Select Yourdon - [P31.DAT]        │
│ ─│ File  Edit  Project  Dictionary  Window  Help          │
│ @IN  = CHEQUE BOOK REQUEST                                │
│ @IN  = CUSTOMER DETAILS                                   │
│ @OUT = ORDER CHEQUE BOOK                                  │
│                                                           │
│ @PSPEC ORDER CHEQUE BOOK FROM BANK                        │
│ On receipt of a CHEQUE BOOK REQUEST, do:      Edit the body│
│ -- CUSTOMER DETAILS                                       │
│ -- ORDER CHEQUE BOOK                                      │
│ @                                                         │
```

Edit a PSpec.

Copy the other details that appeared on the original P31.DAT.

G.3   Checking a PSpec

From the **File** menu
Choose **Check**

See the check report in *Preview of diagram consistency checks* box.
SELECT Yourdon will check the PSpec for the following details:

- All input and output flows on the parent process must appear in the header section.

- The direction of flows in the header section must be defined as the same as on the parent process.

- All flows in the header section must be used in the processing in the same way as described in the body section.

- The system will not be able to check Structured English to verify the direction of the flows in the processing description. You must read the description to make the check.
Close the *Preview of diagram consistency checks* box.

G.4   Conclusions

The exercises in this chapter have introduced the PSpec. PSpecs are a fundamental feature of all the software development techniques discussed in the book.

CASE tutorial:

State transition diagrams

H.1   Introduction

In the following exercises you will use the state transition diagram (STD) editor of the CASE tool.

The exercises assume that you have installed the CASE tool as described in Appendix A, and are familiar with the basic operation of the software; the best way to gain such experience is to complete the general tutorial (Appendix D) before you attempt the exercises in this chapter.

The tutorial will use the sample project 'Bank Service Till' which will, by default, have been installed in the directory `c:\select\system\example`. You need to open this project before continuing.

H.2   Opening an existing STD

Like other editors in the CASE tool, the state transition diagram editor is based on nodes and flows. States are represented by nodes; transitions between states are represented by flows.

In the following examples you will look at state transition diagram S5.DAT, which is a child of dataflow diagram D0.DAT in the Example project.

Open the Example project
Select **File** menu
Choose **Open**
In the *Diagram File Selector*
Select S5.DAT
Choose *Open*

See diagram S5.DAT on-screen.

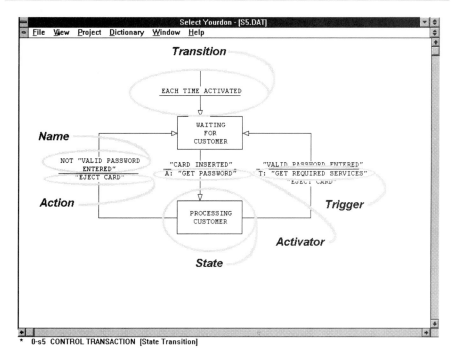

State transition diagram.

H.3   Edit STD

Before you start the following exercises, print a copy of the diagram. This will help you to restore it after you have finished the editing practice.

H.3.1   State

A state represents a stable condition for a system. The name of a state describes its behaviour, for example: WAITING FOR CUSTOMER.

> With S5.DAT on-screen
> Click on the empty space to the right of EACH TIME ACTIVATED
>
> From the menu, choose **State**
> In **Enter Name**, type OUT OF SERVICE

See a new state has been added to the diagram.

> Click on state WAITING FOR CUSTOMER
> From menu, choose **Add Flow**

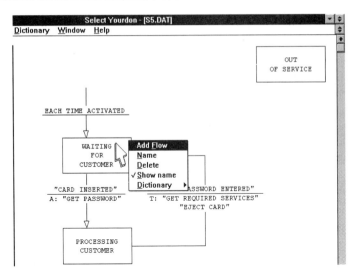

New State added.

Link the flow to state OUT OF SERVICE
In **Enter Name**, type OUT OF CASH

See the transition OUT OF CASH drawn on the diagram.

*At this point you may use **Auto-zoom** to redraw the diagram and allow yourself some more space.*

H.3.2   Transition

A transition indicates the movement from one state to another state. A condition is the event, or events, which cause the transition to occur.

In SELECT Yourdon the name of a transition describes the condition which causes the transition, for example: EACH TIME ACTIVATED.

With S5.DAT on-screen
Click on transition OUT OF CASH

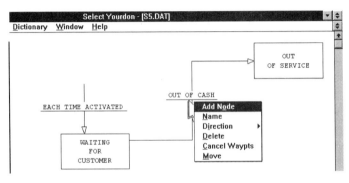

Transition menu.

From the menu, select **Add Node**

See the Node menu. From this menu you can choose the type of node that you want to associate with the transition.

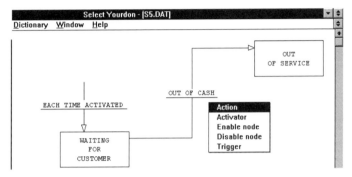

Node menu.

H.3.3   Action

An action is an operation that takes place as the transition occurs. In SELECT Yourdon, an action is recorded as a node that is associated with a transition.

The name of an action is a description of some activity that should be performed. If the action corresponds to an output control flow on the parent, the action name should be written within double quotation marks, for example: NOT "VALID PASSWORD ENTERED". (This will ensure that the diagram will be consistent with the parent when a check report is generated.)

An action may contain a signal, which must be written between double quotation marks, for example: "EJECT CARD".

H.3.4   Trigger

A trigger is a type of process control which causes the specified process to be executed once.

If the diagram is to be consistent with its parent, the name of the trigger must consist of the process name written between double quotation marks.

From the Node menu
Choose **Trigger**

See an *Enter Name* box for you to write the name of the trigger.

In *Enter Name*, type "CLOSE DOWN"

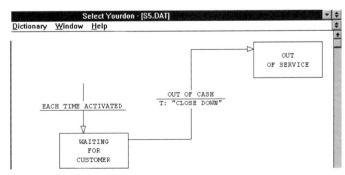

Create new trigger.

On the diagram a trigger is shown with the letter T: as a prefix,
for example: T: "CLOSE DOWN"

H.3.5 Enable/disable

The enable and disable flows represent the types of process control flows which cause a process
to be turned on or off.

Diagram conventions:

- Prefix E: represents Enable
- Prefix D: represents Disable.

H.3.6 Activator

An activator is another type of process switch that is state-specific, that is: the specified process
is an activity performed during a particular state. On the diagram an activator is shown with the
letter A: as a prefix, for example: A: "GET PASSWORD".

H.4 Check STD

If the STD is to check for consistency with its parent, you must verify the following:

- Each state must have a unique name.
- Each state must have an input flow.
- All input control flows on a control process must be present as conditions on the STD.
- All output control flows on a parent node must be present as actions on the STD.
- All flow names and process names that appear on the STD must be written between double quotation marks.
- All flow names and process names that appear on both the STD and the parent must be written in the same type case. (For simplicity, type all the names in CAPITALS.)

H.4.1 Run check

With S5.DAT on-screen
Select **File** menu
Choose **Check**

Wait, then see ***Preview of diagram consistency checks***.

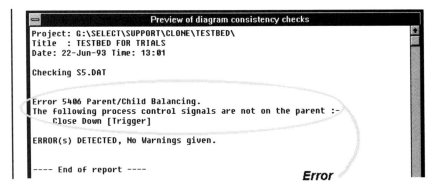

Check report shows an error.

In this example the report says that the process control signal CLOSE DOWN [TRIGGER] is not
on the parent.

This inconsistency happened because you made an alteration to a diagram that is itself the decomposition of another diagram.

You were instructed to type the name of the trigger inside double quotation marks ("CLOSE DOWN") but this assumed that the process control already existed in the parent diagram.

To make your diagram balance you must either amend the parent diagram or edit the node.

H.4.2 Amend parent

With S5.DAT on-screen
Select **File** menu
Select **Parent**
Choose **Open**

See dataflow diagram D0.DAT (the parent of S5.DAT) on-screen.

In D0.DAT
Add a Process CLOSE DOWN
Link CONTROL TRANSACTION to CLOSE DOWN with a trigger

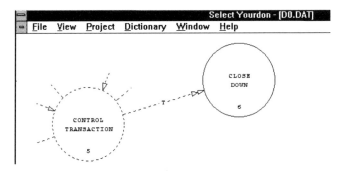

Amend parent diagram.

Open S5.DAT and run the **Check** procedure again; the check report will say that there are no errors.

At the end of the exercise, open D0.DAT and delete CLOSE DOWN.

H.4.3 Edit node

With S5.DAT on-screen
Click on the trigger name CLOSE DOWN

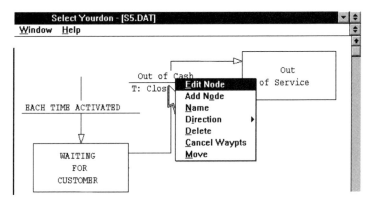

Edit Node menu.

From the menu, select **Edit Node**
Choose **Name**

In **Enter Name**, delete "CLOSE DOWN" and type CLOSE DOWN
Choose **OK**

You have removed the quotation marks because the trigger does not appear on the parent diagram.

Now run the **Check** procedure again; the check report will say that there are no errors.

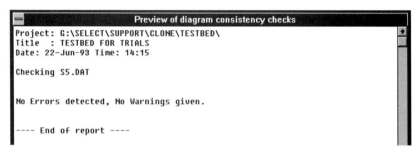

```
─────     Preview of diagram consistency checks      ─────
Project: G:\SELECT\SUPPORT\CLONE\TESTBED\
Title  : TESTBED FOR TRIALS
Date: 22-Jun-93 Time: 14:15

Checking S5.DAT


No Errors detected, No Warnings given.


---- End of report ----
```

Check report, no errors.

H.5 Create STD

You can start to create a new STD from one of two places:

- as a new diagram that you can link, later, with a control process;
- as the child of a control process on a dataflow diagram.

H.5.1   New diagram

Run SELECT Yourdon.

In **File** menu
Select **New**

In **Create New Diagram**
Type BUILDST as **Filename**
Select STATE TRANSITION as **Diagram type**
Choose **Create**

Create new diagram.

Open file BUILDST.DAT

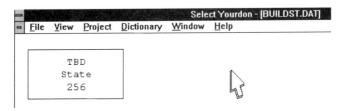

First state on a new screen.

The new state is given the default name TBD.

Click on TBD
From the menu, choose **Name**

In *Enter Name*
Type a new name: WAITING FOR CLIENT

Move the state WAITING FOR CLIENT into the centre of the screen.

Click on the empty space and see a pop-up state menu.

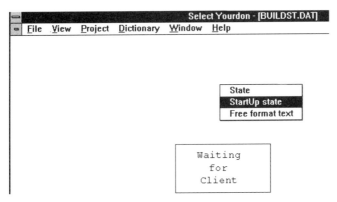

State menu.

Choose **State**
In *Enter Name* box type *state name*

See a new state created on the diagram.

H.5.2 StartUp State

A start-up state represents the initial state of a system as it is switched on. The symbol for a start-up state will disappear from the diagram as soon as it is connected to a transition. Only one start-up state is allowed on an STD.

In this exercise you will link a start-up state to an existing state.

In file BUILDST.DAT
Click in the empty space above WAITING FOR CLIENT
From the menu, choose **StartUp State**

See the start-up state symbol (a small square) on-screen.

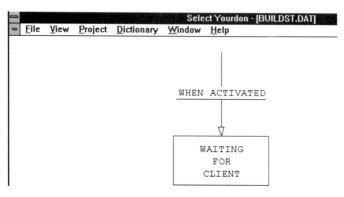

Start-up state linked to state.

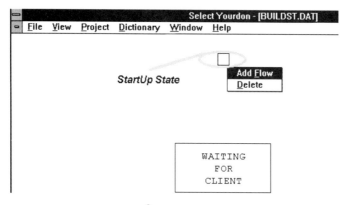

Start-up state.

Click on the start-up symbol
From the menu, choose **Add Flow**

Link the transition to WAITING FOR CLIENT
In **Enter Name**, type WHEN ACTIVATED

See the transition WHEN ACTIVATED linked from a start-up state (that is, from outside the diagram) to the state WAITING FOR CLIENT.

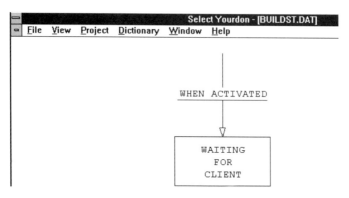

Start-up state linked to state.

Practise adding states and transitions to the diagram, check the consistency of the diagram to ensure that you are following the rules of SELECT Yourdon.

Remember to delete the diagram BUILDST.DAT when you have finished practising with it.

H.5.3   New child diagram

The next exercise will ask you to delete an existing STD diagram.

Before you delete any diagrams you may want to take the following precautions:
(1)   Make a print of S5.DAT diagram.
(2)   Make a clone copy of the existing example project.

In the cloned copy of your project
Delete file S5.DAT.

Use **Purge All** to remove any unwanted references from the dictionary.

Open diagram D0.DAT
Click on CONTROL TRANSACTION
From the menu, select **Child**
Choose **Open**

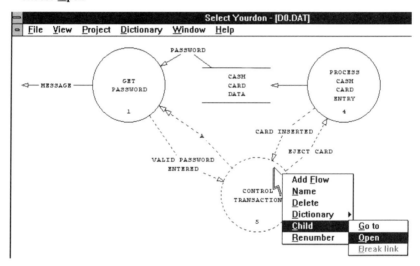

Child menu.

See the question asking if you want to create a new child diagram.

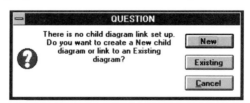

Question: Create new child?

In the *Question* box
Choose *New*

In *Create New Diagram*
Type STD01 as **Filename**

Select STATE TRANSITION as *Type of Diagram*
Choose **Create**

See a new STD diagram, STD01.DAT, on-screen.

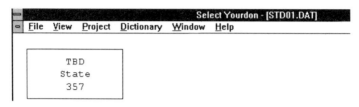

New diagram.

At first the new child diagram has the same appearance as the diagram you created as a NewDiagram. You can continue to develop STD01.DAT in the same way that you developed BUILDST.DAT.

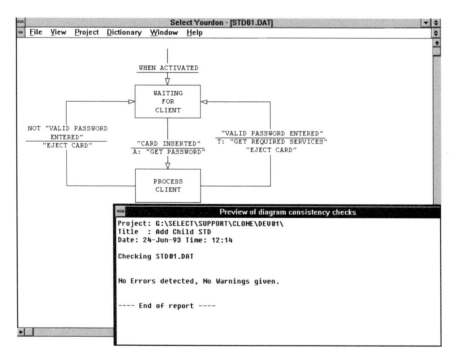

New diagram, fully developed and balanced.

H.6   Parent to child links

You may find it necessary to break a link that exists between a parent and a child diagram, you may also want to set up a link between a parent diagram and another diagram that already exists.

In these exercises you will, first, break the link between the DfD and the STD that you have just created; then you will set the link up again.

H.6.1 Break link

With the diagram STD01.DAT on-screen

Select **File** menu
Choose **Parent**

See diagram D0.DAT on-screen

Click on control process CONTROL TRANSACTION
From the menu, select **Child**
Select **Break Link**

See a message asking if you want to break the link.

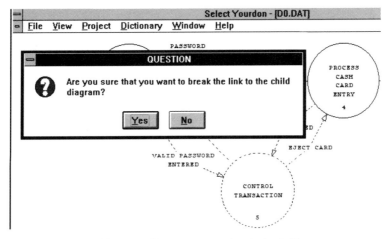

Question: Do you want to break the link?

In the **Question** box
Choose **Yes**

You have broken the link between the two diagrams; if you want to confirm the fact, use the **Child, Go** to option, and see the message that says there is no child diagram link.

H.6.2 Create link

See diagram D0.DAT on-screen

Click on control process CONTROL TRANSACTION
From the menu, select **Child**
Select **Go** to

In the **Question** box
Choose **Existing**

In the **Diagram File Selector**
Select STD01.DAT
Choose **Goto**

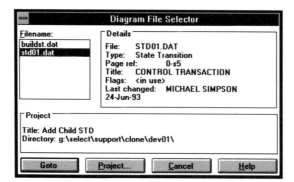

Diagram File Selector.

The diagram STD01.DAT comes on-screen. You have set up a link with its parent, D0.DAT.

Do not forget to delete the cloned project when you have finished practising with it.

H.7 Conclusions

The exercises in this chapter have introduced the STD editor, used in the process-oriented and data-oriented software development techniques discussed in Parts I and II.

CASE tutorial:

Structure charts

I.I   Introduction

A Constantine structure chart can be used to show the architecture, or calling structure, of modules within a project. Such structure charts are based on nodes and flows in a similar way to a dataflow diagram. The nodes are various types of module, and the flows are calls between modules. At the code level, the modules may represent either ordinary functions or member functions.

The exercises assume that you have installed the CASE tool as described in Appendix A, and are familiar with the basic operation of the software; the best way to gain such experience is to complete the general tutorial (Appendix D) before you attempt the exercises in this chapter.

The tutorial will use the sample project 'Bank Service Till' which will, by default, have been installed in the directory `c:\select\system\example`. You need to open this project before continuing.

I.2   Overview

The main components of Constantine structure charts are described in this section.

I.2.1   Modules

- **Module**
  Represents some application-specific function.

- **Sub-system**
  Represents some predefined function, perhaps within the operating system, or language environment.

- **Library**
  Represents a predefined function that may be used across many applications.

- **Contained**
  Represents an in-line function.

- **Data area**
  Represents module that defines data only.

I.2.2   Calls

Calls may be either sequential (solid line), or parallel (dashed line).

You will notice that, because Sub-system and Library modules represent predefined functions, you will not be able to show calling below these modules on the diagram.

I.2.3 Condition

Used to show conditional calls.

The Condition diamond is a node, and you can draw calls to and from the node.

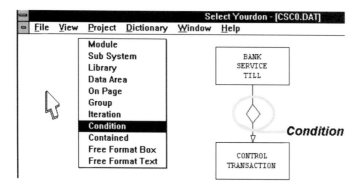

Conditional node.

I.2.4 Iteration

Used to show iterative calls.

The Iteration loop is a node, and you can draw calls to and from the node.

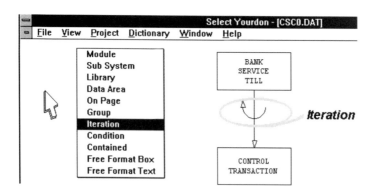

Iteration node.

I.2.5 On-page Connector

Used to avoid crossing call lines on the diagram.

The On-page Connector is a node, and you can draw calls to and from the node.

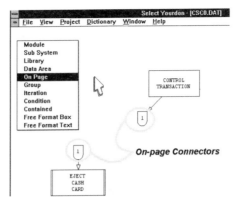

On-page Connectors.

I.2.6   Data Couples and Flags

Data Couples and Flags represent data and control information passed between modules, for example, as parameters.

I.2.7   Decomposition

Modules, Sub-systems, and Library modules may all be decomposed to'child' diagrams.

I.3   Opening an existing structure chart

At the SELECT Yourdon opening window
Select **File** menu
Choose **Open**

In the *Diagram File Selector*
Select CSC0.DAT
Choose *Open*

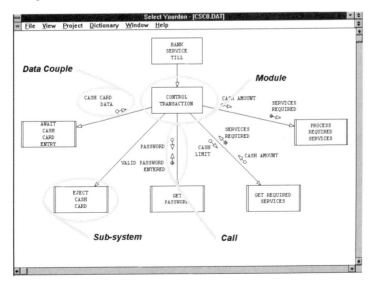

Constantine structure chart.

I.4 Editing a structure chart

If you need basic information on adding, moving and deleting nodes and flows on a diagram, refer to Appendix D.

I.4.1 Adding a data couple

Before you carry out this exercise, make a print of the diagram so that you can restore it later to its original state.

Open CSC0.DAT
Delete the call between
CONTROL TRANSACTION and AWAIT CASH CARD ENTRY

See the diagram with no link between CONTROL TRANSACTION and AWAIT CASH CARD ENTRY.

Click on CONTROL TRANSACTION
From the menu, choose **Add Flow**

Link CONTROL TRANSACTION and AWAIT CASH CARD ENTRY with a call.

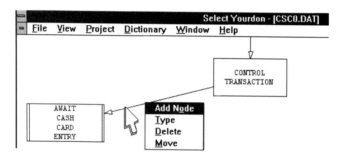

Add Flow to a diagram.

Click on the call
From the menu, select **Add Node**
From the second menu, select **Data Couple**
From the third menu, choose **Output**

In *Enter Name*, type CASH CARD DATA
Choose **OK**

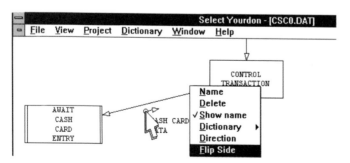

Choose Flip side.

See the data couple CASH CARD DATA drawn on the lower side of the call line. For convenience, you may wish to show the data couple on the other side of the call line.

Click on data couple CASH CARD DATA
From the menu, choose **Flip side**

The data couple will appear on the upper side of the call line.

I.5   Checking a structure chart

Any structure chart can be checked using the **File, Check** option on the menu bar.
The following checks are performed on Constantine structure charts:

I.5.1 Name check

● No modules should still be carrying TBD (to be determined) names.

I.5.2 Node I/O Check

● All nodes must be connected using call flows.

I.5.3 On-page Connector check

● All On-page Connectors must have a matching opposite number on the same diagram.

You will see the check report in the *Preview of Diagram Consistency Checks dialog* box.

I.6   Conclusions

The exercises in this chapter have introduced the structure chart editor. This is a fundamental feature of all the software development techniques discussed in the book.

CASE tutorial:

Entity-relationship diagrams and class-relationship diagrams

J.1 Introduction

In the following exercises you will use the entity-relationship diagram (ERD) and class-relationship diagram (CRD) editor of the CASE tool.

The exercises assume that you have installed the CASE tool as described in Appendix A, and are familiar with the basic operation of the software; the best way to gain such experience is to complete the general tutorial (Appendix D) before you attempt the exercises in this chapter.

The tutorial will use the sample project 'Bank Service Till' which will, by default, have been installed in the directory `c:\select\system\example`. You need to open this project before continuing.

J.2 ERD overview

The components of an entity-relationship diagram (ERD) are **entities** and **relationships** which are connected by **entity links**. The (ERD) editor in the CASE tool supports the Chen method.

ERDs are used for modelling the stored data required within a system, and are useful for analysis and design of relational databases.

The ERD editor is based on the idea of nodes and flows. The nodes represent the entities and relationships and the flows represent the entity links. ERDs can be decomposed into **attribute** and **decomposition** diagrams by using a parent to child structure.

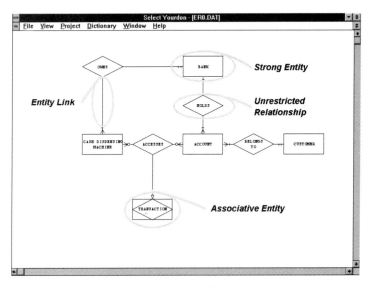

Entity-relationship diagram.

J.3 Editing ERDs

The ERD editor is a context-sensitive working environment, similar to that used in the DfD editor. This means that when you click on an object (or in free space) a pop-up menu of relevant options will appear on the diagram.

For more information on working with nodes and flows, refer to Manipulate a Diagram.

The following illustration shows what happens when you click in open space in the example project ER0.DAT diagram.

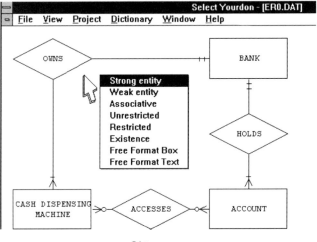

Object menu.

J.4   Creating ERDs

In this exercise you will create a child Attribute diagram from a Strong Entity.

> From the SELECT Yourdon opening window
> Select **File** menu
>
> Choose **Open**
> In the *Diagram File Selector*, select ER0.DAT
> Choose **Open**

See the ER0.DAT diagram on-screen.

> Click on CUSTOMER
> From the menu, select **Child**

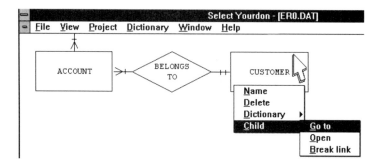

Child menu.

> Choose **Open**

See a *Question* dialog box which gives two options of creating a new child diagram.

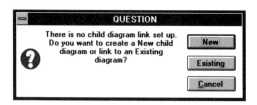

Create child diagram.

- **New**
  Allows you to create a new diagram.
- **Existing**
  Allows you to make a link with a diagram that has already been created.

> Choose **New**

See *Create New Diagram* box

> Type ER2 as *Filename*
> Select ER as *Type of Diagram*
> Choose **Create**

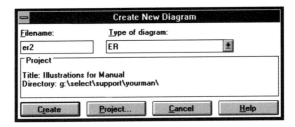

Create New Diagram box.

In *Choose a diagram sub-type* box
Select <u>A</u>*ttribute diagram*
Choose *OK*

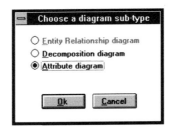

Choose a diagram sub-type.

The child diagram ER2.DAT will be generated showing the Strong Entity box CUSTOMER.

J.5 Developing ERDs

Attributes in an ERD are represented as links between the entity and the domains. All the attribute links have a cardinal value at each end.

In this exercise you will link domains to an entity.

J.5.1 Create domain

Open ER2.DAT
Move the box CUSTOMER to the centre of the screen

Click in the open space below and to the left of customer
From the menu, choose **Domain**

In *Enter Name*, type NAME
Choose *OK*

The domain box NAME will appear on-screen.

J.5.2 Create Attribute Links

Open ER2.DAT
Click on domain box NAME
From the menu, choose **Add <u>F</u>low**
Drag the flow to CUSTOMER

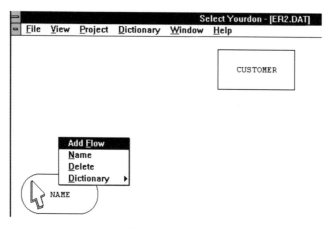

Add Flow menu.

See a menu of cardinality options. Make your choice for the domain end of the link first, then make your choice for the entity end.

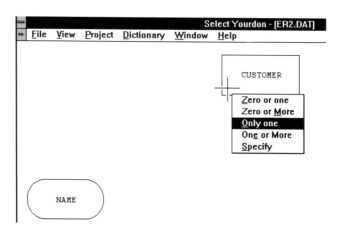

Cardinality menu.

> From the cardinality menu
> Select **Only one**

See the menu appear again.

> Select **Only one**
> In the **Enter Name** box
> Type CUSTOMER NAME
> Choose **OK**

See the link between CUSTOMER and NAME drawn in the diagram.

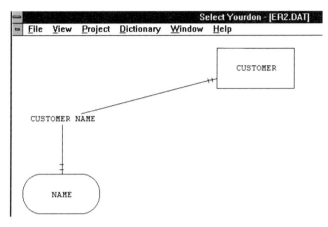

Link drawn.

Use the same procedure to add more domains called ADDRESS, STERLING AMOUNT, and OCCUPATION.

Insert the links between the domains and the entity making them all **Only one** links.
Name the links as follows:

CUSTOMER ADDRESS for DOMAIN ADDRESS
CUSTOMER OCCUPATION for DOMAIN OCCUPATION
CUSTOMER SALARY for DOMAIN STERLING AMOUNT
CUSTOMER CREDIT RATING also for DOMAIN STERLING AMOUNT.

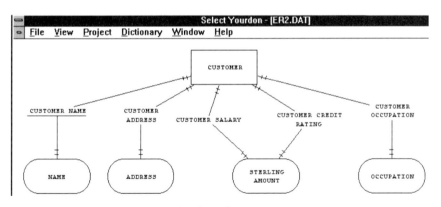

Attribute diagram.

J.5.3 Prime attribute

A prime attribute is an attribute that can be used as a key for a set of attributes. On the diagram, a prime attribute is <u>underlined</u>. Any attribute can be used as the prime attribute.

Open ER2.DAT
Click on attribute CUSTOMER NAME
From the menu, choose **Prime toggle**

See the words CUSTOMER NAME are now underlined.

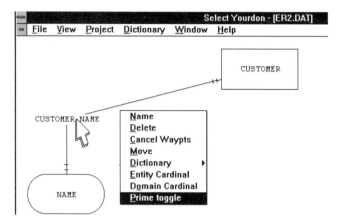

Prime attribute selected.

J.5.4 Check attribute diagram

An attribute diagram must contain a prime attribute. If it does not, the check report will warn you of the omission.

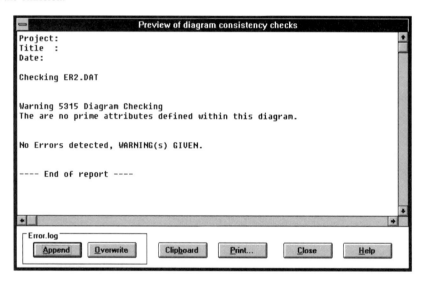

Error report.

J.6 CRDs are 'a kind of' ERD

Class diagrams are a form of entity-relationship diagram, and are created using the same editor in the case tool.

J.7 Conclusions

The exercises in this chapter have introduced the ERD and CRD editor. The use of ERDs is a fundamental feature of the data-oriented software development techniques discussed in Part II, while the CRD is a fundamental tool for object-oriented software development (described in Part III).

APPENDIX

K The origins of SADIE

K.1 Introduction

The first printing of this book ('Edition 1.0') resulted in a number of enquiries about the origins of SADIE. This short appendix has therefore been added to the first reprint ('Edition 1.1') in order to provide some additional information about the roots of the methodology.

K.2 The origins of ISE

In the mid 1980s, Bob Damper and I began work at the University of Southampton on what was to become a long series of detailed computer simulations of areas of the human auditory nervous system. These simulations form one small part of an international effort aimed at improving understanding of the mechanisms of human hearing, and – hence – of developing new ways of alleviating the symptoms of various disorders, including tinnitus, age-related hearing loss, and noise-induced hearing damage (see Pont and Damper, 1991, for further details of this work).

As the simulations grew more detailed, the project expanded and moved first to the University of Sheffield and then to the University of Leicester. As the research section increased in size, more of my time was consumed managing the project, and trying to ensure that the designs, and code, from different team members was compatible with the rest of the elaborate 'jigsaw'. I therefore began to investigate a range of existing software engineering methodologies to see whether these could be used to assist this work. It did not take long to discover that he great majority of existing methodologies support only a single approach: for example, the Yourdon method (Yourdon, 1989) supports process-oriented (P-O) software development, the Chen method (Chen, 1976) supports data-oriented (D-O) development, while the Booch method (Booch, 1994) supports object-oriented (O-O) software development. At the time, there were no methodologies for agent-oriented (A-O) development (but see Pont and Moreale, 1996).

What seemed particularly curious was that many proponents of an O-O approach appeared to make the assumption that, now that 'objects' had been 'discovered', every software team would, overnight, convert to an O-O approach. By contrast, while my research section was indeed working with objects, we were also still developing new simulations using P-O and D-O techniques, as well as looking for ways of maintaining existing systems developed using these 'traditional' approaches. Where we found O-O methodologies particularly lacking was in their support for the integration of traditionally-constructed systems into O-O environments without re-writing all the underlying FORTRAN, C or COBOL code. We also found little support for 'reverse-engineering' existing systems to ease the migration into an O-O or A-O environment where this was felt to be necessary or desirable.

On further investigation, I came to the conclusion that what was needed was a single 'common toolbox' that would support the full range of software projects my research section was involved with. I was already experienced with CASE technology, and was convinced of its value. It was therefore my intention to use the same CASE tool when working, for example, on embedded (process-oriented) systems, implemented in C; on decision support (data-oriented) projects, implemented in SQL and C++; on desktop (object-oriented) systems, implemented in C++ (and using the Microsoft Foundation Class library); and on (agent-oriented) applications for the World Wide Web, implemented in Java.

Since none of the existing methodologies fitted these needs, I assembled the Integrated Software Engineering (ISE) methodology in 1991 (Figure K.1). As with SADIE (see p.11), a major strength of ISE is that much of it has been inspired by, and adapted from, a range of previous methodologies: put another way, where there was a perfectly good wheel in existence, I saw no benefit in creating a new one.

What is new about this methodology is its integrated nature: this provides two particular benefits:

1.   There is a common toolbox, so that all members of a team or company, whatever type of project they are presently working on (P-O, D-O, O-O or A-O), can become familiar with all the tools, and are able to share CASE support.

2.   There is a common repository, for code and designs from all projects, greatly simplifying the processes of method migration (e.g. conversion of a P-O design into an O-O design, or vice versa), and reverse engineering (of code and designs).

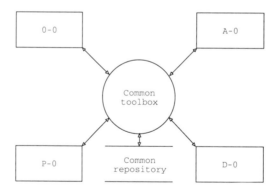

Figure K.1   An overview of the ISE methodology.

Since 1991, the methodology has been refined through the experience of my research section on a wider range of projects. For example, we continue to develop systems in the field of hearing research, and have successfully used ISE in this work (e.g. Pont and Wong, 1994; Sewell and Pont, forthcoming). The methodology has also been applied to good effect in recent medical diagnostic systems on which we have worked (e.g. Jones *et al.*1995).

ISE was created to support the activities of my research section. However, because we found the methodology effective, we began discussing it in the training courses and consultancy activities we ran beyond the confines of Leicester University. As we did so, it became increasingly apparent that software engineers from a range of different backgrounds had experienced similar problems with 'single track' methodologies, and that they too found the integrated nature of ISE valuable. I therefore decided to make the details of ISE available more widely, via this book.

K.3 SADIE versus ISE

This book has described a simplified version of ISE which has been referred to as 'Simple Analysis, Design & Implementation' (SADIE). There are two reasons why I opted not to discuss the full version of ISE here:

1. I see the main audience for the present textbook as university and college students. For such an audience, I find that the 'code first' approach described in this book is effective. By contrast, ISE takes a 'management first' approach, and attaches greater importance to issues such as software size prediction (see Section K.6) and software metrics. In my experience, students – unfamiliar with the problems experienced on large-scale projects – find the importance of management topics less easy to grasp on first exposure to any methodology: the 'code first' approach of SADIE therefore forms a useful basis for early university teaching. Similarly, I find that the techniques of process migration and agent-oriented development are confusing for students on introductory courses: these features were therefore omitted from SADIE. However, having been introduced to software engineering via SADIE, I find that students very quickly adapt to ISE in more advanced classes.

2. As will be clear from the body of the text, I believe that CASE tools are an important component of modern software development activity. I believe that it is particularly important that students (as has already been stated, the main audience for the present textbook) on computer science or software engineering courses have the opportunity to use CASE tools. For a range of technical and legal reasons it was not possible, at the time this book was first planned, to offer the 'ISE Tool' which we use on our own projects with this book. I therefore arranged with SELECT Software Tools to make available their 'Yourdon' product. Some slight adjustments were made to 'Simple ISE' to render it compatible with the tool: the result was SADIE, as described in this book.

Overall, ISE builds on SADIE rather than replacing it (Figure K.2).

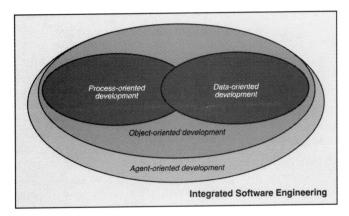

Figure K.2 ISE builds on SADIE, providing (among other features) support for agent-oriented (A-O) development. The A-O approach is described in detail in a technical report available on the CD (Pont and Moreale, 1996).

K.4 An overview of the analysis phase of O-O ISE

The simple six-stage analysis process for O-O development using ISE is outlined below. As will be apparent, the method builds on the simple approach described in Part III.

I 1. **The external objects**

The external objects are identified.

I 2. **The logical interaction ('conversation') diagrams**

An interaction diagram is created, embodying a 'walkthrough'.

I 3. **The system and external messages**

The messages to which the system must respond are identified.

I 4. **The message domain diagram**

The message domain diagram is produced.

I 5. **The data domain diagram**

The data domain diagram is produced.

I 6. **Software size prediction**

The above diagrams may be used to make an initial estimate of the software size, and – hence – the system cost.

To provide an example of the use of O-O ISE, the ATM system (first introduced in Chapter 16) is considered again below.

K.4.1 The external objects

As with any form of analysis, work begins at the boundary of the system. The analyst begins by considering who will use the system, what other systems (e.g. databases) it must interact with, and (in general terms) what type of hardware will be required.

In the case of the bank ATM, a customer is an obvious external entity. The ATM will also be connected to a central bank computer, and it will be switched on and off, I will assume, by an assistant at the bank (Figure K.3).

Figure K.3 The externals for the ATM system.

K.4.2 The logical interaction diagrams

Any accurate model of a software system, whether process-, data-, object- or agent-oriented, needs to include three perspectives: process ('what does it do'), data ('what does it do it to') and control ('when does it do it'). In an object-oriented system, for example, CRDs provide process and data information and, as was discussed in Part III, structure charts can be used to record control information in simple systems. In more complex O-O systems, interaction diagrams (Booch, 1994) provide a more powerful way of representing control and timing information. Typically the provisional interaction diagrams arise as the result of a walkthrough (Norris *et al.*, 1993).

When performing an O-O development using ISE, the interaction between the external objects and the system itself is represented by a **conversation**. For example, suppose it is intended to develop a simple control system for a greenhouse system. An effective way of thinking about the way the system will operate is to consider the 'conversation' between the control system, and the externals (a 'temperature sensor', 'cooler', and 'heater'), as illustrated in Figure K.4.

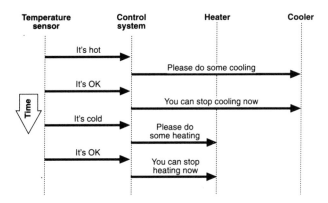

Figure K.4 A 'conversation' between objects in a simple greenhouse control system. This system was first introduced in Chapter 14, where an STD representation of this 'conversation' was presented.

For a more realistic system, an interaction diagram will often be drawn up during the course of a walkthrough, as the operation of the system is considered over a typical period of use: as an example of the end result of this process, Figure K.5 shows how the ATM system might operate while dispensing cash to a customer.

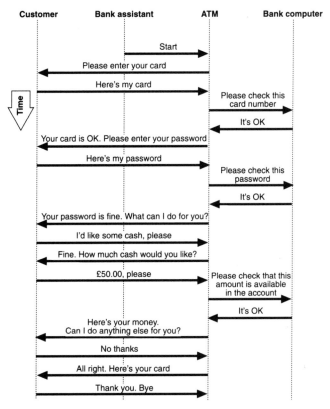

Figure K.5 A logical interaction diagram. It can help to view these as conversations between the various externals and the system itself.

K.4.3 The system and external messages

The next phase in the analysis process involves identifying the key system and external messages: that is, the messages to which the system must respond, and (where appropriate) to which any associated externals must respond.

Examining the various logical interaction diagrams often provides a powerful way of assisting in the identification of important messages. For example, Figure K.6 reproduces Figure K.5, this time with some possible system messages identified. This process would be repeated for any remaining logical interaction diagrams.

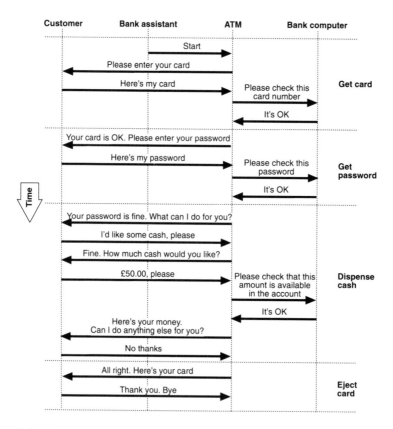

Figure K.6 An annotated logical interaction diagram modelling the 'dispense cash' process.

K.4.4 The message domain diagram

The next analysis stage involves the production of the message domain diagram (MDD), a slightly modified form of context diagram. The MDD summarizes the required system behaviour, from the perspective of the people and other objects with which it must interact.

The finished message domain diagram is shown in Figure K.7.

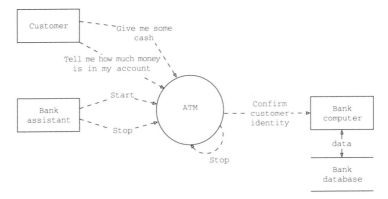

Figure K.7 Message domain diagram for the simple (O-O) ATM. Note that the 'Give me some cash' message would be responded to through the interaction shown in Figure K.6.

K.4.5 The data domain diagram

To complete the 'logical' model of the ATM system, it can also be helpful to include a data domain diagram at the analysis stage.

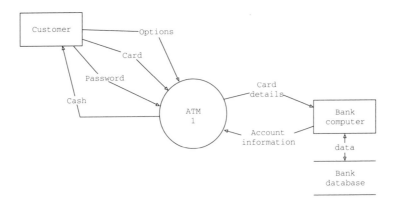

Figure K.8 Partial data domain model (context diagram) for a simple (O-O) ATM system.

K.4.6 Software size prediction

A key cause of failure of many software projects is the difficulty of providing accurate predictions of final software size at an early stage of a project (Boehm, 1983). Such size predictions provide a vital source of data for estimates of project cost and project duration: without accurate figures, cost overruns and late delivery become inevitable. The ideal solution is to have experienced staff available who have 'seen it all before' and can estimate a project size and cost based on past experience: this technique is sometimes referred to as 'expert judgement' (Boehm, 1981). Unfortunately, studies in this area suggest that it takes at least six years to gain the experience necessary to provide such estimates (Hihn and Habib-Agahi, 1991), a fact which makes suitably experienced staff comparatively rare and expensive: furthermore, even after this period of training, such experts are likely to disagree, making it necessary to employ a team to perform this task reliably (Somerville, 1996).

Partly as a result of the cost of the 'expert judgement' approach, various attempts have been made to partially automate the cost estimation process. The seminal work in this area, upon which the method described here builds indirectly, was the study begun at IBM by A. J. Albrecht, on the measurement of software using a 'function point' technique (Albrecht, 1979; Albrecht and Gaffney, 1983). A function point is an abstract surrogate for the standard economic idea of 'goods' produced as the result of an economic activity: it provides a measure of the functionality of the resulting system. FPs are language independent so productivity in different programming languages can be compared.

Function points are generally calculated using the weighted sums of five (or more) different system factors which are of interest to users, such as: Inputs, Outputs, Logical files, Enquiries, and Interfaces. A key feature of this type of approach is that it can be applied not simply at the end of the project to count the number of 'lines of code' written, but also during the analysis phase to predict the final system size, and thus the system cost, timescale and feasibility. A detailed description of the use and measurement of function points is given elsewhere (Jones, 1991). MacDonell (1994) compares and contrasts several different function-based measures.

As far as many users or potential users are concerned the principal drawback with function point analyses is that the various features (such as 'inputs' and 'outputs') are not always obvious, and that counts can be subjective or difficult to obtain. Another significant problem is that the great majority of function point techniques are biased towards information systems or other products developed using a D-O approach (Somerville, 1996). The technique is, for example, rarely used in embedded systems (developed using a P-O approach), and largely unknown in O-O system development.

However, Gaffney and Werling (1991) have considered the estimation of software size by counting system externals, and have applied these techniques to (P-O) aerospace projects. By adapting and extending this approach, a simple set of equations has been derived which allow the prediction of the final software system size (in lines of C++ code) for a range of P-O, D-O and O-O projects with reasonable accuracy (Pont, 1997). For example, consider Figure K.9: this shows the data domain diagram and the message domain diagram developed during the analysis phase of an arbitrary ISE project. It also shows three equations which allow a simple prediction of the number of lines (of C++ code) likely to result from the implementation of a particular pair of domain diagrams. Note that both message domain and data domain diagrams are produced during the analysis phase of all ISE projects: however, the number of lines of code produced depends on the type of design and implementation chosen.

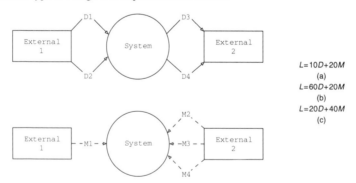

$$L = 10D + 20M$$
(a)
$$L = 60D + 20M$$
(b)
$$L = 20D + 40M$$
(c)

Figure K.9 The data domain diagram (top left) and message domain diagram (bottom left) for an arbitrary ISE project. Also shown (right) are the simple equations allowing provisional estimates of software size (in lines of C++ code) determined by analysis of a number of small projects. Here 'D' refers to the number of 'dataflows' and 'M' to the number of system messages. Equation [a] is appropriate for P-O projects; [b] for D-O projects; and [c] for O-O projects. See Pont (1997) for details.

It should be emphasized that the equations given in Figure K.9 should be fine-tuned to match the styles of analysis, design and coding used in your university or company environment. The exercises at the end of Chapter 19 include some suggestions for carrying out this process.

K.5 Where to find out more

This appendix has outlined the origins of SADIE and ISE. If you are interested in learning more, you will find links to various WWW pages providing further details, including down-loadable reports describing A-O ISE (Pont and Moreale, 1996) and integrated software size estimation (Pont, 1997), on my 'home page': the URL is given at the end of the Preface.

A complete description of ISE, including a series of detailed case studies and a CASE tool, will be available from Addison-Wesley early in 1998, in the form of a book entitled 'Integrated Software Engineering'.

K.6 References

Albrecht, A. J. (1979) Measuring application development productivity, Proceedings of the joint SHARE, GUIDE and IBM Application Development Symposium, October 1979, pp.83–92.

Albrecht, A. J. and Gaffney, J. E. (1983) Software function, lines of code and development effort prediction: a software science prediction, *IEEE Trans. On Software Engineering*, SE-9 (6): 639–47.

Boehm, B. W. (1981) *Software Engineering Economics,* Prentice-Hall.

Boehm, B. W. (1983) The economics of software maintenance, Proceedings of the Software Maintenance Workshop, Washington DC, pp.9–37.

Booch, G. (1994) *Object-Oriented Analysis and Design*, Benjamin Cummings.

Chen, M., Nunamaker, J. F. (Jr.) and Weber, E. S. (1989) Computer-aided software engineering: Present status and future direction, *Database*, **20**: 7–13.

Gaffney, J. E. and Werling, R. (1991) Estimating software size from counts of externals: a generalization of functin points, SPC-91094-N. Hendon, Virginia: Software Productivity Consortium.

Hihn, J. and Habib-Agahi, H. (1991) Cost estimation of software intensive projects: a survey of current practices, Proceedings of the 13th Int. Conf. On Software Engineering, Austin, Texas, pp.276–87.

Jones, C. (1991) *Applied Software Measurement,* McGraw-Hill.

Jones, N. B., Wang, S. and Pont, M. J. (1995) A Framework for Medical Decision Support, in Knepps, P. and Tysler, M. (eds) *Model Based Biomeasurements*, Gupress Bratislava, pp.245–9 [ISBN: 80-967402-0-2]

MacDonell, S. G. (1994) Comparative review of functional complexity assessment methods for effort estimation, *BCS/IEE Software Engineering Journal*, 9(3): 107–17.

Norris, M., Rigby, P. and Payne, M. (1993) *The Healthy Software Project: A Guide to Successful development and management*, John Wiley.

Pont, M. J. (1997) An integrated method for software size estimation, University of Leicester, Department of Engineering, Technical Report 97-1, January 1997. [Available electronically over the WWW via the address given at the end of the Preface.]

Pont, M. J. and Damper, R .I. (1991) A computational model of afferent neural activity from the cochlea to the dorsal acoustic stria, *Journal of the Acoustical Society of America*, **89**: 1213–28.

Pont, M. J. and Moreale, E. (1996) Towards a practical methodology for agent-oriented software engineering with C++ and Java, University of Leicester, Department of Engineering, Technical Report 96-33, December 1996. [A copy is provided on the CD included with this book.]

Pont, M. J. and Wong, K. S. (1994) Computer simulation of auditory evoked responses: a pilot study. *Proceedings of the Institute of Acoustics*, **16**: 147–54.

Sewell, D. R. and Pont, M. J. (forthcoming) An object-oriented model of the transtympanic membrane, *British Journal of Audiology*.

Somerville, I. (1996) *Software Engineering*, (5th edition), Addison-Wesley.

Yourdon, E. N. (1989) *Modern Structured Analysis*, Prentice-Hall.

Index